HANDBOOK OF
RESEARCH-BASED PRACTICE
IN EARLY EDUCATION

Handbook of

RESEARCH-BASED PRACTICE IN EARLY EDUCATION

EDITED BY
D. RAY REUTZEL

THE GUILFORD PRESS
New York   London

© 2013 The Guilford Press
A Division of Guilford Publications, Inc.
72 Spring Street, New York, NY 10012
www.guilford.com

Printed in the United States of America

This book is printed on acid-free paper.

Last digit is print number: 9 8 7 6 5 4 3 2 1

Library of Congress Cataloging-in-Publication Data

Reutzel, D. Ray (Douglas Ray), 1953–
  Handbook of research-based practice in early education / edited by D. Ray Reutzel.
    pages   cm
  Includes bibliographical references and index.
  ISBN 978-1-4625-1018-4 (hardcover)
  1. Early childhood education—Research.   I. Title.
  LB1139.23.R48 2013
  372.21—dc23

                                                    2012043649

To Pam,
teacher of children

—D. R. R.

About the Editor

D. Ray Reutzel, PhD, is the Emma Eccles Jones Distinguished Professor and Endowed Chair of Early Childhood Education at Utah State University. He serves on the Board of Directors of the Literacy Research Association (2012–2015) and is a past president of the Association of Literacy Educators and Researchers and a past board member of the International Reading Association (IRA). A member of the Reading Hall of Fame, Dr. Reutzel received the John C. Manning Public School Service Award from the IRA. He has published more than 200 research reports, articles, book chapters, and books.

CONTRIBUTORS

Samantha B. Berkule, PhD, Department of Psychology, Marymount Manhattan College, and Department of Pediatrics, New York University School of Medicine and Bellevue Hospital Center, New York, New York

Bonnie Brinton, PhD, Department of Communication Disorders, David O. McKay School of Education, Brigham Young University, Provo, Utah

Carolyn Brockmeyer Cates, PhD, Department of Pediatrics, New York University School of Medicine and Bellevue Hospital Center, New York, New York

Douglas H. Clements, PhD, Morgridge College of Education, University of Denver, Denver, Colorado

Shannon T. Dieringer, PhD, School of Physical Education, Sport, and Exercise Science, College of Applied Sciences and Technology, Ball State University, Muncie, Indiana

Douglas Fuchs, PhD, Department of Special Education, Peabody College of Vanderbilt University, Nashville, Tennessee

Lynn S. Fuchs, PhD, Department of Special Education, Peabody College of Vanderbilt University, Nashville, Tennessee

Martin Fujiki, PhD, Department of Communication Disorders, David O. McKay School of Education, Brigham Young University, Provo, Utah

Linda B. Gambrell, PhD, Eugene T. Moore School of Education, Clemson University, Clemson, South Carolina

Claude Goldenberg, PhD, School of Education, Stanford University, Stanford, California

Jacqueline D. Goodway, PhD, School of Physical Activity and Educational Services, College of Education and Human Ecology, Ohio State University, Columbus, Ohio

Steve Graham, EdD, Mary Lou Fulton Teachers College, Arizona State University, Tempe, Arizona

Karen R. Harris, EdD, Mary Lou Fulton Teachers College, Arizona State University, Tempe, Arizona

Bridget E. Hatfield, PhD, Center for Advanced Study of Teaching and Learning, Curry School of Education, University of Virginia, Charlottesville, Virginia

Kellyanne M. Healey, MEd, Graduate School of Education, Rutgers, The State University of New Jersey, New Brunswick, New Jersey

Judy Hicks, MEd, School of Education, Stanford University, Stanford, California

Marcia B. Imbeau, PhD, Department of Curriculum and Instruction, College of Education and Health Professions, University of Arkansas, Fayetteville, Arkansas

Abigail M. Jewkes, PhD, Department of Child Development and Family Relations, College of Human Ecology, East Carolina University, Greenville, North Carolina

Cindy D. Jones, PhD, School of Teacher Education and Leadership, Utah State University, Logan, Utah

Laura M. Justice, PhD, Children's Learning Research Collaborative, College of Education and Human Ecology, Ohio State University, Columbus, Ohio

Judith E. Kieff, EdD, Department of Curriculum and Instruction, University of New Orleans, New Orleans, Louisiana

Susan A. Kirch, PhD, Department of Teaching and Learning, Steinhardt School of Culture, Education, and Human Development, New York University, New York, New York

Linda D. Labbo, PhD, Department of Language and Literacy Education, College of Education, University of Georgia, Athens, Georgia

Jihyun Lee, PhD, School of Physical Activity and Educational Services, College of Education and Human Ecology, Ohio State University, Columbus, Ohio

Linda S. Levstik, PhD, Department of Curriculum and Instruction, College of Education, University of Kentucky, Lexington, Kentucky

Ira Lit, PhD, School of Education, Stanford University, Stanford, California

Lea M. McGee, EdD, School of Teaching and Learning, College of Education and Human Ecology, Ohio State University, Columbus, Ohio

Michael C. McKenna, PhD, Department of Reading Education, Curry School of Education, University of Virginia, Charlottesville, Virginia

Alan L. Mendelsohn, MD, Department of Pediatrics, New York University School of Medicine and Bellevue Hospital Center, New York, New York

Amanda C. Miller, PhD, Department of Special Education, Peabody College of Vanderbilt University, Nashville, Tennessee

Lesley Mandel Morrow, PhD, Graduate School of Education, Rutgers, The State University of New Jersey, New Brunswick, New Jersey

Sylvia Munsen, PhD, School of Teacher Education and Leadership, Utah State University, Logan, Utah

Susan B. Neuman, EdD, Department of Educational Studies, School of Education, University of Michigan, Ann Arbor, Michigan

Silvia Noguerón-Liu, PhD, Department of Language and Literacy Education,
College of Education, University of Georgia, Athens, Georgia

John C. Ozmun, MS, PED, Division of Health and Human Performance,
Indiana Wesleyan University, Marion, Indiana

Christina Yeager Pelatti, PhD, Children's Learning Research Collaborative, College of Education
and Human Ecology, Ohio State University, Columbus, Ohio

Robert C. Pianta, PhD, Center for Advanced Study of Teaching and Learning,
Curry School of Education, University of Virginia, Charlottesville, Virginia

Ruth Alfaro Piker, PhD, Department of Teacher Education, College of Education,
California State University, Long Beach, California

Douglas R. Powell, PhD, Department of Human Development and Family Studies,
Purdue University, West Lafayette, Indiana

M. Deanna Ramey, MAT, Eugene T. Moore School of Education, Clemson University,
Clemson, South Carolina

D. Ray Reutzel, PhD, School of Teacher Education and Leadership, Utah State University,
Logan, Utah

Kathleen A. Roskos, PhD, Department of Education and Allied Studies, John Carroll University,
University Heights, Ohio

Olivia N. Saracho, PhD, Department of Teaching, Learning, Policy, and Leadership,
College of Education, University of Maryland, College Park, Maryland

Julie Sarama, PhD, Morgridge College of Education, University of Denver, Denver, Colorado

Mary Beth Schmitt, MS, Children's Learning Research Collaborative, College of Education
and Human Ecology, Ohio State University, Columbus, Ohio

Timothy Shanahan, PhD, Department of Curriculum and Instruction, University of Illinois
at Chicago, Chicago, Illinois

Carol Ann Tomlinson, EdD, Curry School of Education, University of Virginia,
Charlottesville, Virginia

Jessica R. Toste, PhD, Department of Special Education, Peabody College
of Vanderbilt University, Nashville, Tennessee

Sharon Walpole, PhD, School of Education, University of Delaware, Newark, Delaware

PREFACE

K nowledge in the field of early childhood education has undergone a veritable explosion in the past decade, taking center stage in national and state educational theory, research, and policy discussions (Pianta, Barnett, Justice, & Sheridan, 2012; Spodek & Saracho, 2006). The renewed and extended emphasis on early childhood programs such as Even Start, Head Start, Early Reading First, and others has been publicly and privately funded in the hope that doing so would produce a host of anticipated benefits in the long run. Research evidence, now more than ever, points to the distinctive importance of the early years in a child's life and the plethora of returns associated with early intervention programs in arresting common academic, economic, and social maladies. Knowledge derived from research, policy, and theory in the field of early childhood education not only has generated considerable excitement in related fields of education, human development, human services, policy studies, prevention sciences, and medicine, but also has led to a need to undertake more frequent syntheses of that knowledge to keep it up to date and make it more universally accessible.

In 2012, Robert C. Pianta (a contributor to this volume) and his colleagues published the *Handbook of Early Childhood Education,* which synthesized and summarized the state of the field in early childhood education theory, policy, and research. That volume was very much needed to update and extend the knowledge derived from early childhood theory, research, and policy since the 2006 publication of the *Handbook of Research on the Education of Young Children* (edited by Bernard Spodek and Olivia N. Saracho). These two handbooks provided a solid and current knowledge base from which to propel the work of scientists, researchers, and policymakers into a future that enjoyed an even greater enlightenment and access to up-to-date information than ever before. Even with the timely publication of these two excellent handbooks, there was nonetheless something missing, namely, an accessible translation of the current findings of early childhood theories, research, and policy into research-based professional practices for those who exert the largest influence on young children's early educational experiences: early childhood professionals.

Atul Gwande (2007, 2009) brilliantly underscores the pivotal role of the professional in translating and enacting research into everyday medical practice. In his book *Better: A Surgeon's Notes on Performance*, Gwande (2007) reports a study of his hospital's infectious disease control team. The focus of this study was on the well-established and evidence-based practice of hand washing and the continuing failure of medical practitioners to disinfect their hands adequately. The disease control team tried everything to get the professionals to implement evidence-based practices. They repositioned sinks and had new ones installed. They bought $5,000 "precaution carts" to make washing, gloving, and gowning easy and efficient. They posted admonishing signs, and issued hygiene "report cards." They even gave away free movie tickets as an incentive for cleaning up. Nothing worked!

Gwande (2007, p. 19) laments:

> Compliance rates for proper hand hygiene improved substantially from 40 percent to around 70 percent. But—and this is the troubling finding—hospital infection rates did not drop one iota. Our 70 percent compliance just wasn't good enough. If 30 percent of the time people didn't wash their hands, that still left plenty of opportunity to keep transmitting infections. Indeed, rates of resistant Staphylococcus and Enterococcus infections continued to rise. . .

Consequently, hospital statistics everywhere indicate that doctors and nurses wash their hands about one-third to one-half as often as they should.

So what is the message of Gwande's (2007) work for the field of early childhood education? The degree to which we help the early childhood professional understand and diligently implement evidence-based practices into everyday teaching practices promises to threaten or empower the eventual success of the work in early childhood education. Failure to bridge the world of research, theory, and policy with the world of practice and the practitioner will most likely result in a failure of research, theory, or policy to have any noticeable impact on the children themselves or on society as a whole.

On a related note, one cannot discount questions about the adequacy of the preparation of early childhood professionals. Early childhood education is a patchwork of programs, schools, day care centers, home care centers, and public, private, and religiously affiliated facilities and programs, each with varying requirements for those who are hired to provide both early education and care. It is widely known that early care and education providers' professional preparation can vary dramatically from only a high school diploma and a few days or weeks of training per year to postgraduate degrees and many years of experience and professional learning opportunities. Perhaps nowhere else in the educational system does the level of professional preparation and, as a consequence, the level of professional knowledge vary as greatly as it does in early care and educational settings.

The significance of a professional's specialized knowledge about effective instruction should not be underestimated in relation to how well research, theory, or policy will impact the experiences of young learners in early education. The amount of knowledge generated from research and theory necessary to instruct young students adequately has grown exponentially over the years, as previously noted. But one must question whether or not the knowledge resulting from research, theory, and policy has been translated or communicated in such a way that teachers, teacher educators, professional developers, coaches, supervisors, directors, administrators, or others charged with the professional growth of early childhood teachers can make use of it. Although all of us want to honor the knowledge, skills, and professionalism of early education teachers, we nevertheless cannot afford to ignore how much knowledge the typical early childhood teacher must have to be adequately prepared and effective in educating young students for a rapidly changing, digitally connected, information-saturated brave new world.

The *Handbook of Research-Based Practice in Early Education* was conceived to translate theory, research, and policy of early childhood education into research-based practices for the multiple stakeholders who must make sense of and implement these practices in the everyday educational experiences of young children. It is our hope, as a group of early childhood researchers, teacher educators, advocates, and authors, that this volume will not become one more handbook gathering dust on a research university's library shelf, but rather will be a well-worn, frequently used desk reference, a veritable *vade mecum*, for teacher leaders, administrators, curriculum developers, publishers, and teacher educators to use when translating the recent explosion of knowledge in early childhood education into research-based practices that are implemented with due diligence in early childhood educational settings.

This handbook is divided into four major parts. Part I tackles issues associated with policies, policymakers, educational leaders, and others who influence and have a stake in the quality of early childhood teachers and the outcomes of young children's early educational experiences. It is widely known that young children benefit from high-quality, research-based early educational experiences provided in homes, preschools, and in early care centers by highly qualified professionals. In the first chapter, Neuman discusses how leaders in early education can change the odds for at-risk young children so that they get the educational experiences they need to grow, develop, and learn successfully. Next, Roskos expands on this idea by discussing the kinds of professional development support early childhood teachers need to learn, what the research evidence has to offer, and how to put this knowledge to work in classrooms. Saracho describes the initial preparation of early childhood teachers while offering clear, concise, and useful principles for improving early childhood teacher education programs. Powell discusses research and practices that have been effective when used to engage parents, caregivers, and the community in the education of the young. Kieff describes principles and practices that early childhood professionals need to advocate effectively for the educational, economic, social, and physical needs of young children.

Part II addresses the theme "one size doesn't fit all," speaking to the assertion that to be effective and research based, early educational experiences should be responsive and flexible, and meet the multifaceted needs of a diverse population of young children. To this end, Reutzel and Jones describe how to design and manage effective early childhood classroom learning environments. Morrow, Berkule, Mendelsohn, Healey, and Cates discuss the critical role of play in the educational experiences provided to young children. Tomlinson and Imbeau describe the elements, principles, and practices that are necessary to differentiate instructional experiences to meet the diverse needs of young learners. Goldenberg, Hicks, and Lit review the research on teaching young English learners and how to best serve their particular and important needs in early childhood classrooms. Miller, Toste, Fuchs, and Fuchs bring the research on response-to-intervention models into focus and describe how providers of educational programs for young children can respond to the diverse needs of at-risk students. Labbo and Noguerón-Liu transport the readers of this handbook into the research about young digital natives—children who are as at home in a digital environment as they are in the real world—and discuss how teachers of young children can effectively integrate digital pedagogies into their daily instruction. Ramey and Gambrell wrap up this section with a synthesis of research on motivation and engagement, and describe how early childhood educators can capture and sustain the interests, imagination, and attention of their young learners.

Part III focuses on those day-to-day elements that shape the teaching in early childhood classrooms: standards, curriculum, and assessment. Shanahan leads off with a historical and contemporary discussion of the Common Core State Standards and how these are influencing the world of early childhood education. McKenna and Walpole describe the features, characteristics, and content of effective programs of instruction and curricula for early childhood education programs. Brinton and Fujiki follow up with a discussion of how early childhood education providers can enhance the social and emotional learning experience of young children. Piker and Jewkes explain the problems and solutions for assessing learning to guide instruction in early education classrooms. Finally, Hatfeld and Pianta illuminate the reader on how to assess the quality of early childhood instruction and educational environments, segueing into the final section of the *Handbook,* focused on effective, research-based instruction.

In Part IV, Goodway, Ozmun, Dieringer, and Lee provide a compelling case for physical activity in the daily educational experiences of young children. Munsen makes an equally compelling case for inclusion of the arts in the instruction of young students in early educational settings. Kirch describes the structure of scientific disciplines and how to induct the young novice learner successfully into the world of science. Clements and Sarama follow up with a teachers' guide for making mathematics exciting, fun, and understandable for young children. McGee describes the process of nurturing young students' curiosity about print through reading books aloud. Graham and Harris describe how to support young students' acquisition of the ability to write and a love for writing. Levstik artfully weaves a social studies narrative about how to help young children learn the skills of dialogue, discussion, negotiation, and democracy in the classroom. Finally, Pelatti, Schmitt, and Justice bring it all together in a lively and useful rendering of how early childhood educators can support their young students' acquisition of oral language speaking and listening skills through talking.

In closing, this handbook brings under one cover a comprehensive collection of research syntheses in early childhood education and translates them into practices that early childhood educational researchers, policymakers, leaders, teacher educators, professional developers, and, most of all, classroom teachers will be able to apply in making "research-based" early education a reality for young children. This handbook provides a long-awaited bridge from the ethereal realms of research, theory, and policy to the messy and wondrous realities of practice over which the inquiring professional practitioner may tread to survey the extraordinary landscape of early education.

REFERENCES

Gwande, A. (2007). *Better: A surgeon's notes on performance.* New York: Picador.

Gwande, A. (2009). *The checklist manifesto: How to get things right.* New York: Metropolitan Books.

Pianta, R. C., Barnett, W. S., Justice, L. M., & Sheridan, S. M. (Eds.). (2012). *Handbook of early childhood education.* New York: Guilford Press.

Spodek, B., & Saracho, O. N. (2006). *Handbook of research on the education of young children* (2nd ed.). Mahwah, NJ: Erlbaum.

ACKNOWLEDGMENTS

In 1159, John of Salisbury observed, "Bernard of Chartres used to say that we are like dwarfs on the shoulders of giants, so that we can see more than they, and things at a greater distance, not by virtue of any sharpness of sight on our part, or any physical distinction, but because we are carried high and raised up by their giant size." And so it has been for me. I stand on the shoulders of giants, both historical and contemporary. No work of this magnitude could have ever been accomplished alone.

Furthermore, this handbook would never have been realized if it had not been for the relentless pestering of Craig Thomas, my editor at The Guilford Press, who persuaded me to undertake this momentous project. His encouragement, confidence, and sage counsel made the ultimate realization of this project possible.

As for the authors of these chapters, I can only step back and say, "These are they, the very giants upon whose shoulders I humbly stand!" These are the names of the researchers and early childhood education scholars upon whose work I have relied throughout the entire length of my 35-plus-year career in education. In fact, I look at the list of names in the table of contents and have to wonder why a group of this stature would willingly respond to my invitation to write a chapter for this handbook given their already busy scholarly schedules and lives. These scholars are deeply and passionately committed to the improvement of the early educational experiences for young children everywhere. I believe their generous motives will be key to any future praise or success associated with this volume.

This incredible group of authors cheerfully worked through feedback, nagging, and revisions, often on tight deadlines, in a timely fashion and with unparalleled quality. Their chapters stand as examples of top-notch integrative and teaching scholarship that achieves that rare goal of making the often esoteric findings of research truly accessible to the end users—the early childhood professionals who work tirelessly every day to provide research-based educational experiences to our youngest children.

To the many staff members of The Guilford Press, I offer my sincere gratitude for the excellent professional services, advice, and encouragement that each offered in his or her own way along the pathway of completing this project. I could not have asked for more efficient, effective, or responsive assistance.

I need to pay special tribute to my benefactor, the Emma Eccles Jones Foundation, and to Utah State University, which provided me with the working conditions and economic support needed to make this contribution to the profession possible. I am ever grateful to that wonderful kindergarten teacher, Emma Eccles Jones, who has given so generously to my endowment, building, and college for many years, making much of the work in early childhood education possible in the state of Utah and beyond. I also offer appreciation to my Dean, Beth Foley, and my administrative assistant, Nissa Boman, for their constant support, encouragement, and assistance.

I also express thanks to my colleagues in higher education at Utah State and throughout the nation for their continued collegial support and intellectual inspiration. To those teachers in early childhood education who have contributed to my growing knowledge and understanding of this field in myriad ways, I am also most grateful.

Finally, I owe my greatest tribute to my favorite kindergarten teacher, closest friend, and spouse of 38 years, Pamela, who teaches me every day not only how to love and teach children but also how to become a better person and live life more joyfully and abundantly.

D. RAY REUTZEL, PhD

CONTENTS

PART III. EFFECTIVE TEACHING STANDARDS, CURRICULA, AND ASSESSMENT

PART IV. EFFECTIVE INSTRUCTION ACROSS THE CURRICULUM

PART I

ALL STAKEHOLDERS
ON DECK

CHAPTER 1

HOW WE CAN CHANGE THE ODDS FOR CHILDREN AT RISK
Principles for Effective Leadership in Early Childhood

SUSAN B. NEUMAN

America's poor children do not fare well in our society. The odds are if a child is born poor, he's likely to stay poor. He'll probably live in an unsafe neighborhood, landscaped with little hope, with more neighborhood bars on corners than quality day care or afterschool programs. As he makes his way up through the local school system, he'll likely find his schools dilapidated; the playgrounds distant memories where equipment once laid; and the teachers, though earnest, ready to throw in the towel. As the have-not among the haves, he'll find that his skills are hopelessly behind those of his peers, and only drop further as academic demands get higher, with options increasingly narrowed to staying behind, giving up, or dropping out. And perhaps the most tragic element of all is that this cycle of disadvantage is likely to repeat itself over and over again, until we are determined to do something about it.

This chapter describes how early interventions can break this cycle. It reviews seven principles that have been shown to be essential in effective interventions that influence children's achievement not only immediately but also over time. Together, these principles should be considered in developing new interventions that can effectively change the odds for children at risk.

Each year policymakers are faced with a bewildering array of choices on which programs to fund that may benefit poor children. In this era of fiscal restraint, policymakers must make critical decisions on how many children will receive benefits and which ones they will receive. Some programs, such as Medicaid, are entitlements, which mean that every child whose family meets the criteria for the program is entitled to receive benefits. Other programs such as Early Head Start have never been funded at a level that allows all eligible families to be served. The choices have not been easy, and frequently no clear-cut solutions have been offered by social scientists responsible for evaluating these programs.

As a result, decisions are often made stochastically, as opined by then-Senator Walter Mondale in an address to the American Psychological Association almost a half-century ago:

> What I have not learned from researchers [about improving the odds for poor children] is what we can do about these problems. . . . For every study, statistical or theoretical, that contains a proposed solution or recommendation, there is always another, equally well documented, challenging the assumptions or conclusions of the first. No one seems to agree with anyone else's approach. . . . As a result, I must confess, I stand with my colleagues confused and often disheartened. (Currie, 2005, p. 114)

Many would argue that little has changed in these subsequent years. Today, the reauthorization and appropriation process—decisions that set budgets, benefit levels, and program rules—seems as perplexing as ever. Programs are funded, then defunded and reintroduced all over again, producing discontinuities in services and diminishing any consolidated effort to provide a foundational safety net for children in the early years. Those who stand to be recipients of this disarray, unfortunately, are the most at risk children and their families.

Ideally, of course, policymakers should make decisions based on evidence of what works—on the principles and practices of programs that are likely to achieve positive outcomes for poor children at reasonable costs (Neuman, 2009). In this scenario, priorities would be established, evidence would be carefully weighed, budgets would be allocated appropriately, and programs monitored to ensure implementation fidelity. This would mean a very different process both in setting priorities and funding programs. Essentially, those programs that fundamentally achieve results—changing the lives of children at risk—would set the course of action, providing a guide for further actions. Just consider the advances we might make in helping children to achieve at a price we can afford.

In this spirit, this chapter highlights an evidence-based approach, first describing programs shown to have promise in improving the futures of high-risk children. It then looks within these programs, emphasizing specific factors that seem to cut across them, suggesting that critical features of interventions can remove some of the early risk factors associated with poor achievement. This new knowledge can become the foundation on which leaders and policymakers construct policies that radically reduce the occurrence of adverse outcomes.

WHAT RESEARCH SAYS ABOUT PROGRAMS THAT WORK

The neurobiological, behavioral, and social sciences have seen an explosion of research on children's development over the last several decades (Shonkoff & Phillips, 2000). These scientific advantages have dramatically increased our capacity to intervene and support highly vulnerable children. Scientific studies now show that under the right conditions, early intervention can dramatically improve the prospects of children growing up in poverty (Olds, Kitzman, et al., 2004; Ramey et al., 2000). Take, for example, the stunning evidence of the long-term benefits of the Chicago Parent–Child Centers, funded by Title I, that Arthur Reynolds has documented in extraordinary detail over the years. His findings indicate that at age 26, students are likely still to reap the benefits of early education in terms of their employment status, overall quality of life, and social status

(Reynolds, Temple, White, Ou, & Robertson, 2011), with a return to society of $10.83 for every dollar invested (18% annual return).

Findings like these led me to search the literature for other effective programs—programs that have not only immediate but also long-term benefits sustained over time. With funding from the Spencer Foundation, I visited these programs across the country, chronicling the stories of their success, and culling lessons about what has worked in the past and what is likely to work in the future. In fact, I found in a cross-sectional analysis of these studies remarkable consistencies in the ingredients that have made all these successful programs work.

Take the 15 most-cited interventions in the early childhood literature (Karoly, Kilburn, & Cannon, 2005), for example (see Table 1.1). Recognized for the quality of their experimental or quasi-experimental design, these evaluations address interventions related to child outcomes and school readiness; use reasonable samples sizes for statistical analyses; and are published by peer-reviewed journals or books. Four of the interventions have been subject to cost–benefit analyses.

The interventions fall into two distinct patterns and program approaches. The first set of programs, such as the Infant Health and Development Program (Brooks-Gunn et al., 1994) and Early Head Start (Love et al., 2002), delivers services primarily to the parent either through home visits or parent education. These programs strengthen family resources to help parents provide greater nurturance, health, attachment, and stimulation to their children. The second set of programs emphasizes services to children through early care and education programs. Programs such as the Perry Preschool Project (Weikart, Bond, & McNeil, 1978), the Abecedarian (Campbell & Ramey, 1995), Chicago Parent–Child Centers (Reynolds, 2000), Bright Beginnings (Smith, Pellin, & Agruso, 2003), and the Brookline Early Education Program (BEEP; Hauser-Cram, Pierson, Walker, & Tivnan, 1991) emphasize early childhood education and school readiness. But make no mistake about it—all involve parent education and parent support as a critical feature in their intervention.

All of these programs have shown promise in improving the futures of high-risk children—additional corroboration that their successes are not based on chance. And the story that they reveal is striking: Children who receive responsive and consistent caregiving in settings that are safe and stimulating can make a remarkable recovery from the devastations of poverty. They can learn how to form healthy relationships with others, they become eager to learn, and they develop the skills and knowledge necessary to be able to finish school and earn a productive income. Providing some of the strongest evidence to date, these programs show that we can do what needs to be done to ensure that poor children have opportunities to learn.

But the subplot in this story is equally important. Looking "inside the black box" of these interventions, an extraordinary convergence in the qualities of these programs has made them successful. The most effective interventions demonstrating sizable, robust, and educationally meaningful results follow seven essential principles.

WHAT IS THE SCIENTIFIC EVIDENCE?

Listed below are principles derived from these research syntheses, based on studies of children from economically impoverished families, children with combined environmental and biological risks, and children with disabilities. Figures 1.1a and 1.1b highlight the commonalities across these effective programs.

TABLE 1.1. Key Dimensions of Effective Intervention Programs

Program	Brief description	Outcomes	Currently operating?
	Programs with a strong evidence base		
Abecedarian (Ramey et al., 2000)	Comprehensive early education program for young children at risk for developmental delays and school failure. Program operated in North Carolina from 1972–85, and involved full-day, full-year, center-based care, starting from infancy up to 6 years of age.	Positive results on children's IQ (short term) and achievement; declining enrollment in special education; grade retention	No
Brookline Early Education Project (BEEP; Hauser-Cram et al., 1991)	Comprehensive school-based early intervention program for children birth until kindergarten. Designed as a demonstration project, three levels of service to families ranging from extensive to minimal amounts were offered. Services included home visits and prekindergarten program until entrance into kindergarten.	Positive results on children's social skills and academic skills; limited educated families benefited most; the most intensive services had greater effects	Yes
Chicago Parent–Child Centers (Reynolds, 2000)	Center-based preschool program for high-poverty children in Chicago since 1967. School-year program provides a structured part-day program for children ages 3 and 4, along with required family participation.	Positive results on children's achievement; declining enrollment in special education; reduction in crime and delinquency	Yes
Early Training Project (Gray, Ramsey, & Klaus, 1982)	Implemented in Murfreesboro, Tennessee, the demonstration project was designed to improve the educability of young children from very low-income homes. The program consisted of a 10-week summer preschool for two or three summers prior to first grade, and weekly home visits during the remainder of the year.	Positive results on children's IQ (short-term) and achievement; declining enrollment in special education	No
Infant Health and Development Program (Brooks-Gunn et al., 1994)	Targeted intervention to infants born prematurely, the comprehensive intervention consisted of family support services tailored to reduce health and developmental problems. Program provided home visiting, parent group meetings, and a center-based child development program from the neonatal nursery until 36 months of age.	Positive results on children's IQ (short-term); no differences in grade repetition or special education	No
Milwaukee Project (Garber, 1988)	Beginning during the 1960s, the project focused on an intensive intervention from infancy through early childhood to minimize the statistical effect of heredity of high-risk children from mentally retarded mothers.	Positive results on children's IQ and school achievement (short-term); declining enrollment in special education	No
Nurse–Family Partnership Program (Olds, Kitzman, et al., 2004)	Provides intensive and comprehensive home visitation by public health nurses to low-income first-time pregnant women and mothers of any age. The visits begin during pregnancy and continue through the child's second birthday. The program is intended to help women improve their care of infants and toddlers and their own development.	Positive short- and long-term advantages for both mothers and children. Fewer reported acts of child abuse, lower levels of criminal activity; fewer behavioral impairments due to alcohol and drugs; fewer subsequent pregnancies and births; children had fewer arrests	Yes
Perry Preschool Project (Weikart et al., 1978)	Center-based early childhood education program designed to promote children's intellectual, social, and emotional learning and development. The program, conducted from 1962–67, targeted 3- and 4-year-old children living in poverty with low IQs.	Positive results on children's IQ (short-term) and achievement; declining enrollment in special education, higher employment rates; decreases in teen pregnancy; higher rates of marriage	No

6

Programs with a promising evidence base

Avance (St. Pierre, Layzer, & Barnes, 1995)	Established in the late 1970s to reduce the disproportionately high dropout rate among Mexican American populations, the program provides a yearlong parenting and parent education program, toy-making activities, home visits and a child development program for children, birth through age 3.	Carnegie report findings show a decrease in high school dropouts, increase in college enrollments, decrease in crime; slight increases in children's social skills and school readiness
Bright Beginnings (Smith et al., 2003)	Starting in 1996, a literacy-focused preschool program for low-income children in Charlotte–Mecklenburg, NC. Program consists of a full-day program for 4-years olds, parent involvement, community support and collaboration, professional development and ongoing research and evaluation.	Positive impacts on school performance; educationally most needy children were ready to learn in kindergarten; African American and other minority groups were more proficient in literacy and math than control groups; decreases in grade retention
Early Head Start (Love et al., 2002)	A federally funded community-based program that provides children and their families developmental services to low-income pregnant mothers with infants and toddlers up to age 3. Program includes home visiting, child development, parent education, nutrition and health care referrals, and family support.	Positive statistically significant impacts on children's cognitive development (age 3); positive impacts on language development; favorable impacts on social–emotional development; some progress on parents' efforts toward self-sufficiency
Head Start (Zigler & Valentine, 1979)	A federally funded comprehensive, community-based preschool program initiated in 1960s to improve school readiness skills for 3- and 4-year-olds.	First year findings from the Head Start impact study indicate small to moderate statistically significant positive impacts in prereading, vocabulary, but no significant impacts on oral language, phonological awareness, math; no findings on social skills
Oklahoma PreK (Gormley, Gayer, Phillips, & Dawson, 2005)	Since 1998, the state of Oklahoma has provided a voluntary half-day or full-day prekindergarten program to all 4-year-olds in participating school districts. Credentialed teachers with required ratio of 10 children per adult.	Positive impacts for Hispanics, blacks, whites, and Native American children on letter knowledge, math, and spelling. No language measure was accessed
Parent–Child Home Program (Levenstein, Levenstein, & Oliver, 2002)	Started in the late 1960s, the mother–child home program focuses on developing verbal interaction for families in high-risk groups. Intervention program begins when child is about 2 years old and centers around a parent education program through toys and books of high quality.	Positive short-term cognitive gains; gains on preliteracy skills and social–emotional competence
Reach Out and Read (Needlman, Klass, & Zuckerman, 2006)	A national program that promotes reading aloud to young at-risk children by using the pediatric office as a site for education and intervention. Doctors and nurses give new books to children at each well-child visit from 6 months to 5 years and accompany books with developmentally appropriate advise to parents on how to read to children.	Positive impacts on frequency of reading aloud to children, promoting positive attitudes about books, and stimulating vocabulary growth; most effective for children at greatest risk

Programs with Strong Evidence Base	Principles						
	Targeting	Developmental Timing	Intensity	Professional Development	Coordinated Services	Compensatory Instruction	Accountability
1. Abecedarian							
2. Brookline Early Education Project							
3. Chicago Parent/ Child Centers							
4. Early Training Project							
5. Infant Health and Development Program							
6. The Milwaukee Project							
7. Nurse-Family Partnership Program							
8. Perry Preschool Project							

Legend:

■ Positive evidence of principles present

▨ Mixed findings

□ No evidence found

FIGURE 1.1a. Early childhood programs with a strong research base.

Programs with Promising Evidence Base	Principles						
	Targeting	Developmental Timing	Intensity	Professional Development	Coordinated Services	Compensatory Instruction	Accountability
1. Avance							
2. Bright Beginnings							
3. Early Head Start							
4. Head Start							
5. Oklahoma Pre-K							
6. Parent/ Child Home Program							
7. Reach Out and Read							

Legend:

■ Positive evidence of principles present

▨ Mixed findings

□ No evidence found

FIGURE 1.1b. Early childhood programs with a promising research base.

The Targeting Principle

Children who are most likely to benefit from interventions are those at greatest risk. For both biologically and environmentally vulnerable populations of children, program impacts are *greatest* for the more disadvantaged children and families in these interventions.

For example, an analysis of findings from the Perry Preschool Project (Schweinhart, 2004), an intervention program, revealed that the children who showed the greatest relative gains (compared to a control group) were most at risk, with receptive language skills more than two standard deviations below average. Similarly, children of higher risk participants in the Nurse–Family Partnership program (Olds, Robinson, et al., 2004), a home-visiting program targeting the health and parent education for first-time mothers, benefited more than those in the lower-risk groups. These gains translated into important cost benefits in this program (Bruner, 2004): An analysis indicated that the public saved $6.92 for every $1 invested in the program for those at higher risk; for those at lower risk, the public saved only $1.43 for every $1.

Why is targeting so important? Focusing on children with the greatest need, targeted programs are able to work with small numbers of children. Smaller teacher–child ratios enable programs to individualize their service delivery. For example, Early Head

Start (Raikes et al., 2006), a program emphasizing parent education in the very earliest years, works on the basis of parent and child individual needs while it conforms to overall program standards. Weekly visits focus on helping families reach overall benchmarks, specially tailored to the most crucial needs of the family.

Programs thwarted by inadequate resources and professional inertia have often worsened the situation for poor children. Targeted programs allow intervention specialists to serve these children without diluting quality by spreading resources too thin.

The Developmental Timing Principle

Developmental timing refers to the actual onset of intervention (Shonkoff & Phillips, 2000). Clearly, early identification and timing of intervention are critically important for some conditions and particular circumstances.

Circumstances that call for early diagnosis and treatment are chronic health issues. Conducting early and periodic assessments of children to monitor their development, BEEP (Hauser-Cram et al., 1991), a school-based PreK program, helped to head off health problems for children shortly after birth until entry into kindergarten. These early diagnostic screenings reduced the adverse effects of hearing loss due to chronic ear infections on communication skills and cognitive abilities. Similarly, Avance, a multifaceted intervention targeted to parent health, education, and support for new Latina parents (Rodriquez, 1999) had its greatest impact in preventing early developmental concerns from becoming more serious problems later on.

Educational leaders and policymakers should consider several important guidelines when weighing the costs and benefits of when to begin intervention:

- Programs that provide direct services to parents should begin as early as the prenatal period, or within a few weeks of birth.
- Programs that provide early and periodic screening, health, nutrition, and tactile/kinesthetic stimulation to children should also begin as early as possible. These programs have the potential to improve maternal and child health, and can significantly reduce health costs.
- Programs that provide direct services in early care and education settings should begin before children enter formal schooling in the late toddler, early preschool years.

There is no doubt that—in many cases—the earlier children receive help, the better. It is far more efficient to prevent reading difficulties early on (Snow, Burns, & Griffin, 1998), for example, than to wait until more serious problems occur and costly remediation becomes necessary. Nevertheless, intervention *too early* on may lead to overdiagnosis of problems. The overidentification of learning disabilities, for example, has sky-rocketed in special education (Lyons, Fletcher, & Barnes, 2003). In addition, overidentification can lead to engaging children in developmentally inappropriate activities. Drilling alphabet skills to very young children, who are only beginning to explore what these symbol systems, can be costly in other ways as well, affecting children's interest and motivation to read later on (Neuman, 2006b).

The Intensity Principle

The third essential relates to the intensity of the intervention. The equation in this third essential is simple: *More powerful interventions equal better effects*. Because change for highly vulnerable families is gradual, fragile, and often reversible, disadvantaged children and their families typically need extensive support and specific knowledge to assume their new roles and responsibilities.

Operationally defined by a term usually used in medicine, *dosage*, intensity typically refers to the amount of professional time—hours per day, days per week, weeks per year—spent with children and/or parent support. Programs that are more intensive produce larger positive effects (Halle et al., 2010); similarly, children and parents who participate most actively and regularly show the greatest overall progress.

But dosage—or the time devoted to the intervention—is only one characteristic of the intensity principle. Intensity also relates to *how* the time is used in the program. Intensive programs are *highly focused*, using their time with children and parents as if it were a limited resource. Bright Beginnings (Smith et al., 2003), for example, is highly focused on children's cognitive, language, gross motor, fine motor, visual–motor skills that are critical to school readiness. Teachers meet with diagnostic specialists on a regular basis and work with individual children who might need additional attention.

Intensity can be examined by asking the question: What specific interventions are being "added" to the child's regular early childhood program—how often, for how long, with how many other children, and with whom? Children who receive daily additional (above and beyond the usual) help for a substantial time on a one-to-one basis or in a small group with a highly trained professional are likely progress. However, if they receive services only infrequently, such as a visit once a month or a class one day a week for several hours, or if there are frequent interruptions in service, then the program is likely to be inadequate for our most needy children.

The Principle of Professional Training

Quality programs are defined by not only the services delivered but also the staff that delivers them. Working in challenging situations with young children from highly distressed communities requires talent, skills, and commitment that only a *highly trained staff*, the fourth essential, can adequately provide. A substantial body of research bears this out (Bowman, Donovan, & Burns, 2000): Programs that have shown demonstrable, significant, long-term life-changing effects for our most disadvantaged children have all involved professionals, not paraprofessionals or volunteers.

There is no substitute for the knowledge, ability, and commitment that define well-trained staff and professionals. Best-evidence syntheses, for example, have repeatedly shown the benefits of highly qualified teachers (Barnett, 1995). The extent to which these professionals have the knowledge, skills, and abilities to interact with their target population is fundamental to the success of the intervention.

Quick-fix training programs have repeatedly been shown not to work (Halpern, 1994). Rather, we must recognize that nothing less than the most excellent teachers and service providers—caring, competent, flexible, and highly-trained individuals—are needed to benefit our most at-risk children (Hanushek, 2010).

The Coordinated Services Principle

More often than not, families and children with the greatest need for early intervention struggle with persistent health problems, poor nutrition, and a high degree of stress in their lives (Halpern, 1999). Collectively, these problems cannot possibly be solved with isolated fragments of help that focus in one particular area alone (Neuman, 2006a).

Therefore, programs that help to *coordinate a spectrum of services*, the fifth essential, generally produce the most robust effects.

Clearly a leader in establishing comprehensive services, Head Start, from its very inception (Zigler & Styfco, 2004), provided badly needed health, nutrition, and help to families with a variety of concrete problems. In fact, one of its most important contributions has been an emphasis on the "whole child"—recognizing that the health, education, and well-being of young children are integrally connected, and that effective intervention is best accomplished through family and community involvement. Following Head Start's lead, a number of programs have adapted this model, demonstrating powerful, long-term effects on children's development later on.

The Parent–Child Centers (Reynolds, 2000), for example, set in the most impoverished areas of Chicago now for over 30 years, provide skills-based early childhood programs, along with comprehensive services for families, including health and social services, and parent involvement. Community-based programs and health and nutritional specialists are located on site, offering a wide array of programs to support family life.

The essential features of the principle of coordinated services include (1) providing health and developmental screening and monitoring to children; (2) supporting families through direct and indirect services; and (3) connecting family support with a strong educational intervention for children through information and parent education. The extent to which a program treats families with dignity and respect, and is sensitive to their cultural and socioeconomic circumstances, will determine the degree to which services are used and ultimately effective.

Successful programs that have changed the odds for children reach beyond traditional professional boundaries, helping to coordinate health, social services, and education for families that must often deal with tremendous obstacles. These programs recognize that children learn best when they are healthy, safe, and in close and enduring relationships with family, caregivers, and teachers.

The Compensatory Instructional Benefits Principle

In the early years, children rapidly develop the foundational capacities on which their subsequent development builds. In addition to their rapid growth in the linguistic and cognitive domains (Gopnik, Meltzoff, & Kuhl, 1999), they develop critical dispositions for learning—motivation, curiosity, and problem-solving skills. All of these dimensions of development can be seriously compromised by social and economic disadvantage.

Consequently, children who come from disadvantaged circumstances often lack rich opportunities to learn, *not* the ability to learn (Neuman, 2003). A striking disparity between what they know and what they can do means that they need to catch up, and quickly. Interventions that provide *compensatory instructional benefits*, the sixth essential, have greater effects on children's achievement than do interventions with a weaker focus.

In compensatory programs, it is depth, not breadth that matters and makes a significant difference for children's learning. In the Abecedarian (Campbell & Ramey, 1995), an early intervention program, for example, special emphasis is placed on language development and giving caregivers and teachers intensive inservice training in ways to foster sociolinguistic competence in the children. The language program, a regular feature of the entire day, focused on pragmatic features rather than syntax, and emphasized the contingent and interactive features of adult–child language. Four-year-olds were provided individual sessions that focused on prephonics skills twice weekly for 45 weeks.

Compensatory programs include two essential features: (1) Recognizing that children's progress must be accelerated, instruction has to be of higher quality and faster paced than that for more advantaged children; and (2) programs must focus on specific learning goals that make high rates of progress possible. Activities that make up programs must answer the question: How well does this type of experience lend itself to rapid learning for acquiring and processing information? How well does it help children to master the cognitive uses of language: the ability to treat language more flexibly and to master the use of structural words and inflections necessary for the expression and manipulation for establishing logical relationships?

Spending funds on programs that ignore children's significant difficulties in favor of programs that attempt to mimic the same kinds of experiences in which average preschoolers might engage may merely intensify the differences between children in different social classes. Compensatory programs, through their intensity, focus, and accountability, eliminate the miracle cure in favor of data indicating powerful and lasting effects on achievement.

The Accountability Principle

Determining whether or not programs are accomplishing their goals demands *greater accountability*, the seventh and final essential. Programs that monitor progress, provide careful oversight, create clear expectations, and evaluate their effects have shown dramatic results in changing the trajectory from failure to success for disadvantaged children.

Accountability, to some, may have negative connotations, similar to being audited for taxes. However, it is actually in the interest of the program designer. Measures of accountability provide helpful information on the quality of the services (are they occurring with the intensity that was intended?); whether services are being rendered (are they true to their intention?); and whether adjustments are needed to enhance the program's effects (Schorr, 1991). Rather than continue to repeat the mistakes of the past, accountability mechanisms provide a much-needed record for what works under what conditions, building a powerful knowledge base of effective intervention strategies that work for high-risk children and families.

Accountability helps to make the process of teaching and learning a dynamic one, engaging everyone as a community in continuous improvement. It should not be used as a crude evaluation tool for teachers or children. Instead, accountability is designed to improve programs. It is about using data to make better decisions in pursuit of better results, knowing that children's earliest years are precious and cannot be replayed or simply revised.

REFLECTIONS AND NEW DIRECTIONS: WHAT EDUCATIONAL LEADERS AND POLICYMAKERS CAN DO TO IMPROVE CHILDREN'S LIVES

Recent research syntheses (Neuman, 2009; Shonkoff & Phillips, 2000) for economically disadvantaged children, early learning environments, and basic learning strategies provide us with a rich set of clues about what facets of interventions may be critically important to improve children's development. Together, these essentials, representing a rigorous evidentiary base, indicate that high-quality early educational interventions can profoundly affect the developmental outcomes for disadvantaged children and their families. These essentials provide a road map, a set of strategies for policymakers and community leaders to adopt practices that are effective, as well as to generate new programs that may replace those that are not achieving their objectives.

These practical guidelines for enhancing children's daily environments can change the trajectory from *beating the odds* to *changing the odds*, turning highly predictive failure and despair to life-changing success and achievement. Together, they combine the lessons of research and practice to explode the myth that "nothing works." They show what needs to be done—and what can be done—fundamentally to change the odds for economically disadvantaged children.

REFERENCES

Barnett, W. S. (1995). Long-term effects of early childhood programs on cognitive and school outcomes. *The Future of Children, 5,* 25–50.

Bowman, B., Donovan, S., & Burns, M. S. (2000). *Eager to learn: Educating our preschoolers.* Washington, DC: National Academy Press.

Brooks-Gunn, J., McCarton, C., Casey, P., McCormick, M., Bauer, C., Bernbaum, J., et al. (1994). Early intervention in low-birth-weight premature infants: Results through age 5 years from the Infant Health and Development Program. *Journal of the American Medical Association, 272,* 1257–1262.

Bruner, C. (2004). *Many happy returns: Three economic models that make the case for school readiness.* Washington, DC: State Early Childhood Policy Technical Assistance Network.

Campbell, F., & Ramey, C. (1995). Cognitive and school outcomes for high-risk African-American study at middle adolescence: Positive effects for early intervention. *American Educational Research Journal, 32,* 743–772.

Currie, J. (2005). Health disparities and gaps in school readiness. *The Future of Children, 15,* 117–138.

Garber, H. (1988). *The Milwaukee project.* Washington, DC: American Association on Mental Retardation.

Gopnik, A., Meltzoff, A., & Kuhl, P. (1999). *The scientist in the crib.* New York: Morrow.

Gormley, W., Gayer, T., Phillips, D., & Dawson, B. (2005). The effects of universal pre-k on cognitive development. *Developmental Psychology, 41*(6), 872–884.

Gray, S., Ramsey, B., & Klaus, R. (1982). *From 3 to 20.* Baltimore: University Park Press.

Halle, T., Zaslow, M., Tout, K., Starr, R., Wessel, J., & McSwiggan, M. (2010). Beyond how much: What we are learning about structuring effective early childhood professional development. In S. B. Neuman & M. Kamil (Eds.), *Preparing teachers for the early childhood classroom* (pp. 175–188). Baltimore: Brookes.

Halpern, R. (1994). *Rebuilding the inner city: A history of neighborhood initiatives to address poverty in the U.S.* New York: Columbia University Press.

Halpern, R. (1999). *Fragile families: Fragile solutions.* New York: Columbia University Press.

Hanushek, E. (2010). The economic value of higher teacher quality [NBER, Working Paper No. 16606]. Cambridge, MA: National Bureau of Economic Research.

Hauser-Cram, P., Pierson, D., Walker, D., & Tivnan, T. (1991). *Early education in the public schools.* San Francisco: Jossey-Bass.

Karoly, L., Kilburn, M. R., & Cannon, J. (2005). *Early childhood intervention.* Santa Monica, CA: RAND Corporation.

Levenstein, P., Levenstein, S., & Oliver, D. (2002). First grade school readiness of former participants in a South Carolina replication of the Parent–Child Home Program. *Journal of Applied Developmental Psychology, 23,* 331–353.

Love, J., Kisker, E., Ross, C., Schochet, P., Brooks-Gunn, J., Paulsell, D., et al. (2002). *Making a difference in the lives of infants and toddlers and their families: The impacts of Early Head*

Start: Executive summary. Washington, DC: Administration on Children, Youth, and Families, U.S. Department of Health and Human Services.

Lyons, G. R., Fletcher, J., & Barnes, M. (2003). Learning disabilities. In E. J. Mash & R. A. Barley (Eds.), *Child Psychopathology* (pp. 520–587). New York: Guilford Press.

Needlman, R., Klass, P., & Zuckerman, B. (2006). A pediatric approach to early literacy. In D. Dickinson & S. B. Neuman (Eds.), *Handbook of early literacy research* (Vol. II, pp. 333–346). New York: Guilford Press.

Neuman, S. B. (2003). From rhetoric to reality: The case for high-quality compensatory prekindergarten programs. *Phi Delta Kappan, 85,* 286–291.

Neuman, S. B. (2006a). The knowledge gap: Implication for early literacy development. In D. K. Dickinson & S. B. Neuman (Eds.), *Handbook of early literacy research* (pp. 29–40). New York: Guilford Press.

Neuman, S. B. (2006b). N is for nonsensical. *Educational Leadership, 64*(2), 28–31.

Neuman, S. B. (2009). *Changing the odds for children at risk: Seven essential principles of educational programs that break the cycle of poverty.* New York: Teachers College Press.

Olds, D., Kitzman, H., Cole, R., Robinson, J., Sidora, K., Luckey, D., et al. (2004). Effects of nurse home-visiting on maternal life course and child development: Age 6 follow-up results of a randomized trial. *Pediatrics, 114,* 1550–1559.

Olds, D., Robinson, J., Pettit, L., Luckey, D., Holmberg, J., Ng, R., et al. (2004). Effects of home visits by paraprofessionals and by nurses: Age 4 follow-up results of a randomized trial. *Pediatrics, 114,* 1560–1568.

Raikes, H., Green, B., Atwater, J., Kisker, E., Constantine, J., & Chazan-Cohen, R. (2006). Involvement in Early Head Start home visiting services: Demographic predictors and relations to child and parent outcomes. *Early Childhood Research Quarterly, 21,* 2–24.

Ramey, C. T., Campbell, F., Burchinal, M., Skinner, M. L., Gardner, D., & Ramey, S. (2000). Persistent effects of early intervention on high-risk children and their mothers. *Applied Developmental Science, 4,* 2–14.

Reynolds, A. (2000). *Success in early intervention.* Lincoln: University of Nebraska Press.

Reynolds, A., Temple, J., White, B., Ou, S., & Robertson, D. (2011). Age 26 cost–benefit analysis of the Child–Parent Center early education program. *Child Development, 82*(1), 379–404.

Rodriquez, G. (1999). *Raising* nuestros ninos, *bringing up Latino children in a bicultural world.* New York: Simon & Schuster.

Schorr, L. B. (1991). Effective programs for children growing up in concentrated poverty. In A. Huston (Ed.), *Children in poverty* (pp. 260–281). New York: Cambridge University Press.

Schweinhart, L. (2004). *The High/Scope Perry Preschool Study through age 40: Summary, conclusions, and frequently asked questions.* Ypsilanti, MI: High/Scope Educational Research Foundation.

Shonkoff, J., & Phillips, D. (Eds.). (2000). *From neurons to neighborhoods.* Washington, DC: National Academy Press.

Smith, E., Pellin, B., & Agruso, S. (2003). *Bright Beginnings: An effective literacy focused prekindergarten program for educationally disadvantaged four-year-old children.* Arlington, VA: Educational Research Service.

Snow, C., Burns, M. S., & Griffin, P. (1998). *Preventing reading difficulties in young children.* Washington, DC: National Academy Press.

St. Pierre, R., Layzer, J., & Barnes, H. (1995). Two-generation programs: Design, cost, and short-term effectiveness. *The Future of Children, 5,* 76–93.

Weikart, D. P., Bond, J. T., & McNeil, J. T. (1978). *The Ypsilanti Perry Preschool Project.* Ypsilanti, MI: High/Scope.

Zigler, E., & Styfco, S. (Eds.). (2004). *The Head Start debates.* Baltimore: Brookes.

Zigler, E., & Valentine, J. (Eds.). (1979). *Project Head Start: A legacy of the war on poverty.* New York: Macmillan.

CHAPTER 2

EVERY TEACHER LEARNING

Professional Development Design in P–3 Literacy Practice

KATHLEEN A. ROSKOS

Aun aprendo [I am still learning].
—FRANCISCO JOSÉ DE GOYA

In 1998 Carol Vukelich and I coauthored a chapter titled "How Do Practicing Teachers Grow and Learn as Professionals?" (Neuman & Roskos, 1998). It was Chapter 13 at the tail end of a dozen chapters on best practices in early literacy. And that's about where professional development stood in relation to other educational priorities back then—an afterthought. The real work of helping and supporting teachers to provide effective reading instruction for young learners in a new century lay before us. As evidence mounts, pointing to teacher quality as a key factor in student achievement and life success (Chetty, Friedman, & Rockoff, 2011; Stein, Smith, & Silver, 1999; Yoon, Duncan, Lee, Scarloss, & Shapley, 2007), the role of professional development is shifting from afterthought to *first* thought in educational reform initiatives (e.g., No Child Left Behind Act of 2001). At the core of teacher change and the linchpin of standards reform and student achievement, professional development is increasingly viewed as an important intervention for teaching improvement (and maybe even teaching satisfaction), although current economics pose tough challenges. In this chapter I briefly survey the emergence of professional development as an approach to professional learning, then examine the design features of professional development that create conditions for teacher learning, provide an instance (less than perfect) of design in action, and close with a few thoughts on the way forward.

WHAT RESEARCH SAYS ABOUT PROFESSIONAL DEVELOPMENT RISING

The *idea* of professional development in early childhood education is rooted in a far older idea referred to as inservice training. The older term means what it says: training in a specific approach, technique, or material that takes place *after* an individual begins work responsibilities—a broad, simple definition that emphasizes training (skill) over development (potential). Generally inservice training for early childhood educators is conducted outside the workday (e.g., a workshop), and is episodic and singularly focused, with minimal follow through in the actual workplace. It works best when it augments what individuals already know and do well in practice (e.g., classroom management). It works less well when the goal is professional learning to understand complex pedagogies (e.g., response to intervention [RTI]) and adapting instructional strategies to address novel or complex instructional problems, primarily because it is intended to be *short and sweet*, with fingers-crossed that practitioners will transfer the information to their existing practice. By its very design (short, constrained, episodic, detached), inservice training is a limited form of professional development for building early childhood teachers' capacity as knowledgeable, skilled practitioners, although it suffices in rather narrowly defined areas of teaching work, such as "how to" operate an iPad.

Alert to the drawbacks of inservice training as a context for early childhood teacher development and learning, especially in light of increasing demands on teaching that yields high student achievement, teacher education reformers in the late 1990s argued vigorously for a more substantive model of *inservice professional learning* that engaged teachers in (1) studying their own teaching, (2) collaborating with colleagues, (3) learning about their own learning, and (4) participating actively in a learning community (Ball, 1996; Little, 1993; Sykes, 1996). They rested their argument on nearly two decades of research that pointed to a more potent professional development approach for supporting and improving teachers' pedagogy in practice (Hawley & Valli, 1999; Joyce & Showers, 2002). To wit: When *content* is focused on the essential tasks of teaching for student learning (assessment, instruction, environment), *contexts* are job-embedded, collaborative, and collegial, and *learning activities* are authentic (interactive, meaningful, engaging, sustained), professional development has more influence on early childhood teachers' practice, with potential benefits for young students' achievement. Rich, relevant, participatory, challenging and coordinated professional development approaches, in summary, improve conditions for professional learning that promote developmental change.

This core finding at the start of the 21st century gave rise to a new view of professional development, first described in a set of standards from the National Staff Development Council (NSDC; 2009) related to content, context and process, then articulated in a new definition of professional development as "a comprehensive, sustained, and intensive approach to improving teachers' and principals' effectiveness in raising student achievement" (Wei, Darling-Hammond, & Adamson, 2010, p. 4). Quality indicators of content, for example, included clear evidence of equity (reaching all students), quality teaching (using evidence-based techniques) and family involvement (see Wei, Darling-Hammond, Andree, Richardson, & Orphanos, 2009, p. 12, for the complete set of standards and indicators). The new definition identified features of professional development that support teacher learning, such as alignment with state academic standards, quality of professional development providers, frequency of sessions, and job-embedded coaching, among others. In particular, professional learning experiences that are intense and focus on the work of teaching appear to promote teacher growth and change.

A new definition, as we might expect, generated a new, pressing question: To what extent does *comprehensive, sustained, intensive* professional development actually improve educator effectiveness in raising student achievement? So defined, what professional development opportunities are available for teacher learning? Put another way, if teachers are to learn to improve their effectiveness, with the hope of impacting student achievement, what opportunities do they have to do so?

To answer this question, the NSDC (Wei et al., 2009) and the School Redesign Network at Stanford University initiated a three-phase, multiyear research initiative to shed light on the landscape of professional development opportunities that support and nurture teacher learning. Their initial report, *Professional Learning in the Learning Profession: A Status Report on Teacher Development in the United States and Abroad* (Wei et al., 2009), reviewed research on effective professional development, identified effectiveness criteria, and evaluated the current status of professional learning in the United States compared to other countries (*www.nsdc.org/stateproflearning.cfm*). The report produced a yardstick for measuring professional development quality (Table 2.1), and when applied, found that U.S. teachers had fewer opportunities for high-quality professional development supportive of teacher learning compared to their peers in most high-achieving nations. Time was a telltale factor: In most European and Asian countries teachers spend 15–20 hours per week in joint planning, professional exchange, and collegial interaction, whereas U.S. teachers spend 3–5 hours per week planning, usually alone.

The Phase II report, *Professional Development in the United States: Trends and Challenges* (Wei et al., 2010) updated the research base and further catalogued opportunities for effective professional development over the past decade (*www.nsdc.org/stateproflearning.cfm*). It contained good news: States made progress in supporting beginning teachers (nearly 75% participate in induction programs) and providing access to professional development related to one's teaching content. And it contained bad news: U.S. teachers had fewer opportunities to engage in sustained professional development (defined as more than 8 hours) than they had 4 years earlier; they were only half as likely in 2008 (at 16%) to report collaborative efforts in their schools as in 2000 (when 34% did so); and they reported limited time to engage in collaborative work (average 2.7 hours per week). For the most part, the ambitious reach for more robust professional development in schools retracted, perhaps due to the economic downturn, even as research on high-quality professional development advanced. New studies provided scientific evidence of positive effects of grade-level teams on student achievement (Saunders, Goldenburg, & Gallimore, 2009), and correlational evidence of the effects of peer learning (Jackson & Bruegmann, 2009) and literacy coaching (Biancarosa, Bryk, & Dexter, 2010; Walpole, McKenna, Uribe-Zarain, & Lamitina, 2010) on teacher learning influential in student achievement.

The third technical report, *Professional Development in the United States: Case Studies of State Policies and Strategies* (Jaquith, Mindich, Wei, & Darling-Hammond,

---

TABLE 2.1. Criteria for Effective Professional Development

- Extensive opportunities for both formal and informal inservice development
- Time for professional learning and collaboration built into teachers' work hours
- Professional development activities that are embedded in teachers' contexts and ongoing over a period of time
- School governance structures that support the involvement of teachers in decisions regarding curriculum and instructional practice
- Teacher induction programs for new teachers with release time for new teachers and mentor teachers, and formal training for mentors

---

Note. Based on Wei, Darling-Hammond, Andree, Richardson, and Orphanos (2009).

2010), presented case studies of four professionally active states—Colorado, Missouri, New Jersey, and Vermont (*www.nsdc.org/stateproflearning.cfm*). Selected as "pockets of promise," these states had made significant gains on the National Assessment of Educational Progress, scoring above the national average, and demonstrated evidence of high levels of teacher participation in professional development that promotes teacher learning. The case studies revealed that high-quality professional development opportunities are nested in a statewide standards-based framework and infrastructure that supplies policies, strategies, and structures for educators' active engagement in professional learning at local levels. Effective professional development "at home," so to speak, is more likely when sociopolitical conditions "out there" support it (e.g., regional/state reforms and initiatives).

The trilogy of reports commissioned by the NSDC thoroughly documented professional development opportunity to learn in the United States and delivered a wealth of information to guide professional development design. Complete with criteria, facts and exemplars, a new, more sophisticated definition of professional development gained a foothold in the field—one better matched to the demands and rigors of professional teaching than the earlier, simpler (and easier) idea of inservice training.

CATALYZING LEARNING

A new definition of professional development focused new attention on its design. What should professional development for teacher learning look like? While research yields several high-level design principles (see Table 2.2), details of design that *pull teacher development forward to higher levels of performance* are less clear.

In general, the professional literature indicates a stage-growth theory of teachers' developing pedagogical thought, reasoning, and reflective judgment, from lower- to higher-order thinking with experience (Kagan, 1990; King & Kitchener, 1994). Studies of teachers' lesson planning, for example, show that experts have more elaborate cognitions and superior pedagogical reasoning than novices, whose thinking tends to be concrete, lockstep, and incomplete (Borko & Livingston, 1989; Roskos, 1996). Still, what teachers know and do does not tell us how they got to be high quality and expert. We know, in fact, embarrassingly little about how teachers develops expertise across the different phases of their careers (Wilson, Floden, & Ferrini-Mundy, 2001). From a

---

TABLE 2.2. High-Level Design Principles for Effective Professional Development

- Focused on specific curriculum content and pedagogies needed to teach that content effectively
- Offered as a coherent part of a whole-school reform effort, with assessments, standards, and professional development seamlessly linked (to the curriculum)
- Designed to engage teachers in active learning that allows them to make sense of what they learn in meaningful ways
- Presented in an intensive, sustained, and continuous manner over time
- Linked to analysis of teaching and student learning, including the formative use of assessment data
- Supported by coaching, modeling, observation, and feedback
- Connected to teachers' collaborative work in school-based professional learning communities and learning teams

Note. Based on Wei, Darling-Hammond, and Adamson (2010).

design perspective, this is a problem because the conditions that catalyze learning and understanding are uncertain. Professional development that reflects high-level design principles, in short, is no guarantee that teacher learning improves student achievement because it may not afford enough fine-grained opportunities for deliberate practice. Professional development in reading is no exception.

Considering this problem, some propose a dynamic model of teacher learning in which professional knowledge not only increases with experience but also changes qualitatively through interaction within teaching–learning contexts (Dall'Alba & Sandberg, 2006; Snow, Griffin, & Burns, 2005). As teachers learn, their less to more mature forms of knowing *develop* in their teaching, so that they evolve toward more expert problem solving and decision making. So, for example, a beginning teacher may *know that* phoneme awareness is critical in learning to read but not *know how* or *when* to intervene effectively with children who falter, whereas a more knowledgeable teacher *knows that* this is critical, and also *how* and *when* to implement appropriate techniques; however, that teacher may not use this knowledge adaptively or analyze it critically in light of broader educational outcomes.

The effective design of professional development, therefore, is twofold: It must consider not only high-level design principles but also the salient details that make lofty principles endure in teachers' hearts and minds. It must impart/share knowledge *of* practice in ways that develop pedagogical content knowledge *in* practice. The *sharing of* part is easier than the *developing in* part, although two *developing in* structures and strategies look promising:

1. Grade-level teams (mentioned earlier) that focus on student work and use explicit protocols, facilitated by well-prepared leaders and supported by the broader leadership to improve student achievement (Gallimore, Ermeling, Saunders, & Goldenberg, 2009), using *cause–effect reasoning* that over time appears critical in developing teachers' thinking to focus "*on figuring out* an instructional solution that produces a detectable improvement in learning, not just *trying out* a variety of instructional activities or strategies" (p. 544).
2. School-based literacy coaching, with reading-certified coaches who spend enough time with teachers in specific literacy coaching activities and content that predicts K–3 student reading gains (Elish-Piper & L'Allier, 2011); this *differentiated literacy coaching* includes conferencing, assessing, modeling lessons, and observing teachers to meet specific needs that make a difference.

For Instance . . .

A real-world example brings into sharper focus the design challenge that a new definition of professional development presents. My case in point involves an Early Reading First (ERF) project in a large, urban Head Start agency. Its clientele is diverse, as is its staff, bringing to bear a range of educational credentials, from associate degrees to master's degrees in early childhood education. While the basic design of professional development is partially dictated by ERF requirements (Table 2.3), its particulars are pretty much project-specific as described below.

The project designed within the ERF framework is a professional development approach based on an assisted performance model (Ermeling, 2010; Goldenberg, 2004; Tharp & Gallimore, 1988), in which a highly knowledgeable university/agency team assists the learning of literacy coaches, who in turn assist the teaching teams (teacher/

TABLE 2.3. ERF Requirements for Professional Development Design

Design consideration	Design content
Based on scientifically based reading research knowledge of early language and reading development	Research literature
Assist in developing preschool age children's early literacy skills	Alphabet knowledge
	Phonological awareness
	Vocabulary; oral comprehension
	Print knowledge
Provide teacher mentoring	Structured guidance; ongoing support
	Assistance from experts
	Coaching; observation; team teaching; reduced teaching loads (optional)
	Partnerships (optional)

Note. Adapted from *www2.ed.gov/programs/earlyreading/2009-359a.pdf.*

teacher assistant). Structures and strategies for teacher/assistant professional learning were organized around a three-part cycle that occurred monthly each program year over a 3-year period. (See Figure 2.1.)

Whole-group instruction (teachers + assistants) was conducted in monthly, all-day sessions facilitated by the university/agency team and coaches. A variety of instructional formats (e.g., modeling; case studies; small-group problem solving; online activities) were used to teach participants early literacy content, instructional sequences, and techniques. *Small-group instruction* comprised monthly, 1-hour tutorials led by literacy coaches with their respective teacher cohorts (*n* = 4 teachers per coach). These sessions focused on teacher goal setting based on assessment data and observational feedback gathered weekly. *In-class coaching* focused on modeling, gathering assessment information, observing the implementation of teacher goals, and analyzing instruction, with one-to-one follow-through coaching conversations and feedback. In addition, all ERF staff members had free access to specially designed early literacy college coursework outside their job responsibilities. All learning opportunities were grounded in a professional

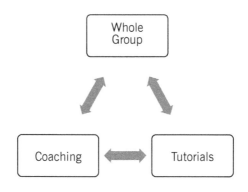

FIGURE 2.1. Three-part cycle.

development curriculum that mapped the professional learning goals, core content, key learning activities, and teacher/teacher assistant assessments over the 3-year period.

So far, so good. The design (on paper) for the most part reflected research-based design principles of professional development in terms of context, content, and process for staff learning. (See Table 2.4.)

However, design (the plan) is one thing; its dynamics (the implementation) are quite another. While the science behind effective professional development designs (e.g., principles, structures, and strategies) has certainly improved, science related to implementing designs lags far behind. Simply put, we know more about what to do, but far less about how to do it.

In a superior review of the literature on implementation (programs, approaches, interventions), Fixsen, Naoom, Blasé, Friedman, and Wallace (2005) describe the importance of (1) a coordinated framework for implementation, (2) a set of core implementation components, and (3) the influential role of sociopolitical external factors in implementation. Effective implementation, they found, is practice-centered and multi-tiered across administrative levels, from boardroom to classroom. Staff selection, staff training/coaching, and facilitative administrative supports are essential components of successful implementation. Similarly, external influences, such as ongoing funding of key activities, agency regulations, and labor relations, must be taken into account and addressed to support and sustain implementation.

Truth be told, the ERF design lacked an appreciation of the complexities of implementation in these critical areas—and, as we might expect, its quality suffered which in turn weakened participants' opportunities for learning. Not that the ERF design once

TABLE 2.4. Evidence of Research-Based Principles

High-level design principle	Evidence
Focused on specific curriculum content and pedagogies needed to teach that content effectively	Curriculum based on scientifically based reading research knowledge of early language and reading development
Offered as a coherent part of a whole school reform effort, with assessments, standards, and professional development seamlessly linked	Assist in developing preschool age children's early literacy skills
Designed to engage teachers in active learning that allows them to make sense of what they learn in meaningful ways	Ongoing opportunities for learning in different formats and through varied activities
Presented in an intensive, sustained, and continuous manner over time	Monthly structure for ongoing professional development activities
Linked to analysis of teaching and student learning, including the formative use of assessment data	Teacher goal setting in tutorial sessions
Supported by coaching, modeling, observation, and feedback	In-classroom coaching that included modeling, observations with feedback, and assistance with assessments
Connected to teachers' collaborative work in school-based professional learning communities and learning teams	Monthly tutorials with colleagues facilitated by a coach

implemented was a failure (it wasn't), but its potential for changing practice was indeed compromised. Here, briefly summarized, are a few reasons why.

Not Practice-Centered Enough

While the design carefully coordinated whole-group, small-group, and coaching professional development content, namely, science-based techniques (e.g., shared book routines), it did not embed enough instruction–practice–feedback loops in training or demand enough in-class coaching to achieve more skilled performance. Too many full-day sessions allocated too many hours to *tell and show* and not enough time to *show, try, and assess* tasks that pressed for the integration of thinking and doing. Why? Preparation and delivery of authentic practice tasks are time-consuming and difficult for professional development providers, requiring an accurate and thoughtful understanding of learning goals; also, participants who don't always want to work that hard on their day out of the classroom tend to resist challenging learning activities. Along these same lines, too much coaching time was squandered on administrative and curriculum matters, and not enough time was devoted to teaching and reinforcing skills, and how to use them flexibly in instruction. Why? The design underestimated the time needed for curriculum redesign to accommodate early literacy instruction in the Head Start classroom and lacked strategies to deal with Head Start regulations that reduced coaching opportunities (e.g., enough time for coach–teacher debriefings).

Knowledge Taken for Granted

The design did not anticipate literacy coaches' learning needs for their role. While all were early childhood educators with experience in early literacy teaching, none held a reading credential that provided in-depth knowledge of reading process, development, assessment, and instruction. As a result, the time allocated to professional development for coaches was heavily weighted to building content knowledge, leaving precious little time for developing coaching skills. At the beginning, coaches often found themselves *just one step ahead* of professional development sessions for staff, and unsure of the key facts, procedures, and concepts of early literacy instruction they needed to explain and unpack. Moreover, the design lacked information to help coaches know what to do and say with confidence in coaching situations with adult learners. Although the monthly tutorial session had a framework for teacher goal setting, it did not provide sufficient guidance in how to differentiate instruction to meet individual teacher needs. Likewise for in-classroom coaching: Modeling, assessing children, and observing activity occurred regularly, but the dynamics of interaction lacked a strategy to ensure ongoing, meaningful learning experiences for staff. Why? There are two practical realities that impact design relevant to coaching, no matter how well conceived. One is the lack of early childhood educators with advanced reading credentials who are willing to accept a coaching position that pays "soft" money; the demand for early literacy coaches with reading knowledge, in short, often outstrips the available pool in a particular region. Another is the genuine lack of evidence-based guidance (structures and strategies) on the functional components of coaching that actually make a difference in teacher learning and lead to better student learning (Fixsen et al., 2005). Coaching to reinforce and support best practices remains an emphasis on form over function (i.e., a focus on structure over process in pulling–pushing teacher professional development forward).

Spheres of Influence Ignored

The design overlooked the pivotal role of supervisors as midlevel managers in the agency organization, thus failing to garner their support as allies for change. This was a major design flaw, lodged in the failure to allocate enough resources (expertise, time, materials) for supervisors' professional development in early literacy assessment and instruction. While the design accommodated biannual meetings with supervisors for purposes of orientation, updates, and assessment reviews, it did not allow for more in-depth regular meetings with project staff where supervisors might acquire content knowledge in early literacy development and curriculum, observe high-quality early literacy instruction, discuss staff needs and issues, and develop strategies to link their roles and responsibilities with ERF program activities (e.g., using common observation protocols). Only toward the end of the program did the ERF leadership actively seek ways to meet more regularly with the supervisors, explain core concepts of early literacy instruction, address curriculum issues (e.g., more time-efficient daily schedules), and plan for sustainability. This was, however, too little too late, even though the supervisors were keenly interested in the ERF program and wanted to know more about how to implement its components at their sites. They were not, in short, resistant, but there simply was not enough time left to prepare them properly for a more active role in promoting staff learning. Why this oversight, when the need to communicate and collaborate with site supervisors seems so obvious? No compelling reason, except perhaps the intense focus on implementing ERF requirements at the classroom level with fidelity, may have led to tunnel vision that was difficult for project leaders to overcome. They had a job to do and only a few years in which to do it; thus, they focused their energies on the near environment of the classroom.

Enough said at this point to reveal the fault lines in the ERF design that threatened its potential for catalyzing learning. Did the professional development design influence classroom practice? It sure did, based on the staff performance data and child outcomes, but not as much as it might have given a "smarter" design implemented in a broader agency environment hospitable to learning, including an informed management team and strong parental involvement.

DESIGNING FROM ABOVE AND BELOW

A basic principle of design is that *form follows function*. Applied to professional development, its approach (form) should afford educator learning that raises student achievement (function). In the case of the ERF design, its form, although worthy, was incomplete, overlooking details of implementation that rendered it less functional for teacher learning. What's the design lesson here?

It is, I think, that the design of professional development for professional learning is harder than we thought; that it requires more planning than we thought; that it involves a design process more complex than we thought. More robust design models are needed to formulate professional development approaches from above, using high-level principles that shape teacher learning, and from below, using structures and strategies that afford deliberate practice *in* practice. This is not unique to the field of education. Medicine also faces an equally wide science-to-service gap, with only 1% of the total medical research budget devoted to learning how to implement therapies safely with patients (Fixsen et al., 2005, p. 74).

In education we might consider, for example, "backward design" (Wiggins & McTighe, 2006) as a framework for organizing the professional development design process and blueprinting the implementation of a more aligned approach. Progressing from Stage 1 (identifying desired results) to Stage 2 (determining acceptable evidence) to Stage 3 (planning experiences and instruction) addresses the critical considerations of professional development (e.g., standards, learning goals) from above and below, yet reduces the complexity of design work. Assisted performance (Ermeling, 2010; Rosemary, Roskos, & Landreth, 2007; Tharp & Gallimore, 1988) is another example, with emphases on (1) developing knowledge of and in practice; (2) creating favorable conditions for learning; and (3) building professional relationships. The design model focuses on establishing a conceptual framework that specifies "terminals of deliberation" for pedagogical growth and change (Dewey, 1964); creating learning networks for coordinating sociopolitical relationships toward desired goals; and implementing robust learning activities that support deliberate practice at evidence-based "terminals" with fidelity across tiers of intervention (district, school, classroom).

REFLECTIONS AND NEW DIRECTIONS

It rests with today's educators to envision and make way for a future in which all early childhood educators have access to high-quality, well-designed professional development in their practice—where all have opportunities to learn and improve, and experience the power and joy of teaching as authentic achievement in service of student learning. Professional development providers need to ask what they can do to "design well, with distinction, refinement and grace" (McLean, 2003, p. 2). And practitioners who participate need to ask what they can do to learn well, with intellectual integrity, courage, and humility, what they can do to remain open to continuous learning.

To address these questions effectively requires more than a roster of professional development activities for implementation. Rather it needs the benefit of laser-like professional attention that carefully articulates the "it" of professional development (e.g., evidence-based literacy programs and practices), determines the effectiveness of designs as actually implemented in districts and schools, obtains independent evaluations of professional development program implementation, and describes the organizational and sociopolitical contexts that afford environments for professional learning.

REFERENCES

Ball, D. (1996). Teacher learning and the mathematics reforms: What we think we know and what we need to learn. *Phi Delta Kappan, 77*(7), 500–508.

Biancarosa, G., Bryk, A., & Dexter, E. (2010). Assessing the value-added effects of literacy collaborative professional development on student learning. *Elementary School Journal, 111*(1), 7–34.

Borko, H., & Livingston, C. (1989). Cognition and improvisation: Differences in mathematics instruction by expert and novice teachers. *American Educational Research Journal, 26*, 473–498.

Chetty, R., Friedman, J. N., & Rockoff, J. E. (2011). *The long-term impacts of teachers: Teacher value-added and student outcomes in adulthood.* Cambridge, MA: National Bureau of Economic Research.

Dall'Alba, G., & Sandberg, J. (2006). Unveiling professional development: A critical review of stage models. *Review of Educational Research, 76*(3), 383–412.

Dewey, J. (1964). *John Dewey on education: Selected writings* (R. D. Archambault, Ed.). New York: Modern Library.

Elish-Piper, L. A., & L'Allier, S. K. (2011). Examining the relationship between literacy coaching and reading gains in grades K–3. *Elementary School Journal, 112*(1), 83–106.

Ermeling, B. (2010). Tracing the effects of teacher inquiry on classroom practice. *Teaching and Teacher Education, 26*(3), 377–388.

Fixsen, D. L., Naoom, S. F., Blasé, K. A., Friedman, R. M., & Wallace, F. (2005). *Implementation research: A synthesis of the literature* (Publication No. 231). Tampa, FL: Louis de la Parte Florida Mental Health Institute.

Gallimore, R., Ermeling, B. A., Saunders, W. M., & Goldenberg, C. (2009). Moving the learning of teaching closer to practice: Teacher education implications of school-based inquiry teams. *Elementary School Journal, 109*(5), 537–553.

Goldenberg, C. (2004). *Successful school change: Creating settings to improve teaching and learning.* New York: Teachers College Press.

Hawley, W., & Valli, L. (1999). The essentials of effective professional development: A new consensus. In L. Darling-Hammond & G. Sykes (Eds.), *Teaching as the learning profession* (pp. 127–150). San Francisco: Jossey-Bass.

Jackson, C. K., & Bruegmann, E. (2009). Teaching students and teaching each other: The importance of peer learning for teachers. *American Economic Journal: Applied Economics, 1*(4), 1–27.

Jaquith, A., Mindich, D., Wei, R. C., & Darling-Hammond, L. (2010). *Teacher professional learning in the United States: Case studies of state policies and strategies.* Oxford, OH: Learning Forward.

Joyce, B., & Showers, B. (2002). *Designing training and peer coaching: Our needs for learning.* Alexandria, VA: ASCD. See also *http://literacy.kent.edu/coaching/information/research/randd-engaged-joyce.pdf.*

Kagan, D. (1990). Teacher cognition. *Review of Educational Research, 60*(3), 419–470.

King, P., & Kitchener, K. (1994). *Developing reflective judgment: Understanding and promoting intellectual growth and critical thinking in adolescents and adults.* San Francisco: Jossey-Bass.

Little, J. W. (1993). Teachers' professional development in a climate of education reform. *Educational Evaluation and Policy Analysis, 15*, 129–152.

McLean, J. (2003, Summer). 20 considerations that help a project run smoothly. Retrieved February 2012, from *www.finehomebuilding.com/how-to/departments/commentary/considerations-that-help-a-project-run-smoothly.aspx.*

Neuman, S. B., & Roskos, K. (Eds.). (1998). *Children achieving: Best practices in early literacy.* Newark, DE: International Reading Association.

No Child Left Behind Act of 2001. Pub. L. No. 107-110, § 115, Stat. 1425 (2002).

Rosemary, C. A., Roskos, K. A., & Landreth, L. K. (2007). *Designing professional development in literacy: A framework for effective instruction.* New York: Guilford Press.

Roskos, K. (1996). When two heads are better than one: Beginning teachers' planning processes in an integrated instruction planning task. *Journal of Teacher Education, 47*(2), 120–129.

Saunders, W. M., Goldenberg, C. N., & Gallimore, R. (2009). Classroom learning: A prospective, quasi-experimental study of Title I schools. *American Education Research Journal, 46*(4), 1006–1033. Retrieved December 1, 2009, from *http://aer.sagepub.com/cgi/content/abstract/46/4/1006.*

Snow, C., Griffin, P., & Burns, M. S. (2005). *Knowledge to support the teaching of reading.* San Francisco: Jossey-Bass.

Stein, M. K., Smith, M. S., & Silver, E. A. (1999). The development of professional developers:

Learning to assist teachers in new settings in new ways. *Harvard Educational Review, 69*(3), 237–269

Sykes, G. (1996). Reform of and as professional development. *Phi Delta Kappan, 77,* 464–467.

Tharp, R., & Gallimore, R. (1988). *Rousing minds to life.* New York: Cambridge University Press.

Walpole, S., McKenna, M. C., Uribe-Zarain, X., & Lamitina, D. (2010). The relationships between coaching and instruction in the primary grades: Evidence from high-poverty schools. *Elementary School Journal, 111*(1), 115–140.

Wei, R. C., Darling-Hammond, L., & Adamson, F. (2010). *Professional development in the United States: Trends and challenges.* Dallas, TX: National Staff Development Council.

Wei, R. C., Darling-Hammond, L., Andree, A., Richardson, N., & Orphanos, S. (2009). *Professional learning in the learning profession: A status report on teacher development in the United States and abroad.* Dallas, TX: National Staff Development Council.

Wiggins, G., & McTighe, J. (2006). *Understanding by design* (2nd ed.). Upper Saddle River, NJ: Pearson.

Wilson, S. M., Floden, R. E., & Ferrini-Mundy, J. (2001). *Teacher preparation research: Current knowledge, gaps, and recommendations* (Executive Summary). Seattle, WA: Center for the Study of Teaching and Policy.

Yoon, K. S., Duncan, T., Lee, S. W.-Y., Scarloss, B., & Shapley, K. (2007). Reviewing the evidence on how teacher professional development affects student achievement (Issues & Answers Report, REL 2007-No. 033). Retrieved January 2012, from *http://ies.ed.gov/ncee/edlabs/regions/southwest/ pdf/REL_2007033.pdf.*

CHAPTER 3

THE PREPARATION
OF EARLY CHILDHOOD TEACHERS

Fundamental Components
of a Teacher Education Program

OLIVIA N. SARACHO

> Every experience is a moving force. Its value can be judged
> only on the ground of what it moves toward and into. . . .
> It is the business of the educators to see in what direction
> and experience it is heading . . . so as to judge and direct it.
> —JOHN DEWEY (1938, p. 39)

When teachers learn how to use instructional knowledge in their classroom practice, they are able to (1) select and sequence instructional strategies, (2) develop children's educational goals, and (3) understand and assume their multifaceted roles in the classroom. For example, teachers assume the role of storyteller when they read or tell a story while the children listen, discuss, and make appropriate responses to teachers' inquiries. They motivate children to predict or sequence events, identify the main ideas, recognize the characters, and describe the setting, as in the following example.

One morning Mrs. Grey and the children are sitting in the library area. She shows the children a big book about a picnic and says, "Today we are going to be reading another big book." She begins reading the big book and the children smile as the teacher continues.

After Mrs. Grey reads the story, she puts on a pair of oversized reading glasses that have a moustache and a large nose attached. The children chuckle. Mrs. Grey continues, "Now, with my looking glasses, I can see so much more. Let me tell you what I see on the cover of the book." Mrs. Grey describes the book's cover in minuet detail and explains that the glasses help her to see all the details. Then she asks, "Who would like to come up and put on the looking glasses and tell me what you see in the first page?" James quickly volunteers. When he puts on the glasses, everyone says, "Turn around so that we can see you." He does, and the children laugh. James describes the first page of the book.

JAMES: I see a mother and a father and a dog and a little boy. They have a picnic basket. Their car is in the picture so maybe they are going to drive to the picnic.

MRS. GREY: What kind of day does it appear to be?

JAMES: It looks like it is warm. They don't have coats on.

James gives the glasses back to Mrs. Grey and sits down. Mrs. Grey begins to read the story. For the first few pages she invites a child to wear the looking glasses and describe what is in the picture. When the family arrives at its picnic and sets up, it begins to get invaded by a number of unwanted guests:

Ten black ants.

Nine red ladybugs.

Eight blue birds.

Seven green caterpillars.

Six yellow butterflies.

Mrs. Grey points to the number words and the color words that many of the children recognize and recite with her. After she finishes reading the book, Mrs. Grey and the children discuss and plan the picnic that they are going to have on Friday in their classroom (Saracho, 2004, p. 204).

In the role of storyteller, the teacher introduces and reads the book to the children. She uses authentic picnic items to teach the children about the picnic and what takes place in a picnic. She also uses the picnic experience to teach or reinforce number concepts.

During the discussion, the teacher encourages children to think, plan, and discuss their picnic event on Friday, and to foresee what might happen that can affect the picnic, such as weather or ants.

A professional teacher has a broad repertoire of classroom behaviors and skills that are grounded in professional and academic knowledge. Teacher education programs need to help teacher candidates develop classroom behaviors and skills in their teaching performance through practice.

WHAT RESEARCH SAYS ABOUT THE PREPARATION OF EARLY CHILDHOOD EDUCATORS

Throughout the United States, implementation of standards-based accountability education reforms, such as the federal government's No Child Left Behind Act of 2001 (NCLB), is generating a new set of challenges in early childhood education (Brown, 2011) to redefine the teachers' profession (Cochran-Smith, 2006) and reform the field of teacher education (Wepner, 2006). The National Association for the Education of Young Children (NAEYC), the world's largest organization of early childhood professionals, is an important leader in this reform. In addition, NAEYC is a constituent member of the National Council for Accreditation of Teacher Education (NCATE), an organization that accredits schools, colleges and departments of education that prepare teachers and other school specialists. In 2009, NAEYC published a position statement titled *Preparing Early Childhood Professionals: NAEYC Standards for Early Childhood Preparation Programs*. Early childhood faculty members and representatives from NCATE and NAEYC Early Childhood Associate Degree Accreditation (ECADA) systems contributed to the development of the NAEYC standards. The position statement provides a continuous foresight to the field of early childhood education, but particularly to the programs that prepare professionals to assume their role as teachers. The NAEYC standards are part of the NCATE accreditation of teacher preparation programs that guide in the initial or advanced teacher licensure. Both accreditation systems use these standards.

Later in 2011 this position statement was revised to respond to new knowledge, research, and situations; at the same time it continues to be faithful to fundamental values and principles of the founders of the profession. Several institutions in the field use the NAEYC position statement to support critical policy structures, including state-approved early childhood teacher education programs and agreements between different levels and kinds of professional development programs (NAEYC, 2009, 2011). Development of teacher education programs is based on NAEYC standards. The purpose of this chapter is to describe the preparation and professional development of effective teachers based on a framework that comprises six components.

TEACHER EDUCATION PROGRAM COMPONENTS

Teacher education programs prepare potential teachers to have the knowledge, skills, and attitudes they need to educate young children. They design learning experiences based on research, theory, and practice. Knowledge of the field of early childhood education derives from an integration of theory, research, and practice. For example, the development of knowledge is initiated through identification of a problem or issue that is investigated through research; this research is based on theory and practice. The outcomes may modify theory and practice, which then guide future research studies (Saracho & Spodek, 2012). Teacher education programs are based on research, theory, ethical considerations, and practice. An early childhood teacher education program has six components: *recruitment and selection, general education, professional foundations, instructional knowledge* (Saracho & Spodek, 2003), *field experiences and clinical practice*, and *program evaluation*. Although most teacher education programs have these components, their content and components of their whole program may vary except for the field experiences and clinical practice component.

Recruitment and Selection

Recruiting and selecting teacher candidates are related means to attract and assess applicants. The worth and nature of early childhood programs are fundamentally contingent upon the quality and character of the teachers who staff them. Recruitment and selection of teacher candidates need to be based on a specific set of criteria. The selection processes in teacher education programs range from open admissions to using a long-term set of standards.

The NCATE (2010), an organization that helps institutions to build high-quality teacher preparation programs, encourages the improvement of candidate selection. It recommends that teacher education programs become more selective and diverse by including in their criteria both test scores and important characteristics of effective teachers. Some teacher preparation programs select teacher candidates based on their grade point average, standardized test scores, written profiles, letters of recommendation, and both individual and group interview performance (Casey & Childs, 2007). However, Clark (2010) shows that grade point average or standardized test scores are not as good at predicting effective teachers as other information, such as providing evidence of leadership, interpersonal, and communication skills. Some researchers (e.g., Da Ros-Voseles & Fowler-Haughey, 2007) suggest other characteristics (e.g., patience, authenticity, a love of learning, perseverance, risk taking, pragmatism). Although these personal characteristics lack support in empirical research, they seem important for effective teaching. Also, the University of Chicago Urban Teacher Education Program requires that selected teacher candidates have "a strong commitment to educational equality to work in underserved urban public schools" (NCATE, 2010, p. 13). Such personal characteristics are frequently based on feelings and beliefs that are difficult to identify. However, Colker (2008) believes that combining these characteristics with both knowledge and skill can create an excellent teacher. Aspiring teachers are able to develop knowledge and skills, but their personal characteristics are embedded in their feelings and beliefs, which cannot be directly observed or assessed. These qualities are considered to be worthwhile, but teacher preparation programs seldom use them in their selection procedures. Collecting information that indicates teacher candidates' personal characteristics is costly, such as interviews and observations. In addition, assessment of these characteristics is subjective in nature and may clearly be disputed by applicants who are rejected.

Criteria for Diverse Candidates

Most 4-year teacher preparation programs select teacher candidates based on their secondary school grades and scores on achievement tests, which can hardly be used to predict success in teaching, and the standard is often modified, especially for several populations. Many times, minority teacher candidates are refused admittance into teacher preparation programs due to their low standardized test scores. This selection criteria are insufficient to identify teacher candidates who will be effective teachers (Bennett, McWhorter, & Kuykendall, 2006) and conflict with the recruitment of minorities into teaching (Goldhaber & Hansen, 2010). Such documented achievement disparity needs to be modified to attract teacher candidates from minority groups. García (1986) proposes that the selection process be modified to guarantee that minority teacher candidates have equal opportunities of being accepted. He recommends that decisions about the selection of teacher candidates should include skills and abilities, such as language and cultural knowledge.

Shortage of Teachers

A shortage of early childhood teachers influences the selection criteria and standards are lowered. Although the admission standards for 2-year associate degree programs are usually less, they typically parallel the admission procedures of 4-year programs. Many 2-year programs use an "open admissions" policy, where all teacher candidates with a high school diploma or an equivalent (e.g., a GED) are admitted. Each program has a certain system of "rolling selection" process, where teacher candidates successfully complete the previous teacher education components before they are admitted into the next level of the program (Saracho & Spodek, 2003).

This position is an important means for offering high-quality education to all students and enhancing school performance. The appearance of standards-based accountability reforms in early childhood education has generated new challenges for the field (Brown, 2011). Since the increase in accountability forces schools to generate high student achievement, most teacher education programs are compelled to graduate teacher candidates who will become highly effective teachers. Government mandates and legislation at both federal and state levels examine not only how teachers are prepared but specifically how teacher candidates are selected into teacher preparation programs. When teacher candidates graduate, they become overwhelmed, which compels teacher preparation program personnel to make critical decisions on the selection of teacher candidates. The selected teacher candidates must be able to manage challenging situations and solve problems that go beyond their preparation. Teacher education programs' selection and acceptance of teacher candidates into their program basically predict and gamble on which candidates will become highly effective teachers *after* they have completed the teacher education program (Clark, 2010). Numerous teacher education programs continue to select early childhood teacher candidates based on a grade point averages and scores on a standardized test. Many challenge the reliability of these indicators in the selection process, but the objectivity of these criteria motivates institutions to use them. Some programs include individual and group interviews to identify early childhood teacher candidates' most important characteristics, such as basic communicative, affective, and leadership skills. Farnsworth, Benson, Peterson, Shaha, and Hudson (2003) indicate that teacher candidates who have these characteristics perform well in a professional program. However, these personal characteristics need further support from empirical research; therefore, only some programs include them.

General Education

General education is useful because it helps practitioners with the required background to make use of a conceptually rich curriculum. Essential concepts from general education coursework are applied to early childhood practice (NAEYC, 2009, 2011). In both 2- and 4-year programs, general education is essential to teacher education. However, 2-year programs use general education for different purposes. The Associate of Arts (AA) degree usually focuses on the arts, humanities, and social sciences; normally, three-fourths of the coursework required is general education. The Associate of Sciences (AS) degree usually requires one-half of the general education coursework, with extensive work in mathematics and science. The Associate in Applied Science (AAS) degree provides preparation for direct employment; therefore, one-third of the coursework is in general education. Many teacher candidates who obtain an AAS degree do not foresee transferring to a 4-year program, but the coursework for these degrees can be transferred (NAEYC, 2009, 2011) to a 4-year institution. "The [A.A.S.] degree programs must be designed to recognize this dual possibility and to encourage students to recognize the long-term career possibilities that continued academic study will create" (American Association of Community Colleges, 1998). General education in both 2- and 4-year programs helps teacher candidates become knowledgeable and well educated.

Teachers need to be well-educated individuals. In teacher candidates' general education, each subject area offers a unique concept, style of thinking, structuring of concepts, and preparation. General education for teacher candidates, including early childhood teachers, is merged with disciplines (e.g., language, social studies, science, communication, humanities, health and physical education, mathematics, biological and physical sciences, social sciences, history, fine arts). Children's literature is a facet of literature as a whole, just as art and music for children are similar to the art and music content areas. A discipline that is comparable to children's literature or children's music requires that teacher candidates have knowledge of the fundamental foundation of literature and music to help them to understand and relate the content they teach to children. The essence of early childhood education is selected from these disciplines in general education because they provide the core of the field's content knowledge. Simply providing a range of separate subject courses is not an adequate general education for early childhood teachers. Knowledge must be integrated and understood to create a broad perspective and should relate to the general conditions of human life (Saracho & Spodek, 2003).

The American Association of Colleges for Teacher Education (1977), in its standards for accreditation of teacher education programs, suggests that "general education should include the studies most widely generalizable. General studies is taught with emphasis upon generalization rather than academic specialization as a primary objective" (p. 4). The process of professional accreditation of schools, colleges, and departments of education guarantees that teachers are well prepared to provide high-quality teaching (NCATE, 2010). In a recent set of standards, NCATE (2008) defines general education as the "theoretical and practical understanding generally expected of a liberally educated person. General education includes developing knowledge related to the arts, communications, history, literature, mathematics, philosophy, sciences, and the social studies, from *multicultural* and *global* perspectives" (p. 87, original emphasis). In relation to young children, the Association for Childhood Education International (ACEI; 1998) states that general education helps teacher candidates to assist young children in exploring and interpreting their world in a way that makes sense to them; therefore, teachers need to acquire a broad and liberal education. General education helps teacher candidates to develop the following:

- An acquaintance with great music, art and literature
- A knowledge of health, safety and nutrition

- An understanding of the physical and biological aspects of the world and the universe
- A knowledge of mathematical concepts
- An ability to articulate one's thoughts orally and in writing
- An ability to read with comprehension, then to analyze, interpret and judge a wide range of written material
- A knowledge of technology as an educational resource, instructional tool and curriculum component
- A comprehension of the variety and complexity of communication patterns as expressed by people of differing cultural and socioeconomic backgrounds in a global context
- A knowledge and understanding of differences and similarities among societies and cultures, both at home and abroad
- An awareness of the social, historical and political forces affecting children and the implications for education within individual nations and world contexts (ACEI, 1998, p. 2).

Recently, technology use has become part of general education. Teacher preparation programs need to include technology in their general education component. McGee and colleagues (2001) believe that teachers need to be computer literate to succeed in their work environment. Lumpkin and Clay (2001) describe basic operations, cultural issues, tools for productivity, communication, and research to find solutions to problems and to make decisions when using technology. Although 99% of full-time, regular public school teachers know how to use computers and the Internet, only one-third of these teachers have the competency to use computers and the Internet for instruction. Therefore, general education needs to provide teacher candidates with technology and instructional technology training (Jones, 2001). Teachers need to learn (1) how to use computers to keep up with the current digital age, and (2) how to motivate children so that both teachers and children use computers expressively and in creative ways. However, they need to focus on the operation or development of new devices. They need to learn to develop a framework that offers social support for learning and new structures at both the micro and macro levels of the educational system (Bers & Kazakoff, 2012).

Professional Foundations

The term *professional foundations* refers to those facets of history, philosophy, sociology, economics, psychology, politics, and anthropology that are the source of education. Linguistics is also recognized as a foundation, especially for multicultural education. Professional foundations relate to the pursuit of knowledge *about* education instead of professional strategies (Peters, 2010). According to the ACEI (1998), teacher preparation programs provide experiences that help to explain the philosophical, historical, psychological, cultural, social, and ethical foundations of early childhood education. Early childhood teacher candidates need to develop a personal philosophy and method of approaching the learning–teaching process based on contemporary research and education theories.

Traditionally, teacher candidates learn instructional strategies from a classroom with experienced practitioners instead of educational theory (Peters, 1977/2010). In their teaching, they use skilled techniques instead of knowledge and understanding. Presently, theory is learned in foundation courses that frequently are miscellaneous points of reference. Such foundation courses can provide teacher candidates a basis for their decisions and actions (Saracho & Spodek, 2003).

Teacher candidates need to have a broad foundation of knowledge. They need to know the history and traditions of early childhood education. It is essential that they know the principles of child growth and development, learning theory, and different contexts such as cultural, social, and political contexts (Saracho & Spodek, 2003). The ACEI (1998) states:

> Teachers of young children should possess a broad synthesis of knowledge of child development principles derived from studying research in the social and behavioral sciences that influence learning (i.e., biology, physiology, psychology, sociology and anthropology). In addition to knowledge of child development theory and research, teachers should study children in a variety of situations to understand better the meaning and degree of variation and exceptionality among individuals. Moreover, techniques for observing and recording such behavior need to be developed in accordance with research and theory. (p. 2)

Child development is a fundamental realm that has earned distinguished recognition in early childhood education because its developmental stages establish young children's learning ability and the selection of developmentally appropriate materials and practices. The NAEYC recommends that *developmentally appropriate practices* be used as a best-practice framework of principles and guidelines for young children's (birth through age 8) *optimal* learning and development (Copple & Bredekamp, 2009). Early childhood teacher candidates need to have comprehensive knowledge of child development to understand the developmental nature within phases of early childhood and the stages that precede and follow each other. They need to be aware of the variance within these developmental patterns, how stages emerge, their predecessors, and the reality that they must combine different developmental domains to recognize and acknowledge the range of children's individual differentiations within their classrooms. Associate degree programs typically provide less content in professional foundation courses, but require child development knowledge in the teacher candidates' field of studies.

Federal NCLB legislation requires that early childhood education programs have "highly qualified teachers." Therefore, teachers of young children need to learn and understand the continuum of the young children's (birth to age 8) development and learning. They need to use this knowledge to develop effective curricula and instruction for young children (Copple & Bredekamp, 2009; NAECTE, 2009). In addition, teacher candidates need to have knowledge of children's cultures and languages as well as the principles that motivate language and language acquisition. Such knowledge is obtained through general education but placed in proper perspective through the professional foundations courses.

Instructional Knowledge

Instructional knowledge is the knowledge that teachers apply in classroom practice, planning, and evaluation. It provides teacher candidates the knowledge to select and sequence strategies and methods of instruction, in addition to developing educational goals for children. Although researchers recognize three areas of teacher knowledge—content-area knowledge, pedagogical content-area knowledge, and general pedagogical knowledge (König, Blömeke, Paine, Schmidt, & Hsieh, 2011), instructional knowledge teaches teacher candidates knowledge of both teaching theories and teaching methods.

Whereas many teacher education programs offer the elements of instructional knowledge in separate courses, others merge this knowledge into integrated courses. Instructional knowledge provides to teacher candidates information on how to (1) organize and prepare instructional plans; (2) assess children and learning; (3) recognize individual differences; (4) become culturally sensitive; (5) understand children; (6) manage educational resources; and (7) establish educational policies and practices (Shulman, 1986). Saracho (1984) uses the classroom environment to understand professional knowledge, and to learn and understand the roles of the teachers.

Instructional knowledge helps teacher candidates in their classroom practice, planning, and assessment. For instructional knowledge, Saracho (1984) identifies six roles teachers assume in a classroom environment:

1. *Curriculum designer* describes how teachers develop their curriculum based on theories and practices of early childhood education and community interests.
2. *Decision maker* describes how the teachers continuously make decisions about children, materials, activities, and goals.
3. *Organizer of instruction* describes how the teachers use educational goals and related available resources to plan long- and short-range classroom experiences.
4. *Manager of learning* describes how the teachers use the learning environment to provide learning experiences based on young children's interests.
5. *Diagnostician* describes how the teachers assess young children's strengths and needs to design appropriate and successful learning experiences for them.
6. *Counselor/advisor* describes how teachers continuously interact, emotionally support, and provide appropriate guidance to young children.

The aforesaid roles identify early childhood teachers' instructional purpose and responsibilities. To function effectively in each role, they need to acquire an extensive range of knowledge, skills, and attitudes to successfully apply the principles and practices of early childhood education in the learning process.

The learning process needs to focus on the role of the teacher as facilitator. All developmental areas (e.g., cognitive, physical, social, emotional, aesthetic, moral, ethical) need to be included. Teacher candidates need to study how learning takes place, factors that influence learning; climates for learning; and modifications based on children's needs (e.g., individual needs, interests, attitudes, motivations). In addition, they need to know curriculum content and instructional strategies that motivate young children to become interested in learning in multiple education contexts as well as use developmentally appropriate practices to teach young children. Teacher preparation programs need to integrate methods that parallel Saracho's (1984) roles for the following:

- Planning that integrates young children's needs and developmental stages with the teacher's education philosophy as well as local, state/province and national mandates
- Selecting and evaluating prepared materials and creating new materials consistent with stated goals and objectives
- Adopting a variety of curriculum models to meet individual as well as group needs
- Creating learning environments that foster creativity, healthy self-concepts and regard for others, and intellectual and physical growth in balanced proportions
- Integrating play, a growth process, as an integral part of a child's intellectual, social/emotional, physical and aesthetic development
- Implementing a program of learning for young children that includes all curriculum areas such as language (oral and written, literature, reading), mathematics, use of technology, science (physical, life, earth and space, science and technology), social studies (geographical, political, historical, economical, cultural, anthropological), performing and visual arts (music, dance, theater, art, film) and physical education

- Recognizing the potential and need to integrate content across the curriculum, where appropriate, in varied education contexts
- Developing classroom management and guidance techniques for children
- Implementing appropriate roles for teachers, parents and peers in social contexts to encourage responsible social development
- Recognizing and responding to families (traditional and diversified) in school/parent/community relationships that involve them in the educational process
- Assessing and evaluating children's total development (intellectual, social/emotional, aesthetic, physical) using authentic, performance-based assessment
- Working with paraprofessionals and community organizations
- Developing leadership ability for appropriate contexts (ACEI, 1998, p. 3).

In addition, teacher candidates, similar to practicing teachers, may misjudge the realities of their own classroom behaviors, which can generate conflict between their assumed beliefs and their actual practice. Distinguishing between the realities of teachers' experiences and their supposed impressions of themselves is essential to assist teacher preparation programs to acquire insight about the nature of teaching and the roles of teachers (Ben-Peretz, 2001).

Field Experiences and Clinical Practice

Teacher preparation programs need to move away from a norm that focuses on academic preparation and coursework that is barely related to school-based experiences. Instead, they need to shift to programs based more intensively in field experiences and clinical practice, and intertwined with academic content and professional courses. Such a challenging clinically based approach provides different and wide-ranging opportunities for teacher candidates to associate and implement the knowledge they obtain in courses while being guided by knowledgeable and skilled clinical educators. Teacher candidates are able to merge practitioner knowledge with academic knowledge as they learn by doing. In addition, they improve their practice when they attain new knowledge and information about their students' learning (NCATE, 2010).

Field experiences and clinical practice are important in an early childhood teacher preparation program. They include collaboration, accountability, and an environment and practices related to professional learning. Field experiences correspond to a mixture of early and ongoing school-based opportunities where teacher candidates observe, help, tutor, instruct, engage in service learning projects, or conduct applied research. Clinical practice comprises student teaching and internships that offer teacher candidates experiences that permit them to immerse themselves completely in the learning community, providing candidates the opportunity to demonstrate proficiencies in the professional roles for which they are preparing. In clinical practice, teacher candidates also interact with the children's families and communities in ways that reinforce their learning. In addition, clinical practice encourages teacher candidates to learn to use information on technology in teaching, learning, and other professional duties (NCATE, 2008). According to NAEYC (2011), field experiences and clinical practice include field observations, fieldwork, practica, student teaching, and other "clinical" practice experiences, including home visiting. A designed series of these experiences helps teacher candidates develop understanding, competence, and dispositions in a specialized area of practice. In addition, they learn the knowledge, skills, and professional dispositions that are essential in promoting the young children's development and learning across the complete developmental period of early childhood in at least two of the three early childhood age groups (birth to age 3, ages 3 to 5, ages 5 to 8) *and* in different early childhood education settings (e.g., primary school grades, child care centers and homes, Head Start programs).

The NCATE Blue Ribbon Panel report (NCATE, 2010) showed that clinical preparation is inadequately defined and ineffectually supported. The Panel recommended 10 key principles in planning effective, clinically based preparation programs:

1. Student learning is the focus.
2. Clinical preparation is integrated throughout every facet of teacher education in a dynamic way.
3. A candidate's progress and the elements of a preparation program are continuously judged on the basis of data.
4. Programs prepare teachers to become an expert in content and how to teach it, and also innovators, collaborators, and problem solvers.
5. Candidates learn in an interactive professional community.
6. Clinical educators and coaches are rigorously selected and prepared, and drawn from both higher education and the prekindergarten to 12th-grade (P–12) sector.
7. Specific sites are designated and funded to support embedded clinical preparation.
8. Technology applications foster high-impact preparation.
9. A powerful research and development (R&D) agenda, and systematic gathering and use of data support continuous improvement in teacher preparation.
10. Strategic partnerships are imperative for powerful clinical preparation.

The National Research Council (2010) asserts that improving the clinical practice of educators can improve P–12 learning and achievement. It recognizes clinical preparation (or field experience) as one of the three "aspects of teacher preparation that are likely to have the highest potential for effects on outcomes for students, along with content knowledge and the quality of teacher candidates" (p. 180). The NCATE (2010) cites studies that indicate how teachers benefit from preparation programs that offer well-supervised field and clinical experiences (equivalent to medical school internships) that are compatible with candidates' ultimate teaching experience and include a culmination assignment, which usually is a portfolio indicating teacher candidates' development of practice and evidence of their students' learning. They also report studies of professional development schools and urban teacher residencies that indicate higher retention rates and greater teacher efficacy of new teachers prepared in these rigorous clinically based programs. Research on teacher effectiveness that examines the relationship of particular instructional practices and students' achievement supports the importance of clinical preparation (NCATE, 2010).

The NCATE (2010) calls for an improved selection of field placements. It recommends that states and the federal government offer opportunities for teacher candidates to work in hard-to-staff schools, such as the ones from the American Association for Medical Colleges, in which medical school graduates are assigned to teaching hospitals for internships and residencies. NCATE requests that clinical internships occur in structured school settings that have staff members who support teacher learning and student achievement. In addition, NCATE recommends that states and school districts request that effective practitioners, coaches, and clinical faculty supervise and mentor teacher candidates. Clinical faculty from higher education and the P–12 area need to contribute to the decision on whether teacher candidates are ready to enter the classroom on the basis of their own performance and their students' outcomes.

The Professional Development School movement identifies and collaborates with high-quality field placements in which teacher candidates develop or refine their skills with competent mentorship and supervision. This movement is supported by the National Network for Educational Renewal (NNER), which is dedicated to the concurrent renewal of P–12 and teacher education. NNER's founding principles were developed by John Goodlad and his colleagues. According to Goodlad, "School university partnerships in general and partner schools specifically are the essential vehicles through which we may bring about simultaneous renewal" (NNER, 2010).

Many teacher education programs are consciously offering clinical field experiences in high-need/low-resource schools. If the field placement is chosen for other purposes, the quality of the site may be unimportant. The most important criterion in this selection is the quality of the candidates' opportunities to learn and practice rather than the quality of the site itself. The study by Huang, Invernizzi, and Drake (2012) indicates that pre-kindergarten programs have a differential impact that continues over time. This impact includes children who are at risk, children from different ethnic groups (e.g., black and Hispanic), and children with disabilities. Therefore, at least one site in a diverse urban setting is required (NAEYC, 2009, 2011). Supplementary exemplar field placements can help to reach the goal of preparing well-educated and socialized new teachers. Bullough and colleagues (2002) state, "Recognizing the powerful influence school context plays on beginning teacher development. Better schools create better teachers and better teacher education" (p. 68).

Program Evaluation

Program evaluation is a critical element in any teacher education program because it offers tools to evaluate and improve the program. Evaluating a program is an effective way to develop more teachable learning environments to help all students and their teachers to improve their performance in several educational contexts. Program evaluation focuses on effectiveness to improve children's education. Although evaluation is essential for the effectiveness of a program, the approach, design, and methods may differ significantly based on the program (Koga & Hall, 2010). Assessment of design and experiences needs to be integrated into pedagogy through numerous stages that challenge teacher candidates' thinking, self-awareness, personalization, ownership, and self-generated feelings of responsibility. Norsworthy (2010) recommends that teacher education programs have well-designed assessment tasks that are natural elements of the program's pedagogy.

During the last two decades, teacher education programs have initiated several forms of teacher assessment, usually referred to as "performance assessment." This new assessment focuses on the formative function of assessment, in which outcomes help teachers to continue their professional development. These perceptions of teaching have led to new assessment methodologies that include teachers' work samples and organized teacher portfolios, explicitly video portfolios. In this new assessment that concentrates on collecting and judging evidence, teachers carefully select samples of instructional activities from one of their curricular units. This assessment also uses open-ended and complex tasks in a variety of contexts. The different types of evidence refer to the same set of instructional situations that purposely set out to achieve specified learning objectives. Assessors evaluate teachers' performance based on the following design principles of teacher performance assessments (Bakker et al., 2011).

- Criteria and performance levels integrate theoretical and practice-based perspectives on competent teaching.
- Criteria and performance levels describe critical facets of professional performance in relation to what professional teachers need to know and be able to do.
- Criteria and performance levels accepts any teaching style.
- Multiple approaches are used for the various teaching components.
- The assessment is conducted in a context that is similar to the real teaching context.
- Assessment assignments relate to the complexity of teaching.
- The scoring method is systematic and clear.

Video portfolios are based on the principles that can be scored. In addition to the video portfolios, interviews that are conducted examine teachers' experiences in scoring and judging the video portfolios.

Pragmatically, all assessment procedures have advantages and disadvantages. Nonstandardized assessments (e.g., work sampling) provide more flexibility and detailed information, but the absence of standardized scoring protocols creates problems, and it is impossible to make comparisons. Standardized assessments make it easy to compare children, classrooms, and programs, although they frequently do not offer real-time, detailed information. In addition, several assessors (e.g., teachers vs. independent or external assessors) may be effective based on both the method of the assessment and the stakes. It makes little sense to have external assessors administer work sampling assessments or make observations when they are unaware of the situations. Similarly, when teachers administer standardized assessments in high-stakes settings, their lack of objectivity may prejudice any decisions based on the assessment results (Waterman, McDermott, Fantuzzo, & Gadsden, 2012).

Educational evaluation studies need to focus on practice, to search for new procedures to identify issues, and to consider influences of outside policies and procedures. For example, the medical field concentrates on (1) understanding the success of particular medical treatments and procedures (i.e., methods in evaluation), (2) the importance of several doctor–patient interactions, and (3) the impact of pharmaceutical marketing of the doctors' prescription practices (i.e., political context). Thus, research on medical practice informs medical practitioners, develops new guidelines, and guides forthcoming medical training. Educational evaluations that parallel medical evaluations can be used to develop training and educational programs (Azzam & Szanyi, 2011). In addition, evaluation results provide evidence that help determine the success of an educational program (Hashimoto, Pillay, & Hudson, 2010; Saracho & Spodek, 2003; Scriven, 2007; Stake, 2004a, 2004b; Wiliam, 2011). Such evaluations focus on the need to assess the merit, worth, and value of a program or a project.

Program evaluation uses information to determine the program's worth, practicality, and effectiveness. The *worth* of a program refers to both fundamental values of the program and the evaluator's values. The program's practical characteristics can be determined through observations when activities correspond to the program's goals. The program's effectiveness is established through evidence obtained from the results.

Evidence-based policy has become a catch phrase and is rapidly expanding throughout the world. The evidence-based movement is derived from experimental methods that encourage the broader treatment of randomized controlled trials and methodological thoroughness. However, a growing discomfort has emerged because many consider this procedure to be the norm. Qualitative methods and more descriptive types of research are acknowledged as an appropriate alternative method (Abma, 2005). The evaluation literature sometimes focuses its attention on the methodological competence of particular evaluations or evaluation elements; sometimes it points to specific links related to the field's professional standards, whereas at other times the networks are implicit. Evaluators and stakeholders select the methodologies and make decisions that affect the quality and use of the information that is gathered and reported. In certain instances, authors harshly criticize these choices. Evaluators conduct systematic, data-based inquiries. They are responsible for designing and conducting evaluations that are technically sensible and effectively concentrate on the evaluation questions guiding the project (Morris, 2011).

The interpretive issue is preferred in the assessment process or system. The evaluation needs to include detailed descriptions of the evaluation design and methodology in the responses and descriptions that help to identify trends in the educational program. This process requires the use of a mixed-methods design that concomitantly uses both qualitative and quantitative measures to indicate the validity of program outcomes. Evaluators who use experimental designs usually have a contingency plan in case that there are problems with their design (Azzam & Szanyi, 2011).

An evaluation needs to take advantage of the resources used in its processes. Its stakeholders need to be actively present in defining the evaluation scope (before), conducting the evaluation (during), and exploring its results (after). This claim is completely grounded in Patton's (2011) ``intended uses by intended users'' perspective, which is supported by Stake's (2004a, 2004b) proposed richness of the evaluation environment. Both Patton and Stake believe that the inclusion of the intended users helps to frame a better purpose of the evaluation because it sets the stage for better evaluation questions and evidence-related processes. This suggests that those involved in the program are able to acquire knowledge about its worth and effectiveness. Cornachione, Trombetta, and Nova (2010) suggest that two theoretical evaluation methods be used to improve the evaluation design. Combining both Patton's instrumental concept (involvement and utility) and Stake's contextual point of view (aiming at a more in-depth program quality representation, responsive in nature) enhances the evaluation and its results.

Responsive evaluation concentrates on a program's experiences instead of its purposes. It identifies what people do naturally. Observations and responses are the foremost ways of gathering data. The evaluator records individuals' perceptions and values, inspects records, and presents a report formally or informally, orally or in writing, and in different forms (e.g., brief narratives, portrayals, product displays, graphs) depending on the needs of the audience.

The evaluator's most important responsibility is to use several ways of sharing enough information about the program to help others have a basis for making decisions. The evaluator's role is to share information on the worth of the program rather than to judge how the program needs to be changed. The evaluator needs to avoid making judgments about the program because of a lack of knowledge concerning the program's operation or the consequences of the decisions. Besides, if an evaluator takes on the role of judge, the accessibility of information may diminish (Stake, 1974, 1976). The evaluators' most important function is to present to those in the program enough information that they can use as a source for making decisions about the program. Guba and Lincoln (2004) recommend the use of running notes, field experience logs, chronologies, context maps, taxonomies or category systems, observation schedules, sociometries, panels, and debriefing questionnaires. Many strategies are suggested, but to be able to conduct a thorough evaluation the evaluator has the freedom to develop different means to record any type of information.

RESEARCH INTO PRACTICE

Research has a vital role. Teacher education programs can examine the variation within and across the continuum, including relationships between studies that (1) investigate teachers instead of programs to understand how the programs interact with other programs and teacher contexts; (2) chart the teachers' theoretical and empirical learning through programs and across specific amalgamations of programs; (3) explain the disparity within a program, such as examining the way a program is not (necessarily) massive; and (4) assess the strength of the different theories that currently are used to guide teacher development opportunities. Systems need to focus on teacher quality and its relationship to teacher preparation and professional development. Many advocate the construction of a system of support that promotes teacher quality for both individuals and the entire profession. Wilson, Rozelle, and Mikeska (2011) believe that to advance toward national standards and curriculum for teacher learning opportunities, when asked, "What do we now know about how and when and under what conditions teachers at different stages of their careers learn?" a proper response requires thoughtful research and sound metrics that focus on building a system that is rational and influential.

REFLECTIONS AND NEW DIRECTIONS

Teacher education programs make difficult decisions in designing curriculum, clinical experiences, and assessment systems to prepare teachers to work across the full spectrum with children in the age range from birth to age 8. It is also problematic when state classifications of the early childhood age span and its subdivisions differ to a great extent and are modified with frequency. Even programs that focus on the upper end of the age range may inefficiently prepare teacher candidates in the critical content or subject (e.g., literacy) matter areas that young children need for academic success. In addition, teacher education programs offer insufficient consideration of children's critical early years, particularly from birth to age 3. Teachers who work in infant/toddler care and lack preparation with this age group may be unable to promote children's learning and development. They may have learned only curriculum and teaching strategies for older children (NAEYC, 2009). Evidence on the effectiveness of an early childhood teacher education program can be obtained through research evaluation studies.

PROFESSIONAL DEVELOPMENT ACTIVITIES

Teacher preparation programs provide teacher candidates with basic knowledge. Beginning teachers need to increase their knowledge in several areas (e.g., discipline, classroom management techniques, curriculum, organized learning centers, early literacy, language development). Professional development at any level is a long-range activity that continues throughout the teacher's entire career; therefore, professional development is essential. Various schools offer the following professional development activities to help teachers expand their knowledge and skills:

- Help teachers organize their own in-service training programs;
- Help teachers attend conferences and receive publications developed by professional organizations;

- Cooperate with other schools or other school systems to create professional development activities; and/or
- Support teachers who enroll in college or university courses. (Spodek & Saracho, 1994, p. 370)

Teachers are ultimately responsible for their own professional development. They use their own resources to

- Participate in the inservice training that is available to them;
- Continue their formal education through university programs;
- Become involved in professional organizations, and/or
- Independently seek the range of educational resources available (Spodek & Saracho, 1994, p. 370).
- Participate in inservice programs that support the teachers' professional development such as in-service meetings, teacher-directed inservice programs, teacher study groups, observing other teachers, mentoring and networking, using technology, and college/university courses.
- Engage in action research.

In addition to the above, teachers can engage in professional development in many ways. Teachers can improve the quality of their teaching through staff meetings, listening to invited speakers, viewing films, or participating in workshops. Several schools support the teachers' attendance to community workshops, conferences (local, regional, and national), and college/university courses to encourage their professional development. Teachers can also exchange ideas such as share with each other craft activities, songs, or action plays. They can use their own experience and their fellow teachers' experiences in their learning. Early childhood education is continuously changing. Early childhood teachers have the responsibility to keep up-to-date to continue their professional development throughout their teaching career. Therefore, it is essential that teachers have knowledge about the current literature, information sources, major organizations and agencies, and the dissemination systems in the early childhood education field (Spodek & Saracho, 1994).

REFERENCES

Abma, T. A. (2005). Responsive evaluation: Its meaning and special contribution to health promotion. *Evaluation and Program Planning, 28*, 279–289.

American Association of Colleges for Teacher Education. (1977). *Standards and evaluative criteria for the accreditation of teacher education: A draft of the proposed new standards with study guide*. Washington, DC: Author.

American Association of Community Colleges. (1998). *AACC position statement on the Associate degree*. Retrieved from *www.aacc.nche.edu/about/positions/pages/ps08011998.aspx*.

Association for Childhood Education International (ACEI). (1998). *Preparation of early childhood education teachers ACEI position paper*. Olney, MD: Author.

Azzam, T., & Szanyi, M. (2011). Designing evaluations: A study examining preferred evaluation designs of educational evaluators. *Studies in Educational Evaluation, 37*(2/3), 134–143.

Bakker, M. E. J., Roelofs, E. C., Beijaard, D., Sanders, P. F., Tigelaar, D. E. H., & Verloop, N. (2011). Video portfolios: The development and usefulness of a teacher assessment procedure. *Studies in Educational Evaluation, 37*(2/3), 123–133.

Bennett, C., McWhorter, L., & Kuykendall, J. (2006). Will I ever teach?: Latino and African American students' perspectives on Praxis I. *American Educational Research Association Journal, 43*(3), 531–575.

Ben-Peretz, M. (2001). The impossible role of teacher educators in a changing world. *Journal of Teacher Education, 52*(1), 48–56.

Bers, M. U., & Kazakoff, E. R. (2012). Techno-tykes: Digital technologies in early childhood. In O. N. Saracho & B. Spodek (Eds.), *Handbook of research on the education of young children* (3rd ed., pp. 197–205). New York: Routledge.

Brown, C. (2011). Searching for the norm in a system of absolutes: A case study of standards-based accountability reform in pre-kindergarten. *Early Education and Development, 22*(1), 151–177.

Bullough, R. B. Jr., Young, J., Erickson, L., Birrell, J. R., Clark, D. C., Egan, M. W., et al. (2002). Rethinking field experience: Partnership teaching versus single-placement teaching. *Journal of Teacher Education, 53*(1), 68–80.

Casey, C. E., & Childs, R. (2007). Teacher education program admissions criteria and what beginning teachers need to know to be successful teachers. *Canadian Journal of Educational Administration and Policy, 67*, 1–18.

Clark, S. (2010). *Putting it to the test: Examining the use of standardized test scores to select teacher candidates into preparation programs.* Presented at the First Biannual Conference of the World Federation of Associations for Teacher Education on Teacher Education in a Global Context: Challenges and Opportunities, Chicago, IL. Retrieved from *www.wfate. org/papers/teacher_candidate_selection_criteria.pdf.*

Cochran-Smith, M. (2006). *Policy, practice, and politics in teacher education.* Thousand Oaks, CA: Corwin Press.

Colker, L. J. (2008). Twelve characteristics of effective early childhood teachers. *Young Children, 63*(2), 68–73.

Copple, C., & Bredekamp, S. (Eds.). (2009). *Developmentally appropriate practices in early childhood programs.* Washington, DC: National Association for the Education of Young Children.

Cornachione, E. B., Jr., Trombetta, M. R., & Nova, S. P. C. (2010). Evaluation use and involvement of internal stakeholders: The case of a new non-degree online program in Brazil. *Studies in Educational Evaluation, 36*, 69–81.

Da Ros-Voseles, D., & Fowler-Haughey, S. (2007). The role of dispositions in the education of future teachers. *Young Children, 62*(5), 90–98.

Dewey, J. (1938). *Experience and education.* New York: Collier Books.

Farnsworth, B. J., Benson, L. F., Peterson, N. L., Shaha, S. H., & Hudson, L. A. (2003). Selecting the best teacher candidates: Can a group interview help? *Education, 124*, 341–360.

García, P. A. (1986). The impact of national testing on ethnic minorities: With proposed solutions. *Journal of Negro Education, 55*(3) 347–357.

Goldhaber, D., & Hansen, M. (2010). Race, gender, and teacher testing: How objective a tool is teacher licensure testing? *American Educational Research Journal, 47*(1), 218–251.

Guba, E., & Lincoln, Y. (2004). The roots of fourth generation evaluation: Theoretical and methodological origins. In M. Alkin (Ed.), *Evaluation roots: Tracing theorists' views and influences* (pp. 225–241). Thousand Oaks, CA: Sage.

Hashimoto, K., Pillay, H., & Hudson, P. (2010). An evaluation framework for sustaining the impact of educational development. *Studies in Educational Evaluation, 36*(3), 101–110.

Huang, F. L., Invernizzi, M. A., & Drake, E. A. (2012). The differential effects of preschool: Evidence from Virginia. *Early Childhood Research Quarterly, 27*(1), 33–45.

Jones, C. A. (2001). Tech support: Preparing teachers to use technology. *Principal Leadership, 9*, 35–39.

Koga, N., & Hall, T. (2010, October 25). *Curriculum modification* (National Center on Accessing the General Curriculum, National Center on Accessible Instructional Materials). Wakefield, MA: Cast, Inc. Retrieved from *http://aim.cast.org/learn/historyarchive/backgroundpapers/ curriculum_modification.*

König, J., Blömeke, S., Paine, L., Schmidt, W. H., & Hsieh, F. (2011). General pedagogical knowledge of future middle school teachers: On the complex ecology of teacher education in the United States, Germany, and Taiwan. *Journal of Teacher Education, 62*(2), 188–201.

Lumpkin, A., & Clay, M. N. (2001). A college of education's technology journal: From neophyte to national leader. *Action in Teacher Education, 23*(3), 20–26.

McGee, C. D., Wavering, M. J., Imbeau, M. B., Sullivan, E. P., Morrow, L. R., Lefever-Davis, S., et al. (2001). ATE distinguished programs in teacher education award 2001: Preparing scholar-practitioners in the 21st century. *Action in Teacher Education, 23*(3), 5–15.

Morris, M. (2011). The good, the bad, and the evaluator: 25 years of AJE ethics. *American Journal of Evaluation, 32*(1), 134–151.

National Association of Early Childhood Teacher Educators. (2009). Position statement on early childhood certification for teachers of children 8 years old and younger in public school settings. *Journal of Early Childhood Teacher Education, 30*(2), 188–191.

National Association for the Education of Young Children (NAEYC). (2009). *NAEYC Standards for early childhood professional preparation programs: A position statement of the National Association for the Education of Young Children.* Washington, DC: Author.

National Association for the Education of Young Children (NAEYC). (2011). *2010 NAEYC Standards for initial and advanced early childhood professional preparation programs: Associate, baccalaureate and graduate degree programs.* Washington, DC: Author.

National Council for Accreditation of Teacher Education (NCATE). (2008). *Professional standards for the accreditation of teacher preparation institutions.* Washington, DC: Author.

National Council for Accreditation of Teacher Education (NCATE). (2010). *Transforming teacher education through clinical practice: A national strategy to prepare effective teachers.* Washington, DC: Author.

National Network for Educational Renewal. (2010). Overview. Retrieved from *www.nnerpartnerships.org/about/overview.html.*

National Research Council. (2010). *Preparing teachers: Building evidence for sound policy.* Washington, DC: National Academies Press.

Norsworthy, B. (2010). *Assessment as pedagogy: A means not an end.* Presented at the First Biannual Conference of the World Federation of Associations for Teacher Education on Teacher Education in a Global Context: Challenges and Opportunities, Chicago, IL. Retrieved from *www.wfate.org/papers/assessment_as_pedagogy.pdf.*

Patton, M. Q. (2011). *Developmental evaluation: Applying complexity concepts to enhance innovation and use.* New York: Guilford Press.

Peters, R. S. (2010). *Education and the education of teachers.* New York: Taylor & Francis. (Original work published 1977)

Saracho, O. N. (1984). Perception of the teaching process in early childhood education through role analysis. *Journal of the Association for the Study of Perception, International, 19*(1), 26–29.

Saracho, O. N. (2004). Supporting literacy-related play: Roles for teachers of young children. *Early Childhood Education Journal, 31*(3), 203–208.

Saracho, O. N., & Spodek, B. (2003). The preparation of teachers for the profession in early childhood education. In O. N. Saracho & B. Spodek (Eds.), *Studying teachers in early childhood settings* (Vol. 4, pp. 1–28). Greenwich, CT: Information Age.

Saracho, O. N., & Spodek, B. (2012). Introduction: A contemporary researcher's *vade mecum (redux).* In B. Spodek & O. N. Saracho (Eds.), *Handbook of research on the education of young children* (3rd ed., pp. 1–15). New York: Routledge.

Scriven, M. (2007). Key evaluation checklist (KEC). Retrieved from *www.wmich.edu/evalctr/archive_checklists/kec_feb07.pdf.*

Shulman, L. S. (1986). Those who understand: Knowledge growth in teaching. *Educational Researcher, 15*(2), 4–14.

Spodek, B., & Saracho, O. N. (1994). *Dealing with individual differences in the early childhood classroom.* New York: Longman.

Stake, R. E. (1974). *SAFARI project: SAFARI, innovation, evaluation, research and the problem of control: Some interim papers.* Norwich, UK: Center for Applied Research in Education, University of East Anglia.

Stake, R. E. (1976). *Evaluating educational programmes: The need and the response.* Paris: Organisation for Economic Cooperation and Development.

Stake, R. E. (2004a). Stake and responsive evaluation. In M. C. Alkin (Ed.), *Evaluation roots: Tracing theorists' views and influences* (pp. 203–217). Thousand Oaks, CA: Sage.

Stake, R. E. (2004b). *Standards-based and responsive evaluation.* Thousand Oaks, CA: Sage.

Waterman, C., McDermott, P. A., Fantuzzo, J. E., & Gadsden, V. L. (2012). The matter of assessor variance in early childhood education—or whose score is it anyway? *Early Childhood Research Quarterly, 27,* 46–54.

Wepner, S. B. (2006). Teaching gone amok: Leave no teacher candidate behind. *Teacher Education Quarterly, 33,* 135–149.

Wiliam, W. (2011). What is assessment for learning? *Studies in Educational Evaluation, 37*(1), 3–14.

Wilson, S. M., Rozelle, J. J., & Mikeska, J. M. (2011). Cacophony or embarrassment of riches: Building a system of support for quality teaching. *Journal of Teacher Education, 62*(4) 383–394.

CHAPTER 4

INVOLVING PARENTS
AND COMMUNITY MEMBERS
Coming Together for Children

DOUGLAS R. POWELL

In a goal-setting meeting at the beginning of the school year, the director and teachers of the Shady Grove early childhood program agreed to work on improving parent and community involvement. Several weeks after the meeting, the director distributed a survey to all parents, asking for suggestions on how the program could strengthen communications with parents, opportunities for involvement at the center, and supports for families. About 70% of parents returned the anonymous survey. A small number of parents indicated they were pleased with current arrangements and offered no suggestions. Most parents offered one or more suggestions. Many parents wanted more frequent communication about their child's experiences and progress in the program, with one parent indicating she felt like she was "bothering my child's teacher when I ask how my child is doing." Some parents expressed a concern that teachers didn't always seem interested in talking or hearing a parent's ideas. Other parents indicated they'd like to help out in the program but did not have time for an ongoing time commitment. Still others asked for a workshop or group discussion on topics such as kindergarten readiness. During a monthly staff meeting devoted to discussion of parents' survey responses, the Shady Grove program director and teachers considered ways to act on many of the suggestions. One teacher said, "Maybe we need to reflect on the word *our* when we say 'our classroom' or 'our program.' Who does *our* include?" Another teacher expressed concern about the 30% of parents who did not respond to the survey. "Do they not care? Are they too busy to respond? Are there cultural misunderstandings? How do we reach out?"

This vignette illustrates important steps toward improved opportunities for parent involvement in children's learning. The Shady Grove early childhood program established a goal of improving parent involvement, parents were invited to offer suggestions for better home–school relationships, and the program staff thoughtfully explored some meanings of parents' feedback. There are opportunities as well as challenges in the parents' responses. Some suggestions appear relatively easy to pursue, whereas other patterns of parent responses may require further information and careful interpretation. Promising signs in the Shady Grove staff discussion of parents' suggestions include an open versus defensive reaction to parent concerns and a view of parent involvement as forming and maintaining high-quality relationships with families rather than offering disconnected events for parents to attend.

This chapter provides an overview of best practices toward realizing the early childhood field's long-standing goal of involving parents and community members in young children's learning and development. The commitment to parent involvement has deep roots in early childhood education and in the past two decades has moved beyond narrow approaches that emphasized one-way, program-to-parent communications (Powell, 2001). The chapter's use of the term *parent* is meant to embrace all primary adult caregivers in a child's family.

WHAT RESEARCH SAYS ABOUT PARENT INVOLVEMENT

The early childhood field's understanding of parent involvement has matured since the mid-1990s. There is now recognition of distinct types of parent involvement and the value of mobilizing community resources on behalf of family well-being and early childhood program services (Epstein, 1996). There is growing clarity in nationally recognized standards regarding the value of reciprocity and genuine collaborations in parent–teacher relationships (Copple & Bredekamp, 2009; Sandall, Hemmer, Smith, & McLean, 2005). Recent studies point to parent involvement as a dynamic versus static construct, with parents increasing or decreasing their involvement in different types of support for their children's learning over time, perhaps in response to changes in children's development and age-graded expectations at school (Powell, Son, File, & Froiland, 2012; Son & Morrison, 2010). Recent research also indicates that the extent of early childhood centers' outreach to families (e.g., invitations to participate in school activities) is positively linked to the amount of parent involvement at home and at school (Hindman & Morrison, 2011).

A growing research literature points to three forms of parent involvement as predictive of young children's academic and social outcomes: (1) home–school communication, (2) parental involvement at school, and (3) parental involvement in their children's learning at home and in the community (e.g., Fantuzzo, Tighe, & Childs, 2000). Figure 4.1 provides a summary of these three approaches. Key findings of research on each of these forms of parent involvement are discussed below.

Home–School Communication

Parent involvement in this dimension of the home–school relationship includes participation in written (e.g., notes, e-mails), telephone, and in-person (e.g., parent–teacher conferences) communication with the child's teacher and, when appropriate, other school personnel. Although research suggests that home–school communication is beneficial for children (Marcon, 1999), research on the distinctive contribution of home–school communication to children's outcomes has been limited. Some studies include parent–teacher conferences as an element of school-based involvement (e.g., Powell, Son, File, & San Juan, 2010) or examine parent–school communication along with other forms of parent involvement (Marcon, 1999). One study found that home–school conferencing and school-based involvement did not predict children's outcomes when considered simultaneously with a measure of home-based involvement (Fantuzzo, McWayne, Perry, & Childs, 2004).

Facilitating Home–School Communication
- Emphasize two-way communication about a child's learning and development
- Provide individualized meetings with parents that reflect a collaborative approach
- Use one-way communication methods to keep parents informed of classroom activities
- Establish communication channels early

Supporting School-Based Involvement
- Provide welcoming physical space for families at the program site
- Involve parents and community members as volunteers in the program, classroom, or on a project
- Take steps to learn the views of parents who may not readily respond to typical invitations for parent participation at school

Promoting Home-Based Involvement
- Use parent-friendly strategies for offering information to parents on supporting their child's learning at home
- Model recommended practices with children in person or via video clips
- When appropriate, offer individualized feedback to parents on their implementation of recommended practices
- Help parents tailor learning experiences to their child's interests and abilities
- Offer opportunities for guided discussion of recommended practices
- Facilitate access to community-based services and resources

FIGURE 4.1. Summary of key approaches to effective parent involvement.

Recent research involving public school PreK classrooms suggests that parents' perception of their child's teacher as responsive to the child and to information from the parents is positively related to children's early reading and social skills, and negatively related to problem behaviors (Powell et al., 2010). Teachers show responsiveness when they "meet families where they are" (Christenson, 2004, p. 93). This includes a teacher communicating openness to new information, suggestions, and other forms of feedback about the classroom, and maintaining a welcoming, supportive stance toward parents (Powell, 2001). Parents' perception of teacher responsiveness may contribute to the frequency and flow of parent–teacher interactions that affect the child (Powell et al., 2010).

Parental Involvement at School

This form of parent involvement includes participation in school activities, such as volunteering or observing in the classroom; serving on planning or advisory committees; and attending workshops, presentations, or social events at school. One study found that classroom volunteering was the most common form of school-based involvement among Head Start parents (Castro, Bryant, Peisner-Feinberg, & Skinner, 2004). Classroom-level involvement provides participants with information about children's learning and development and, for parents, may provide insight into a child's abilities that leads to improvements in how parents promote school-related abilities at home (Powell, 2001). Parent or community member participation at school also may send messages to children about the importance of school (Pomerantz, Moorman, & Litwack, 2007) and familiarize volunteers with school goals and function.

A recent study in state-funded PreK classrooms in a large urban school district found that parental school involvement positively predicted children's social skills and mathematics skills, and negatively predicted problem behaviors (Powell et al., 2010). Another recent study involving a national Head Start sample found that school-based involvement, particularly volunteering, was positively associated with children's vocabulary development (Hindman & Morrison, 2011). The findings of these two studies are generally consistent with results of some (Marcon, 1999; Miedel & Reynolds, 1999) but not all (Fantuzzo et al., 2004; Mantzicopoulos, 1997) prior investigations of associations between school-based involvement and children's outcomes. Research on effects of the Chicago Child–Parent Centers, a comprehensive early intervention and family support program, shows that the program increased parent involvement, which in turn was linked long term to higher rates of educational attainment and lower rates of juvenile arrest (Reynolds, 2000; Reynolds, Ou, & Topitzes, 2004).

Parental Involvement at Home and in the Community

One of the rationales for promoting parent–teacher collaboration is the expectation that children will experience similar goals and practices at home and at school. In addition to shared goals for a child, professional standards call for early childhood programs in particular (Sandall et al., 2005) and schools in general (National Parent Teacher Association, 1997) to promote positive parenting knowledge and skills. A robust scientific literature guides program practices focused on this dimension of home–school relationships. More research has been conducted on parental involvement in children's learning at home than on other forms of parental involvement.

Current research and theory tell us to pay attention to different dimensions of family learning environments. The provision of learning resources at home (e.g., children's books) represents a basic dimension of parent involvement that contributes to children's outcomes (e.g., early literacy skills) (Payne, Whitehurst, & Angell, 1994). Parents' teaching practices are another central aspect of parents' home-based involvement. For example, children's home experiences in playing number board games is linked to children's numerical knowledge (e.g., Ramani & Siegler, 2008), and parent–child reading interactions are associated with children's early literacy skills (e.g., Hindman & Morrison, 2011). Parents' support of children's experiences in the neighborhood and community (e.g., visits to parks, museums, libraries) is yet another dimension of home-based parent involvement. A recent study found an association between children's variety of out-of-home experiences and growth in mathematics skills (Powell et al., 2012).

Another line of research that informs best practices in promoting parents' home-based involvement pertains to outcome studies of relatively brief programs that teach parents how to support their children's learning and development. Results of three intervention studies, each addressing a different developmental domain and conducted in the context of an early childhood program, illustrate the benefits of helping parents improve patterns of instruction or interaction with their children. First, parent–child book reading is a common family activity that one set of researchers was able to improve by showing parents how to involve their child actively in the reading process. Rigorous studies of the dialogic reading program have shown positive effects of middle-income (Arnold, Lonigan, Whitehurst, & Epstein, 1994) and lower-income (Whitehurst et al., 1994) parents on children's language skills. Second, parental support of preschool children's mathematics skills has been improved by a program that provides parents with information and interactive materials for engaging their children in mathematics activities at home (Starkey & Klein, 2000). A third example of positive effects of targeted work with parents comes from the Incredible Years program, whose aim is to prevent conduct problems in children. An outcome study found that program participants demonstrated more positive parenting practices at home, and their children exhibited improved behavior in the classroom (Webster-Stratton, 1998). The mathematics and Incredible Years programs were implemented with Head Start parents.

In addition to identifying the benefits of parent training, researchers have found that child outcomes are stronger when both teachers and parents receive training in dialogic reading (Lonigan & Whitehurst, 1998) or the Incredible Years (Webster-Stratton, Reid, & Hammond, 2001) program. For example, children who were read to by both teachers and parents using dialogic reading methods had larger gains than children who were read to by teachers only (Whitehurst et al., 1994).

RESEARCH INTO PRACTICE

Facilitating Home–School Communication

Best practices in facilitating home–school communication emphasize *two-way communication* about a child's learning and development throughout the school year and the importance of sharing both positive news and concerns when they arise. *Individualized meetings* with parents should reflect a collaborative approach to supporting a child's learning. *One-way communication* methods are appropriate for keeping parents informed of classroom activities, including individual children's experiences. *Communication channels should be established early* in the home–school relationship.

Two-Way Communications

A two-way flow of information between teacher and parent is essential to realizing the goal of establishing and maintaining reciprocal relationships with parents. Methods of two-way communication include telephone conversations; e-mail exchanges; written notes that include a response; and in-person contacts through home visits, parent participation at school, and parent–teacher conferences (described below). E-mail is not recommended for communicating about complex or difficult topics because there is limited opportunity to ensure that written words or messages are being received in their intended way. Face-to-face meetings include nonverbal messages that can provide important information when interpreted in a culturally respectful manner. Programs serving English learners should provide ready access to an interpreter or cultural mediator, at a minimum, and ideally employ teachers who speak the home language of children and their parents. Recent evidence shows that increases in Mexican American families' involvement in school-based activities from kindergarten through third grade was greater for children who consistently had bilingual teachers than for children who did not (Tang, Dearing, & Weiss, 2012).

Individualized Meetings

Parent–teacher conferences are a central element of two-way communication. They work best as a collaborative conversation focused on a child's learning and development. Parents' insights into their child's strengths and needs should help teachers improve their work with the child, and teachers' information about the child's progress should help parents support their child's learning at home. Parent–teacher conferences are commonly held twice a year, in the fall and often toward the end of the school year, but should occur as frequently as needed.

The Harvard Family Research Project (2010) has developed tip sheets for teachers, parents, and principals on how to maximize the potential of parent–teacher conferences (*www.hfrp.org*). Teachers are encouraged to use examples of a child's work to discuss progress and growth; ask questions and actively listen to parents' views of their child's strengths and needs; offer suggestions for activities and strategies that families can use at home to support their child's learning; emphasize how "we" (family and school) can work together to resolve any problems; develop an action plan of how family and school will support the child; and describe plans for follow-up communication with the family. Parents are actively encouraged to ask questions and provide information in each of the areas emphasized in the tips for teachers, including making a plan for how the school and family will support the child. Principals are encouraged to share guidelines with both families and teachers about the goals and logistics of parent–teacher conferences; provide professional development to teachers on best practices in conducting effective conferences; create a welcoming school environment; and be visible and available during the days of conferences (i.e., walk through the building, introduce themselves to parents, communicate school appreciation for families who take time to attend).

Collaborative relationships with parents are central to the principle of family-centered practices in serving children with disabilities, including the planning process for an individualized family service plan (IFSP) for children through age 2 years and an individualized education program (IEP) for young children age 3 years and older. Experts recommend a number of practices to ensure a truly collaborative planning process (Byington & Whitby, 2011). First, it is appropriate for a professional who is familiar with IFSP/IEP procedures to offer to meet with parents prior to their first IFSP or IEP meeting to familiarize parents with the IFSP/IEP process, including all forms to be used at the meeting and common special education terms. Parents should be encouraged to organize photographs, scrapbooks, portfolios, or other forms of sharing personal information about their child at the meeting. Second, a collaborative process should be used with parents to develop a meeting agenda, prepare a list of questions and concerns to bring to the meeting, and identify a convenient meeting time. Parents may wish to bring an advocate to the meeting. Third, experts recommend that the initial IFSP or IEP meeting should begin with a blank document, in order to make clear that there are no preconceived ideas about goals to be met or services to be provided. The meeting room should be comfortable and inviting, with name tags for all participants and a seating arrangement that prevents power imbalances (use a round or U-shaped table) and encourages parents to sit next to the team facilitator.

One-Way Communication

There are many options for keeping parents informed about school and classroom activities, especially children's curriculum experiences. Simple newsletters at the classroom or school level can be sent home with children or issued electronically on a regular basis to parents who have Internet access. Parents appreciate descriptions of recent and planned activities that involve their child, as well as notices of important school dates. Some teachers send home short notes aimed at prompting parent–child discussion of a school event (e.g., "Ask me about the new hermit crabs in the classroom"; Berger & Riojas-Cortez, 2012, p. 114) or issue individualized notes (e.g., "happygrams") that briefly report a child's accomplishment. Bulletin boards are a conventional way to describe a class-room's activities. Some schools or classrooms maintain a website or blog to keep parents informed of activities. Schools or classrooms that rely on Web-based technologies for one-way communications to parents need to ensure that Internet access is readily available to all families. A handbook issued to parents at the beginning of the year is another form of one-way communication that is especially important in setting forth school policies, programs, practices, and expectations. It is essential that all written communications to parents appear in the language used by parents. Procedures should be in place to ensure the accuracy and cultural sensitivity of translated material. A common practice in trans-lating documents, known as *back translation*, is for a translator not involved in the first translation to translate the item back to the source language to ensure accuracy. Efforts also should be made to have one or more native language speakers review the translated material with regard to the meaning and cultural sensitivity of words and concepts.

Establishing Communication Channels

Teachers should strive to establish personal contact with parents at the beginning of the school year and not wait until there is a problem to initiate communication with a parent. Some programs such as Head Start use home visits at the start of the school year to estab-lish a connection between a teacher and a family. School open houses are a common event at the beginning of the program year that can help families become familiar with school staff and facilities. Teachers can set the stage for productive relationships with families by sending a friendly letter that welcomes the classroom community to a new school year and establishes a posture of openness to parent perspectives and a commitment to form-ing and maintaining genuine partnerships with parents.

Supporting School-Based Involvement

It is beneficial to offer a range of options for parents to spend meaningful time at their child's school. Parents vary considerably in their interests, availability, and level of com-fort with schools. Some parents may wish to observe occasionally in their child's class-room, whereas others may seek ongoing volunteer roles in the classroom or participation in program-level policy or advisory councils. Volunteers from the community, including businesses, service clubs, and nonprofit organizations, may respond best to well-defined opportunities, such as contributing to a special project or reading with individual or small groups of children on a regular basis. Best practices are described below for provid-ing welcoming physical space for families; involving volunteers in the school; involving volunteers in project work; and learning the perspectives of parents who may not readily respond to typical invitations for parent participation at school.

Space for Families

The arrangement of an early childhood program's physical environment should convey a welcoming message to parents. The arrival space should be adequate for several parents and their children to arrive and say good-bye to one another at the same time, and the center's reception area should include furniture that invites adults to sit comfortably. Early childhood programs also can welcome families with bulletin board displays of photographs and text that explicitly and implicitly communicate the program's values and approach to working with families and their children, such as pictures that represent diversity in racial/ethnic background and family structure (Keyser, 2006).

Some early childhood programs provide designated space for parent information, such as a library of books, videos/DVDs, and parent–child activity bags that parents can borrow (Keyser, 2006). A central feature of the Chicago Child–Parent Centers is a parent resource room that provides school–community outreach. Located adjacent to classrooms, the parent room offers a range of activities aimed at supporting parents' educational and personal development, such as parent reading groups, craft projects, classes or workshops in child and family topics (e.g., financial management), and referrals to community-based services. It is staffed by a certified teacher (Reynolds, 2000).

Volunteering at School

Opportunities for participation at school should be offered to parents and community volunteers at several levels. Direct involvement in a classroom has the potential to enrich children's experiences and increase a volunteer's understanding of developmentally appropriate practices with young children (Powell et al., 2010). Classroom volunteer activities may include reading stories to individual or small groups of children, changing bulletin boards, arranging games or other activities for children who complete assignments early, listening to children describe their experiences, working on a classroom newsletter, chaperoning field trips, and helping children in an activity center (Reynolds, 2000). It is important for teachers to make volunteers feel welcome, to explain classroom routines and rules, and to recognize and respect volunteers' contributions (Berger & Riojas-Cortez, 2012). School volunteer work may also take place at a program or center level through contributions to advisory or policy councils, fund-raising efforts, bulletin boards and other forms of communication with parents, and assistance with special school events. The provisions for welcoming volunteers, explaining procedures, and recognizing and respecting their contributions, noted earlier relative to classroom participation, also apply to program- or school-level involvement.

Involving Volunteers in Project Work

Projects are highly conducive to the involvement of community members and families. For example, developing and maintaining a garden offers many opportunities for community and extended family members to participate, as well as hands-on experiences for children's learning. One gardening project at an early childhood center attracted the ongoing contributions of a master gardener who solved the problem of "teacher garden phobia" by helping staff become familiar and comfortable with gardening (Starbuck & Olthof, 2008, p. 76). For this garden project, a local nursery contributed many plants, a community member built a trellis house, one mother found a company willing to donate unused bricks for the garden pathway, another mother painted signs to label the different gardens, a father tilled the land, and fathers and children hauled wheelbarrows of soil. An advisor from a gardening club or local Cooperative Extension office can offer expertise on a range of gardening issues (e.g., why there are holes in the bean leaves). Gardens can be an important springboard for learning more about a culture, such as Native American connections with the earth (McWilliams, Maldonado-Mancebo, Szczepaniak, & Jones, 2011), and the involvement of family members in harvesting a garden's yield can provide valuable insights into diverse uses of different foods (Starbuck & Olthof, 2008).

Learning about Parents' Perspectives

Early childhood programs may need to include targeted outreach to learn about the goals and concerns of parents who do not participate in traditional forms of school-based involvement. Parent focus groups have been used to reach all parents by FirstSchool, an innovative approach to education from PreK through third grade that involves a collaborative partnership among families, schools, communities, and institutions of higher education (Gillanders, Mason, & Ritchie, 2011). For example, a series of three focus group meetings with Latino mothers conducted by a Spanish-speaking facilitator revealed that the mothers often did not participate in family involvement activities at school because they did not speak English. They wanted more information about how to help their children succeed in school but often could not understand material offered by the school. They also were interested in opportunities to connect with other parents in the school. In response to this information, the school conducted a Latino parent night in Spanish, during which school staff members asked parents what they wanted to know about the school's policies and practices. In addition, the school provided more information on children's placements in English as a second language classes. One of the ways the school disseminated this information was through a Family Night session conducted in Spanish (Gillanders et al., 2011).

Promoting Home-Based Involvement

Effective educational programs for parents of preschool-age children use one or more of the following strategies to support parents' home-based involvement: providing a parent-friendly organization of information on child development and parenting; modeling desired practices with children; offering individualized feedback to parents on their implementation of recommended practices; helping parents tailor learning experiences to their child's interests and abilities; offering opportunities for guided discussion of recommended parenting practices; meeting in comfortable settings at convenient times; providing learning materials for parents to use at home with their child; and facilitating access to community-based family services and resources. In addition, effective programs typically provide in-depth training and support for staff members who work with parents. In some cases, early childhood programs also ensure that teachers use practices recommended to parents, so that children experience continuity of support between home and school. Below are illustrations of each of these practices from effective parenting programs, including programs cited in the research section of this chapter.

Parent-Friendly Organization of Information

Effective programs of support for parents present information in meaningful units that reflect responsiveness to parents' concerns. For example, the Incredible Years program frames its content from the perspective of parents. The topics include how to play with your child, help your child learn, use praise and encouragement to bring out the best in your child, how to set limits and handle misbehavior effectively, and how to teach your child to problem solve (Webster-Stratton, 1998). Note the use of accessible language and the absence of technical terminology.

Some programs use acronyms to help parents remember key parenting practices. The dialogic reading program employs two acronyms to provide a summary of reading techniques emphasized in the program (Zevenbergen & Whitehurst, 2003). One is the

PEER sequence, which is used on nearly every instance of shared book reading except the first. The acronym stands for Prompt, Evaluate, Expand, and Repeat. The parent or adult prompts the child to say something about the book, evaluates the child's response, expands the child's response by rephrasing and adding information, and repeats the prompt–evaluate sequence to ensure that the child has learned from the expansion. The program offers the acronym CROWD to help parents remember five types of questions that initiate a PEER sequence: Completion, Recall, Open-ended, Wh- (what, where, why), and Distancing (relating the book content to an aspect of the child's life outside the book).

Modeling Desired Practices

Modeling is a powerful tool for illustrating recommended actions. In the family mathematics classes offered in the Starkey and Klein (2000) program, parents and their children sat at tables (two to three dyads per table) to engage in up to three manipulative activities. At the beginning of each activity, two teachers demonstrated how the activity works, with one teacher playing the role of the parent and the other, the role of the child. Each of the teachers' demonstrations emphasized how to set up the activity's materials, how to present the task or activity to the child, and different ways to check the child's solutions. Some parenting programs offer video demonstrations of recommended practices (e.g., Arnold et al., 1994). For example, video training resources based on the dialogic reading program are available from Washington Learning System in a number of different languages, including Spanish, Mandarin, Vietnamese, and Korean (*www.walearning.com*).

Offering Individualized Feedback

Parents often welcome constructive guidance from an expert who observes their attempts in a recommended practice. After the two teachers in the family mathematics program demonstrated a manipulative activity to parents, they moved from table to table while parent–child dyads were engaged in the activity. The teachers monitored parents during the activity and offered feedback when necessary. In the early class sessions, for example, teachers found that some parents did not clear the table of extraneous items (e.g., kit bags) and needed a reminder on the importance of an uncluttered learning area on the table (Starkey & Klein, 2000). For families with good computer resources, the National Library of Virtual Manipulatives, based at Utah State University, offers interactive, Web-based manipulatives for children to learn and strengthen their mathematics skills (*www. nlvm.usu.edu*). The library's Pre–2 resources include learning tools related to geometry (e.g., building similar triangles by combining sides and angles), measurement (e.g., programming a ladybug to hide behind a leaf), and numbers and operations (e.g., arrange colors to complete a pattern), among other areas.

Helping Parents Tailor Learning Experiences

Teachers who demonstrated activities in the family mathematics program (Starkey & Klein, 2000) gave tips on how to identify aspects of an activity that might be difficult for a child, and how to decide whether an activity needs to be extended to either a more advanced or a less challenging level. While parents were engaged in an activity with their child during the class session, the "roaming" teachers offered individualized guidance to parents on how to gauge the appropriateness of a more or less challenging version of a task for their child. For example, teachers noticed that some parents tended to push their children to more advanced problems, even when they had been unable to solve a less challenging problem (Starkey & Klein, 2000). Helping parents attend to and build on their child's description of a story is integral to training in dialogic reading. In particular, parent evaluation of a child's response and understanding is a core part of the program's PEER sequence described earlier. In addition to watching and critically discussing videotapes, parents in dialogic reading classes participated in one-on-one role plays with the trainer, who functioned as the child. The trainer presented various examples of child behavior and gave each parent feedback on his or her use of the dialogic reading approach (Whitehurst et al., 1994).

Offering Opportunities for Guided Discussion

Guided discussion is a common element of work with parents in a group setting, such as workshops and classes, or in a one-to-one arrangement, such as a home visit. A typical goal of a semistructured discussion is to help parents incorporate new information by exploring and potentially altering existing ideas about their child and parenting practices. Open-ended questions can help parents consider possible uses of practices recommended in a parenting workshop or class (Powell & Peet, 2008). For example, a book club program for low-income parents included a choral reading of a children's book and discussion of three questions after the reading: What would you want your child to take away from this book? What kinds of questions or comments would you use to stimulate a discussion of the story? How would you help your child revisit this book? (Neuman, 1996). Guided discussion also may help parents reflect on modeled parenting practices. In the Incredible Years program, for example, parents viewed 2-minute videos of recommended parenting skills and participated in a focused discussion of the parent–child interactions featured in each of the brief vignettes. Discussion leaders encouraged parents to engage in problem solving related to the video vignette (Webster-Stratton, 1998). A training video for the dialogic reading program included illustrations of adult–child book reading that exemplified both the program's approach and inappropriate adult–child book reading. Parents were invited to identify inappropriate actions in the videos and to describe what the adult should have done differently in response to the child (Whitehurst et al., 1994).

Meeting in Comfortable Settings at Convenient Times

Effective programs meet with parents in familiar, comfortable settings at times that are compatible with family schedules. For example, the family mathematics classes for Head Start parents and their children met every other Saturday morning in a classroom at the local Head Start center. There was an opening activity that accommodated early or late arrivals prior to the introduction of individual activities. Lunch was provided at the end of each class (Starkey & Klein, 2000). The Incredible Years program for parents of preschool-age children offered home-based training to parents unable to attend four booster classes in the kindergarten year, to help them with the transition to kindergarten (Webster-Stratton et al., 2001).

Providing Learning Materials for Use at Home

It is common for early childhood programs to lend or give learning materials to families for use at home. Effective programs typically provide materials as a follow-up to training.

The family mathematics program offered a lending library of mathematics kits for family use at home between class sessions. The contents of the kits were the focus of activities featured in the classes. Parents could borrow up to three mathematics kits at a time. Across the 8-week program, parents borrowed an average of 11 kits (Starkey & Klein, 2000). Developed by Neuman (1996), each participating parent was given a copy of the book read in choral unison at the group session (discussed earlier). The books included library pockets and small index cards for parents to write questions they believed would be useful for guiding discussions about the book with their child. The dialogic reading program provided parents a guide that explained the purpose of recommended books and offered hints for how to introduce and read the book. Books were given to parents to keep (Whitehurst et al., 1994). The Home Instruction of Parents of Preschool Youngsters (HIPPY) home visiting program, which provides learning materials and concrete guidance to parents on how to support their children's learning experiences at home, is associated with improvements in the third-grade mathematics achievement of children from low-income Spanish-speaking families (Nievar, Jacobson, Chen, Johnson, & Dier, 2011).

Facilitating Access to Community-Based Resources

It is challenging for parents faced with stressful circumstances to support their child's learning and development appropriately. There also are lost opportunities when parents do not make use of resources that support their child's development or pursue their own goals (e.g., further education or job training) because they lack information about, or access to, community services. For these reasons, nationally recognized standards call for early childhood programs to connect families with resources based on their priorities and needs (Copple & Bredekamp, 2009; Sandall et al., 2005). A core program practice here is to maintain up-to-date lists of agencies and contact information for help with basic family functioning, such as housing, utilities, food, physical and mental health care, and recreation. Simply providing the name, address, and telephone number of a community agency may be an insufficient referral approach for parents coping with highly stressful situations or facing language barriers in accessing services. A program staff member, such as a family services coordinator, may find it helpful to contact an agency prior to making a referral, to ensure the agency is a good fit with a family's specific circumstance. It also may be useful for community-based service providers to make presentations about services available to families during parent meetings at the school (McWilliams et al., 2011).

Training and Support for Staff

Effective educational programs focused on home-based parent involvement usually offer in-depth support for staff members who work with parents. Teachers in the family mathematics program received a manual of curriculum activities and instruction in how to use the activities with parents (Starkey & Klein, 2000). In research on the Incredible Years program, classes were led by Head Start family service workers who participated in a 4-day workshop and received weekly supervision as part of their training to lead classes. The group leaders worked from a program manual that specified the content of each class session, the videotaped vignettes to be shown, discussion questions for the vignettes, recommended role-play activities, and homework assignments. Parents who emerged as natural leaders in a first round served as group co-leaders when the program was offered to parents in a second cohort (Webster-Stratton, 1998).

Teachers' Use of Practices Recommended to Parents

As noted earlier, there are benefits for children when parents and teachers use the same targeted strategies at home and school. This can be accomplished by providing training with the same content to both parents and teachers. For example, to ensure that teachers understood and appropriately implemented the techniques promoted in the Incredible Years program, they received a series of six monthly, one-day workshops (a total of 36 hours) focused on positive management and discipline strategies, and promoting social competence in the classroom. Teachers viewed videotapes of other classroom teachers and participated in group discussion of teacher–student interactions featured in brief videotaped vignettes (Webster-Stratton et al., 2001). This training for teachers paralleled the content of the Incredible Years training received by parents, as described earlier.

REFLECTIONS AND NEW DIRECTIONS

The lifestyles and structural characteristics of families currently served by early childhood programs call into question some parent involvement practices developed in an era dominated by stay-at-home mothers and two-parent families. As well, the growing racial, ethnic, and linguistic diversity of families requires that early childhood programs look carefully at how well existing opportunities for parent involvement engage families. The Shady Grove teachers, introduced at the outset of this chapter, are moving in a potentially productive direction by pondering the meaning of "*our* program" and how to reach the 30% of parents who did not respond to the program's survey. Their questions speak to challenges facing the field of early childhood programs regarding ways to deepen and broaden methods to promote reciprocal relationships with increasingly diverse families.

PROFESSIONAL DEVELOPMENT ACTIVITIES

- Engage in programwide planning to improve relations with families and the surrounding community. Conduct a survey of parents as part of this process (see opening vignette), and involve parents and community representatives in the decision making.

- Offer a workshop or other form of training resource for all program staff based on implications of rapidly changing family characteristics (e.g., single parents, cultural and linguistic minority families) relative to early childhood programs. Include an interactive component that helps participants apply the information to their situations.

- Carefully review all written information for parents, including application forms, letters, and bulletin boards, to ensure inclusive approaches to diverse family forms. For example, is there an assumption that all children come from intact, two-parent families? What races, ethnicities, and abilities are represented in photographs and other visuals?

- Assess how the physical setup of the center and each classroom might be tweaked or reworked to provide a fully welcoming environment for parents and other visitors. Is there adequate space for adults to gather without interfering with other functions? Are there comfortable places to sit? Do bulletin boards and other visuals provide up-to-date information?

▪ Provide inservice training on how teachers can effectively engage parents as full partners and facilitate a two-way flow of information about a child during parent–teacher conferences, written communications, and informal in-person exchanges.

REFERENCES

Arnold, D. H., Lonigan, C. J., Whitehurst, G. J., & Epstein, J. N. (1994). Accelerating language development through picture book reading: Replication and extension to a videotape training format. *Journal of Educational Psychology, 86*, 235–243.

Berger, E. H., & Riojas-Cortez, M. (2012). *Parents as partners in education: Families and schools working together* (8th ed.). Upper Saddle River, NJ: Pearson.

Byington, T. A., & Whitby, P. J. S. (2011). Empowering families during the early intervention planning process. *Young Exceptional Children, 14*, 44–56.

Castro, D., Bryant, D. M., Peisner-Feinberg, E. S., & Skinner, M. L. (2004). Parent involvement in Head Start programs: The role of parent, teacher, and classroom characteristics. *Early Childhood Research Quarterly, 19*, 413–430.

Christenson, S. L. (2004). The family–school partnership: An opportunity to promote the learning competence of all students. *School Psychology Review, 33*, 83–105.

Copple, C., & Bredekamp, S. (2009). *Developmentally appropriate practice in early childhood programs* (3rd ed.). Washington, DC: National Association for the Education of Young Children.

Epstein, J. L. (1996). Perspectives and previews on research and policy for school, family, and community partnerships. In A. Booth & J. F. Dunn (Eds.), *Family–school links: How do they affect educational outcomes?* (pp. 209–246). Mahwah, NJ: Erlbaum.

Fantuzzo, J., McWayne, C., Perry, M. A., & Childs, S. (2004). Multiple dimensions of family involvement and their relations to behavioral and learning competencies for urban, low-income children. *School Psychology Review, 33*, 467–480.

Fantuzzo, J., Tighe, E., & Childs, S. (2000). Family involvement questionnaire: A multivariate assessment of family participation in early childhood education. *Journal of Educational Psychology, 92*, 367–376.

Gillanders, C., Mason, E., & Ritchie, S. (2011). FirstSchool: An approach that prepares pre-k to 3 educators to effectively interpret and respond to school data. *Young Children, 66*, 12–19.

Harvard Family Research Project. (2010). *Parent–teacher conference tip sheets for principals, teachers, and parents.* Cambridge, MA: Author. Retrieved from *http://hfrp.org/publications-resources*.

Hindman, A. M., & Morrison, F. J. (2011). Family involvement and educator outreach in Head Start: Nature, extent, and contributions to early literacy skills. *Elementary School Journal, 111*, 359–386.

Keyser, J. (2006). *From parents to partners: Building a family-centered early childhood program.* St. Paul, MN: Redleaf Press.

Lonigan, C. J., & Whitehurst, G. J. (1998). Relative efficacy of parent and teacher involvement in a shared-reading intervention for preschool children from low-income backgrounds. *Early Childhood Research Quarterly, 13*, 263–290.

Mantzicopoulos, P. Y. (1997). The relationship of family variables to Head Start children's preacademic competence. *Early Education and Development, 8*, 357–375.

Marcon, R. A. (1999). Positive relationships between parent school involvement and public school inner-city preschoolers' development and academic performance. *School Psychology Review, 28*, 395–412.

McWilliams, M. S., Maldonado-Mancebo, T., Szczepaniak, P. S., & Jones, J. (2011). Supporting

Native Indian preschoolers and their families: Family–school–community partnerships. *Young Children, 66,* 34–41.

Miedel, W. T., & Reynolds, A. J. (1999). Parent involvement in early intervention for disadvantaged children: Does it matter? *Journal of School Psychology, 37,* 379–402.

National Parent Teacher Association. (1997). *National standards for parent–family involvement programs.* Chicago: Author.

Neuman, S. B. (1996). Children engaging in storybook reading: The influence of access to print resources, opportunity, and parental interaction. *Early Childhood Research Quarterly, 11,* 495–513.

Nievar, M. A., Jacobson, A., Chen, Q., Johnson, U., & Dier, S. (2011). Impact of HIPPY on home learning environments of Latino families. *Early Childhood Research Quarterly, 26,* 268–277.

Payne, A. C., Whitehurst, G. J., & Angell, A. L. (1994). The role of home literacy environment in the development of language ability in preschool children from low income families. *Early Childhood Research Quarterly, 9,* 427–440.

Pomerantz, E. M., Moorman, E. A., & Litwack, S. D. (2007). The how, whom, and why of parents' involvement in children's academic lives: More is not always better. *Review of Educational Research, 77,* 373–410.

Powell, D. R. (2001). Visions and realities of achieving partnership: Parent–school relationships at the turn of the century. In A. Göncü & E. L. Klein (Eds.), *Children in play, story, and school* (pp. 333–357). New York: Guilford Press.

Powell, D. R., & Peet, S. H. (2008). Development and outcomes of a community-based intervention to improve parents' use of inquiry in informal learning contexts. *Journal of Applied Developmental Psychology, 29,* 259–273.

Powell, D. R., Son, S.-H., File, N., & Froiland, J. M. (2012). Changes in parent involvement across the transition from public school prekindergarten to first grade and children's academic outcomes. *Elementary School Journal, 113,* 276–300.

Powell, D. R., Son, S.-H., File, N., & San Juan, R. R. (2010). Parent–school relationships and children's academic and social outcomes in public school pre-kindergarten. *Journal of School Psychology, 48,* 269–292.

Ramani, G. B., & Siegler, R. S. (2008). Promoting broad and stable improvements in low-income children's numerical knowledge through playing number board games. *Child Development, 79,* 375–394.

Reynolds, A. J. (2000). *Success in early intervention: The Chicago Child–Parent Centers.* Lincoln: University of Nebraska Press.

Reynolds, A. J., Ou, S., & Topitzes, J. W. (2004). Paths of effects of early childhood intervention on educational attainment and delinquency: A confirmatory analysis of the Chicago Child–Parent Centers. *Child Development, 75,* 1299–1328.

Sandall, S., Hemmer, M. L., Smith, B. J., & McLean, M. E. (2005). *DEC recommended practices: A comprehensive guide for practical application in early intervention/early childhood special education.* Longmont, CO: Sopris West.

Son, S.-H., & Morrison, F. J. (2010). The nature and impact of changes in home learning environment on growth of language and academic skills in preschool children. *Developmental Psychology, 46,* 1103–1118.

Starbuck, S., & Olthof, M. R. (2008). Involving families and community through gardening. *Young Children, 63,* 74–79.

Starkey, P., & Klein, A. (2000). Fostering parental support for children's mathematical development: An intervention with Head Start families. *Early Education and Development, 11,* 659–680.

Tang, S., Dearing, E., & Weiss, H. B. (2012). Spanish-speaking Mexican-American families' involvement in school-based activities and their children's literacy: The implications of having teachers who speak Spanish and English. *Early Childhood Research Quarterly, 27,* 177–187.

Webster-Stratton, C. (1981). Videotape modeling: A method of parent education. *Journal of Clinical Child Psychology, 10*, 93–98.

Webster-Stratton, C. (1998). Preventing conduct problems in Head Start children: Strengthening parent competencies. *Journal of Consulting and Clinical Psychology, 66*, 715–730.

Webster-Stratton, C., Reid, M. J., & Hammond, M. (2001). Preventing conduct problems, promoting social competence: A parent and teacher training partnership in Head Start. *Journal of Clinical Child Psychology, 30*, 283–302.

Whitehurst, G. J., Arnold, D. S., Epstein, J. N., Angell, A. L., Smith, M., & Fischel, J. E. (1994). A picture book reading intervention in day care and home for children from low-income families. *Developmental Psychology, 30*, 679–689.

Zevenbergen, A. A., & Whitehurst, G. J. (2003). Dialogic reading: A shared picture book reading intervention for preschoolers. In A. van Kleeck, S. A. Stahl, & E. B. Bauer (Eds.), *On reading books to children: Parents and teachers* (pp. 177–200). Mahwah, NJ: Erlbaum.

CHAPTER 5

ADVOCACY FOR YOUNG CHILDREN
Engaging with Policymakers and the Politically Powerful

JUDITH E. KIEFF

> Never doubt that a small group of thoughtful committed citizens
> can change the world. Indeed, it is the only thing that ever did.
> —MARGARET MEAD

It is January and at Royal Castle Child Care Center in New Orleans, Louisiana, Director Pearlie Harris is organizing the refundable School Readiness Tax Credit (SRTC) vouchers to distribute to her staff, to the families of children enrolled in the center, and to the businesses that have supported the center over the last year. In 2009, Louisiana legislation, authored by Senator Ann Duplessis, created four separate, refundable SRTC vouchers. To receive these tax credits, Royal Castle Child Care Center participates in Louisiana's Quality Rating and Improvement System (QRIS) and recently earned a 5-star (out of 5 stars) rating. A refundable tax credit is available to taxpayers even if it is greater than their tax liability; therefore, the families associated with this care center have much to celebrate. Not only are Royal Castle Child Care Center children receiving high-quality care and education, but their families are also being rewarded for their choice to enroll them in such a program. Teachers, administrators, and businesses that support the center are also rewarded for the work they do to improve the quality of child care in their community. The collaboration between Senator Duplessis, a politically powerful individual, and the advocacy efforts of countless early childhood professionals across the state of Louisiana represents a win–win situation because high-quality child care and early education foster success for all children and families, to say nothing of the future cost savings in social support programs for the state.[1]

---

[1] As of August 2011, of the 28 states that have tax credits tied to Quality Rating Scales, 14 are refundable (Karolak, 2011). For more information regarding use of tax credits to promote quality early care and education, see Stoney and Mitchell (2007).

Senator Duplessis authored and championed the Louisiana SRTC legislation. Although she sponsored this legislation, she would be the first to tell you that she not only did not do this alone but she also could not have done it without the help of early childhood professionals who advocated tirelessly for this law. These grassroots advocates developed the initial ideas for the legislation, researched its feasibility, consulted with members of the state's executive branch of government, drafted then redrafted the bill countless times, then sold the idea not only to other legislators but also the general public. After the Louisiana SRTC legislation was passed, advocates continued to spread the word about positive effects of the legislation and maintained vigilance to protect it during subsequent economic downturns and budget cuts. Who were these grassroots advocates? They included financial experts, lawyers, and community activists, but those who ignited and sustained the movement from idea to legislation to implementation were the early childhood education professionals, professors, community nonprofit organization administrators, center directors, teachers, and parents. Many of these supporters would probably not see themselves as advocates involved in formulating public policy. In their minds, they were just working together, each contributing his or her own special skills, to bring about better opportunities for the citizens in their communities. Several key strategies and tactics have proven effective over time and through experience when planning and guiding successful advocacy efforts such as the one described here. The purpose of this chapter is to describe how they can be used to collaborate with the politically powerful and formulate public policy that supports young children and their families.

WHAT RESEARCH SAYS ABOUT ADVOCATING FOR PUBLIC POLICY CHANGES

History tells us that when early childhood professionals and elected officials work together to produce public policy, good things can happen for children and families. One notable example of federal legislation that has had a far-reaching effect on children and families is the Individuals with Disabilities Education Act (IDEA). This law ensures that children with disabilities receive needed services. IDEA provides funding and guidelines for states and all public agencies that deliver early intervention, special education, and other services to millions of infants, toddlers, children, youth, and their families. Another federal law that has had a profound effect on infants, toddlers, children, and their families is the Family and Medical Leave Act of 1994. Under this federal provision, eligible employees are able to take an unpaid, job-protected leave with continued health insurance for specific medical reasons. For example, a parent, male or female, can take up to 12 weeks maternity or paternity leave when a new baby is born or adopted. Also, a leave can be granted under this law if an employee's child, spouse, or parent has a serious medical condition that requires constant care.

Even though both of these examples represent federal legislation, their effects are felt at a local level. In fact every piece of legislation, federal or state, has local implications and is often based on local needs (National Center for Learning Disabilities, 2009). Most often, laws begin as a grassroots effort of an individual or group that sees a specific unmeet need in the community. These individuals or groups inform policymakers about that need, then work together with policymakers to find a resolution.

This is exactly how advocacy efforts to develop and pass the Louisiana SRTC legislation began. After Hurricane Katrina, the child care community in metropolitan New

Orleans was devastated when 70% of the child care centers were destroyed. As center directors began the process of rebuilding the child care network, they collaborated with community leaders, many of whom were also early childhood professionals, to develop strategies for rebuilding a system of high-quality, sustainable early childhood care and education centers that would be accessible to all in the community. Leaders of these disparate groups were aware of work in other parts of the country related to the use of quality rating scales to evaluate and improve centers, and tax incentives to foster improvements. They studied these ideas and began to craft legislation that was unique to Louisiana. They searched for someone to support and champion this legislation and found that in Senator Ann Duplessis from the New Orleans area. Senator Duplessis and her staff worked with these grassroots advocates to formulate the legislation, sponsor it, and move it through the legislative process to become law. Somehow in this process, the community leaders who were working to rebuild a high-quality child care system unwittingly became public policy advocates.

The Role of Evidence in Policymaking

When considering policy or program decisions, policymakers often rely on their own political or ideological viewpoint, on the opinions of the few whom they consider to be experts, or on factors related strictly to economic efficiency. However, the results of decisions based on these factors alone may not prove to be in the best interest of either the intended population or the public in general. Program and policy decisions based on evidence derived from well-conceived research will have the greatest positive effect on all affected populations. Basing policy and program funding decisions on empirical evidence is most important when it comes to funding programs for the nation's most vulnerable populations, including young children, children with special needs, and their families (Urban Institute, 2003). Therefore, it is vitally important that policymakers consider all evidence available related to program/policy outcomes, feasibility, and/or impact on multiple segments of the population before making decisions.

Evidence-based policymaking is based on the study of carefully created and analyzed quantitative and qualitative data that addresses four basic questions:

1. What is the problem?
2. What are the possible ways to solve the problem?
3. What are the impacts of this solution on the intended population and the general population?
4. What political and social values do the proposed options reflect? (Urban Institute, 2003)

Evidence of successful programs and policies comes from empirical research studies, analysis of previous research, public opinion surveys, statistical studies, and economic impact data.

The Multifaceted Roles of Early Childhood Advocates

When working in the area of public policy development, early childhood professionals have many roles to play. A major role for advocates is to gather or, in some cases, create, interpret, and bring this evidence to policymakers' attention. Advocates must show those in decision-making positions empirical evidence of both the positive and negative impact of proposed programs or policies. In some cases, advocates may need to bring this same evidence to the general public in order to gather wide support that will in turn influence the decisions of policymakers.

Other important roles for advocates include collaborating with policymakers to develop new bills or amend/repeal existing bills. It may also include working with policymakers to fund existing policies fully, providing expert testimony before legislative committees, reviewing proposals and providing "policy" briefs and research, as well as educating and informing both policymakers and the general public about the potential positive or negative effects of new or existing policies. Advocates also rally support of the public for the passage, repeal, or modification of specific policies. Finally, they keep issues in front of the policymakers and the public until they are resolved through our democratic process.

For example, early childhood advocates within a school district might determine that they need to bring information about the success of inclusion programs in other districts to the attention of their local principals or district administrators. Advocates may include parents, teachers, and interested citizens from all sectors of the community. These advocates work to schedule an opportunity to provide testimony to the school board regarding Public Law 94-142 and/or how inclusive classrooms fulfill district obligations to observe the letter and spirit of this law. Advocates may also inform and educate other teachers and the parents of all children who share a common concern as to the positive effects of inclusive education for all children. In this way advocates rally community support for more inclusive learning opportunities for children with disabilities. And finally, advocates work relentlessly to keep the issue alive and on the *front burner* of the policymakers. This is a vital role because policies often get bogged down in government bureaucracies. Certainly, advocates need to be flexible and engage in the art of compromise, but persistence and focus are key to bringing about positive change for children and families.

Working Effectively in the Political Arena

Many early childhood professionals feel inadequate to delve into the world of politics and would prefer to stay out of it altogether because, unfortunately, the world of politics has acquired such a negative image in recent years. Politics is often seen as being populated by power-hungry individuals who employ corrupt practices to maintain their power, often for personal gain. Also, politicians are frequently portrayed in the media as arrogant, unwilling to compromise, and not wanting to give credit to others through collaborative efforts. One cannot deny that these individual politicians exist, but they are certainly not the majority. Most elected officials recognize their role as representatives of those who elected them, and they welcome the ideas and help of their constituents in formulating and passing useful legislation that best serves their community.

Politics employs a process through which groups of people make decisions for the society as a whole. Local, state, and federal politicians are elected officials who have a responsibility to represent their constituent's interest. To become political means to become active in civil, state, and public affairs. Public participation in political decision making is a fundamental principle of a democratic society. When individuals from many perspectives and areas of expertise collaborate in social decision making, the result is often better conditions for all. Therefore, public participation in decision making in a democracy is not only a right and privilege but it is also a requirement for developing effective public policy. Thus, *advocacy* is defined as follows: "Public policy advocacy is the process of taking action, using instruments of democracy to create new public spaces and a more just society. Politics is the only discipline through which it is possible to change and improve something in society, including the status of women and children" (Kevatin, 1998, p. 25).

Public Policy Advocacy as an Ethical Responsibility

Early childhood professionals are in a unique position to see and understand conditions that adversely affect growth, development, and learning, as well as poverty, abuse, or injustice because they work directly with children and families. They recognize issues, situations, policies, and practices that may harmful to families or inhibit children's optimal growth and development. This is a perspective that many policymakers may not have. It is therefore incumbent on the early childhood professional to speak out and work with policymakers to create conditions in society conducive to the optimal growth and development of all children and families (National Association for the Education of Young Children [NAEYC], 2011).

It is because of this unique perspective that the NAEYC has established *The Code of Ethical Conduct and Statement of Commitment* (2011) to encourage advocacy as an ethical responsibility for those working in the profession. Principle 1.3 of the Code of Ethics states:

> We shall not participate in practices that discriminate against children by denying benefits, giving special advantages, or excluding them from programs or activities on the basis of their sex, race, national origin religious beliefs, medical conditions, disability, or marital status/family structure, sexual orientation, or religious beliefs or other affiliations of their families. (Aspects of this principle do not apply in programs that have lawful mandates to provide services to a particular population of children.) (NAEYC position statement, retrieved February 1, 2012, from *www.naeyc.org*)

This principle implies that among the most important responsibilities of early childhood professionals is the recognition of practices and policies that maybe be harmful, the rejection of these practices and policies, and the formulation of more equitable practices and policies. Therefore, early childhood professionals are called to action, to advocate not just within the confines of their jobs but also in the context of their communities, state, country, and globally (Kieff, 2009).

Advocating for Appropriate Levels of Funding

Ensuring adequate funding for programs that support infants, toddlers, young children, and their families is a critical aspect of public policy advocacy that early childhood professionals must assume. One reason is that many federal programs are passed with unfunded or partially funded mandates. For example, the Head Start program has never been fully funded by the federal government. In other words, many more children and families are eligible for Head Start programs than can be accommodated with existing funding. Another example of unfunded mandates or inadequate funding is the Federal Resource and Referral Act of 1982. This federal legislation mandated the creation of child care resource and referral agencies within each state without providing funding. Early childhood advocates worked diligently with policymakers and in 1985 small amounts of federal funds were provided through the federal Dependant Care Block Grant program to states. As a result, some states began to fund resource and referral programs, but early childhood advocates continued to work with policymakers to secure full federal funding. In a push to get increased funding for child care and resource and referral agencies, local child care providers created a national coalition with a powerful voice, and in 1990, the Child Care and Development Block Grant (CCDBG) legislation was passed (Karolak, 2011). Through this legislation, funds were allocated for not only resource and referral agencies but also to improve the quality of child care and education. This was a major victory for early childhood advocates. However, advocacy work is never done because the funding of programs is constantly in jeopardy when new legislators, with new priorities, are elected. Early childhood advocates must constantly work to build relationships with new legislators by sharing their unique perspectives and the reasons for funding the programs in the first place.

Another reason why program funding is at the center of early childhood advocacy efforts is that birth to age 5 programs and K–12 public education programs are funded differently. For birth to age 5 programs, funding comes directly from fees paid by families for child care and education. In K–12 public education, funding is provided through the collection of local, state, and federal tax dollars. This funding disparity is changing due to the growth in recent years of state funded PreK and federal block grant money intended to increase the quality and accessibility of child care services (NAEYC, 2012). However, early childhood advocates need to remain vigilant and alert, particularly during city-, state-, and federal-level budget-cutting discussions that may threaten these funding streams.

In addition to funding direct services to children and families through block grants and PreK programs, state and federal funds support a wide variety of services that support children and families. Programs such as Medicaid and food stamps not only provide a needed social safety net for families but also serve as economic stabilizers because they put money back into the local economy (NAEYC, 2012). This is another reason why early childhood professionals need to be aware of local, state, and federal policies, and to make their voices heard by working with policymakers.

RESEARCH INTO PRACTICE: UNDERSTANDING THE LEGISLATIVE PROCESS

Early childhood advocates need to engage in substantial research to determine who within the current political structure has the potential power to develop supportive policies, to understand how the policymaking procedure works, and to learn how best to develop policy. The persons identified as potential policymakers in early childhood education vary at different levels of government. In public schools, school board members are most often responsible for the development of policy. Because most school board members are elected, they are therefore obligated to be responsive to their constituents. In city government, city council members are often ultimately responsible for the development and passage of policy because they, too, are elected and obligated to be responsive to their constituents.

Policy development at the state and federal level is a function of the Executive branch of government. Although there are some differences between how each state's Legislative branch is set up, the procedures for policy development at state and federal levels are similar. What follows is an overview of the federal legislative process as it relates to policy development, with examples of the roles early childhood advocates can play and strategies that can be used at each step of the legislative process. It is important to note that any bill can change significantly as it passes through various committees in each chamber of the legislature. This point emphasizes how important it is for early childhood advocates to track legislation continually so that they are aware of changes to policies and bills throughout the legislative process.

Step 1: Development and Introduction of a Bill

The first step is to develop the idea for the bill. Ideas come from many sources, including the general public. Early childhood advocates work together to research issues and develop solutions for issues affecting children and families. When they feel they have a viable plan, they choose a legislator to sponsor the bill and become its champion. This legislator and his or her staff work with the advocate or advocacy group to develop the plan further and formulate the initial bill. Early childhood advocates are often called upon to provide research-based documentation and impact statements related to the bill. When the bill is ready, it is given a number and introduced at the beginning of the legislative session by the sponsor. Knowing the number of the bill is vital to being able to track the bill effectively as it moves through the process of becoming law. There are two chambers of Congress: the House of Representatives and the Senate. Bills introduced in the House of Representatives are given a number preceded by the letters *HR*, and bills introduced in the Senate have a number preceded by the letter *S*.

Step 2: Committee Referral

Each chamber of the Legislative branch has standing committees that specialize in different areas, such as foreign relations or agriculture. The revenue committee and the education committee often hear legislation that directly impact children and families. The new bill is assigned to the appropriate committee, placed on its calendar, and carefully reviewed by a subcommittee. Public hearings may be held, and early childhood advocates may be called upon as experts to testify as to the soundness of the bill. Or if a bill has been introduced that advocates feel will negatively impact children and families, they may be asked to testify and explain the possible consequences of the bill. During committee referral, advocates can rally support for the bill (or support for the defeat of a bill) by launching e-mail or letter writing campaigns in which citizens contact committee members and express their opinions. Advocates can also write letters to the editor or opinion editorials for the local newspaper or disseminate public service announcements (PSAs) to public radio and television stations to educate the public and keep the issue in the forefront.

Step 3: Floor Action

After the hearings are completed, the subcommittee *marks up* the bill. This means that the subcommittee makes changes to the original bill based on the feedback gathered from hearings and public input. The subcommittee then votes to recommend the legislation to the full committee. If the subcommittee votes not to recommend the legislation, the bill dies in committee, but if the bill advances, the full committee may hold more public hearings and subsequently make additional changes to the bill. At some point, if the committee votes to recommend the bill, it is sent back to the full House or Senate for consideration. If the committee fails to pass the bill, then it dies, but if it votes to pass the bill back to the full House or Senate, the committee chairperson instructs staff to prepare a written report that includes the purpose of the bill, the position of the Executive branch, views of dissenting members of the committee, the impact on existing laws, budgetary consider- ations, and any new taxes or increases in taxes that would be required. This point in the process is a good time for early childhood advocates to influence passage of the bill by both working with the staffers as they write the final report and maintaining a campaign to keep the public informed and involved with bill. When the report is ready, it is placed on the legislative calendar for *floor action*, where it is debated by the full membership of the originating legislative chamber. Once the debate has ended and any amendments to the bill have been approved, the full membership votes for or against the bill. If the bill is approved, it is sent to the other chamber of Congress, where it generally follows the same route through committee and floor action.

Step 4: Conferencing

As the bill passes through committee in the second chamber, it may be approved, rejected, or tabled, in which case it will die. It may also be changed. If only minor changes are made in the second chamber, the bill goes back to the originating chamber for concur- rence. If the second chamber changes the bill significantly, a conference committee made up of members of both chambers meet to reconcile the differences. If the committee can- not agree on the changes, then the bill will die. If the conferencing committee agrees on a compromised version of the bill, a conference report is prepared describing the recom- mended changes. Both chambers must approve of the conference report before it is sent to the President. Again, early childhood advocates can work with committee staffers to provide needed information and expertise. They also work to maintain the public's focus on the bill and garner support for its passage through e-mail and letter writing campaigns between the public and its representatives.

Step 5: Executive Action

If the President approves the new legislation, he or she signs the bill and it becomes law. If the President takes no action for 10 days while Congress is in session, the bill automati- cally becomes law. The President can veto the bill outright or take no action on the bill for 10 days after the Congress adjourns. If this happens, the bill dies. Congress may attempt to override the veto by a roll call vote. Two-thirds of the members present (the sufficient number for a quorum) must approve the bill for it to become law.

The process of developing ideas into legislation is indeed quite complicated. The writers of the Constitution intended to allow many opportunities for public input. Each step of the process provides an opportunity for early childhood advocates to support or refute pending legislation through direct input to those formulating the bill and through more indirect means of educating the public, keeping the public informed of the progress of the bill, and rallying support for its passage (or defeat).

Tracking Legislation through Action Alerts

In order to effectively influence the legislative process, an advocate must read and under- stand the proposed bill and track it through the legislative process. Tracking is important because advocates need to know what changes are being made and when the bill is sched- uled for hearings and debate. Advocates can then launch public letter writing or e-mail campaigns to rally public support for the passage or defeat of the bill. For federal bills, advocates can use the U.S. Congress's website, called Thomas (after Thomas Jefferson; *http://thomas.loc.gov*), to get information about the status of bill as it moves through the legislative process. When you look up the bill using its designated call number, you see the bill itself, the names of its sponsors, the committee to which it has been assigned, and the dates of hearings as they are scheduled.

Another way to track legislation is through websites sponsored by various advocacy groups. Specialized sections on the website explain the organization's advocacy agenda; provide information about pending or upcoming legislation that relates to the agenda; and give information on when to act, whom to contact, and what message to give. The NAEYC operates the Children's Champion Network that includes an "action alert" system. Members can join a list-serve and receive regular updates regarding pending legislation. The following sites have advocacy links that provide alerts of pending legislation, as well as valuable resource information related to their advocacy agenda:

- Alliance for Children and Families
  http://www.alliance1.org; click on Public Policy, then Policy Alerts
  The Alliance tracks federal legislation on child abuse prevention and intervention, social services for low-income families, mental health, and other family supports.
- Children's Defense Fund
  http://www.childrensdefense.org; click on Take Action
  The Children's Defense Fund analyzes the impact of proposed federal legislation on ensuring that every child has a healthy start, head start, fair start, safe start, and a moral start.
- Families USA
  http://www.familiesusa.org; click on Action Center
  Families USA keeps track of funding and policy decisions that make a difference for children's health care.

THE IMPORTANCE OF RELATIONSHIPS FOR EFFECTIVE ADVOCACY

An advocate's role in public policy development is first to inform public officials of the needs of their communities. If no one tells school board members, city council members, or state or federal legislators about the negative impact of pending legislation or existing policies, they will not be aware that a problem exists. When legislators and civic leaders understand how policies affect people's lives, they are better able to develop, revise, and/ or fund projects that foster the well-being of their constituents. It is therefore vital to develop and maintain positive relationships with policymakers (Benson, 2000; NAEYC, 2004). The first step in building a positive relationship with policymakers is to know who they are and their perspectives regarding issues related to children and families. Early childhood advocates should be aware of who represents them on their school board, in city and county government, in the state legislature, and in the two chambers of Congress. The names, background and contact information, and voting records of elected officials can be located using a simple Internet search. This information helps advocates to understand the policymakers' perspectives, which in turn helps them frame the advocacy message to be delivered when they meet with legislators or other policymakers in person.

The second way to establish a relationship with a policymaker is to meet face-to-face (Benson, 2000). This can be done at political rallies or public meetings held by the policymaker. Your time will be very limited, so you do need to prepare in advance and be ready to deliver your advocacy message quickly. Establish early in the conversation that you are a constituent and an early childhood educator. Know the names and numbers of any pending bills you are advocating for (or against) and be ready to state your perspective and exactly what you want the policymaker to do. End by thanking the official for his or her work as it relates to children and families. Be specific. Let the official know that you know his or her voting record. This short brief message is often referred to as the *elevator speech* because it can be delivered in the time it takes to ride up several floors in an elevator. Here is a sample elevator speech for early childhood advocates:

"Hello, Senator Smith, I am Betty Jones, the director of ABC Child Care, which is in your district. I see firsthand how important refundable tax credits are to families and to my staff. My families are delighted that their choice of high-quality child care is noticed and rewarded. My staff feels appreciated for its work to deliver quality education and care to young children. I know you supported House Bill 223 when funding for this program was authorized. I am looking for your support of House Bill 312, which will continue this funding. Thank you for your continued support of children and families in our district."

Because most policymakers are either elected or appointed, they are obligated to meet with their constituents to hear their views. Advocates can also establish a relationship with public officials by meeting with them in their headquarters. It is an advocate's right to schedule a meeting and share expertise and concerns regarding existing policies or upcoming legislation. Advocates have more time in this scheduled meeting than at a public event, but careful preparation is still a must. The following are guidelines for meeting with elected officials in their offices:

- Make an appointment with the official's aides and let them know who is coming and the purpose of the meeting.
- Bring a carefully selected delegation with you. Include in your delegation someone who will be directly affected by the pending or existing legislation you are there to discuss. Prepare that person to tell his or her story. It is important for public officials to hear the stories of their constituents and attach these stories to real faces. This is known as *putting a face on an issue*.
- Be on time, but be prepared to wait. Elected officials are very busy, with meetings and events that often run over the scheduled time.
- Introduce the members of your delegation, and let the official know their relationship to pending or existing legislation that is the focus of your visit.
- Deliver a clear and succinct message. It should address why the policymaker should care and how you want him or her to act. Have facts from reputable sources to back up what you are saying. Connect these facts to the stories of constituents; again, put a *face on the issue*.
- Politely guide the conversation. It is easy to get drawn *off message*, but remember what you came for and stay focused on your goal. Diplomatically move the conversation where you want it to go.
- Listen to the policymaker's response. Answer any questions and make a note of further information that might be needed. Stay open-minded. Working to understand

opposing points of view will help you craft a stronger message (National Center for Learning Disabilities, 2009).

- Make *the hard ask* (i.e., "Can we count on you to support Senate Bill 332?").
- Thank the policymaker for his or her time, regardless of the response. Offer your expertise as a resource and invite him or her to visit your program or school to meet other constituents.
- Leave an information kit that outlines your position in more detail and provides resource materials that support your position. Include in the kit contact information for members of your delegation.
- Follow up within a few days with a thank-you note that summarizes your visit and provides further materials to answer questions or concerns raised during the meeting; thank the policymaker for the time and effort he or she extended with regard to the issue.

At times you will not be able to meet directly with the policymaker because of schedule conflicts. Ask to meet with the staff member who is working on the particular issue or legislation about which you are concerned. Do not be disappointed because staff members have significant influence with policymakers and often welcome your input. Making a good impression on a staff member will further your cause.

A third way to establish relationships with policymakers is to invite them to your school or program for a special event. These visits can raise their awareness of critical issues related to children and families, and if the media are invited, also raise the awareness of the general public (NAEYC, 2004). Plan the event to reinforce your advocacy message. For example, in 2011, First Lady Michelle Obama attended an event at Royal Castle Child Care Center in New Orleans to celebrate the center's 5-star status. As part of the event, children and families engaged in music and movement activities and received nutritious snacks. Consequently, the event showcased both Ms. Obama's personal advocacy efforts to combat childhood obesity and local early childhood advocates' agenda to showcase quality child care and education programs for young children.

Certainly much advanced planning goes into any visit or media event involving a public official. Schedules need to be carefully coordinated. Media need to be notified, and often security must be arranged. Parents and teachers at the program site should be given an opportunity to interact with the policymaker and convey a focused advocacy message. At the conclusion of the visit, give the policymaker an information kit and ask him or her directly to support children and families through support of specific legislation.

BUILDING AND MAINTAINING
EFFECTIVE ADVOCACY AGENDAS

"Advocacy is a proactive stance taken by individuals in response to particular issues that concern them" (Kieff & Casbergue, 2000, p. 13). It involves representing the needs of infants, toddlers, and young children, and articulating these needs to policymakers and to the general public through education, lobbying, and conducting and/or sharing relevant research findings. Each early childhood professional should develop an advocacy agenda that speaks to the needs of the children and families within his or her sphere of influence. An effective advocacy agenda involves the development of both strategies and tactics. *Strategies* are the general plans you develop and use to put forward your message and reach your objective. *Tactics* are the specific actions, tools, or procedures you use to attain your desired goals (Kevatin, 1998).

DEFINING THE FOCUS OF ADVOCACY

The first phase in developing an effective strategy for an advocacy agenda is to clearly define the issue, condition, or concern you want to address. Advocacy, however, because it takes much time and sustained energy, is most effective when the issue has personal meaning to the advocate (Goffin & Lombardi, 1988). For example, when her daughter was killed in a car accident involving a drunk driver, Candy Lightner channeled her grief into establishing Mothers Against Drunk Drivers (MADD). This advocacy organization is responsible for creating national and state laws that have changed how our society thinks about drinking and driving.

To define the focus of your advocacy efforts, remember that all policy development begins at the local level. Look within your own sphere of influence, the children and families close to you, to determine specific issues that negatively affect them or specific needs they have, in order to develop and learn at an optimal level. It might be that a child, niece, nephew, or student in your program has a chronic illness. In working with this child or family you become aware of gaps in community services, and you are energized to do something about it through advocacy. You may know a child who is a member of a military family. You see firsthand the effect having a family member on active duty has on the child. You see gaps in community services that need to be filled. Or you might see policies in your organization, community, or state that are preventing the delivery of these services. There might be good policies in place, but they are not being enforced or funded at an adequate level to serve the children and families. All of these are good reasons to develop an advocacy agenda.

BECOMING AN INFORMED ADVOCATE

When you identify specific program or policy needs or deficiencies, the focus of your advocacy agenda becomes clear. The next step is to become well informed about this issue. Certainly, you will have your own training and experience on which to draw, but being an informed advocate implies that you have gone beyond your own general knowledge set and studied the issue from multiple perspectives (Kieff, 2009). If you feel that there are policies or practices in place that inhibit a group of children or families, then you need to find out the original intent of the policy, how that intent has been diverted, and who among existing policymakers has the authority to correct this. If the focus of your advocacy is on creating a policy that enables a certain population, you must make sure you understand that population's perspective. It may be somewhat different than your own. When you begin to develop your message, it is important that you put an authentic *face* on it.

You may also need to do some research to find out where jurisdiction for the policy lies, that is, which policymakers you need to work with to bring about the desired goal, whether it is to develop a new policy, or repeal or modify an existing one. It is also important at this stage in the development of your advocacy agenda to find out who else may be working in this particular area of advocacy. What other groups or coalitions have focused on this issue? They will have both expertise and materials to share with you. Voices are stronger and more powerful when advocates coalesce to support an issue.

DEVELOPING ADVOCACY STRATEGIES AND CHOOSING TACTICS

After you thoroughly research your advocacy issue and have become informed about its many aspects, it is now time to develop the strategies and select the tactics to further your agenda. There are several sets of guiding questions you need to address continually as you develop and work through your agenda. Figure 5.1 presents these question sets. It is important to understand that the answers to each of these questions constantly change as you research your issue and develop more and more relationships with coalitions and policymakers who can influence the issue. Advocacy agendas are dynamic working documents.

Once you have developed your strategies, you can choose from a wide range of tactics, such as organizing a letter writing campaign, working with coalitions, and/or working with the media to reach your ultimate goal. There are three broad categories of tactics: (1) educational, (2) persuasive, and (3) mobilizing (see Figure 5.2). Educational tactics inform others about an issue and raise the awareness of both policymakers and the general public. Persuasive tactics convince others that certain policies need to be passed, modified or repealed. Mobilization tactics encourage the public to contact the appropriate elected official and state an opinion. It is in the development and use of tactics that every early childhood professional can utilize his or her own special skills and talents, or even develop new ones.

---

1. Describe the issue that concerns you.

2. What is it, exactly, that you want to obtain? Effect? If you get your way, what will the end result look like?

3. Who are the stakeholders? That is, whom do you want to affect? What populations of children and/or families need to be supported through this advocacy effort? How can you describe this group? What is their perspective regarding the issue?

4. Who is the audience in your advocacy efforts? Who has the power to make the changes needed? Toward whom should you address your actions? Who are the key policymakers responsible for the action, policy, or the lack thereof? Among the policymakers, who would likely be a champion for your cause? Who might be an opponent?

5. Who can help you effect change? Who might be your allies? With whom can you connect? What other groups or coalitions have been working on this issue or are also concerned with it? What already has been done to effect change in this area?

6. What messaged do you want your audience to hear? Who should transmit this message?

7. How can the message be delivered?

8. What have you already achieved? What are your resources? What do you still need to develop? How will you begin? What will be the next step?

FIGURE 5.1. Worksheet for developing advocacy strategies.

Tactics are the specific actions you take or materials you develop and use as you implement your advocacy agenda. Tactics are used to educate or inform, persuade, or mobilize others to support or defeat pending legislation. Certainly, any of the listed tactics can be used for more than one of these purposes.

Educational Tactics: Designed to raise awareness and to inform
　　Fact sheets
　　Websites
　　Position papers
　　Information kits
　　Letters to the editor
　　Opinion editorials
　　Multimedia presentations
　　Testimony

Persuasive Strategies: Designed to promote or dissuade the development of specific rules or policies
　　Visits to policymakers
　　Letter-writing or e-mail campaigns
　　Phone calls
　　"Life stories" to put a face on an issue
　　Public service announcements (PSAs)

Mobilizing Tactics: Designed to get the message to the public and keep it alive
　　Network with others
　　Form advocacy groups
　　Join coalitions
　　Conduct media events

FIGURE 5.2. Advocacy tactics.

REFLECTIONS AND NEW DIRECTIONS

Early childhood professionals have an ethical responsibility to advocate for causes that affect the well-being of young children and their families. In recent years, the actual practice of advocacy has changed dramatically with the advent of new technologies that make it easy to connect with other advocates. These emerging technologies can be used to raise public awareness of pending legislation that supports or detracts from the well-being of children and families. Technology can also be used to sway the opinion of policymakers. Advocacy is easier today because a strong body of research underscores the importance of how the early years of life relate to positive emotional, social, intellectual, physical, and social outcomes (Karolak, 2011). However, because funding for early childhood programming is frequently in jeopardy, early childhood professionals need to constantly engage in advocacy for children and families.

Even with technological advances, what effectively propels advocacy efforts are the relationships formed between advocates and advocacy group and policymakers. Characteristics of effective advocacy include all of the following:

- Advocates recognize issues, situations, policies, and/or practices that cause harm or otherwise create barriers that prevent optimal development of infants, toddlers, and young children (Hyson, 2003).
- The optimism of advocates who believe that one person can make a difference for one child and a coalition of advocates can make a difference for many children (Kieff, 2009).
- Advocates are curious and able to examine an issue from multiple perspectives (Goffin & Lombardi, 1988).
- Advocates communicate effectively to a wide range of individuals (Hyson, 2003).
- Advocates have a vision and are able to articulate this vision to others (Hyson, 2003).
- Advocates are risk takers. They put themselves out there; that is, they speak up even if there might be negative consequences (Kieff, 2009).
- Advocates set realistic goals, and when they reach them they set new goals. They have stamina and perseverance (Goffin & Lombardi, 1988).
- Advocates are aware of a broad range of educational, persuasive, and mobilization tactics, and know when to use them (Kieff, 2009).
- Advocates work tirelessly and consider defeat not as an end result but as an obstacle to overcome (Kieff, 2009).

The first step in developing advocacy capacity is to assess one's own skills as they relate to the characteristics described here. As you develop your advocacy skills, you will find your own voice in a cause that is near to your heart. It might be maintaining funds for programs that support inclusion or working to bring about quality health care legislation for all children. But remember, it is important to understand that everyone can do something to advance improved and supportive conditions for children and their families. When we work together, we are a most powerful force!

PROFESSIONAL DEVELOPMENT ACTIVITIES

- Log onto the National Council for State Legislatures website (*www.ncsl.org*) and navigate the site to find all the information you can about your state. Or use *http://thomas.loc.org* to find pending legislation at the federal level. Review relevant legislation that is now pending. How does this legislation affect children and families in your community? Where do you stand on these legislative initiatives? What advocacy roles are you ready to take on regarding this legislation? What tactics will be most effective in supporting (or defeating) this pending legislation?

- Review websites for Alliance of Children (*http://alliance1.org*), Children's Defense Fund (*www.childrensdefense.org*), Families USA (*http://familiesusa.org*), and the National Association for the Education of Young Children (*www.naeyc.org*). Read legislative alerts and calls for action. Follow through on suggested activities. Write a report reflecting your experiences and detailing your actions.

- Working in groups, define a specific issue that affects infants, toddlers, young children, and families in your community. Draft an advocacy agenda using the sets of questions outlined in Figure 5.1. Suggest multiple tactics that are useful to develop relationships with policymakers and to mobilize your message. Reflect on your advocacy agenda by describing your current capacity to take on the agenda and what you need to build.

What are you willing to do right now? What are you willing to learn to do to further your agenda? Share your agenda with other members of your class and revise according to their feedback.

▨ Examine your current capacity for advocacy by reviewing the characteristics of effective advocates listed in the "Reflections and New Directions" section. What characteristics do you feel you currently possess? What experiences have enabled you develop these strengths? What characteristics do you need to develop to become an effective advocate? How can you challenge yourself to develop these characteristics? Set three goals for yourself and develop a plan and time line to meet those goals.

REFERENCES

Benson, P. (2000). *ECSC's role in shaping policy: A practical guide to changing minds and saving lives.* Washington, DC: Emergency Medical Services for Children (EMSC) National Resource Center.

Goffin, S. G., & Lombardi, J. (1988). *Speaking out: Early Childhood Advocacy.* Washington, DC: NAEYC.

Hyson, M. (Ed.). (2003). *Preparing early childhood professionals: NAEYC's standards for programs.* Washington, DC: NAEYC.

Karolak, E. (2011). Changes in the policy and advocacy landscape: A conversation with Helen Blank. *Exchange, 200,* 4320000.

Kevatin, M. (1998). *Public policy advocacy: Women for social change in the Yugoslav successor states.* Washington, DC: STAR Project, Delphi International.

Kieff, J. (2009). *Informed advocacy in early childhood care and education: Making a difference for young children and families.* Upper Saddle River, NJ: Pearson.

Kieff, J., & Casbergue, R. (2000). *Playful learning and teaching: Integrating play into preschool and primary programs.* Needham Heights, MA: Allyn & Bacon.

National Association for the Education of Young Children (NAEYC). (2004). *Affiliate public policy tool kit.* Washington, DC: Author.

National Association for the Education of Young Children (NAEYC). (2011). *The Code of Ethics and Statement of Commitment: Revised April 2005, Reaffirmed and Updated May 2011.* Washington DC: NAEYC. Retrieved from *www.naeyc.org.*

National Association for the Education of Young Children (NAEYC). (2012). Why is it so important to contact members of congress? *Young Children, 67*(1), 63.

National Center for Learning Disabilities. (2009). Working with policymakers. Retrieved December 28, 2011, from *www.ncld.org/at-school/your-childs-rights/advocacy-selfadvocacy/working-with-policymakers.*

Stoney, L., & Mitchell, A. (2007). *Using tax credits to promote high quality early care and education services.* Washington, DC: The Partnership for America's Economic Success.

Urban Institute. (2003). *Beyond ideology, politics, and guesswork: The case for evidence-based policy.* Washington, DC: Author.

PART II

ONE SIZE DOESN'T FIT ALL

CHAPTER 6

DESIGNING AND MANAGING EFFECTIVE EARLY CHILDHOOD CLASSROOM ENVIRONMENTS

D. RAY REUTZEL
CINDY D. JONES

> The classroom environment can work for us or against us, which is why
> it is first, last, and always among pedagogical concerns.
> —KATHLEEN A. ROSKOS AND SUSAN B. NEUMAN (2011)

Ms. Raines, a veteran kindergarten teacher, received word as the school year ended that she was being transferred to a new kindergarten classroom in a school across the city due to demographic shifts in district kindergarten enrollments. Ms. Raines had been in the same classroom and school for many years. Consequently, she had collected a great deal of "teaching stuff" to instruct her young students. As she contemplated the move to the new classroom, she realized that she had not thought about how to design a new classroom environment from the ground up for many years. Faced with an empty classroom, questions about classroom design now occupied her thoughts as she turned the key to open the door to her new kindergarten classroom.

WHAT RESEARCH SAYS ABOUT DESIGNING AND MANAGING EFFECTIVE EARLY CHILDHOOD CLASSROOM ENVIRONMENTS

It is accepted as nearly axiomatic among contemporary scholars that the physical environment of the classroom plays a decisive role in the learning and behavior of young children. Teachers evidence instinctive concern for the effect of the ecology of the classroom on children's learning and behavior as they design, organize, decorate, and manage their classrooms. Throughout history philosophers, educators, and scientists have observed the "press" or coercive influence that physical environments exert upon human behavior and thinking (Gump, 1989). Research into the role of the classroom environment has in recent decades become a topic of increasing interest in early childhood education. In this chapter, we discuss historical, ecological, educational, and assessment research on the role of the classroom environment in the education of young children. We begin with a discussion of the historical role of classroom environments in the educational experiences of young children.

Historical Views on Classroom Environment

Friedrich Froebel (1974), a German educator and father of the modern day kindergarten, originally studied architecture. His study of architecture undoubtedly laid the foundation for a later focus on organizing learning environments for young children that stimulated their drive toward creative, self-directed activity (Broman, 1982). Later, John Dewey, in his 1887 publication "My Pedagogic Creed," noted that one role of school was to interpret a child's classroom environment into the simplest terms and concepts to support learning. Maria Montessori (1965) advocated for classroom environments that were carefully prepared to promote learning. In 1914, she wrote, "The care and management of the environment itself affords the principal means of motor education, while sensory education and the education of language are provided for by my didactic material" (M. Montessori, 1965, p. 50). In 1912, Montessori devoted an entire section of her method to "Environment: Schoolroom Furnishings" (p. 80) with specific attention to the creation of adequate open-air spaces, little chairs and tables, lowered chalkboards, windows, storage shelves, and so forth.

Stormz and McKee (1928), in their book *The Progressive Primary Teacher*, devoted an entire chapter to a critique and redesign of the primary-grade classroom environment. They observed, "Similarly, in business or industry, materials and activities are organized. In every grouping of this sort the organization is dominated by the purposes involved— efficiency, convenience, comfort, attractiveness. In school work our aim should be primarily to interest the children in a variety of educative activities" (p. 10).

Following World War II, inhabitants of Villa Cella, Italy, constructed a "school of the people" using a small government grant for rebuilding the community. Loris Malaguzzi became the driving force behind the educational approach that eventually became known as Reggio Emilia (Wurm, 2005). The "Reggio" approach to early childhood education placed special emphasis on design of the space and the classroom environment. *Space* refers to the physical features of the place where teachers and children work and the inherent values these features reveal. *Environment*, or *ambience* as in Italian, refers to the way the physical space is organized, decorated, lived in, and changed over time. Reggio Emilia schools carefully consider the answer to the question, "What are you unconsciously communicating about your values of the child based on the spaces you create?" (Wurm, 2005, p. 27). From this brief review, it is clear that philosophers, educators, and scientists throughout history have understood and validated the power of environment to shape, influence, and mold the learning and lives of young children.

Ecological Research on Classroom Environment

Barker's (1968, 1978) pioneering work in ecological psychology determined that human behavior is directly related to environments in lawful and predictable ways.

He summarized these changes in human behavior in three succinct generalizations: (1) Human behavior changes from setting to setting to meet the requirements of each setting; (2) the behavior of people in each setting is more similar than different; and (3) each person's behavior tends to be consistent over time in the same or similar setting.

Cambourne (2002) asserted that classroom settings also elicit predictable human behaviors. These behaviors in classrooms, however, are influenced by three essential and interlocking characteristics: (1) *access* to and *organization* of space and inanimate physical objects; (2) familiar activity routines; and (3) settings that beckon teachers and students to socially interact and cognitively engage. Our review is organized around these three essential, interlocking characteristics that influence human behavior in classroom environments.

Access to adequate physical space to accommodate the number of students within a classroom is a precondition for encouraging high-quality social interactions and heightened cognitive activity among the occupants (Roskos & Neuman, 2001). The way classroom space is *organized* also influences students' behaviors and learning. Open spaces suggest freedom and fluidity of student movement. Spatial and physical boundaries help students self-regulate and guide their behavioral and activity choices, as well as indicating specific functional locations within the classroom (Roskos & Neuman, 2001). Organization of learning tools, props, objects, or materials in classrooms also has consequences for young students (Reutzel & Jones, 2010; Wolfersberger, Reutzel, Sudweeks, & Fawson, 2004).

As Roskos and Neuman (2001, 2011) point out, patterns, structure, and organization of activities in the classroom environment are often invisible to the mind's eye but are essential elements of designing effective classroom learning environments. These near-transparent organizational structures, patterns, or routines give form, order, quality, and meaning to the activities within a classroom. For example, classroom rules for student conduct need to be explicitly taught, sufficiently concrete, of high utility, and integrated into the very fabric of the classroom routine (Reutzel & Clark, 2011; Reutzel & Jones, 2010; Reutzel & Morrow, 2007). Classroom procedures comprise ways to take care of repetitive student actions such as lining up, taking bathroom breaks, moving among activities, or sharpening a pencil. Routines are established when procedures, rules, and schedules are taught and rehearsed over and over again. Yinger (1979, 1980) states that the routinization of classroom rules and procedures leads to fewer interruptions of the flow and sequence of classroom events and interactions. According to Doyle (2006), "Routines provide a continuous signal for organizational and interpersonal behavior" (p. 108). Similarly, managing time well means minimizing transition times between activities to maximize learning time, maintaining a brisk pace of activity, and encouraging a sense of orderliness in the classroom environment.

The physical spaces themselves and the arrangement of learning materials within physical spaces should invite teachers and young students to engage socially and cognitively in the classroom environment. Classroom spaces should provide students access to organized learning materials to encourage activities among inhabitants of the classroom environment that are productive, imaginative, and authentic. Unfortunately, research reveals little about how to create effective and engaging "setting–object–action" relationships in early childhood classroom environments. Consequently, we need a much more complete and exacting description of the complex relationships that exist among agents, objects, and settings within the classroom environment than is currently available (Roskos & Neuman, 2001).

Education Research on Classroom Environments

Past educational research on classroom environment and its effects on student behaviors, activities, interactions, and learning has largely focused on the physical arrangement of classroom spaces and learning materials. One of the earliest studies of this type was Morrow and Weinstein's (1982, 1986) study of classroom libraries. These researchers made the library more visible by giving it clear boundaries as a separate space in the classroom. They also infused the library center with comfortable furnishings; well-organized access to many and varied books; and materials for responding to books, such as puppets, writing supplies, and listening centers. As a result of these design changes, they found that students used the library corner more frequently. Similarly, other researchers who have replicated these findings show that design changes in classrooms that divide or partition off specific spatial settings for clearly identified purposes, and infuse novel and interesting learning props, objects, and materials into the classroom, result in enhanced social interactions, language use, focused and sustained attention, and increased learning (Hall, 1987; Morrow, 1990; Neuman & Roskos, 1989, 1992; Vukelich, 1991, 1994).

In a second focus of educational research on the effect of classroom environments, researchers have investigated the role of instruction. Although classroom environments influence or "press" inhabitants to behave in predictable ways, interaction of the inhabitants within the environment can also influence behaviors and outcomes. Researchers have found that the interaction between teachers, mentors, parents, and other students within the classroom affects student engagement, language use, persistence, attention, and learning outcomes (McGill-Franzen, Allington, Yokoi, & Brooks, 1999; Neuman & Roskos, 1992, 1997; Paley, 1994; Rowe, 1999; Tharpe & Gallimore, 1988; Vukelich, 1994).

In summary, as Roskos and Neuman (2001, p. 290) indicate,

> We need to better articulate and explain the concept of the . . . environment as a "pattern of relations" for teachers and their professional work. Much emphasis has been placed on creating the "print-rich environment" and "flooding" classroom with books and print. . . . An essential understanding for teachers is *how* to design the organization of activity to create patterns that steadily enliven and invigorate children's . . . learning in the classroom.

ASSESSMENT OF CLASSROOM ENVIRONMENTS

In this section, we describe three widely used, valid, and reliable assessment tools for evaluating early childhood classroom environments. These assessments represent a culmination of decades of research into what makes an effective classroom environment. Consequently, an examination of classroom environment assessments serves to synthesize and crystallize the essential elements associated with effective classroom environments.

We have selected three, well-known, well-researched classroom environment assessment instruments for review: (1) the Early Childhood Environment Rating Scale (ECERS-R; Harms, Clifford, & Cryer, 1998); (2) the Classroom Literacy Environmental Profile (CLEP; Wolfersberger et al., 2004); and (3) the Classroom Assessment Scoring System (CLASS; Pianta, LaParo, & Hamre, 2008). After describing each of these instruments, we look across the collective dimensions assessed for shared themes and categories that inform later recommendations for creating and maintaining effective classroom environments in early childhood education.

Early Childhood Environment Rating Scale

The ECERS (Harms et al., 1998) has been widely used and has proved to be a reliable means for assessing early childhood programs and classroom environments. The ECERS contains a total of 43 items distributed across seven environmental subscales: (1) Space and Furnishings, (2) Personal Care Routines, (3) Language-Reasoning, (4) Activities, (5) Interaction, (6) Program Structure, and (7) Parents and Staff. Each subscale contains a number of quality indicators. The scoring sheet records the ratings for quality indicators, items, subscale, and total scale, along with a space for observer comments. The indicator responses—*yes, no,* and *not applicable*—score individual items on a scale of 1 (*inadequate*) to 7 (*excellent*). The ECERS can be scored two ways. First, one can score the number of the highest quality indicators with affirmative responses. Second, one can score each item on a scale from 1 to 7. Using the latter scoring method extends the observation time from 2 to 5 hours. A profile sheet is also included to display the scoring information visually to identify strengths and weaknesses.

Harms and colleagues (1998) report subscale internal consistency (Cronbach's alphas ranging from .71 to .88) with total scale internal consistency at .92. Interrater reliability was $r = .92$. Predictive validity of the ECERS was shown to be good in a study by Peisner-Feinberg and Burchinal (1997).

Classroom Literacy Environmental Profile

Wolfersberger and colleagues (2004) developed the CLEP, which is a tool for examining the "print richness" of early childhood and elementary classrooms. They identified, defined, and organized into categories the characteristics of print-rich classroom environments through a systematic and extensive review of the literature, classroom observations, and teacher focus group discussions, using formative data to write and review the initial items of the CLEP instrument. In generalizability and dependability studies, classrooms and items on the CLEP evidenced large variance components, indicating that the degree of implementation in print-rich classroom environments could be reliably discriminated with the CLEP instrument.

When using the CLEP instrument, users rate classroom literacy environments on a 7-point Likert rating scale containing descriptors or written anchors under points 1, 3, 5, and 7. The CLEP instrument allows raters to evaluate 33 aspects of classroom literacy environments using two subscales: *Identifying Literacy Tools for Use in Literacy-Rich Classroom Environments* and *How to Use Literacy Tools or Props to Support Such an Environment.* Areas examined using the CLEP are shown in Table 6.1.

Wolfersberger and colleagues (2004) assert that the CLEP is a valid and reliable tool for evaluating the print richness of early childhood and elementary classrooms to enrich, refine, research, and redesign classrooms to foster engaged literacy learning for all children. A generalizability and dependability study reveals a phi coefficient of .87 when the CLEP is used by two raters, on two occasions to assess the classroom literacy environment. The CLEP serves as a reliable guide for educators to apply what Neuman and Roskos had earlier called "a more calculated approach to the design of literacy enrichments in early childhood and elementary classroom environments" (1992, p. 221).

**TABLE 6.1. Classroom Literacy Environment Profile (CLEP):
Areas Assessed in Subscales**

Subscale 1: Identifying Literacy Tools for Use in Literacy-Rich
Classroom Environments

1. Quantity of literacy tools
2. Utility of literacy tools
3. Appropriateness of literacy tools
4. Quantity of text materials (including books, magazines,
   newspapers, etc.; count multiple copies as one)
5. Genres of text materials
6. Levels of text materials
7. Format and content of text materials
8. Print used for classroom organization
9. Classroom literacy product displays
10. Reference materials
11. Written communications
12. Writing utensils
13. Writing surfaces
14. Publishing materials
15. Technological resources to support literacy events
16. Furnishings to support literacy events
17. Storage and display containers to support literacy events
18. Accessories to support literacy events

Subscale 2: How to Use Literacy Props or Tools to Support
a Literacy-Rich Classroom Environment

19. Location of classroom areas
20. Boundaries of classroom areas
21. Size of classroom areas
22. Types of classroom areas
23. Classroom library
24. Grouping of literacy tools
25. Accessibility of literacy tools
26. Participation in literacy events in encouraged
27. Participation in literacy events is Inviting
28. Authentic literacy settings
29. Authentic literacy events
30. Interactions with literacy tools
31. Record-keeping of literacy interactions
32. Variety of literacy products
33. Sharing literacy products

Classroom Assessment Scoring System

The CLASS, developed by Pianta and colleagues (2008), can be purchased for two levels
of observations: PreK and K–3. Rather than focusing primarily on the physical environment of the classroom or the curriculum, the CLASS focuses on the interactions between
teachers and their students. Three major areas of classroom characteristics are included
in the CLASS assessment: (1) emotional support, (2) classroom organization, and (3)
instructional support. The CLASS assesses 10 key dimensions of teacher–student interactions: Positive Climate, Negative Climate, Teacher Sensitivity, Regard for Student Perspectives, Overcontrol, Behavior Management, Productivity, Learning Formats, Concept
Development, Quality of Feedback, and Language Modeling.

    LaParo, Pianta, and Stuhlman (2004) report reliability and validity data for the
CLASS using a principal components factor analysis with varimax rotation. The CLASS

instrument accounted for 72% of the variance associated with teacher–student interactions using a two-factor solution: Emotional Support and Instructional Support. The internal consistency of the subscales within Emotional Support was alpha = .85. The internal consistency of the subscale within Instructional Support was alpha = .88. The two factors of the CLASS show statistically significant correlations with the ECERS total score: Emotional Support CLASS score with ECERS total = .52, $p < .0001$; Instructional Support CLASS score with ECERS total = .40, $p < .0001$. In summary, the CLASS is particularly useful for examining the emotional and instructional environment of early childhood classrooms for purposes of determining accountability, identifying professional development needs, and program planning.

As we examined commonalities among these classroom environmental assessment tools and analyzed the historical, educational, and ecological literature reviewed in this chapter, five overarching themes or categories emerged in relation to establishing and maintaining effective classroom learning environments: (1) positive emotional climate, (2) supportive physical environment, (3) efficient management and organization, (4) effective curriculum programs and instructional practices, and (5) high-quality teacher–student interactions. In the next section of this chapter, we describe how early childhood teachers can establish effective classroom environments.

RESEARCH INTO PRACTICE

The thoughtful design of classroom space can create educational environments that actively exert a positive and pervasive influence on students' motivation and learning. First, we discuss the spatial design of the classroom, including the arrangement and organization of learning materials and furnishings to create inviting and structured settings for learning activities. Second, we discuss designing a classroom management plan that gives structure and order to the activities that play out within that environment.

Designing the Spatial Layout of the Classroom

Research has shown that the physical or spatial design of early childhood classrooms exerts a powerful influence on student learning (Reutzel & Clark, 2011; Reutzel & Jones, 2010; Roskos & Neuman, 2011). Research has also shown that preschool-age children evidence a keen awareness of their classroom environment (Holmes & Cunningham, 1995). Young children, when shown photographs of classroom spaces, can describe appropriate activities for each area, as well as draw activity spaces found in their own classrooms. Kershner and Pointon (2000) surveyed seventy 5- and 6-year-old children about their classrooms. These young children expressed preferences for specific grouping and seating arrangements, interesting and informative wall displays, general tidiness of the space, low noise levels, and the opportunity to choose to work alone or with others.

According to research by Wolfersberger and colleagues (2004), designing classroom space to support effective instruction involves (1) planning the spatial layout of the classroom; (2) selecting, arranging, and organizing materials and furnishings; and (3) preparing a management plan to give structure and order to the learning activities to be carried out in the classroom. The model shown in Figure 6.1 begins with the structuring of various classroom spaces to support learning activities. Next, it directs attention to "provisioning" the classroom spaces with necessary furnishings and learning supplies. The model then speaks to the need to design routines that support interactive relationships

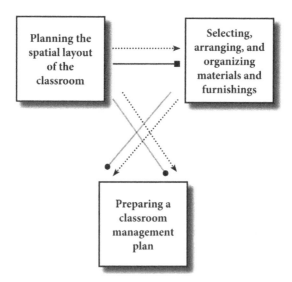

FIGURE 6.1. Designing effective classroom learning environments. Each combination of symbols (●, ■) and line types (continuous, dotted) represents a hypothetical decision to be made in creating an effective classroom environment.

between the furnishings and learning supplies, and the children and teachers who use them.

Drawing a Floor Plan of Classroom Spaces

Spending adequate time to prepare the classroom for its eventual occupants—young children—pays large learning and management dividends later on. A good place to begin is determining whether the classroom provides sufficient area for its intended occupants. Adequate classroom space, as determined by major several professional associations and government agencies, is approximately 35 square feet per child (National Association for the Education of Young Children [NAEYC], 2012). Classroom spaces that are either too crowded or too expansive may invite a litany of student behavior, classroom management, and teaching-learning problems (Smith & Connolly, 1980). Once the adequacy of space is determined, the next logical step is to design carefully the spatial layout of the classroom. Decisions about the design of classroom space typically focus on two major concerns: (1) spatial design to support the various learning activities to be carried out in the classroom, and (2) access to and organization of learning materials within each designed space in the classroom.

Typically speaking, early childhood classroom space is divided into activity spaces that support whole-class, small-group, and individual/independent teaching–learning arrangements. To get started, we recommend that teachers draw a classroom floor plan. Teachers should think about their instructional goals. Spaces should align well with the curriculum to be taught and the goals of instruction (Roskos & Neuman, 2011). Teachers should also consider where and how they want to conduct whole-class instruction, as well as small-group or individual activities.

Teachers are sensible to locate whole-group learning spaces on the floor plan near whiteboards, projector screens, or interactive computer whiteboards, well away from areas in the classroom designated for quieter activities (Reutzel & Cooter, 2012). A large, well-padded carpet can comfortably seat an entire group of young children in a whole-group space. For management purposes, the carpet or "rug" area should be divided into individual spaces or squares so that each child has an assigned place during "rug time." Also, locating tables around the "rug" offers additional seating options for the whole group. When planning whole-group instructional areas, teachers should locate this area where children can see and interact with the teacher and audiovisual aids and technologies during demonstrations or modeling of skills, concepts, processes, or strategies.

Small-group and individual instruction and activity areas in the classroom pose similar challenges when planning classroom space. How many spaces and what types should there be to support small-group and independent activities? How many small group areas can the teacher reasonably design and manage? Many early childhood teachers prefer setting up small-group or independent activity areas of the classroom as "centers," which can be either teacher-directed or independent. Small-group areas can focus student activity on exploration of content subjects, skills, or strategy practice in basic skills areas, and on dramatic play and performances. Procedures for entering, using, and cleaning up centers should be posted and practiced under the guidance of the teacher. Objectives, rules for behavior, and tasks to be completed should also be clearly displayed in effectively designed classroom learning or activity centers.

Learning centers should have clear boundaries signaled by furnishings that contain learning supplies specific to that area (Morrow, Reutzel, & Casey, 2006). All small-group or independent learning spaces or centers should be clearly labeled and their materials stored on tables, on shelves, in boxes, or displayed on a bulletin board. Equipment or other supplies in centers should have their own designated locations, so that teachers can direct children to them, and children can easily find and return the items. At the beginning of each school year, centers provide access to only a small number of items; new materials may be added gradually as the year progresses. The teacher should introduce the purposes, uses, and placement of each item in learning centers. In classrooms too small to designate areas of floor space for small-group or independent activities, materials for "centers" can be placed into transportable baskets to be brought to student tables in the classroom.

Examples of learning centers or activity areas may include a classroom library and content-area learning centers. A classroom library, or reading nook, is a place where books and young children come together. In classroom libraries, take-home, checkout, book trading, and book-ordering processes should be well planned and practiced with children. Well-designed classroom libraries serve five important functions (Reutzel & Fawson, 2002): (1) to support instruction, (2) to facilitate learning about books and print, (3) to organize the storage of classroom books, (4) to provide resources for content-area learning, and (5) to provide a location for student talk and interaction around books. The classroom library is a vital center or activity area in effective classroom environments. Content-area learning spaces are of particular importance in an era of Common Core State Standards (CCSS; National Governors Association Center for Best Practices & Council of Chief State School Officers, 2011; Reutzel & Morrow, 2007). All content-area learning centers—music, art, blocks, science, social studies, and drama centers—should include books and writing materials.

Seating arrangements in small-group centers is an important consideration. Hasting and Schwieso (1995) investigated the effects of various seating arrangements on primary-grade students' task engagement. Results indicated that 76% of children preferred being seated in groups rather than rows. On the other hand, when students were asked to complete individual learning tasks, measures of on-task behaviors increased when the seating arrangement was changed from groups to rows. This was particularly true with the lowest quartile cohort of children. As a result, Hasting and Schwieso recommended that group-seating arrangements be used when interaction, discussion, and collaboration are needed to complete a task or project. However, when learning tasks require individual work, seating in rows leads to improved on-task behaviors among young children. In summary, these researchers recommend that teachers should "consider the design of physical environments in the context of pedagogical purposes" (p. 290).

Small-group or independent learning centers should be designed and located to create relatively quiet academic areas, with other places reserved for more active play or performances. For example, the literacy center that houses the classroom library, writing areas, and oral language areas might be next to the math center because these areas generally house activities that require relative quiet. Alternatively, art, music, dramatic play, woodworking, and block play tend to be noisier activities, so they are placed at the opposite end of the room from the quiet areas. The small-group instruction table is situated in a quiet area that allows the teacher a commanding view of the entire classroom. While the teacher is involved in small-group or individualized instruction, the rest of the class is working either in small groups or independently. A classroom floor plan of the physical environment designed for many preschool and kindergarten classrooms, and some first- and second-grade classrooms, is shown in Figure 6.2.

Arranging and Organizing Learning Materials within Classroom Spaces

Past national surveys have indicated lack of *access* to a rich array of learning materials in early childhood classrooms, including learning tools as basic as books (Fractor, Woodruff, Martinez, & Teale, 1993; McGill-Franzen et al., 1999; Morrow, 1990; Neuman, 1999). Access to print is unevenly distributed across socioeconomic levels in the United States (Neuman, 1999; Neuman & Celano, 2001). Research has shown that access to learning materials and tools positively influences children's persistence and engagement in play as well as learning activities (Fernie, 1985; Neuman & Roskos, 1990). Arrangement, grouping, appropriateness, authenticity, utility, proximity, portability and variety of learning materials in classrooms affect student choices, behaviors, and learning outcomes (Neuman & Roskos, 1993; Reutzel & Cooter, 2012). Research has shown that smaller, well-defined niches and nooks often encourage greater language use and social collaboration among younger students (Morrow, 1988; Neuman & Roskos, 1997). On the other hand, small-group and independent classroom spaces that are too private do not allow for adequate teacher monitoring and supervision.

When small-group or independent center spaces are organized so that naturally related learning tools are clustered together, younger children become more involved in sustained play and learning. For example, Neuman and Roskos (1993) placed learning tools associated with mailing letters together in a play post office setting (e.g., envelopes, writing instruments, stamps, and stationery). Doing so led to longer play episodes than when these props were scattered throughout the room. Furthermore, learning tools, objects, or props that were authentic, familiar, and useful in familiar environmental contexts (e.g., telephones in the kitchen area or mailboxes in the office area) encouraged more complex language and social interactions. Roskos and Neuman (2011) have recently also encouraged "greening" the classroom space as prescribed in LEED (Leadership in Energy and Environmental Design) certified schools, in which classroom spaces

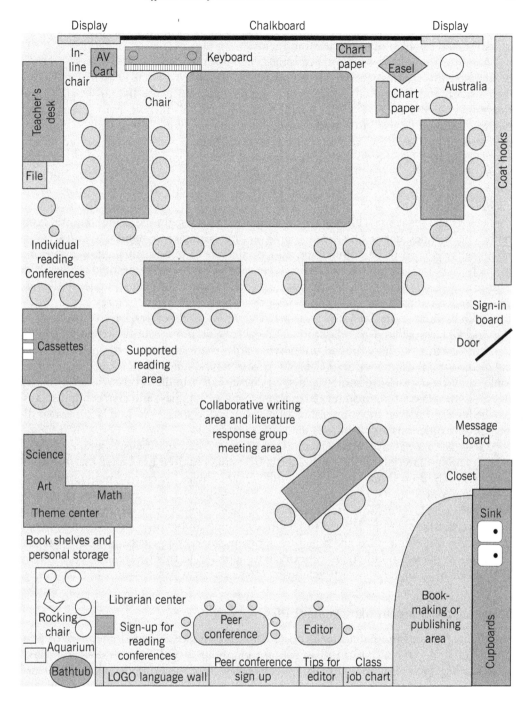

FIGURE 6.2. Example of a classroom floor plan. From Ray D. Reutzel and Robert D. Cooter, *Teaching Children to Read: From Basals to Books, 2nd Edition*, © 1996, p. 190. Reprinted by permission of Pearson Education, Inc., Upper Saddle River, NJ.

provide adequate natural and artificial lighting; improved air quality, ventilation, and acoustics; and removal of toxic cleaning agents.

No dimension of classroom space is more taken for granted or less understood than the walls in classrooms (Roskos & Neuman, 2011). Research has shown that colors, open spaces, and functional organization of wall space influence human learning and functioning (Ceppi & Zini, 1998; Lackney, 2003). Roskos and Neuman (2011) assert that walls should be used to showcase what students know and are learning. Wall displays should be appealing, varied, and interactive. Display areas can be located almost anywhere in the classroom—on walls, windows, floors, doors, and ceilings (Reutzel & Cooter, 2012). Where possible, displays should be coproduced, with teachers and students sharing responsibility. A *message board* is an example of a wall display where teachers and students can communicate with each other. A *sign-in board*, another wall display, encourages young children to write their names to begin the school day and gives the teacher a quick check on students' progress in writing their names. *Window writing*, using pens with water-soluble ink, allows students to publish their finished writing products on the window glass. An *environmental print wall* can be devoted to display of print examples children bring from home (e.g., labels from cans, cereal boxes, old packages, bumper stickers, and newspaper advertisements). Useful and interesting information, such as rules, calendars, lunch menus, TV guides, and posters, can be displayed in prominent places around the classroom. Likewise, classroom routines, time schedules, hints for figuring out how to read unknown words, the writing process (including steps and media for publishing writing), lists of favorite insects, songs the students like, favorite books, and so on, can be information displays in the early childhood classroom. Concrete objects in the classroom, including furnishings, school supplies, and classroom displays, may be labeled for even the youngest of students. Signs, charts, lists, and labels also indicate specific functions and locations within the classroom.

Designated areas of the classroom need to be devoted to efficient storage of classroom learning materials. Because the needs of young children are better met by tables than desks, children should be provided individual cubbies for storing individual work. When arranging staplers, paper punches, construction paper, and unlined paper for students' daily use, keep in mind easy accessibility and cleanup. The proper location for each item in centers needs to be labeled to facilitate cleanup and maintenance. Each item can be labeled with both a word and a picture. Crayons, markers, pencils, pens, erasers, and chalk can be placed in individual containers for storage. In this way, children can easily sort and clean up materials scattered during busy activity times.

Designing a Classroom Management Plan

The topic of classroom management brings to mind the often-quoted aphorism of Benjamin Franklin, "If you fail to plan you are planning to fail." Of all concerns classroom teachers have about designing an effective classroom environment, classroom management tops the list. What is *classroom management*? It is everything a teacher does to organize students, classroom resources, time, and classroom space so that effective instruction can take place.

Wang, Haertal, and Walberg (1994) examined 11,000 research reports to determine the factors that most influence student learning in school classrooms. They identified 28 factors, the most significant of which was classroom management. They concluded that a teacher who is "grossly inadequate in classroom management skills is probably not going to accomplish much" (Wong & Wong, 1998, p. 84). Gunning (2010) described effectively managed classrooms as places where there is purpose and order, an expectation of high student effort and engagement, a balance of cooperation and competition, and students who are trained to be independent and capable learners.

Classroom Rules and Consequences

Teachers need to determine rules and consequences for failing to obey the rules in the classroom. Teachers should not fall into the trap of negotiating rules with students because they are ultimately responsible for maintaining order and a positive learning climate in classrooms. Although students can be encouraged to ask questions for clarification about rules and consequences, they do not set the rules for behavior in the classroom. Teachers should also plan mechanisms for sharing classroom rules and expectations with parents and soliciting their support.

Managing consequences of student disruptions and inappropriate behavior should be planned such that it minimizes interruptions to classroom instruction and activity. A classroom management chart using green, yellow, and red cards can be used for this purpose. When students misbehave, they are told to replace a green with a yellow card on the classroom management chart, along with knowing and accepting the consequences. This plan allows teachers to respond to student misbehavior calmly and confidently while maintaining the flow of classroom activity.

Training Students to Engage the Classroom Environment Effectively

Allowing children to independently engage the multiple activity spaces, furnishings, and learning materials at the beginning of the academic year is an invitation for disaster. Teachers should plan how to explicitly train students to use these activity spaces, furnishings, and learning materials! For this purpose, Reutzel and Morrow (2007) developed a training process to help teachers train young students to engage effectively the multiple activity spaces, furnishings, and learning materials throughout the classroom.

Start the year by conspicuously labeling the small-group or independent literacy spaces or centers, including furnishings and materials in these spaces, as *closed* or *under construction*. (We have even seen teachers use yellow crime scene plastic tape for this purpose. It really gets the students' attention!) Mention to students that within a few weeks they will be working more often in the activity spaces set up around the classroom, but before they can do so, there is much they need to learn. Take a few minutes each day to explain to students what each activity space is intended to accomplish.

During the first and second weeks, teachers should practice transition procedures by moving students from their tables to the rug, lining up for recess, and so forth. According to Doyle (1984), effective transitions are accomplished when teachers signal the onset of transitions, actively structure and monitor transitions, and strive to minimize both the time involved in transitions and the loss of instructional momentum in the classroom. Ardoin, Martens, and Wolfe (1999) found that the use of three rapidly presented directions (e.g., touch your nose, scoot in your chair, walk quietly to the rug) with which young children can easily comply is helpful in achieving maximum compliance from children during transitions. Also, experience has taught us the value of using timers or stop watches to motivate children to accomplish transitions briskly and without dallying. A worthwhile goal is to reduce transition times between activities and movements to other classroom spaces to a single minute, so that the bulk of classroom time is spent on teaching and learning. We use three steps to make this happen (Reutzel & Morrow, 2007).

First, we use a consistent signal such as a hotel registration bell or turning off the lights to alert children to stop what they are doing or to freeze and listen for directions. Second, we provide three rapid, sequenced directions that can be coupled with written directions and pictures on cue cards. Children look, listen, and read directions to accomplish what is directed. Third, we use our signal device to alert children to follow the directions given and in the correct sequence. During these procedural practice times, any student who fails to follow directions as stated causes the group to stop and repractice the expected procedures.

In the third week, select one or two classroom activity spaces to explain and model. For example, model how students are to enter the science exploration center. Model how a team leader, appointed by the teacher, will lead the group in reading aloud the rules and directions displayed in the science exploration center. Model how students are to seat themselves comfortably to read alone or with a partner. Discuss expectations that assigned daily tasks in this center will be completed in the time allotted. Explain the displayed consequences for failure to follow directions and obey the rules. Last, model the cleanup process of the science exploration center. This may involve ringing a bell or some other signaling device to alert students that the activity has ended. Model how to freeze quietly in place to listen for directions. Then when another signal is given, students have 15–30 seconds to tidy up their learning centers. A final signal alerts them when they are to move to another center or return to their assigned seats.

This training process is repeated at a slightly accelerated pace over the next several weeks (Weeks 4–6) until all classroom activity spaces have been explained, modeled, and role-played. Role playing the use of the learning spaces and materials around the classroom is a critical final step. Remaining firm about children meeting expectations as they role-play use of these activity spaces and learning materials will save many management problems later. Of course, as students role-play, they are becoming more excited and motivated to use these learning centers. Digital photographs of students properly engaged in the various learning spaces are helpful reminders for students. Train students to move efficiently into and out of various classroom center spaces between activities. Use timers or stopwatches to motivate students to accomplish tasks briskly.

Planning Effective Classroom Routines

Yinger (1979, 1980) indicates that turning classroom rules, schedules, activities, and procedures into well-practiced and familiar routines leads to fewer interruptions of the flow and sequence of classroom events and interactions. Children develop a sense of security when the events of the school day revolve around a sequence of anticipated activities. Although variety is the spice of life, children often find comfort in familiar instructional routines and predictable schedules (Holdaway, 1984). There are any number of ways to organize the activities and instruction of the school day. However, it is important that young children experience a variety of interactive settings within the whole class, in small groups, and individually each day. Grouping arrangements should be flexible, meet the needs of the students, and involve the "best practices" of effective instruction. To help young children gain a sense of classroom routine, teachers can post and review daily a schedule of learning activities (see Figure 6.3) as a part of the opening exercises for each new school day (Morrow et al., 2006).

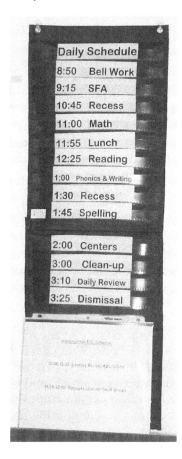

FIGURE 6.3. Example of a daily schedule of learning activities.

Planning a Supportive Classroom Climate

Finally, teachers should pay meticulous attention to planning a supportive psychological climate for the classroom—one that communicates high expectations and personal warmth (Pressley et al., 2003). Teachers need to encourage students to perform well, and communicate expectations that students can and will do so (Brophy & Good, 1986). Students need to feel accountable to someone for doing their best work (Brophy, 2006). According to research, many children who live in poverty or lack resources in their lives do not receive positive reinforcements and praise in their out-of-school lives. Hart and Risley (1995) found that the average child in a professional family received 32 affirmations and five prohibitions per hour, resulting in a ratio of six encouragements to one discouragement per hour. On the other hand, a child in a welfare family accumulated five affirmations and 11 prohibitions an hour—a ratio of two discouragements to one encouragement per hour. Teachers need to engage regularly in communicating praise, compliments, encouragement, warmth, care, and concern to young students (Pressley et al., 2003). Young children who feel worthwhile, encouraged, and accountable in their classroom are motivated to respond more appropriately, which results in wasting less instructional time because of behavioral interruptions or social disruptions.

REFLECTIONS AND NEW DIRECTIONS

Early theorists and philosophers who studied early childhood development emphasized the significant role the physical environment plays in young children's learning and development. Contemporary educators and researchers have empirically demonstrated the effect of the ecology of the classroom on young students' learning, behavior, language use, development, and motivation. As a result, other researchers have worked to develop and validate a variety of instruments to assess the content, design, and human interaction patterns that occur in early childhood classroom environments.

Although much research has focused on, clarified, and validated knowledge about the physical design, arrangement, organization, and content of classroom environments, much less is known about the patterns of interactions and relationships that occur within this environment. Researchers need to focus future efforts on describing and manipulating aspects of the classroom to understand interactions and relationships among teachers, learners, and the environment that can lead to optimal student outcomes. Teachers need to know specifically how and why the classroom environment—content, spaces, arrangement, rules, routines, and so forth—operates to facilitate or inhibit student interactions with other students, the teacher, and physical surroundings within the classroom that result in improved or decreased student learning, motivation, and development. This is especially true with regard to how the classroom environment affects teachers' abilities to manage the classroom and its occupants. Without adequate classroom management, teachers are hard-pressed to provide high-quality, effective instruction.

Future research needs to describe meticulously and determine how changes in elements of physical space and human interaction patterns within the classroom environment affect student behavior, learning, and motivation. Educators and researchers need to develop a more detailed understanding of why and how specific spatial, content, and organizational dimensions of classroom environment design operate to influence the behaviors, outcomes, and motivation of teachers and students alike. So we end as we began, by reiterating Roskos and Neuman's (2011, p. 110) recent observation, "The classroom environment can work for us or against us, which is why it is first, last, and always among pedagogical concerns."

PROFESSIONAL DEVELOPMENT ACTIVITIES

- Administer the ECERS, CLEP, or CLASS with a colleague in your own classroom. Determine strengths and weaknesses. Write up a 5-year plan to redress identified weaknesses.

- Draw a floor plan for your current classroom. Write your rationale for the spaces you have created in your classroom. Do you see any areas that may not support your curriculum, instruction, or management purposes? If so, how would you make changes and why?

- Plan a small-group learning center to support one area of the curriculum and instruction offered in your classroom. Draw the floor plan for furnishings; list contents of the center, objectives, rules for behavior, and possible tasks to be accomplished. Describe how you will organize the center to make the contents accessible to students for use and cleanup.

- Survey the wall space and the uses to which you put this space in your classroom. After reading this chapter, in what ways would you change use of the wall space in your classroom? Draw four panels representing your classroom walls, show what you will use the wall space for in the future, and explain why you made these choices.

REFERENCES

Ardoin, S. P., Martens, B. K., & Wolfe, L. A. (1999). Using high-probability instruction sequences with fading to increase student compliance during transitions. *Journal of Applied Behavior Analysis, 32,* 339–351.

Barker, R. G. (1968). *Ecological psychology.* Stanford, CA: Stanford University Press.

Barker, R. G. (1978). Stream of individual behavior. In R. G. Barker (Eds.), *Habitats, environments, and human behavior* (pp. 3–16). San Francisco: Jossey-Bass.

Broman, B. L. (1982). *The early years in childhood education* (2nd ed.). Boston: Houghton Mifflin.

Brophy, J. (2006). History of research on classroom management. In C. Weinstein & C. Evertson (Eds.), *Handbook of classroom management: Research, practice, and contemporary issues* (pp. 17–43). Hillsdale, NJ: Erlbaum.

Brophy, J., & Good, T. (1986). Teacher behavior and student achievement. In M. Wittrock (Ed.), *Handbook of research on teaching* (3rd ed., pp. 328–375). New York: Macmillan.

Cambourne, B. (2002). Conditions for literacy learning. *The Reading Teacher, 55*(4), 358–360.

Ceppi, G., & Zini, M. (1998). *Children, spaces, relations: Meta-project for an environment for young children.* Milan, Italy: Domus Academy Research Center.

Dewey, J. (1887, January). My Pedagogic Creed. *School Journal, 54,* 77–80.

Doyle, W. (1984). How order is achieved in classrooms: An interim report. *Journal of Curriculum Studies, 16*(3), 259–277.

Doyle, W. (2006). Ecological approaches to classroom management. In C. Weinstein & C. Evertson (Eds.), *Handbook of classroom management: Research, practice, and contemporary issues* (pp. 97–125). Hillsdale, NJ: Erlbaum.

Fernie, D. (1985). The promotion of play in the indoor play environment. In J. L. Frost & S. Sunderlin (Eds.), *When children play* (pp. 285–290). Wheaton, MD: Association for Childhood Education International.

Fractor, J. S., Woodruff, M., Martinez, M., & Teale, W. H. (1993). Let's not miss opportunities to promote voluntary reading: Classroom libraries in the elementary school. *The Reading Teacher, 46,* 476–484.

Froebel, F. (1974). *The education of man.* Clifton, NJ: August A. Kelly.

Gump, P. V. (1989). Ecological psychology and issues of play. In M. N. Bloch & A. D. Pellegrini (Eds.), *The ecological context of children's play* (pp. 35–56). Norwood, NJ: Ablex.

Gunning, T. (2010). *Creating literacy instruction for all students* (7th ed.). Boston: Allyn & Bacon.

Hall, N. (1987). The literate home corner. In P. Smith (Ed.), *Parents and teachers together* (pp. 134–144). London: Macmillan.

Harms, T., Clifford, R. M., & Cryer, D. (1998). *Early Childhood Environment Rating Scale, Revised Edition.* New York: Teachers College Press.

Hart, B., & Risley, T. R. (1995). *Meaningful differences in the everyday experience of young American children.* Baltimore: Brookes.

Hasting, N., & Schwieso, J. (1995). Tasks and tables: The effects of seating arrangements on task engagement in primary classrooms. *Educational Research, 37*(3), 279–291.

Holdaway, D. (1984). *Stability and change in literacy learning.* Portsmouth, NH: Heinemann.

Holmes, R., & Cunningham, B. (1995). Young children's knowledge of their classrooms: Names, activities, and purposes of learning centers. *Education and Treatment of Children, 18*(4), 433–443.

Kershner, R., & Pointon, P. (2000). Children's views of the primary classroom as an environment for working and learning. *Research in Education, 64,* 64–78.

LaParo, K. M., Pianta, R. C., & Stuhlman, M. (2004). The Classroom Assessment Scoring System: Findings from the prekindergarten year. *Elementary School Journal, 104*(5), 409–426.

Lackney, J. A. (2003). 33 principles of educational design (School Design Research Studio). Retrieved August 2006, from *engr.wisc.edu/eeprincples.html.*

McGill-Franzen, A., Allington, R. L., Yokoi, L., & Brooks, G. (1999). Putting books in the classroom seems necessary but not sufficient. *Journal of Educational Research, 93*, 67–74.

Montessori, M. (1964). *The Montessori method*. New York: Schocken. (Original work published 1912)

Montessori, M. (1965). *Dr. Montessori's own handbook: A short guide to her ideas and materials*. New York: Schocken. (Original work published 1914)

Morrow, L. M. (1988). Young children's responses to one-to-one readings in school settings. *Reading Research Quarterly, 23*(3), 89–107.

Morrow, L. M. (1990). Preparing the classroom environment to promote literacy during play. *Early Childhood Education Research Quarterly, 5*, 537–554.

Morrow, L. M., Reutzel, D. R., & Casey, H. (2006). Organizing and managing language arts teaching: Classroom environments, grouping practices, exemplary instruction. In Carolyn M. Evertson & Carol S. Weinstein (Eds.), *Handbook of classroom management: Research, practice, and contemporary issues* (pp. 559–581). Hillsdale, NJ: Erlbaum.

Morrow, L. M., & Weinstein, C. S. (1982). Increasing children's use of literature through program and physical design changes. *Elementary School Journal, 83*(2), 131–137.

Morrow, L. M., & Weinstein, C. S. (1986). Encouraging voluntary reading: The impact of a literature program on children's use of library corners. *Reading Research Quarterly, 21*(3), 330–346.

National Association for the Education of Young Children (NAEYC). (2012). Standard 9: NAEYC accreditation criteria for physical environment standard. Retrieved January 2012, from *http://oldweb.naeyc.org/academy/standards/standard9/standard9C.asp*.

National Governors Association Center for Best Practices & Council of Chief State School Officers. (2011). Common Core State Standards Initiative. Retrieved December 20, 2011, from *www.corestandards.org*.

Neuman, S. B. (1999). Books make a difference: A study of access to literacy. *Reading Research Quarterly, 34*, 286–311.

Neuman, S. B., & Celano, D. (2001). Access to print in low-income and middle-income communities: An ecological study of four neighborhoods. *Reading Research Quarterly, 36*, 8–26.

Neuman, S. B., & Roskos, K. (1989). Preschoolers' conceptions of literacy as reflected in the spontaneous play. In S. McCormick & J. Zutell (Eds.), *Cognitive and social perspectives for literacy research and instruction* (pp. 87–94). Chicago: National Reading Conference.

Neuman, S. B., & Roskos, K. (1990). The influence of literacy-enriched play settings on preschoolers' engagement with written language. *National Reading Conference Yearbook, 39*, 179–187.

Neuman, S. B., & Roskos, K. (1992). Literacy objects as cultural tools: Effects on children's literacy behaviors in play. *Reading Research Quarterly, 27*, 202–225.

Neuman, S. B., & Roskos, K. (1993). *Language and literacy learning in the early years: An integrated approach*. New York: Harcourt Brace Jovanovich.

Neuman, S. B., & Roskos, K. (1997). Literacy knowledge in practice: Contexts of participation for young writers and readers. *Reading Research Quarterly, 32*(1), 10–33.

Paley, V. (1994). *The boy who would be a helicopter*. Cambridge, MA: Harvard University Press.

Peisner-Feinberg, E., & Burchinal, M. (1997). Relations between preschool children's child care experiences and concurrent development: The cost, quality and outcomes study. *Merrill–Palmer Quarterly, 43*(3), 451–477.

Pianta, R. C., LaParo, K. M., & Hamre, B. K. (2008). *Classroom Assessment Scoring System (CLASS), PreK–3*. Baltimore: Brookes.

Pressley, M., Dolezal, S. E., Raphael, L. M., Mohan, L., Roehrig, A. D., & Bogner, K. (2003). *Motivating primary-grade students*. New York: Guilford Press.

Reutzel, D. R., & Clark, S. (2011). Organizing literacy classrooms for effective instruction: A survival guide. *The Reading Teacher, 65*(2), 93–105.

Reutzel, D. R., & Cooter, R. B. (2012). *Teaching children to read: The teacher makes the difference* (6th ed.). Boston: Pearson Education.

Reutzel, D. R., & Fawson, P. C. (2002). *Your classroom library: New ways to give it more teaching power.* New York: Scholastic Professional Books.

Reutzel, D. R., & Jones, C. D. (2010). Creating and sustaining effective preschool literacy classroom environments. In S. M. C. McKenna, S. Walpole, & K. Conradi (Eds.), *Promoting early reading: Research, resources, and best practices* (pp. 175–198). New York: Guilford Press.

Reutzel, D. R., & Morrow, L. M. (2007). Promoting and assessing effective literacy learning classroom environments. In J. R. Paratore & R. L. McCormick (Eds.), *Classroom literacy assessment: Making sense of what students know and do* (pp. 33–49). New York: Guilford Press.

Roskos, K., & Neuman, S. B. (2001). Environment and its influences for early literacy teaching and learning. In S. B. Neuman & D. K. Dickinson (Eds.), *Handbook of early literacy research* (pp. 281–294). New York: Guilford Press.

Roskos, K., & Neuman, S. B. (2011). The classroom environment. *The Reading Teacher, 64*(2), 110–114.

Rowe, D. (1999). The literate potentials of book-related dramatic play. *Reading Research Quarterly, 33,* 10–35.

Smith, P. K., & Connolly, K. J. (1980). *The ecology of preschool behavior.* Cambridge, UK: Cambridge University Press.

Stormz, M. J., & McKee, J. W. (1928). *The progressive primary teacher.* Boston: Houghton-Mifflin.

Tharpe, R., & Gallimore, R. (1988). *Rousing minds to life—teaching, learning and schooling in social context.* Port Chester, NY: Cambridge University Press.

Vukelich, C. (1991). Materials and modeling: Promoting literacy during play. In J. F. Christie (Ed.), *Play and early literacy development* (pp. 215–231). Albany: State University of New York Press.

Vukelich, C. (1994). Effects of play interventions on young children's reading of environmental print. *Early Childhood Research Quarterly, 9*(2), 153–170.

Wang, M. C., Haertal, G. D., & Walberg, H. J. (1994). What helps students learn? *Educational Leadership, 51*(4), 74–79.

Wolfersberger, M. E., Reutzel, D. R., Sudweeks, R., & Fawson, P. C. (2004). Developing and Validating the Classroom Literacy Environmental Profile (CLEP): A tool for examining the "print richness" of early childhood and elementary classrooms. *Journal of Literacy Research, 36*(2), 211–272.

Wong, H. K., & Wong, R. T. (1998). *How to become an effective teacher: The first days of school.* Mountain View, CA: H. K. Wong Publications.

Wurm, J. P. (2005). *Working the Reggio way: A beginner's guide for American teachers.* St. Paul, MN: Red Leaf Press/NAEYC.

Yinger, R. J. (1979). Routines in teacher planning. *Theory Into Practice, 18*(3), 163–169.

Yinger, R. J. (1980). A student of teacher planning. *Elementary School Journal, 80,* 107–127.

CHAPTER 7

LEARNING THROUGH PLAY

LESLEY MANDEL MORROW
SAMANTHA B. BERKULE
ALAN L. MENDELSOHN
KELLYANNE M. HEALEY
CAROLYN BROCKMEYER CATES

> Play is the child's work.
> —MARIA MONTESSORI

Ms. Healey's kindergarten class was learning about different cultures. They sang songs from the countries they learned about, read stories, and learned about important places to visit. They also learned about their food. This week's featured country was Italy. Ms. Healey created an Italian restaurant in her room with menus, order pads, bills, and so forth. Ethan was a waiter today, and Jovanna and Tiarra, customers coming for dinner, looked at the menu, which had pictures and words. On the menu were pizza, pasta with tomato sauce, macaroni and cheese, salad, bread, and milk and water. Ethan came by and asked what they wanted. Jovanna said, "I want one piece of pizza with broccoli on the top." Ethan wrote it down.

Tiarra said, "I want the same thing but I want mushrooms on top of mine."

Ethan said, "I'm sorry, we don't have mushrooms."

Tiarra said, "Oh, I really wanted mushrooms."

Ethan suggested, "How about olives?"

Tiarra made an ugly face and said, "Yuk! I don't like olives."

Ethan got a little angry, "Well, what do you want?"

"Oh," said Tiarra, "I'll just have it plain."

The play continued with salad, drinks, and dessert. As the girls ate, they talked about how good everything was but Tiarra still complained about not having mushrooms. When they finished, Ethan brought the check and the children figured out the amount to pay with play money.

Dramatic play and other types of play have long been considered an important part of early childhood instruction. The National Reading Panel report (2000), the National Early Literacy Panel report (2010), No Child Left Behind (2001), and Race to the Top

(2011), are policy initiatives and research that suggest the necessity for acquisition of specific language and literacy skills in early childhood. There is a tendency with so many mandates to think that the way children learn this best is through the use of explicit instruction. Often the result is neglect or deciding that there is no time for or benefit in play.

Preschool and some kindergarten programs recognize the importance of play to develop cognitive skills. However, the primary grades are not allotting time for play except for physical education and on the playground. The Common Core State Standards (CCSS; National Governors Association Center for Best Practices & Council of Chief State School Officers, 2010) call for integration of content areas such as science and social studies to develop literacy skills, possibly leading to more project- and inquiry-based instruction. Here we refer to the activities that occur in this type of instruction as *guided play*. We discuss the value of both dramatic play and guided play in this chapter. *Dramatic play* is defined as play in which children symbolically represent life and experiences. Guided play makes use of project-based, hands-on activities in service of learning goals and objectives.

The National Association for the Education of Young Children (NAEYC; 2009) has affirmed the importance of play in its accreditation standards. Teachers in grades PreK–3 need to know how play enhances school readiness, language, literacy, and general cognitive development. In the first section of this chapter, we address this need by reviewing theoretical perspectives on play. We then turn to studies that have examined the relationship of play to learning, language, and literacy development. We review (1) studies that have involved literacy behavior of children in their spontaneous dramatic play; (2) studies of the effects of access to literacy-enriched environments on children's literacy development; and (3) studies of the added benefit to children's engagement when an adult mediates, converses with, and supports literacy related play.

A Brief History of Theories about Play

Prior to the 1970s, psychoanalytic theory dictated the use of play in classrooms. As a result, teachers limited their involvement in children's play so as not to interfere with their emotional problem solving (Johnson, Christie, & Yawkey, 1987). Piaget's (1945/1962) theory of play, which augmented the psychoanalytic view, stressed play's relationship to cognition. Piagetian theorists noted that younger children would pretend to eat or drink, activities in which they engaged in real life. However, older children might pretend to be firefighters, doctors, or nurses, all roles the child had observed but never occupied in reality. The Piagetian view of play demonstrates the relationship between pretend play and overall cognitive and language development. Vygotsky's (1933/1967, 1978) theory of cognitive development gives a central role in play to a more experienced partner. The partner can be an adult, an older child, or a more skilled peer. The partner, however, should release control as the child's play matures.

What Research Says about Young Children Learning through Play

One approach to examining the relationships between play and cognitive development has been taken by researchers interested in language development. This work, which is consistent with Vygotskian theory, has examined sociodramatic play during which children enact scenarios they create and negotiate themselves, using knowledge of real-life situations they have experienced or observed. Investigators who have observed preschool children's in such play have concluded that engagement in sociodramatic play prompts children to use language to convey meaning, interpret ideas, and appreciate the perspective of others (Bodrova, 2008; Dickinson & Tabors, 2001; Heath, 1983; Pellegrini & Galda, 1993).

Studies have demonstrated that, aside from improved language ability, encouraging preschoolers to engage in dramatic play is associated with facilitated literacy learning. One large-scale study of a group of preschools found that preschool classroom enhancements designed to encourage literacy during play resulted in increased child literacy behaviors during dramatic play. For example, during dramatic play, children played in a veterinarian's office designed by the teacher. They role-played reading in the waiting room and writing down appointments for patients. The researchers found that adult support in the literacy-enriched play setting enhances children's literacy learning (Morrow, 1990; Morrow & Rand, 1991).

Another study was conducted with two groups of children in one preschool classroom. Three play settings were created: a doctor's office, a restaurant, and a post office. This study indicated that literacy-enriched dramatic play areas are not only contexts in which to learn what children know about literacy but also places where children can practice what they already know, in addition to participating in literacy activities (Neuman & Roskos, 1997).

In studies of children in primary school grades, results demonstrated the value of using play-based approaches to encourage cognitive development in the elementary school. For example, Flint (2010) found that the use of "buddy reading" pairs in a first-grade classroom enhanced shared reading, play interactions, and social–emotional development. In a related study, Kamii and Kato (2005) found that 5- and 6-year-old Japanese children playing a card game in a naturalistic play setting, rather than a structured didactic setting, demonstrated gains in logical–mathematical knowledge.

Another study with first- and second-grade children found that children who were trained in imaginary play experienced gains in their ability to plan imaginary activities. They also had significantly higher scores on measures of positive emotional expression than children who were not in this group (Moore & Russ, 2008). Guthrie (2011) has reviewed classroom approaches for literacy learning that incorporate play-based activities, noting that when students are provided opportunities to interact with concrete objects, such as experimenting with science materials, they demonstrate enhanced problem solving and are motivated to engage in reading to find out more.

Several intervention studies have looked at the role of parents during play. The Video Interaction Program (VIP) comes from work by pediatric primary care physicians to enhance the interaction between parent and child during play to enhance language development. The relationship and support created during play enhance cognitive, language and social–emotional development (Mendelsohn, Dreyer, Brockmeyer, Berkule-Silberman, & Morrow, 2011; Mendelsohn et al., 2005, 2007). Other researchers have found that when adults provide interactive participation and modeling, the symbolic quality of children's play is enhanced (Fein & Fryer, 1995; Haight & Miller, 1992). Studies also reveal an important role for adults during play. The best type of adult participation is to scaffold behaviors but not predetermine roles, content, or direction of play. The adult should pay attention to what happens, and facilitate and stimulate children to develop play scripts or themes by themselves. There should be reciprocal verbal interaction (Bondioli, 2001;

Bornstein & Tamis-LeMonda, 1995; Haight & Miller, 1992; Peterson, Jesso, & McCabe, 1999; Smilansky & Shefatya, 1990).

As children move ahead in school, they seem to lose the enthusiasm they once had for play in the primary grades. School often becomes a collection of skills to be learned using one worksheet after another. However, programs that include thematic instruction with interesting and relevant inquiry-based activities that are interactive and playful can motivate the curiosity and enthusiasm once found in PreK and kindergarten children. Thematic instruction with specific content to learn with language and literacy skills embedded can include hands-on active projects that have the qualities of engaging in play. When theme topics are relevant they can motivate and engage children in language, literacy, developing cognitive skills and content information. To do this teachers need to use real world materials, provide choices, give children responsibility, as well as provide activities for problem solving, challenges, collaborating with each other and success (Guthrie, Wigfield, & Perencevich, 2004; Manning, Manning, & Long, 1994; Walmsley, 1994).

For example, Ms. Tracey's second-grade class was studying Colonial Williamsburg. She coordinated with the librarian, and the music and art teachers. Part of the content to be learned was the names and purposes of the buildings in the town. James selected the church, and his assignment was to re-create the building. He first got a photo from the Internet. Then, he read a lot about the church. This was important because he had to write and present a report. The children used the Internet as their textbook, as a source of children's literature about Colonial times, and as information to be retrieved about the town of Williamsburg. When the buildings and written reports were done, the students arranged them according to a map of the town. They prepared Colonial cookies and drinks, and presented their work to another class in the school.

In this project there were choices, such as which building to recreate. Hands-on activities to help children decide how to make the structure involved math, art, and problem-solving skills. Reading and writing were involved in preparation of the report. There was the challenge to get the project done, and a feeling of success when it was finished.

The results of many studies indicate that children's play goes through predictable developmental stages and enhances cognitive growth. Research illustrates that play promotes descriptive language and enhances memory, self-regulation, and gains in executive functioning skills, including memory and cognitive flexibility. Researchers have also found that cognitive development in play is further enhanced when adults model behavior for children during play (Bodrova & Leong, 2007; Diamond, Barnett, Thomas, & Munro, 2007).

A CLASSROOM ENVIRONMENT THAT ENHANCES PLAY

The physical environment of a classroom, including arrangement in space, choice of materials, and the aesthetic quality, is an essential ingredient for learning through play in early childhood. The play-oriented, literacy-rich classroom promotes meaningful language experiences and contains materials that encourage exploration (Morrow, 2012). Preparing a classroom's physical environment is often overlooked in instructional planning. We concentrate on lesson planning and forget to give similar consideration to spatial arrangements in which teaching and learning occur. It is crucial that the curriculum and environment be coordinated to promote the most effective instruction. By synthesizing research on expert teachers, we are able to describe an exemplary, literacy-rich classroom environment that promotes symbolic and project-based play (Pressley, Rankin, & Yokoi, 1996).

A classroom that fosters dramatic and guided play is student-friendly. A variety of accessible materials, stored for easy access both visually and physically, meet different interest and achievement levels. Classroom tables and desks are arranged to encourage social interaction, so that four to five students sit close to each other. The room has provisions for whole-group instruction with students sitting at tables or desks, or on a rug in the literacy center. The area for whole-group meetings contains an electronic whiteboard, a pocket chart, and an easel with chart paper. The teacher uses a rocking chair during whole-class mini-lessons or when reading stories to the class. Children utilize the rocking chair when they role-play the teacher reading to the other children.

The classroom has functional print centers to communicate information. For example, the Notice Board is a place where children can leave messages for each other. In addition, Word Walls have children's names on them, in addition to words dealing with current themes (e.g., the word *tractor* from the unit "The Construction Zone"). Other materials in the room represent children's literature, books made by the class, artwork, and so forth.

To accommodate small-group, symbolic, and project-based play, there are learning centers, each labeled according to its content area. The centers integrate play into literacy learning and content areas by featuring reading and writing activities. Thematic projects with embedded literacy skills development have more meaning when integrated into content areas. Therefore, it is common to find paper and pencils in the block and dramatic play areas, and books in the art and music centers. Themes such as "My Family, My Community" and "Animals Everywhere" foster the development of new vocabulary, ideas, and experiences, creating a purpose for reading and writing. Each center has not only general materials that are typical of the content it represents, but also special materials that encourage symbolic play linked to the current topic of study. Different centers are described below.

Dramatic Play Center

Depending on the grade, this area includes dress-up clothing, a telephone and phone book, stuffed animals, a mirror, food cartons, plates, silverware, newspapers, magazines, books, cookbooks, notepads, and a kitchen setting with a table and chairs. The area also has a broom, a refrigerator, storage shelves, and materials relative to the current theme. For example, when learning about different cultures, one classroom set up a restaurant in the dramatic play area, as mentioned earlier. One week the restaurant had food from India; the next week, Chinese food was on the menu. In the restaurant were recipes, a cash register, play money, and checks. In the center, items are added and removed depending on the topic of study.

The Music Center

This area includes a piano, a guitar, or other real instruments. Rhythm instruments such as bells, triangles, rhythm sticks, and cymbals represent an effort to feature musical instruments from different countries, such as maracas from Mexico and a Caribbean steel drum. There are CD players with musical links to themes, such as songs about the different seasons when studying that topic.

The Art Center

This center includes multiple types of paper in different sizes. There are colored pencils, markers, watercolors, collage materials (e.g., pipe cleaners, foil paper, and wool), and string and fabrics for all types of creative artwork. Depending on the theme, different materials are added. One example is Play-Doh for the "Animals" unit. Students can use books that illustrate works of art by well-known artists for reading and reference.

The Social Studies Center

This center is particularly important to themes such as "Ready for PreK," "My Family and Friends," "States in the United States," and "Learning about Other Countries." These themes focus on getting along with others, recognizing and appreciating differences and likenesses in friends and family, developing respect for self and others, and developing a community of learners. There are appropriate books accompanying these ideas. In addition, general social studies materials include maps, a globe, flags and artifacts from various countries, community figures, and traffic signs.

The Science Center

This always popular center has interesting objects with which to explore and experiment, such as magnets, simple machines, and plants. Other equipment includes an aquarium, a terrarium, a thermometer, a compass, a prism, shells, rock collections, a stethoscope, a kaleidoscope, and a microscope. Some themes require additional materials for exploration, such as "The Five Senses," "Animals Everywhere," or "Growing Healthy and Strong."

The Math Center

Children may find an abacus, various types of currency, scales, rulers, measuring cups, clocks with movable parts, a stopwatch, a calendar, a cash register, a calculator, a number line, a height chart, an hourglass, different types of manipulative numbers (felt, wood, magnetic), fraction puzzles, and geometric shapes in their math center. Different themes encompass math concepts, and appropriate materials are added.

The Block Area

There are blocks in PreK classrooms and some kindergartens, but they are seldom found in first- and second-grade classrooms. So much can be learned in first and second grade from playing with blocks of many different sizes, shapes, and textures. If the theme is "The Construction Zone," children can build houses, roads, bridges, and tunnels. Relevant thematic books in the center enrich the topic. Paper and pencils are needed as well.

The Literacy Center

The literacy center is a focal point in an early childhood classroom. It should give the message that literacy is so important that it needs a special center to provide space for writing, reading, oral language, listening, comprehension, word study materials, and puppets and props for acting out stories and retelling them.

The Author's Spot

A portion of the literacy center is set aside and includes a table, chairs, and writing materials, such as colored markers, crayons, pencils, chalk, a stapler, a hole punch, a chalkboard, and various types and sizes of paper. Some classrooms have bookbinding machines for making class books. Children are provided journals and directions on how they are to be used. Index cards are used for recording children's "Very Own Words," which are stored in index boxes. Folders, one for each child, are used to collect writing samples. Classrooms have at least two or three computers for writing and reading activities.

Teachers prepare blank books in which children write on topics related to themes being studied. For example, there are different animal-shaped books when studying animals or books shaped like snowmen, flowers, and so forth, to represent different seasons for that topic of study. There is a place for children to display their written work, and a mailbox, stationery, envelopes, and stamps so that children can write to each other and to pen pals.

The Library Corner

This area contains a rocking chair and a rug because many activities in this center take place on the floor, when the teacher has group meetings, lessons, and story time. Pillows and stuffed animals add an element of softness.

Books are stored in open shelves to display titles representing the themes studied. These books are changed according to themes and featured special selections. Books are also stored in plastic baskets labeled by genre (animals, seasons, poetry, families, etc.). Pictures accompany the labels in PreK and kindergarten.

Well-stocked classroom libraries have five to eight book selections per child at three or four different levels of difficulty. The books included in the center are picture storybooks, poetry, informational books, magazines, biographies, cookbooks, joke books, folktales, fairy tales, e-books on the computer, and so forth. Children enjoy informational and narrative stories. These rooms have equal amounts of fiction and nonfiction. The teachers rotate their books regularly to maintain children's interest in them. Children can check books out of the classroom to read at home. Literacy manipulatives such as puppets, taped stories with headsets, and felt boards with story characters, costumes and electronic stories, are included in the literacy center. These materials encourage the dramatic play about stories.

Everything in these rooms has a function, a purpose, and a place to be stored. The teacher models new materials, their purposes, how they are used, and where they belong. Early in the school year, there are only a few items in the centers, so children can learn to use them properly. The teacher adds to them slowly as different themes and skills are studied.

STORYTELLING TECHNIQUES
THAT ENCOURAGE DRAMATIC PLAY

Storytelling strongly attracts children to books (Ritchie, James-Szanton, & Howes, 2003). It allows the storyteller to use creative techniques and to be close to the audience. Telling a story produces an immediate response in the audience and is one of the surest ways to establish rapport between listeners and the storyteller. Storytelling is an important technique for classrooms of children from diverse backgrounds. Many of these children come from cultures in which storytelling, as opposed to storybook reading, is more the norm. When retelling, teachers and children do not need to memorize the story to know it well. They use catchphrases and quotes that are important to the story. Have the original book at hand when you have finished telling a story, so that the children can see it and enjoy again its pictures and printed text.

Creative techniques help storytelling come alive. They excite the imagination, involve the listeners, and motivate children to try storytelling themselves and create their own techniques. Clues for creative techniques are taken from the story. Some stories lend themselves to the use of puppets; others are perfect for the felt-board; still others can be worked up as chalk talks.

Felt-Boards with Story Characters

Felt-boards with story characters are a popular and important tool in a classroom. One can make characters or purchase them. Prepare your own with construction paper covered with clear contact or laminate. Attach strips of felt or sandpaper to the backs of the cutouts, so that they cling to the felt-board. Narrative and expository texts that lend themselves to felt-board retelling are those with a limited number of characters or ideas throughout the story. A magnetic board featuring figures with magnets glued to their backs is similar to a felt-board with felt figures.

Puppets

Puppets are used with stories rich in dialogue. There are many kinds of puppets, including finger, hand, stick, and face puppets. Shy children often feel secure telling stories with puppets. Stories such as *The Gingerbread Boy* (Galdone, 1983) and *The Little Red Hen* (Pinkey, 2006) are appropriately told with puppets because they are short, have few characters, and repeat dialogue. An informational book can be retold using a puppet as well. The day in the life of a policeman or a woman can be told with puppets or props, and a shark stuffed animal can be used to retell facts from a book about sharks.

Sound Story

Sound-story techniques allow both audience and storyteller to provide sound effects when they are called for in a book. The sounds can be made with voices, rhythm instruments, or music. When preparing to tell such a story, first select those parts of the story for which sound effects will be used. Then decide on each sound to be made and who will make it. As the story is told, students and storyteller chime in with their assigned sounds. Record the presentation, then leave the recording in the literacy center with the original book. Among books that adapt easily to sound-story techniques are *Too Much Noise* (McGovern, 1995) and *Mr. Brown Can Moo! Can You?* (Seuss, 1998).

Prop Stories

Using props to tell a story is easy. Simply collect stuffed animals, toys, and other articles that represent characters and objects in a story. Display the props at appropriate times during the storytelling. Three stuffed bears and a yellow-haired doll aid in telling

Goldilocks and the Three Bears (Daly & Russell, 1999). Several toy trains aid in telling *The Little Engine That Could* (Piper, 1990), or relating an informational book about trains might use the same props as used in *The Little Engine That Could.*

Chalk Talks

Chalk talks are another technique that attracts listeners. The storyteller draws the story while telling it. Chalk talks are most effective with a large chalkboard, so the story moves in sequence from beginning to end. The same technique can be carried out on mural paper, hung across a wall; the storyteller simply uses crayons or felt-tip markers instead of chalk. The chalk-talk technique can also be adapted to easel and chart paper or an overhead projector. Choose a story with simple illustrations. Draw only a select few pictures as you tell the story. There are stories that have been written as chalk talks, including an entire series, *Harold and the Purple Crayon* (Johnson, 1981). Children are anxious to try chalk talks.

Stories Using Computers

The computer can do many things with stories, including scan books onto the computer using PowerPoint or Presi, and add music, sound effects, animation, and interesting transitions. It provides a model for children to create their own stories, pictures, and effects.

All materials need to be modeled for children, then placed in the literacy center for them to use. Children can create stories and a technique, and present the project to the class. Storytelling activities involve children in literal comprehension because they must know the sequence, details, and elements of the story. They must problem-solve as they create the materials, deciding what parts of the story to include or delete. They interpret voices of characters as they make a presentation of their finished project to the class.

Mrs. Lynch had a literacy center as the one described earlier. She had done an excellent job of modeling the use of the materials for the children. During center time on any given day you are likely to see sociodramatic play with children's literature in her classroom.

> Tesha and Tiffany were on the floor with a felt-board and character cutouts from *The Gingerbread Boy*, alternately reading and manipulating the figures: Tesha and Tiffany chanted, "Run, run as fast as you can! You can't catch me, I'm the Gingerbread Boy!" As they chanted this phrase from the story, Tiffany held the Gingerbread Boy and moved him up and down and around the board to make him look like he was running.
>
> Tyrone had a big book of *The Little Red Hen* and gave several smaller-size copies of the same story to a group of children he gathered together. He sat in the classroom rocking chair. Role playing a teacher, he said, "Now boys and girls, let's read the title and the name of the author together," which they did. He would occasionally stop and ask a question about the story, such as "What do you think will happen next?" and at the end he said, "Was the hen right when she didn't give the animals any of the bread she baked?"
>
> Rosa and Jovanna were doing a chalk talk of *Harold and the Purple Crayon.* One drew as the other told the story. When the girls finished the story they started to make up more episodes and draw them as well. A half-hour later they finally finished and had drawn in every bit of space on two large whiteboards on the wall in the room.

One other group was acting out the story *Caps for Sale*. There were caps in the center for role playing and monkey puppets for the other children participating. One person, the storyteller, used the book to help narrate the story.

Much of the information discussed here is the results of studies that involved K–2 classroom observation and intervention. Children in these classrooms participated in literacy programs that included activities described here. These youngsters scored significantly better than children in classrooms that did not participate in the program on tests of reading comprehension, the ability to retell and rewrite stories, and the ability to create original oral and written stories by including elements of story structure. Children in the treatment classrooms also showed significant improvement in vocabulary and language complexity (Morrow, 1990, 1992; Morrow, O'Connor, & Smith, 1990).

RESEARCH INTO PRACTICE:
PLAY IN CONTENT AREAS IN EARLY CHILDHOOD CLASSROOMS

Early childhood educators realize the value of play for social, emotional, and physical development. In the past, play has not been viewed as the place or time to motivate literacy. Play has gained greater importance as a medium for practicing literacy behaviors because it provides repeated, meaningful, functional social settings. Literacy development involves a child's active engagement in cooperation and collaboration with peers, builds on what the child already knows, and thrives on the support and guidance of others. Play provides this setting. During observations of children at play, one can see the functionally relevant uses of literacy that children incorporate into their play themes. Children have been observed to engage in emergent and conventional reading and writing in collaboration with other youngsters (Morrow, 1990, 1992; National Governors Association Center for Best Practices & Council of Chief State School Officers, 2010; Roskos & Christie, 2000).

To observe the interactive nature of literacy development, we visited a classroom where the teacher, Ms. Hart, has designed a veterinarian's office to go along with an animal theme concentrating on pets. In her classroom, the dramatic play area was designed as a waiting room: chairs; a table filled with magazines, books, and pamphlets about pet care; posters about pets; office hour notices; a no-smoking sign; and a sign advising visitors to "Check in with the nurse when arriving." On a nurse's desk were patient forms on clipboards, a telephone, an address and telephone book, appointment cards, a calendar, and a computer for recording appointments and patient records. The offices contained patient folders, prescription pads, white coats, masks, gloves, cotton swabs, a toy doctor's kit, and stuffed animals as patients. Ms. Hart guided the use of the various materials in the veterinarian's office by reminding the children to read to pets in waiting areas, fill out forms with prescriptions or appointment times, or fill out forms with information about an animal's condition and treatment. Ms. Hart also modeled behaviors by participating in play with the children when the materials were first introduced.

The following anecdotes relate the types of behavior witnessed in this setting—a setting that provided a literacy-rich environment with books and writing materials, teacher modeling of reading and writing that children could observe and emulate, the opportunity to practice literacy in real-life situations that have meaning and function, and children collaborating in reading and writing with peers.

Jessica was waiting to see the doctor. She told her stuffed animal dog, Sam, not to worry; the doctor wouldn't hurt him. She asked Jenny, who was waiting with her stuffed kitten, Muffin, what the problem was. The girls agonized over the ailments of their pets. After a while, they stopped talking, and Jessica picked up a book from the table and pretended to read *Are You My Mother?* to Sam. Jessica showed Sam the pictures as she read.

Jennie ran into the doctor's office shouting, "My dog got run over by a car!" The doctor bandaged the dog's leg. Then the two children decided that the incident must be reported to the police. Before calling the police, they got out the telephone book and turned to a map to find the spot where the dog had been hit. Then they called the police on the toy phone to report the incident.

Preston examined Christopher's teddy bear and wrote a report in the patient's folder. He read his scribble writing out loud and said, "This teddy bear's blood pressure is 29 points. He should take 62 pills an hour until he is better and keep warm and go to bed." While he read, he showed Christopher what he had written, so he would understand what to do. He asked his nurse to type the notes into the computer.

The type of play discussed here sets the stage for excellent opportunities for English learners (ELs) and children from diverse backgrounds. They learn about functioning in real settings with other children. With the props and the informal nature of the experience they feel more comfortable participating.

Additional classroom play settings to create that encourage reading and writing at different grade levels follow:

1. *Newspaper Office:* Includes telephones, directories, maps, computers, paper, pencils, and areas that focus on sports, travel, general news, and weather.
2. *Supermarket or Local Grocery Store:* Can include labeled shelves and sections, food containers with their labels left on, a cash register, telephone, computers, receipts, checkbooks, coupons, and promotional flyers.
3. *Post Office:* Can be used to mail children's letters and needs to include paper, envelopes, address books, pens, pencils, stamps, cash registers, computers, and mailboxes. A mail carrier hat and bag are important props for a child delivering the mail by reading names and addresses.
4. *Airport:* Can be created with signs posting arrivals and departures, tickets, boarding passes, luggage tags, magazines and books for the waiting area, safety messages on the plane, and name tags for the flight attendants. A computer is used to get onto the Internet to make plane reservations.
5. *Gas Station and Car Repair Shop:* Can be designed in the block area. Toy cars and trucks can be used for props. There can be receipts for sales, road maps to help with directions to different destinations, auto repair manuals for fixing cars and trucks, posters that advertise automobile equipment, and empty cans of different products sold in stations (Morrow & Rand, 1991).
6. *Travel Agency:* This area needs a map of the world as a background. There are also flyers from all over the world, tickets, passports, printed travel plans for different places, and pictures of special placed in the world to visit.

To use materials to their fullest potential, teachers need to use props from the child's environment. The materials in the setting created must serve a real function and be familiar to children. Do not set up several dramatic themes at once. Have the dramatic play area match a theme being studied. Change the area when you begin to study a new theme (Barone, Mallette, & Xu, 2004; Neuman & Roskos, 1993).

The materials in dramatic play areas should be clearly marked and accessible. All levels of literacy development should be accepted, and reading or writing attempts should be recognized as legitimate literacy behaviors. Teachers might find it useful to record anecdotes about literacy activities in which children engage and note their language, literacy, science, and social studies activities.

Play is typically thought of as a preschool and kindergarten activity; however, play can be used with first, second, and third graders. Older children engage in more sophisticated literacy behaviors in play. Play in the primary grades is important to help accomplish the Common Core State Standards that include the development of reading, oral language and writing skills. In Mr. Kunz's third-grade class, students studied how to keep the environment clean, how to conserve energy, water, and other resources. The content to be learned for science and the literacy skills involved research, writing an informational piece about conservation of one kind or another, and doing an oral presentation in front of the class (National Governors Association Center for Best Practices & Council of Chief State School Officers, 2010). The following anecdote illustrates guided play in science in the primary grades.

Mr. Kunz read an informative piece of literature about keeping our environment clean. It was short, with wonderful photographs. Then he asked the children to create inventions that would help the environment. The students brainstormed as a whole about how to keep our environment clean and were told to search the Internet and read more about this. The teacher had lots of books for the children. They also had their textbook and the Internet. He had the children work in pairs, letting them choose their partners, since he found that collaboration motivated them more than working alone. After about 20 minutes of having the children talk and research, he met with the pairs to talk about their ideas. Each day, the children had time to learn about the environment and plan their invention to share with the class when complete. When it was time for presentations there was a lot of excitement and talk in the room.

Jack and Jaydon were selected to begin. Jack started the discussion. He said, "Our invention is to help conserve water when watering grass. What we made is a Nonwasteful Water Sprinkler. It is made from a shoebox and we covered it with yellow paper so it would look nice. There is tubing inside and out to control the flow of water." Jaydon took over the conversation. Pointing to the drawing on the box and to a tube on the outside of the box, he said, "The important parts of this sprinkler is the timer that is set for the time needed to sprinkle the garden it was purchased for. The nozzle keeps it from sprinkling too much water and adjusts for just the right amount of water for the garden you want to water. This is a very good item to have at your house so we don't get water shortages. It only costs $9.99 but after Labor Day it will be $5.99 and if you have a coupon it will only be $4.99. This is a bargain, it is really worth it." According to Mr. Kunz, children were more engaged in this playful, project-based activity than if they had just to talked and read about a topic. It created enthusiasm, a sense of pride, and success. The collaboration of partners enhanced the experience.

A vignette in social studies follows:

Second-grade social studies students in Ms. Stone's class take virtual field trips every year by using the Internet. One class visited Egypt and Israel. They dramatized being on the airplane, and being the pilot and the crew. The flight attendant went over the safety rules as the passengers reviewed the chart. When they arrived via the Internet, they visited the pyramids, then Israel to see the Masada and were told the story about what happened there thousands of ago. They went to the Wailing Wall and left messages they hoped would come true. Ms. Stone had Egyptian friends with whom they were able to Skype and to talk. Her Egyptian friend told them what it was like to live in Egypt. She talked about her work and her children's school, and the children all said hello. Ms. Stone's friend helped to partner her class with pen pals from an Egyptian school where she taught.

Prior to their journey, they read informational stories about Israel and Egypt. They went on the Internet, each with a different assignment to find out information about the countries. According to Ms. Stone, children were more engaged in this playful project-based activity than if they had just talked about a topic. It created enthusiasm, a sense of pride and success, and the collaboration of partners enhanced learning.

Concept-Oriented Reading Instruction

Concept-oriented reading instruction (CORI; Guthrie et al., 2004), an evidence-based research approach, motivates children to read and write in an engaged manner. The program involves children studying relevant, real-world information. Activities include social interaction, scaffolding, studying interesting text, building background knowledge, motivating children, and enhancing literacy strategies. In a classroom where CORI is used to teach literacy skills there is a lot of activity. The topic usually deals with science, and there is lots of children's literature of all kinds and levels. There are novels, biographies, informational literature, textbooks, newspapers, pamphlets, poetry, fables, folktales, and more.

> At the beginning of the unit "Habitats Where Birds Live," the teacher brought in a parakeet as a class pet. She hung posters about birds, showing different types and where they live. There were beautiful peacock, ostrich, and pheasant feathers on a table, labeled with the type of bird from which they came, many informational books about birds, and narratives such as "Owl Moon." After a conversation about the topic, the teacher suggested that the class take a walk in the woods behind the school and take notes about the plants, animals, and birds they saw. They were also to pick up artifacts such as sticks, seeds, leaves, and so forth. Before they left, they wrote down their predictions of what they would see. The purpose of the walk was to see the habitat of the birds in their area, what they may eat, and where they live to survive. Students brought their journals to record their observations and a plastic baggie to collect artifacts. They saw flowers, seeds, grass, bugs, nuts, pinecones, spiders, caterpillars, and a big bird in a tree and bird feathers on the ground. In their classroom, they talked about their findings and made lists of questions about their walk they wanted to answer, then dug into books to find out what they want to know. Another activity in which they engaged while studying this topic was to dissect owl pellets. In the pellets, they found animal bones, which enabled them to identify animals the owls had eaten. There was a lot of hands-on activity and engaged reading and writing.

Play and Literature

There has been less emphasis on play in content areas and in the primary grades than in PreK and kindergarten. We also need to be sure that our literacy instruction will be as engaging as in content areas. The following classroom demonstrates guided play in first-grade language arts.

> In Ms. Bushell's first-grade class, students were learning about characters in books. They talked about what they looked like and how they acted. They made a Venn diagram to list similarities and differences in the characters. Ms. Bushell asked each child to select a character from one of the books he or she had read. The assignment was to become like the character by dressing up and using props from the classroom. The teacher conferred with each child to help him or her select a book, a character, and how he or she might dress. The children were allowed to bring some things from home for their outfits, but they were to use them together with classroom dress-ups or things they had made. After creating their characters, each child had to act like his or her character and say things he or she thought the character would say. On the day of the presentations, Ms. Bushell asked Natalie to begin by acting like her character. Natalie walked to the front of the room holding her book and said, "I have on a tutu skirt, and have butterfly wings on my back. I have a tiara on my head and a wand in my hand. I am wearing sparkly red shoes from my Halloween costume when I was Dorothy from *The Wizard of Oz*, and I have on lots of bracelets I made that I brought from home. I dress like this all the time and I speak fancy like I dress. I say I look fantastic in my fabulous clothes. Who am I?"
>
> One child said, "Dorothy in *The Wizard of Oz*?" Natalie said, "No, not Dorothy." Someone else said, "Pinkalicious!" Natalie said, "No, that's not right either." Then one little girl shouted out," I know! You are Fancy Nancy." And Natalie said, "That's right! I am Fancy Nancy. I am very fancy. I wear fancy clothes and I say big, fancy words. Fancy Nancy would say that you are spectacular to figure out who I am." Natalie held up the book to show a few pages to the class, and everyone applauded.

Play Involvement with Parents and Children

Teachers and parents must work on communicating and collaborating to contribute to children's literacy growth. This is very important for students from diverse populations who need to learn to understand each other (Casanova, 1987; Chavkin & Gonzalez, 1995; Wasik, 2004). Helping parents understand what they can do to help is valuable. However, it must be enjoyable for both parent and child. When parents and children read together at home and it is a pleasurable experience, children are motivated to read and write voluntarily. We wanted children to see literacy as both a solo activity and a social activity with family members.

The BELLE and VIP Projects and Play

The VIP, a study initiated by pediatricians, psychologists, and researchers from New York University School of Medicine (Mendelsohn et al., 2005), is currently being conducted with 0- to 5-year-olds and their parents in the context of a child development study, the Bellevue Project for Early Language, Literacy, and Education Success (BELLE; Mendelsohn et al., 2005, 2007, 2011). The goal of the researchers has been to enhance parent and child interactions during storybook reading and play, subsequently improving language, cognitive development, and school readiness. The intervention occurs during primary pediatric care appointments at an urban public hospital that serves ethnically diverse, low socioeconomic status (SES), at-risk families. VIP is an individualized, relationship-based program to improve language and literacy through the utilization of learning materials and the review of videotaped parent–child interactions. The session lasts about 30–45 minutes. The core component of VIP involves videotaping the parent and child for 5–7 minutes; the videotape is watched by the mother and the child development specialist (CDS) to identify strengths and promote other positive interactions. The CDS gives each family the toy and the book in the video to use at home. The families are also given the video itself. The CDS models interactive talk and play in storybook reading and during play. The book and toys are thematically related. To succeed in this project, those working with the families make continuous phone calls so that parents remember their appointments and come for the session. The program has successfully increased interaction between parent and child in storybook reading and during play.

The program we are talking about here is an adaptation of VIP carried out in a preschool with 3- to 4-year-old children from low-SES families. The preschool implementation closely follows BELLE model, aiding parents in social interactions with their children. The reasons for the success are as follows:

- The activities were easy to understand and initiate.
- The activities took a short time to carry out.
- The activities brought about results quickly.
- Parents felt empowered by knowing how to work with their children.
- The families enjoyed receiving the books and toys.
- Children's school readiness in language development and early literacy behaviors were enhanced; therefore, there was satisfaction and success.

The following vignette describes a play period between a father and his daughter. Together, they read a story about a child and grandmother, and used a shopping basket and plastic food to simulate grocery shopping in a supermarket. They were also given a pad and pencil on which to write items they planned to purchase. This session was recorded after several weeks of working with the CDS. Of note is a lot of parent–child interaction, with a relationship in which they tease each other a lot. They roughhouse a bit with language, and although they sound confrontational with each other, it is their way of having a meaningful exchange.

> After the story reading, the father and child sat down to play on the floor. The father held the notepad and pencil, while the daughter sat next to him, looking through the different foods.
>
> DAUGHTER: That's chocolate? Yum.
>
> FATHER: That's chocolate . . . Kit Kat or, uhh, Hershey? Which one is that? A Kit Kat or a Hershey?
>
> DAUGHTER: Uh . . . chocolate.
>
> FATHER: (*nodding*) Chocolate. A Kit Kat or a Hershey?
>
> DAUGHTER: Kit Kat.
>
> FATHER: Ah. That's a good choice, getting some Kit Kat. How many you wanna get, one?
>
> DAUGHTER: Um . . . no more.
>
> FATHER: You got money on you, right?
>
> DAUGHTER: (*looking at her father as if the answer is obvious*) No.
>
> FATHER: No?

DAUGHTER: No!

FATHER: How you gonna pay for it if you don't have money?

DAUGHTER: (*looking at the food*) No! You got money, you the dad.

FATHER: You got money in your bank at home.

DAUGHTER: No. No, you gotta pay for it.

FATHER: Me? (*looking playfully appalled at his daughter's suggestion*) How am I going to pay for it?

DAUGHTER: You . . . you got a lot of money! You work.

FATHER: You got money, too! You got money at home, too, in your piggy bank. How much you got? Like three dollars?

DAUGHTER: I ain't gonna tell you.

FATHER: You ain't gonna tell me? You little diva.

DAUGHTER: No, I ain't.

FATHER: What else you got over in there?

DAUGHTER: Chips and cookie and doughnuts!

FATHER: Doughnuts, too?

DAUGHTER: Yeah.

FATHER: All right.

DAUGHTER: (*looking at the doughnut box in her hand*) They is purple . . .

FATHER: (*surprised*) Purple?

DAUGHTER: (*looking at Father*) Yeah.

FATHER: (*sing-song*) Woooo. . . . We're gonna have purple doughnuts. Well, you gonna pay?

DAUGHTER: No, if you don't, then we stole 'em.

FATHER: I'll pay this time cause we don't steal, but next time we bring your bank.

Their banter continues. The daughter keeps filling the basket with more and more food.

Although father and daughter have an unusual rapport, it is a definitively positive one. The father likes to tease, and his daughter reacts to his play style in the same way. Both seem to enjoy it and really like to get into it.

REFLECTIONS AND NEW DIRECTIONS

In planning school activities, the CCSS is moving us in the direction of teaching literacy and other skills through content areas. It is an excellent opportunity to engage in inquiry-based, active projects. We are losing our "at-risk" children after early childhood as schools lose their relevance and playfulness. Researchers have demonstrated that play is valuable for developing cognitive skills, engagement, and motivation. Sometimes the playful activities may not seem to provide enough explicit instruction, but there needs to be a balance between play activities and explicit instruction. Professional development is necessary to help teachers deal with this. Play of the nature described here, when spontaneous activity transpires or children are given the opportunity to create and problem-solve, has been replaced with video games, the computer, and TV. During these games, there is little ongoing problem solving, creative spontaneous behavior, or interactions among those who are playing. Learning must be relevant, engaging, fun, and experimental, yet guided by goals. The type of play described in this chapter is crucial to keep students motivated. Children need to be immersed in some types of play during the school day, whether it be completely spontaneous or partially planned.

PROFESSIONAL DEVELOPMENT ACTIVITIES

- Make a list of the cognitive, language, and literacy values of engaging children in play.
- Prepare a lesson using a content area and embed project-based learning.
- Go into a first-grade class and look for materials that encourage dramatic play. What did you find?
- Assume that you teach second grade. Your children are engaging in project-based learning when they are creating a Mexican feast. At the feast they sing Spanish songs, dance Spanish dances, and wear appropriate costumes. They prepare and eat Spanish food, and beat a *piñata*. If a parent questions what the children are learning in these activities, provide an answer that justifies the value of project-based playful activities in second grade.
- Select two of the anecdotes in this chapter. Using a copy of the CCSS, find the standards used in these activities.

REFERENCES

Barone, D. M., Mallette, M. H., & Xu, S. H. (2004). *Teaching early literacy: Development, assessment, and instruction.* New York: Guilford Press.

Bodrova, E. (2008). Make-believe play versus academic skills: A Vygotskian approach to today's dilemma of early childhood education. *European Early Childhood Education Research Journal, 16*(3), 357–369.

Bodrova, E., & Leong, D. J. (2007). *Tools of the mind: The Vygotskian approach to early childhood education* (2nd ed.). Upper Saddle River, NJ: Pearson/Merrill Prentice Hall.

Bondioli, A. (2001). The adult as a tutor in fostering children's symbolic play. In A. Göncü & E. L. Klein (Eds.), *Children in play, story, and school* (pp. 107–131). New York: Guilford Press.

Bornstein, M. H., & Tamis-LeMonda, C. S. (1995). Parent–child symbolic play: Three theories in search of an effect. *Developmental Review, 15,* 382–400.

Casanova, U. (1987). Ethnic and cultural difference. In V. Richardson-Koehler (Ed.), *Educator's handbook* (pp. 379–393). New York: Longman.

Chavkin, N., & Gonzalez, D. L. (1995). *Forging partnerships between Mexican American parents and the schools.* Washington, DC: Office of Educational Research and Improvement (ERIC Document Reproduction Service No. 388 489)

Diamond, A., Barnett, W. S., Thomas, T., & Munro S. (2007). Preschool program improves cognitive control. *Science, 318,* 1387–1388.

Dickinson, D., & Tabors, P. (2001) *Beginning literacy with language: Young children learning at home and at school.* Baltimore: Brookes.

Fein, G. G., & Fryer, M. G. (1995). Maternal contributions to early symbolic play competence. *Developmental Review, 15,* 367–381.

Flint, T. K. (2010). Making meaning together: Buddy reading in a first grade classroom. *Early Childhood Education Journal, 38*(4), 289–297.

Guthrie, J. T. (2011). Best practices in motivating students to read. In L. M. Morrow & L. B. Gambrell (Eds.), *Best practices in literacy instruction* (4th ed., pp. 177–198). New York: Guilford Press.

Guthrie, J. T., Wigfield, A., & Perencevich, K. C. (Eds.). (2004). Motivating reading comprehension: Concept oriented reading instruction. New York: Erlbaum.

Haight, W., & Miller, P. J. (1992). The development of everyday pretend play: A longitudinal study of mothers' participation. *Merrill–Palmer Quarterly, 38*(3), 331–394.

Heath, S. B. (1983). *Ways with words.* Cambridge, UK: Cambridge University Press.

Johnson, J. E., Christie, J. F., & Yawkey, T. D. (1987). *Play and early childhood development.* Glenview, IL: Scott, Foresman.

Kamii, K., & Kato, Y. (2005). Fostering the development of logico-mathematical thinking in a card game at ages 5–6. *Early Education and Development, 16*(3), 367–384.

Manning, M., Manning, G., & Long, R. (1994). *Theme immersion: Inquiry-based curriculum in elementary and middle schools.* Portsmouth, NH: Heinemann.

Mendelsohn, A. L., Dreyer, B. P., Brockmeyer, C. A., Berkule-Silberman, S. B., & Morrow, L. M. (2011). Fostering early development and school readiness in pediatric settings. In S. B. Neuman & D. K. Dickinson (Eds.), *Handbook of early literacy research* (Vol. 3, pp. 279–294). New York: Guilford Press.

Mendelsohn, A. L., Dreyer, B. P., Flynn, V., Tomopoulos, S., Rovira, I., Tineo, W., et al. (2005). Use of videotaped interactions during pediatric well-child care to promote child development: A randomized controlled trial. *Journal of Developmental and Behavioral Pediatrics, 26*(1), 34–41.

Mendelsohn, A. L., Valdez, P., Flynn, V., Foley, G., Berkule, S., Tompoulos, S., et al. (2007). Use of videotaped interactions during pediatric well-child care: Impact at 33 months on parenting and child development. *Journal of Developmental and Behavioral Pediatrics, 28*(3), 206–212.

Moore, M., & Russ, S. W. (2008). Follow-up of a pretend play intervention: Effects on play, creativity, and emotional processes in children. *Creativity Research Journal, 20*(4), 27–436.

Morrow, L. M. (1990). Preparing the classroom environment to promote literacy during play. *Early Childhood Research Quarterly, 5,* 537–554.

Morrow, L. M. (1992). The impact of a literature-based program on literacy achievement, use of literature, and attitudes of children from minority backgrounds. *Reading Research Quarterly, 27,* 250–275.

Morrow, L. M. (2012). *Literacy development in the early years: Helping children read and write* (7th ed.). Needham, MA: Allyn & Bacon.

Morrow, L. M., O'Connor, E. M., & Smith, J. (1990). Effects of a story reading program on the literacy development of at-risk kindergarten children. *Journal of Reading Behavior, 20*(2), 104–151.

Morrow, L. M., & Rand, M. K. (1991). Promoting literacy during play by designing early childhood classroom environments. *The Reading Teacher, 44*(6), 396–402.

National Association for the Education of Young Children. (2009). NAEYC standards for the early childhood professional preparation programs. Retrieved from *www.naeyc.org/files/naeyc/file/positions/profprepstandards09.pdf.*

National Early Literacy Panel. (2008). *Developing early literacy: Report of the National Early Literacy Panel.* Washington, DC: National Institute for Literacy.

National Governors Association Center for Best Practices & Council of Chief State School Officers. (2010). *Common Core State Standards.* Washington, DC: Author.

National Reading Panel. (2000). *Teaching children to read: An evidence-based assessment of the scientific research literature on reading and its implications for reading instruction. Reports of the subgroups.* Bethesda, MD: National Institutes of Health. Available from *www.nichd.nih.gov/publications/nrp.*

Neuman, S. B., & Roskos, K. (1993). Descriptive observations of adults' facilitations of literacy in young children's play. *Early Childhood Research Quarterly, 8,* 77–97.

Neuman, S. B., & Roskos, K. (1997). Literacy knowledge in practice: Contexts of participation for young writers and readers. *Reading Research Quarterly, 32*(1), 10–32.

No Child Left Behind Act of 2001. Retrieved February 7, 2012, from *www.govtrack.us/congress/bill.xpd?bill=h107-1.*

Pellegrini, A. D., & Galda, L. (1993). Ten years after: A reexamination of symbolic play and literacy research. *Reading Research Quarterly, 28*, 162–175.

Peterson, C., Jesso, B., & McCabe, A. (1999). Encouraging narratives in preschoolers: An intervention study. *Journal of Child Language, 26*, 49–67.

Piaget, J. (1962). *Play, dreams, and imitation in childhood.* New York: Norton. (Original work published 1945)

Pressley, M., Rankin, J., & Yokoi, L. (1996). A survey of the instructional practices of outstanding primary-level literacy teachers. *Elementary School Journal, 96*, 363–384.

Race to the Top Act of 2011. (2011). Retrieved February 7, 2012, from *www.govtrack.us/congress/bill.xpd?bill=s112-8.*

Ritchie, S., James-Szanton, J., & Howes, C. (2003). Emergent literacy practices in early childhood classrooms. In C. Howes (Ed.), *Teaching 4- to 8-year-olds* (pp. 71–92). Baltimore: Brookes.

Roskos, K. A., & Christi, J. F. (Eds.). (2000). *Play and literacy in early childhood: Research from multiple perspectives.* Mahwah, NJ: Erlbaum.

Smilansky, S., & Shefatya, L. (1990). *Facilitating play: A medium for promoting cognitive, socio-emotional and academic development in young children.* Gaithersburg, MD: Psychosocial and Education Publications.

Vygotsky, L. (1967). Play and its role in the mental development of the child. *Soviet Psychology, 5*, 6–18. (Original work published 1933)

Vygotsky, L. (1978). *Mind in society: The development of higher psychological processes.* Cambridge, MA: Harvard University Press.

Walmsley, S. A. (1994). *Children exploring their world: Theme teaching in the elementary school.* Portsmouth, MA: Heinemann.

Wasik, B. H. (2004). *Handbook of family literacy.* Mahwah, NJ: Erlbaum.

CHILDREN'S LITERATURE REFERENCES

Daly, A., & Russell, C. (1999). *Goldilocks and the three bears.* London: Ladybird Books.

Eastman, P. D. (1960). *Are you my mother?* New York: Random House.

Galdone, P. (1983). *The gingerbread boy.* Boston: Houghton Mifflin.

Johnson, C. (1981). *Harold and the purple crayon.* New York: Harper & Row.

McGovern, A. (1995). *Too much noise.* Boston: Houghton Mifflin.

Pinkey, J. (2006). *The little red hen.* New York: Dial Books.

Piper, N. (1990). *The little engine that could.* New York: Platt & Munk.

Seuss, T. S. (1998). *Mr. brown can moo! Can you?* New York: Random House.

Slobodking, E. (1968). *Caps for sale.* New York: Scholastic.

CHAPTER 8

DIFFERENTIATING INSTRUCTION

CAROL ANN TOMLINSON
MARCIA B. IMBEAU

> People differ in their gifts and talents. To teach them,
> you have to start where they are.
>   —CONFUCIUS

Mrs. Gilewicz stood at the window of her classroom and looked at the students as they exited the school bus. It was easy to spot the students who would enter her room once the bell rang to begin the day. She knew them well. She thought to herself, "The sign on the door says 'Second Grade.' I wonder what that is supposed to mean!" It was true that the kids were approximately the same age, but what did that have to do with anything? Maria, Alfredo, and Joshua were essentially sixth graders—except that they weren't tall enough. Javier and Tanka were new to English and struggled with all things related to reading— Javier because he had never learned to read, since his dad moved a lot for work; Tanka because the Japanese script he was learning when his father joined the faculty at a university in the United States was a poor match for the books that lined his new classroom.

Brian was a very quick learner but engaged in a constant struggle with his emotions and was easily distracted, whatever the task at hand. Isabella loved to read anything that had print on it but became combative when math time rolled around. She was clearly afraid of making errors, and math was still unpredictable to her. Tommy had a mom who loved him very much but didn't really know how to be a mom, so that Tommy often came to school tied in knots or angry, or both. On those days, it took much of the morning for him to settle into classroom routines. Shawnice had a clever mind and a quick wit, but she was frequently hungry and sleepy when she showed up at the door, and she seemed to need to stay close to her teacher most of the time. Porter had acute asthma and missed a lot of school. Leandra had a diagnosed learning disability. Kelly, Bridgett, and Teddy were undiagnosed but had an equally difficult time with reading and writing. Max knew a lot about bugs and planets and wanted only to read and write about these two things.

Ms. Gilewicz took a very deep breath. In just minutes, the group of 27 "second graders" would come together in her room. She couldn't teach them like they were a "matched set." That had never made sense to her—and had never worked. "I wonder," she said aloud and to no one, "why they put that sign on the door!"

WHAT RESEARCH SAYS ABOUT DIFFERENTIATION

Differentiated instruction, a way of thinking about teaching and learning, is designed to assist teachers in recognizing, understanding, and addressing student differences that are inevitable in virtually all classrooms. It is not a synonym for *individualization*, which calls on teachers to craft unique lessons for each learner in the classroom. Rather, differentiation asks teachers to look for meaningful patterns of difference among students in the classroom and to plan instruction in ways that can attend to those patterns.

The model of differentiation on which this chapter is based (Tomlinson, 1995, 1999, 2003; Tomlinson, Brimijoin, & Navarez, 2008; Tomlinson & Imbeau, 2010) stresses the interdependence of five key classroom elements (supportive learning environment, quality curriculum, assessment, instruction, and classroom leadership/management) as they relate to student growth and achievement, and the need for teachers to attend to all of these elements in mutually reinforcing ways to address learner variance (see Figure 8.1). This model of differentiated instruction establishes a series of principles to guide teacher thinking and instructional planning. Research on differentiation has addressed the five key classroom elements and the model's six principles as well as to the model as a whole. The fundamental principles that inform differentiation are also found in current *NAEYC Standards for Early Childhood Professional Preparation* (National Association for the Education of Young Children, 2009). The following summary of the five key classroom elements in the differentiation model provides a brief look at research from these perspectives and is based on both educational research in general and research specifically related to early childhood education.

Supportive Learning Environment

The learning environment is key to everything that takes place in the classroom and invites or undermines student learning and positive teacher–student relationships (Buyse, Verschueren, Doumen, Van Damme, & Maes, 2008; Chetty, Friedman, & Rockoff, 2011; Palmero, Hanish, Martin, Fabes, & Reiser, 2007; Pianta, Steinberg, & Rollins, 1995; Pianta & Stuhlman, 2004). Hattie's synthesis of meta-analyses (2009) suggests that such a relationship is one of the strongest predictors of student achievement, with an effect size of 0.72. Looking specifically at early childhood, it appears that teacher emotional support—including warmth and respect between teacher and students, and among students; enthusiasm of teacher and students during learning activities; and teacher responsiveness to students' level of academic and emotional functioning—is a particularly powerful predictor of student academic achievement (Hamre et al., 2012). Among principles emphasized by differentiation and affirmed by research related to environment are the importance of teacher beliefs about the capacity of each student to achieve success as a learner (Dweck, 2000) and the need for each student to experience success, affirmation, challenge, and a sense of collegiality and community in the classroom.

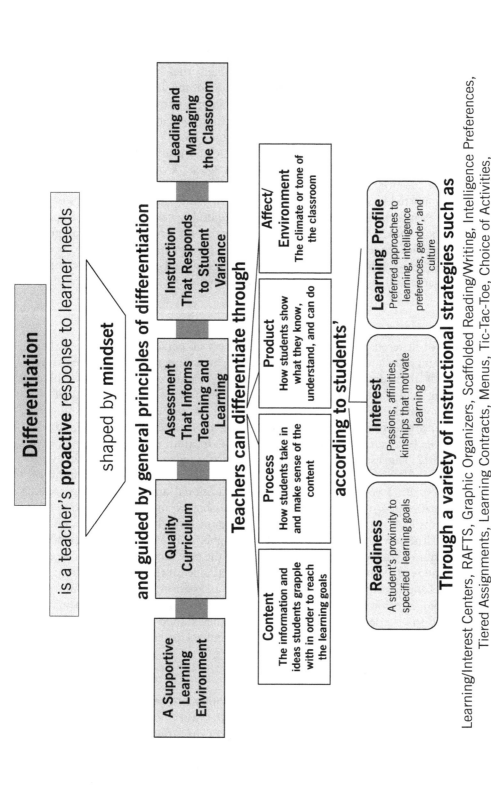

Differentiation

is a teacher's **proactive** response to learner needs

shaped by **mindset**

and guided by general principles of differentiation

| A Supportive Learning Environment | Quality Curriculum | Assessment That Informs Teaching and Learning | Instruction That Responds to Student Variance | Leading and Managing the Classroom |

Teachers can differentiate through

Content
The information and ideas students grapple with in order to reach the learning goals

Process
How students take in and make sense of the content

Product
How students show what they know, understand, and can do

Affect/ Environment
The climate or tone of the classroom

according to students'

Readiness
A student's proximity to specified learning goals

Interest
Passions, affinities, kinships that motivate learning

Learning Profile
Preferred approaches to learning, intelligence preferences, gender, and culture

Through a variety of instructional strategies such as

Learning/Interest Centers, RAFTS, Graphic Organizers, Scaffolded Reading/Writing, Intelligence Preferences, Tiered Assignments, Learning Contracts, Menus, Tic-Tac-Toe, Choice of Activities, Independent Projects, Expression Options, Small-Group Instruction, etc.

FIGURE 8.1. A concept map of differentiated instruction showing its key elements and their relationship to one another.

Quality Curriculum

A second key classroom element requiring attention in the model of differentiation is a quality curriculum, which provides access to rich content that helps students to build foundational knowledge, as well as understand the nature of the disciplines. This element also involves teacher clarity regarding what students should know, understand, and be able to do as a result of student engagement with relevant content across the disciplines (Milligan & Wood, 2010; Salmon, 2008; Simon, 2006). Such a curriculum pays each child the compliment of being a thinker and problem solver. It also prepares children to succeed in those roles (Clements, Sarama, Spitler, Lange, & Wolfe, 2011; Katz, 2008; Pianta, LaParo, & Hamre, 2007; Wang, Kedem, & Hertzog, 2004). A quality curriculum is further supported in a joint position statement by early childhood leaders of the NAEYC and the National Association of Early Childhood Specialists in State Departments of Education (NAECS-SDE), stating that effective curriculum "has clear goals shared by teachers and students, engages children, uses investigation and focused teaching to share valued content, builds on students' prior learning and experiences, is comprehensive, is evidence-based, and is validated by professional standards" (NAEYC, 2009)

Assessment

A third element of differentiation requires that teachers be persistent students of their own students. This necessitates the systematic use of preassessment and formative assessment that is tightly aligned with specified curricular goals as the compass for daily planning in a differentiated classroom rather than for the purpose of grading (Pianta et al., 2007). Pre- and formative assessments are particularly powerful contributors to student achievement when students also participate in thinking about assessment results and setting personal goals to ensure continuing progress toward and beyond content requirements. Hattie (2012) suggests that "we must know what students already know, know how they think, and aim to then progress all students towards the success criteria of the lesson" (p. 39). All forms of assessment (both traditional and performance preassessments, formative assessments, and summative assessments) may be differentiated to ensure that students have maximum opportunity to demonstrate their knowledge, understanding, and skill (Snow, 2011; Tomlinson & McTighe, 2006). Effective assessments hold steady in terms of students' criteria for success, while providing flexibility in aspects such as student mode of expression, amount of time available for the task, scaffolding for the task, degree of sophistication in the language of the assessment, and so on (Tomlinson & McTighe, 2006). Specific feedback providing targeted guidance on what students are doing well related to criteria for success, and actions they should take to continue their growth with those criteria, enhance the power of the feedback to support student success.

Instruction

Fourth, as teachers systematically study students' proximity to essential learning goals, it quickly becomes evident that it is also necessary to address variance in student readiness, interests, and approaches to learning, in order to support the growth of each child. High expectations for understanding, application, and transfer of content should be evident for each student. This sort of "teaching up" aligns with the development of a "growth mindset" in teachers and students alike. Planning instruction with student readiness in mind is essential for academic growth. When learning tasks are consistently too difficult or too easy for students, growth does not occur (Byrnes, 1996; Vygotsky, 1978, 1986). Programs of learning that direct teachers' understanding of how to select materials, present ideas, design tasks, and give feedback based on students' stages of development have a strongly positive impact on student achievement (Hattie, 2009; National Research Council, 2000). In an effectively differentiated classroom, flexible instructional groups with materials that are responsive to the needs of students within the group are strong contributors to student success (Hattie, 2012).

Planning that effectively addresses student interests is likely to increase student motivation to learn, increase focus on learning, help students develop a sense of self-determination as learners, and increase task-persistence (Csikszentmihalyi, Rathunde, & Whalen, 1993; Fulk & Montgomery-Grymes, 1994; Zimmerman & Martinez-Pons, 1990). In addition, ways in which students approach learning, or their *learning profiles*, can impact efficiency of learning. A learning profile can be affected by a student's gender, culture, intelligence, and preferences, among other factors. Experts recommend against categorizing a student as a particular type of learner and instead favor providing multimodal instruction and multiple ways to make sense of and express learning (Coffield, Moseley, Hall, & Ecclestone, 2004; Hattie, 2009, 2012; Lisle, 2006; Pashler, McDaniel, Rohrer, & Bjork, 2008; Willis, 2006, 2007).

Classroom Leadership/Management

Finally, it is critical for teachers to feel competent and confident in orchestrating a classroom in which flexible but orderly routines support students' increasing independence as learners, so that more than one thing at a time can take place in the classroom, thus increasing student opportunity to learn in appropriate ways and at appropriate levels (Pianta et al., 2007). This allows the teacher time to work with small groups and individuals, and allows students' work to target varied learning needs. Furthermore, there is a strong relationship between a teacher's confidence in leading such a classroom, and competence in developing and guiding routines and procedures that support flexibility and the teachers' capacity to teach intellectually rich content. Such flexibility is necessary for student thought and problem solving, and it is likely that teachers who value "tight control" in favor of orderly flexible classrooms create and deliver lower level and routinized curriculum and tasks that do not require student discussion, use of varied materials, higher level thinking, and student decision making for completion (McNeil, 2000). It appears likely that teachers who approach classroom management from the perspective of creating positive and effective learning environments, including attributes such as acceptance, trust, relationships, respect, flexibility, and student self-determination, are more successful than those who emphasize teacher authority (Agne, Greenwood, & Miller, 1994; Brophy, 1998).

STUDIES ON DIFFERENTIATION

Differentiation, with its many facets, is a complex model to research. A number of studies in recent years, however, have examined at least some of its aspects applied in classrooms. Several of the studies have a specific focus on the elementary school years. Brimijoin's (2001) dissertation presents evidence of strong achievement gains on a State Standards Test for students in an effectively differentiated elementary classroom. Marulanda, Giraldo, and Lopez (2006) report that first-grade children in Colombia whose reading instruction utilized the model of differentiating content, process, and product in response to student readiness, interest, and learning profile over a 4-month period had fewer oral reading errors, higher comprehension scores, fewer students scoring below grade level, and more students scoring above grade level than control students. Beecher and Sweeny (2008) report that the achievement score gap between white students and low-income students of color was drastically reduced in math, reading, and writing in an elementary school that used enriched curriculum and differentiation with all students. In addition, achievement gains occurred across student groups, and attitudes about school improved as well. Finally, Tomlinson and colleagues (2008), who conducted a multiyear study of the implementation of differentiation in an elementary school, found positive and sustained achievement gains throughout a 7-year period for students in all segments of the achievement spectrum. Similar gains did not occur in peer schools in which differentiation was not implemented.

RESEARCH INTO PRACTICE

Children come to a classroom needing affirmation, contribution, power, purpose, and challenge (Tomlinson, 2003). *Affirmation* occurs when the child feels safe, accepted, valued, heard, understood, and knows that others believe in his or her capacity to succeed. The need for *contribution* is satisfied when the child feels that he or she makes a difference in the way the classroom works and in the success of others—when each student sees that his or her strengths, experiences, and perspectives are called upon to strengthen the group. A child's *power* stems from understanding how the classroom works and what is expected of him or her, what quality work looks like and how to move in that direction, and knowing that there is support for the learning journey, that what he or she learns is quickly useful in his or her world, and that he or she can make choices that contribute to success. *Purpose* results when the learner genuinely understands content rather than merely parroting it, when he or she sees how ideas and skills make a difference in the world at large, and particularly in his or her slice of the world, and when he or she is absorbed in the work of learning. *Challenge* occurs when a student senses a match between his or her abilities and the work to be done, when he or she feels stretched by work that is difficult but achievable with effort, and responsible for contributing to positive learning outcome and knowledgeable about how to do that.

A key premise of the model of differentiation discussed in this chapter is that the classroom elements (supportive environment, quality curriculum, assessment, instruction, and classroom leadership/management) are avenues through which teachers respond to student needs. Furthermore, the elements are interdependent. When one of the elements is strengthened, all of them benefit. When one is weak, all of the elements suffer. Thus, it is important to understand that teachers can craft each element to be responsive to learners' needs and also understand how the elements impact one another. The sections that follow provide both guidance on effective implementation of each of the five elements and a brief examination of some ways the five model elements impact one another.

A Supportive Learning Environment

Mrs. Winston sat at a table in the first-grade classroom with five students who were writing about an experience the class had just shared. William, one of the five, however, was making no progress. She guided him in thinking and planning what he would write, but as she turned her attention to other students briefly, William wiggled, twirled his paper with the tip of his pencil, and leaned back in his chair. William was always a mover and shaker. When Mrs. Winston turned back to William, she said with warmth and an edge of surprise, "William, where is that idea you were going to write down? I don't see it!"

He shrugged and looked away. "I can't do it. I'm no good at writing."

Mrs. Winston's eyes were wide as she got close to him and spoke in a hushed voice. "Do you know why you think you can't write, William," she asked, as though revealing an important secret.

"No," he said in a hush that matched his teacher's, "Why?"

Now very close to him with a conspiratorial whisper, she said, "There's a gremlin on your shoulder telling you that you can't write. But they never tell the truth!" Giving an appropriate gesture on her own shoulder, she said, "Flick that gremlin off right now!" William did. Then he looked around on the floor for evidence of a gremlin, picked up his pencil, and wrote.

Four decades ago, Haim Ginott (1972) made the often cited comment that his mood created the classroom "weather" and his response to every classroom situation was the determining factor in whether a child was humanized or dehumanized. It *is* the case that a teacher is key to everything that takes place in the classroom—including, but not limited to, the nature of the environment in which we ask students to learn.

There are at least three components in creating a classroom environment that actively supports a child's growth as a learner and as a human being: (1) the teacher's beliefs and attitudes, (2) the teacher–student connections, and (3) the teacher's ability to build community connects students with one another. The goal is to create a community of learners—a family- or team-like setting in which students consistently experience affirmation, contribution, and power, and are provided a sense of purpose and a support system for challenge.

Teacher Beliefs and Attitudes That Support a Positive Environment for Each Child

Among teacher beliefs that support a positive learning environment, effective differentiation, and subsequently student success, are noted in Figure 8.2. Teachers make those beliefs clear to students both explicitly and in more subtle ways. It is important for teachers to express to students how they have every confidence that students will succeed at a task, that they are working energetically to support students' learning and are pleased when students work hard to support their own success. It makes sense to talk about how much more interesting it is when students approach tasks in different ways than when everyone thinks exactly alike.

Positive beliefs develop over time in teachers, as well as students. Therefore, it is important for teachers continually to examine beliefs that underlie their professional actions, and to be reflective about the disparities between what they may currently believe and what they aspire to believe about children, teaching, and learning. A teacher who firmly believes these statements is positioned to shape each of the classroom elements in ways that empower every child as a learner and as a person. A teacher who works consistently to *develop* these beliefs is growing in the direction of effective teaching, including effective differentiation.

- Every child is valuable, irreplaceable, and worthy of respect.
- Every child needs/deserves the highest quality learning experiences a school can offer.
- Student differences are inevitable, positive, and significant in student learning.
- Effective teaching includes instructional planning with these differences in mind.
- Children are worthy of our trust and can learn to do whatever is necessary to succeed and contribute to the success of others in the classroom.
- Effort rather than innate ability determines how much a child can learn.
- One role of a teacher is to elicit the student's effort. Another is to make consistently evident the teacher's effort on behalf of the student's success.
- Virtually every student in a classroom can learn what he or she needs to learn to succeed with a given topic or content area.
- It is the teacher's responsibility to understand each student's progression in learning and to ensure that each learner takes his or her next steps in learning every day.

FIGURE 8.2. Teacher beliefs in a differentiated classroom.

Teacher–Student Connections

Many, if not most, learners who arrive at school are less concerned about the content they will study than about how they will fare with the teacher and classmates. Especially with young learners, school can feel unfamiliar and even frightening. The teacher's skill and will in connecting with students, and sustaining those connections over time, are critical in helping young learners feel safe, affirmed, and significant—an important step toward taking the risk of learning. Figure 8.3 suggests several actions teachers can take to connect with students.

- Without exception, treat each child with respect and dignity.
- Make it a goal to understand each child more fully every day. Find time each day to talk with students individually and in small groups. Listen carefully to what students say—both words and meaning.
- Show pleasure in talking with and listening to the student.
- Use what you hear to develop interest-based or culturally relevant learning opportunities or examples when sharing content, or to engage in conversation with a child later in the day or week.
- When a student exhibits effort or growth, or makes a contribution to the class in some way, be specific in letting the student know what you saw and why you feel it is worth noting.
- Be enthusiastic about meaningful work students do.
- Be a source of encouragement and support when work or other aspects of school are difficult for a child.
- Trust students to do the right things and to do things right—and provide direction and scaffolding to support the trust.

FIGURE 8.3. Actions teachers take to connect with their students.

When a teacher consistently demonstrates interest and belief in a child, it is far more likely that the child will develop trust in the teacher. As the child finds the teacher trustworthy, the child feels safer in taking the risk to learn. To optimize the learning environment, however, each child needs to feel seen, valued, and trusted not only by the teacher, but also by peers with whom he or she will learn.

Building Community

A teacher who believes in the capacity of each child to succeed and systematically demonstrates that belief to individual students has already begun helping students connect to one another. Children, of course, observe and interpret the teacher's interactions with peers, just as they attribute meaning to their own interactions with the teacher. When it is clear that the teacher respects every student, is enthusiastic in supporting the success of each student, sees each student as a contributor to the welfare of the group, and notes the growth of each child, it seems appropriate to students also to respond in kind to one another. In Patricia Polacco's (1998) book about a teacher who transformed a child's experience of school, *Thank You, Mr. Falker,* the young girl who is the main character explains that no matter how hard you tried, you just couldn't figure out who Mr. Falker liked best. Mrs. Winston is a practitioner of that belief. She lets William know that she does not accept the idea that he cannot write. Later in the class period, she asks him to help her recall the hand motions to a song she wants to use with the class—signaling the rest of the class that this wiggly little boy who has trouble focusing can teach them all a thing or two. In a class where there are no winners and losers, favored and less favored, first- and second-class members, students learn to value, trust, and support one another just as they are valued, trusted, and supported. This opens the way to develop a community or team of learners in which students are willing and able to help the teacher and one another succeed. Figure 8.4 suggests actions teachers can take to build a community or team of learners.

- Talk with students regularly about the benefits of having the class work like a good team or a strong family in which members pull together to help everyone do his or her best.
- Teach students how to help one another, when to help one another, and the difference between help that makes us stronger and help that makes us weaker.
- Give students frequent opportunities to work together to make decisions and solve problems.
- Use specific criteria to help students reflect on the effectiveness of the ways they work in pairs and small groups, so that they grow in their understanding of meaningful collaboration.
- Involve students in refining guidelines for working with peers, so that rough spots are eliminated and collaborations become more effective.
- When students work together on shared tasks, be sure that each student in the group has a meaningful role to play in effectively doing the work that other students in the group could not do as effectively (Cohen & Benton, 1988).
- Help students develop a vocabulary for talking about and reflecting on the varied strengths and experience they and their peers contribute to the class.

FIGURE 8.4. Actions teachers can take to build community.

In much the same way that very thoughtful parents work from a set of beliefs that guides their words, actions, reactions, and decisions with their children, so do teachers who consistently strive to create a classroom environment that enables children to grow as much as possible as learners and individuals. The analogy is an apt one. Max van Manen (1991) reminds us that parents and teachers share the pedagogy of teaching young people to take responsibility for themselves, for one another, and for the welfare of the world.

Quality Curriculum

At Franklin Primary School this year several evening events have been planned for students and their families to learn more about the curriculum used in their children's classrooms. Mrs. Harris, the school principal, works with every grade-level team to provide guidance and resources to support the teachers' work. Tonight is devoted to the kindergarten curriculum, and she is pleased to see many children and their families moving to the classroom stations set up in the library. Students in each classroom have an important role in this event, and Mrs. Harris sees José excitedly tell his mom about what they are learning in his classroom. Standing near him, the principal overhears him explain about their unit "Plants, A Study in Cycles." She smiles as he tells about the experiments the class has conducted "because that's what scientists do" and how he had to be "very careful" to record what he observed each day and "think really hard" to discover what "a plant needed to grow and suburvive" [survive]. She tried not to giggle when she saw him hit himself in the head with his hand and say, "Oh, and I almost forgot—did you know that plants are a cycle just like you and me?"

Effective teachers of young children in a differentiated classroom plan curriculum that emphasizes student understanding and is developmentally appropriate, relevant, and engaging. Tomlinson (2003) indicates that quality curriculum is also the following:

- *Important*—Students are involved with learning tasks essential to build understanding of the topic and the discipline.
- *Focused*—All learning experiences are aligned with what teachers want their students to know, understand, and be able to do as a result of the learning experience.
- *Demanding*—Learning and behavior expectations are high, and all students are expected to complete tasks whose difficulty is just beyond what they can currently do independently.
- *Scaffolded*—A variety of resources and supports are provided along with specific criteria for quality work to assist each student in taking his or her next step with the learning targets and to do so successfully.

In primary-grade classrooms it is often the case that teachers plan units of study with others at their grade level using state or district standards or guidelines. Most states have adopted the Common Core State Standards (*www.corestandards.org/in-the-states*), so many teachers likely align their ideas for units of study with these new standards. However, standards alone do not guarantee development of a curriculum that results in understanding, appropriateness, relevance, or engagement. In a differentiated classroom, teachers plan curriculum based on what they want their students to come to Know, Understand and be able to Do (KUD). The kindergarten team at Franklin Primary School knew that the garden, the greenhouse, and the compost pile in the outdoor classroom fascinated their students. Students had observed a pumpkin growing in the outdoor class-room in the fall and had made predictions about how big it would become while learning that seasons change the weather of a region, and the climate and geography of a region affect what can grow there. The teachers decided to teach a unit on plants that would allow more student involvement in the outdoor classroom and also more opportunity for students to use knowledge and skills they had practiced in earlier units. They wanted their unit on plants to be a study in cycles because that concept would help their students see the connection between plants and their own lives. Figure 8.5 provides the KUD for the plant unit.

Once team members determined the unit's focus, they used the remaining curriculum planning time to design learning experiences that aligned with the unit's KUD and to organize them in a logical sequence to help young learners construct the knowledge, skills, and understanding. Lessons cast all students as leaders and problem-solvers as they learned about plant cycles. Because the team knew the students would differ in readiness to learn, interests, and learning preferences, they built in lessons to address those areas of variance. Nonetheless, they planned curriculum to "teach up"; that is, they designed learning experiences that would engage their most advanced learners, then planned to differentiate to enable all learners to work with those high-level, meaning-rich tasks. José clearly knew about his classroom's study. His clarity about the meaning of the content and the complexity of the tasks he describes suggest a classroom in which each student finds the support necessary to learn at a high level and experience power, purpose, and challenge.

Assessment to Inform Teaching and Learning

First-grade teachers discussing an upcoming lesson on symmetry were confident that they knew who might already understand the concept, who might grasp the concept readily, and who would struggle with it. Nonetheless, they agreed to preas-sess students after a brief introductory lesson on the concept, just to be sure they were right. The assessment involved finding a few minutes over a 2-day period to sit with each student. They asked students to draw three cutout figures from a teacher-made grab bag, to tell whether each figure was an example of symmetry or asymmetry, and to explain why they answered as they did. When the teachers met again to plan, each was surprised that the preassessment revealed students they had "miscategorized." It was very clear in talking with the students individually, they concluded, that student vocabulary played a much larger role than they had expected in student understanding of the concept of symmetry.

- **Know**—Parts of a plant (seed, root, stem, flower, leaf); organisms, living and nonliving; and soil, light, water, food.
- **Understand**—*Scientists carefully record what they see in order to make predictions and draw conclusions. Living things differ from nonliving things. Plants grow from seeds and need water, soil, light, and food to grow. The details of a cycle are different for different organisms.*
- **Be Able to *Do***—Conduct an experiment, make predictions, record observations, think at high levels, work cooperatively.

FIGURE 8.5. KUD for the plant unit.

Teachers sometimes see assessment as a chore at best and a necessary evil at worst. Much of the negativity that surrounds assessment stems from viewing assessment as judging and categorizing children. That stance feels oppositional to the desire of many teachers to be mentors and advocates for their students, particularly in the early childhood years.

A very different and far more satisfactory view of assessment positions it as a vehicle for fueling student success. This latter view aligns with not only the principles and practices of differentiation but also current best thinking about the role of assessment in teaching and learning. This approach to assessment emphasizes the power of preassessment and formative assessment not only to help teachers more effectively guide each learner toward success but also to help learners take increasing control of their success. Thus, assessment that functions as formative to the extent that evidence about student performance is elicited, interpreted, and used by teachers, learners, or their peers to make decisions about next steps in instruction is likely to be better grounded than an assessment made in the absence of that evidence (Wiliam, 2011). This approach also stresses the power of carefully focused feedback that helps a particular student move his or her position forward on a learning trajectory and deemphasizes grades or judgment. If teachers want to increase student learning, they need to be sure their responses to students' work elicit a cognitive rather than emotional reaction (Wiliam, 2011). Some important guidelines for use of formative assessment in an effectively differentiated classroom can be found in Figure 8.6.

Instruction That Responds to Student Variance

Mr. Rojas took his kindergarten students on a science walk. They talked about what a scientist does and what it means to gather data. The students gathered items from nature that were interesting to them as they walked and stored their "data" in the various pockets of carpenter aprons. When the students returned to class, Mr. Rojas asked them to put their items in small boxes so that each box contained things that were alike. As the students worked, he walked among them, asking them questions about their classification decisions. Based on what he noted during that time and on recent assessments of shapes, sizes, and colors, the next day he assigned students to one of three classification stations. At the first station, students classified nature objects by color and size. At the second, they classified the objects by size and shape. At the third station, students classified the objects by shape and two other criteria of their choosing—other than color or size. The whole class then came together to share some items they classified and explain how they thought about their classifications. They also talked about ways in which their work might be similar to the work of a scientist.

There are three areas of student variance that can impact learning: readiness, interest, and learning profile. In each instance, when teaching and learning opportunities match a student's needs in those areas, learning is likely to proceed more effectively and efficiently, and students are more likely to derive a sense of power, purpose, and challenge.

There are at least four important instructional planning principles or guidelines for addressing student readiness, interest, and learning profile. The first principle, *respectful tasks*, implies that each student's work should look equally appealing and important compared to the work of their peers. In other words, it should not be the case that some

- Preassessments and formative assessments should be directly aligned with specified goals in the portion of curriculum being assessed. In other words, assessments should directly mirror the KUD for a particular segment of learning.

- Preassessments can be formal (e.g., asking students to draw or write answers; interviewing students to determine their knowledge, understanding, and skill; using a checklist of indicators to monitor student understanding while students perform a task) or informal (e.g., jotting notes as students work or play; asking students to give a thumbs-up sign if they understand how to do a math computation).

- While the learning targets (KUDs) should remain constant for all students (with the exception of students with individualized education plans [IEPs] indicating otherwise), it is fine for students to be able to express their knowledge in different formats (e.g., writing, drawing, creating a diagram, dictating an answer in English or in another first language). The goal of an assessment is to determine what students actually know, understand, and can do. When the format of the assessment makes it more difficult for a student to express learning, the assessment is not doing its job.

- Preassessments should examine prerequisite knowledge, understanding, and skills that a teacher assumes students will bring to the classroom with them, as well as check for common misunderstandings about a topic.

- It is also helpful to use surveys, drawings, open-ended questions, and observation to understand students' particular interests.

- If a teacher aspires to help students understand essential ideas and to develop the skills of thinking and problem solving, pre- and formative assessments should require those abilities and not focus solely on repetition of knowledge or using skills out of context.

- Students should understand what the learning targets (KUDs) are at any point and be sure that what they practice and what the teacher assesses match those targets.

- Help students articulate what they think is going to be assessed on a particular pre- or formative assessment so that they develop the habit of being conscious of learning goals and you can determine the degree to which they understand the assessment process.

- Invest in helping students understand that learning nearly always involves making mistakes, and that people learn by figuring out why they made a mistake so they don't continue making it. If people don't make mistakes, they don't learn.

- Give students feedback on assessments specifically focused on specified learning targets and criteria for quality work. Avoid grading pre- and formative assessments.

- Help students examine their own work according to specified criteria for success so they learn to identify gaps between their own work and quality work.

- Be sure students learn to make specific plans to trace the effectiveness of the work they do and to narrow or eliminate the gaps.

- Guide students in developing the skills of reviewing one another's work to find these gaps and assist one another in narrowing or eliminating them.

- Be sure students learn to say what supports or resources they will need to continue growing in a particular area.

- Help students understand that the teacher uses student assessments to understand what each student needs to do to grow in learning—to take his or her next step of growth in a particular area. In other words, help them to understand that assessment helps you know how to help them become successful learners. This is an important element in student understanding of differentiation.

FIGURE 8.6. Guidelines for using assessment.

students consistently work with low-level drill-and-practice tasks while others consistently use important ideas and skills to solve problems or create products for meaningful audiences. Every student's work should be centered on essential understanding of the lesson, use essential knowledge and skills to explore or apply this understanding, and call on the student to be a thinker.

The second overarching principle that applies to differentiation for readiness, interest, and learning profile is *flexible grouping*, which has to do with a teacher's mindful planning of student grouping arrangements and giving each student the opportunity to work with a broad range of peers within a relatively short period. There are times, of course, when it is important to have students work with peers at a similar point of readiness on a given task. There are also times when it makes good sense to have students work with peers with different readiness levels, similar or varied interests, and preferred approaches to learning, and those who come at a task in a variety of ways. There are times when a teacher should absolutely be the architect of the student groupings, and other times when students should have the opportunity to select working partners and learn what makes a particular learning context effective or ineffective for them.

The third principle is the reminder that *differentiation* is not a synonym for *different*. The goal of differentiation is not to provide a range of dissimilar tasks for students, but to provide varied avenues to accomplish the same critical learning outcomes. Sometimes students need different knowledge and skills (K and D) to progress. (For example, a first grader who spells like a fifth grader likely needs a more advanced spelling or vocabulary approach than some other peers. A second grader who does not grasp the idea of addition will likely need to continue with that concept in order to understand subtraction.) Thus, teachers in differentiated classrooms sometimes teach forward and backward simultaneously as they work to help students progress from their varied points of entry into a content area. All students, however, should work consistently with the essential understandings. That work may be scaffolded in various ways based on student needs, but everyone should be a participant in making meaning of essential ideas and applying or transferring them.

Finally, it is important for teachers to develop a broad repertoire of *instructional strategies* that invite attention to students' varied learning needs, and to become skilled in selecting instructional strategies that align with both student needs and the nature of the current content and learning goals. Strategies such as learning centers, interest centers, learning contracts, tiered assignments, small-group instruction, math and vocabulary games, book boxes, book circles, varied modes of expressing learning, and many others, can help all students focus on critical outcomes in ways that address their particular readiness, interest, and learning profile needs.

Differentiating Student Readiness

The term *readiness* refers to a student's current position relative to a particular set of learning outcomes or KUD. It is not a synonym for *ability*. Although ability is not a fixed entity, we tend to feel that it is. Readiness is quite fluid and should change regularly for any child. Differentiating student readiness implies understanding the learning targets (KUD), the prerequisite knowledge a student needs to move ahead in a particular topic or discipline, and the sequence of learning for a particular topic (including steps that come both before and after what the teacher is teaching, where a particular student is in the learning sequence at a given time, and what that student needs at that time to move ahead confidently). Of course, effectively differentiating student readiness also requires effective use of preassessment and formative assessment, as well as alignment of KUD, assessments, and instructional plans.

The goal of readiness differentiation of *knowledge and skill* is to have students work at a degree of difficulty that's just a little too hard, with content that represents the "next step" in a sequence of learning with support from peers, teachers, volunteers, or teaching assistants, so that students can successfully master that step and move ahead again. For example, in kindergarten during math time, some students may work with number awareness and recognition by counting specified items in a classroom and labeling them with numbers; others may be counting students and representing classmates who are and are not wearing jeans; and still others may be representing students who are present–absent on a given day in class.

The goal of readiness differentiation of *understanding* is to have all students work with the same essential understanding(s) at a degree of difficulty that is just a little too hard, and with scaffolding or support that enables students to apply or extend the understanding. For example, all students in a first-grade class may work with the understanding that scientists classify animals by using patterns. All students may classify dinosaurs by patterns related to eating and movement. Some of the students might work in pairs, using a teacher-created chart with two cells completed and a box of eight dinosaur models to classify according to eating and movement. Seven other students may meet with the teacher as a group to discuss how to classify four dinosaur models, then work in pairs or triads to classify the other four. The teacher might then lead a whole-class discussion in which students have the opportunity to discuss a dinosaur they classified, explain how they made the decision about the classification, and get feedback from classmates on their decisions.

Differentiation for Student Interest

Interest-based differentiation allows young students to connect what they need to learn with things about which they care. It also enables them to extend current interests. Both increase student motivation to learn and make school learning more natural and relevant for young learners. For example, one second-grade teacher set up a part of the room as an "I Want to Know" area. As students posed questions about topics they were studying or something outside the bounds of those topics, the teacher would often challenge them to be "information detectives" who seek answers to their own questions. They had a guide for finding sources to learn about their topics, a structured log to keep track of what they were learning, and a variety of ways they could share what they learned. The teacher met with individuals and small groups of students during their explorations to guide their thinking and planning. A first-grade teacher encouraged her students to develop their own word collections about topics of interest. Some students collected words about trucks and cars, others about dogs, still others about outer space, and so on. Some students continued to focus on the same topic over an extended period of time. Others changed topics as their interests changed. The teacher made time for students to share new words in their collections during morning circle, at end-of-the-day meetings, or in a few spare minutes before lunch, and so on. Students could create word boxes, word cards, or work scrapbooks and also use one another's collections, housed in a special place in the room, to get ideas for writing.

Differentiation for Student Learning Profiles

The goal of learning profile differentiation is twofold: (1) to enable students to approach learning in a way that is comfortable and effective for them; and (2) to guide students in developing awareness of ways they can approach learning and varying their approach to learning when it might benefit them to do so. Culture and gender impact the ways in which students approach learning, as do what we call learning style and intelligence preference.

While it is certainly not correct that all individuals from a given culture approach learning in the same way or that all male students, for example, learn in the same way, there are some culture-and gender-shaped patterns. Many boys, for instance, learn better when they can move as they learn. So do some girls. Students from some cultures may, for example, be more inclined to work collaboratively and to see the group as a sort of family, while students from another culture may see learning more as an individual pursuit. The point is not to categorize individuals by culture or gender and assign them tasks accordingly. Rather, a thoughtful teacher studies a range of learning patterns and makes options available to students based on those patterns, talking with students about their choices and whether the choices are serving them well as learners.

Similarly, current thinking cautions against categorizing students by a particular learning style or intelligence preference. Rather, it seems better to teach using a variety of modes (e.g., speech, images, written words, drawings, demonstrations, role play) and to offer various modes of learning and expression to students—once again, helping them become aware that they can approach learning in a variety of ways, and that when they sense that they are not making progress in learning, they can switch to another approach. It is also important, especially in the early childhood years, to understand and accommodate for the reality that different children learn at different rates. Some students may need additional time to learn a concept or skill that is difficult for them. Others may need additional time because they want to know more about a topic. Still others may require more time because conditions at home are unsettling and they need a classroom where they can "collect themselves" in order to learn well.

A first-grade teacher was working with her students to build a model of their community. Among ways she attended to learning preferences were the following. Some of the options have implications for readiness and interest as well. All students were part of the community research team, charged with finding out about the area in which their school was located. However, some students chose to be print researchers, others to be interview researchers, and still others to be observation researchers. They shared and compiled what they learned about how to build the community model. In addition, students could work on the design team, the engineering team, or the architecture team. Each team had a different role in bringing the model to life, but conversation and collaboration among teams was important as well.

Leadership/Management of a Differentiated Classroom

> Dale kept adding tasks to his "to do" list as he reflected about what he wanted to accomplish during the new school year. He knew it was essential to prepare his classroom to be inviting to his incoming first graders, but he also knew that this new school had several students from challenging home situations, so it was likely that many of his children would have lots on their minds as they entered each day. But what should he do first? What was most important? These questions reminded

him of a conversation he had with Mrs. Bass, a veteran teacher who was seen by everyone as intelligent, insightful, wise, compassionate, and no-nonsense. She had emphatically told him, "You may not be able to change that child's home situation, but I can guarantee you feeling sorry for the child will not help him. Make sure he learns all he can and has a sense of how important he is. Let him see that working hard helps him achieve success and that you are here to see that he is successful." So Dale decided he wanted a classroom where children felt safe and invited, where each one felt valued and accepted, so he began to list ways he could help students envision and contribute to a classroom in which everyone could succeed. He also knew that establishing classroom agreements and implementing strategic routines and procedures with his young learners would help him to accomplish the vision of the classroom he believed would work best for the very important people he served.

Like many teachers who work to prepare their classrooms at the beginning of the school year, Dale might organize several ideas to help him accomplish this task. He needs to determine carefully where he stands on a number of issues. He knows that many teachers think they need to "control" students in order for learning to occur, but he believes this kind of management is more often about power and authority and not cooperation. Dale sees the young people entrusted to his care as children from his own family, and he asks himself how he would want them to be treated. He senses that he should first *lead* his students, then *manage* the details and processes of the classroom. Leading students requires teachers to do the following:

- Be aware of your beliefs about human potential and the role of those beliefs in helping young people realize their potential.
- Have a vision of how you think the classroom should operate and ideas for how to enlist the students in making that vision happen.
- Help students work as an effective team that focuses on success for all its members.
- Reflect on decisions you make to ensure that the practice aligns with your beliefs, and make adjustments if you find they are off course.
- Celebrate group and individual contributions to making the classroom work effectively for all its members.

Leadership calls on teacher competence and confidence in the ability to create a classroom community where everyone is treated with dignity and respect, where people feel safe and valued, and where cooperation with others is a prerequisite for growth. While this kind of leadership is people-focused, it nonetheless offers important guidance for how routines and procedures in the classroom should support the vision a teacher is trying to achieve. Management of processes and routines in a differentiated classroom should send a clear message that students are capable and can assist with the operation of their class. Schedules, materials, furniture, routines, and procedures should ensure that each student has the necessary structure and freedom to learn effectively and efficiently.

Organizing the classroom's physical space is important, allowing students to work in a number of configurations throughout a day, week, or month. Students need to learn that they can go to various places within the classroom to work by themselves, or work as a whole class, with partners, or in small groups or at learning stations. Effective teachers teach children efficient ways to move from one group configuration to another through practice and reinforcement.

Teachers take care to arrange furniture and materials so that students access them safely and without disturbing others, allowing for productive movement throughout the day. They also implement procedures for how students line up; where coats, backpacks, and lunch boxes are stored; and where school supplies can be retrieved. These details take on importance and are easily observed in effective classrooms, but they can just as readily be a problem for students when a teacher forgets to think about how best to handle these details. Additional elements of managing a differentiated classroom include teaching children what to do when they need help and the teacher is working with another child or small group; deciding with students where they should put work and supplies when they are finished; implementing signals that remind students about appropriate noise levels and transition procedures; giving directions to students that are efficient and effective; developing a system of keeping track of student progress and needs; organizing special places for ongoing projects, experiments, student-accessible materials, and so forth; and providing guidelines or hints for students to consult if they forget important information they need to complete a task.

Managing the details of the classroom is accomplished by teachers who are clear about why these routines and procedures are in place and how they help to promote independence of the students for whom they were designed. They are important for students at any age but are particularly helpful for young children who are learning that they can make important decisions about their lives, giving them a sense of ownership of success and self-efficacy as learners.

REFLECTIONS AND NEW DIRECTIONS

Frameworks for early childhood education, such as the NAEYC standards, and instructional models, such as differentiation, provide a solid foundation for teaching and learning that no doubt benefits the increasingly diverse population of young children in the United States. Nonetheless, the gap between a vision and implementation of that vision into classroom reality is vast. This gap provides opportunity in the areas of research and practice alike.

Practitioners need intelligent, sustained, classroom-focused support to understand and implement recommended practices that enable learning environment, curriculum, formative assessment, responsive instruction, and classroom/leadership and management to function at a level of best practice and in concert with one another in ways that maximize the potential of each child in a classroom. Researchers need to examine directly teachers' thinking and classroom practices with a two-pronged intent. One of these is to understand more fully the concerns, perceptions, and needs of teachers of young children—particularly as these relate to academically diverse student populations. A second important focal point is to describe and report effective classroom practices in ways that enable other teachers to translate research findings into their own work with academically diverse learners. Thus, in addition to studies that suggest practices and constellations of practices that benefit student academic and affective growth, there is also a great need for qualitative studies that add dimensionality to necessarily less narrative and descriptive quantitative work. Supporting teachers in conducting sound action research in their own classes, as well as sharing, in rigorous ways, practices they have observed to be effective with academically diverse young children, action research also provides foundational understanding that allows all students to have equal access to excellent learning opportunities throughout their school years.

PROFESSIONAL DEVELOPMENT ACTIVITIES

- Offer book/lesson study options on differentiation for faculty; allow teachers to decide the professional activity they believe best suits their next step.

- Schedule curriculum planning days [either during the school year or summer] for grade-level teams to work on shared units of study that have a quality KUD, along with differentiated learning experiences and formative assessments.

- Work with age/grade-level colleagues to plan classroom routines that will be supported throughout a grade level or the school.

- Utilize observation and interview protocols to be used by classroom teachers, specialists, and/or administrators that reveal important data to guide differentiation.

- Have teachers regularly share ideas for curriculum, differentiated instruction, formative assessment, and classroom leadership/management at faculty and staff meetings.

- Encourage teachers and staff to observe in other classrooms or schools where effective differentiation is taking place.

REFERENCES

Agne, K., Greenwood, G., & Miller, L. (1994). Relationship between teacher belief systems and teacher effectiveness. *Journal of Research and Development in Education, 27*(3), 141–152.

Beecher, M., & Sweeny, S. (2008). Closing the achievement gap with curriculum enrichment and differentiation: One school's story. *Journal of Advanced Academics, 19,* 502–530.

Brimijoin, K. (2001). *Expertise in differentiation: A preservice and inservice teacher make their way.* Doctoral dissertation, Curry School of Education, University of Virginia, Charlottesville, VA.

Brophy, J. (1998). Classroom management as articulating students into clearly articulated roles. *Journal of Classroom Interaction, 33*(1), 1–4.

Buyse, E., Verschueren, K., Doumen, S., Van Damme, J., & Maes, F. (2008). Classroom problem behavior and teacher–child relationships in kindergarten: The moderating role of classroom climate. *Journal of School Psychology, 46,* 367–391.

Byrnes, J. (1996). *Cognitive development and learning in instructional contexts.* Boston: Allyn & Bacon.

Chetty, R., Friedman, J., & Rockoff, J. (2011). The long term impacts of teachers: Teacher value-added and student outcomes into adulthood. Retrieved January 6, 2012, from *http://obs. rc.fas.harvard.edu/chetty/value_added.pdf.*

Clements, D., Sarama, J., Spitler, M., Lange, A., & Wolfe, C. (2011). Mathematics learned by young children in an intervention based on learning trajectories: A large-scale cluster randomized trial. *Journal for Research in Mathematics Education, 42*(2), 127.

Coffield, F., Moseley, D., Hall, E., & Ecclestone, K. (2004). *Should we be using learning styles?: What research has to say to practice.* London: Learning and Skills Research Centre.

Cohen, E., & Benton, J. (1988). Making groupwork work. *American Educator, 12*(3)10–17, 45–46.

Csikszentmihalyi, M., Rathunde, K., & Whalen, S. (1993). *Talented teenagers: The roots of success and failure.* New York: Cambridge University Press.

Dweck, C. (2000). *Self-theories: Their role in motivation, personality, and development.* Philadelphia: Psychology Press.

Fulk, B., & Montgomery-Grymes, D. (1994). Strategies to improve student motivation. *Intervention in School and Clinic, 30,* 28–33.

Ginott, H. (1972). *Teacher and child: A book for parents and teachers.* New York: Macmillan.

Hamre, B., Pianta, R., Burchinal, M., Field, S., Lo-Casale-Crouch, J., Downer, J., et al. (2012). A course on effective teacher–child interactions: Effects on teacher beliefs, knowledge, and observed practice. *American Educational Research Journal, 49*(1), 88–123.

Hattie, J. (2009). *Visible learning: A synthesis of over 800 meta-analyses relating to achievement.* New York: Routledge.

Hattie, J. (2012). *Visible learning for teachers: Maximizing impact on learning.* New York: Routledge.

Katz, L. (2008). Another look at what young children should be learning. *Exchange*, pp. 53–56.

Lisle, A. (2006). Cognitive neuroscience in education: Mapping neuro-cognitive processes and structures to learning styles, can it be done? Retrieved December 28, 2010, from *www.leeds. ac.uk/educol/documents/157290.htm.*

Marulanda, M., Giraldo, P., & Lopez, L. (2006). *Differentiated instruction for bilingual learners.* Presentation at Annual Conference of the Association for Supervision and Curriculum Development, San Francisco.

McNeil, L. (2000). *Contradictions of school reform. Educational costs of standardized testing.* New York: Routledge.

Milligan, A., & Wood, B. (2010). Conceptual understandings as transition points: Making sense of a complex social world. *Journal of Curriculum Studies, 42*(4), 487–501.

National Association for the Education of Young Children (NAEYC). (2009). NAEYC standards for early childhood professional preparation programs. Retrieved January 5, 2012, from *www.naeyc.org/files/naeyc/file/positions/profprepstandards09.pdf.*

National Association for the Education of Young Children (NAEYC). (2009). Where we stand NAEYC/NAECS/SDE on curriculum, assessment and program evaluation. Retrieved February 17, 2012, from *www.naeyc.org/files/naeyc/file/positions/standcurrass.pdf.*

National Research Council. (2000). *How people learn: Brain, mind, experience and school.* Washington, DC: National Academies Press.

Palmero, F., Hanish, L. D., Martin, C., Fabes, R., & Reiser, M. (2007). Preschoolers' academic readiness: What role does the teacher–child relationship play? *Early Childhood Research Quarterly, 22*, 407–422.

Pashler, H., McDaniel, M., Rohrer, D., & Bjork, R. (2008). Learning styles: Concepts and evidence. *Psychological Science in the Public Interest, 9*(3), 106–119.

Pianta, R., LaParo, K., & Hamre, B. (2007). *Classroom Assessment Scoring System (CLASS).* Baltimore: Brookes.

Pianta, R., Steinberg, M., & Rollins, K. (1995). The first two years of school: Teacher–child relationships and deflections in children's classroom adjustment. *Development and Psychopathology, 7*, 295–312.

Pianta, R., & Stuhlman, M. (2004). Teacher–child relationships and children's success in the first years of school. *School Psychology Review, 33*, 444–458.

Polacco, P. (1998). *Thank you, Mr. Falker.* New York: Philomelo.

Salmon, A. (2008). Promoting a culture of thinking in young children. *Early Childhood Education Journal, 35*, 457–461.

Simon, M. (2006). Key developmental understandings in mathematics: A direction for learning and establishing learning goals. *Mathematical Thinking and Learning, 8*(4), 359–371.

Snow, K. (2011). *Developing kindergarten readiness and other large-scale assessment systems: Necessary considerations in the assessment of young children.* Washington, DC: NAEYC.

Tomlinson, C. (1995). *How to differentiate instruction in mixed ability classrooms.* Alexandria, VA: ASCD.

Tomlinson, C. (1999). *The differentiated classroom: Responding to the needs of all learners.* Alexandria, VA: ASCD.

Tomlinson, C. (2003). *Fulfilling the promise of the differentiated classroom: Strategies and tools for responsive teaching.* Alexandria, VA: ASCD.

Tomlinson, C., Brimijoin, K., & Navarez, L. (2008). *The differentiated school: Making revolutionary changes in teaching and learning.* Alexandria, VA: ASCD.

Tomlinson, C., & Imbeau, M. (2010). *Leading and managing a differentiated classroom.* Alexandria, VA: ASCD.

Tomlinson, C., & McTighe, J. (2006). *Integrating differentiated instruction and understanding by design: Connecting content and kids.* Alexandria, VA: ASCD.

van Manen, M. (1991). *The tact of teaching: Toward a pedagogy of thoughtfulness.* Albany: State University of New York.

Vygotsky, L. (1978). *Mind in society.* Cambridge, MA: Harvard University Press.

Vygotsky, L. (1986). *Thought and language* (A. Kozulin, Trans. & Ed.). Cambridge, MA: MIT Press.

Wang, X., Kedem, Y., & Hertzog, N. (2004). Scaffolding young students' reflections with student-created power point presentations. *Journal of Research in Childhood Education, 19*(2), 159–174.

Wiliam, D. (2011). *Embedded formative assessment.* Bloomington, IN: Solution Tree.

Willis, J. (2006). *Research-based strategies to ignite student learning: Insights from a neurologist and classroom teacher.* Alexandria, VA: ASCD.

Willis, J. (2007). *Brain-friendly strategies for the inclusion classroom.* Alexandria, VA: ASCD.

Zimmerman, B., & Martinez-Pons, M. (1990). Student differences in self-regulated learning: Relating grade, sex, and giftedness to self-efficacy and strategy use. *Journal of Educational Psychology, 82,* 51–59.

CHAPTER 9

Teaching Young English Learners

CLAUDE GOLDENBERG
JUDY HICKS
IRA LIT

Rhonda, a preschool teacher for nearly 30 years, looks around her classroom at the end of a bright spring day. Her gaze settles on her classroom library, and she thinks back to something that happened only hours earlier. During Circle Time, Rhonda had shared with the children that Lyly, new to the class, had just moved to the United States from Vietnam. Rhonda had shared that, like Duong, a friendly little boy in the class, Lyly speaks Vietnamese at home. After Circle Time, Adriana, born in the United States to Mexican parents, had taken Lyly by the hand and marched her new friend over to one of the class-made books. The book was hand-bound, large, and laminated, produced from a child-inspired unit on bread and bread-making back in January. Adriana was eager to show the newcomer her contribution to that book—a drawing of Adriana, her parents, and her two sisters kneading dough. The words *pan* and *Adriana* were written with painstaking care next to and beneath the crayon drawing. Adriana picked up a plastic loaf of bread from a bin in the dramatic play area, pretending to eat it. Lyly watched and giggled. Adriana then returned to the book and deliberately moved through the pages, a mix of children's illustrations and photographs that featured breads from around the world. She passed *bao, chapati,* and *arepas* before she arrived at the page with a photograph of Duong eating *bánh mì.* Adriana had done her best to pronounce this Vietnamese word for bread—had she remembered it from that unit?— and Lyly, who had spoken not a word these 3 days, smiled shyly and corrected her. Rhonda thinks back to her first years in the classroom, when nearly all of her students were native English speakers. Over the years, the faces of her students had changed as first Latino, then Asian and Pacific Island immigrants populated the neighborhood. Her colleagues have always regarded Rhonda as an effective preschool teacher, but more and more she wonders if she is meeting the needs of such a linguistically and culturally diverse group.

The population of students who come to school without a firm command of English—children known as English learners (ELs)[1]—has grown considerably over the

---

[1]Numerous terms have been used to designate the population of children we address in this chapter, each emphasizing different aspects of children's language characteristics. We use the term *English learners,* or ELs, to signify children who probably have age-appropriate language proficiency in their home language but limited proficiency in English. For additional terms and discussion, see *http://cecerdll.fpg.unc.edu* and *www.ncela.gwu.edu/files/rcd/be021775/glossary_of_terms.pdf.*

past several decades. The number of ELs in K–12 public schools in the United States has increased 150% in the last two decades, while the student population has increased only 20% (Goldenberg & Coleman, 2010). ELs speak more than 400 different home languages; approximately 75% speak Spanish (Russakoff, 2011). Projections vary but the numbers and percentages are virtually certain to grow. Complicating this picture is the fact that many of the ELs in the United States come from families in poverty and attend lower-resource schools (Li, 2005). Head Start and Early Head Start—serving almost exclusively families in poverty—have an enrollment that includes more than 30% ELs (Administration for Children and Families, 2008).

While a large majority of U.S. children attend some type of preschool, children of immigrant parents attend preschool at a lower rate than do children of nonimmigrant parents (Turney & Kao, 2009). Among children ages 3–5, 73% of European American and 76% of African American children attend center-based care; in contrast, only 57% of Latino children are in center-based care (U.S. Department of Education, 2000). Children who attend preschool during the year before kindergarten have an advantage in reading and math over peers who are not enrolled in center-based care (Magnuson, Lahaie, & Waldfogel, 2006; Rumberger & Tran, 2006). In other words, attending preschool provides academic benefits that children of immigrants—large numbers of whom are ELs—are disproportionately missing (Karoly & Gonzalez, 2011). We return to this point later in the chapter.

Early educators must be informed by what research has to say about creating optimal learning environments for children with limited English proficiency. Concern over the achievement of this population of students has led to a large number of recent research reviews and professional publications aimed at improving their educational opportunities. While much of the current literature is based on investigations of school-age children and youth, several recent publications focus specifically on early childhood education (e.g., Center for Early Care and Education Research–Dual Language Learners, 2012; Espinosa, 2010). Overall, a growing body of research can inform educators responsible for creating settings for young English learners. Our goal in this chapter is to survey this research and suggest its implications for early childhood educators.

WHAT RESEARCH SAYS ABOUT EDUCATING YOUNG ELS

We organize our review of the research by addressing four key topics:

1. Children's home language in the early childhood curriculum
2. Similarities and differences in effective practices for ELs and English speakers in English-only programs
3. Promotion of children's language development in English and the home language
4. Parent and home involvement

Children's Home Language in the Early Childhood Curriculum

The language of instruction issue—otherwise known as the great "bilingual education" debate—has been the most controversial aspect of the education of ELs for more than the past half-century and continues to be politically charged (e.g., Gándara & Hopkins, 2010). Bilingual education's basic premise is that students should be taught academic skills in their home language as they learn and acquire skills in English. According to this view, instruction in the home language strengthens the home language and creates a more solid foundation for cognitive and academic growth in English; moreover, promoting bilingual competence is valuable in its own right. Opponents of bilingual education argue that instruction in students' home language delays ELs' entrance into the academic and social mainstream, and depresses English achievement; bilingualism might be fine, but the school should focus on rapid and effective English learning. Others have also raised concern about the resources required to fund bilingual programs and whether the benefits justify the costs (Jiménez-Castellanos & Topper, 2012; Parrish, 1994), a debate inherently entangled with questions about the value of the home language maintenance and the contribution home language instruction makes to academic achievement in English. Crawford (2004) provides an excellent history of the many political, ideological, and educational debates around bilingual education.

The strongest research evidence we have for the efficacy of home language instruction comes from experimental studies conducted mostly in elementary schools. Findings overall suggest that ELs' learning to read in their home language can help boost their reading skills *in English*. Not surprisingly, studies consistently find that learning to read in the home language also maintains and strengthens home language literacy skills; there is no controversy about this. The effects of bilingual instruction on home language literacy are large; the effects on English literacy are more modest (see Goldenberg & Coleman, 2010, Chap. 2). The most recent study to date, a fully randomized experiment and probably the strongest methodologically, reached a somewhat different conclusion. In first grade, children in all-English instruction did significantly better in English achievement than did children in bilingual education. By fourth grade, however, English immersion students' scores were not significantly higher than those of students in the bilingual program. Spanish achievement was far higher for the bilingual education students throughout all years of the study (Slavin, Madden, Calderón, Chamberlain, & Hennessy, 2011).

Preschool studies tend to support the same conclusion: At best, instruction in the home language contributes to growth in both English and home language skills; at worst, there is no difference in English achievement but an advantage in home language achievement (Barnett, Yarosz, Thomas, Jung, & Blanco, 2007; Bernhard et al., 2006; Campos, 1995; Durán, Roseth, & Hoffman, 2010; Farver, Lonigan, & Eppe, 2009; Winsler, Díaz, Espinosa, & Rodríguez, 1999). In addition to promoting bilingual language and literacy skills, instruction in the home language can also have psychological and social benefits that immersion in a second language cannot offer. Chang and colleagues (2007) found that Spanish-speaking children who experienced Spanish interactions with their teachers were more likely to engage in more complex interactions than children who experienced only English interactions with their teachers. Use of Spanish was associated with teacher ratings of greater frustration tolerance, assertiveness, and peer social skills. The correlational design leaves open the possibility of alternative interpretations, but we can say that use of Spanish during classroom interactions was associated with more favorable language learning and sociopsychological conditions for children.

Teachers can also use the students' home language in various ways that support their learning, even when instruction is essentially in English. Lugo-Neris, Jackson, and Goldstein (2010), for example, found that teaching vocabulary during English storybook reading produced greater gains in vocabulary learning when teachers embedded Spanish explanations in storybook reading in English. We do not necessarily suggest that code switching during English read-alouds is an effective strategy. Code switching as an instructional strategy is controversial but advocated by some educators (Faltis, 1989).

Rather, we are referring to supplementing the reading with explanations or brief clarifications in the home language or pointing out a *cognate* (e.g., "Do you know what a market is? It sounds like *mercado*, right?"), which can make texts in English more accessible to ELs and possibly make them aware of linkages across languages.

Similarities and Differences in Effective Practices for ELs and English Speakers in English-Only Programs

Studies of effective early childhood curricula have shown cognitive and social benefits for ELs that may be comparable to or greater than those for non-EL counterparts. Researchers in Nebraska, for example, found that a professional development literacy workshop series (*HeadsUp! Reading*) for early childhood educators was equally effective in promoting early literacy skills for children from English-speaking and Spanish-speaking homes (Jackson et al., 2006). In Oklahoma, one of the pioneers of universal high-quality PreK education, preschools produce developmental gains across various demographic groups, including Latinos, approximately 70% of whom come from predominantly Spanish-speaking homes. Gains for these students (in English) were stronger than those for students from English-speaking homes (Gormley, 2008; Gormley & Phillips, 2005). The Spanish-speaking students begin at far lower English levels than the other students, so this could help explain their greater growth. There were apparently no special modifications for EL students, although as Gormley (2008) speculates, "it is possible that gains would be even greater . . . if teachers spoke Spanish more often, especially in their interactions with English language learners" (p. 4).

Studies also illustrate the value of well-known elements of effective teaching for young ELs, such as explaining vocabulary words encountered during reading and using them in different contexts (Collins, 2005). In other words, successful teaching and curricula seem to be successful for most children, suggesting that there is probably considerable overlap between effective practices for ELs and for students already proficient in English (August & Shanahan, 2008; Goldenberg & Coleman, 2010).[2] EL children have also been taught to "learn how to learn." Pasnak, Greene, Ferguson, and Levit (2006) successfully taught EL Head Start children how to solve seriation and oddity problems through what was presented as a series of games. These "playful learning" early childhood environments are associated with not only positive cognitive outcomes but also social–emotional and motivational benefits for children—less stress, more positive attitudes toward school, mastery of social skills, higher levels of persistence at difficult tasks, and more independence (Hirsch-Pasek, Golinkoff, Berk, & Singer, 2009; Stipek et al., 1998). "Playful learning" appears to be a way to take into account not only the cognitive child, but the whole child (Hirsh-Pasek et al., 2009), whether the child is an EL or not.

Regardless of their level of English development, young ELs who are working to master the rudiments of English probably need additional supports to help them participate fully in classroom learning activities if the activities are in English. This is suggested by Collins's (2005) finding that while preschool ELs benefit from explanations about the meaning of words (just as English speakers do), children who began with lower English scores learned less than children with higher English scores. Roberts and Neal (2004) found that pictures helped Spanish-speaking preschoolers with low-level oral English

---

[2]The caveat here is that ELs have tended to score lower in preliteracy and premath measures prior to the curricular interventions.

skills learn story vocabulary (e.g., *dentist, mouse, cap*), suggesting that *visual representations*, not just *explanations*, provided these children with additional support for learning.

Researchers have identified other possible means of additional support for ELs. For example, Silverman and Hines (2009) report that "multimedia-enhanced instruction" (videos) helped to make read-aloud instruction more effective for preschool to second-grade ELs. The ELs who saw the videos as part of their science lessons about "habitats" learned more target words and made greater gains on a general vocabulary measure than ELs who did not. The videos had no impact on the learning of the non-ELs and therefore helped either to diminish greatly or eliminate the gap in ELs' and non-ELs' vocabulary knowledge.

So far, however, attempts to incorporate additional supports such as these into comprehensive programs and curricula have had mixed success. Buysse, Castro, and Peisner-Feinberg (2010) evaluated a professional development program that comprised instructional practices designed to complement effective early childhood education core practices with scaffolding strategies designed for ELs. The strategies included visual cues and props, prereading activities, and the systematic observation of second language learning. The study found gains in the instructional activities and classroom environment, but the only beneficial child outcomes observed by the researchers were some of the phonological awareness measures.

The key message is that what we know about effective instruction in general is the foundation of effective instruction for ELs. "Generic" effective instruction, however, is probably not sufficient to promote accelerated learning among ELs, although it is almost certainly a necessary base. What goes atop this base? We have some intriguing clues from studies (e.g., Roberts & Neal, 2004; Silverman & Hines, 2009), but we are less certain about how to incorporate these supports into comprehensive programs, delivered in English, that optimize developmental outcomes for ELs.

Promotion of Children's Language Development in English and the Home Language

Language development is, of course, a high priority in early childhood programs. English language development is critically important, but so is promoting development of the home language. Developing the home language is important in its own right *and* as a means of promoting other important cognitive and social outcomes (Genesee, Paradis, & Crago, 2004).

In her volume, *One Child, Two Languages* (2008), Patton Tabors describes the sequence that most young children follow as they begin learning a second language in preschool:

- First, young children often attempt to use their home language.
- Then, when they realize their home language is not working in this context, they tend to become silent. English Learners listen and observe, gaining an understanding of the classroom language.
- Next, they begin to "go public," testing out some new words and phrases.
- Finally, they begin to produce the new language, using phrases and then sentences. (p. 37)

Children may approach English learning differently, so this developmental sequence is not universal and invariant. But when teachers are aware of the general sequence, they have the opportunity to support ELs most effectively. For example, it is important to be able to recognize and respond to children's nonverbal requests and protests. A silent child has needs that must be met, and the teacher can couple meeting those needs with introducing new phrases. Additionally, children who are not yet communicating verbally can be encouraged to build relationships through shared interests (e.g., working with a partner on a puzzle or dressing dolls) and through humor. Children can also be provided the space and time both to act as *spectators* and to *rehearse* what they hear and want to repeat. Furthermore, models of pragmatically appropriate phrases—that is, appropriate to the particular situation in which the word or phrase is used—can be very useful for children who are just starting to "go public" with their new language.

English language development (ELD) instruction supports ELs as they develop English skills and knowledge in increasingly sophisticated ways (Saunders & Goldenberg, 2010). ELD strategies can include explicit teaching of features of the second language (e.g., vocabulary, grammar, and pragmatics); scaffolding of language using sentence frames; making connections between the home language and the second language; engaging the whole body in learning; providing engaging and motivating contexts that encourage interactions in English and multiple opportunities for oral language practice within a relatively low-stress environment (García & Jensen, 2007). We know surprisingly little, however, about the relative effects, benefits, and disadvantages of different approaches to promoting ELD for ELs in early childhood settings and K–12 schools. There is considerable research on second language instruction in older populations learning a foreign language for professional or academic reasons, but far less on young children and students whose second language is the majority language of the school and the society.

In early elementary settings, a separate block of ELD instruction during the school day (as opposed to incorporating ELD into content instruction) is somewhat more effective than only integrating ELD into the day (Saunders, Foorman, & Carlson, 2006), although there certainly should be EL learning opportunities throughout the day as well. There is also evidence in the preschool context for a separate block of language development in the home language. For Spanish-speaking children in an English immersion preschool, researchers found that a 30-minute block of Spanish language development led to significant gains in children's oral proficiency in Spanish (Restrepo et al., 2010).

Perhaps the most fundamental controversy in the ELD field is whether a second language should be *acquired* through authentic communicative use or *learned* through organized instruction focusing on language forms and conventions. The best evidence to date suggests that both are necessary: Second language instruction should provide opportunities for meaningful communication in the target language, and instruction and feedback on use of conventional forms such as correct syntax, grammar, and vocabulary (Lightbown & Spada, 2006; Saunders & Goldenberg, 2010). It is likely that this balance shifts depending on the learner's developmental level. In early childhood, the balance might tilt toward authentic and communicative language use rather than formal organized instruction. But at the same time, organized learning opportunities can help children acquire English language skills, at least for children in kindergarten and first grade. Tong, Lara-Alecio, Irby, Mathes, and Kwok (2008) found that providing kindergarten and first-grade students with an English-oracy intervention using a published ELD program with elements such as daily English lessons, storytelling and retelling, and academic oral language activities resulted in more accelerated ELD growth, compared to students in control schools who received typical "English as a second language (ESL) instruction."

Parent and Home Involvement

Most ELs who do attend preschools and early childhood centers are from low SES families. More than half of 4-year-olds from immigrant families who are in some sort of early childhood center live below the poverty line and have parents with less than a high school education (Karoly & Gonzalez, 2011). Family income and parent education are known to predict children's language development and academic learning (Mistry, Biesanz, Chien, Howes, & Benner, 2008; Payne, Whitehurst, & Angell, 1994; Wood, 2002), which means that children from low SES homes are at risk for poor school outcomes.

Because there is considerable variability within any group—low SES or otherwise—we should not assume all ELs or all low-SES ELs have the same home learning environments (Farver, Xu, Eppe, & Lonigan, 2006). Moreover, despite risk factors such as those associated with parents' low levels of formal schooling, EL parents consistently show interest in their children's education and are highly motivated to provide their support (Goldenberg & Gallimore, 1995; Perry, Kay, & Brown, 2008; Schaller, Rocha, & Barshinger, 2007). The problem is that teachers often underestimate language-minority parents' interest and ability to help their children succeed in school (Brooker, 2002; Goldenberg, 1987). Yet parents are responsive to focused and sensitive efforts to help them play an active role in supporting their children's earliest school success. As Schaller and colleagues (2007) note, "As early childhood educators, we can take advantage of the positive attitude amongst immigrant parents; if we partner with them while their children are still young, we can help them make their educational vision a reality" (p. 355).

However, researchers have found variability in the impact of home intervention programs on children's academic learning, perhaps due to the range of design and implementation features of various programs. Several studies that have demonstrated promising results focus on encouraging parents to use particular literacy learning techniques (Lim & Cole, 2002; Mendelsohn et al., 2001). Others have reported mixed or inconsistent results (e.g., Baker, Plotrkowski, & Brooks-Gunn, 1998). Taking a somewhat different tack, Perry and colleagues (2008) found that Hispanic parents were able to incorporate school-related literacy activities successfully into their home routines; the authors note that parents made adjustments to those routines to suit family and cultural contexts. In a study with complementary findings, Kenner (1999) reported the case study of a 4-year-old Gujarati speaker in a preschool in which the teachers actively incorporated materials, literacy activities, and artifacts from children's homes into the class. Kenner documented how the multilingual children in the class, with the support of parents and the teacher, built upon and incorporated materials and activities from the home and community into their language and literacy activities in both English and children's home languages. The Perry and colleagues and Kenner studies suggest the possibility that rather than implementing preprepared parent involvement programs, teachers who seek collaborations with parents, supporting the creation of learning opportunities for children that bridge their experiences at home and in school, might be more successful.

An important issue for both parents and teachers is whether parents of ELs should use the home language with children exclusively or try to encourage more English use. Research (and experience) has established that children can learn more than one language, either simultaneously or sequentially, with no adverse effect (Genesee et al., 2004). In fact, there are potential cognitive and other advantages to growing up bilingual (Bialystok, 2001; Kuhl, 2004). Yet many parents—and teachers—assume that speaking more English at home is common sense and promotes higher levels of English proficiency for children. Correlational studies do tend to corroborate these language-specific intuitions: Use of any language at home is positively associated with children's learning outcomes in that language, and negatively associated with outcomes in the other language. But findings are mixed, and correlational studies offer a poor basis for recommending practices (Goldenberg, Rueda, & August, 2006). Moreover, Hammer, Davison, Lawrence, and Miccio (2009) found that increased use of English by Spanish-speaking mothers did not accelerate children's English growth but did decelerate Spanish vocabulary growth.

Two experimental studies suggest that promoting first language literacy in the homes of young ELs can have a positive effect on second language (English) early literacy development (Hancock, 2002), whereas promoting second language literacy in the home has minimal impact (Koskinen et al., 2000). Roberts (2008) found that home storybook reading in either the home language or English can promote Hmong and Spanish-speaking children's English vocabulary learning. As a whole, studies suggest that the home language environment can support development of both the home language and English, just as Barnett and colleagues (2008), Winsler and colleagues (1999), and others have shown that bilingual preschool environments can promote development in both languages. Bilingual language development, in other words, need not be a zero-sum game, and parents should not feel that use of the home language undermines children's English language development. Maintenance of the native language may also be important for other reasons in addition to the cognitive and linguistic benefits, such as maintenance of cultural and family values and communication.

RESEARCH INTO PRACTICE: EDUCATING YOUNG ELs

Effective early childhood programs for ELs begin with a foundation of what we understand about good practice to support young learners more generally. But because young ELs (and their teachers) face the added challenge of learning a new language and, in many cases, different norms and expectations, early educators must go beyond just "good practice." The recommendations offered below in support of ELs in early childhood classrooms thus build on the core elements of effective practice for young learners elaborated throughout this volume. (For more extensive suggestions and recommendations for educating young ELs, readers are urged to consult Espinosa [2010], especially Chapter 6, "Promising Curriculum, Instructional, and Assessment Strategies for Young English Language Learners.")

Home Language in the Classroom

Programs for young ELs ideally should support growth in both the home language and English. Illinois, for example, has been a leader in this regard (Severns, 2012). Unfortunately, bilingual preschool programs, and the resources and staff required to run them, are not universally available. We therefore follow these suggestions favoring bilingual classrooms and teachers with suggestions for early educators who work in English-only classrooms.

Dual-Language Programs

A range of school programs—referred to as transitional, maintenance, developmental, dual-language, or dual-immersion programs—provide opportunities for children to develop language proficiency in both a home language and English. (See Severns [2012], "Structuring the Classroom: Illinois's Models of Instruction," p. 9, and references cited for additional information on program models.) While the research does not offer precise prescriptions for how much or what portion of the day, or what percentage of interactions with children should be in their home language, the evidence strongly suggests the benefits of fostering development of the home language while supporting children's English development. Appropriate selection and implementation of program models and curricula depend on goals for children's learning, available staff, and other resources. A fully trained bilingual staff, dedicated to promoting dual-language growth, of course, provides maximum flexibility. For example, instruction can be organized primarily in one language in the morning and in the other in the afternoon, with support available in the other language at all times, if staff members are bilingual. Alternatively, specific activities throughout the day (or half-day) can be offered in specified languages. If language resources of the staff are more limited, then program design must take this into account, for example, by accessing community and family resources. Teachers and paraprofessionals take on responsibilities for which they have the requisite language skills, building on strengths and available resources.

Home Language in English Curriculum and Instruction

Bilingual instruction programs are not always practical or feasible, but there are numerous ways the home language can be incorporated into preschool programs relying principally on English language instruction, for example:

- Teachers, aides, parents, or community volunteers can read to children from books in the children's home language(s). These books may be part of the classroom library, brought in by parents, or borrowed from a library.
- Children, parents, and teachers can work together to create individual and class books in the child's home language.
- Children can be taught rhymes and letters in their home language. This will help to develop children's *phonological awareness*—the understanding that words are made up of sounds—using words and sounds that are familiar to them and to lay the foundation for learning to read in either the home language or English (ideally, both).
- Numeracy (e.g., counting to 20 and creating patterns) can be taught in the home language.

- Other content can also be taught in the home language; concepts taught in the home language about any subject are learned more readily and can become the basis for English language development lessons (see below) in which the focus becomes learning vocabulary and other aspects of language related to these concepts.

Home Language as a Strategic Support

The home language may also be utilized as a strategic support for instruction that is primarily in English, for example:

- When reading a book or story in English, teachers can embed explanations or definitions of new words in children's home languages. Pointing out cognates (e.g., *elefante* in Spanish, *elephant* in English; *komiputa* in Tongan, *computer* in English) might especially help children make connections between the home language and English. After reading, children should be provided opportunities to use those words in either or both languages.
- Similarly, when teaching a lesson or introducing a new activity in English, teachers can scaffold new vocabulary or concepts by first introducing and exploring them in the home language. However, teachers should avoid simultaneous (or sequential) translation, since there is a danger that children—just like adults—can "tune out" when the language they do not fully comprehend is being spoken, particularly if they have already heard it or know they will hear it in the language they understand easily.

In addition to teaching and learning interactions such as those listed earlier, children should have other opportunities to use the home language in the classroom. Educators can engage young ELs by using their home language to promote language, cognitive, and social development, for example,

- Teaching all of the children in the class the greeting from each of the home languages represented in the classroom.
- Ensuring that the teachers who speak a child's home language have ample opportunities to interact with that child.

Language, Literacy, and Content Instruction

Preschool teachers can use a number of strategies to support EL children's learning of English language, literacy, and subject-matter content (e.g., social studies, science, math). Some of these strategies are intended for more explicit instruction, others may be incorporated into less structured discussions and conversations, and still others may be used in both situations.

English Language Development

There should be a separate block of time during the day, perhaps 20–30 minutes, when English language development is the principal focus. This block of time would include a mix of explicit teaching of features of the language and ample opportunity for using oral language for authentic and communicative purposes. It would also include learning songs, poems, and chants. There should also be plenty of physical activity in support of English language development, including acting out actions or concepts and manipulating objects and pictures of the words children are learning.

Children may be grouped by language level during this time, so that support is offered at the appropriate level, but children should be in heterogeneous language-level groups for most the day. For children in the very early stages of language learning, teachers might accept nonverbal responses only, such as pointing to a picture of a word the children are learning. As children progress to higher levels of English proficiency, the teacher can expect one- to three-word responses; they can also provide for students models of sentences [e.g., "Hello. My name is _____."] for students to use as frames for their own responses. As children develop more background knowledge and vocabulary in the second language, sentence frames might still be provided, but more sophisticated oral language would be expected ["That's not a _____, that's a _____!"]. These types of leveled interactions can also be used when asking questions of children.

> In Alveena's preschool classroom, asking and answering questions is an integral part of each day. Most of Alveena's children are ELs, and she provides English sentence frames for them to use. During snack time at their tables, children are encouraged to use and can be heard asking: "Would you like some _____?" and "May I please have the _____?" Alveena has taught the children these frames during ELD time by modeling them and having the students practice with each other. Alveena has little songs that help children remember the sentence frames. A visitor to Alveena's classroom will be greeted with "My name is Oscar. What's yours?" and "I live in Hillsdale. Where do you live?" As children become more comfortable with English, they no longer need the scaffolding that the frames provide. In the meantime, the scaffolds provide access to language structures and vocabulary, and an entrée into conversations and relationships.

Ongoing Support for General Language Development

During unstructured or free-choice time, teachers must look for strategic opportunities to develop children's language, and wherever possible build on and extend the concepts and language children are learning at other times of the day. When possible, teachers can teach key vocabulary in the home language and in English.

Interactive reading—in which an adult engages children in discussion of a book before, during, and after reading the book aloud—has benefited children in learning vocabulary and developing critical thinking. Interactive reading in the classroom may be in English or the home language, and in the home language at home. Dialogic reading (Whitehurst & Lonigan, 1988), a particular kind of interactive reading, is structured by a series of prompts. Whitehurst and Lonigan (1988) suggests five types: (1) completion prompts, in which the child essentially fills in the blank; (2) recall prompts to help children think about plot; (3) open-ended prompts that focus on the illustrations; (4) *wh-* prompts (what, where, when, why, how) that focus on the pictures; and (5) distancing prompts to help the child form a connection between the world and the book. By engaging in these interactions throughout a read-aloud, children can develop receptive and expressive vocabulary and make connections between books and their own lives. Although some practitioners have found success using dialogic reading with ELs (Doyle & Bramwell, 2006), this remains a promising but not yet well-researched topic.

Language Supports for Content Learning

Finally, during class time, when all children are learning the same material, such as a social studies or science activity, some strategies that can be effective for EL students can also help English speakers, or at least do not detract from the learning of native speakers. Using visuals—either photographs or realia—when introducing new words or concepts provides useful nonverbal support. When talking about different insects, for example, showing a photograph or plastic specimen of a bee and a spider and using these as the basis of a lesson or discussion comparing the two allows for a frame of reference that is not dependent on language. Multimedia-enhanced teaching (CDs, DVDs, video) helps to build or create background knowledge that is a basis for concept development. While a teacher can bring shaved ice into a classroom to replicate snow, an interactive video that shows a blizzard can supplement the tactile experience in important ways. Coupled with the vocabulary of blizzards, this type of hands-on multimedia lesson can build background knowledge that supports concept development and retention of vocabulary.

Whole-class time is also ideal for promoting strategic partnerships between children. Children who are paired together have the opportunity to develop new relationships and learn from one another. By pairing ELs with native speakers, both groups have the opportunity to interact with and learn from one another. Care must be taken to ensure that both children are valued members who make important contributions to the partnership. For example, pairs of children may be given a puzzle to complete together or a science investigation to explore. Language proficiency is neither correlated with success on the task nor necessary in the task completion; rather, communication and teamwork are important. In mixed-age classrooms, older native speakers may be paired with younger ELs to "read" a wordless picture book. Spaces should be made available for quiet personal time or for two-person extended interactions. These spaces should be equipped with learning materials connected to the classroom themes and lessons and open-ended materials for exploration.

Positive Environments for Language Learning

It is essential that teachers create low-stress but appropriately challenging and engaging language learning environments in their classrooms. If children feel excessive anxiety around using language, they are more likely to shut down and remain quiet. Using whole-class rhymes and songs, so that children's voices can meld into a "class voice," is one way of reducing possible anxiety. Another strategy is to create and reinforce a classroom in which taking risks and trying new things—rather than perfection—are rewarded. Individualized, casual conversations in which teachers get down to the level of the children (either by sitting or by kneeling) also take the pressure off children by not making them "perform" in front of other children, or by providing ample practice time before "going public." Finally, engaging children's bodies in language learning is effective in terms of not only retaining vocabulary but also reducing anxiety. Children who are moving and smiling are likely to remain engaged and ready to learn.

Families as Resources

Parents as Invested Partners in Educational Outcomes

Parents are a vital resource for preschool teachers; there are numerous ways that early childhood educators can take advantage of this resource for the benefit of children. The first and most fundamental way is to remember that parents are deeply interested in their children's well-being in general and their school success in particular. Parents see schooling as the primary means of social and economic mobility for their children and consider the preschool years important and potentially formative. The most common mistake of EL educators at all levels is to assume that parents are not interested in their children's education for any of several reasons, such as economic stress, job obligations, or failure to see the value of education. It is true that from the perspective of some teachers, at times parents behave in ways that seem to indicate a lack of interest or ability to support their children as they begin their school careers. This can be due to factors such as not feeling comfortable talking to educated professionals (e.g., teachers), not understanding the language, or coming from a country or culture in which there is no tradition or expectation of home–school collaboration. In addition, sometimes work or child care responsibilities do interfere with scheduled meetings or activities at school. Nonetheless, the vast majority of parents are willing and able to support their child's success in preschool and beyond. Early educators can and should support parents in this effort. Teachers should also work to understand the diverse perspectives and approaches to education shared by the families in their care.

Creating Opportunities for Parental Participation in the Preschool

For parents who do not work during the day, participation at the school or center is an excellent way to learn more about their child's program, which parents generally appreciate knowing, while providing teachers the support of additional adults in the room. In addition, children generally love having their parents come to the class. The experience offers the child an opportunity to demonstrate pride in his or her family, the parent an opportunity to reinforce the value of the school experience, and generally fosters a positive home–school relationship. Parents can play many roles in the classroom, including the following:

- Bring literacy materials from home, such as letters from relatives or books and magazines in English, their native language, or both.
- Help to supervise activities or centers, such as the block area, the play kitchen, or the painting easel.
- Share a skill, a craft, or a recipe with groups of children.
- Tell or read a favorite story to the class or a small group of children.

Some parents might need support from the teacher to identify age-appropriate materials, but all parents have something important they can share with a class of preschoolers.

In Sukkyung's classroom, children take home a survey at the beginning of each school year to ascertain parents' availability to help out and share in the classroom. A variety of options are provided, including volunteering on a weekly or biweekly basis, volunteering for special occasions, or helping to prepare materials at home (for parents who work full time but still want to help out). Parents are invited to do things such as read to children; prepare a presentation; help at literacy, math, or art centers; or help to prepare a snack. Although it is time-consuming, this survey is translated into all students' home languages. Sukkyung has found that she gets a great return on this investment of time—most of the parents respond, and more than half of the parents each year engage actively and consistently in the classroom.

Many more come to the classroom for a day to share a skill with the children, such as making tortillas or birdhouses. Sukkyung makes a point of meeting with the parents before these presentations to make sure they are comfortable with presenting and familiar with the routines in the classroom, and she offers to help translate when it would be useful. She also has a list of pointers that she hands out (e.g., keep your talk to less than 5 minutes; bring photographs or other visuals, if possible; try to do something hands-on so that every child has a turn). Sukkyung lets parents know how much she appreciates their time, help, and expertise, and a "Wall of Volunteers" in the classroom displays photographs and descriptions of parents' contributions. An added bonus of this parent participation is that the children get to know each other's parents, and parents get to know each other, too. The classroom community extends beyond the walls of Room 2 because parents who otherwise might not have had the opportunity to meet end up setting up playdates and picnics on weekends and during school vacations.

Extending Preschool Learning Opportunities into the Home

To extend preschool-based learning opportunities there are numerous things teachers can do. For example, they can send home the following:

- Books for children and parents to read together; if the teacher sends home books the children have heard in class, children usually enjoy showing off what they have learned.
- Papers with pictures or concepts (e.g., numbers, colors, shapes) children are learning about, that they can talk about at home with parents.
- Products that the children have made, so they can share and discuss the activities and creations with their parents.

In all of these cases, teachers should include a brief explanation of what the child is bringing home and offer guiding questions parents can use to encourage dialogue about the activities and products. To support home–school communication, teachers can also provide a place for parents to indicate, either by signing or writing a brief note, that their child showed them and explained whatever he or she took home. There should also be opportunities for parents to ask questions or write longer notes to the teacher. This is accomplished by leaving space on materials that go home, via a daily teacher–parent "check-in" slip, or by sending home an interactive journal for more extensive communications. To prevent loss of materials and forms, teachers might consider having parents provide backpacks. If that is not feasible, laminated colorful folders, sealed on the sides, work well. It is also helpful to punch a hole at either end of the folders and tie a length of yarn to the ends, so that children can put the yarn loop over their heads, with folder hanging in front of them (see Figure 9.1). Let parents know to expect the folder each day with materials and activities for home, and a form to sign and return in the folder (or backpack).

Recognizing That Parents Want to Help Their Children, but Acknowledging the Diversity of Perspectives and Experiences Related to Education

In addition to extending learning opportunities from the preschool to the home, teachers should also realize the possible differences in how parents view the relationship among schools, teachers, and parents. Teachers must be aware of and sensitive to the possibility of differences in values and perceptions. If, for example, some parents view the classroom as the location for education and teachers as the experts, they may not place a priority on bringing what are seen as "school practices"—such as reading books with children or using letter magnets on the refrigerator to spell words—into the home.

Sensitivity to parents' perspectives is always important, but teachers should also realize that to help their children succeed, parents are open to learning about practices that might vary from their own experiences. In fact, we have found that practices and perspectives do change as parents move and adapt to a new country and ways of doing things. Practices and perspectives are not likely to change radically, but neither are they static. There are both continuities and discontinuities across cultures and generations (Goldenberg & Gallimore, 1995). In other words, the home–school partnership is a two-way street.

It is also important for educators to be wary of stereotyping and overgeneralizing. Although different cultures might have somewhat different norms or behavioral expectations, it is not clear how these differences impact the educational process, or how educators should factor them into educational programs or interactions with children and parents (Goldenberg et al., 2006). The best rule of thumb is that all parents should be treated respectfully and never patronized, with the assumption that they want what is best for their children and are willing to work with and support educators' efforts in this regard. Early childhood educators should get to know each child and his or her family, and to tap the knowledge and resources that different families possess. This can be done through home visits, surveys, conferences, and informal conversations. When Rhonda, the teacher in the vignette at the beginning of this chapter, invited parents to the classroom to share their ways of making different types of bread, she was tapping into what Moll, Amanti, Neff, and Gonzalez (1992) call "funds of knowledge." By inviting families to share their cultures, skills, and knowledge in the classroom, Rhonda's classroom community can become more inclusive and a richer learning environment for the children.

FIGURE 9.1. Claire's folder.

Home Language Practices

Some ELs' parents will continue to develop the first language at home; others may believe that developing the home language will interfere with English learning. There are several things early educators can do to promote productive language practices in children's homes:

- Teachers can speak with parents and provide information about the cognitive and cultural benefits of maintaining the home language.
- As much as possible, teachers can demonstrate the value of the home language by encouraging young children to share their language with their classmates and teachers, and by making connections between the home language and English.
- Teachers can reiterate to parents that learning to read in the home language helps to maintain the home language and support the development of reading in English.
- Parents can also look for opportunities to speak or read with their children in English, and children can be encouraged to show off their developing English skills by reading familiar texts they bring home from school, sharing vocabulary, and offering descriptions of classroom activities and school products. Maintaining the home language and promoting opportunities to develop English skills are not mutually exclusive.

Preschool teachers should encourage parents to read aloud or tell oral stories to their children in either the home language or English. Read-aloud experiences offer opportunities for physical closeness and connection between a child and a caring other, as well as an opportunity for children to develop a love of books and reading. Beyond those interpersonal and motivational benefits are specific benefits to early reading, namely, children learn concepts of print from read-alouds, and they build background knowledge and vocabulary. But parents, like teachers, generally need some training to get academic benefit from read-alouds.

- Parents can choose books of particular interest to their children. Most community libraries have a children's book collection, and children can choose the books they would like to check out. Teachers can provide suggestions for books that supplement what is being learned at school, and that preschool-age children tend to enjoy.
- Parents who explicitly point out concepts of print (e.g., how words are separate entities, the direction of the print, how the illustrations relate to the words, how letters make up words) bring children's attention to those concepts. A quick "There is the word *bus*, b-uh-sss. I see the letters *b*, *u*, *s*. Where is the *b*? Oh, look, here is a picture of a bus" does not detract from the enjoyment of reading; rather, it injects a lesson into the reading. Over time, these lessons enhance children's understanding of how books and text work.
- Parents can choose one or two words from a read-aloud book to talk about in more depth. By introducing those words before reading, parents can have children listen for the words in the story, then discuss with children what the words mean in that context.
- Parents have the added benefit of being fluent in the home language. As much as possible, parents can build their children's English vocabulary by connecting English words to words in the child's oral vocabulary in the home language. The Portuguese-speaking parent, for example, can make the connection between what

may be a new English word (e.g., *fish*) with what is likely a familiar Portuguese word (*peixe*, pronounced pee shee).

These are all strategies that effective preschool teachers use when they do interactive read-alouds. When parents also engage in these practices, children get additional exposure to the concepts and background knowledge that will aid them as they move toward becoming readers themselves.

REFLECTIONS AND NEW DIRECTIONS

There is much to build on as we work to create effective programs for young ELs. A good knowledge base about effective early childhood programs generally should be the basis for effective programs for ELs. Beyond this, we know that ELs' home languages are *resources to build on* rather than *handicaps to overcome*; children can maintain and develop their home language while developing English language skills, thereby promoting bilingual development. When participating in learning activities in English, teachers can provide support to help students understand and engage fully. We also know that because parents and families are valuable resources, early childhood educators should create collaborative relationships with families to support children's growth and learning.

Of course, there is a great deal of work still to be done in the field. In particular, we need to recruit, prepare, support, and retain many more effective bilingual teachers who speak the variety of languages that children speak at home. These bilingual teachers need to be able to provide native language instruction and support for the ELs in their classrooms. Equally important, we need to recruit, train, support, and retain effective early childhood educators who know how to promote children's English language development and teach a comprehensive preschool curriculum to children with varying degrees of English proficiency. One of the stumbling blocks in this process, however, is that we do not yet know precisely what ideal practice looks like for ELs. Nor do we have enough data to draw conclusions based on different home languages or different English proficiency levels.

Therefore, the research and practitioner communities must continue to grapple with important questions: What is the ideal balance—or *is* there an ideal balance—between home language and target language instruction? What is the ideal balance between more and less structured teaching? How is that balance struck in early childhood settings? And how does it differ for different developmental levels? In working with families, how do we take advantage of parents' interest and motivation relative to their children's schooling? What are effective ways to engage parents in collaborative relationships with early educators to promote children's cognitive, linguistic, academic, and personal development?

As we begin to combine answers to these questions with answers about best practices in early childhood settings more generally, we will be able to provide high-quality preschool experiences for *all* children that appropriately support, challenge, and nurture the whole child—experiences that effectively prepare all children for future schooling and life.

PROFESSIONAL DEVELOPMENT ACTIVITIES

- Training, based on what we know so far, to meet the needs of ELs in a variety of languages and developmental levels.

- Working with colleagues and supervisors to reflect on practice, to discuss challenging situations, and to plan curriculum.
- Training on incorporating families into the preschool classroom.
- Engaging in action research or partnering with outside researchers to examine teachers' own practices and share them with both practitioner and research communities.

ACKNOWLEDGMENTS

Our thanks to Linda Espinosa and Ray Reutzel for their very helpful comments and suggestions. All errors of commission and omission are, of course, strictly the authors' responsibility.

REFERENCES

Administration for Children and Families. (2008). *Dual language learning: What does it take?: Head Start dual language report.* Washington, DC: U.S. Department of Health and Human Services.

August, D., & Shanahan, T. (2008). *Developing reading and writing in second-language learners: Lessons from the report of the National Literacy Panel on language-minority children and youth.* New York: Routledge.

Baker, A. J. L., Plotrkowski, C. S., & Brooks-Gunn, J. (1998). The effects of the Home Instruction Program for Preschool Youngsters (HIPPY) on children's school performance at the end of the program and one year later. *Early Childhood Research Quarterly, 13*(4), 571–588.

Barnett, W., Jung, K., Yarosz, D., Thomas, J., Hornbeck, A., Stechuk, R., et al. (2008). Educational effects of the Tools of the Mind curriculum: A randomized trial. *Early Childhood Research Quarterly, 23*(3), 299–313.

Barnett, W., Yarosz, D., Thomas, J., Jung, K., & Blanco, D. (2006). Two-way and monolingual English immersion in preschool education: An experimental comparison. *Early Childhood Research Quarterly, 22,* 277–293.

Bernhard, J. K., Cummins, J., Campoy, F. I., Ada, A. F., Winsler, A., & Bleiker, C. (2006). Identity texts and literacy development among preschool English language learners: Enhancing learning opportunities for children at risk for learning disabilities. *Teachers College Record, 108*(11), 2380–2405.

Bialystok, E. (2001). *Bilingualism in development: Language, literacy, and cognition.* Cambridge, UK: Cambridge University Press.

Brooker, L. (2002). "Five on the first of December!": What can we learn from case studies of early childhood literacy? *Journal of Early Childhood Literacy, 2*(3), 292–313.

Buysse, V., Castro, D., & Peisner-Feinberg, E. (2010). Effects of a professional development program on classroom practices and outcomes for Latino dual language learners. *Early Childhood Research Quarterly, 25,* 194–206.

Campos, S. J. (1995). The Carpenteria preschool program: A long-term effects study. In E. E. García & B. McLaughlin (Eds.), *Meeting the challenge of linguistic and cultural diversity in early childhood education* (pp. 34–48). New York: Teachers College Press.

Center for Early Care and Education Research–Dual Language Learners (CECER-DLL). (2011). Research briefs 1–8. Retrieved July 31, 2011, from *http://cecerdll.fpg.unc.edu.*

Chang, F., Crawford, G., Early, D., Bryant, D., Howes, C., Burchinal, M., et al. (2007). Spanish-speaking children's social and language development in pre-kindergarten classrooms. *Early Education and Development, 18,* 243–269.

Collins, M. (2005). ESL preschoolers' English vocabulary acquisition from storybook reading. *Reading Research Quarterly, 40,* 406–408.

Crawford, J. (2004). *Educating English learners: Language diversity in the classroom* (5th ed.). Los Angeles: Bilingual Education Services.

Doyle, B., & Bramwell, W. (2006). Promoting emergent literacy and social–emotional learning through dialogic reading. *The Reading Teacher, 59*, 554–564.

Durán, L. K., Roseth, C. J., & Hoffman, P. (2010). An experimental study comparing English-only and transitional bilingual education on Spanish-speaking preschoolers' early literacy development. *Early Childhood Research Quarterly, 25*, 207–217.

Espinosa, L. (2010). *Getting it right for young children from diverse backgrounds: Applying research to improve practice.* Upper Saddle River, NJ: Pearson.

Faltis, C. (1989). Code-switching and bilingual schooling: An examination of Jacobson's new concurrent approach. *Journal of Multilingual and Multicultural Development, 10*, 117–127.

Farver, J., Lonigan, C., & Eppe, S. (2009). Effective early literacy skill development for young Spanish-speaking English language learners: An experimental study of two methods. *Child Development, 80*(3), 703–719.

Farver, J. M., Xu, Y., Eppe, S., & Lonigan, C. J. (2006). Home environments and young Latino children's school readiness. *Early Childhood Research Quarterly, 21*, 196–212.

Gándara, P., & Hopkins, M. (Eds.). (2010). *Forbidden language: English Learners and restrictive language policies.* New York: Teachers College Press.

García, E. E., & Jensen, B. (2007). Helping young Hispanic learners. *Educational Leadership, 66*(7), 8–13.

Genesee, F., Paradis, J., & Crago, M. (2004). *Dual language development and disorders: A handbook on bilingualism and second language learning.* Baltimore: Brookes.

Goldenberg, C. (1987). Low-income Hispanic parents' contributions to their first-grade children's word-recognition skills. *Anthropology and Education Quarterly, 18*, 149–179.

Goldenberg, C., & Coleman, R. (2010). *Promoting academic achievement among English learners: A guide to the research.* Thousand Oaks, CA: Corwin.

Goldenberg, C., & Gallimore, R. (1995). Immigrant Latino parents' values and beliefs about their children's education: Continuities and discontinuities across cultures and generations. In P. R. Pintrich & M. Maehr (Eds.), *Advances in motivation and achievement: Culture, ethnicity, and motivation* (Vol. 9, pp. 183–228). Greenwich, CT: JAI Press.

Goldenberg, C., Rueda, R. S., & August, D. (2006). Sociocultural influences on the literacy attainment of language-minority children and youth. In D. August & T. Shanahan (Eds.), *Developing literacy in second-language learners: Report of the National Literacy Panel on Language-Minority Children and Youth* (pp. 269–318). Mahwah, NJ: Erlbaum.

Gormley, W. (2008). *The effects of Oklahoma's Universal Pre-Kindergarten program on Hispanic children.* Washington, DC: Center for Research on Children in the U.S. Policy Brief. Available at *www.crocus.georgetown.edu*.

Gormley, W., & Phillips, D. (2005). The effects of universal pre-K in Oklahoma: Research highlights and policy implications. *Policy Studies Journal, 33*, 65–82.

Hammer, C. S., Davison, M. D., Lawrence, F. R., & Miccio, A. W. (2009). The effect of maternal language on bilingual children's vocabulary and emergent literacy development during Head Start and kindergarten. *Scientific Studies of Reading, 13*(2), 99–121.

Hancock, D. R. (2002). The effects of native language books on the pre-literacy skill development of language minority kindergarteners. *Journal of Research in Childhood Education, 17*(1), 62–68.

Hirsch-Pasek, K., Golinkoff, R., Berk, L., & Singer, D. (2009). *A mandate for Playful Learning in preschool: Presenting the evidence.* New York: Oxford University Press.

Jackson, B., Larzelere, R., St. Claire, L., Corr, M., Fichter, C., & Egertson, H. (2006). The impact of *HeadsUp! Reading* on early childhood educators' literacy practices and preschool children's literacy skills. *Early Childhood Research Quarterly, 21*, 213–226.

Jimenez-Castellanos, O., & Topper, A. (2012). The cost of providing an adequate education to English language learners: A review of the literature. *Review of Educational Research, 82*, 179–232.

Karoly, L. A., & Gonzalez, G. C. (2011). Early care and education for children in immigrant families. *The Future of Children, 21,* 71–101.

Kenner, C. (1999). Children's understandings of text in a multilingual nursery. *Language and Education, 13,* 1–16.

Koskinen, P. S., Blum, I. H., Bisson, S. A., Phillips, S. M., Creamer, T. S., & Baker, T. K. (2000). Book access, shared reading, and audio models: The effects of supporting the literacy learning of linguistically diverse students in school and at home. *Journal of Educational Psychology, 92*(1), 23–36.

Kuhl, P. (2004). Early language acquisition: Cracking the code. *Neuroscience, 5*(11), 831–843.

Li, R. (2005). *Childhood bilingualism: Current status and future directions.* Workshop summary. Washington, DC: Office of Special Education and Rehabilitative Services and Office of English Language Acquisition (U.S. Department of Education) and National Institute of Child Health and Human Development and National Institutes of Health (U.S. Department of Health and Human Services).

Lightbown, P., & Spada, N. (2006). *How languages are learned* (3rd ed.). Oxford, UK: Oxford University Press.

Lim, Y. S., & Cole, K. N. (2002). Facilitating first language development in young Korean children through parent training in picture book interactions. *Bilingual Research Journal, 26*(2), 367–381.

Lugo-Neris, M. J., Jackson, C. W., & Goldstein, H. (2010). Facilitating vocabulary acquisition of young English language learners. *Language, Speech, and Hearing Services in Schools, 41*(3), 314–327.

Magnuson, K., Lahaie, C., & Waldfogel, J. (2006). Preschool and school readiness of children of immigrants. *Social Science Quarterly, 87*(5), 1241–1262.

Mendelsohn, A. L., Mogilner, L. N., Dreyer, B. P., Forman, J. A., Weinstein, S. C., Broderick, M., et al. (2001). The impact of a clinic-based literacy intervention on language development in inner-city preschool children. *Pediatrics, 107*(1), 130–134.

Mistry, R. S., Biesanz, J. C., Chien, N., Howes, C., & Benner, A. D. (2008). Socioeconomic status, parental investments, and the cognitive and behavioral outcomes of low-income children from immigrant and native households. *Early Childhood Research Quarterly, 23*(2), 193–212.

Moll, L., Amanti, C., Neff, D., & Gonzalez, N. (1992). Funds of knowledge for teaching: Using a qualitative approach to connect homes and classrooms. *Theory Into Practice, 31*(2), 132–141.

Parrish, T. (1994). A cost analysis of alternative instructional models for limited English proficient students in California. *Journal of Education Finance, 19,* 256–278.

Pasnak, R., Greene, M. S., Ferguson, E. O., & Levit, K. (2006). Applying principles of development to help at-risk preschoolers develop numeracy. *Journal of Psychology, 140,* 155–173.

Payne, A. C., Whitehurst, G. J., & Angell, A. L. (1994). The role of home literacy environment in the development of language ability in preschool children from low-income families. *Early Childhood Research Quarterly, 9,* 427–440.

Perry, N. J., Kay, S. M., & Brown, A. (2008). Continuity and change in home literacy practices of Hispanic families with preschool children. *Early Child Development and Care, 178,* 99–113.

Restrepo, M. A., Castilla, A. P., Schwanenflugel, P. J., Neuharth-Pritchett, S., Hamilton, C. E., & Arboleda, A. (2010). Effects of supplemental Spanish oral language program on sentence length, complexity, and grammaticality in Spanish-speaking children attending English-only preschools. *Language, Speech, and Hearing Services in Schools, 41,* 3–13.

Roberts, T. (2008). Home storybook reading in primary or second language with preschool chlordane: Evidence of equal effectiveness for second-language vocabulary acquisition. *Reading Research Quarterly, 43,* 103–130.

Roberts, T., & Neal, H. (2004). Relationships among preschool English language learners' oral proficiency in English, instructional experience and literacy development. *Contemporary Educational Psychology, 29,* 283–311.

Rumberger, R. W., & Tran, L. (2006). *Preschool participation and the cognitive and social development of language minority students* (Technical report). Los Angeles: UCLA, Center for Research and Evaluation, Standards, and Student Testing.

Russakoff, D. (2011). *PreK–3rd: Raising the educational performance of English language learners* (Policy to Action Brief No. 6). New York: Foundation for Child Development.

Saunders, W. M., Foorman, B. R., & Carlson, C. D. (2006). Is a separate block of time for oral English language development in programs for English learners needed? *Elementary School Journal, 107,* 181–197.

Saunders, W. M., & Goldenberg, C. (2010). Research to guide English language development instruction. In D. Dolson & L. Burnham-Massey (Eds.) *Improving education for English learners: Research-based approaches* (pp. 21–81). Sacramento, CA: CDE Press.

Schaller, A., Rocha, L., & Barshinger, D. (2007). Maternal attitudes and parent education: How immigrant mothers support their child's education despite their own low levels of education. *Early Childhood Education Journal, 34,* 351–356.

Severns, M. (2012). *Starting early with English language learners: First lessons from Illinois.* Washington, DC: New America Foundation.

Silverman, R., & Hines, S. (2009). The effects of multimedia-enhanced instruction on the vocabulary of English-language learners and non-English-language learners in pre-kindergarten through second grade. *Journal of Educational Psychology, 101,* 305–314.

Slavin, R., Madden, N., Calderón, M., Chamberlain, A., & Hennessy, M. (2011). Reading and language outcomes of a multiyear randomized evaluation of transitional bilingual education. *Educational Evaluation and Policy Analysis, 33,* 47–58.

Stipek, D., Feiler, R., Byler, P., Ryan, R., Millburn, S., & Salmon, J. M. (1998). Good Beginnings: What difference does the program make in preparing young children for school? *Journal of Applied Developmental Psychology, 19*(1), 41–66.

Tabors, P. O. (2008). *One child, two languages: A guide for early childhood educators of children learning English as a second language.* Cambridge, MA: Brookes.

Tong, F., Lara-Alecio, R., Irby, B., Mathes, P., & Kwok, O. (2008). Accelerating early academic oral English development in transitional bilingual and structured English immersion programs. *American Educational Research Journal, 45,* 1011–1044.

Turney, K., & Kao, G. (2009). Pre-kindergarten child care and behavioral outcomes among children of immigrants. *Early Childhood Research Quarterly, 24,* 432–444.

U.S. Department of Education, National Center for Educational Statistics. (2000). *Statistics in brief—March 2000: Home literacy activities and signs of children's emerging literacy.* Washington, DC: U.S. Government Printing Office.

Whitehurst, G., & Lonigan, C. (1988). Child development and emergent literacy. *Child Development, 69,* 848–872.

Winsler, A., Díaz, R. M., Espinosa, L., & Rodríguez, J. L. (1999). When learning a second language does not mean losing the first: Bilingual language development in low-income, Spanish-speaking children attending bilingual preschool. *Child Development, 70*(2), 349–362.

Wood, C. (2002). Parent–child preschool activities can affect the development of literacy skills. *Journal of Research in Reading, 25*(3), 241–258.

CHAPTER 10

TIMELY SUPPORT
FOR STRUGGLING LEARNERS
Response to Intervention

AMANDA C. MILLER
JESSICA R. TOSTE
DOUGLAS FUCHS
LYNN S. FUCHS

> We can whenever and wherever we choose successfully teach all
> children whose schooling is of interest to us. We already know
> more than we need in order to do this. Whether we do must finally
> depend on how we feel about the fact that we haven't so far.
> —RONALD EDMONDS (1973)

Chris is a first-grade student in a school district that implements the response-to-intervention (RTI) framework as a method of preventing and identifying learning difficulties. Chris is given a reading screening measure in the fall of first grade, and his performance is below the district's set benchmark. Based on this information, Chris's teacher identifies him as being "at risk" for reading difficulties. Chris's teacher closely monitors his reading progress over the next 6 weeks to see whether he will respond to her classroom instruction, which is referred to as Tier 1 prevention in the RTI framework. If not, he will need more intensive, supplemental instruction to enable him to attain satisfactory academic performance. Approximately 6 weeks later, Chris's progress-monitoring data indicate that he is not learning at a satisfactory rate and is falling behind his peers. He is in need of additional instruction to help him develop his decoding and fluency skills in particular. The classroom teacher decides that Chris will require Tier 2 prevention to build these skills.

Tier 2 prevention provides supplemental instruction aimed at building Chris's decoding and fluency skills in a small group with three other students. The group meets with its teacher three times a week for 30 minutes. This direct, teacher-led instruction takes place in student learning centers. Each week, Chris's teacher closely monitors his progress on reading assessments. At the end of the 8 weeks, Chris's teacher uses the data she collected to determine that Chris is still not exhibiting satisfactory reading performance; Chris is in need of Tier 3 instruction, the most intensive instruction available.

Chris's teacher collaborates with the school's reading specialist and special education teacher to design an individualized program that targets Chris's areas of greatest need. One-on-one instruction is implemented by the special education teacher four times per week for 45 minutes each day. The teacher carefully monitors Chris's progress, and during this intervention, Chris makes tremendous gains. Chris's special education teacher examines his progress-monitoring data and concludes that he has reached the reading achievement goals set at the beginning of the intervention. At this point, the intensity of Chris's instruction is decreased to Tier 2. The teacher will continue to monitor his progress carefully. If Chris continues to flourish, and his reading development remains on target, the supplemental Tier 2 instruction will discontinue; however, if Chris fails to meet academic goals, he will again transition into Tier 3 instruction. Chris's experience exemplifies an RTI model that both identifies him as a struggling learner and serves as an intervention to get him back on track and allow him to make the desired academic gains.

TIMELY SUPPORT FOR STRUGGLING LEARNERS: RTI

Educators, parents, and policymakers alike are concerned about students who struggle academically and fail to reach educational milestones. Substantial evidence suggests that early identification of children who are at risk for academic difficulties leads to early intervention that enhances the likelihood of positive learning outcomes. However, this presents two challenges:

1. What means should be used in the identification process?
2. What type of intervention should be provided?

One science-based practice that has effectively addressed these issues is RTI, which departs from previous models of general education and presents a multi-tiered system oriented toward early intervention and prevention (D. Fuchs, Fuchs, & Compton, 2012). It shifts the focus in delivery of school services toward assessing risk and providing targeted instruction, and away from determining failure.

We begin this chapter by describing the basic tenets of the RTI framework. Then we present evidence that suggests that RTI serves as an effective tool for both identifying and mitigating learning disabilities (LD). The majority of the chapter describes putting this research into practice by providing a concrete framework of the implementation of RTI, as well as clear illustrations of RTI's best practices. Finally, we evaluate issues currently surrounding RTI and discuss its future.

WHAT IS RTI?

RTI is unique in that it is simultaneously an assessment and an intervention process. In an RTI framework, students' level or rate of learning is systematically monitored, typically through weekly assessments referred to as *progress monitoring*. Progress-monitoring data are used to make decisions about the student's future course of instruction, such as whether instructional modifications are necessary or intensified services should be provided (Johnson, Mellard, Fuchs, & McKnight, 2006). The Individuals with Disabilities Education Improvement Act (IDEA; 2004) acknowledged RTI as a method that can be used to identify children with LD, and a number of school districts have begun to implement RTI in classrooms. Despite its increased use in areas of both intervention and identification of children with LD, no set guidelines delineate how districts, schools, evaluation teams, and teachers should implement the RTI framework. Fortunately, recent research has informed our educational system about RTI best practices and increased the likelihood that RTI serves as an effective tool to help struggling learners succeed.

The RTI framework is a multi-tiered system that typically is organized within three tiers of service delivery, although some researchers have proposed two- or four-tier models. Each tier represents a continuum of prevention and intervention; the nature of the academic intervention becomes more intensive at each tier. A brief overview of what goes on in each of the three tiers follows, but a more complete and practical description of the instruction is provided later in the "Research into Practice" section.

The first tier is considered primary prevention, where all students receive high-quality, science-based classroom instruction. One aim of primary prevention is to help distinguish between two possible explanations of poor academic growth: inadequate instruction versus student characteristics and/or disability. If a child does not make adequate progress when receiving classroom instruction that appears to benefit most students, then this provides some evidence that a disability, rather than instructional quality, may be the source of low achievement (D. Fuchs, Fuchs, & Vaughn, 2008). On the other hand, if nearly all students in the classroom fail to reach academic milestones, this might point to ineffective classroom instruction. Students who fail to respond to this primary prevention are identified as being at risk and in need of additional instruction and support.

Tier 2, or secondary prevention, increases the level of intensity by providing direct and explicit skills-based instruction, generally in a small-group format. Tier 2 instruction relies on effective, empirically validated programs. Across domains, most students respond favorably to the instruction administered in secondary prevention. Nonetheless, a significant minority of students, the equivalent of approximately 2–6% of the general population, does not respond to Tier 2 prevention (Al Otaiba & D. Fuchs, 2002; D. Fuchs, Fuchs, & Compton, 2012; Mathes, Howard, Allen, & Fuchs, 1998; Torgesen, 2009). These children are typically referred to as "nonresponders," and they will require more intensive, individualized intervention.

Tier 3, or tertiary prevention, is the most intensive instructional tier. Students who do not respond to previous instruction receive individualized, Tier 3 intervention, implemented as special education. As with Tiers 1 and 2, the child's progress is closely monitored. Because Tier 3 is the most intensive option, it is also the most resource-dependent. Once children achieve an adequate level of performance at this tier, instructional intensity is decreased to Tier 2 or Tier 1. Progress monitoring continues across all three tiers (see Figure 10.1); instructional intensity is increased or decreased as needed in order to promote positive long-term outcomes.

WHAT RESEARCH SAYS ABOUT RTI

Implementation and Effectiveness

Many schools across the nation have adopted the RTI process, and a handful of studies indicates that its implementation is improving learning outcomes. For example, Torgesen (2009) measured its effectiveness by comparing the percentage of students who had significant reading difficulties (defined as children who scored below the 20th percentile

Tier 1
- **Universal Screening** to identify children at risk of academic difficulties
- **General Education** using science-based practices
- **Progress Monitoring** of at-risk students—do they respond to this level of instruction?

Tier 2
- **Tier 1 Nonresponders** receive supplementary, more intense instruction
- **Small Groups,** typically of three to four children
- **Progress Monitoring** of at-risk students—do they respond to this level of instruction?

Tier 3
- **Tier 2 Nonresponders** receive intensive, one-on-one intervention that targets each student's learning needs
- **Progress Monitoring** of at-risk students
- **If Tier 3 is ineffective**, teacher adapts the intervention and Tier 3 instruction continues
- **If Tier 3 is effective,** instructional intensity is decreased to Tier 1 or Tier 2

FIGURE 10.1. Summary of the RTI framework.

on a group-administered measure of reading comprehension) before and after RTI implementation. Identification rates of students with reading difficulties dropped dramatically over 3 years of RTI implementation in 318 schools. For example, the first year of the study, approximately 25.1% of kindergarteners finished the year with significant difficulties in reading; however, after the third year of RTI implementation, this percentage dropped to 14.9%. First, second, and third graders exhibited comparably reduced rates of reading difficulty. The percentage of students who received LD diagnoses also decreased significantly. In the study's first year, 2.1% of kindergartners were identified as LD; in the third year, only 0.4% of kindergartners were identified. Again, similar reductions were observed among first-, second-, and third-grade students. These data support the use of an RTI framework to provide timely support to struggling learners in early childhood education.

Assessment and Identification of LD

In addition to serving as a framework for intervention, RTI can also be used to identify students who are at risk for learning difficulties. Heller, Holtzman, and Messick (1982) originally conceptualized intervention responsiveness as a framework for identifying students with LD. Students with LD exhibit unexpected underachievement and respond poorly to the instructional practices that benefit the majority of students. The RTI framework enables teachers to identify accurately which students are at risk for LD and to monitor the progress of these students. RTI allows the identification process to occur early in the child's schooling, as opposed to traditional models of identification that depend on postfailure referral in the later elementary grades (Fletcher & Vaughn, 2009).

Early identification of LD is critical because it means that children can receive supplemental instruction prior to experiences of academic failure.

There is considerable evidence of the effectiveness of an RTI framework in identifying learning difficulties in both reading (Fletcher & Vaughn, 2009; Speece & Case, 2001; Vellutino et al., 1996) and math (L. S. Fuchs et al., 2005). For example, Vellutino and colleagues (1996) studied a group of first-grade children identified by their teachers as having reading problems. The researchers provided 16 weeks of daily tutoring to a subset of these children and assessed each child's degree of responsiveness based on reading growth. They identified one group of children as difficult to remediate, and argued that treatment response served as a useful means of distinguishing between learners with and without disabilities.

Similarly, an RTI framework is useful in identifying students with math-related learning difficulties. L. S. Fuchs and colleagues (2005) conducted a randomized field trial across multiple first-grade classrooms in multiple schools. One purpose of the study was to measure each child's responsiveness to intervention in order to identify children with mathematics disabilities. They compared identification accuracy using an RTI approach with two other identification approaches: IQ–achievement discrepancy and low achievement with average IQ. L. S. Fuchs and colleagues concluded that RTI proved to be a promising approach for identifying students at-risk for math difficulties.

RESEARCH INTO PRACTICE

The following section provides a more detailed overview of the procedures that typically occur at each tier of the RTI framework. Within this discussion are boxes that lay out steps to follow in implementing an RTI framework for reading instruction using the field's "best practices" (D. Fuchs & Fuchs, 2005).

Primary Prevention

The Basics

An important practice of primary prevention is assessment and universal screening. In the first month of the school year, students are screened to identify those who, without special attention, are in danger of reading failure.

STEP 1: SCREENING

Assess all students using a brief screening tool known to reliably predict performance on state assessments of reading. The Dynamic Indicators of Basic Early Literacy Skills (DIBELS) is the most frequently used screening tool in the United States. DIBELS designates three cutoff scores that can be used to identify students who are "at risk," "at some risk," or "at low risk" for reading failure in the fall of kindergarten or first grade (D. Fuchs et al., 2008). Because no screening measure is perfect, either over- or underidentifying students as being at risk, D. Fuchs and colleagues (2008) recommend casting a wide net (e.g., students below the 50th percentile) to select all students "suspected" to be at risk.

Primary prevention, or Tier 1, is implemented by providing high-quality instruction to all students in the general classroom. The efficacy of this instruction must be supported by sound, science-based research. The central goal of primary prevention is to reduce the number of students who ultimately are identified as struggling by providing support before students begin to fall behind. As such, effective classroom instruction is a critical element in the RTI framework (Taylor, 2008).

Other Considerations

In Tier 1, teachers implement core instructional programs designed using science-based research that should meet the needs of approximately 75–85% of students. In order to ensure that students are receiving adequate classroom instruction, teachers should ask whether the core program is meeting the needs of the majority of students. If it is not, we must ask ourselves why—for example, weakness of the program or fidelity of implementation. Monitoring the effectiveness of the core instructional program over time is essential to ensuring that students are receiving high-quality classroom instruction. In addition, differentiated instruction should be implemented. This requires the teacher to adapt classroom instruction to meet the learning needs and ability level of individual students. Rather than a "one size fits all" approach, differentiated instruction allows students to encounter information in a manner that maximizes their learning potential. That said, there are few research-validated approaches to differentiating instruction at Tier 1.

STEP 2A: CLASSROOM INSTRUCTION

School districts provide teachers with science-based curricula and instruction, as well as professional development opportunities. Teachers' fidelity of implementation is documented.

Progress Monitoring

Students who are identified as being at risk for learning difficulties in the initial fall screening should be carefully monitored in the area of academic risk. The goal of progress monitoring is to identify a subset of students that responds inadequately to general education.

STEP 2B: PROGRESS MONITORING

Every week for 6–8 weeks, students suspected of being at risk are assessed in the area of risk with brief monitoring tools. Their scores are graphed against time, and the weekly rate of increase (i.e., the slope) is calculated to quantify the rate of learning. Adequate Tier 1 response is operationalized with the use of normative estimates for the slope or criterion-referenced figures for weekly improvement.

Secondary Prevention

The Basics

The aim of secondary prevention is to help students raise their academic performance to the level of their peers' in a relatively brief amount of time. Typically, the instruction in secondary prevention lines up with that of primary instruction, but with increased intensity. Instructional intensity may be increased in a number of ways, such as by forming groups that range from three to five students per teacher. Other methods include grouping students according to their level of achievement or skills deficits; increasing the duration and frequency of the instructional sessions; and providing explicit, targeted instruction that allows for ample practice opportunities with immediate feedback (Vaughn & Denton, 2008).

STEP 3A: TARGETED, TIER 2 INTERVENTION

At-risk students receive instruction in groups of three to five students of similar ability. The group completes at least three 30-minute sessions per week for 10–20 weeks, and students are instructed by a certified teacher or aide, who implements an evidence-based standard tutoring protocol.

Other Considerations

Tier 2 prevention involves implementing a problem-solving approach, standard instructional protocols, or a combination of the two.

PROBLEM SOLVING

The problem-solving approach involves collaboration of the child's parent(s), teacher, and school support team to try to resolve academic problems. Practitioners determine the magnitude of the problem, analyze its causes, design a goal-directed intervention, conduct it as planned, monitor student progress, modify the intervention based on student responsiveness, evaluate its effectiveness, and plot future actions. Great emphasis is placed on monitoring the student's progress and comparing it to that of other students; the student's relative classroom performance, rather than test performance, determines responsiveness and, eventually, Tier 3 eligibility. The problem-solving approach is popular with practitioners due to its individualized nature; however, this can also be an inherent weakness because it presupposes that practitioners have the necessary expertise to assess students' skills levels and develop effective, individualized interventions. Problem-solving practitioners must also be knowledgeable in many types of assessment and intervention; possess the clinical judgment to know which assessments and interventions to use; and have the knowledge, discipline, and opportunity to measure accurately the effectiveness of interventions, which are sometimes a unique hybrid of two or more evidence-based practices that, in combination, have no track record (D. Fuchs & Fuchs, 2006).

STANDARD TREATMENT

Whereas the problem-solving approach differs from child to child, a standard treatment protocol does not. Implementation usually involves an intervention of fixed duration (e.g., 10–20 weeks) delivered in small groups or individually (e.g., Al Otaiba & Fuchs, 2006; McMaster, Fuchs, Fuchs, & Compton, 2005; Vaughn, Linan-Thompson, & Hickman, 2003; Vellutino et al., 1996). If students respond to the treatment, they are seen as remediated, and they discontinue supplemental Tier 2 instruction. However, if they show *insufficient* progress at Tier 2, a disability is suspected and further evaluation is warranted.

If students receive different treatments, as in the problem-solving approach, it is difficult to compare one student's progress to another's and to make decisions based on the student's relative progress. The use of standard treatment protocols implemented with high fidelity increases the validity of the intervention-as-test design of the RTI framework. Consider the case in which a standard treatment protocol effectively improves the performances of Student A, Student B, and Student C, but the same treatment protocol does not benefit Student D. By comparing the relative gains of Student D to those of the other three students, we see that Student D is in need of Tier 3 instruction. Using a standard treatment protocol, all practitioners know what to implement because there is only one protocol, which makes fidelity of implementation easier to assess and ensure (D. Fuchs & Fuchs, 2006).

Progress Monitoring

Response to the Tier 2 diagnostic trial is monitored to identify the subset of students who respond inadequately (i.e., "nonresponders"). Parental feedback is provided by a written report, a telephone call, or a face-to-face meeting.

STEP 3B: PROGRESS MONITORING

Students are assessed every week of secondary prevention in the area of risk with brief monitoring tools. Adequate response is determined by use of local–national normative estimates for weekly improvement *or* criterion-referenced figures for weekly improvement.

Tertiary Prevention

The Basics

Although the learning outcomes of many at-risk students improve with high-quality primary and secondary intervention, this is not enough for approximately 2–6% of the student population (L. S. Fuchs et al., 2008; Vaughn et al., 2010). The RTI model recommends these nonresponders take part in the most intensive instruction available: Tier 3.

Compared to secondary prevention, tertiary prevention is provided in longer, more frequent sessions and in very small groups or, preferably, one-on-one. Whereas secondary prevention is implemented by individuals with varying degrees of expertise, tertiary prevention is typically provided by the special education teacher or reading specialist. Additionally, intervention at this tier is specialized and modified to meet individual student needs, as assessed by ongoing progress-monitoring data (Vaughn & Denton, 2008).

Other Considerations

Tier 3 provides special education services that complement general education instruction and contribute to prevention efforts. As of this writing, there is disagreement about whether special education should have a role in RTI. Some wish it would become the most intensive instructional tier. Others say it should exist outside RTI or become a component only after it has been redefined and "blurred" with general education (cf. D. Fuchs, Fuchs, & Stecker, 2010). In this chapter we take the former approach. Special educators should be charged with delivering tertiary prevention to students who have not been helped by prior tiers of instruction. This belief is based on the assumption that special education provides more specialized expertise for struggling learners.

STEP 4: REFERRAL FOR SPECIAL EDUCATION SERVICES

Tier 2 nonresponders receive an individualized, comprehensive evaluation that addresses all eligibility determination, evaluation, and procedural safeguards specified in IDEA. Written parental consent is obtained. The evaluation team (including the special education teacher and other qualified professionals) designs an evaluation that rules out mental retardation as an alternative diagnosis, using a brief intellectual assessment, and eliminates other diagnostic possibilities, such as emotional disturbance or visual disabilities.

D. Fuchs, Fuchs, and Compton (2012) put forth several recommendations regarding tertiary prevention. They suggest that experimental teaching be employed to target each student's learning needs, and that teachers set year-end goals to match these needs. Teachers should use their clinical experience and judgment to modify the treatment components on a student-by-student basis—what is referred to as *experimental teaching*. This individualized instruction may address foundational skills to help students catch up on prerequisite skills that allow them eventually to perform satisfactorily on grade-appropriate material. Tier 3 teachers may begin with a more intensive version of the standard protocol used in secondary prevention (e.g., longer or more frequent instructional session, or smaller and more homogeneous groups) but must be quick to modify this treatment if a student's ongoing progress monitoring does not indicate he or she is likely to attain learning goals. Importantly, the teachers never become complacent with their instruction; rather, they continue to monitor progress and evaluate student performance in relation to goals, and to modify instruction if a student is unlikely to attain his or her goals. Research indicates that experimental teaching accelerates academic performance of students in special education (D. Fuchs et al., 2010; L. S. Fuchs & Fuchs, 1998; Stecker, Fuchs, & Fuchs, 2005).

STEP 5: TIER 3 INSTRUCTION

The child's teacher, reading specialist, and special educators work together to design an instructional plan and set concrete goals by which to monitor the child's growth and achievement. The instructor provides individualized instruction using an experimental teaching approach. The child's progress should be carefully monitored, and adaptation of the instruction should be based on the child's performance.

D. Fuchs, Fuchs, and Compton (2012) also emphasize that there should be flexible guidelines with respect to entering and exiting Tier 3. Movement in and out of tertiary prevention should be strategic and based on the needs of the student at a given time, or as measured across time, as disabilities may change. Educators should recognize that students may have (or even are likely to have) uneven profiles of academic development. In other words, one student who requires primary prevention for learning some academic skills may require tertiary prevention for learning other skills. Maintaining flexibility in moving students across the three prevention tiers is an important aspect of RTI.

REFLECTIONS AND NEW DIRECTIONS

Fine-Tuning RTI as an Instrument for Identification and Intervention

Studies have recently targeted ways to (1) increase the accuracy with which RTI identifies at-risk children, and (2) permit children to obtain the appropriate level of supplemental instruction sooner rather than later. We now present current RTI approaches aimed at addressing each of these issues.

Two-Step Screening

Educators must identify accurately and early the children who will likely go on to express learning difficulties. Most practitioners are aware of the consequences of "false-negative" classifications. Misclassifying children as typically developing when in fact they are at risk for LD means that children in need of services go without. However, false *positives* (i.e., students who appear to be at risk for LD but are not) present a different challenge to the RTI framework. Most schools rely on one-time, brief screening measures that often produce high rates of false positives. These misclassifications result in schools investing valuable resources into secondary prevention efforts for children who, in reality, do not require them to succeed. One way to improve the accuracy of identifying at-risk children is to follow up the initial, brief screening measure (i.e., universal screen) with a second round of screening measures.

The universal screen should be used to exclude children who clearly are not at risk, and the second-stage screen should target only those students who did not meet the screen's benchmark and whose risk status is thus uncertain. The second stage is a more thorough assessment designed to discriminate false positives from those who are actually at risk. D. Fuchs, Fuchs, and Compton (2012) present an analogous situation: Doctors do not recommend treatment based on a single, elevated blood pressure measurement or a suspicious mammogram because both tests produce high rates of false positives. Instead, these initial screenings are followed by second-stage screens, which generally are more expensive but also more accurate.

There is evidence that a two-stage screening process improves the accuracy of identifying at-risk students (Compton et al., 2010; D. Fuchs, Compton, et al., 2012; L. S. Fuchs et al., 2011). For example, D. Fuchs, Compton, and colleagues (2012) explored the degree to which a two-stage screen administered in the first grade could predict which children would go on to express reading disability in fifth grade. In 42 first-grade classrooms, 783 students completed a Stage 1, universal screen. Then all children who fell below the benchmark on the Stage 1 screen completed a second stage of cognitive assessments. The researchers followed the children for 4 years and identified which children expressed grade 5 reading disability. They then compared how accurately they could predict which children expressed fifth-grade reading disability using data from the initial Stage 1 screen alone versus data from the Stage 1 and Stage 2 screens combined. Using data from the Stage 1 screen alone resulted in a large number of false positives: 195 students were identified as being at risk, but only 36 actually went on to exhibit reading difficulties in grade 5. In other words, 159 children would have been needlessly tutored. In contrast, using the more precise, two-stage screening process, only 65 students would have been tutored, including only 29 false positives. You can see that the two-stage screening process decreased the number of children who received unnecessary tutoring; this allows the school's resources to be allocated to the truly at-risk children who benefit from such services.

Circumventing the "Wait-to-Fail" Approach

A second challenge to the RTI framework is providing a child with the appropriate intensity of instruction. Students in RTI systems almost always participate in less intensive tiers of prevention before receiving the most intensive instruction available. In a three-tier system, students identified as being at risk for inadequate response to Tier 1 are eligible for Tier 2; those who do not respond to Tier 2 are eligible for Tier 3. Most at-risk students make adequate academic gains in Tier 2; however, a subset of children fails to respond to Tier 2 prevention and, only after this multi-tiered failure, is referred for Tier 3 intervention. Thus, the majority of RTI systems use a "wait-to-fail" approach: Children must fail to respond to Tiers 1 and 2 before they begin to receive the appropriate tier of instructional intensity, Tier 3. D. Fuchs, Fuchs, and Compton (2012) suggest that a better approach is to use Tier 1 data to predict which children will likely fail to respond to Tier 2 prevention (i.e., become nonresponders), before they have a chance to fail. Children who will likely become nonresponders should jump straight to Tier 3 rather than floundering for up to 30 weeks in Tier 2 instruction that inevitably will not meet their academic needs. In summary, predicting nonresponders in Tier 1 spares these students from "waiting to fail" before they are allowed to receive appropriate services.

Several studies support the feasibility of predicting Tier 2 nonresponders and fast-tracking them to Tier 3 instruction (Compton et al., 2012; D. Fuchs, Fuchs, McMaster, Yen, & Svenson, 2004). For example, Compton and colleagues (2012) gave a sample of 427 first-grade students a screening battery to identify students at risk for reading difficulties. At-risk students received 14 weeks of Tier 2 prevention, and their progress was monitored throughout. Compton and colleagues determined which students benefited from the Tier 2 prevention (i.e., responders) and which students did not (i.e., nonresponders). They then demonstrated that they could predict with 90% accuracy which children would become nonresponders, based only on the initial screening measures administered in the fall of first grade alone (independent of the Tier 2 progress-monitoring data). This means that 90% of the children for whom Tier 2 instruction would be ineffective could be fast-tracked to Tier 3, where the more intense instruction would, we hope, meet their learning needs.

Based on the results of this study and others, D. Fuchs, Fuchs, and Compton (2012) urge practitioners to use a multistage screening process within primary prevention to identify children who are unlikely to respond to secondary prevention, and thereby circumvent the "wait-to-fail" approach. This extra step on the front end pays dividends in the long run: It benefits at-risk students by enabling them to receive the instructional intensity that they require sooner rather than later, and it conserves the school's valuable resources by avoiding implementation of instruction that will prove futile for some students.

ISSUES AND CHALLENGES RTI MUST ADDRESS

Over the past decade, RTI has been adopted as a school service delivery model in many school districts across the country. Although they share the goal of providing more efficient and effective support for struggling readers, RTI systems differ in a variety of ways across districts—the number of tiers of prevention, the types of interventions and protocols employed, and who delivers the interventions. As such, a number of questions remain unanswered and are of utmost concern to researchers and practitioners alike.

How Do We Define *Unresponsiveness*?

One challenge that RTI must face is the question of how to define *unresponsiveness*? A variety of measures are currently used to index student performance, and varying criteria are used to define *responsiveness*. Because progress monitoring is a core tenet of the RTI framework, the field must continue to collaborate and evaluate progress-monitoring measures to ensure that they are valid and reliable. Practitioners' decisions about which measures to employ should be guided by technically sound, empirical evidence. Practitioners should also realize that no progress-monitoring measure can be used for all educational purposes; rather, measures are designed to tap specific academic skills, and it is up to the educator to tune into available resources, such as the National Center on Student Progress website (*www.studentprogress.org*), to stay abreast of current research and inform these important decisions (D. Fuchs et al., 2008).

The Role of Special Education

A second question is: At what point should prevention become special education (D. Fuchs et al., 2004)? If a child fails to respond to instruction in the first two tiers but shows reading improvement after Tier 3, one-on-one tutoring, should the student then return to the general classroom? Or does responsiveness to this intensive instruction signal a need for special education? Will the student who returns to the general classroom be able to progress with his or her peers? Will the teacher be capable of sustaining the instruction he or she needs? Relatedly, if the student is placed in special education, will the special educator be able to provide the instruction he or she needs (D. Fuchs et al., 2004)? If Tier 3 is not considered special education, will the schools be able to find individuals with the expertise required to implement experimental teaching? Who are we training to work in this model—teachers, special educators, or school psychologists?

Do the Benefits of Tier 3 Outweigh Its Costs?

Given the high cost of tertiary prevention, it is appropriate to question whether this third tier is necessary. Do the educational benefits outweigh the costs? To date, little research has addressed this question; one thing that is certain, however, is that primary and secondary prevention are not enough for a significant minority of students. Providing the most intensive, individualized instruction available seems like the most logical solution, but again, additional studies that assess the long-term outcomes of Tier 3 prevention are necessary (D. Fuchs, Fuchs, & Compton, 2012).

Closing Remarks

RTI, in principle, provides a framework for making efficient use of school resources, while maximizing students' opportunities for success. Through practices that focus on prevention and early intervention, academically at-risk students receive the effective instruction they require without waiting months, or even years, to qualify for special education services. RTI provides individualized and intensive instruction to struggling students and distinguishes students with disabilities from those who perform poorly because of inadequate prior instruction (D. Fuchs et al., 2008).

Although RTI faces challenges, it is an evolving process that offers considerable promise. RTI is a versatile framework, capable of serving as both a multilevel intervention and a method of making data-based decisions to identify struggling learners. Because of this, RTI is proving to be a useful framework for many schools and districts. Importantly, the RTI process leaves room for innovation, which allows it to be a sustainable model that will likely continue to meet the needs of schools and districts in the future.

PROFESSIONAL DEVELOPMENT ACTIVITIES

- How does RTI address some of the difficulties with our current school services delivery model?
- What are the benefits or limitations of using an RTI model for LD identification?
- How do you already see some elements of RTI applied in your school?

REFERENCES

Al Otaiba, S., & Fuchs, D. (2006). Who are the young children for whom best practices in reading are ineffective?: An experimental and longitudinal study. *Journal of Learning Disabilities, 39*(5), 414–431.

Compton, D. L., Fuchs, D., Fuchs, L. S., Bouton, B., Gilbert, J. K., Barquero, L. A., et al. (2010) Selection at-risk first-grade readers for early intervention: Eliminating false positives and exploring the promise of a two-stage gated screening process. *Journal of Educational Psychology, 102*(2), 327–340.

Compton, D. L., Gilbert, J., Jenkins, J. R., Fuchs, D., Fuchs, L. S., Cho, E., et al. (2012). Accelerating chronically unresponsive children to Tier 3 instruction: What level of data is necessary to ensure selection accuracy? *Journal of Learning Disabilities, 45*(3), 204–216.

Fletcher, J. M., & Vaughn, S. (2009). Response to intervention: Preventing and remediating academic difficulties. *Child Development Perspectives, 3*(1), 30–37.

Fuchs, D., Compton, D. L., Fuchs, L. S., Bryant, V. J., Hamlett, C. L., & Lambert, W. (2012). First-grade cognitive abilities as long-term predictors of reading comprehension and disability status. *Journal of Learning Disabilities, 45*(3), 217–231.

Fuchs, D., & Fuchs, L. S. (2005). Responsiveness to intervention: A blueprint for practitioners, policymakers, and parents. *Teaching Exceptional Children, 38*(1), 57–61.

Fuchs, D., & Fuchs, L. S. (2006). Introduction to response to intervention: What, why, and how valid is it? *Reading Research Quarterly, 41*(1), 93–99.

Fuchs, D., Fuchs, L. S., & Compton, D. L. (2012). Smart RTI: A next-generation approach to multi-level prevention. *Exceptional Children, 78*(3), 263–279.

Fuchs, D., Fuchs, L. S., McMaster, K. L., Yen, L., & Svenson, E. (2004). Nonresponders: How to find them? How to help them? What do they mean for special education? *Teaching Exceptional Children, 36*(6), 72–77.

Fuchs, D., Fuchs, L. S., & Stecker, P. M. (2010). The "blurring" of special education in a new continuum of general education placements and services. *Exceptional Children, 76*, 301–322.

Fuchs, D., Fuchs, L. S., & Vaughn, S. (2008). *Response to intervention: A framework for reading educators.* Newark, DE: International Reading Association.

Fuchs, L. S., Compton, D. L., Fuchs, D., Hollenbeck, K. N., Hamlett, C. L., & Seethaler, P. M. (2011). Two-stage screening for math problem-solving difficulty using dynamic assessment of algebraic learning. *Journal of Learning Disabilities, 44*(4), 372–380.

Fuchs, L. S., Compton, D. L., Fuchs, D., Paulsen, K., Bryant, J. D., & Hamlett, C. L. (2005). The prevention, identification, and cognitive determinants of math difficulty. *Journal of Educational Psychology, 97*(3), 493–513.

Fuchs, L. S., & Fuchs, D. (1998). Treatment validity: A unifying concept for reconceptualizing the identification of learning disabilities. *Learning Disabilities Research and Practice, 13,* 204–219.

Fuchs, L. S., Fuchs, D., Craddock, C., Hollenbeck, K. N., Hamlett, C. L., & Schatschneider, C. (2008). Effects of small-group tutoring with and without validated classroom instruction on at-risk students' math problem solving: Are two tiers of prevention better than one? *Journal of Educational Psychology, 100,* 491–509.

Heller, K. A., Holtzman, W. H., & Messick, S. (Eds.). (1982). *Placing children in special education: A strategy for equity.* Washington, DC: National Academy Press.

Individuals with Disabilities Education Act [IDEA], 20 U.S.C. § 1400 *et seq.* (2008).

Johnson, E., Mellard, D. F., Fuchs, D., & McKnight, M. A. (2006). *Responsiveness to intervention (RTI): How to do it.* Nashville, TN and Lawrence, KS: National Research Center on Learning Disabilities.

Mathes, P., Howard, J., Allen, S., & Fuchs, D. (1998). Peer-assisted learning strategies for first-grade readers: Responding to the needs of diverse learners. *Reading Research Quarterly, 33*(1), 62–94.

McMaster, K. L., Fuchs, D., Fuchs, L. S., & Compton, D. L. (2005). Responding to nonresponders: An experimental field trial of identification and intervention methods. *Exceptional Children, 71*(4), 445–463.

Speece, D. L., & Case, L. (2001). Classification in context: An alternative approach to identifying early reading disability. *Journal of Educational Psychology, 93*(4), 735–749.

Stecker, P. M., Fuchs, L. S., & Fuchs, D. (2005). Using curriculum-based measurement to improve student achievement: Review of research. *Psychology in the Schools, 42,* 795–820.

Taylor, B. M. (2008). Tier 1: Effective classroom reading instruction in the elementary grades. In D. Fuchs, L. S. Fuchs, & S. Vaughn (Eds.), *Response to intervention: A framework for reading educators* (pp. 5–25). Newark, DE: International Reading Association.

Torgesen, J. K. (2009). The response to intervention instructional model: Some outcomes from a large-scale implementation in reading first schools. *Child Development Perspectives, 3*(1), 38–40.

Vaughn, S., Cirino, P. T., Wanzek, J., Wexler, J., Fletcher, J. M., Denton, C. A., et al. (2010). Response to intervention for middle school students with reading difficulties: Effects of a primary and secondary intervention. *School Psychology Review, 39,* 3–21.

Vaughn, S., & Denton, C. A. (2008). Tier 2: The role of intervention. In D. Fuchs, L. S. Fuchs, & S. Vaughn (Eds.), *Response to intervention: A framework for reading educators* (pp. 51–70). Newark, DE: International Reading Association.

Vaughn, S., Linan-Thompson, S., & Hickman, P. (2003). Response to instruction as a means of identifying students with reading/learning disabilities. *Exceptional Children, 69,* 391–409.

Vellutino, F. R., Scanlon, D. M., Sipay, E. R., Small, S. G., Pratt, S., Chen, R., et al. (1996). Cognitive profiles of difficult-to-remediate and readily remediated poor readers: Early intervention as a vehicle for distinguishing between cognitive and experiential deficits as basic causes of specific reading disability. *Journal of Educational Psychology, 88*(4), 601–638.

CHAPTER 11

DIGITAL READING AND WRITING
Pedagogy for the Digital Child

LINDA D. LABBO
SILVIA NOGUERÓN-LIU

> The media that children use and create [will be] integral to their growing sense of themselves, of the world, and of how they should interact with it.
> —CENTER FOR MEDIA AND CHILD HEALTH AT CHILDREN'S HOSPITAL (2008)

It is center time in Ms. Bailey's kindergarten classroom. Gerald, Marie, Sara, and Damon are the first students to arrive in the digital stories center. Gerald and Sara, both "digital children," have grown up playing with apps and e-books on iPads and iPhones at home. Marie and Damon watch their friends navigate through the screen pages and start the story narration. In a few minutes, all of the children are touching, shaking, tapping, giggling, and swiping their way across text, illustrations, narration, animations, and special effects. They have entered into the world of *Toy Story Showtime!** This app "features Buzz Lightyear as he sets out to impress Jessie the Cowgirl in a talent show; readers . . . assist him with his comedy and juggling acts while they discover new vocabulary words through context and story-based repetition" (*www.disneydreaming.com/2011/12/28/disney-app-toy-story-showtime*). By the end of the story, Buzz learns he can dance, and the children enjoy an activity to choreograph his dance routine. Eager to write about the story, Marie and Gerald hurry to the digital writing center, where they are met with an array of digital tools—a storyboard, clip art, and music. Sara and Damon visit the dramatic play center to stage their own talent show and reenact Buzz's dance.

In many fundamental ways for emerging readers and writers are living in a new era. Mobile device ownership among children ages 4–14 has grown exponentially since 2005, and 93% of 6- to 9-year-olds live in a home with a cell phone (MacArthur Foundation Report, 2009). More recently, in the Nielsen Report (2012), "according to a Nielsen survey of adults with children under 12 in tablet-owning households, in Q4 [Quarter 4] 2011 seven out of every 10 children in tablet-owning households used a tablet computer—a nine percent increase compared to Q3 2011."

While these family-oriented statistics indicate growing acceptance of technologies at home, most kindergarten and primary-grade classroom teachers have not integrated digital media into the literacy curriculum because they lack training, access, or experience (Chen & Chang, 2006; Labbo, Eakle, & Montero, 2002). Fortunately, many educators are ready for research-based ideas for building bridges between children's out-of-school digital experiences and in-school practices. Our purpose in this chapter is to shed light on how teachers like Ms. Bailey can create pedagogical and technological "zones of possibility" (Moll & Greenberg, 1990) to expand young children's opportunities to engage in digital reading and writing. In these zones, teachers mobilize resources between home and school to support children's emergent understandings of digital texts in both settings.

What Research Says
about the Digital Child, Technology, and Literacy

It is beyond the scope of this chapter to explore the wide range of digital media present in children's lives (video games, MP3 players, social networking sites for children, etc.). We focus on pedagogies related to reading and writing digital texts. Additionally, we discuss what teachers like Ms. Bailey know about (1) the digital child; (2) relevant research and practice on digital reading; and (3) relevant research and practice on digital writing. We close with reflections on future directions and ideas for professional development.

Digital children, sometimes called *digital natives*, have never known a world without computers, cell phones, handheld tablets, and the expectation that digital media will continuously evolve (Prensky, 2001). For over 30 years, educators have taken a sociocognitive perspective (Vygotsky, 1978) to understand how young children develop literacy before they enter kindergarten (Clay, 1975). Informal interactions with caregivers around literacy events provide children with foundational literacy insights (Rowe, 1998). Today, many children enter kindergarten with technology-related literacy concepts because literacy events at home involve playing with digital media (Blanchard & Moore, 2010). Computers are playgrounds for digital kids (Labbo, 1996) and as Salonius-Pasternak and Gelfond (2005) note, this form of play is "the first qualitatively different from of play that has been introduced in the last several hundred years" (p. 6). Playing is "an essential and integral part of all children's healthy growth, development and learning" (Isenberg & Quisenberry, 2002, p. 33) because doing so assists their cognitive and emotional development (Verenikina, Herrington, Peterson, & Mantei, 2010). Glaubke (2007) notes that 64% of 3- to 5-year-old children can point and click with a mouse, 56% can use a computer independently, and 37% can turn on a computer by themselves. This technological infusion at home requires a parallel pedagogical shift for teachers' understanding of the emerging digitally literate child at school. Equally important is the need for schools to bridge the digital divide for children like Marie and Damon, who come from homes where parents either do not have handheld tablets or limit children's access to mobile devices.

The National Council of Teachers of English, (NCTE; 2008) recognized that including developmentally appropriate information and communication technologies (ICTs) in the primary classroom can support beginning readers development of both traditional and digital literacy skills (Roschelle, Pea, Hoadley, Gordin, & Means, 2000). Digital media is clearly at the center of our research and guidelines for practice. For purposes of this chapter, we adopt Blanchard and Moore's (2010, p. 2) definition of digital media:

"Digital media" . . . [are] both the technology tools and the media that infuse life into the tools. This definition acknowledges a continuum of interactivity for digital media bracketed by young children being passive observers or listeners on one end and active participants on the other. Interactivity would be judged by the extent to which young children have control over content or communication through responsive interaction in a verbal or nonverbal fashion. (Calvert, Rideout, Woodard, Barr, & Strouse, 2005; Glaubke, 2007; Johnson, Bruner, & Kumar, 2006)

RELEVANT RESEARCH BASE FOR DIGITAL READING

"A picture storybook is one in which the text and the illustrations work together to amplify each other. . . . Combined they tell a story that goes beyond what each one tells alone" (Temple, Martinez, & Yokata, 2011, p. 67). Teacher read-alouds and comments about the interplay of a book's language and artistry enrich children's engagement and response (Temple et al., 2011). While e-books build on the rich tradition of picture storybooks, they offer a unique reading experience whether they are coviewed (Takeuchi & Stevens, 2011) or read independently (Labbo & Kuhn, 2000). E-books use multimedia to support text through visual, auditory, and animation effects (Roskos, Brueck, & Widman, 2009). On the surface, e-books are physically different from picture books and require cognitively different attention and strategies (e.g., display screens involve page turning movements of pointing–holding–clicking, or swiping rather than grasping–lifting–turning–releasing; Roskos et al., 2009). Thus, by interacting with e-books many children acquire navigational aspects of multimodal, new literacies (Lankshear & Knobel, 2003). On a deeper level an e-book is one that can amplify a story by giving the reader control over how it unfolds. The visual and auditory elements of e-books contribute to high levels of motivation, reading engagement (Lewis, 2000), and playful interactions.

Research suggests that when caregivers read e-books with emergent readers, the nature of talk is qualitatively different than that when reading print versions of the same books. For example, de Jong and Bus (2002) noted that e-books, when compared to print versions, create unique opportunities for focusing on vocabulary, occasions for children to initiate more questions, and time for making more complex connections to the story. Research also indicates that independently reading e-books can promote young children's development of early literacy concepts (de Jong & Bus, 2002); literacy skills, such as word recognition, phonological awareness, and fluency (Plowman & Stephen, 2003; Van Kleeck, 2008); and story comprehension (Doty, Popplewell, & Byers, 2001; Pearman, 2008). Most of the extant research has focused on e-books as presented on computer screens. As a result, children's interactions have involved moving a cursor, pointing, clicking, and so forth, with a computer mouse. Handheld tablets are changing the ways children interact with e-books. For example, as portable as books, iPads enable children to view e-books anywhere and anytime. Indeed, since 2010, researchers have begun to explore the affordances of touch screens and accelerometers. An *accelerometer* is an internal sensing device that responds to physical movements of a tablet (Revelle, 2009). This flexibility serves as an alternative interface, whereby children can shake, tilt, or even blow on the tablet while playing games and reading e-books. This kinesthetic and tactile interface presents more benefits for children's interactions and engagements with e-texts than do mouse-driven programs (Couse & Chen, 2010).

RESEARCH INTO PRACTICE: READING DIGITAL TEXTS

In this section we draw on sociocognitive theory and relevant research to suggest three things teachers should know as they integrate e-books into the classroom: (1) categories of e-books; (2) joint media engagements (JMEs) with e-books (Takeuchi & Stevens, 2011); and (3) differentiated instruction with e-books.

Categories of E-Books

It is important for educators to understand that e-books come in unique categories that offer potentially different literacy experiences. Grimshaw, Dungworth, McKnight, and Morris (2001) found that story comprehension for children who heard story narration was significantly higher than that for those who did not hear narration. Narration may reduce the cognitive load on working memory and provide support for children who have trouble decoding. On the other hand, Labbo and Kuhn (2000) noted that interactive screen animations, hot spots, may be *considerate*, supporting children's affective/playful comprehension of story, or *inconsiderate*, detracting from the comprehension of the story. Highlighted text draws attention to concepts of print, such as left-to-right directionality. Clearly, e-books provide a rich context for children's playful, active engagement with stories. This interactivity may focus children's attention on words—touch for a definition; main characters' activities—glowing spots prompt animation; cause and effect—swiping action to see the result of an action; and navigation—menu, arrows (Labbo & Kuhn, 2000).

In this section we include an initial list of e-book categories: Traditional e-books, Gamified e-books, Media-Related e-books, and Internet e-books (see Table 11.1). Traditional e-books include storybooks in print, such as fairy tales or fables, that have been converted as e-texts. Gamified e-books specifically aim to engage children in game-like interactions with a story as they solve problems and create linear or nonlinear paths through text. The lines between games and books blur "with games to be read and books to be played" (Neary, 2012). Media-inspired e-books include familiar characters and offer high-quality graphics and stories drawn directly from animated movies, cartoons, social networking sites, and so forth. See Figure 11.1 for an illustration of e-book screen features from *Toy Story Showtime!*

Children make sense of everyday events by playfully acting them out (Vygtosky, 1967), and animated TV series, movies, and cartoons are part of their daily experiences. Children enjoy extending digital play from on-screen to off-screen role playing and other activities (Verenikina & Kervin, 2011). Internet e-books do not all adhere to expected e-book components. For example, some Internet e-books offer static text and illustrations, with the only digital feature being an audio narration of the story. In the same way educators make decisions about traditional print books to develop a skill or evaluate picture books, this same reflective practice should apply to the selection of e-books in reading instruction.

Joint Media Engagements

JMEs refer to spontaneous and designed experiences of people using media together. JMEs can happen anywhere and anytime multiple people are interacting together with media. Modes of JMEs include viewing, playing, searching, reading, contributing, and

TABLE 11.1. Categories of E-Books

Category	Description	Example	Features
Traditional e-books	Classic books repackaged	*Green Eggs and Ham* (Oceanhouse Media)	• Original artwork and text • Read to me/read myself/auto play • Highlighted text • Hot spots—animation
Gamified e-books	Narrative and navigation may not be linear	*Spot the Dot* (Rukus)	• Interactions shape, tell or transform the story • Follow directions or prompts for hot spot locations • iPad or iPhone
Media-inspired e-books	Spinoff from other media (TV shows, movies, cartoons)	*Toy Story Showtime!* (Disney Learning)	• Familiar characters • Highlighted text • Definitions on demand/touch • Learn by doing and exploring hot spots • Extended learning activities • iPad/iPhone app
Internet e-books	May offer traditional tales or unpublished author stories	*www.childrenstory. info/childrenstories/ thegingerbreadman. html*	• Static text • Static illustrations • No highlighting of text • Audio reading of text

Note. Based on *www.wired.com/geekdad/2011/10/making-sense-of-digital-books-for-kids-part-2.*

 Buzz is proud of his stunt. But Rex and Trixie aren't so happy. They have to fix all the stars he knocked down.

FIGURE 11.1. Interactivity and an e-book screen. Glowing areas—guide exploration. Menu—provides navigational choices. Arrows—turn pages. Retrieved from *http://itunes.apple.com/us/app/toy-story-showtime!id479272579?mt=8.* Copyright Disney/Pixar. Reprinted by permission.

creating, with either digital or traditional media. JMEs can support learning by provid-ing resources for making sense and making meaning in a particular situation, as well as future situations (Stevens & Penuel, 2010).

When teachers share group JMEs with children around e-books, they not only make meaning together but they also help children build schemas for future interactions with media. During JMEs, teachers demonstrate, explain, model, wonder, and collaborate with children to weave together multimedia content (Labbo, Phillips, & Murray, 1995–1996). Teachers may find similar opportunities that the mothers in de Jong and Bus (2002) study found to expand children's vocabulary, talk, and story engagement. The goal of JMEs is that teachers create opportunities for children to share access to the screen, socially mediate decision making, discuss media, and play through story paths (Takeuchi & Stevens, 2011).

Group JMEs involve before, during, and after e-reading activities. *Before e-reading*—For a large group, display the e-book on a large TV monitor or Smartboard (see *http:// ipadacademy.com/2011/08/how-to-use-the-ipad-with-a-smart-board-connecting-the-ipad-and-smart-board*). For a small group, gather around the iPad screen in a comfort-able location. Discuss the title and ask children to predict what the story is about. Guide children in combining clues from the title, illustrations, music, animations, and narration on the introductory screen and perhaps the first screen page. For example, in the media-inspired e-book app, *Toy Story Showtime!*, children combine what they know about *Toy Story* movies with their guesses about the meaning of showtime. Next, turn off the sound and take a picture walk (Temple et al., 2011), navigating through each screen page with-out reading the text. Asking children what they notice in the illustrations, animations, or words can lead to more story predictions. As children picture-walk through *Toy Story Showtime!* they may notice that all of the characters seem to be talking to Buzz Light-year. The teacher may ask why Buzz Lightyear always looks so puzzled. Use the menu to navigate back to the title screen and begin a shared reading.

- *During e-reading*—Children will take turns interacting with the multimedia. Invite brief comments as to how specific multimedia components enhance under-standing, enjoyment, or progress through the story. For example, while viewing Buzz's interactions with other characters across screens, students may notice that his movements are like dance steps.
- *After e-reading*—Explore e-extension or e-games. In a well-crafted e-book such as *Toy Story Showtime!*, children choreograph a dance for Buzz by helping him use all of the leaping, sliding, hopping moves he learned in the story. Finally, cre-ate off-screen activities for children to continue engagement with the story. For example, students could create an impromptu talent show or try their own hand at choreographing dance movements.

Whereas these examples focus on the genre of fiction, further research explores the potential of digital and interactive texts to enhance informational texts. One area of pos-sibility is promoting collaboration across grade levels, where upper elementary students design and share interactive e-books with students in lower grade levels. Hodgson (2009) worked with sixth graders in the design of science-focused interactive picture books that introduced concepts through images, text, and hyperlinks. These books were shared and evaluated by second and third graders, and these interactions provided valuable lessons about content and affordances of digital texts for all groups of students. Examples of these interactive science books and other digital text projects are available at the National

Writing Project's (2008) *Profiles in Practice: Digital Storytelling with Teacher Consultants* site. Teacher-designed interactive informational texts can also be shared and created with Smartboard and iPad tools. Such texts can provide early scaffolding in navigation through hyperlinked media, as well as instruction in content area–specific concepts.

Opportunities for Differentiated Instruction

When teachers give children opportunities to read e-books independently during center time, they expect an e-book to scaffold learning by making specific components of literacy noticeable and memorable (see Labbo, 2000). In order to differentiate learning opportunities (Edyburn, 2007; Gregory & Chapman, 2006), it is important for teachers to match the type the e-book with the specific needs of the students. See Table 11.2 for examples of the alignment of key factors in matching e-books to children's literacy needs for phonemic awareness, fluency, comprehension, and vocabulary. Children who are English learners (ELs) benefit from engagement with multimedia technologies and multimodal resources (Leu et al., 2005). Some ELs benefit from teacher support during initial e-book interactions (see Segers, Takke, & Verhoeven, 2004); however, selecting e-books and online texts with animations, word-level support, and translations in a child's heritage language helps to make the content more accessible and may help ELs

TABLE 11.2. Matching E-Books to Children's Instructional Area: A Sample

Child's instructional focus	E-book category and example	Activity
Phonemic awareness	Traditional e-books: *Green Eggs and Ham* (Oceanhouse Media)	Identify rhyming words (see Ehri & Nunes, 2002)
Fluency	Traditional e-books: *PopOut! The Tale of Peter Rabbit* (LoudCrow Interactive, Inc.)	Repeated readings (may involve two or more turns in a listening center) • First, listen to narration and enjoy the artistry of the animations) • Second, echo read • Third, chorally read • Last, turn off "read to me" and read text aloud independently (see Labbo, 2000; National Reading Panel, 2000)
Comprehension	Media-inspired e-books: *Toy Story Showtime!* (Disney Learning)	• Before reading, child draws on media background knowledge of the movie or cartoon to predict who and what the story is about • After reading child reenacts the e-story in the sociodramatic play center (see Labbo, 2000; Pearman, 2008)
Vocabulary	Movie- and cartoon-inspired e-books: *Toy Story Showtime!* (Disney Learning)	• During reading the child interacts with animations to learn action words from the text that turn into animated dance moves. The child can also click on special vocabulary words (e.g., *impressed*) that are unknown to hear definitions • After reading children complete story a extension activity using vocabulary words learned in the story (see Reinking et al., 2000; Van Kleek, 2008)

acquire vocabulary. For example, *RyeBooks: The Beast Nian* by Rye Studio (*http://itunes.apple.com/us/app/ryebooks-the-beast-nian-by/id396384621?mt=8*) offers English, Basque, Chinese, Dutch, French, German, Japanese, Korean, Spanish, and Vietnamese translations. Additionally, if a teacher knows a student is struggling with literacy development, such as in the area of fluency, he or she might select a traditional e-book, such as *PopOut! Peter Rabbit* (*http://itunes.apple.com/us/app/popout!-the-tale-peter-rabbit/id397864713?mt=8*), for a multiday series of repeated readings (National Reading Panel, 2000). Using e-book activities to support fluency provides models of fluency, word-level support, and more time than teachers usually have available to listen to children's repeated readings. First, the child listens to the narrated story, following along with highlighted text, and enjoying the artistry of the animations. Second, the child echo reads then chorally reads (Cunningham & Allington, 1998) the narrated text. Finally, the child reads the text aloud independently (see Labbo, 2000; National Reading Panel, 2000).

RELEVANT RESEARCH BASE FOR DIGITAL WRITING

As the materials, spaces, and audiences of composition continue to evolve and diversify—from paper and pen to the affordances of the screen—we need to develop and support models to teach and assess new ways to write (Yancey, 2009). The National Writing Project (2010) defines *digital writing* as "created with, and oftentimes for reading or viewing on, a computer or other device that is connected to the Internet" (p. 7). Text created in this way is different in important ways: (1) It allows for wider, instant circulation through networked connectivity, and (2) it gives digital writers a large repertoire of resources (beyond print) for composition (National Writing Project, 2010). These two affordances of digital text are also considered in the NCTE's *21st Century Curriculum and Assessment Framework* (2008). These guidelines recommend fostering skills to help students be both critical *consumers* and *creators* of multimedia text. They should be able to assess the ways multimodal texts communicate information to different audiences, and to evaluate the effect of visual, audio, or hyperlinked elements on text meanings.

In addition, shifts toward digital writing-online spaces are facilitated by the spread of Web 2.0 tools that support a more participatory in and collaborative community of authors (Kang, Chen, & Kidd, 2009). Web content is no longer constrained to a narrow group of users: Platforms such as blogs, social networks, or wikis allow accessible ways to publish content. These tools have the potential to create socially authentic and collaborative writing experiences for students (Hicks, 2009). For instance, by using blogs as tools for writing, young children develop a sense of audience (Lapp, Shea, & Wolsey, 2011), whether blog entries are directed to their peers, their parents, other classrooms, or the public beyond the classroom walls. In addition, by scaffolding students' understanding of social media at an early age, teachers and students can have conversations about risks, safety, and respect for others in online interaction (Kist, Doyle, Hayes, Horwitz, & Kuzior, 2010). These early lessons help children to be aware of the ways texts can circulate and be accessed in online spaces.

Some research studies explore digital writing by looking at the ways students transform text from one meaning-making system to another. This process has been referred to as *transmediation* (Mills, 2011) and *transduction* (Marsh, 2006). When children use storyboards, short films, animations, or digital comics to produce a story, they "go beyond the simple reproduction of literary content to the transformation of meaning and knowledge" (Mills, 2011, p. 64). They become aware of the message and additional meaning conveyed by images, sounds effects, or transitions in a multimodal text. These emergent notions help children construct identities as text designers, in addition to becoming readers and writers (Marsh, 2006).

The composition of digital stories also expands the writing process to make students mindful of the purposeful use of multiple modalities. In the production of short films, young children develop a script and create a storyboard to plan the integration of audio, video, and sound effects in their text. In her digital storytelling guide for elementary school teachers, Miller (2010) notes the benefits of digital story composition, including the potential to engage and empower reluctant readers and writers who engage in a revision process that integrates various elements beyond print, keeping in mind the end product (a short film production). She also highlights the impact of thinking about a larger audience within and outside the classroom. Engaging in digital story production also can become a project across the curriculum, applicable to content areas and genres beyond the writing of personal narratives.

RESEARCH INTO PRACTICE: WRITING DIGITAL TEXTS

Writing with digital media integrates multiple meaning-making systems into one text. Through the production of digital images, digital stories, or short films, students are applying "traditional" elements of writing and thinking about the potential of other mediums to enhance and transform a story (Hicks, 2009). A good approach to integrate digital projects in a literacy curriculum is to think of effective writing practices that can be supported and enhanced by a digital component. In the following sections, we showcase successful implementation of digital writing projects. In particular, we take a closer look at (1) children as digital photographers, (2) multimodal composition through digital stories, and (3) online publishing of students' work.

Children as Digital Photographers

A first step to integrate digital composition is through the production of digital photography. Digital images can be components of digital language–experience approaches (D-LEAs; Labbo et al., 2002) to help young students notice the potential of multimodal texts. Labbo, Love, and Ryan (2007) used this method to promote vocabulary development in a kindergarten classroom. Through the representation of oral language experiences in digital images, students were able to transform information into a new sign system. The steps of this activity comprised (1) setting up a language experience in the form of a read-aloud in which students noticed key words and connections to text, and self and other words; (2) photographing the experience, having students reenact words through performance/staging; (3) composing a multimedia photo story through small group retellings and sharing these computer-generated compositions; and (4) following up with discussion and sharing of the D-LEA text by distributing print copies to take home. In this project, children contributed to digital image production in the planning of key themes (choosing the vocabulary words) and decided on the photo content by staging images taken by their teacher. The final product was a collaborative digital text that was also available as tangible copies students could share at home.

Another approach to incorporate digital photography is to engage children directly in the craft of photo composition. Blagojevic and Thomes (2008) collaborated in a Young

Photographers project, where they planned developmentally appropriate ways to introduce the use of digital and disposable cameras in a PreK classroom. In the first stage of their project, students had supervised and teacher-directed access to a digital camera in the classroom; in the second phase, they had access to a disposable/unbreakable camera to take home and the freedom to experiment with composition in multiple contexts. During the first stage, children were guided to compose stories to go along their digital images by audio recording or dictating their stories for instructors to type. They also received instruction in composition techniques; the different perspectives of multiple camera angles; learning the specialized language photographers use, such as *shutter release, focus,* or *viewfinder.* Experiences in projects such as these expose children to visual "grammar" as they make sense of the ways photographers can tell stories, frame experiences, and communicate meaning through images.

Multimodal Composition through Digital Stories

In the production of digital stories, children integrate digital photos, a narrated script or captions, and audio and transition effects into a short film. In the following two projects, teachers integrated the digital story production process with the study of fairy tales and folktales, and with the examination of primary documents during a thematic unit. In both cases, the creation of the story was a group effort that recruited the expertise of other adults (parents, assistants, or older students) to assist students in the use of software and the translation of texts to students' home languages. Lotherington, Holland, Sotoudeh, and Zentena (2008) report the use of digital stories in multilingual K–1 classrooms in the Toronto area. Their aim was to have students craft digital retellings and transformation of fairy tales and folktales. After reading the story, teachers led and modeled the planning of a short film using a storyboard. In one classroom, students used Play-Doh figures to recreate *The Three Little Pigs,* brainstorming different settings and characters for their retelling. The teacher photographed each segment of the students' re-creation of action (following their storyboard), then students' read-alouds of their retelling were audio recorded. In another classroom, students used a picture-creation software to compose their illustrations (Kid Pix) for a retelling of *The Lion and the Mouse* (Aesop's fable). In small groups, students produced their stories using slide show software with audio attachments or captions of their retelling. Because of the multicultural composition of the groups, teachers recruited parents and bilingual educational assistants to translate the stories. The end products were multilingual and multimodal retellings, collaboratively produced, that honored children's diverse backgrounds and integrated multiple ways to make meaning.

In a similar effort to craft a group digital story, Fuhler (2010) describes how primary documents can help students learn and reflect on historical events, and empathize with somebody else's circumstances. In a sample lesson aimed at elementary students, the teacher first presented "intriguing photographs" from a particular time period (the Dust Bowl era). The teacher built students' background on this topic by discussing these photographs and listening to a read-aloud of related picture books. Students then jotted down their thoughts and responses to the photographs, which depicted children and places during this time period. After exploring examples of digital stories about other topics and making connections with the layout of picture books, the teacher guided students to collaborate in small groups to write scripts. Using storyboards, students utilized their own original drawings and the photographs they examined to illustrate their script. To support the production of a group digital story, Fuhler recommends the involvement of parents, technology coordinators, or upper-grade students who are familiar with movie-making software. At the end of their production, students shared their stories in front of an audience, and had the time to self-evaluate their learning.

In spite of the heavy focus of digital storytelling literature on the genre of personal narratives, the project described by Fuhler (2010) showcases an inquiry approach to produce an informational text about the Dust Bowl era. The use of images to support the process of writing similar pieces can be applied to the writing of biographies, family history and genealogy, and community history projects (see Frazel, 2010; Van Horn, 2008). Digital projects can also include how-to manuals and tutorials. For instance, a student digital project featured in Miller (2010) demonstrates how an apple is made into applesauce, narrated from the apple's perspective (see "Sarah and Apple"). Under the Common Core State Standards for K–5 (National Governors Association Center for Best Practices & Council of Chief State School Officers, 2010, p. 10), these types of informational texts are included in the range for these grade levels. Students can watch and critique digital and multimodal compositions, and work collaboratively to create their multimodal project, with the intended purpose of showcasing the history and practices of their local community, or their own family traditions, history, recipes, or diverse cultural backgrounds.

Online Publishing of Students' Work

The circulation of students' texts via online communication (e.g., e-mail) and publishing (e.g., through classroom blogs) opens new possibilities for writing instruction. As done by the teachers working with digital stories, blogs and e-mail can be managed as a whole-group project. It is relevant to note the importance of informing both children and parents about online safety, privacy, and audience when students' writing goes online.

E-mail is one of the ways early elementary students can start to develop a sense of audience. Young digital writers can make sense of the differences and similarities of e-mail, letter writing, and other forms of social exchange (Mavers, 2007). Because e-mail writing is a common practice observed in households, children can also understand its potential to reach remote audiences (e.g., relatives or friends who are away). In school settings, pen pal projects can enrich students' discussions and retellings of texts. As part of a larger project to support literacy instruction (Teale & Gambrell, 2007), students were paired with adult pen pals in the community, with whom they exchanged messages in discussing a book both had read. Students (as young as second graders) participated in a writer's workshop approach to craft these messages. Benefits of this project included increases in students' engagement, participation in authentic communication experiences, and a sense of belonging to a learning community of readers beyond the classroom walls.

Another way to engage students in digital writing is through classroom blogs. There are several free blog providers (e.g., Wordpress and Blogger) with privacy settings that allow teachers to control who views and comments on students' entries. The Edublogger site (*theedublogger.com*) has resources shared by teachers who use blogs in their instruction, with useful recommendations for beginners. Kist and colleagues (2010) report the use of blogs in a first-grade classroom, where students posted entries with creative writing exercise, book talks, and math problems, both at home and at school. Their teacher modeled logging-in and logging-out steps, and started their blog activities with entries in which students described everyday events. This was followed by a morning routine of reading their peers' entries and extended to parents being able to write messages as well. At a second-grade classroom, Kist and colleagues provide a glimpse of the use of Twitter for home–school communication during the day. They started with an initial orientation for parents to discuss this space, and to address safety concerns and guidelines (e.g., not using students' real names) and privacy features to keep the account restricted to approved viewers only. Lapp and colleagues (2011) highlight the potential of students' classroom blogs to receive peer feedback, through comments in blog entries—such as "praise" and encouragement to fellow writers, or "pushing" to help writers improve their craft. Students who learned how to give feedback to their peers using these ideas during their regular writer's workshop applied these practices to their feedback in blog comments.

As these classroom experiences demonstrate, digital writing can enrich already existing practices, activities, and centers in early childhood classrooms. Adding digital images to a language experience approach activity, creating digital stories to retell or transform a folktale, or using blogs to view and publish peers' feedback are examples of a digitally enhanced writer's workshop. It is important to note that digital writing can also be a useful vehicle to establish home–school partnerships, in which parents collaborate at home or at school to support students, and also communicate and clarify any concerns about children's participation in online platforms.

ASSESSMENT OF DIGITAL PROJECTS

When we think about integrating digital writing projects with already existing classroom practices, assessment should take a similar approach. The production of digital texts can nicely align with skills and practices evaluated in the traditional writer's craft. However, digital writing also develops new skills of multimedia composition that expand the focus of assessment to modalities beyond print (Hicks, 2009). Also, since digital texts can reach readers beyond the classroom, the quality of students' writing should also achieve its intended purpose and resonate with its intended audience (National Writing Project, 2010). Instruction and assessment of digital projects should then take in to consideration how these projects inform and enhance traditional forms of writing, while developing new ways of thinking about composition in online spaces.

Several authors working with digital media explain how these projects align with national standards for language arts and technology. These include the National Council of Teachers of English/International Reading Association Language Arts standards (NCTE/IRA; 1996) and the National Educational Technology Standards for Students (International Society for Technology in Education, 2007). With digital storytelling, Ohler (2008) and Miller (2010) note how the development of a script and narrative is essential for the project to be effective. For instance, a closer look at the following NCTE/IRA (1996) standards illustrates their argument:

- *Standard 1.* Students read a wide range of print and non-print texts to build an understanding of texts, of themselves and of the culture of the United States and the world; to acquire new information; to respond to the needs and demands of society and the workplace; and for personal fulfillment. Among these texts are fiction and non-fiction, classic and contemporary work. (p. 19)
- *Standard 4.* Students adjust their use of spoken, written and visual language (e.g., conventions, style, vocabulary) to communicate effectively with a variety of audiences and for different purposes. (p. 24)

Ohler (2008) and Miller (2010) point to the potential of reading and writing digital texts to meet these standards. By looking at digital stories and e-books from e-writer or designer perspectives, students note that they can apply digital authors' craft to their own projects. In digital stories, students' scripts, art, and images together can effectively communicate their narratives, if used strategically. By analyzing mentor texts, drafting, and revising and reviewing, students enhance their writing skills and become familiar with the grammar of new composition practices.

In addition, the Common Core State Standards Initiative also integrates digital texts within English language arts standards. Digital tools are included as resources for reading and writing to select when they align with students' communication goals. For instance, in grades K–2, students are expected to engage in scaffolded exploration of technology for the production and distribution of writing: "With guidance and support from adults, [students] explore a variety of digital tools to produce and publish writing, including in collaboration with peers" (p. 19).

For purposes of formative and summative assessment of digital writing, the use of rubrics according to the goals and purposes of the assignment is recommended. Some authors and practitioners assess the elements of the finalized project. For instance, Allison (2009) developed a rubric to guide students in the reading, drafting, revising and publishing of blog entries, by focusing on each the blog entry elements and modes: text, images, links, or audio podcasts. Miller (2010) describes a rubric developed by Kevin Hodgson (2009), evaluating elements of digital stories. The rubric focuses on (1) point of view/purpose; (2) voice/pacing; (3) images; (4) economy; and (5) grammar. Others assess the different stages of digital story production. Frazel (2010) uses separate rubrics for (1) the preparation of the story (creating the script, storyboards, narrative); (2) the production (e.g., selecting images, assembling, editing); and (3) the story presentation. If digital stories are approached as group projects, these rubrics can be adapted to assess the segments or production stages to which each student contributes. Because these rubrics focus on multiple modalities, teachers can include handwritten or drawn storyboards, journal entries, voice recordings, and other pieces and artifacts that support digital writing processes. It is worth noting that the elements assessed focus on both digital and nondigital pieces, which do not require students to type their entries or to evaluate their keyboarding skills.

REFLECTIONS AND NEW DIRECTIONS

In this chapter, we presented some directions for rethinking emergent reading and writing in early childhood classrooms, by expanding our vision to the ways young children engage in digital text consumption and production. Through the reading of e-books, interaction with handheld tablets, and production of digital stories, young children develop an understanding of the multimodal nature of digital text and its circulation in networked spaces. As "early adopters" of new technologies (Wohlwend, 2011), young children are exploring the affordances of new, multimodal media in playful ways, and developing understanding about technology-mediated literacy. While we have provided recommendations for reading and writing practices in separate sections, we have also called for a digital literacy pedagogy in which processes and activities inform each other. We should not only focus on the potential of computers and mobile devices as "deliverers" of literacy instruction but also explore how they can become a medium for meaning making in which children produce texts and publish them online (Burnett, 2010).

It is our hope that this chapter invites you to reflect on your existing classroom practices and consider how technology integration can add to your literacy perspectives.

Drawing on our existing knowledge of the reading and writing workshop, we can find ways to mobilize best practices in the reading and writing of digital texts (Hicks, 2009). We can guide students to notice the differences and similarities between e-books and traditional print books, and the types of skills and strategies that work for both kinds of texts. The close analysis of digital stories, blog entries, video games, or e-mails as mentor texts can help students note the purpose, audience, modalities, and choices digital authors make; and these can inform students' own composition of digital texts. For instance, in a project introducing blogs in second grade (Lapp et al., 2011), the teacher had students brainstorm their ideas about what blogs are; they were exposed to various mentor-text blogs to understand them as a genre and as a platform for publishing. They created a Venn diagram comparing their writing "on paper" versus their writing "on blog." This kind of scaffolding expands students' horizons to build a repertoire of literacy practices, tools for meaning making, and communication.

New technologies at home and at school are changing the ways we interact with texts and with each other. In this chapter, we have provided some guidelines for reading and writing practices young children may encounter at home and at school. By building technological "zones of possibility" in online and face-to-face conversations with family members, educators can support children's consumption and production of digital media at an early age. We recommend sharing information about the e-books and print books children are reading and discussing, the digital writing projects students are working on, and involving parents as collaborators in these digital practices, in ways similar to how they are engaged in print-book read-alouds. Through joint engagement in digital reading and writing, educators, parents, and children together can navigate the affordances of digital texts, and work to bridge home and school technology experiences.

PROFESSIONAL DEVELOPMENT ACTIVITIES

- Incorporate mobile, multifunctional, handheld devices into classrooms. "Because of their relatively low cost and accessibility in low-income communities, handheld devices can help advance digital equity, reaching and inspiring populations 'at the edges'—children from economically disadvantaged communities and those from developing countries" (Shuler, 2009, p. 4).

- Work with another teacher at your grade level to design and conduct JME e-book read-alouds in your classrooms. Discuss how you selected the e-book. Reflect on how you shared interactivity and meaning making with your students. Share how specific multimedia e-book features combined with text to result in a compelling story experience.

- Try your hand at differentiating literacy instruction with e-books. Keep anecdotal notes to help you write a reflection about sessions. Think about the role you played in supporting children's successful digital reading.

- Create your own photograph-based, multimodal composition about a topic or thematic unit of study. Share your composition with your class as part of the unit. Reflect on your creative composition experience as a step in supporting your students' multimedia composition.

- Focus on ways to unite the digital reading workshop with the digital writing workshop. In what ways can an e-book serve as a mentor text for children's writing? Design a digital reading and writing learning experience that capitalizes on their interest in interactivity and playful digital media engagements.

■ Explore the potential of social media and Web 2.0 tools to join or create professional networks interested in early childhood digital literacy. You can find a wide range of teacher blogs in *theedublogger.com*, or follow other teachers, professional organizations, events, and scholars on Twitter.

■ Reflect on the ways you live the digital "writerly life" (Calkins, 1994) and seek opportunities to expand your own ways of meaning making for creative writing or self-expression, through blogging, tweeting, or composing digital films for friends and family. How can these experiences inform and connect with the reading and writing in your classroom?

REFERENCES

Allison, P. (2009). Be a blogger. In A. Herrington, K. Hodgson, & C. Moran (Eds.), *Teaching the new writing: Technology, change and assessment in the 21st century classroom* (pp. 75–91). New York: Teachers College.

Blagojevic, B., & Thomes, K. (2008). Young photographers. *Young Children, 63*(5), 66–72.

Blanchard, J., & Moore, T. (2010). *The digital world of young children: Impact on emergent literacy*. Research presented by the Pearson Foundation. Retrieved from *www.pearsonfoundation.org/downloads/emergentliteracy-whitepaper.pdf*.

Burnett, C. (2010). Technology and literacy in early childhood educational settings: A review of the research. *Journal of Early Childhood Literacy, 10*(3), 247–270.

Calkins, L. M. (1994). *The art of teaching writing*. Portsmouth, NH: Heinemann.

Calvert, S., Rideout, V., Woodard, J., Barr, R., & Strouse, G. (2005). Age, ethnicity and socioeconomic patterns in early computer use: A national survey. *American Behavioral Scientist, 48*(5), 590–607.

Chen, J. Q., & Chang, C. (2006). Using computers in early childhood classrooms: Teachers' attitudes, skills, and practices. *Journal of Early Childhood Research, 4*(2), 169–188.

Clay, M. (1975). *What did I write?* Portsmouth, NH: Heinemann.

Couse, L. J., & Chen, D. W. (2010). A tablet computer for young children?: Exploring its viability for early childhood education. *Journal of Research on Technology in Education, 43*(1), 75–98.

Cunningham, P., & Allington, D. (1998). *Classrooms that work*. Reading, MA: Addison-Wesley.

de Jong, M., & Bus, A. (2002). Quality of book-reading matters for emergent readers: An experiment with the same book in a regular or electronic format. *Journal of Educational Psychology, 94*(1), 145–155.

Doty, D. E., Popplewell, S. R., & Byers, G. O. (2001). Interactive CD-ROM storybooks and young readers' reading comprehension. *Journal of Research on Computing in Education, 33*(4), 374–384.

Edyburn, D. L. (2007). Technology enhanced reading performance: Defining a research agenda. *Reading Research Quarterly, 42*(1), 146–152.

Ehri, L. C., & Nunes, S. R. (2002). *The role of phonemic awareness in learning to read: What research has to say about reading instruction*. Newark, DE: International Reading Association.

Frazel, M. (2010). *Digital storytelling: Guide for educators*. Eugene, OR: International Society for Technology in Education.

Fuhler, C. (2010). Using primary-source documents and digital storytelling as a catalyst for writing historical fiction in the fourth grade. In B. Moss & D. Lapp (Eds.), *Teaching new literacies in grades K–3: Resources for 21st-century classrooms* (pp. 134–148). New York: Guilford Press

Glaubke, C. (2007). *The effects of interactive media and preschoolers' learning: A review of the research and recommendations for the future*. Oakland, CA: Children Now.

Gregory, G. H., & Chapman, C. (2006). *Differentiated instructional strategies: One size doesn't fit all* (2nd ed.). Thousand Oaks, CA: Corwin Press.

Grimshaw, S., Dungworth, N., McKnight, C., & Morris, A. (2001). Electronic books: Children's reading and comprehension. *British Journal of Educational Technology, 38*(4), 583–599.

Hicks, T. (2009). *The digital writing workshop.* Portsmouth, NH: Heinemann.

Hodgson, K. (2009). Digital picture books: From flatland to multimedia. In A. Herrington, K. Hodgson, & C. Moran (Eds.), *Teaching the new writing: Technology, change and assessment in the 21st century classroom* (pp. 55–74). New York: National Writing Project/Teachers College.

International Society for Technology in Education. (2007). National Educational Technology Standards for Students. Retrieved from *www.iste.org/standards/nets-for-students/nets-student-standards-2007.*

Isenberg, J., & Quisenberry, N. (2002). Play: Essential for all children (A position paper of the Association for Childhood Education International). *Childhood Education, 79*(1), 33–39.

Johnson, G., Bruner, G., & Kumar, A. (2006). Interactivity and its facets revisited. *Journal of Advertising, 35*(4), 35–52.

Kang, T. P., Chen, J., & Kidd, T. (2009). The trend of Web 1.0, Web 2.0, Web 3.0 and beyond. In T. Kidd & I. Chen (Eds.), *Wired for learning: An educator's guide to Web 2.0* (pp. 3–19). Charlotte, NC: Information Age.

Kist, W., Doyle, K., Hayes, J., Horwitz, J., & Kuzior, J. T. (2010). Web 2.0 in the elementary classroom: Portraits of possibilities. *Language Arts, 88*(1), 62–68.

Labbo, L., & Kuhn, M. (2000). Weaving chains of affect and cognition: A young child's understanding of CD-ROM talking books. *Journal of Literacy Research, 32*(2), 187–210.

Labbo, L., Phillips, M., & Murray, B. (1995–1996). "Writing to read": From inheritance to innovation and invitation. *The Reading Teacher, 49*, 314–321.

Labbo, L. D. (1996). A semiotic analysis of young children's symbol making in a classroom computer center. *Reading Research Quarterly, 31*(4), 356–385.

Labbo, L. D. (2000). 12 things young children can do with a talking book in a classroom computer center. *The Reading Teacher, 53*(7), 542–546.

Labbo, L. D., Eakle, A. J., & Montero, K. M. (2002). Digital language experience approach (D-LEA): Using digital photographs and creativity software as LEA innovation. *Reading Online: Electronic Journal of the International Reading Association.* Retrieved from *www.readingonline.org/default.asp.*

Labbo, L. D., Love, M. S., & Ryan, T. (2007). A vocabulary flood: Making words "sticky" with computer-response activities. *The Reading Teacher, 60*(6), 582–588.

Lankshear, C., & Knobel, M. (2003). *New literacies: Changing knowledge and classroom learning.* Buckingham, UK: Open University Press.

Lapp, D., Shea, A., & Wolsey, T. D. (2011). Blogging and audience awareness. *Journal of Education, 191*(1), 33–44.

Leu, D., Castek, J., Coiro, J., Gort, M., Henry, L., & Lima, C. (2005). Developing new literacies among multilingual learners in the elementary grades. Retrieved from *www.newliteracies.uconn.edu/pub_files/developing_new_literacies_among_multicultural.pdf.*

Lewis, H. (2000). Exploring the effects of talking book software in U.K. primary classrooms. *Journal of Research in Reading, 23*(12), 149–157.

Lotherington, H., Holland, M., Sotoudeh, S., & Zentena, M. (2008). Project-based community language learning: Three narratives of multilingual story-telling in early childhood education. *Canadian Modern Language Review, 65*(1), 125–145.

MacArthur Foundation Report. (2009). Exploring digital media and learning. Retrieved from *www.macfound.org/atf/cf/%7bb0386ce3-8b29-4162-8098-e466fb856794%7d/dml_buff.pdf.*

Marsh, J. (2006). Emergent media literacy: Digital animation in early childhood. *Language and Education, 20*(6), 493–506.

Mavers, D. (2007). Semiotic resourcefulness: A young child's email exchange as design. *Journal of Early Childhood Literacy, 7*(2), 155–176.

Miller, L. (2010). *Make me a story: Teaching writing through digital storytelling.* Portland, ME: Stenhouse.

Mills, K. (2011). "I'm making it different to the book": Transmediation in young children's multimodal and digital texts. *Australasian Journal of Early Childhood, 36*(3), 56–65.

Moll, L. C., & Greenberg, J. M. (1990). Creating zones of possibilities: Combining social constructs for instruction. In L. C. Moll (Ed.), *Vygotsky and education: Instructional implications and applications of sociohistorical psychology* (pp. 319–348). New York: Cambridge University Press.

National Council of Teachers of English (NCTE). (2008). 21st century curriculum and assessment framework. Retrieved from *www.ncte.org/positions/statements/21stcentframework.*

National Council of Teachers of English/International Reading Association (NCTE/IRA). (1996). *Standards for the English Language Arts.* Newark, DE/Urbana, IL: Authors.

National Governors Association Center for Best Practices & Council of Chief State School Officers. (2010). Common Core State Standards. Washington, DC: Author. Retrieved from *www.corestandards.org/assets/ccssi_ela%20standards.pdf.*

National Reading Panel. (2000). Report of the National Reading Panel: Teaching children to read. Retrieved from *www.nichd.nih.gov/publications/nrp/smallbook.cfm.*

National Writing Project. (2008). Profiles in practice: Digital storytelling with teacher consultants for the National Writing Project: Kevin Hodgson. Retrieved from *http://pearsonfoundation.org/NWP/ProfilesInPractice/2008/kevin-hodgson/related-links.html.*

National Writing Project. (2010). *Because digital writing matters: Improving writing in online and multimedia environments.* San Francisco: Jossey-Bass.

Neary, L. (2012). Children's book apps: A new world of learning. Retrieved from *www.npr.org/2011/03/28/134663712/childrens-book-apps-a-new-world-of-learning.*

Nielsen Report. (2012). American families see tablets as playmate, teacher, and babysitter. Retrieved from *http://blog.nielsen.com/nielsenwire/online_mobile/american-families-see-tablets-as-playmate-teacher-and-babysitter.*

Ohler, J. (2008). *Digital storytelling in the classroom: New media pathways to literacy, learning and creativity.* Thousand Oaks, CA: Corwin Press.

Pearman, C. (2008). Independent reading of CD-ROM storybooks: Measuring comprehension with oral retellings. *Reading Teacher, 61*(8), 594–602.

Plowman, L., & Stephen, C. (2003). A "benign addition"?: Research on ICT and pre-school children. *Journal of Computer Assisted Learning, 19*(2), 149–164.

Prensky, M. (2001). Digital natives, digital immigrants, part 2: Do they really think differently? *On the Horizon, 9*(6), 1–6. Retrieved from *www.twitchspeed.com/site/prensky%20-%20digital%20natives,%20digital%20immigrants%20-%20part2.htm.*

Reinking, D., Labbo, L. D., & McKenna, M. C. (2000). From assimilation to accommodation: A developmental framework for integrating digital technologies into literacy research and instruction. *Journal of Reading Research, 23*, 110–122.

Revelle, G. (2009). Mobile technologies in support of young children's learning. In A. Druin (Ed.), *Mobile technology for children: Designing for interaction and learning* (pp. 265–284). Burlington, MA: Morgan Kauffmann.

Roschelle, J. M., Pea, R. D., Hoadley, C. M., Gordin, D. N., & Means, B. M. (2000). Changing how and what children learn in school with computer-based technology. *Children and Computer Technology, 10*(2), 76–101.

Roskos, K., Brueck, J., & Widman, S. (2009). Investigating analytic tools for e-book design in early literacy learning. *Journal of Interactive Online Learning, 8*(3), 218–240.

Rowe, D. (1998). The literate potentials of book-related dramatic play. *Reading Research Quarterly, 33*(1), 10–35.

Salonius-Pasternak, D. E., & Gelfond, H. S. (2005). The next level of research on electronic play:

Potential benefits and contextual influences for children and adolescents. *Human Technology: An Interdisciplinary Journal on Humans in ICT Environments, 1*(1), 5–22.

Segers, E., Takke, L., & Verhoeven, L. (2004). Teacher-mediated versus computer-mediated storybook reading to children in native and multicultural kindergarten classrooms. *School Effectiveness and School Improvement, 15*, 215–226.

Shuler, C. (2009). *Pockets of potential: Using mobile technologies to promote children's learning.* New York: Joan Ganz Cooney Center at Sesame Workshop.

Stevens, R. R., & Penuel, W. R. (2010, October). *Studying and fostering learning through joint media engagement.* Paper presented at the Principal Investigators Meeting of the National Science Foundation's Science of Learning Centers, Arlington, VA.

Takeuchi, L., & Stevens, R. (2011). *The new coviewing: Designing for learning through joint media engagement.* New York: Joan Ganz Cooney Center at Sesame Workshop and LIFE Center.

Teale, W. H., & Gambrell, L. B. (2007). Raising urban students' literacy achievement by engaging in authentic, challenging work. *The Reading Teacher, 60*(8), 728–739.

Temple, C., Martinez, M., & Yokata, J. (2011). *Children's books in children's hands: An introduction to their literature* (4th ed.). Boston, MA: Pearson.

Van Horn, L. (2008). *Reading photographs to write with meaning and purpose: Grades 4–12.* Newark DE: International Reading Association.

Van Kleeck, A. (2008). *Research on book-sharing: Another critical look.* Mahwah, NJ: Erlbaum.

Verenikina, I., Herrington, J., Peterson, R., & Mantei, J. (2010). Computers and play in early childhood: Affordances and limitations. *Journal of Interactive Learning Research, 21*(1), 139–159.

Verenikina, I., & Kervin, L. (2011, October). iPads, digital play and pre-schoolers. *He Kupu: The Word, 2*(5), 4–19. Retrieved from *www.hekupu.ac.nz/journal%20files/issue5%20october%202011/ipads%20digital%20play%20and%20preschoolers.pdf.*

Vygotsky, L. S. (1967). Play and its role in the mental development of the child. *Soviet Psychology, 5*(3), 6–18.

Vygotsky, L. S. (1978). *Mind in society: The development of higher psychological processes* (M. Cole, V. John-Steiner, S. Scribner, & E. Souberman, Eds.). Cambridge, MA: Harvard University Press.

Wohlwend, K. (2009). Early adopters: Playing new literacies and pretending new technologies in print-centric classrooms. *Journal of Early Childhood Literacy, 9*(2), 117–140.

Yancey, K. (2009, February). *Writing in the 21st century: A report from the National Council of Teachers of English.* Urbana, IL: National Council of Teachers of English.

CHAPTER 12

MOTIVATING AND ENGAGING CHILDREN IN EARLY CHILDHOOD SETTINGS

M. DEANNA RAMEY
LINDA B. GAMBRELL

A ll children are born with an innate curiosity to learn about their world. The children in the following vignette are in the midst of a complex block construction project, and are determined to solve a problem they encounter while building.

Center time in Mrs. Logan's preschool class is a 90-minute period of exploration in the dozen centers around the room. This morning, classmates Evy and Connor are headed straight to the block area. The day before, they had started construction on a group of elaborate structures for their toy forest animals and were anxious to add to their buildings. Central to their plan was building a bridge to connect the animal school with the animal palace, both of which are elevated. Evy and Connor notice that the longest block available will not connect the span between the structures. Undeterred, the children try to solve their dilemma in a variety of ways, thinking aloud as they come up with new bridges to test. Evy continues to work toward a solution even when two of her friends invite her to join them in one of her favorite centers, the dramatic play area. After 25 minutes of trial and error Evy and Connor succeed, and a parade of forest animals marches back and forth between the palace and school on a sturdy new bridge. Excitedly, Evy asks Mrs. Logan to come and see their animal city. Mrs. Logan smiles broadly as Evy and Connor enthusiastically explain what they had to do to build the bridge.

Evy and Connor's attention and persistence in solving the task at hand was for them a complex problem, reflecting their engagement in the chosen activity. They were genuinely interested in building a bridge for their animals and intended to do just that. Evy and Connor were intrinsically motivated to improve their work. But from where does this motivation and earnest engagement in discovery arise, and how can educators and caregivers of young children nurture this natural inclination for learning in all children?

In this chapter, we examine the factors associated with motivation. Next, we discuss the ways in which motivation and engagement are operationalized in early childhood research, and address ways both motivation and engagement are fostered and inhibited in young children. Last, we describe strategies that teachers of young children can implement to encourage and support their students in becoming motivated and engaged learners.

WHAT RESEARCH SAYS ABOUT MOTIVATION

Healthy children are born into the world as engaged learners—naturally curious, persistent, resilient and intrinsically motivated to master their environment. Even as infants, children act on their surroundings not for rewards or other external inducements but because of interest and pleasure, reasons that emanate from self. Thus, children are born wired with a desire to learn. Connell (1990) suggests that individuals engage in an appraisal of self in relation to their activity, the motivational component of what he terms the *self-system processes.*

Key to motivation and engagement within the self-system processes are three essential psychological needs: competence, autonomy, and relatedness. Valeski and Stipek (2001), speaking specifically about young children, draw on the work of Connell (1990) and Connell and Wellborn (1991), citing theory and research that suggest children are motivated to engage enthusiastically in learning behaviors when essential psychological needs are met (Connell, 1990; Connell & Welborn, 1991; Valeski & Stipek, 2001). The children in Figure 12.1 exemplify this motivation to learn. Furthermore, the core needs of competence, autonomy, and relatedness are the central components of self-determination theory for motivation proposed by Deci and Ryan (1985). These needs have different weights and values, and are met in different ways depending on the developmental stage of an individual and the "cultural enterprise" in which that individual is engaged (Connell, 1990). This is especially true when considering early childhood, a period of rapid growth and development in which children transition from complete dependency on others to increasing competence and autonomy. It is also a time when influential relationships in a child's life expand from parents and family to include caretakers, teachers, and peers.

Competence has been identified as a fundamental human need, and in the context of motivation, there is a particular emphasis on the importance of experiencing competent interactions with one's environment (Connell, 1990; Deci, 1975). If an individual is able to achieve positive outcomes successfully while avoiding negative ones, the need for

FIGURE 12.1. These preschoolers are involved in a long-term project about South American rainforests. They are highly engaged in the study and, during center time, have chosen to represent the plants and animals they are learning about through their drawing and writing.

competence is fulfilled. Deci, Vallerand, Pelletier, and Ryan (1991) broaden the notion of competence to include dimensions beyond the achievement of outcomes. In their view, competence also involves understanding how to identify outcomes, both internal and external, and having the capability to achieve them. For very young children, actual competence may not be as important as perceived competence. While all children may have a need to feel competent, the nature of the task and the relationship between task and child determine how significant competence is as a motivational influence.

Autonomy is another influential need in human motivation and engagement. Connell (1990) defines *autonomy* as "the experience of choice in the initiation, maintenance, and regulation of behavior, and the experience of connectedness between one's actions and personal goals and values" (pp. 62–63). In other words, it is the child's sense that he or she has ownership of the decision to engage or not engage in a particular behavior. Autonomy is also sometimes conceptualized as self-determination (Deci et al., 1991), a crucial component of motivated actions versus those activities in which an individual is compelled to participate. In self-determination theory, the extent to which a behavior is self-determined, as measured by an individual's perceived locus of control, dictates how closely external motivation approximates intrinsic motivation (Ryan & Deci, 2000). In the case of young children, the nature and meaning of autonomy evolves as children gain a growing sense of separateness between themselves and their parents and caretakers (Carlton & Winsler, 1998).

Last, there is the fundamental need for relatedness. Deci and his colleagues (1991) suggest that relatedness "involves developing secure and satisfying connections with others in one's social milieu" (p. 327). Relatedness is also considered to be an intrapersonal construct affiliated with self-esteem. Connell (1990), for example, suggests that feeling related, in addition to signifying a secure attachment to the social environment, means that an individual considers him- or herself "worthy and capable of love" (p. 63). In other words, in addition to having a significant connection with others, or another in one's surroundings, a person who has fulfilled the need of relatedness also possesses high self-esteem. Furthermore, Furrer and Skinner (2003) found relatedness to be a key factor in children's motivation and achievement in school. Again, this core need will look very different for an infant or toddler in whom appropriate relatedness is manifested by a secure attachment with their caregiver, as compared to a second grader who experiences relatedness because of both a warm relationship with their teacher and a sense of belonging within the classroom community.

Motivation and Engagement in Early Childhood Settings

Motivation and engagement are similar constructs; however, there are basic and important differences between the two. *Motivation to learn* can be defined as the likelihood of choosing to engage in learning tasks and activities (Gambrell, 2009, 2011; Guthrie & Wigfield, 2000). Therefore, motivation represents the internal, unobservable drive to learn. *Engagement* refers to observable behaviors associated with motivation to learn, such as sustained engagement in a task.

The engagement perspective is linked to motivation and has strong implications for practice (Guthrie & Humenick, 2004; Guthrie & Wigfield, 2000; Tracey & Morrow, 2006). This perspective articulates the differences between "engaged" and "disengaged" learners, and focuses on the characteristics of the motivated or engaged learner. In keeping with this perspective, engaged learners are intrinsically motivated to achieve a variety of personal goals and are strategic in their behaviors, knowledgeable in their construction of new understandings, and socially interactive about their learning. Therefore, promoting intrinsic motivation should be a high priority across all stages of development. In the following section, we describe how motivation and engagement are operationalized with respect to developmental stages for infants, toddlers, preschoolers, kindergartners, and primary-grade children.

Motivation and Engagement for Infants

During infancy, though their repertoires of behaviors may be limited, babies endeavor to control their environment. They are intrinsically motivated to explore their surroundings, to seek out challenges, and to develop competence in their ability to impact their environment. They are engaged, not out of compliance or promise of reward, but because they are curious and find pleasure in such behavior. Seeing the results of their actions encourages continued engagement, and consequently supports intrinsic motivation (Carlton & Winsler, 1998). For an infant, motivation of this nature is largely regarded as *mastery motivation*, which, according to Morgan, Harmon, and Maslin-Cole (1990), involves one's attempt independently to master a skill or task of moderate challenge with focus and persistence. Mastery motivation is an expression of active participation rather than passive observation (Barrett & Morgan, 1995). In his classic article, White (1959) characterized this drive for mastery as an intrinsic competence motive, born of human need to improve adaptively upon managing one's environment.

In the course of a year or so, infants make tremendous gains in their range of skills, progressing, for example, from the uncoordinated movement of limbs to rolling, crawling, cruising, then walking. It is the innate motivation for mastery that spurs the infant to engage the muscles, marshal the coordination, and exert the mental energy needed to propel this metamorphosis. Social relationships also play a large part in an infant's motivation. Babies' exploratory behaviors are supported and scaffolded by parents and caregivers. Research suggests that infants who enjoy secure relationships with caregivers are most like likely to exhibit patterns of engagement rather than patterns of disaffection (Ainsworth, 1979; Connell, 1990). Research also suggests that one's motivational orientation and subsequent disposition for engagement or disaffection is established at an early age (Carlton & Winsler, 1998). Furthermore, early mastery motivational patterns are linked to later cognitive competence (Barrett & Morgan, 1995). Though infants are naturally inclined to learn the world and the ways in which the actions they control affect themselves and their surroundings, and individual dispositions toward learning may vary from child to child, parents and caregivers can play an instrumental role in fixing positive orientations toward mastery motivation and patterns of engagement in very young children.

Motivation and Engagement for Toddlers

The world expands dramatically for the infant, who, after a bit of growth and much persistence, becomes a mobile toddler. Surroundings are viewed from new perspectives as toddlers spend more time on their feet walking, running, and climbing. Encountering a widening field of exploration, toddlers impact their environment in more significant ways than they were able to as infants as they continue to add to their repertoires of physical and cognitive skills. Consistent with an increase in cognitive capacity, Barrett and Morgan (1985) suggest that toddlers are developing the ability to make choices about which actions they will employ to achieve a particular goal. For the most part, motivation for toddlers is still very much intrinsic and focused on mastery. Carlton and Winsler (1998) note that in the case of toddlers, success is not influenced by extrinsic factors because caregivers are likely to praise all efforts regardless of their outcome. At this stage of development, relatedness continues to be fundamental to the support of positive motivation and engagement behaviors.

Although toddlers benefit from close relationships with parents and significant caregivers, and are reliant on these adults as a secure base from which to explore, there is a growing awareness by toddlers of separateness between themselves and their caregivers (Sroufe, 1990). This awareness of self prompts within the toddler a need to individuate (Connell, 1990). Autonomy and self-direction therefore begin to play a greater role in impacting the intrinsic motivation of children in this age group. This is supported by Carlton and Winsler's (1998) assertion that toddlers tend to engage in exploratory behaviors leading to mastery of a task when there is minimal interference in such exploration by parents and caregivers.

Motivation and Engagement for Preschoolers

Ruff and Rothbart (1996) suggest that during the preschool years children are involved in more self-directed, self-planned activity. At this stage, children's attention, once largely focused by parent- or teacher-driven choices, becomes increasingly self-determined. Such a shift may help to explain a preschooler's newfound ability to engage in activities requiring a series of planned actions in order to achieve a desired goal (Carlton & Winsler, 1998). As they approach the age of 3, preschoolers, now more verbal, often demonstrate their engagement in a task or activity through their private speech, or *self-talk*. Such private speech, which helps to scaffold preschoolers' behavior and guide their actions when encountering a challenging task (Berk & Winsler, 1995), also enables children to assume the responsibility of self-regulation once held by parents and caregivers (Carlton & Winsler, 1998). Feelings of competence are also on the rise as newly self-regulated preschoolers begin to feel an expanded sense of autonomy and control over their surroundings. Though more independent than they were as toddlers, warm relationships with parents and caregivers remain important in supporting the motivation and engagement for learning among preschoolers.

Engagement in activities stemming from mastery motivation is still present in preschoolers, particularly when they are permitted free exploration and offered open-ended activities. Frequently, however, preschool-age children, having a greater likelihood of being in school, child care, or other group settings, are asked to perform tasks or activities they do not necessarily find intrinsically motivating. In such situations, promoting autonomy-oriented extrinsic motivation may approximate intrinsic motivation. Ryan and Deci (2000) conceptualized these more autonomous forms of extrinsic motivation as *identified* and *integrated regulation*. Defined by *perceived locus of causality* (the degree to which control is perceived to be external or internal) and *relevant regulatory processes*, children may engage in the mastery motivation behaviors typical of intrinsic motivation if they feel they have at least some control over the action, and the action is valued or, even better, fully assimilated.

Motivation and Engagement for Children in Kindergarten and Primary Grades

The kindergarten and primary grades are academic enterprises. Many consider kindergarten to be the beginning of a child's formal education. As such, expectations for what children should be learning are evidenced by individual state standards, and more recently, the Common Core State Standards (National Governors Association Center for

Best Practices & Council of Chief State School Officers, 2010). Generally, children in kindergarten have less autonomy than they did as preschoolers, and this is even truer for children in the primary grades. For the most part, learning activities in these grades are required and driven primarily by teachers.

Primary school students continue to exhibit some behaviors of mastery motivation similar to preschoolers; however, intrinsically motivated learning behavior tends to wane as children are presented with achievement or "performance goals" for which they may lack an innate interest. Ames (1992) suggests that in the case of mastery goals, students are motivated to learn new skills or improve ability as measured by their own internal standard of evaluation. In contrast, the outcomes of performance goals focus on students' skills level and feelings of self-worth; success is therefore measured by an individual's ability to outperform peers or complete a task with little effort. Bodrova and Leong (2007) contend that "successful achievement is crucial for the development of motivation" (p. 172). Feelings of competence, if not actual competence, therefore play an increased role in determining the quality of motivation and engagement for learning. Extrinsic rewards (or punishment) given to induce achievement "are generally ineffective for sustaining much excitement and passion for learning over the long haul" (Ryan & Powelson, 1991, p. 50). Mastery goals are preferred because such a motivation orientation increases the quality of learning engagement (Ames, 1992), perhaps suggesting a more sustainable enthusiasm for learning. As in the case of preschoolers, a mastery orientation might be obtained if students perceive autonomous regulation (Ryan & Deci, 2000). Relatedness, as in the younger years, is of great importance to motivation and engagement, and is expanded beyond parents and teachers to include peers. Feeling strongly connected to the classroom community and internalizing the values of the community encourage engagement in the classroom enterprise and strengthen motivation (Connell, 1990).

RESEARCH INTO PRACTICE

Children are born with an intrinsic desire to learn and to engage in exploratory and mastery activities and behaviors that bring pleasure, promote healthy growth and development, and in turn expand cognitive abilities. There is consistency in the research regarding the necessity to fulfill the fundamental needs of competence, autonomy, and relatedness in order to support motivation. However, because of developmental and cognitive changes, and ever-widening demands on behavior from infancy to school age, the essence, impact value, and instrumentality of these needs are not static. In order to create engaging learning environments for children, it is important for caregivers and teachers to implement strategies that support these key psychological needs, while recognizing the changing nature of the interaction of these needs. With this in mind, those who work with young children are in an optimal position to foster the intrinsic motivational orientations of young children and promote autonomous extrinsic motivation, both of which are most likely to result in more active and enthusiastic engagement in learning.

In the following section, we describe four research-based instructional elements that can be implemented in early childhood settings to promote motivation and engagement in learning: creating a child-centered environment; scaffolding; using external motivators appropriately and effectively; and promoting warm relationships. In addition, each section concludes with a brief checklist to stimulate reflection and discussion about how these instructional elements support and nurture young children's motivation and engagement in learning.

Creating a Child-Centered Environment

Young children are more likely to have feelings of competence and autonomy, thereby engaging in behaviors that promote strong and lasting learning, when the learning environment is child-centered. In a child-centered setting children have some say about the activities they do, the length of time they have to do them, and the way the activities are evaluated. This is not to say that the children make every decision about what occurs in the class or that there are no expectations or boundaries for behavior. Ideally, there is balance between structure and freedom of choice, as well as consideration of developmentally appropriate practices relevant to the age of the children in the environment. Berk and Winsler (1995), for example, suggest that preschool classrooms in which children enjoy independence, while being supported by responsive adults in a moderately structured environment, may be an exemplar for fostering feelings of competence and intrinsic motivation.

Children in a child-centered environment are more responsible for making decisions about their actions and therefore have greater feelings of autonomy. Stipek, Feiler, Daniels, and Milburn (1995) found that kindergartners and first graders in child-centered programs scored higher than children from didactic programs in most measures of motivation. Additionally, confirming findings in earlier studies, they added the following:

> In educational contexts that allowed children considerable freedom to initiate tasks and complete them without pressure to conform to a particular model or get right answers, children selected more challenging tasks, were less dependent on an adult for approval, and evidenced more pride in their accomplishments. (p. 220)

These benefits translate into increased competence and greater autonomous regulation, both of which support motivation. Research on slightly older children (fourth through sixth grade) demonstrated that autonomy-supportive classrooms are more associated with students' stronger orientation for mastery motivation and greater ability to achieve learning goals than are classrooms that rely heavily on teacher control (Ryan & Grolnick, 1986).

Checklist for Child-Centered Classroom

- Are meaningful choices of activities available?
- Do materials and activities provide challenge and promote curiosity?
- Are children given an appropriate amount of time to explore activities and interact with materials, thereby promoting persistence and flexibility in problem solving?
- To the extent possible, given the child's age and development, are learning goals emphasized more than performance or achievement goals?

Scaffolding

Scaffolding is a now familiar term in education. Wood, Bruner, and Ross (1976) suggest that scaffolding is "a process that enables a child or novice to solve a problem, carry out a task or achieve a goal which would be beyond his unassisted effort" (p. 90). With scaffolding, an adult or more capable other assumes control of the features of a task that a child is not yet competent to do, thus enabling the child to focus on aspects of the task in which he or she is competent. Gradually, expert support is withdrawn, until the child can perform the task or solve the problem independently. Scaffolding is important in promoting motivation and engagement in young children because it fosters a sense of competence and supports the development of autonomy needed for self-determined behavior.

Scaffolding may take many forms as children move from infanthood to grade school. For instance, in the case of a young baby wanting to roll from her back to her stomach, a parent may serve as a guide, mimicking the motion needed to make the transition. For a toddler attempting to stack a pile of blocks, a caregiver might help to position them so that they stay balanced as the tower grows. A preschool child might need to be scaffolded by a teacher as he endeavors to solve a new jigsaw puzzle. A parent assisting a young child learning to ride a bike is a classic example of scaffolding. While the child concentrates on pedaling and steering, the parent scaffolds the child's effort to ride by providing the balance and initial momentum needed to propel the bike forward. After some practice, the support of the parent is no longer needed and the child, now competent and autonomous, rides off on her own.

A form of scaffolding that is particularly helpful when children become verbal is *private speech*. Private speech, also called *self-talk*, is crucial to the development of children's self-regulation (Carlton & Winsler, 1998). In private speech children talk themselves through difficult situations or complicated problems. Similar to the way that adults scaffold children through "joint problem solving," private speech enables children to scaffold their own behavior (Winsler, Diaz, & Montero, 1997). Though this type of scaffolding actually comes from within the children themselves, teachers and caregivers can support this internal scaffolding by modeling private speech and encouraging children to use it.

Checklist for Scaffolding
- Has the child been provided an appropriate amount of support for the task?
- Has support been gradually withdrawn until the child has complete control of the activity?
- Has private speech been modeled and encouraged in students as a form of self-scaffolding?

Using External Motivators Appropriately and Effectively

Commencing in first grade, if not kindergarten, children transition into more formal school settings and have less choice regarding their learning. Goals and desired behaviors, to a large extent, are decided for them. Though some of the activities children are asked or required to do may have intrinsic interest for them, it is likely that participation in such activities is more extrinsically driven. In order to promote real engagement in learning activities rather than mere compliance, teachers and caregivers can encourage motivation that is autonomously regulated.

The use of rewards as an external motivator has been hotly debated. It had been assumed for years that rewarding behavior that is naturally, intrinsically motivating undermines such intrinsic motivation (Deci, 1975). Cameron and Pierce (1994) roundly dispute that, insisting that, except in very specific and avoidable situations, rewarding students has no impact on intrinsic motivation one way or another. Though the argument continues, the dust has somewhat settled, and researchers are finding a middle ground regarding use of rewards to encourage motivation. Two things that may be beneficial for motivating and engaging young children are praise and proximal rewards.

Praise of student achievement is a popular means for motivating and encouraging children. Though it can have detrimental effects if the recipient perceives it as insincere, praise can be an effective tool for fostering intrinsic motivation and encouraging autonomous forms of extrinsic motivation. Brophy (2004) suggests guidelines for using praise as a motivator for student learning. His suggestions include the following: praise should be simple, straightforward, and sincere. Further, students should be praised privately, an indication that the praise is genuine.

Tangible rewards are another external motivator that can be used effectively with young children. Gambrell (1996) theorized a "reward proximity hypothesis," suggesting that rewards that are closely related to the desired task or behavior can promote intrinsic motivation. Research in the area of literacy supports this theory. Marinak and Gambrell (2008) found that in the case of motivation to read the reward of a book supports intrinsic motivation to read. Furthermore, they suggest that "[u]sing literacy-related rewards may increase students' sense of personal competence and signals task mastery, thereby increasing the likelihood of sustained reading engagement" (p. 23). It therefore follows that use of rewards proximal to the activity that children are asked to do may increase their motivational orientation for that activity.

Checklist for Use of External Motivators

- Have external motivators been used judiciously?
- Have the chosen external motivators fostered intrinsic motivation or encouraged autonomously regulated forms of extrinsic motivation rather than those that simply control behavior or induce compliance?
- Has praise, when used as a motivator, been sincere, specific, and sufficient?
- Have tangible rewards been used sparingly, and are they closely related to the desired behavior or task?

Promoting Warm Relationships

As discussed earlier, relatedness is an essential psychological need related to motivation and engagement. Though it is always important, the meaning of relatedness shifts as children progress through different stages of development. Few would dispute that infants and toddlers need to feel secure in their relationships with parents and caregivers for optimal development. Reinforcement of babies' exploratory actions and behaviors by close and caring adults encourages motivation for, and engagement in, further learning activities. Though children grow and mature as they become more independent, the need for warm, caring relationships with caregivers and teachers remains important. Valeski and Stipek (2001) state that "close supportive relationships with the teacher help children to feel socially connected, and are presumed to promote academic engagement" (p. 1198). Furthermore, they assert that a comfortable relationship with a teacher may be even more critical given that young children are more accustomed to viewing adults as caregivers than as academic instructors.

Another way of encouraging motivation and engagement of young learners is to promote and support warm peer relations. As children approach school age their needs regarding relatedness shift and expand (Connell, 1990). One way this is manifested is in the growing importance of positive peer relationships. In their study of peer interactions, Coolahan, Fantuzzo, Mendez, and McDermott (2000) found that children who were involved in interactive play ventures showed active engagement in learning activities in the classroom. These children also "displayed higher levels of competence, motivation, persistence, and a positive attitude toward learning than did children who were less engaged in peer play" (p. 462). Furthermore, children who showed a tendency for disconnected peer play were viewed by their teachers as passive and lacking motivation. It follows then that fostering positive relationships among children can promote motivation and encourage engagement in learning.

Checklist for Promoting Warm Relationships
- Are you cognizant of your dual role as teacher and nurturer?
- Do you recognize that the need for close and warm relationships continues as young children grow older?
- Have you supported strong, positive peer relationships?

REFLECTIONS AND NEW DIRECTIONS

Good teaching practices should encourage motivation and inspire engagement to learn. It is the role of the teacher or caregiver to nurture in each child that innate curiosity, interest, and intent to act that we conceptualize as motivation. All children are born with an intrinsic motivation to master their world. Ideally, children would sustain this natural propensity to engage in activities that facilitate learning throughout their lives. We must consider, however, that as children grow, they are subject to an ever-widening world with increasing external demands.

While intrinsic motivation and mastery goals can be nurtured, it is not realistic given the demands of formal education to think that children, even young children, will have intrinsic motivation for everything they will be asked to do. Extrinsic motivation is not necessarily in opposition to intrinsic motivation, which in general is more highly valued. It is possible to promote real and long-lasting engagement in learning activities, even when children are extrinsically motivated, assuming that teachers and caregivers avoid implementing practices that are simply meant to control behavior or induce compliance with a demand. If the goal is for young children to be engaged learners, teachers and caregivers can use the same strategies that support innate intrinsic motivational orientations to foster more internally regulated extrinsic motivation. Creating environments and implementing practices that encourage positive motivation orientations for our youngest children sets the stage for engagement in learning activities well into the future.

PROFESSIONAL DEVELOPMENT ACTIVITIES

- In early childhood the setting, or learning environment, plays an important role in the development of children's intrinsic motivation and engagement. Research suggests that teachers' and caregivers' efforts should be deliberate, to nurture children's motivation to learn. What activities or learning centers in your classroom are designed to increase students' motivation and engagement in learning? What are the features of these activities or centers that promote motivation and engagement? Consider ways you design your early childhood setting or classroom environment to support and increase students' motivation to learn?

- A checklist appears at the end of the sections in this chapter on creating a child-centered environment, scaffolding, using external motivators appropriately and effectively, and promoting warm relationships. Use the checklist in your own classroom as a springboard for reflecting on how your classroom promotes a learning environment that nurtures and supports the development of motivated and engaged learners.

■ Start a relationship log for your class. Take some time to appraise your relationship with each of your students. Once a month, revisit your log and make a note about ways in which these relationships have grown or changed. You will likely find that you are connecting with most of your students, but perhaps there is there one that you realize you tend to avoid, or another who is just "off your radar." Borrowing from a popular confidence-boosting strategy, try to "fake it till you make it." Make an effort to embrace those hard-to-love children as if you adore them, even if the feelings are not there at first. While this may seem insincere, after a while, as these children begin responding to your efforts, the positive feeling you may have been fudging at first may become genuine.

REFERENCES

Ainsworth, M. M. S. (1979). Infant–mother attachment. *American Psychologist, 34*(10), 932–937.

Ames, C. C. (1992). Classrooms: Goals, structures, and student motivation. *Journal of Educational Psychology, 84*(3), 261–271.

Barrett, K. C., & Morgan, G. A. (1995). Continuities and discontinuities in mastery motivation during infancy and toddlerhood: A conceptualization and review. In R.H. MacTurk & G. A. Morgan (Eds.), *Mastery motivation: Conceptual origins and applications* (pp. 57–93). Norwood, NJ: Ablex.

Berk, L. E., & Winsler, A. (1995). *Scaffolding children's learning: Vygotsky and early childhood education.* Washington, DC: National Association for the Education of Young Children.

Bodrova, E., & Leong, D. J. (2007). *Tools of the mind: The Vygotskian approach to early childhood education* (2nd ed.). Upper Saddle River, NJ: Prentice-Hall.

Brophy, J. E. (2004). *Motivating students to learn.* Mahwah, NJ: Erlbaum.

Cameron, J., & Pierce, W. D. (1994). Reinforcement, reward, and intrinsic motivation: A meta-analysis. *Review of Educational Research, 64*(3), 363–423.

Carlton, M. P., & Winsler, A. (1998). Fostering intrinsic motivation in early childhood classrooms. *Early Childhood Education Journal, 25*(3), 159–166.

Connell, J. P. (1990). Context, self, and action: A motivational analysis of self-system processes across the life span. In D. Cicchetti & M. Beeghly (Eds.), *The self in transition* (pp. 61–97). Chicago: University of Chicago Press.

Connell, J. P., & Wellborn, J. G. (1991). Competence, autonomy, and relatedness: A motivational analysis of self-system processes. In M. R. Gunnar & L. A. Sroufe (Eds.), *Self processes and development* (pp. 43–77). Hillsdale, NJ: Erlbaum.

Coolahan, K. C., Fantuzzo, J., Mendez, J., & McDermott, P. (2000). Preschool peer interaction and readiness to learn: Relationships between classroom peer play and learning behaviors and conduct. *Journal of Educational Psychology, 92*, 458–465.

Deci, E. L. (1975). *Intrinsic motivation.* New York: Plenum Press.

Deci, E. L., & Ryan, R. M. (1985). *Intrinsic motivation and self-determination in human behavior.* New York: Plenum Press.

Deci, E. L., Vallerand, R. J., Pelletier, L. G., & Ryan, R. M. (1991). Motivation and education: The self-determination perspective. *Educational Psychologist, 26*(3), 325.

Furrer, C., & Skinner, E. (2003). Sense of relatedness as a factor in children's academic engagement and performance. *Journal of Educational Psychology, 95*, 148–162.

Gambrell, L. B. (1996). Creating classroom cultures that foster reading motivation. *The Reading Teacher, 50*, 14.

Gambrell, L. B. (2009). Creating opportunities to read more so that students read better. In E. H. Hiebert (Ed.), *Read more, read better* (pp. 251–266). New York: Guilford Press.

Gambrell, L. B. (2011). Motivation in the school reading curriculum. In T. Rasinski (Ed.), *Developing reading instruction that works* (pp. 41–65). Bloomington, IN: Solution Tree Press.

Guthrie, J. T., & Humenick, N. M. (2004). Motivating students to read: Evidence for classroom practices that increase motivation and achievement. In P. McCardle & V. Chabra (Eds.), *The voice of evidence in reading research* (pp. 329–354). Baltimore: Brookes.

Guthrie, J. T., & Wigfield, A. (2000). Engagement and motivation in reading. In M. L. Kamil, P. B. Mosenthal, P. D. Pearson, & R. Barr (Eds.), *Reading research handbook* (Vol. III, pp. 403–424). Mahwah, NJ: Erlbaum.

Marinak, B. B. A., & Gambrell, L. B. (2008). Intrinsic motivation and rewards: What sustains young children's engagement with text? *Literacy Research and Instruction, 47*(1), 9–26.

Morgan, G. A., Harmon, R. L., & Maslin-Cole, C. A. (1990). Mastery motivation: Definition and measurement. *Early Education and Development, 1*, 318–339.

National Governors Association Center for Best Practices & the Council of Chief State School Officers. (2010). *Common Core State Standards Initiative: Common Core State Standards for English language arts & literacy in history/social studies, science, and technical subjects.* Washington, DC: Author.

Ruff, H. A., & Rothbart, M. K. (1996). *Attention in early development: Themes and variations.* New York: Oxford University Press.

Ryan, R. M., & Deci, E. L. (2000). Self-determination theory and the facilitation of intrinsic motivation, social development, and well-being. *American Psychologist, 55*(1), 68–78.

Ryan, R. M., & Grolnick, W. (1986). Origins and pawns in the classroom: Self-report and projective assessments of individual differences in children's perceptions. *Journal of Personality and Social Psychology, 50*(3), 550–558.

Ryan, R. M., & Powelson, C. L. (1991). Autonomy and relatedness as fundamental to motivation and education. *Journal of Experimental Education, 60*(1), 49–66.

Sroufe, L. A. (1990). An organizational perspective on self. In D. Cicchetti & M. Beeghly (Eds.), *The self in transition* (pp. 281–307). Chicago: University of Chicago Press.

Stipek, D., Feiler, R., Daniels, D., & Milburn, S. (1995). Effects of different instructional approaches on young children's achievement and motivation. *Child Development, 66*(1), 209–223.

Tracey, D. H., & Morrow, L. M. (2006). *Lenses on reading.* New York: Guilford Press.

Valeski, T. N., & Stipek, D. J. (2001). Young children's feelings about school. *Child Development, 72*(4), 1198–1213.

White, R. R. W. (1959). Motivation reconsidered: The concept of competence. *Psychological Review, 66*(5), 297–333.

Winsler A., Diaz, R., & Montero, I. (1997). The role of private speech in the transition from collaborative to independent task performance in young children. *Early Childhood Research Quarterly, 12*(1), 59.

Wood, D. D., Bruner, J. S., & Ross, G. (1976). The role of tutoring in problem solving. *Journal of Child Psychology and Psychiatry, 17*(2), 89–100.

PART III

EFFECTIVE TEACHING STANDARDS, CURRICULA, AND ASSESSMENT

CHAPTER 13

COMMON CORE STATE STANDARDS
Educating Young Children for Global Excellence

TIMOTHY SHANAHAN

> The Common Core State Standards provide a consistent, clear understanding
> of what students are expected to learn, so teachers and parents have a
> roadmap for what they need to do to help them.
> —STEVE PAINE, president of the Council of Chief State School Officers

Mrs. Jones's second graders were crowded around their desks in groups of three. Each group was examining intently two books they had just read: *The Three Little Pigs* (by Stephen Kellogg) and *The True Story of the Three Little Pigs* (by Jon Sciezka). One child in each group was recording information on a chart that compared the settings, characters, problems, attempts, and outcomes of the two stories. The other boys and girls were looking up information to be used as evidence for the comparisons. Soon they were going to write comparisons of how the pigs and the wolf responded to their problems.

In 2010, the National Governors Association (NGA) and the Council of Chief State School Officers (CCSSO) issued the Common Core State Standards (CCSS), and since that time 45 states, the District of Columbia, and the Virgin Islands have adopted those standards as their learning goals in the English language arts and mathematics. All but Alaska, Texas, Nebraska, and Virginia have signed on; Minnesota adopted the language arts standards but not the math standards. This represents the first time in U.S. history that there has been such a widespread commitment to coordinate curriculum decisions across the states. Almost 90% of teachers and students in the United States will now attempt to reach common educational goals.

Not only do the CCSS represent the most extensive agreement ever concerning what students should know and be able to do, but these new standards also are markedly more demanding than past standards in terms of what they expect students to accomplish (American College Testing [ACT], 2010; Carmichael, Wilson, Porter-Magee, & Martino, 2010). In the past, standards have usually been written from the ground up; that is, kindergarten standards would be written, then first-grade standards would be grafted on top of those, and so on. With the CCSS, the designers began by specifying what they expected of college- and career-ready high school seniors (both from analyses of the demands of colleges and workplaces, and considerations of international standards), then built down from there. Thus, whereas past standards have represented what educators thought they could accomplish, the CCSS describe what students need to learn if they are to leave school with the ability to participate in U.S. society and compete globally by working or continuing their education. Thus, while these standards are more demanding, they represent a more honest representation of student needs. Nevertheless, these standards will likely place greater pressure on school administrators and teachers, and, at least initially, fewer students can be expected to meet these higher goals.

The purpose of this chapter is to examine these new standards with regard to preschool and primary education, particularly with regard to the English language arts standards. Although the math standards receive some attention here, they do not appear to require changes as fundamental as those required by the English language arts standards at primary-grade levels, nor have the primary-grade math standards been especially controversial (Stotsky & Wurman, 2010); most of the public discussion of math has focused on the upper grades. Of course, although nothing can replace the careful reading and diligent study of the standards themselves (*www.corestandards.org*), this chapter should provide some useful explanation and guidance for the implementation of these standards. But first, let's take a brief detour to consider existing early childhood and primary school curricula, the ones the CCSS is replacing. By contextualizing the common core in this way, I hope that educators will have a clearer idea of the implications of these new learning standards.

WHAT RESEARCH SAYS ABOUT THE CCSS

In the United States, each state has been responsible for public instruction within its borders. In other words, unlike in most countries, education in the United States has been treated as largely a local issue (Shanahan, 2010). While this is a fair description of the legal status of U.S. education, which is one reason that universal adoption of common standards is such a big deal, the actual curricula that teachers and children have worked with in the recent past is actually not as fractionated as this implies. The various forces that have shaped education choices in the states are many of the same forces that led to the creation of the CCSS.

During the 1800s, textbook companies were small, local businesses (Venezky, 1987), and there were many alternatives from which to choose. This diversity of choices changed during the 20th century with the rapid growth of school populations, improvement of transportation systems (which allowed books to be shipped easily), and growth of the modern corporation. These changes, and others, transformed textbook publishing from a patchwork, mom-and-pop enterprise to one driven by major international corporations. As competition has heightened, fewer and larger companies have been producing textbooks, a winnowing process that has helped to bring about an unofficial standardization of the K–3 curriculum. With only a handful of textbook alternatives and steep competition among these companies, instructional programs have become more homogenized (Hiebert, Martin, & Menon, 2005).

Of course, not all primary grade teachers use textbooks, and even fewer preschool teachers do, but the market penetration of these programs is sufficiently extensive to suggest that U.S. education is not as disparate as has been presumed (Gamse, Jacob, Horst,

Boulay, & Unlu (2008). Furthermore, the same forces that shaped the design of these core programs have been at work within teacher education, assessment, and other aspects of pedagogy, which means that even schools without textbook programs have gravitated toward analogous instructional goals across the states. Thus, textbooks have provided a base—albeit a partial one—of curricular consistency with regard to reading and mathematics education in the primary grades.

This unification of instruction has been strengthened even more by federal efforts to reform education during the past couple of decades. As a result of educational controversies such as the "reading wars" (Taylor, 1998), the U.S. Congress and the U.S. Department of Education have formed various research review panels over the past 15 years: The National Reading Panel (National Institute of Child Health and Human Development [NICHD], 2000) considered reading instruction in grades K–12; the National Literacy Panel for Language-Minority Children and Youth (August & Shanahan, 2006) explored literacy development and instruction for second-language learners from birth to age 18; the National Early Literacy Panel (2008) looked at beginning literacy learning for preschoolers and kindergartners; and the National Mathematics Advisory Panel (2008) looked at K–12 math education. The purpose of these panels was to determine what research has to say about teaching reading and math, and they have been widely shaping influential public policy and pedagogical practice.

The influence of the National Reading Panel (NRP; NICHD, 2000) has had a particularly profound effect (Swanson & Barlage, 2006). The NRP found that providing phonemic awareness training to young children was beneficial, as was the explicit teaching of phonics, oral reading fluency, vocabulary (word meaning), and comprehension strategies. (The two later panels on literacy—one aimed at preschool literacy instruction and the other at second-language literacy learning—though adding important insights about effective literacy teaching, generally concurred as to the value of the explicit teaching of these NRP-identified components of literacy.) These research findings were not only quickly adopted by commercial programs but also strongly encouraged by the federal government through No Child Left Behind (e.g., Reading First, Early Reading First), including far-reaching policy and legislative changes to Title I and Head Start.

These recent policy efforts have served to reduce further the amount of disparity evident in early education standards across the states. Thus, the adoption of the CCSS is just another step in a long process of standardization and unification aimed at providing all children in the United States a more equal and effective opportunity to learn. (It is also worth noting that the developers of the CCSS were directly influenced by these earlier research reports and policy efforts, which means that the specific changes many schools have adopted during the past decade should be somewhat consistent with the new CCSS.)

One final force for such unification has been previous standards development efforts that have taken place in the states. In 1989, the NGA officially adopted the idea of each state establishing educational standards or goals. During the 1990s, the NGA helped to create Achieve, Inc. (*www.achieve.org*), a nonprofit agency that helps states to set quality standards. Since that time, states that have revised their standards have usually worked with Achieve, using its model standards as a template for their local efforts. Because of this, there has been growing similarity among the state standards, and this is especially true for states that have developed new standards over the past few years.

The point of this brief analysis is to point out that the distance between current practices and the new CCSS is likely to be varied. For teachers who work in states with relatively new state standards or use newer commercial instructional programs, the shift to the common core will likely be less unsettling. However, even states whose current standards and materials are contemporaneous will discover that some sizable shifts need to be accommodated, and as noted earlier, this is especially true for the language arts. The newer CCSS demands within the math curriculum are more evident in the upper grades, so this discussion focuses on only changes to the English language arts curriculum in the early school years (as with math, the sizable changes in the English curriculum in the upper grades are not covered here). The National Council of Teachers of Mathematics (NCTM; 2010) released a statement indicating its support for the CCSS but expressed various concerns. Relevant to the primary grades: Too much attention to fractions in the early grades does not allow sufficient time to explore place value, addition, and subtraction in grades K–3; by third or fourth grade, there should be some attention to statistics which there is not; and, overall, throughout the math standards document, there is too little emphasis on connections among the standards and technology.

RESEARCH INTO PRACTICE: THE CCSS AND EARLY EDUCATION

The CCSS for math and the English language arts do not directly address any learning requirements for the preschool years. The CCSS standards start out in kindergarten and proceed through grade 12. The standards documents contain no explanation for this omission, nor have any public explanations been provided by the standards creators themselves. Nevertheless, the changes to primary-grade literacy instruction are extensive enough that they require some realignments of the various state education documents that dictate preschool education policies (Zubrzycki, 2011).

The CCSS English language arts standards are expressed not as a single list of standards but are organized into a series of sections or sets of standards. The reading standards for K–5 are listed in three sets: reading standards for literature, reading standards for informational text, and foundational skills. Additionally, there are writing standards, speaking and listening standards, and language standards.

The reading standards are the most extensive and put forth some of the most far-reaching changes to current practice. Basically, there are 10 reading comprehension standards laid out for each grade level, but each of these standards is articulated in two different forms—for literary text and for informational text. For example, first graders are to "retell stories, including key details, and demonstrate understanding of their central message or lesson" with literary texts (NGA CCSSO, 2010, p. 11), and they are, analogously, to "identify the main topic and retell key details of a text" with informational text (p. 13).

Most, perhaps all, past state standards started with the foundational skills, such as phonological awareness, letter-name knowledge, and phonics and decoding, *then* listed the standards that focused directly on reading comprehension. The CCSS standards are organized differently. They start out with the comprehension standards, which continue on through high school, while the foundational skills are tucked into the document *after* the reading comprehension standards—and only in the K–5 section of the document. The foundational skills in CCSS include an ambitious schedule for phonics and word recognition development, and for *fluency* (reading text accurately, at an appropriate rate, and with appropriate expression). It is important to note the emphasis on these basic skills, since some educators may misinterpret (or miss altogether) the placement of these standards. Given the heavy emphasis on such skills in federal programs such as Reading First, this shift has led to some mistaken claims that these skills are no longer of importance, or that teachers can safely turn their attention elsewhere (Shanahan, 2011). CCSS developers were careful to follow the research evidence cited earlier to ensure that young children receive sufficient attention in these reading (and writing) basics.

Another important difference in the structure of the standards is that the reading and writing standards have a thematic or categorical internal organization. Although there are only 10 standards per grade level, the reading standards for literature and informational texts are each divided into four categories: key ideas and details (Items 1–3); craft and structure (Items 4–6); integration of knowledge and ideas (Items 7–9); and range of reading and level of text complexity (Item 10). This structure not only makes it easier for teachers to remember the standards, but it also carries important information about the goals for readers. For example, the key ideas and details sections focus heavily on understanding what a text says, so these items emphasize retelling, answering and asking questions about main ideas, details, and similar abilities. Craft and structure standards focus on developing awareness of how a text works, that is, how it communicates information, and awareness of the author (e.g., being able to describe the structure of a story or distinguishing the author from the characters); integration of knowledge and ideas emphasizes making information and ideas comparisons and connections across multiple texts; and, finally, range of reading and text complexity specifies the difficulty level (or readability) of the texts that have to be read at each grade level.

Remarkably, when one considers the deep separations evident in reading and writing standards in earlier state documents, the writing standards are organized in a similar fashion, with 10 items per grade level, and with four categories (text types and purposes, production and distribution of writing, research to build and present knowledge, and range of writing). The writing categories are analogous to the reading categories, focusing on communicating ideas (Items 1–3), author craft (Items 4–6), the synthesis of information from multiple sources (Items 7–9), and complexity of text that students should be able to produce (Item 10). This similarity in structure and focus should facilitate instructional efforts aimed at exploiting the shared knowledge underlying reading and writing to connect these instructional emphases more effectively (Fitzgerald & Shanahan, 2000; Graham & Hiebert, 2010; Shanahan, 1984; Tierney & Shanahan, 1991). Although the speaking and listening standards are not organized in the same way, connections between these and the reading and writing standards are easy to see as well because the processes or skills included are analogous to those in the reading and writing sections.

The language standards, like past state standards, emphasize the development of mechanics, usage, grammar, and spelling skills in oral and written language. These standards are very similar to those of many states, so they should not pose much of a new challenge to primary-grade teachers. One other inclusion in this section of the standards is noteworthy, however. Vocabulary learning is often emphasized either within reading comprehension or on its own. In the CCSS standards, "vocabulary acquisition and use" is in the language section. This may be confusing to some educators because the literary and informational text reading standards also have many items about the interpretation of word meanings and authors' word choices within text; thus, it is easy to overlook this separate information concerning the importance of building vocabulary knowledge, awareness of the nuances in word meanings, and understanding the relationships among words. Thus, the standards really emphasize vocabulary in two markedly different ways: Within reading, writing, speaking, and listening, students are expected to be able to use and interpret vocabulary, or rather diction, on the fly—while trying to make sense of an author's or speaker's message, and while trying to speak or write to others effectively. But the idea of building up one's vocabulary through more concentrated study is also emphasized, in this case, within the language section of the document.

Text Complexity

The CCSS pose many important changes for which educators need to account; perhaps none is more far-reaching than the emphasis on text complexity. In the past, standards have generally focused on the cognitive skills students needed to demonstrate. Thus, standards have tended to be verb-centric, emphasizing that students need to *recall, infer, predict, summarize, compare, analyze,* and so on, while neglecting the nature of the texts in which students are to implement these skills. The problem is that text difficulty is central to how well students engage in these processes or actions. Thus, students may struggle to infer or analyze with harder texts but be able to engage successfully in these same cognitive processes in easier materials (ACT, 2006). The past neglect of text difficulty in standards has allowed both teachers and test makers to convince themselves that students are learning the standards, even when actual reading performances were far below grade level.

What is text difficulty? Many factors can make a text difficult (Shanahan, Fisher, & Frey, 2012), including vocabulary and grammar or *syntax* (how complicated the sentences are). Other aspects of text that influence how well or how easily readers understand the text include the cohesiveness of the text (e.g., the clarity of the connections among nouns, pronouns, synonyms), tone (Is the text serious? Funny? Ironic? Is the author's message to be taken literally or is he or she using hyperbole or irony?), the complexity or subtlety in the relationships among the ideas and characters, and how the text is organized. Some text complexity factors are not entirely situated within the text itself, such as whether a text presupposes an awareness of particular knowledge or experiences on the part of the reader, or how interested a reader is likely to be about the text content. All of these factors can play some role in how well readers comprehend a text.

Despite the numerous text complexity variables, the quantitative measurement of text complexity is a somewhat simpler matter, at least beyond beginning-reading levels. Early researchers who studied readability tried to identify all of the factors in text complexity but soon settled on smaller sets of predictor variables that could be measured consistently enough to allow the efficient placement of texts onto a scale of complexity (Klare, 1984). These days, most readability measures focus on only two factors: measures of vocabulary difficulty (e.g., abstractness, length of words in letters or syllables, word frequency) and of sentence complexity (e.g., average sentence length, inclusion of certain kinds of clauses or phrases). It is not that these are the only features of text that can interfere with or complicate reader understanding, but that only two variables are usually sufficient to provide an accurate specification of text difficulty levels. Due in part to the fact that many of these different aspects of text complexity are highly interrelated, it might look the like readability formula includes only vocabulary and grammar, but since these are so closely connected with the other factors, it provides a "good enough" estimate of the overall text difficulty. However, in using such partial means to estimate text complexity, these same scales are not very useful for explaining why someone might struggle to understand a particular text.

The CCSS make text complexity central to the classroom equation as they specify readability levels that must be accomplished by students in grades 2–12. The CCSS identify these readability levels in terms of Lexiles (Lennon & Burdick, 2004). The Lexile measure, developed with funding from the NICHD, represents the best validated and most accurate, reliable estimate of text complexity currently available. Despite the quality of the Lexile measure, it can still over- or underestimate the difficulty of some books, so the CCSS suggest using it in combination with other measures and with consideration of local factors, such as student knowledge or interest.

It should be noted that the Lexile levels that the CCSS specify are somewhat harder than earlier specifications of Lexiles (thus, in the past, second- and third-grade readers would have been placed in texts in the Lexile ranges of 450L–725L, while in the CCSS plan these students would be placed in materials that could range up to 790L). The reason for this discrepancy is because Lexiles have traditionally based grade-level text matches on comprehension levels (specifying the grades at which students are expected to understand a text written in a particular Lexile range with 75% reading comprehension), while the CCSS based these matches on the back-mapping noted earlier. If students are to reach the high school graduation levels envisioned, they have to hit higher Lexile levels along the way; within the CCSS, this stretching begins in grade 2. Thus, the texts that second- and third-grade students will be asked to read under the common core are harder to read than those used in the recent past.

However, the specification of any text level for use at particular grade levels poses another important challenge for teachers because of long-standing pedagogical practices in which teachers have tried to minimize the challenge level that text poses to students. The idea has been that students have an "instructional level" in reading; that is, there is a text level that, if used, will facilitate the greatest amount of learning, and these instructional levels have generally been set to minimize text challenges (the most popular approach to instructional level assigns texts based on the prediction that students will be able to read these texts with an oral reading accuracy of 95% and a comprehension level of at least 75%). Various schemes exist for teaching students from leveled materials (*leveled* just means that the texts have been arrayed on some complexity continuum, and that students then move along this continuum, reading such materials in a sequence, from easier to harder, starting with the level thought to be the instructional level). This shift of emphasis away from working with an instructional-level text to one in which teachers intentionally attempt to stretch students to fit harder books is a great one that may possibly confer learning advantages. However, to make this approach workable, teachers will need to increase the amount of scaffolding, support, and motivation they provide to students, to ensure that learning accrues from these harder texts (Fisher, Frey, & Lapp, 2012; Shanahan et al., 2012).

Serious concerns about the implications of the CCSS for beginning readers have been expressed (Hiebert, 2011/2012). The challenge level of beginning reading materials has been noted as a potential impediment to learning (Hiebert, 1999). However, research shows that with sufficient amounts of scaffolding—such as repeated reading—students as early as second grade can make big learning gains from markedly harder texts (Morgan, Wilcox, & Eldredge, 2000). There is no such evidence with younger children, however, and it should be remembered that the CCSS does not specify text levels for kindergarten and grade 1. Readability instruments do not provide sufficiently reliable estimates of text difficulty at these levels (instruments for such use are now under study). Given the concerns noted, it would be prudent for teachers to delay ramping up text difficulty in kindergarten or grade 1. At these beginning levels, students have to figure out how decoding works, abstracting key principles and relationships from the texts that they read. If beginning texts are too complex (or distract students too much from the decoding aspects of reading), then early progress may be slowed or interrupted. Thus, keeping the texts simple early on is important, even if it requires a greater pivot to more complex text once students are reading at about second-grade level.

Close Reading of Text

The common core calls for an emphasis on *close reading*, the basic idea that reading needs to focus on *extracting ideas from text*, and that all other emphases should be minimized. Students need to think deeply about what a text says, how the text says it, and the meaning or the implications of the information. That means that in shared reading lessons, when teachers read to students, or in guided reading lessons, when students read a text with the assistance and support of a teacher, the emphasis is largely or entirely on the text being read. Contrast this approach with that taken in many reading lessons with a heavy emphasis on reviews of students' background knowledge, extensive previews of the text prior to reading (e.g., picture walks, predictions), purpose setting for reading by the teacher, and often, many teaching asides throughout the selection in which teachers introduce various instructional supports (e.g., emphasis on how to decode words, extensive discussion of particular word meanings, explanation of a grammar rule). These "help" to make the reading somewhat easier, but often by revealing a good deal of information from the text before children have had any opportunity to make sense of it themselves through reading.

What kinds of reading lessons does the common core envision? Initially, two of the CCSS authors, David Coleman and Susan Pimentel, issued "advice to publishers," recommending that all of the prereading previews and prior discussions of text content be banned from classrooms. However, this advice proved controversial, and they quickly reversed themselves (*www.achievethecore.org/downloads/publishers%20criteria%20 for%20literacy%20for%20grades%20k-2.pdf?20120412*).

These controversies aside, the basic idea of close reading, according to the common core, is that reading lessons should focus heavily on reading and interpreting the ideas in a text, an approach that has been found effective in fostering reading comprehension in the elementary grades (McKeown, Beck, & Blake, 2009). Not only does the common core discourage revealing much information from text prior to the reading, and digressions away from the text during reading (skills teaching can take place afterwards), but it also emphasizes the value of "text-dependent questioning" that focuses student attention on collecting and using information from the text rather than other sources such as prior knowledge. Text-dependent questions are those that would be impossible to answer correctly without actually reading the text.

What about the teaching of strategies such as summarizing, predicting, using text structure, and asking one's own questions? Where do they fit within the common core generally and in close reading specifically? The common core does not specify that any reading comprehension strategies need to be taught. The emphasis of the common core is on the reading outcomes (what the students are able to gain from reading the text); strategies may, as such, be useful in helping to effect such outcomes, but whether they are learned or not is not a matter of public concern, so they are not included in the standards themselves. Thus, teachers can teach comprehension strategies if they find it useful to do so, and they can ignore such instruction if they choose. It is important to note that research clearly supports the teaching of comprehension strategies in the primary grades (Shanahan et al., 2010), though the emphasis on close reading may seem to preclude that possibility. However, experts on the teaching of comprehension strategies have long stressed the importance of emphasizing the text content thoroughly, even when strategies are being taught (e.g., Pressley et al., 1992); strategy teaching may—but does not necessarily have to—distract attention from a text-content focus. If it does, then such strategies would not be consistent with the common core, and if the teaching of these strategies helps students to make greater sense of specific challenging texts they are being asked to read, then their use would be CCSS-appropriate.

Informational Text

The common core emphasizes the reading of informational text and encourages the reading of literary texts (e.g., stories and poems); the CCSS requires the introduction of informational text on an equal footing from kindergarten up. *Informational text* refers to those texts that "convey information about the natural or social world" (Duke & Bennett-Amistead, 2003, p. 16); precluding biographies (about individuals) or how-to manuals and directions (aimed at guiding someone to do something rather than conveying information); the distinction being made is not fiction versus nonfiction. Historically, U.S. core reading programs—whether provided by commercial publishers or assembled by teachers themselves—have usually been slanted toward the reading of literature, particularly in the lowest grades (Venezky, 1983). As recently as 2002, studies showed that about 80% of the selections in core reading programs were literary in nature (Moss & Newton, 2002), and one study found first-grade students working with informational texts for only about 3.6 minutes per day (Duke, 2000). Nevertheless, that imbalance has been reduced over the past decade as more informational texts become available for young readers.

Why is the common core emphasizing informational text to such a degree? Because U. S. fourth-graders read literary text significantly better than informational text, and their informational text reading lags behind that of students in 17 other countries (Mullis, Martin, Kennedy, & Foy, 2007). Further bolstering this emphasis, research that reveals young children's strong interests in science, history, technology, and the arts, and their tendency to prefer informational texts over literature (Mohr, 2006).

The benefit to teaching with informational text is that it exposes children to many text structures, language, and print conventions that are uncommon in literature. Thus, informational texts expose students to a rich array of text structures or organizational schemes (e.g., enumeration, compare–contrast, non-time sequence, cause–effect, problem–solution), text features (e.g., tables of contents, preface, appendices), print conventions (e.g., bold print, italics, bullets, headings/subheadings), and graphics (e.g., charts, tables, projections). Of course, not all informational text is high quality, and unless texts are carefully selected they will not serve as sound exemplars of these varied features. Fortunately, given the increases in the availability of informational text for preschool and primary-grade students, there are high quality resources available for supporting such teaching (Duke & Bennett-Armistead, 2003; Shanahan et al., 2010). Also, this substantial emphasis on informational text provides greater opportunity for curricular integration and connections across content and disciplinary areas of study.

Writing about Reading

CCSS writing standards require students to write about what they read. Often—in the earliest grades especially—students are asked to write about what they know (e.g., to write about family or about a place that is special). Much of the writing in which young children engage tends to be memory writing (the so-called "bed-to-bed" story: "Today I got up and . . ."); journaling; and writing with an immediate, contextualized, interpersonal communicative purpose, such as the "I love you" note or the "no trespassing" sign. This shift to writing about information drawn from texts is an important one. A recent meta-analysis of studies of older students, fourth grade and up, found that to combine reading and writing by having students write about what they read improves reading achievement (Graham & Hebert, 2010), and we have long known that reading and writing are connected, even in the primary grades (Fitzgerald & Shanahan, 2000; Shanahan, 2006; Tierney & Shanahan, 1991).

Reading and writing share a great deal of knowledge: sound–symbol relationships underlie both decoding and spelling; vocabulary knowledge is required for both reading and writing; and the same can be said for knowledge of syntax and text structure. But this knowledge can only be shared, or be mutually beneficial, when both reading and writing are available to students, and the more closely connected reading and writing are in use, the more likely that sharing takes place (Shanahan & Lomax, 1986). Thus, these studies show that writing about text improves reading achievement more effectively than having students reread the text or discuss it, perhaps because writing requires a more thorough and explicit engagement with the text information.

Accordingly, the standards ask students to review books and to summarize information from texts in kindergarten and first grade, and these writing-about-reading efforts are then expected to increase in sophistication and independence as students progress through the grades. Students are even expected to collect information from multiple sources, including texts, through research, and to assemble some of that information through their writing throughout the primary-grade years. Writing about reading may require summarization of the information from a text, modeling (trying to duplicate some text feature in one's own writing), analysis of the information in text, critical responses to text, and the collection and synthesis of information from multiple sources.

What about Preschool?

As has been noted, the common core does not include preschool standards. However, this does not mean that the standards do not have implications for preschool classrooms. There are many things that preschool teachers can do to put children on track toward early success with the common core standards.

One area in which preschool teachers can get students off to a good start is the foundational skills of reading. The National Early Literacy Panel (NELP; 2008) conducted an extensive meta-analysis of studies on the teaching of early literacy skills. In one analysis of 299 studies that measured early skills, then correlated them with later literacy achievement (decoding, reading comprehension, and spelling), NELP found that alphabet knowledge and *phonological awareness* (the ability to hear and manipulate the sounds within words separate from meaning) were big predictors of later success in decoding, reading comprehension, and spelling. These variables continued to exert an impact on later literacy achievement even when researchers controlled for other variables such as IQ or socioeconomic status. Clearly, these early skills—with *early* referring to those skills developed during the preschool years—will continue to matter later on, when students are in the common core grades.

Furthermore, the NELP examined 78 studies that considered the effectiveness of explicit efforts to teach these decoding skills (e.g., alphabet knowledge, phonological awareness, early phonics skills such as letter sounds) during the preschool and kindergarten years. This analysis revealed moderate-to-large learning effects on not only phonological awareness and letter names (not surprising given that these skills were being taught explicitly) but also conventional measures of reading, such as decoding and reading comprehension. Virtually all of the code-focused interventions for these years included phonological awareness training. These activities generally required children to detect or manipulate units of sounds in words; few of the studies focused on rhyming. In general, instructional activities that combined phonological awareness training and training on print-related activities (e.g., working with letters and sounds) yielded larger effects across outcome measures. There was no evidence that the effectiveness of this instruction was influenced by children's ages or developmental levels; thus, 4-year-olds were as able to learn from such interventions, as were kindergartners. However, this does not mean that students received identical training in the various studies. Generally, instruction aimed at the youngest children focused on the grossest or largest units of sound, beginning with hearing the separation between words, syllables, onsets–rimes (b-ig) and finally phonemes (the smallest meaningful sound differences in words /c/-/a/-/t/).

The successful code-focused instruction in these studies was delivered to young children either one-to-one or in small groups (there were no studies of code-focused interventions at these levels in which teaching was delivered to larger groups or whole classes). These activities tended to be systematic (following a planned curriculum), teacher-directed, and focused on helping children learn these skills by using them.

NELP found that other aspects of preschool and kindergarten instruction were valuable as well. The NELP analysis that examined early predictors of later literacy achievement considered the role of early oral language development in later literacy learning. In the initial attempts to answer this question the results weren't very promising. Preschool oral language measures were found to explain less than 10% of the variation in later literacy achievement, and early language learning appeared to be no more connected to reading comprehension than to decoding skills—a puzzling result.

The panel decided to divide up the analyses based on measures of young children's oral language. Tests that measured only expressive or receptive vocabulary knowledge during the preschool years (e.g., the widely used Peabody Picture Vocabulary Test) explained about 6–9% of variance in later decoding performance, and even less in students' later reading comprehension levels. However, the results were quite different with more complex measures of early oral language, such as listening comprehension or vocabulary measures that required young children to define or explain vocabulary words rather than just name them or point to pictures, or more comprehensive batteries of oral language measures such as the Preschool Language Scale or the Clinical Evaluation of Language Fundamentals: Preschool. When such measures were used, preschool language performance explained as much as 49% of later reading achievement. Furthermore, with these more powerful early language measures, the correlations with later decoding and reading comprehension diverge, with oral language being significantly more closely related to reading comprehension than to decoding.

These correlational findings suggest that to enhance student performance in later reading comprehension (and probably speaking, listening, and writing as well), preschools should make the effort to enhance the sophistication of young children's oral language development. NELP looked at experimental studies of programs aimed at enhancing young children's language learning. For example, it looked at 16 studies in which children were read to in various ways. These studies showed that a clear and powerful impact of being read to had on the young children's oral language development (usually measured with vocabulary tests). Although the studies didn't contribute significantly higher effects for *dialogical reading* (reading to children, then talking with them about the text, usually through questioning) than for reading alone, it should be noted that in the studies of dialogical reading, the control group or comparison children were usually being read to, while in studies that just looked at reading to children (without the dialogical involvement), the comparison kids were typically not read to at all. Rather than comparing the impacts of these approaches to language development, these effects should be combined: Reading to children seems to improve their language, and reading to them and engaging them in conversations about the texts seem to provide an added boost to language learning. Unfortunately, these studies did not differentiate among texts that were read to children, but it seems reasonable that preschoolers would enjoy and benefit as much from informational text as their slightly older siblings. Including informational texts in read-alouds and book-sharing sessions seems like an appropriate adjustment to facilitate CCSS implementation.

Of course, there are programs that aim more directly at teaching language, and these too had powerful effects on children's language learning, measured in multiple ways. Typically, oral language instructional programs try to enhance student use and understanding of particular words (e.g., the prepositions *in, on, under, over*), or particular sentences types (e.g., comparisons, questions). Such efforts seemed to be most effective the younger the children were, but they were equally effective with children across a range of demographic characteristics.

The CCSS does not establish learning goals for preschool children, but that does not mean these standards are not relevant to preschool teaching. If the goal is to help children to reach higher levels of literacy than they do now, then it is imperative that children start progressing along the literacy-learning continuum as early as possible. These studies suggest the potential effectiveness of a two-pronged approach to supporting young children's literacy and preliteracy development. On the one hand, helping children to develop predecoding skills by teaching letter names, phonological awareness, and early decoding skills (e.g., the sounds of the letters), print concepts (e.g., directionality), and early writing skills (e.g., name writing and invented spelling) can provide a significant boost to early literacy development. On the other hand, reading to children, engaging them in discussions about text, and explicitly guiding them to use their language in more sophisticated ways creates a language context in which later reading comprehension can flourish. The common core does not detail these outcomes for preschoolers, but it creates a context in which such early learning opportunities can make a big contribution to getting students off on the right foot.

REFLECTIONS AND NEW DIRECTIONS

This chapter described the CCSS for the English language arts and shows how these standards are a reasonable next step in the long journey toward standardization of learning opportunities in U.S. education. However, while many of the new CCSS items are really not that different from the various sets of state standards being replaced, in some areas the standards represent surprisingly big breaks with the past. Most specifically, primary-grade teachers, specifically in grades 2 and 3, are going to be asked to work with more difficult and more challenging texts (rather than aiming at the child's "instructional level"), which will require them to provide more skillful scaffolding and motivation that allows children to make sense of these texts, without reading to the children or telling them what the texts say. Similarly, the standards encourage greater exposure and involvement of children with informational texts and writing about the ideas in text.

These changes will require teachers to shift not only what they teach but also how they teach it. One of these changes is to engage children in close reading, in which attention is focused heavily on the text (rather than on student background or teacher purpose), with a great emphasis on figuring out and talking about what texts say, how they say it, and what they mean. The organization of the standards described here, and the heavy focus on writing and talking about text, open up valuable opportunities for combining or integrating reading and language arts instruction; thus, separate reading and writing blocks might not be such a good instructional idea going forward. Similarly, the heavy emphasis on informational texts and the use of multiple texts opens up avenues to integration across the language arts, social studies, and science.

Finally, although the CCSS does not include preschool, it is evident that preschool children can be put on a good path toward early success with the common core. Research has shown that preschools can develop children's understanding of the alphabetic code by teaching the ABCs, phonological awareness, print concepts, and letter sounds, while they simultaneously build students' oral language sophistication and knowledge of the world. The earlier children make progress in these areas of learning, the more likely that they will reach the heights of attainment envisioned by the common core.

PROFESSIONAL DEVELOPMENT ACTIVITIES

- Divide teachers into teams. Have each team follow one or more standards progression, such as examining all of the Reading Standards #1, from K–12, then report back to the other teachers on what they learned. Pay specific attention to any qualitative changes that take place in a standard as it develops.

- Compare the reading and writing standards, and look for connections that can be made through instruction. Do the same thing with the speaking and listening standards.

- Identify books, articles, and stories at your grade levels Lexile span. Then read the materials to examine what aspects might make them hard to understand, including vocabulary, sentence structure, student knowledge, structure or organization, and cohesion.

- Practice creating standards-relevant questions and tasks. Take a reading selection and write questions about the text based on the reading standards. Then try to design a writing assignment based on the standards that require students to write about the text.

REFERENCES

American College Testing (ACT). (2006). *Reading between the lines.* Iowa City: Author. Retrieved from *www.act.org/research/policymakers/pdf/reading_report.pdf.*

American College Testing (ACT). (2010). *A first look at the common core and college and career readiness.* Iowa City: Author. Retrieved from *www.act.org/commoncore/pdf/firstlook.pdf.*

August, D., & Shanahan, T. (2006). *Developing literacy in second-language learners.* Mahwah, NJ: Erlbaum.

Carmichael, S. B., Wilson, W. S., Porter-Magee, K., & Martino, G. (2010). *The state of state standards—and the common core—in 2010.* Washington, DC: Thomas B. Fordham Institute. Retrieved from *www.edexcellence.net/publications/the-state-of-state.html.*

Duke, N. K. (2000). 3.6 minutes per day: The scarcity of informational texts in first grade. *Reading Research Quarterly, 35,* 202–224.

Duke, N. K., & Bennett-Armistead, S. (2003). *Reading and writing informational text in the primary grades: Research-based practices.* New York: Scholastic.

Fisher, D., Frey, N., & Lapp, D. (2012). *Text complexity: Raising rigor in reading.* Newark, DE: International Reading Association.

Fitzgerald, J., & Shanahan, T. (2000). Reading and writing relations and their development. *Educational Psychologist, 35*, 39–50.

Gamse, B. C., Jacob, R. T., Horst, M., Boulay, B., & Unlu, F. (2008). *Reading First Impact Study Final Report* (NCEE 2009-4038). Washington, DC: National Center for Education Evaluation and Regional Assistance, Institute of Education Sciences, U.S. Department of Education.

Graham, S., & Hebert, M. (2010). *Writing to read: Evidence for how writing can improve reading.* New York: Carnegie Corporation of New York.

Hiebert, E. H. (1999). Text matters in learning to read. *The Reading Teacher, 52*, 552–566.

Hiebert, E. H. (2011/2012). The common core's staircase of text complexity: Getting the size of the first step right. *Reading Today, 29*(3), 26–27.

Hiebert, E. H., Martin, L. A., & Menon, S. (2005). Are there alternatives in reading textbooks?: An examination of three beginning reading programs. *Reading and Writing Quarterly, 21*, 7–32.

Klare, G. R. (1984). Readability. In P. D. Pearson, R. Barr, M. L. Kamil, & P. Mosenthal (Eds.), *Handbook of reading research* (pp. 681–744). New York: Longman.

Lennon, C., & Burdick, H. (2004). *The Lexile framework as an approach for reading measurement and success.* Raleigh, NC: MetaMetrics. Retrieved from *www.lexile.com/m/uploads/ whitepapers/lexile-reading-measurement-and-success-0504_metametricswhitepaper.pdf.*

McKeown, M. G., Beck, I. L., & Blake, R. G. K. (2009). Rethinking comprehension instruction: Comparing strategies and content instructional approaches. *Reading Research Quarterly, 44*(3), 218–253.

Mohr, K. A. J. (2006). Children's choices for recreational reading: A three-part investigation of selection preferences, rationales, and processes. *Journal of Literacy Research, 38*, 81–104.

Morgan, A., Wilcox, B. R., & Eldredge, J. L. (2000). Effect of difficulty levels on second-grade delayed readers using dyad reading. *Journal of Educational Research, 94*, 113–119.

Moss, B., & Newton, E. (2002). An examination of the informational text genre in basal readers. *Reading Psychology, 23*, 1–13.

Mullis, I. V. S., Martin, M. O., Kennedy, A. M., & Foy, P. (2007). *PIRLS 2006 International Report: IEA's progress in international literacy study in primary schools in 40 countries.* Boston: TIMMS & PIRLS International Study Center, Lynch School of Education, Boston College.

National Council of Teachers of Mathematics (NCTM). (2010). NCTM public comments on the Common Core Standards for Mathematics. Retrieved from *www.nctm.org/about/content. aspx?id=25186.*

National Early Literacy Panel (NELP). (2008). *Developing early literacy: Report of the National Early Literacy Panel.* Washington, DC: National Institute for Literacy. Retrieved from *http:// lincs.ed.gov/publications/pdf/nelpreport09.pdf.*

National Governors Association Center for Best Practices & Council of Chief State School Officers [NGA CCSSO]. (2010). *Common core state standards.* Washington, DC: Author.

National Institute of Child Health and Human Development (NICHD). (2000). *Report of the National Reading Panel: Teaching children to read: An evidence-based assessment of the scientific research literature on reading and its implications for reading instruction* (NIH Publication No. 00-4769). Washington, DC: U.S. Government Printing Office. Retrieved from *www.nationalreadingpanel.org/publications/summary.htm.*

National Mathematics Advisory Panel. (2008). *Foundations for success: The final report of the National Mathematics Advisory Panel.* Washington, DC: U.S. Department of Education. Retrieved from *www2.ed.gov/about/bdscomm/list/mathpanel/report/final-report.pdf.*

Pressley, M., El-Dinary, P. B., Gaskins, I., Schuder, T., Bergman, J. L., Almasi, J., et al. (1992). Beyond direct explanation: Transactional instruction of reading comprehension strategies. *Elementary School Journal, 92*, 513–555.

Shanahan, T. (1984). Nature of the reading–writing relation: An exploratory multivariate analysis. *Journal of Educational Psychology, 76*, 466–477.

Shanahan, T. (2006). Relations among oral language, reading, and writing development. In C. A.

MacArthur, S. Graham, & J. Fitzgerald (Eds.), *Handbook of writing research* (pp. 17–183). New York: Guilford Press.

Shanahan, T. (2010). Education policy and the language arts. In D. Lapp & D. Fisher (Eds.), *Handbook of research on teaching the English language arts* (pp. 152–158). New York: Routledge.

Shanahan, T. (2011). Comparing common core and Reading First. Retrieved from *www.shanahanonliteracy.com/2011/06/comparing-common-core-and-reading-first.html*.

Shanahan, T., Callison, K., Carriere, C., Duke, N. K., Pearson, P. D., Schatschneider, C., et al. (2010). *Improving reading comprehension in kindergarten through 3rd grade: A practice guide* (NCEE 2010-4038). Washington, DC: National Center for Education Evaluation and Regional Assistance, Institute of Education Sciences, U.S. Department of Education. Retrieved from *http://whatworks.ed.gov/publications/practiceguides*.

Shanahan, T., Fisher, D., & Frey, N. (2012). The challenge of challenging text. *Educational Leadership, 69*(6), 58–62.

Shanahan, T., & Lomax, R. (1986). An analysis and comparison of theoretical models of the reading–writing relationship. *Journal of Educational Psychology, 78*, 116–123.

Stotsky, S., & Wurman, Z. (2010). *Common core's standards still don't make the grade.* Boston: Pioneer Institute.

Swanson, C. B., & Barlage, J. (2006). *Influence: A study of the factors shaping educational policy.* Bethesda, MD: Editorial Projects in Education. Retrieved from *www.edweek.org/media/influence_study.pdf*.

Taylor, D. (1998). *Beginning to read and the spin doctors of science: The political campaign to change America's mind about how children learn to read.* Urbana, IL: National Council of Teachers of English.

Tierney, R. J., & Shanahan, T. (1991). Research on the reading–writing relationship: Interactions, transactions, and outcomes. In R. Barr, M. L. Kamil, P. Mosenthal, & P. D. Pearson (Eds.), *Handbook of reading research* (Vol. 2, pp. 246–280). Mahwah, NJ: Erlbaum.

Venezky, R. L. (1983). The origins of the present-day chasm between adult literacy needs and school literacy instruction. *Visible Language, 16*, 113–136.

Venezky, R. L. (1987). A history of the American reading textbook. *Elementary School Journal, 87*, 247–265.

Zubrzycki, J. (2011, December 7). Educators walk a tightrope between academics and young children's developmental needs. *Education Week.* Retrieved from *www.edweek.org/ew/articles/2011/12/07/13prek_ep.h31.html?tkn=wzsfpcfbwhh%2bv%2bfqbtt77ye%2bjen24usf39wo&cmp=clp-edweek*.

CHAPTER 14

EFFECTIVE PROGRAMS OF INSTRUCTION FOR ALL STUDENTS

MICHAEL C. MCKENNA
SHARON WALPOLE

> The real reform agenda is societal development. Not in an abstract sense, but empirically. Not in broad strokes, but through identifying precise themes and their consequences for better or for worse.
> —MICHAEL FULLAN (2006)

Cathy Ross had been a literacy coach for 9 years in two different elementary schools. She had a master's degree in reading, and her efforts to work with teachers and principals had been largely successful. When she was summoned to a meeting with the district language arts coordinator a week before the start of school, she had little idea what to expect but hoped privately that her work would be praised. She was right. The coordinator extolled her efforts and revealed a surprising knowledge of what she had accomplished at her schools. As a "reward," she was to be transferred to the district's most ailing school, Hamilton Elementary. Hamilton had failed to meet state and district standards for 4 consecutive years, and it now had just 2 years left before a management team from the state department of education took control. Cathy's job was to size up the situation as quickly as possible, make an ambitious plan for effecting change, and begin to implement it. The principal was understandably desperate for help and had promised to support her. Cathy arrived during preparations for the new school year and was able to meet with teachers and grade-level groups, confer with the principal and specialists, inspect the schedule, survey materials in use, and examine assessment data. Once school began, she carried out observations systematically, guided by achievement histories. At the end of the second week of school, she had learned a great deal about Hamilton and the professionals who worked there. Crafting a realistic but aggressive plan for change was the next order of business. In order to develop such a plan, Cathy started by comparing the situation at Hamilton with her vision of an effective program of instruction. Points at which the reality at Hamilton differed from that vision would become legitimate targets for collaborative efforts. Below we summarize the research that instructional leaders in situations similar to Cathy's should know and be able to use.

WHAT RESEARCH SAYS
ABOUT AN EFFECTIVE PreK–3 INSTRUCTIONAL PROGRAM

To what extent have researchers been able to clarify a vision of an effective instructional program? This is a broad question, and to address it we have attempted to distill some of the key lessons provided by research. We have organized these key lessons around the essential components of an effective literacy instructional program.

Instruction Must Reflect Evidence-Based Practice

Instructional approaches vary in their effects on learning. The abundance of research conducted to identify the most effective methods is so extensive that summaries are needed. Two of the most important are the reports of the National Reading Panel (National Institute of Child Health and Human Development, 2000) and the National Early Literacy Panel (2008). These reports concur in recommending instruction that is explicit and systematic in each of the major components of reading (comprehension, vocabulary, oral reading fluency, word recognition, and phonological awareness). Our review of the research since the National Reading Panel's report (Walpole & McKenna, 2013) found no evidence that contradicts the findings of either panel; to the contrary, subsequent studies have simply tended to provide nuance and elaborate on those findings. The task for schools is to determine how to implement the findings specifically. Our own work has led us to view this task as having two parts. First, we must choose a small number of the most effective approaches; then we must provide guidance in how to employ them (Walpole & McKenna, 2009b). This guidance is a form of professional development, and one that is especially well suited to coaching.

Coaching Can Influence Teachers' Choices of Instructional Methods

Research into what constitutes effective reading instruction can provide a blueprint of what should be happening in classrooms. At first blush, informing teachers about effective approaches would appear to be a simple matter of professional development. In our review of the research on literacy coaching (Walpole & McKenna, 2009a), we suggested that the rationale for coaching rests on four assumptions:

1. The instructional methods teachers employ influence student achievement.
2. Variations in the methods themselves and in the quality of teacher implementation are considerable.
3. Coaching can help teachers implement specific methods and abandon others; coaching can help teachers improve the quality of their work.
4. The effect of coaching can be gauged by changes in student achievement as a result of this altered practice. (p. 25)

The difficulty lies in the third assumption. To be sure, coaches can help teachers implement evidence-based approaches, but their efforts are sometimes resisted (Matsumura, Garnier, & Resnick, 2010; McKenna & Walpole, 2008). Taylor (2008), while acknowledging that coaching has the potential to change teacher beliefs, points out that coaching exists in a context where other factors also influence teacher behavior, such as alternative guidance, peer beliefs, community norms, and school and district policies.

Administrative Support Is Indispensible

For coaching to be effective, school administrators must make clear to teachers that their participation is expected. As we have remarked elsewhere, "The principal, in whom real power resides, is in a position either to further the coach's efforts, to limit them through indifference, or to overtly challenge them. It is up to the coach to craft a relationship in which the principal's actions are not only supportive but are *seen* as supportive by teachers" (Walpole & McKenna, 2013, p. 220, original emphasis). One of the surest ways a coach can foster a principal's support is by working to improve the principal's knowledge of reading. There is a relationship between the level of a principal's expertise in reading and the level of reading achievement in the school (Murphy, 2004). We suspect that the two are connected because knowledgeable principals have a clear idea of which practices to advocate and which to discourage. For this reason, the school principal is arguably the most important individual to coach.

Appropriate Materials Must Be Available to Support Instructional Goals

On its face, this statement may seem self-evident, but there is considerable debate about which materials are truly appropriate. Core programs remain standard fare in most schools, but they lack the indispensable quality once ascribed to them. Regardless of whether a core is in place, a key consideration is whether teachers have available to them an abundance of engaging trade books at a wide range of levels, a balance of fiction and information text (Duke, 2000), big books and predictable books for teaching concept of word, and decodable books for practice in applying newly acquired word recognition skills (Walpole & McKenna, 2009b). As early as preschool, children should also begin to encounter digital materials (Labbo & Noguerón-Liu, Chapter 11, this volume; Morrow, 2010). Because immersion in an abundance of materials will not advance literacy by osmosis, teachers must organize them for easy access and employ routines for their regular use (Reutzel & Jones, 2010).

Assessment Data Must Inform Decisions about Instruction

The focus on response to intervention (RTI) has sharpened our appreciation of the fact that assessments can and must be used to plan instruction and monitor its effects (Miller, Toste, Fuchs, & Fuchs, Chapter 10, this volume). With a surprisingly small set of measures, teachers can screen for areas of difficulty, diagnose specific targets, and monitor the progress of children toward benchmark status. We recommend a lean, mean assessment approach following the Cognitive Model of Reading Assessment (McKenna & Stahl, 2009; Stahl, Kuhn, & Pickle, 1999), which guides teachers toward the most important instructional targets with the least amount of assessment. The school's assessment system should also embody a means of plotting trajectories for individual students through the course of a year, and from grade to grade. It should permit a coach to aggregate data at classroom and grade levels in order to identify trouble spots.

Instruction Must Be Differentiated to Address the Needs of All Children

Imagine a classroom where all children receive exactly the same instruction. Conducting assessments to screen and diagnose problems and to monitor progress toward remedying those problems is not required. Only outcome assessments are necessary, in order to assign grades. However, when assessment informs instructional planning, differentiation is the inevitable result. Research has long established the need for a combination of whole-class and small-group instruction within a literacy block (Connor et al., 2011; Taylor, Pearson, Clark, & Walpole, 2000), and populating small groups is the first step toward effective differentiation. And it is a step that should address the needs of both proficient students and those who struggle (Tomlinson & Imbeau, Chapter 8, this volume; Walpole & McKenna, 2009b).

Addressing the Needs of Children Who Struggle Requires Intensive Interventions

An assessment system should give teachers the information they need to form small, flexible groups with a targeted and temporary focus. It should also signal when small-group instruction is not working, so that more intensive approaches can be tried. This is the rationale of RTI, and it has occasioned considerable reflection on what effective interventions should look like, who should deliver them, and how long they should last before a child is formally considered for special education. In the case of commercial intervention programs, objective reviews are available through a number of sources, such as the What Works Clearinghouse (*www.whatworks.ed.gov*), the Center on Instruction (*www.centeroninstruction.org*), the Best Evidence Encyclopedia (*www.bestevidence.org*), and the National Center on Response to Intervention (*www.rti4success.org*). Choosing an intervention with a research pedigree is not a guarantee that it will work as planned, however. Implementing it with fidelity can be problematic. Dickinson, Freiberg, and Barnes (2011) concluded that one of the reasons interventions are so often ineffective is that the teachers who deliver them do not receive adequate professional development.

Specialists and Classroom Teachers Must Work in a Coordinated Way

Tiered instruction, planned to provide increasing levels of intensity and focus, cannot be accomplished by one teacher working alone. It requires the systematic efforts of classroom teachers and specialists, with guidance from coaches and support from administrators. Reading specialists and special educators who once worked independently now often work together at more than a single of tier of instruction. They may move together from one classroom to the next, for example, teaching within a small-group rotation. At other times, they may provide intensive instruction to individual students.

Scheduling Must Ensure Efficiency and Lighten the Instructional Burden

Employing specialists in this manner presents considerable scheduling challenges. We have argued that is should begin with a controlled heterogeneous assignment of children to homerooms, so that there is a range of proficiency in each but not the full range for any teacher (Walpole & McKenna, 2013). This policy helps to reduce the number of small groups and leads to better use of the brief time during which specialists are available. It also eliminates the need for large numbers of children to migrate to other classrooms during the literacy block. Such interclass regrouping made sense in an era when core programs were structured differently, but it may now waste valuable instructional time, prevent teachers from gaining insights into the needs of some of their students, and threaten collaboration with specialists and grade-level colleagues.

Collaboration Is Crucial

The coordination of classroom teachers and specialists has yet another consequence. It requires collaboration among professionals. The era when specialists provided instruction that was unconnected to children's classroom experiences is, we hope, drawing to a close. RTI demands that teachers jointly plan and regularly inspect the data gathered for that purpose. At first, such collaboration may evoke anxiety. "Many teachers have shared with us," Joyce and Showers (2002) observe, "the difficulty they experience in jointly performing an activity that traditionally they have done independently" (p. 92). But this anxiety is alleviated when a supportive climate is established. "People want to work together," Kanter (2004) observed. "People are willing to help others and give them a chance to excel" (pp. 46–47). Bean (2012) observes that one of the surest ways to promote collaboration is to distribute leadership. She summarizes research evidence "that student achievement in schools is enhanced when leadership is shared" (p. 17). Shared leadership begins with ensuring that all teachers are given responsibilities that bring them into close association with others. Ideally, these responsibilities will be related to areas of expertise.

Curricular Coherence across Grades Is Essential

Developmental models of reading acquisition (e.g., Chall, 1983/1996; Ehri, 1999) indicate that a coordinated sequence of instruction matters. The developers of core programs have attempted to embody evidence-based sequences into their materials, but this does not mean that instructional sequences are perfect. And when a core is not in place, instructional planning that is mindful of the increased demands of achievement over time is often in jeopardy. A related problem is the interface between preschool and kindergarten because of frequent discontinuities in assessment and curriculum (Beauchat, Blamey, & Walpole, 2010). Because classroom teachers are primarily (and understandably) concerned with a single grade level, it is essential that instructional leaders be familiar with the core materials, and their scope and sequence throughout the primary grades (Walpole & McKenna, 2013). If a core is not in place, standards must be used to guide choices, especially with respect to the foundational and grade-level skills addressed in the Common Core State Standards (see Shanahan, Chapter 13, this volume).

A related problem can occur when intervention programs are poorly aligned with the core. Two commercial programs, though each may incorporate evidence-based practice, do not necessarily dovetail in a consistent manner. In a recent experimental study, Wonder-McDowell, Reutzel, and Smith (2012) compared the effects of two types of supplemental instruction provided by reading specialists to struggling second graders in 11 schools. One type was closely aligned with the core program in terms of the order of decoding skills, the themes of text selections, and other characteristics. The other type was unaligned with the core; the specialists simply followed the protocol of a commercial intervention program. Inconsistencies consequently arose, such as decoding instruction that followed a different sequence. Although both groups of children made significant progress on a variety of measures over the course of the 10-week study, those who received the aligned instruction outperformed the unaligned instruction group.

The School Culture Should Foster Both Proficiency and Motivation

Too often, in the press for proficiency, we lose sight of the fact that "the central and most important goal of reading instruction" is "to foster the love of reading" (Cramer &

Castle, 1994, p. v). It is true that proficiency is necessary for motivation to read, but it is not always sufficient. A comprehensive program of instruction must embrace motivation as a central, not a peripheral, component. In addition to guiding young readers toward greater proficiency, it must afford choices among an abundance of engaging materials (Guthrie & Wigfield, 2000). It must also offer opportunities for children to interact in meaningful ways during small-group work and read-alouds (Beauchat, Blamey, & Philippakos, 2012; Beck & McKeown, 2001). Finally, the importance of attitudes and motivation means that these dimensions of literacy development must be represented among the assessments teachers administer (Afflerbach & Cho, 2011).

RESEARCH INTO PRACTICE

For Cathy, realizing these lessons was easier said than done. Her initial goal of identifying differences between the situation at Hamilton and the ideal program was simple enough because the differences were so glaring. Accordingly, she developed a 12-point plan, constructing a rubric for each point. In effect, she was using an approach called innovation configuration (IC; Hall & Hord, 2001; Roy & Hord, 2003). In IC, each dimension is described in terms of likely stages, from minimal to full implementation. Her IC appears in Table 14.1. She also shared the IC with the principal, and the two worked in concert to reach consensus about where they believed Hamilton Elementary to be with respect to each of the 12 dimensions.

Cathy and the principal then met to outline steps they would take to move the school in the direction of full implementation of each key dimension. They worked with other building leaders to consider these steps and garner support for them.

Effective Practice

Cathy made a list of *some* of the approaches specifically identified as effective in research reviews. She did not attempt to be comprehensive because she realized that she would have to focus on a small number of highly effective approaches at first. For example, in comprehension, she listed student-generated questions and tied their use to a book study on question–answer relationships (Raphael, Highfield, & Au, 2006). For vocabulary, she focused on teaching Tier 2 words for fiction (Beck & McKeown, 2001) and Tier 3 content-area words in related clusters, using evidence-based approaches such as concept of definition (Schwartz & Raphael, 1985) and semantic feature analysis (Pittelman, Heimlich, Berglund, & French, 1991). For fluency, she chose repeated readings (Samuels, 1979). For phonemic awareness, she chose a technique called Say It and Move It (Blachman, Ball, Black, & Tangel, 1994). Each of these techniques is simple to use and could provide a foundation for shared instructional innovations within a grade level.

Coaching

As a coach new to the school, Cathy couldn't rest on her laurels. Few of her new colleagues had even met her. She would need to start anew, launching a coaching initiative and building relationships with teachers. She decided to begin by scheduling meetings with grade-level teams, during which she did more listening than talking. She made offers to help the teams plan and review data. She also offered to teach a few small

TABLE 14.1. An Innovation Configuration for the Program of Reading Instruction

Program dimension	Full implementation	Partial implementation		Minimal implementation
	4	3	2	1
Effective practice	Nearly all teachers apply evidence-based instructional approaches with at least adequate quality.	Nearly all teachers apply evidence-based approaches, but implementation quality varies extensively.	Most, but not all, teachers apply evidence-based approaches.	Many teachers apply instructional approaches with weak research support.
Coaching	Coaching has influenced the practice of all teachers.	Coaching has influenced the instruction of many teachers.	Coaching has influenced the instruction of some teachers.	Coaching has failed to influence the instruction of many teachers.
Administrative support	Principal and district leaders are highly supportive of the reform.	Principal and district leaders are interested in the reform and seek understanding.	Principal and district leaders are tolerant of the reform and begin to show interest.	Principal and district leaders are hostile or indifferent toward the reform.
Materials	Teachers have access to organized sets of fiction and information trade books, decodables, software, and support materials.	Teachers have a sufficient number of fiction and information trade books, decodables, software, and support materials, but they are not organized.	Some, but not all, teachers have a sufficient number and variety of books and other materials.	Teachers have an insufficient number and variety of books and other materials.
Assessment	Screening, diagnostic, and progress-monitoring assessments are standard practice and used to plan instruction.	Assessments are valid and systematic, and adequately interpreted but results are largely unused.	Assessments are valid and systematic, but results are largely unused and/or poorly interpreted.	Assessments are haphazard, unsystematic, and/or of questionable validity, and/or results are largely unused and/or poorly interpreted.
Differentiation	Assessments drive a tiered model of instruction, intervention, and acceleration.	Differentiation addresses skills deficits for struggling students but does not serve higher-achieving students.	Differentiation is limited to leveled books and fails to address skills deficits.	Differentiation is not a focus of classroom instruction.
Interventions	Evidenced-based interventions are in place, scheduled logically, and are delivered by knowledgeable providers to children accurately identified.	Interventions are generally high quality and scheduled logically, but providers are inconsistent in their training.	Interventions are generally high quality but require that students be pulled from instruction haphazardly.	Some interventions have limited validation and/or are delivered poorly, and/or their use is not coordinated with classroom instruction.

(continued)

TABLE 14.1. *(continued)*

Program dimension	Full implementation	Partial implementation		Minimal implementation
	4	3	2	1
Collaboration	All classroom teachers co-plan with grade-level colleagues and specialists to provide coordinated instruction.	Most classroom teachers co-plan with grade-level colleagues and specialists.	Some, but not all, classroom teachers co-plan with grade-level colleagues and specialists.	Many classroom teachers do not co-plan with grade-level colleagues and specialists, but instead work independently and their efforts are not coordinated.
Specialists	All specialists constructively embrace their role of working in tandem with one another and with classroom teachers.	Some specialists resist the idea of working closely with one another and/or classroom teachers.	Many specialists resist the idea of working closely with one another and/or classroom teachers.	Most specialists resist the idea of working closely with one another and/or with classroom teachers.
Scheduling	The schoolwide schedule accommodates tiered instruction, optimizes use of specialists, and maximizes instructional time.	The schedule of some grade levels accommodates tiered instruction, optimizes use of specialists, and maximizes instructional time.	The schedule of some grade levels hampers tiered instruction and/or involves wasted time, and/or curtails efficient use of specialists.	The schedule hampers tiered instruction and/or involves wasted time, and/or curtails efficient use of specialists.
Vertical articulation	The entire PreK–3 curriculum adequately reflects a developmental model of reading acquisition.	The curriculum at most grade levels adequately reflects a developmental model of reading acquisition.	The curriculum at some grade levels is not coherently articulated with others.	The PreK–3 curriculum is not coherently articulated across grades.
Motivation	All teachers employ approaches designed to foster positive attitudes and motivation.	Most teachers employ approaches designed to foster positive attitudes and motivation.	Attitude and motivation are not a priority of some teachers.	Attitude and motivation are not a priority of many teachers.

groups, so that she could get to know the children better. She realized that not all of the teachers would respond to these suggestions, but she hoped for a ripple effect when she helped those who did. Cathy's quandary as a coach was the short time that Hamilton had to show improvement. The urgency of the situation meant that she needed to enter reform mode and adopt what we have characterized as a "hard" rather than "soft" model of coaching (McKenna & Walpole, 2008; Mangin & Stoelinga, 2011). Hard coaching required a clear vision of what changes must be made, and the IC had helped her clarify that vision. Cathy's early meetings with grade-level teams and individual teachers help her personalize and differentiate her coaching efforts.

Administrative Support

Cathy's meetings with the principal and other instructional leaders to pace their work highlighted the importance of working with a building leadership team (BLT). They decided to form a team that included representatives of all grade-level teams, specialists, and paraprofessionals. The BLT, through sometimes uncomfortable discussion, realized that collaboration was more than cooperation. It required that individuals learn to air and acknowledge their differences, accommodate them, and find common ground (Walpole & Najera, 2013). Once they agreed that the current situation was not acceptable, and that instruction had to change, Cathy was able to establish her credibility by proposing links among professional development during grade-level team meetings, the formative observations she conducted, and the principal's required evaluations. The principal assured the BLT that evaluation would focus only on implementation of practices that teachers were learning together and for which they had access to individual coaching. This administrative support established the importance of using grade-level time well, and it enhanced Cathy's legitimacy with the teachers.

Materials

To establish instructional consistency and to simplify teachers' planning, Cathy started by specifying that teachers work with grade-level core materials. She created simple, repetitive weekly schedules for whole-group shared reading, employing vocabulary instruction, repeated readings, and comprehension strategy modeling. Her goal was to increase the total number of minutes that children spent each day in supported reading, and to standardize teachers' use of instructional materials within each grade level. Those simple instructional procedures formed the first targets for grade-level team meetings, for coaching, and for the principal's walk-throughs and observations.

Assessment

Cathy had to work quickly to understand the needs of children. Because no criterion-referenced comprehension test was administered until the end of third grade, Cathy began with fluency, which is a good predictor of comprehension (Kim, Petscher, Schatschneider, & Foorman, 2010) and easy to screen. With a reading specialist, a special educator, and a school counselor, Cathy was able to move from classroom to classroom, assessing all children's oral reading fluency. Students with words correct per minute at or above the goals for their grade level needed no further assessment. They would differ in their vocabularies and their comprehension abilities, but they would not need additional fluency work. For those whose fluency was below grade-level expectations, Cathy and her team administered a short, informal phonics inventory. These assessments were scored in grade-level team meetings. Among the children with weak fluency, they clearly identified children with strong decoding knowledge and those with specific decoding deficits. They were prepared, then, to make a differentiation plan (Walpole & McKenna, 2009b). Because fluency benchmarks are not available until the middle of first grade, the special educator and reading specialist collected informal assessments of phonemic awareness and alphabet knowledge in kindergarten, and phonological awareness in preschool. These measures were used to identify children who needed extra assistance from preschool through the middle of first grade. From that point through the end of grade

3 they were used to diagnose specific skills needs when fluency screening indicated a problem.

Differentiation

Cathy knew that some teachers would not be comfortable providing small-group instruction to all children every day; they had to build their classroom management skills first. Teachers used the assessment data they had collected to form groups and agreed to devote 2 weeks to small-group management. The problem was how to engage the rest of the children during small-group time. Teachers agreed that all children would respond to a writing prompt each day, then engage in self-selected reading. Teachers would meet with small groups for just 10 minutes each at first, using the time to discuss the week's core story. Once they were comfortable with the rotation, they would expand the time to 15 minutes per group. For second and third grade, their first differentiation target would be fluency and comprehension. They could use little books from the core series, already leveled by complexity. Cathy knew that she could establish teacher comfort at those grade levels by beginning with fluency, then moving to the more technical differentiation needs in the area of word recognition. For first grade, the initial differentiation focus was decoding. Teachers could use the core intervention lessons for their small groups before beginning a more targeted approach.

Interventions

The history of inconsistent instruction in the school had yielded a large number of struggling readers who would likely respond quickly to intensive interventions. Cathy had to take stock of the school's intervention materials before she could think about how to use them, but she could not do it alone. She asked BLT members to gather data about available resources. Reading teachers, special educators, classroom teachers, and even the after-school program personnel all had some individual stores of commercial intervention materials. The BLT created a spreadsheet to catalog their materials, and the reading teacher took responsibility for researching the materials on the What Works Clearinghouse. They decided they would gather the materials into one space, to evaluate their scope better and to communicate that they would now be shared, rather than personal, resources.

Collaboration

Although the BLT had begun to establish a collaborative climate, the union between new information and existing resources (student achievement data, teacher comfort with differentiation, and intervention resources) required more extensive collaborative thinking and actions. Cathy could continue her work with grade-level teams, perhaps moving beyond her initial work in differentiation. But she could not craft a schoolwide intervention strategy without the help of all members of the BLT, and getting that help would require additional time for collaboration. The principal asked BLT members to agree to a Saturday retreat, where they would have an entire day to brainstorm and problem-solve. In exchange, each could have an additional professional day at a time that they chose. All but one BLT member agreed. The plan they constructed, combining all of the school's specialists into an intervention team, was radically different from the school's previous approach.

Specialists

While all individuals on the Hamilton staff were experiencing shifts in their professional roles and responsibilities, the specialists' worlds would change the most. Rather than assigning children to specialists based on their funding (separating special education and Title I), the BLT recommended that the specialists' individual workloads be combined and redistributed. Although those children with established individual education plans (IEPs) still needed services, those services could be provided to other children with similar needs at the same time. Cathy would provide for the specialists a list of children who needed intervention, divided by grade level and by area of need. She would also give them the combined list of intervention resources currently available in the school. Finally, the principal would reassign three paraprofessionals to work on the intervention team full time, provided that other staff members would provide the training they needed to work with children in the intervention plan. The specialists realized that the only way that they could serve the children who needed intervention was to stagger the reading blocks across the school day, so that only one grade level had small-group instruction each hour.

Scheduling

Over time, the quality of the grade-level team professional support, augmented by Cathy's coaching and the principal's targeted walk-throughs and observations, had engendered increased teacher efficacy. When the BLT presented the specialists' intervention plan to the full staff, everyone could see the logic. If the instructional day were structured so that each grade-level team had small-group instruction at a different hour, the specialists could work as a team and serve as many as five small groups at each grade level for 45 minutes. Because they were confident that the change would increase the quality and amount of intervention services their own struggling readers would receive, teachers were willing to do the very difficult job of adjusting their instructional schedules. As they began that work, some grade-level teachers had another scheduling brainstorm. They requested an hour of grade-level planning at the very end of the school day rather than the 40 minutes captured during their children's specials. The principal was able to free one grade-level team each weekday for the final 20 minutes of the school day by assigning a member of the intervention team to manage end-of-day procedures and dismissal. Teachers, then, stayed slightly later than the time indicated in their contract planning to capture a full hour of grade-level time with Cathy each week.

Vertical Articulation

Vertical articulation of the curriculum occurred fairly slowly during the first year. Cathy's first priority was *horizontal articulation*—coherence *within* each grade level— and she worked to achieve this goal through weekly collaborative meetings. She was able to guide teachers to raise their expectations for student achievement and to compare students' reading achievement data within their grade level. But Cathy also wanted teachers to view the reading program with a broader lens, to see in fact what was occurring at adjacent grade levels, and to contrast those efforts with an understanding of reading development. To ensure *vertical articulation*—coherence *across* grade levels—she guided teachers through a number of activities. They began by examining outcome data across grades to identify achievement trajectories and trouble spots. They shared work samples to understand better the development of spelling and composition. They compared progress of intervention groups and made decisions along with specialists to intensify services for children who were still not thriving. Teachers, finally, were ready to increase their own responsibilities for differentiating their small groups. They agreed to a summer book study on word recognition development so that they could begin the fall with a more focused, classroom-based differentiation plan so that specialists could intensify the services for those children with the most significant needs.

Motivation

Cathy knew that by improving the proficiency of the students, teachers would remove a major barrier to their motivation to read. However, she wanted to take additional steps as well. She persuaded the BLT to administer the Elementary Reading Attitude Survey (ERAS; McKenna & Kear, 1990) to grades 1–5 at the beginning and end of the year. She would then compile the data and track the development of attitudes. She hoped that her periodic reports to teachers would also increase awareness of the affective dimensions of reading. As part of her professional development (PD) efforts, she conveyed to teachers the following suggestions about motivational approaches: (1) promoting room arrangement and décor that advocate reading; (2) emphasizing new, amusing words (onomatopoeias, palindromes, words with weird origins, etc.) designed to build interest in words; (3) establishing for each grade a shared library, with preplanned read-alouds based on highly engaging books recommended by teachers; (4) creating reading journals to collect each student's responses to the writing prompts following read-alouds; (5) exploiting the power of humor through cartoons, jokes, poetry, quotes, and song lyrics; (6) taking advantage of high-interest topics, such as dangerous animals; (7) making time for literature circles; and (8) arranging for occasional cross-grade partnering.

REFLECTIONS AND NEW DIRECTIONS

A program of reading instruction is far more than materials. It has a number of dimensions, each of which must be accounted for if lasting reform is to result. In this chapter, we have described an approach to reform that proceeds along 12 avenues simultaneously. This multidimensional approach may well seem daunting. We have argued, however, that to ignore one or more of these avenues would jeopardize improvements in the others. To organize a reform effort, we have adapted the idea of using an IC to gauge relative progress in multiple dimensions.

Identifying these dimensions and organizing a plan to implement improvements in any one of them is a straightforward first step. To illustrate subsequent steps we have described Cathy's actions to move her school in the direction of a more effective program. Our fictional account is based on the composite experiences of many coaches with whom it has been our honor to work. However, Cathy's example begs a number of questions:

- What if a school does not have a literacy coach to drive the reform effort?
- What if the administration balks at the scope of the initiative and fails to lend a full measure of support?
- What if there are insufficient resources to acquire the materials needed?

These and other questions suggest that Cathy's actions cannot simply be transported to any school context. The plan enacted by a coach (or another literacy leader) must be tailored to the local context, so that it reflects the realities of a particular school. Only when these realities are recognized honestly and addressed creatively can true progress be expected.

In this process it is important to remember that the 12 factors are interconnected in the web of a school's instructional program. To illustrate how they influence one another, we created Figure 14.1. We began by identifying three dimensions that are pivotal to change: administrative support, coaching, and collaboration. Together, these change factors can best enable change when appropriate assessments and materials are in place, when the reading curriculum is vertically articulated, when scheduling is strategic, and when specialists' expertise is optimized. We next identified three factors that have a direct effect on student learning and motivation: whole-class instruction, differentiation, and interventions. These three factors are in turn directly influenced by both change factors and enabling factors. To work effectively, these factors require continual feedback. The right-to-left arrows in Figure 14.1 suggest that student outcomes must inform instructional planning, both by those who provide instruction and by those who are charged with guiding change.

The model we have created may seem at first to be purely theoretical, with little practical relevance to what actually happens in a school. We suggest that it has value as a frame of reference for those endeavoring to guide the change process. As an overview of the various pathways of influence leading to growth in proficiency and motivation, it can be used in tandem with the IC to identify problem areas and to craft workable plans for addressing them.

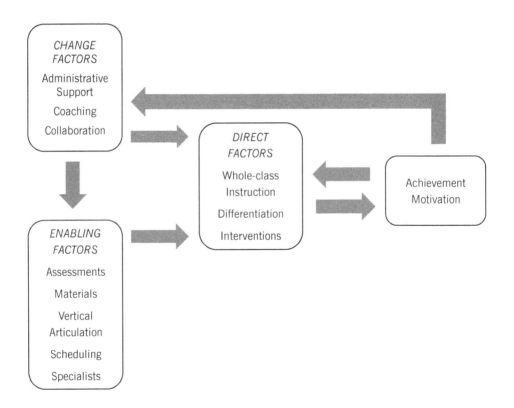

FIGURE 14.1. A model of how key factors influence achievement growth.

PROFESSIONAL DEVELOPMENT ACTIVITIES

- Think through the IC in Table 14.1 as it applies to your school. Which dimensions of your instructional program are closest to optimal implementation? Which dimensions have the farthest to go?

- Space has prevented us from compiling a list of evidence-based instructional approaches. Choose one aspect of instruction (phonics, vocabulary, etc.) and begin such a list. We suggest a three-column chart with these headings:

    Name of Approach

    Description and Steps

    Source of Evidence

- Choose an intervention you are considering and locate the reviews on each of the four sites we mentioned. To what extent do the reviews concur? Are you able to form a reasonable judgment about the intervention?

REFERENCES

Afflerbach, P., & Cho, B. (2011). The classroom assessment of reading. In M. L. Kamil, P. D. Pearson, E. B. Moje, & P. P. Afflerbach (Eds.), *Handbook of reading research* (Vol. 4, pp. 487–514). New York: Routledge/Taylor & Francis.

Bean, R. M. (2012). Literacy leadership in a culture of collaboration. In R. M. Bean & A. S. Dagen (Eds.), *Best practices of literacy leaders: Keys to school improvement* (pp. 3–20). New York: Guilford Press.

Beauchat, K. A., Blamey, K. L., & Philippakos, Z. A. (2012). *Effective read-alouds for early literacy: A teacher's guide for PreK–1.* New York: Guilford Press.

Beauchat, K. A., Blamey, K. L., & Walpole, S. (2010). *The building blocks of preschool success.* New York: Guilford Press.

Beck, I. L., & McKeown, M. G. (2001). Text talk: Capturing the benefits of read-aloud experiences for young children. *The Reading Teacher, 55*, 10–20.

Blachman, B. A., Ball, E. W., Black, R. S., & Tangel, D. M. (1994). Kindergarten teachers develop phoneme awareness in low-income, inner-city classrooms: Does it make a difference? *Reading and Writing, 6*, 1–18.

Chall, J. E. (1996). *Stages of reading development.* New York: McGraw-Hill. (Original work published 1983)

Connor, C., Morrison, F. J., Fishman, B., Giuliani, S., Luck, M., Underwood, P. S., et al. (2011). Testing the impact of child characteristics × instruction interactions on third graders' reading comprehension by differentiating literacy instruction. *Reading Research Quarterly, 46*, 189–221.

Cramer, E. H., & Castle, M. (Eds.). (1994). *Fostering the love of reading: The affective domain in reading education.* Newark, DE: International Reading Association.

Dickinson, D. K., Freiberg, J. B., & Barnes, E. M. (2011). Why are so few interventions really effective?: A call for fine-grained research methodology. In S. B. Neuman & D. K. Dickinson (Eds.), *Handbook of early literacy research* (Vol. 3, pp. 337–357). New York: Guilford Press.

Duke, N. K. (2000). 3.6 minutes per day: The scarcity of information texts in first grade. *Reading Research Quarterly, 35*, 202–224.

Ehri, L. (1999). Phases of development in learning to read words. In J. Oakhill & R. Beard (Eds.), *Reading development and the teaching of reading: A psychological perspective* (p. 79–108). Oxford, UK: Blackwell.

Fullan, M. (2006). *Turnaround leadership.* San Francisco: Jossey-Bass.

Guthrie, J. T., & Wigfield, A. (2000). Engagement and motivation in reading. In M. L. Kamil, P. B. Mosenthal, P. D. Pearson, & R. Barr (Eds.), *Handbook of reading research* (Vol. 3, pp. 403–422). Mahwah, NJ: Erlbaum.

Hall, G., & Hord, S. (2001). *Implementing change: Patterns, principles, and potholes.* Boston: Allyn & Bacon.

Joyce, B., & Showers, B. (2002). *Student achievement through staff development* (3rd ed.). Alexandria, VA: Association for Supervision and Curriculum Development.

Kanter, R. M. (2004). *Confidence: How winning and losing streaks begin and end.* New York: Crown Business.

Kim, Y., Petscher, Y., Schatschneider, C., & Foorman, B. (2010). Does growth rate in oral reading fluency matter in predicting reading comprehension achievement? *Journal of Educational Psychology, 102,* 652–667.

Mangin, M. M., & Stoelinga, S. (2011). Peer? Expert? *Journal of Staff Development, 32,* 48–51.

Matsumura, L., Garnier, H. E., & Resnick, L. B. (2010). Implementing literacy coaching: The role of school social resources. *Educational Evaluation and Policy Analysis, 32,* 249–272.

McKenna, M. C., & Kear, D. J. (1990). Measuring attitude towards reading: A new tool for teachers. *The Reading Teacher, 43,* 626–639.

McKenna, M. C., & Stahl, K. A. D. (2009). *Assessment for reading instruction* (2nd ed.). New York: Guilford Press.

McKenna, M. C., & Walpole, S. (2005). How well does assessment inform our reading instruction? *The Reading Teacher, 59,* 84–86.

McKenna, M. C., & Walpole, S. (2008). *The literacy coaching challenge: Models and methods for grades K–8.* New York: Guilford Press.

Morrow, L. M. (2010). Preparing centers and a literacy-rich environment for small-group instruction in Early Reading First preschools. In M. C. McKenna, S. Walpole, & K. Conradi (Eds.), *Promoting early reading: Research, resources, and best practices* (pp. 124–141). New York: Guilford Press.

Murphy, J. (2004). *Leadership for literacy: Research-based practice, PreK–3.* Thousand Oaks, CA: Corwin Press.

National Early Literacy Panel. (2008). *Developing early literacy: Report of the National Early Literacy Panel.* Washington, DC: National Institute for Literacy.

National Institute of Child Health and Human Development. (2000). *Report of the National Reading Panel. Teaching children to read: An evidence-based assessment of the scientific research literature on reading and its implications for reading instruction* (NIH Publication No. 00-4769). Washington, DC: U.S. Government Printing Office.

Pittelman, S. D., Heimlich, J. E., Berglund, R. L., & French, M. P. (1991). *Semantic feature analysis: Classroom applications.* Newark, DE: International Reading Association.

Raphael, T. E., Highfield, K., & Au, K. H. (2006). *QAR Now: Question answer relationships: A powerful and practical framework that develops comprehension and higher-level thinking in all students.* New York: Scholastic.

Reutzel, D. R., & Jones, C. D. (2010). Assessing and creating effective preschool literacy classroom environments. In M. C. McKenna, S. Walpole, & K. Conradi (Eds.), *Promoting early reading: Research, resources, and best practices* (pp. 175–198). New York: Guilford Press.

Roy, P., & Hord, S. (2003). *Moving NSDC's staff development standards into practice: Innovation configurations, Volume I.* Oxford, OH: National Staff Development Council.

Samuels, S. J. (1979). The method of repeated readings. *The Reading Teacher, 32,* 241–254.

Schwartz, R. M., & Raphael, T. E. (1985). Concept of definition: A key to improving students' vocabulary. *The Reading Teacher, 39,* 198–205.

Stahl, S. A., Kuhn, M. R., & Pickle, J. M. (1999). An educational model of assessment and targeted instruction for children with reading problems. In D. H. Evensen & P. Mosenthal (Eds.), *Reconsidering the role of the reading clinic in a new age of literacy* (pp. 249–272). Stamford, CT: JAI Press.

Taylor, B. M., Pearson, P. D., Clark, K. F., & Walpole, S. (2000). Effective schools and accomplished teachers: Lessons about primary-grade reading instruction in low-income schools. *Elementary School Journal, 101*, 121–165.

Taylor, J. E. (2008). Instructional coaching: The state of the art. In M. M. Mangin & S. R. Stoelinga (Eds.), *Effective teacher leadership: Using research to inform and reform* (pp. 10–35). New York: Teachers College Press.

Walpole, S., & McKenna, M. C. (2009a). Everything you've always wanted to know about literacy coaching but were afraid to ask: A review of policy and research. In K. M. Leander, D. W. Rowe, D. K. Dickinson, R. T. Jimenez, M. K. Hundley, & V. J. Risko (Eds.), *Fifty-ninth yearbook of the National Reading Conference* (pp. 23–33). Milwaukee, WI: National Reading Conference.

Walpole, S., & McKenna, M. C. (2009b). *How to plan differentiated reading instruction: Resources for grades K–3.* New York: Guilford Press.

Walpole, S., & McKenna, M. C. (2013). *The literacy coach's handbook: A guide to research-based practice* (2nd ed.). New York: Guilford Press.

Walpole, S., & Najera, K. (2013). Improving the school reading program: A new call for collaboration. In B. M. Taylor & N. K. Duke (Eds.), *Handbook of effective literacy instruction* (pp. 510–529). New York: Guilford Press.

Wonder-McDowell, C., Reutzel, D. R., & Smith, J. A. (2012). Does instructional alignment matter: Effects on struggling second-grade readers' achievement. *Elementary School Journal, 112*, 259–279.

CHAPTER 15

ENHANCING SOCIAL
AND EMOTIONAL LEARNING

BONNIE BRINTON
MARTIN FUJIKI

Mike, a sixth grader, is excited about J. K. Rowling's Harry Potter books, and he enjoys discussing the ones he has read. Talking with one of his teachers, Mike notes the animosity between Draco Malfoy and Ron Weasley. When asked, "Why does Draco dislike Ron so much?", Mike is puzzled. Although Mike has picked up on the ill-feeling between the characters, he has failed to infer what Draco implies but rarely states outright—that he looks down on Ron's inclusive attitude and family poverty. Mike cannot appreciate the negative emotion Draco conveys in comments such as, "You don't want to go making friends with the wrong sort" (Rowling, 1998, p. 108) or "you couldn't afford half the handle. . . . I suppose you and your brothers have to save up twig by twig" (p. 165), nor can he anticipate Ron's reactions to these insults.

In another instance, Mike, James, and Kevin are pretending to be broadcasters as they sit at a table presenting a newscast in front of a video camera. One boy makes a mild scatological reference and the others chuckle. James and Kevin resume their previous topic, but Mike continues the "potty talk" until James and Kevin nervously shuffle in their seats and tell Mike to "shush." Mike escalates the references, and James and Kevin introduce a safer subject. Mike persists with his talk and eventually leaves the table, sits in another chair, and rotates around, making nonsense noises.

These scenarios seem quite different, but Mike's difficulty in each context stems from common underlying problems. First, Mike has language impairment (LI); that is, he does not understand or produce language as well as other children his age. His LI makes it challenging for Mike to process verbal information in interaction or in text. In addition, Mike lacks the social and emotional competence to perform tasks such as interpreting emotional information, making social inferences, and adjusting his behavior to collaborate with others. As a result, Mike's peer relationships, academic performance, and inclusion in his learning community are all compromised. Like Mike, many children have difficulty with social and emotional learning, particularly if they have associated challenges such as LI, autism spectrum disorder (ASD), or attention-deficit/hyperactivity disorder (ADHD). Even children who do not have developmental problems, however, may lack social and emotional knowledge. These limitations have the potential to impact not only social but also academic functioning.

WHAT RESEARCH SAYS ABOUT SOCIAL AND EMOTIONAL COMPETENCE

Social and emotional competence is a broad concept involving a number of complex processes and behaviors. Voegler-Lee and Kupersmidt (2011) indicated that "social and emotional competence includes the ability to effectively express and regulate emotions, establish positive relationships with peers and adults, and solve personal problems" (p. 605). Social and emotional competence involves several interrelated constructs, processes, and behaviors. For purposes of our discussion we focus on emotional intelligence.

The construct of emotional intelligence was introduced into the academic literature by Salovey and Mayer (1990), and later to the popular press by Goleman (1995). *Emotional intelligence* is "the ability to perceive and express emotions, to understand and use them, and to manage emotions so as to foster personal growth" (Salovey, Detweiler-Bedell, Detweiler-Bedell, & Mayer, 2008, p. 535). Salovey and colleagues (2008) described four overlapping areas that make up emotional intelligence: (1) perception, appraisal, and expression of emotion; (2) emotional facilitation of thinking; (3) understanding and analyzing emotional information; and (4) regulation of emotion (from Figure 33.1, p. 535). Perceiving emotion involves the ability to identify both one's own emotions and those experienced by others. It also includes the ability to express emotion. Accurately perceiving emotion is a basic but necessary step toward emotional intelligence. By way of illustration, children who cannot accurately interpret emotional expressions on the faces or in the voices of others are at a serious disadvantage in social interactions.

Using emotion to facilitate thinking involves the ability to manage emotions to improve cognitive performance. For example, an emotionally sophisticated individual may recognize that certain emotional states facilitate specific abilities and capitalize on those states (e.g., the writer who recognizes that a positive emotional state increases creativity and takes advantage of the mood to enhance performance, or the coach who uses an opponent's negative comments to motivate greater physical effort from players).

Understanding emotions involves a more sophisticated level of interpreting one's own emotions and the emotions of others. For example, as they mature, children learn that one can experience mixed emotions concurrently, such as feeling sad that the family car broke down but delighted that the trip to the dentist must be postponed. By middle childhood they also gain a more sophisticated understanding of complex emotions such as guilt (Harris, 2008).

Finally, regulating emotion involves managing emotion as needed in a given situation (Thompson, 1994). This involves not only moderating but also elevating emotion. For example, an individual may need to calm his or her emotions when taunted by a peer but gear up emotions to persist in a difficult homework assignment. Emotion regulation may be internal or external. Infants are heavily dependent on external regulation, such as being patted and rocked by a caretaker when upset. As children mature they become more capable of internal regulation, such as telling themselves "It's not real" during a frightening movie. It is notable, however, that even adults may draw on external sources for emotion regulation (e.g., seeking out a friend who will provide kind words of encouragement).

These four aspects of emotional intelligence are overlapping. Emotion understanding depends on accurate perception, and regulation involves both perception and understanding. Using emotions to facilitate performance requires accurate perception, understanding, and regulation.

From this discussion we might suppose that emotional intelligence and social competence are separate domains, with emotional intelligence supporting or facilitating our ability to make our way successfully through social interactions with others. In this regard, there is little doubt that successful social behavior is heavily influenced by emotional intelligence. In interactions as diverse as meeting new classmates on the first day of school to saying good-bye to a close friend who is moving away, the way one expresses, understands, and regulates emotions is fundamental. At the same time, however, the relationship between social competence and emotional intelligence is more interactional than unidirectional. Social interactions with other people provide the context in which emotions are experienced. For example, the social relationship between two individuals and the interactional context in which they find themselves play a key role in how they understand their own and each others' emotions. (Compare the emotional expectations of a couple celebrating a wedding anniversary on a weekend getaway to those of a recently divorced couple exchanging the children for the weekend.) As Denham and colleagues (2011) have observed, "The interpersonal function of emotion is central to its expression and experience. Conversely, social interactions and relationships are guided, even defined, by emotional transactions" (p. 414).

Social and Emotional Competence: Why Does It Matter?

Mounting pressure to teach effectively and to demonstrate student progress challenges educators to consider the use of instructional time and resources very carefully. Since student learning is often measured only in terms of specific academic skills, why should teachers spend valuable classroom time focusing on social and emotional competence? The answer can be found in considering Mike, the sixth grader described at the beginning of this chapter. Mike's limited social and emotional competence restricts his ability to establish and maintain personal relationships at home, at school, and in his community. At the same time, Mike's limited social and emotional development compromises his ability to be successful academically. This occurs because social and emotional difficulties can affect his motivation to learn, his inclusion in learning contexts, and his ability to acquire literacy skills. Elaboration of each of these points follows.

Motivation to Learn

Motivation is a multifaceted construct that may stem from both external and internal sources. Children may respond to extrinsic or external sources of motivation such as praise or rewards, but it is internal or intrinsic motivation that drives learning most effectively. For example, intrinsic motivation is essential to becoming an engaged reader who reads broadly and extensively not to earn praise or stickers but for the sake of reading (Guthrie, Wigfield, & Perencevich, 2004; Wigfield & Wentzel, 2007).

Motivation is central to learning, and emotion is at the heart of motivation. Emotion underlies the deep interest that motivates a child to read late into the night to see whether Harry Potter ultimately defeats Lord Voldemort. By the same token, emotion regulation is critical when learners need to devote considerable time and effort to challenging work.

For example, remaining calm and focused in the face of frustration helps a child to persist in difficult disciplinary literacy tasks.

Motivation is also related to an individual's sense of self-efficacy or belief about what he or she can do. Children form beliefs about their efficacy in learning tasks based partly on their previous experience (Wigfield & Tonks, 2004) and the value they place on the skill they are learning. Children who have difficulty learning to read, for example, may have a store of negative experiences with print, may dislike books, or may have acquired a negative view of their potential as readers. As Wigfield and Wentzel (2007) explain, "It is difficult for students to maintain a strong sense of efficacy when they are not doing well" (p. 193). Likewise, it can be challenging for students to persist in tasks they do not find pertinent or compelling. The value children place on literacy activities, for instance, influences their motivation to learn to read (Wigfield, Hoa, & Klauda, 2008).

It may be particularly challenging for students at risk for learning problems to maintain motivation, but it can also be difficult for typical learners. The positive or negative emotion associated with perceived success or failure can influence successive efforts to learn. In addition, children who enjoy or value an activity are more likely to invest in learning it. Thus, if children do not enjoy literacy activities, it is important to help them "realize that reading has personal relevance and meaning for them" (Paul & Wang, 2012, p. 195). Facilitating social and emotional development can be important in helping children invest in learning tasks, view themselves as successful learners, and maintain motivation to persist in the labor of learning.

Inclusion in Learning Contexts

From infancy on, learning is often a social endeavor. For example, in homes where print is available and valued, most children enjoy settling in with a caretaker to read a storybook. These story-sharing experiences constitute rich learning contexts in which children and more sophisticated readers share focus and exchange thoughts and ideas. When Mike was a preschooler, however, he disliked reading with his mother and would squirm off her lap and find something else to do. His impaired language skills made it difficult for him to participate in the story conversation (e.g., see van Kleeck & Vander Woude, 2003). But Mike's lack of interest was not just a matter of difficulty comprehending the words. He also had difficulty with social and emotional competence.

In addition to understanding the language of stories, children must be able to perceive and understand emotional cues from the reader's tone of voice. They must also be able to make emotional connections with both the reader and the story. Without these emotional connections, there may be no "hook" for children in story sharing, and there may be little motivation to persist with the story. As children grow older, their access to many additional learning contexts may be limited by poor social and emotional development. Children who have difficulty understanding the emotional cues expressed by peers may appear to be nonresponsive in conversational interaction. They may have difficulty appreciating the perspectives of others and may be unable to anticipate or recognize the emotional and social impact of their behavior on others.

Other social and emotional problems may also exclude children from important learning contexts. For example, some shy children come to interactions with an approach–avoidance conflict: They would like to interact with others but are fearful of doing so (Rubin, Bowker, & Kennedy, 2009). These children may lack the strategies needed to enter ongoing play and work groups. Even when involved in peer interactions, they may lack social behaviors that would allow them to make meaningful contributions. When working with peers on assignments or projects, they may remain on the outskirts of the activity. As a result, these children may have difficulty participating fully in classroom collaborations and cooperative learning activities.

It is concerning whenever a child is not fully included in the classroom culture, and it is particularly devastating for learners such as Mike. Students who have language-learning problems may need much more exposure to, and involvement in, learning activities than do less vulnerable learners. Because of social and emotional limitations, however, those who need the most supportive learning environment may get the least. It is important to foster social and emotional development to ensure that all children are included in the classroom culture and have full access to learning contexts.

Ability to Acquire Literacy Skills

The ability to read and write on basic as well as sophisticated levels is influenced by social and emotional development in many ways. As Hogan (2011) noted, "When successful, a literary work produces a complex emotional experience in the reader" (p. 22). A child's social and emotional competencies affect the way that he or she experiences text. Even for preschoolers, the ability to comprehend stories and narratives depends on interpreting the emotions, intentions, and motives of characters. Consider a simple story such as *The Three Little Pigs*. Readers must infer a great deal of social and emotional information that is not explicitly stated in the text. For example, the reader needs to appreciate the excitement and/or trepidation that the pigs might feel in leaving their childhood home and setting out on their own. Even if it is not directly mentioned in the text, the reader needs to understand that the pigs might be somewhat anxious in their new environment. The story is meaningful to the extent that the reader can empathize somewhat with the pigs in their search for safe shelter. The reader also needs to understand that the pigs are afraid when the wolf seeks entry to their homes, even if the text does not state this directly. In some versions of the story, the wolf eats the first two pigs. The reader must infer how the third pig feels about the loss of his siblings, and how this loss might affect his behavior. In versions in which all the pigs survive, the reader is left to infer how the near-death experience of the first two pigs might inform their behavior in the future.

Social and emotional competence is foundational to comprehension of this relatively simple story, and it becomes increasingly important as children encounter more complex narratives. Students who experience difficulty interpreting emotion cues and inferring emotions elicited by events may well have trouble understanding story plots, even if they can decode the words and sentences in the text. This is particularly challenging for vulnerable learners, such as those with language or learning impairments. Many of these children struggle with basic emotion understanding as preschoolers, and they may have lingering difficulty in understanding emotions beyond the basic "happy, mad, sad" as elementary school students. Older students who cannot understand or anticipate more nuanced, complex, or mixed emotions will likely be unprepared to comprehend the stories that comprise chapter books. Indeed, research suggests that emotional intelligence and reading comprehension are associated in children and adolescents with language-learning problems (Angadi, 2011).

Social and emotional learning is important not just to reading comprehension but also to writing. Most written genres involve expressing or sharing emotions either directly or via implication. As Hogan (2011) noted with regard to literature, "a successful work is a work that enhances the reader's emotional response" (p. 25). Students lacking social and emotional knowledge will be hard-pressed to write about people and events in a way that shares perspectives and portrays feelings.

Can We Facilitate Social and Emotional Development?

The previous discussion highlights the central role that social and emotional competence plays in supporting students' relationships, as well as their motivation to learn, their inclusion in important learning contexts, and their access to literacy. Social and emotional learning is essential to students' overall development and should therefore be infused throughout school curricula. As Bernard (2006) explained, "Be aware that the road to raising the achievement of all young people is paved not only with quality academic programs, but also with quality social–emotional–motivational programs" (p. 116).

Social and Emotional Learning in the Classroom

Social and emotional learning is important, but are educational programs that target this area effective and practical to implement in classrooms? Recent research suggests that they are. Durlak, Weissberg, Dymnicki, Taylor, and Schellinger (2011) reported a large-scale meta-analysis of 213 studies of social and emotional learning programs implemented in grades K–12. In comparison to controls, students who participated in these programs showed gains in social and emotional skills (e.g., identifying emotions, perspective taking, conflict resolution), attitudes about themselves and others (e.g., self-perceptions) and positive social behaviors (e.g., cooperating with others). In addition, students showed a decrease in conduct (behavioral) problems and emotional distress. In studies that assessed academic performance, students showed a significant increase in achievement test scores and grades. Voegler-Lee and Kupersmidt (2011) reviewed the outcomes of six programs for children from PreK to sixth grade. They found that children who participated in these programs showed improved social competence, emotion regulation, and prosocial behaviors, along with decreased conduct problems, aggression, and withdrawal.

Programs that enhance social and emotional learning share certain characteristics. Durlak and colleagues (2011) and Voegler-Lee and Kupersmidt (2011) found that effective programs were universal or school based, enjoyed administrative support, and were implemented by school personnel (as opposed to outside consultants). Durlak and colleagues noted that the most effective programs involved SAFE procedures; that is, they were designed in coordinated, Sequences, with small steps leading to more complex behaviors. Programs were Active, in that students had opportunities to engage in and practice specific skills and behaviors. Programs were Focused, in that sufficient time and attention were devoted to instruction, and Explicit in explaining specific behaviors and objectives to students (see Durlak et al., 2011, for examples of programs and their outcomes).

It is notable that social and emotional learning programs are effective in improving emotional and social competence, as well as academic performance, when they are carefully designed and implemented within classrooms and schools. It should be noted, however, that these programs not only effectively improve the behavior and academic skills of children considered to be typically developing but they can also impact the abilities of children with social, emotional, and behavioral problems (Payton et al., 2008). As encouraging as these outcomes are, we also need to consider the needs of students whose limited social and emotional competence is associated with a variety of additional developmental problems.

Social and Emotional Learning in Children with Disabilities

Each child in a classroom has a unique profile of strengths and needs, and particular children may require more support than others. Some children, like Mike, have disabilities that are associated with a variety of challenges in social and emotional learning. Children with ASD, for example, by definition, have problems with social interaction. Many children with LI, learning disabilities, ADHD, or intellectual disability (ID) demonstrate a range of social and emotional difficulties as well. These children constitute a notable proportion of the school-age population. For example, 7% of kindergarteners may present with LI (Tomblin et al., 1997), 5% may present with ADHD (Faraone, Sergeant, Billberg, & Biederman, 2003), 0.06% may present with ASD (Rutter, 2005), and 1% may present with ID (Maulik, Mascarenhas, Mathers, Dua, & Saxena, 2011). Most of these children attend regular classrooms and require careful attention to maximize their growth.

Determining the effectiveness of educational programs in facilitating social and emotional development for children with disabilities has proved difficult, however. For example, Kavale and Mostert (2004) reported a meta-analysis of 53 studies of social skills training programs implemented for children with learning disabilities and found only modest effects. These findings are sobering, but there are a number of considerations. First, investigating the outcomes of social and emotional learning intervention in children with disabilities is challenging work. As Kavale and Mostert pointed out, studies of the efficacy of social and emotional interventions have been plagued by difficulties in measurements, research design, and even in defining targeted behaviors. Children with disabilities often demonstrate slower or subtler changes than do typically developing children, and growth can be difficult to document. Perhaps most importantly, children with disabilities can vary dramatically in their developmental trajectories, and the types of research designs often utilized with large groups of typical learners may not be well suited to characterize their behavior. Research studies that focus more closely on the performance of individual children in response to a specific intervention in carefully described contexts may show more promising results (e.g., see Marchant, Solano, Young, & Renshaw, 2007).

Regardless of any shortcomings of research on the efficacy of social and emotional learning programs for children with disabilities, the fact remains that these children are part of the school population, and they are among the students who most need support in social and emotional development.

RESEARCH INTO PRACTICE: HOW CAN WE BEST FACILITATE SOCIAL AND EMOTIONAL DEVELOPMENT?

Instruction time in school is precious, and it is important to use resources wisely. When planning approaches, programs, or interventions to facilitate social and emotional learning, there are a number of important considerations. As mentioned earlier, programs that have an organized sequence, that encourage active learning, and that are focused and explicit have proven most effective for typical learners (Durlak et al., 2011). It is safe to assume that these characteristics are equally, if not more, important for more vulnerable learners. In addition, other factors influence how well children respond to educational approaches designed to foster social and emotional competence. These factors are particularly critical to the development of children with disabilities.

Accessibility of Instruction

Most programs designed to enhance social and emotional learning are highly dependent on spoken and written language as vehicles of instruction; that is, most instruction is provided through talking, reading, and writing. What's more, the language used to present social and emotional concepts quickly becomes both complex and abstract. Students who can discuss nuances of emotions and have an extensive repertoire of emotion words are likely to do well with such instruction. Conversely, children who have limited language ability (e.g., children with LI, ASD, ID) may struggle to understand and produce the words and the sentence structures involved in such sophisticated talk. They may spend so much effort trying to keep up with the discourse that they may not have much mental energy available to reflect on the concepts being taught. It is important to provide sufficient support to give these children access to the instruction. For example, when introducing important concepts, it is helpful for educators to slow their speech, to use clear sentence structures, to highlight the most important points using vocal stress and intonation, and to repeat important points (educators will find that these adjustments enhance the comprehension of all students). Many students benefit from added visual, tactile, and contextual cues to make abstract concepts more concrete. Many educators also find that it is helpful to seat particular students close by, so that it is possible to monitor their responses to input. Likewise, it is important to monitor how well students understand instruction on an ongoing basis and to make necessary adjustments to clarify. It is also important for educators and other professionals such as speech–language pathologists to collaborate to help children gain access to the language of social and emotional instruction.

Emotion Talk

Interactions between young children and their caregivers provide a foundation for social and emotional learning (Gottman & DeClaire, 1998; Thompson, 2011). By engaging in "emotion talk" with their children in conjunction with everyday activities and conversations, caregivers help their children learn to understand, to regulate, and to display emotion in socially appropriate ways. Emotion talk in the classroom can facilitate social and emotional learning as well. This talk can, and should, take place in the context of everyday activities and interactions. As Pellitteri, Dealy, Fasano, and Kugler (2006) noted, "Every academic task and social interaction can be an opportunity to facilitate emotional awareness in students" (p. 168). By highlighting the social and emotional content of stories, literature, historical events, political issues, and so forth, educators provide rich contexts for social and emotional issues. It is important to make emotional and social information explicit, since many children fail to infer information from subtle or implied references.

Peer interactions at school should provide a rich context for social and emotional learning. Unfortunately, however, such interactions are frequently negative experiences for students with disabilities. Pellitteri and colleagues (2006) pointed out how important it is for educators to structure student interactions by facilitating emotional awareness in a nonpunitive way. They noted, "Teachers have a tremendous responsibility to monitor the group dynamics and the emotional tone of the social interactions, particularly for students with disabilities" (p. 165).

Educational Focus

Children have myriad social and emotional needs. Sometimes these needs are manifest in behaviors that draw negative attention or invite disrespect from peers. It can be tempting to target these behaviors when working with children. It is often the case, however, that a specific behavior simply manifests a deeper underlying issue. For example, if a student makes a rude comment about another child's clothes, it can be tempting to teach that child to pay other children compliments about their clothing. This may be counterproductive, however, if a student proceeds around the classroom saying, "That's a nice shirt," to each of his peers. It is far more productive to focus instruction on understanding the emotions of others, attending to the emotional cues conveyed by others, and anticipating the emotional impact that one's comments elicit. It is important to focus educational interventions on the kinds of social and emotional knowledge that can be expected to generalize to a wide variety of contexts and interactions.

Social Goals

Even though they may not be consciously aware of them, students have social goals that motivate and shape their behavior in individual social interactions (Rose & Asher, 2004). Positive goals include getting to know people, having fun with others, cooperating, sharing ideas and feelings, and forming relationships. When children enter interactions with positive social goals, they attempt to reach out to others in sociable ways. Sometimes, however, children enter interactions with social goals that are less than positive. For example, a child out on the playground may be disposed to aggress, withdraw, or simply protect him- or herself. If children have negative social goals, attempts to teach them strategies to engage with others in felicitous interactions may be doomed. It is impossible to force a social goal on another person. (We are reminded of an exhausted mother of a teenage boy who, after a frustrating day of dealing with adolescent recalcitrance, dropped her son and a friend off at an amusement park with the admonition, "Have fun or I'll kill you!") Children who have had negative or frustrating interactions with peers in the past may not have happy expectations for peer interaction. Simply put, they may not understand that playing and cooperating with others can be pleasant. Although we cannot explicitly teach social goals, it is feasible to guide children toward more positive goals indirectly (Taylor & Asher, 1984). It can be important to draw attention to the fact that children can experience positive emotions while interacting together ("Look at those kids. They are cooperating. They are all smiling. They're having a lot of fun. It's fun to work with other kids"). It is even more important to highlight instances when individual children interact positively with others ("I noticed you were working well with Tim and Pearl at the art table this morning. You were all laughing. That looked like fun"). Gradually, children may learn to adopt underlying social goals that motivate them to seek more sociable interactions.

Time and Intensity of Instruction

Programs designed to foster social and emotional learning in children take time. The effective programs analyzed by Durlak and colleagues (2011) lasted from 1 to more than 2 years, and additional follow-up was recommended. For children with disabilities, an extended period of instruction in social and emotional concepts is indicated in order to effect meaningful change. Indeed, such instruction should constitute part of the ongoing curriculum. For these children, social and emotional learning should be an early priority and a focus that is maintained throughout the school years (Brinton & Fujiki, 2006).

REFLECTIONS AND NEW DIRECTIONS

Social and emotional competence underlies an individual's ability to establish and maintain healthy relationships, to adjust to social contexts, to maintain motivation, and to work and learn with others. Social and emotional competence is manifest in the social behaviors students demonstrate at school, as well as the way they approach classroom tasks and achieve academic learning. There is clear evidence that programs that enhance social and emotional learning in students can yield positive results in social behaviors and attitudes, as well as academic growth. The most effective programs are not haphazard or incidental but are carefully focused and sequenced to build one competency upon another. In addition, successful programs involve students actively and provide opportunities to practice new skills (Durlak et al., 2011).

Successfully navigating even relatively common social interactions requires a good deal of social and emotional competence. Classroom contexts are replete with opportunities to foster social and emotional learning in the course of daily interactions with students. An important principle to remember is that educators need to make implicit information explicit; that is, they need to help students recognize and understand the social and emotional aspects of events, situations, conversations, conflicts, and all kinds of interactions. For example, educators can highlight and explain the emotional information conveyed indirectly or subtly by characters in literature. It can be helpful to draw students' attention to the emotions that certain situations elicit, and to illustrate similarities and connections between characters' reactions and those that students might experience themselves. In addition to emphasizing the emotional content of literature, educators can help students recognize and interpret social and emotional cues conveyed by their peers in classroom interactions. Educators are responsible for setting the emotional tone of their classrooms and fostering respectful and cooperative relationships among their students.

Although supporting social and emotional learning is important for all students, it is particularly essential for students who may have difficulties associated with disabilities. There is a critical need for additional research to demonstrate the best ways to support social and emotional learning in these students. It is particularly important to focus on students' individual needs, give students access to the language of instruction, involve students in a rich context of emotion talk, and guide students toward positive social goals.

PROFESSIONAL DEVELOPMENT ACTIVITIES

- Meet with your administrator (principal) to discuss schoolwide goals and programs to facilitate social and emotional learning in students. If a program is in place in your school, plan ways to implement it in your classroom. In doing this, keep the needs of children with disabilities in mind. If a program is not in place, consider one of the programs described by Durlak and colleagues (2011) and discuss ways you might implement it in your classroom with your administrator.

- Consider the literature units you will teach, and the books and stories you will use in this academic year. Consider the social and emotional content of the literature and plan ways to make that information explicit in your lessons and discussions with students. Plan ways to engage your students in conversations, activities, or projects focusing on the social and emotional content.

- Consider your students and think about any individuals with disabilities and/or weak social skills or limited emotional intelligence. Make a plan to support the social and emotional learning of these students. Your plan might include observing these students carefully in social interaction, grouping these students with peers who tend to be accommodating to them, choosing books and materials that highlight aspects of social and emotional functioning, emphasizing emotion talk, and so forth.

- If you have students who are receiving special services, meet with the service providers (speech–language pathologist, special educator, school psychologist, etc.) to plan ways to support the social and emotional learning of these children in your classroom. Meet with the special service providers regularly to assess student progress.

- Arrange to have yourself video- or audiotaped while you teach a lesson with social and emotional content (literature, history, political science, etc.). Watch or listen to the recording and consider ways you might adjust your language to make it more accessible to students. Examples might include slowing your speech, using stress and intonation to emphasize important points, and defining emotion words. Concentrate on aspects of your language that you can adjust, and record yourself again. Consider how any changes you make may affect your students' responses.

REFERENCES

Angadi, S. G. (2011). A study of emotional intelligence in relation to reading comprehension of secondary school students. *International Research Journal, 3*(28), 19–21.

Bernard, M. E. (2006) It's time we teach social–emotional competence as well as we teach academic competence. *Reading and Writing Quarterly, 22,* 103–119.

Brinton, B., & Fujiki, M. (2006). Social intervention for children with language impairment: Factors affecting efficacy. *Communication Disorders Quarterly, 28,* 39–41.

Denham, S., Warren, H., von Salisch, M., Benga, O., Chin, J.-C., & Geangu, E. (2011). Emotions and social development in childhood. In P. K. Smith & C. H. Hart (Eds.), *The Wiley–Blackwell handbook of childhood social development* (pp. 413–433). Malden, MA: Blackwell.

Durlak, J. A., Weissberg, R. P., Dymnicki, A, B., Taylor, R. D., & Schellinger, K. B. (2011). The impact of enhancing students' social and emotional learning: A meta-analysis of school-based universal interventions. *Child Development, 82,* 405–432.

Faraone, S. V., Sergeant, J., Billberg, C., & Biederman, J. (2003). The worldwide prevalence of ADHD: Is it an American condition? *World Psychiatry, 2*(2), 104–113.

Goleman, D. (1995). *Emotional intelligence.* New York: Bantam Books.

Gottman, J., & DeClaire, J. (1998). *Raising an emotionally intelligent child: The heart of parenting.* New York: Simon & Schuster.

Guthrie, J. T., Wigfield, A., & Perencevich, K. C. (2004). Scaffolding for motivation and engagement in reading. In J. T. Guthrie, A. Wigfield, & K. C. Perencevich (Eds.), *Motivating reading comprehension: Concept-oriented reading instruction* (pp. 55–86). Mahwah, NJ: Erlbaum.

Harris, P. L. (2008). Children's understanding of emotion. In M. Lewis, J. M. Haviland-Jones, & L. Feldman Barrett (Eds.), *Handbook of emotions* (3rd ed., pp. 320–331). New York: Guilford Press.

Hogan, P. C. (2011). *What literacy teaches us about emotion.* New York: Cambridge University Press.

Kavale, K. A., & Mostert, M. P. (2004). Social skills interventions for individuals with learning disabilities. *Learning Disability Quarterly, 27,* 31–43.

Marchant, M. R., Solano, B. R., Young, R. K., & Renshaw, T. L. (2007). Modifying socially withdrawn behavior: A playground intervention for students with internalizing behaviors. *Psychology in the Schools, 44,* 779–794.

Maulik, P. K., Mascarenhas, M. N., Mathers, C. D., Dua, T., & Saxena, S. (2011). Prevalence of intellectual disability: A meta-analysis of population-based studies. *Research in Developmental Disabilities, 32,* 419–436.

Paul, P. V., & Wang, Y. (2012). *Literate thought: Understanding comprehension and literacy.* Sudbury, MA: Jones & Bartlett Learning.

Payton, J., Weissberg, R. P., Durlak, J. A., Dymnicki, A. B., Taylor, R. D., Schellinger, K. B., et al. (2008). *The positive impact of social and emotional learning for kindergarten to eight-grade students: Findings from three scientific reviews*. Chicago: Collaborative for Academic, Social, and Emotional Learning.

Pellitteri, J., Dealy, M., Fasano, C., & Kugler, J. (2006). Emotionally intelligent interventions for students with reading disabilities. *Reading and Writing Quarterly, 22*, 155–171.

Rose, A. J., & Asher, S. (2004). Children's strategies and goals in response to help-giving and help-seeking tasks within a friendship. *Child Development, 75*, 749–763.

Rowling, J. K. (1998). *Harry Potter and the sorcerer's stone*. New York: Levine Books.

Rubin, K. H., Bowker, J. C., & Kennedy, A. E. (2009). Avoiding and withdrawing from the peer group. In K. H. Rubin, W. M. Bukowski, & B. Laursen (Eds.), *Handbook of peer interactions, relationships, and groups* (pp. 303–321). New York: Guilford Press.

Rutter, M. (2005). Incidence of autism spectrum disorders: Changes over time and their meaning. *Acta Paediatrica, 94*, 2–15.

Salovey, P., Detweiler-Bedell, B. T., Detweiler-Bedell, J. B., & Mayer, J. D. (2008). Emotional intelligence. In M. Lewis, J. M. Haviland-Jones, & L. Feldman Barrett (Eds.), *Handbook of emotions* (3rd ed., pp. 533–547). New York: Guilford Press.

Salovey, P., & Mayer, J. (1990). Emotional intelligence. *Imagination, Cognition, and Personality, 9*, 185–211.

Taylor, A. R., & Asher, S. R. (1984). Children's goals in social competence: Individual differences in a game playing context. In T. Field, J. L. Roopnarine, & M. Segal (Eds.), *Friendship in normal and handicapped children* (pp. 53–78). Norwood, NJ: Ablex.

Thompson, R. (1994). Emotion regulation: A theme in search of definition. *Monographs of the Society for Research in Child Development, 59*(2–3), 25–52.

Thompson, R. (2011). *The emotionate child: Building emotional health and compassion in young children*. Paper presented at the Seventh Annual Marjorie Pay Hinckley Lecture, Brigham Young University, Provo, UT.

Tomblin, J. B., Records, N. L., Buckwalter, P., Zhang, X., Smith, E., & O'Brien, M. (1997). Prevalence of specific language impairment in kindergarten children. *Journal of Speech, Language, and Hearing Research, 40*, 1245–1260.

van Kleeck, A., & Vander Woude, J. (2003). Book sharing with preschoolers with language delays. In A. van Kleeck, S. A. Stahl, & E. B. Bauer (Eds.), *On reading books to children: Parents and teachers* (pp. 58–92). Mahwah, NJ: Erlbaum.

Voegler-Lee, M. E., & Kupersmidt, J. B. (2011). Intervening in childhood social development. In P. K. Smith & C. H. Hart (Eds.), *The Wiley–Blackwell handbook of childhood social development* (2nd ed., pp. 605–626). Malden, MA: Blackwell.

Wigfield, A., Hoa, L. W., & Klauda, S. L. (2008). The role of achievement values in the self-regulation of achievement behaviors. In D. H. Schunk & B. J. Zimmerman (Eds.), *Motivation and self-regulated learning: Theory, research, and applications* (pp. 169–195). Mahwah, NJ: Erlbaum.

Wigfield, A., & Tonks, S. (2004). The development of motivation for reading and how it is influenced by CORI. In J. T. Guthrie, A. Wigfield, & K. C. Perencevich (Eds.), *Motivating reading comprehension: Concept-oriented reading instruction* (pp. 249–272). Mahwah, NJ: Erlbaum.

Wigfield, A., & Wentzel, K. R. (2007). Introduction to motivation at school: Interventions that work. *Educational Psychologist, 42*(2), 191–196.

CHAPTER 16

ASSESSING YOUNG CHILDREN'S LEARNING

RUTH ALFARO PIKER
ABIGAIL M. JEWKES

The ultimate use of any assessment data should be aligned with
the stated purpose of the assessment and should cause no harm.
—JACQUELINE JONES (2004, p. 7)

As Ms. Jones and Martha review Martha's work samples from the past few months, the teacher can't help but recall the journey they took to arrive at his moment. Martha, who started first grade as quiet and shy, became an outgoing and verbose young girl. Her ability to use English has drastically increased over the school year, while she still maintains her native language. She enjoys expressing her ideas through drawings and writing, and particularly likes sharing her work with her peers and parents. Her math and writing samples illustrate how Martha is meeting the first-grade state standards in mathematics and language arts. Although this was not always the case, Ms. Jones' persistence and willingness to use multiple assessments clearly have benefited Martha.

Historically, informal assessments, particularly observations, characterized common approaches for evaluating young children's growth and learning (Shepard, Kagan, & Wurtz, 1998). Educators used observations to document children's behavior as they carried out everyday activities. However, passage of the No Child Left Behind Act of 2001 changed the landscape of assessment for young children, leading to increased accountability, higher educational outcomes, and the demand for early childhood assessments (Meisels, 2007). Consequently, children take standardized achievement tests as early as second grade, and states are developing early learning standards for younger and younger ages, resulting in greater academic expectations of young children (McAfee & Leong, 2011; Stipek, 2006) and the development of accompanying assessments. Questions of how students can best demonstrate what they know guide political discussions and federal funding, such as the U.S. Department of Education's Race to the Top—Early Learning Challenge grant and the use of performance assessments at the national level for the Common Core State Standards (National Governors Association Center for Best Practices & Council of Chief State School Officers, 2010).

As these new assessments are created, developers must remember that assessments intended for young children should differ from those for older children (Shepard et al., 1998; Wortham, 2008). Early childhood is a unique time given that young children's development and learning is not linear or narrow; rather, it changes rapidly and differs from growth rates at other ages (Lightfoot, Cole, & Cole, 2012; Meisels, 2007). For example, young children's test scores from one time point may differ from the scores on the same test administered only a month later. Additionally, children enter early learning classrooms—whether preschool, kindergarten, or first grade—with varied cultural, linguistic, and economic experiences (Meisels, 2007), and many early childhood assessments do not account for this diversity (see McAfee & Leong, 2011; Meisels & Atkins-Burnett, 2006). Thus, a standard pencil-and-paper test administered by individuals unfamiliar to the child, using a language the child may not understand, becomes inappropriate for most young children. As a result of being tested in this way, many children are misplaced or mislabeled, which leads to missed learning opportunities (Green, 1997; Samson & Lesaux, 2009; Stiggins, 2002). As assessments are used more frequently with young children and their scores are the basis for educational decisions such as kindergarten entry and promotion to the next grade, careful consideration of how early childhood assessments are used is of utmost importance. Our purpose in this chapter is to review recent research on early childhood assessments and provide practical recommendations regarding their selection, use, and interpretation.

WHAT RESEARCH SAYS
ABOUT THE ASSESSMENT OF YOUNG CHILDREN

Assessment is "almost any form of measurement and appraisal of what children know and can do, including tests, observations, interviews, and reports from knowledgeable sources, and other means" (McAfee & Leong, 2011, p. 2). When designing and selecting early childhood assessments, educators should be guided by simple yet powerful principles (Shepard et al., 1998). First, the assessment must provide a clear benefit for the child, either directly or through program improvement. The results of the assessment must never be used for placement, promotion, or tracking (Meisels & Atkins-Burnett, 2006; National Association for the Education of Young Children [NAEYC], 2003; Shepard et al., 1998). Second, the assessment should be "tailored to a specific purpose and should be reliable, valid, and fair for that purpose" (Shepard et al., 1998, p. 5). A *reliable* assessment produces consistent results that are reproducible at a different time period. An assessment that measures what it is intended to measure is considered *valid*, and a *fair* measure is unbiased, such that some students are placed at a disadvantage due to race, gender, ethnicity, or other factors (Cronbach, 1990; McMillan, 2008). Third, due to the difficulty in obtaining reliable and valid assessment data on and from young children, some assessments should be postponed until the child is older. Fourth, the assessment should be "age-appropriate in both content and the method of data collection" (Shepard et al., 1998, p. 6). Assessments should address the developmental domains and be conducted in contexts familiar to young children. Fifth, the child's first and second language must be considered when identifying culturally and linguistically appropriate assessments and when interpreting results, keeping in mind that all assessments measure language ability (McAfee & Leong, 2011; NAEYC, 2003, 2005). When assessing dual-language and English learners (DLLs and ELs, respectively), qualified assessors should use multiple assessment methods and measures, including both nonverbal and verbal measures, and be bilingual and bicultural (McAfee & Leong, 2011; NAEYC, 2005). Finally, teachers should view parents as a knowledgeable resource and involve them in the ongoing process of assessment; this is particularly true for DLLs and ELs (McAfee & Leong, 2011).

The purpose of an assessment guides decision making that "determines every other aspect of how the assessment is conducted" (Shepard et al., 1998, p. 6), including the content, methods of data collection, technical requirements, and consequences. There are four purposes of assessment: (1) support of learning and instruction, (2) identifying children with special needs, (3) program evaluation and monitoring trends, and (4) high-stakes accountability (Meisels & Atkins-Burnett, 2006; Shepard et al., 1998). Each has an important place and need within the larger context of assessment. Various assessment types with diverse purposes have been developed over time within the field, including standardized tests, play-based assessments, dynamic assessments, performance assessments, observation-based assessments, functional assessments, ecological assessments, and curriculum-based assessments (Gullo, 2006; Mindes, 2007). In the following section, we first explain the four purposes for early childhood assessments, and then describe four commonly used types of assessments in early childhood education: standardized tests, performance assessments, curriculum-based assessments, and observation-based assessments.

Four Purposes of Assessment

Support of Learning and Instruction

One purpose of assessment is "to promote children's learning and development" (NAEYC, 2003, p. 3). Assessment practices should be ongoing within the naturally occurring context of the classroom as children engage in meaningful curricular activities (Gullo, 2006; McAfee & Leong, 2011). Teachers gather information about children and use knowledge of age-appropriate practices and early learning standards to understand what children can do, what they need to learn next, and how to modify curricula to plan instruction that supports children's learning and development. This process creates a relationship between assessment and curriculum that leads to improved instruction and educational outcomes for all children (Gullo, 2006; NAEYC, 2003; Shepard et al., 1998). By also understanding children's language proficiencies and their expectations for how to interact with others and in group settings, teachers provide appropriate instructional opportunities (Gottlieb, 2006; Heath, 1983). Unlike the other purposes of assessment, the primary audience in this case is the teacher. Many teachers implement informal assessments that meet their daily curricular needs, and these may be teacher-developed or curriculum-based. Teacher-developed assessments rarely contain acceptable psychometric properties, such as reliability and validity (Meisels & Piker, 2001). Nevertheless, these teacher-developed assessments provide in-the-moment, meaningful feedback regarding what students can do (Shepard et al., 1998). These assessments must accurately represent children's true abilities (McAfee & Leong, 2011; McMillan, 2008) and provide correct information for teachers to record and refer to when designing the classroom curriculum. Teachers keep and reuse measures whose scores they trust and that provide consistent results over time, while also considering environmental distractions, unexpected events, and children's feelings. Measures that teachers do not find helpful to their everyday planning and instruction are generally discarded or revised. Furthermore, with the number of children from linguistically and culturally diverse backgrounds steadily growing in the United States (Payan & Nettles, 2008), teachers should consider children's language, culture, and experiences when identifying appropriate assessments and interpreting the results. For example, when assessing DLLs and ELs, the assessment context should be familiar; various measures should be used; the home language, English, or a mix of linguistic responses should be acceptable; and results should be interpreted by bilingual and bicultural personnel (Gottlieb, 2006; McAfee & Leong, 2011; NAEYC, 2005). The purpose of supporting learning and instruction is to optimize educational opportunities that lead to academic success.

Identifying Children with Special Needs

Another purpose of early childhood assessments is to identify children with a specific difficulty, such as physical, cognitive, and emotional delays or disabilities that may require additional services (Meisels & Atkins-Burnett, 2006; NAEYC, 2003; Shepard et al., 1998). The two stages for this identification process are screening and diagnosis (Meisels & Atkins-Burnett, 2005). A *screening* assessment is a preventive measure for children who may require additional support and intervention services. Screening measures are typically conducted when a child is not demonstrating age-appropriate behaviors. These assessments are quick and efficient measures whose administration does not require specialized training. The results indicate whether the child is performing within or outside the standard range of development. Based on the results from a screening test, a child may be referred for additional testing that focuses on areas identified by the screening. Only trained professionals conduct *diagnostic* testing. These additional tests may lead to diagnosis of a learning delay or disability and a need for intervention services. Such a diagnosis is only determined after a series of assessments have been completed, never as a result of a single administration of one screening instrument (Meisels & Atkins-Burnett, 2005; NAEYC, 2003). Furthermore, screening and diagnostic assessments must present evidence of satisfactory psychometric properties—specifically, reliability, validity, and generalizability (Kettler & Feeney-Kettler, 2011; NAEYC, 2005). Examples of screening instruments that meet these criteria include the Early Screening Instrument—Revised (ESI-R; Meisels, Henderson, Liaw, Browning, & Have, 1993; Meisels, Marsden, Wiske, & Henderson, 1997), Phonological Awareness Literacy Screening (PALS; Invernizzi, Landrum, Teichman, & Townsend, 2010), and Get Ready to Read—Revised (GRTR-R; Wilson & Lonigan, 2009). The Battelle Developmental Inventory, Second Edition (BDI-2; Newborg, 2004), the Universal Nonverbal Intelligence Test (UNIT; Bracken &

McCallum, 1998), and the Kaufman Assessment Battery for Children, Second Edition (KABC-II; Kaufman & Kaufman, 2004), are examples of diagnostic measures.

Finally, screening and diagnostic instruments should be able to reliably distinguish between children with disabilities and those with cultural and linguistic differences (Gaviria-Soto & Castro-Morera, 2005; Samson & Lesaux, 2009). Assessors of DLLs and ELs should be bilingual, bicultural, and properly trained in first- and second-language development (NAEYC, 2005; see National Research Council, 2008, for a review). For example, Samson and Lesaux (2009) examined the overrepresentation and identification rates of language-minority (LM) students in special education using data from the nationally representative sample of the Early Childhood Longitudinal Study—Kindergarten Cohort. Although LM students were underrepresented in special education in kindergarten and first grade, they were overrepresented in third-grade special education. LM learners placed in special education in third grade had lower teacher ratings in kindergarten and first grade, and lower reading proficiency scores in first grade compared to LM learners not placed in special education. According to the authors, kindergarten and first-grade teachers lacked the knowledge and training to identify properly and refer children with potential disabilities, and instead waited for children to become more English proficient by third grade. This delay in being provided the proper resources and opportunities to learn placed these children at an academic disadvantage, which may have led to their falling further behind in school. Identifying children who require supplemental services early is key to minimizing later academic difficulties.

Program Evaluation and Monitoring Trends

Monitoring a program's performance over time is a third purpose of assessment (Meisels & Atkins-Burnett, 2006; Shepard et al., 1998). Program evaluations or outcomes assessment examine groups of children or program services as a whole rather than focus on individual children or classrooms. One example of this type of assessment is the National Assessment of Education Progress (NAEP) mandated by congressional policymakers to investigate achievement trends over time and across the country. Similarly, large-scale program evaluation studies research the outcomes of specific government-funded programs such as Head Start (U.S. Department of Health and Human Services, Administration for Children and Families, 2010) and Title I (Stullich, Eisner, & McCrary, 2007) programs. Smaller private programs tend to utilize assessments that come with a curriculum. For example, the High/Scope Curriculum has a child outcome assessment, the Child Observation Record (COR; High/Scope Educational Research Foundation, 1992), and a program quality and effectiveness assessment, the High/Scope Program Quality Assessment (PQA; High/Scope Educational Research Foundation, 1998). By combining the PQA and COR responses, the program evaluation offers an overall description of the quality of services (e.g., teacher–child interactions, environment, staff perceptions, and parent feedback) and child developmental outcomes. Evaluating programs and monitoring group trends provide a macro level perspective of how to support children's learning and services.

High-Stakes Accountability

Tests whose results or outcomes are used to make decisions to hold individuals and schools accountable are identified as high-stakes tests (Meisels, 2007). Results of these high-stakes tests influence decisions regarding program or school funding, child placement, retention, school success, and teacher promotion. Common arguments against using high-stakes tests with young children include practical problems with measurement, reduced opportunities to learn, unintended consequences, and reduced variability and predictability (Meisels, 2007; Meisels & Atkins-Burnett, 2006). Because children are unfamiliar with the structure of test questions (e.g., multiple-choice), because they have no or limited experience with taking tests, and because their learning and development differ from the expectations of the items, young children make poor test takers. Children learn in contextual situations, such as walking around the neighborhood to discover the different types of trees or observing the transformation of a silkworm into a butterfly as a real-life example of metamorphosis. They have very limited experience sitting at a table recalling and responding to "Which is a better answer: A, B, or C?" These types of cognitive expectations are challenging for young children, although this, too, is changing because teachers use multiple-choice and fill-in-the-bubble types of responses in the early grades to prepare children for test taking. Behaviors beyond the children's control, such as boredom, hunger, illness, or fatigue, also affect their performance.

Another argument against administering high-stakes tests to young children originates in concerns about adverse effects on children's opportunities to learn. Children enter school with differing experiences, knowledge, and cultural backgrounds. Schooling is a mechanism, in theory, by which children, after a number of years, come to learn the same content and expectations for classroom participation. For example, the Common Core State Standards suggest that all children in a particular grade level across the country know the same information (National Governors Association Center for Best Practices & Council of Chief State School Officers, 2010). Therefore, testing children prior to or early in their schooling experiences on information they are in the process of learning through these schooling experiences is premature and inappropriate. Consequently, scores on these high-stakes tests may lead to unintentional consequences, such as placement of children in lower-achieving groups that affects children's self-worth and self-perception, and negatively influencing instruction by narrowing the curriculum. Finally, making valid predictions of children's future academic performance based on the results of a one-time, one-score test assumes that all children enter preschool, kindergarten, and first grade with the same experiences, knowledge, and family background. Two large-scale studies examining the predictive validity of high-stakes tests for academic success found young children's performance to be unstable and dependent on the situation and skills being assessed (Kim & Suen, 2003; LaParo & Pianta, 2000). Examples of high-stakes tests include the NAEP, kindergarten readiness tests, and the Head Start National Reporting System (NRS; Meisels, 2007). Under No Child Left Behind (U.S. Department of Education, 2001), NAEP scores limit learning opportunities and adversely affect children and schools:

> School districts and schools that fail to make adequate yearly progress (AYP) toward statewide proficiency goals will, over time, be subject to improvement, corrective action, and restructuring measures aimed at getting them back on course to meet State standards. Schools that meet or exceed AYP objectives or close achievement gaps will be eligible for State Academic Achievement Awards. (p. 1)

Because of these possible consequences associated with high-stakes tests, early childhood assessments must be reliable and valid, and not used to evaluate individual children under age 8 (Meisels, 2007).

Types of Assessments Commonly Used in Early Childhood Education

Standardized Tests

Standardized tests are formal assessments that follow established, detailed guidelines as described in *The Standards for Educational and Psychological Testing* (American Educational Research Association/American Psychological Association/National Council on Measurement in Education [AERA/APA/NCME], 1999). Each test has (1) its own manual, with an explanation of how it was designed; (2) a description of the population from which it was developed; (3) how it is to be administered and by whom; (4) a discussion of the test's reliability and validity evidence; and (5) instructions for properly scoring the items. *Reliability* is statistically calculated by identifying the amount of estimated "error" in a score, specifically, calculating the true score, confidence interval, and standard error of measurement (Cronbach, 1990; McMillan, 2008). Combining the information provided by these calculations explains how close the students' scores represent their true ability. There are three common types of test *validity*: content validity, criterion validity, and construct validity. Each approach calculates how well a test is measuring what it is intended to measure (Cronbach, 1990; McMillan, 2008). Standardized tests are meant to measure students' abilities, achievements, and aptitudes (McAfee & Leong, 2011; Wortham, 2008). Two commonly found achievement tests in educational settings are norm-referenced and criterion-referenced tests. A *norm-referenced test* compares how well a student performs in relation to the population for which the test was designed. Examples of norm-referenced tests are the Iowa Test of Basic Skills (ITBS; Hoover, Dunbar, & Frisbie, 2001) and the Comprehensive Test of Basic Skills (CTBS; CTB/McGraw-Hill, 1989). A *criterion-referenced test* uses a preestablished level of mastery, such as state standards, to evaluate a student's knowledge of specific skills or concepts. The Standardized Testing and Reporting (STAR; California Department of Education, 2007) is an example of a criterion-referenced test. The recent focus on school accountability has led to increased use of standardized testing to determine how well children in the early elementary grades are meeting state and national standards. These state-mandated tests are administered as early as second grade. Prior to second grade, standardized tests for young children are used for accountability, screening, and diagnosis of potential learning problems (McAfee & Leong, 2011).

Criticisms of standardized test use with young children are numerous. Young children grow and learn at different rates, and in nonlinear ways. Consequently, calculating test reliability and validity with young children is challenging, with many tests unable to meet the established guidelines (McAfee & Leong, 2011; Wortham, 2008). By definition, all standardized tests must be administered in the same way, even if young children are tired or unable to understand the instructions or questions. Thus, modifications for individual or group needs or learning styles are not allowed (Gullo, 2006), and sociocultural factors are rarely considered (McAfee & Leong, 2011). This is particularly true for children from diverse backgrounds, including DLLs and ELs (Hirsch-Pasek, Kochanoff, Newcombe, & De Villiers, 2005). Standardized test items are based on common practices in school settings that often differ from ethnically, linguistically, economically, and culturally diverse children's backgrounds and experiences. Only standardized tests developed for diverse children who represent the backgrounds of the children being tested should be selected (Gullo, 2006; NAEYC, 2003). Some measures have presented acceptable evidence of validity and reliability when used with diverse young children, such as the Kaufman–II (Dale, McIntosh, Rothlisberg, Ward, & Bradley, 2011), the Peabody Picture Vocabulary Test–III (Dunn & Dunn, 1997; Washington & Craig, 1999), and the Woodcock–Johnson Psycho-Educational Battery–III/Batería Woodcock–Muñoz—Revised (Woodcock & Mather, 2000; Woodcock & Muñoz-Sandoval, 1996).

Another criticism is that standardized tests are only one type of assessment, and their results should be used in conjunction with other measures when evaluating young children (Gullo, 2006; Meisels, 2007). The use of standardized tests may also lead to the narrowing of the curriculum, with a focus on specific discrete skills (Gullo, 2006), commonly referred to as *teaching to the test*. Teachers may emphasize teaching as a model of passive reception, with students perceived as empty vessels needing to be filled with knowledge and a limited set of skills; resulting in a didactic approach to instruction rather than a constructivist approach that views students as active learners constructing their own knowledge (McAfee & Leong, 2011; Meisels, 2007). Despite these criticisms, the results of standardized tests provide information regarding general trends in teaching, assist in modifying instruction to meet the needs of a group of children, help in planning for the following year (McAfee & Leong, 2011), diagnose a child with a special need, and improve program services.

Performance Assessments

Performance assessments are an alternative to standardized tests. On performance assessments, children demonstrate what they know or can do through daily classroom activities. More specifically, Fantuzzo, Hightower, Grim, and Montes (2002) define *performance assessments* as "measures that provide *actual observation* and samples of children's abilities in natural learning environments *over time*" (p. 108, original emphasis). Common methods of data collection include observations, games, projects, portfolios, rubrics, checklists, and work samples (Wortham, 2008). Calfee (1992) offers four criteria for designing performance assessments. They should (1) be integrative, meaning that they include a variety of skills rather than focusing on specific content areas; (2) capture children's top-level competence or their best work; (3) encourage metacognition, whereby children can understand and discuss their thinking and learning; and (4) be guided by developmental standards that consider individual variety in children's learning at particular ages or grades. Furthermore, a growing body of research has demonstrated the validity and reliability of performance-based assessments. For example, one study examining the use of performance assessment in preschool shows that young children's performance is significantly related to teachers' perceptions (Schappe, 2005). Similarly, first-grade teachers' ratings significantly predict children's third-grade achievement in mathematics and language arts (Gallant, 2009). Research shows that ratings on performance-based assessment are comparable to standardized test scores, predict children's academic achievement, and produce positive parental reactions (Fantuzzo et al., 2002; Meisels, Bickel, Nicholson, Xue, & Atkins-Burnett, 2001; Meisels, Liaw, Dorfman, & Nelson, 1995; Meisels, Xue, Bickel, Nicholson, & Atkins-Burnett, 2001; Meisels, Xue, & Shamblott, 2008; Meisels et al., 2003).

Curriculum-Based Assessments

As suggested by their name, curriculum-based (or curriculum-embedded) assessments (CBAs) connect assessment with curriculum content and instructional practices (Gullo, 2006). CBAs provide information about children's abilities and content knowledge that teachers then use to tailor instruction to achieve children's developmental and educational goals (Gullo, 2006; Macy & Bricker, 2006). The results are used as the basis for instruction and for documenting the child's performance over time and across the curriculum. A key component of this approach is assessing children within the learning context of the classroom, therefore enabling teachers to see how children perform within the classroom context and how personal factors may affect children's performance. Gullo (2006) describes a multistep process for CBA that begins with the teacher creating an explicit connection between the classroom curriculum and instruction as a basis for assessing children's learning. The outcomes of curriculum-based assessment are used to modify the overall curriculum or tailor instruction to meet individual needs of the children. One way to do this is through the use of embedded learning opportunities, which are developmentally appropriate activities that target children's specific learning goals (Macy & Bricker, 2006). After implementing these learning activities, teachers administer a follow-up assessment to determine children's performance in learning the intended content. This process continues in a cyclical fashion to assess children's learning in relation to the curriculum. Along with improving early childhood classroom teaching practices (Gullo, 2006), researchers find that this type of assessment is especially beneficial for young children with special needs (Wright, 2010); in addition, CBA can be used for accountability purposes (Fuchs & Fuchs, 2004). CBA is one way to determine kindergartners' readiness skills with reliability and validity (VanDerHeyden, Witt, Naquin, & Noell, 2001). Furthermore, research in Head Start demonstrates how CBAs lead to positive improvements in the language and literacy quality of the classroom (Hallam, Grisham-Brown, Gao, & Brookshire, 2007). CBA approaches create a system of assessment across the early elementary grades for both general and special education classrooms (Fuchs & Fuchs, 2004).

Observation-Based Assessments

Shepard and colleagues (1998) define *observation-based assessment* as "a systematic way to collect data by watching or listening to children during an activity" (p. 38). Direct, systematic observation of young children in early childhood settings has a long tradition as a way to assess learning and development. Current preschool policies in 19 states and many school readiness assessments require the use of observation, although the specific ways in which observation is used may vary widely (Ackerman & Coley, 2012; Daily, Burkhauser, & Halle, 2010). Observation is often viewed as one component of an assessment (Wilson & Adams, 1996), but we separate it into its own assessment type given its relevance and importance for understanding young children. Many published early childhood assessments are observation-based, meaning that they use observations as the primary or sole source of information. Information from observations is commonly recorded in the form of anecdotal notes or checklists (McAfee & Leong, 2011; National Research Council, 2008) and by using technology (audio and video) to capture children in action. Observation is most frequently featured in portfolios and performance assessments (Gettinger, 2001; National Research Council, 2009). Commonly used examples of observation-based assessment include the COR (High/Scope Educational Research Foundation, 1992), the Work Sampling System (WSS; Dichtelmiller, Jablon, Dorfman, Marsden, & Meisels, 2001), the Classroom Assessment Scoring System (CLASS; Pianta, LaParo, & Hamre, 2007), the Creative Curriculum (Dodge, Colker, & Heroman, 2000), the Hawaii Early Learning Profile (HELP; Teaford, Wheat, & Baker, 2010), and California's Desired Results Developmental Profile (DRDP; California Department of Education, 2010).

Similar to other forms of assessment for young children, it is important that observations be conducted by a range of individuals—teachers, parents, and other professionals—and in various contexts—different settings, times of day, and group size (National Research Council, 2009), thus providing evidence of what Pellegrini (2001) calls "ecological sensitivity." Since young children may perform differently in varied situations, for example, during morning group time versus outside playtime, observation for assessment purposes needs to occur multiple times across a variety of settings to obtain a complete and accurate picture of an individual child. Although young children can be observed engaging in numerous types of activities, play is a common context for child observation and active learning. Children engaging in mature play learn literacy, mathematics, and social skills beyond their age (Bodrova, 2008). Interestingly, observation of kindergartners on the playground is a better predictor of first-grade achievement than other standardized achievement scores (Pellegrini, 1992).

With the early childhood care and education field shifting to an academic focus, discussion of observation-based assessments has been growing. One critique of observation-based assessments, their lack of validity and reliability, makes them less systematic and biased (National Research Council, 2008). Nevertheless, preschool teachers report that observation is now used primarily to assess children's academic progress (Hatch & Grieshaber, 2002), and elementary school teachers report using observations as *summative* assessments that provide information over time, such as through portfolios of children's work, rather than as *formative* assessments (information collected informally; e.g., anecdotal notes) (McNair, Bhargava, Adams, Edgerton, & Kypros, 2003). Similarly, research by Bagnato, Smith-Jones, McComb, and Cook-Kilroy (2002) demonstrates that early childhood teachers who receive training in how to use observation-based assessments can do so in reliable ways. The CLASS (Pianta et al., 2007) requires proper training and certification prior to implementation. Furthermore, a recent study shows that 84% of observations conducted as part of the Head Start NRS certified assessors as valid and reliable (Mathematica Policy Research, 2006). For observation-based assessments to be used reliably, there is a need for teacher training, clearly designed rubrics or scoring systems, and ongoing recertification and training (National Research Council, 2008).

RESEARCH INTO PRACTICE: ASSESSMENT AS A DECISION-MAKING PROCESS

Sound assessment practices should highlight children's knowledge, skills, and interests; document children's growth over time; describe children's progress toward specified learning goals; and provide constructive feedback to instructional programs (Jones, 2004; McAfee & Leong, 2011; NAEYC, 2003). Assessments should be age-appropriate, take into account the child's language and cultural background, and be used for their intended purposes (National Research Council, 2008). For young children, all developmental domains should be assessed (Shepard et al., 1998). In addition, children and their families should be part of the assessment process, either directly or indirectly, regardless of the purpose of the assessment. Finally, the results of any assessment should clearly benefit the child (National Research Council, 2008).

We revisit our teacher, Ms. Jones, introduced at the beginning of this chapter. She begins the year with basic information from the school records of each of the 27 children in her class. However, soon after, she begins to gather her own information about each child, using ongoing assessments that provide valuable information regarding what the children know, what to teach next, and how often to review certain concepts. When she feels a child is struggling with particular material, she pays extra attention to see how else she can support the child or whether the child should be evaluated for additional intervention services. The screening and diagnostic evaluations offer another layer of information that Ms. Jones uses to gain a deeper understanding of the children's abilities and needs. Ms. Jones is not the only person interested in how well children are performing. Beginning in second grade, the district mandates the administration of standardized tests that measure how well children across multiple classrooms, grades, and schools are meeting national benchmarks. This way of monitoring student progress at district and state levels is required by federal education laws and tied to school funding. The results of these tests have important implications for the district and state accountability system. Our purpose in this section is to describe Ms. Jones's assessment decision-making process to evaluate and support the growth and learning of one of her students, Martha. Ms. Jones must determine how well Martha is performing academically, then develop a curriculum and instructional plan that supports Martha's continued growth.

Throughout the assessment process, teachers make decisions about the purpose, selection, implementation, and use of assessments (National Research Council, 2008; Shepard et al., 1998), whether they are classroom-based or required by the school district. McAfee and Leong (2011) describe an assessment cycle that demonstrates teachers' major decisions in learning about children's abilities, then providing appropriate instructional opportunities. The steps in the cycle are the why (purpose), the what, the when, and the how (documentation) of assessment information, the compiling and summarizing, the interpreting, and the using of the information. The cycle is appropriate for all children in the classroom. For children who struggle in one area of learning, teachers may repeat the cycle process more often. For this chapter, the cycle has been adapted to provide a broader framework for thinking about early childhood assessment, specifically, as it applies to the four purposes of assessment. The first and most important part of the cycle is the why:

> We assess to determine individual children's developmental status at a given time and other progress and change over time. Status refers to children's current condition or situation with respect to any particular aspect of growth, development, or learning. . . . Status is concerned with "where children are" in their development. This basic information is then used for other purposes. (McAfee & Leong, 2011, p. 31)

The *why* of assessment refers to the purpose; this means supporting children's development and learning, and, for our intent, identifying children who need additional assistance; monitoring instructional and program effectiveness; and examining individual or group score trends (National Research Council, 2009; Shepard et al., 1998). The next step in the cycle is to determine *what* is assessed, either getting to know the individual child or group of children or monitoring children's growth and learning (McAfee & Leong, 2011; National Research Council, 2008). Each group comprises unique children with their own personalities and ways of interacting. A key component of any assessment is the relationship between the teacher and child, which begins with the teacher getting to know the child's personality, strengths, and resources (Jablon, Dombro, & Dichtelmiller, 2007). Children enter school with different knowledge and experiences; to guide the instructional approach, the role of the teacher is to understand what children already know and how they interact. Thus, teachers and children learn about each other in order to develop patterns of behavior and ways of interacting as they learn and work together. Additionally in early childhood education, teachers are expected to support both developmental domains (physical, social, emotional, language, and cognitive) and academic content areas (science, mathematics, language arts, social studies, and the arts).

Therefore, teachers must be familiar with age-appropriate developmental domains and grade-level standards to understand where the children are and what they need to learn next (Shepard et al., 1998). For the third step, teachers should plan *when*, or how often, to assess children and for which purposes, gathering information before the year begins and/or during the year. Teachers may decide to assess daily, periodically, or when problems or concerns arise, depending on specific program and school requirements. Regardless, these decisions should be made prior to the start of each school year.

The next step in the cycle refers to documentation, or the *how* of collecting and recording assessment information. This information can be collected formally, using standardized tests, or informally, through observations, performance assessments, or curriculum-embedded assessments. Methods of collecting assessment information include observing children; eliciting information from children, parents, and other adults; and collecting drawings and work samples. Numerous tools exist for recording the collected information, for example, checklists, anecdotal notes, rubrics, rating scales, matrices, photographs, running records, audio and video recordings, and portfolios. Teachers should select tools that provide the most accurate and reliable information about the child's abilities and performance (McAfee & Leong, 2011; National Research Council, 2008).

As teachers collect and record information about children's knowledge, they need to *compile* and *summarize* the information, which is the next step in the cycle. Teachers gather numerous pieces of information through multiple sources and tools over the course of the year. One approach for compiling the information is the use of portfolios, in which teachers organize and store the information. A portfolio also provides teachers, children, and parents a visual representation of the child's development over time along the domains of development and content standards. Teachers summarize their findings to understand where the child is and where he or she is going. This information, too, is shared with parents and other school personnel as a necessary part of the child's development and learning. These summaries offer a picture from which to reflect and *interpret* what children know and what else they need to know. Teachers then *use this information* to plan curriculum and develop individualized instruction. The assessment cycle provides a framework for teachers when selecting, implementing, and using assessments for various purposes.

Utilizing the assessment cycle (McAfee & Leong, 2011), we illustrate how Ms. Jones makes decisions that support Martha's educational opportunities. First, Ms. Jones uses her ongoing classroom assessments, as she does with all the children in her class, to assist Martha in adjusting to the classroom environment and to plan instruction. What she comes to learn is that Martha is struggling with language arts; therefore, she makes decisions regarding how to further evaluate Martha's true abilities and support her learning. If Ms. Jones feels that Martha requires additional evaluations for possible learning disabilities or intervention services (a second purpose of assessment), she may refer Martha to the school psychologist for testing. Finally, assessments are used to monitor trends and for accountability purposes. Using the assessment cycle, we discuss how Ms. Jones might use the results of such tests to support Martha's educational opportunities, particularly in language arts.

Ongoing Assessment to Support Learning and Instruction

Ms. Jones remembers that when Martha started first grade in the fall, she was quiet, shy, and slow to warm up. Due to Ms. Jones's limited Spanish abilities, she decides to seat Martha next to a girl who is verbose and bilingual. She hopes the other girl will help Martha transition to the English-only classroom and keep her abreast of the classroom activities. As Martha adjusts to the classroom environment, she becomes more outgoing and enjoys talking with her friends. Although she mixes Spanish and English when speaking, she increasingly expresses her needs in English. Recently, Ms. Jones has noted that Martha is not progressing in language arts (*why*). In particular, her fluency is below that of her classmates, and she has difficulty using the story or sentence context to recognize or understand unknown words (*what*). Fluency and vocabulary acquisition are part of the state's content standards, which are aligned with the Common Core Standards. Therefore, because Ms. Jones worries that Martha may fall behind, she decides to conduct more focused assessments to identify strategies that support Martha's learning needs. The next step is collecting and recording more information about Martha's fluency and vocabulary acquisition (*how*). Ms. Jones decides to use performance-based assessments that include observations in the naturally occurring context of the classroom and involve children in the process. She also decides to elicit information from educational professionals who are familiar with Martha's academic performance, and from family members who know Martha outside of the school environment. Ms. Jones understands that this level of in-depth assessment may be time-consuming, yet she also knows that waiting or doing the minimum may lead to Martha falling further behind in language arts.

Observations

As with other forms of assessment, observation requires careful thought and planning. This includes conducting regular observations that provide a complete and accurate picture of the child, finding time throughout the school day to observe, deciding what skills or behaviors to observe, and recording the observations (Jablon et al., 2007). Because Martha struggling with fluency and vocabulary development (*what*), Ms. Jones decides to begin observing her during the language arts instructional times (*when*). She conducts weekly running records with all the children in their small reading groups. Ms. Jones decides to reduce the number of children in Martha's group from five to three in order to provide more individualized attention. As Martha reads aloud in her reading group, Ms. Jones has a checklist of the different levels of books, and she checks off the books Martha reads with fluency. She begins with a level in which she knows Martha is fluent and, over the course of the week, increases the level of difficulty (*how*). Upon analyzing a week's worth of running records and the checklist, Ms. Jones realizes that Martha's errors are frequently with new vocabulary and verb tenses (*interpreting*). Since Martha enjoys writing, Ms. Jones asks the class to create personal dictionaries beginning with all the words they know, including those on the classroom Word Wall. Then, before introducing new reading material, she previews the text with the whole class and specifically asks Martha to identify words that are unfamiliar (*using the information*). They discuss the words, which are added to their dictionary. During small-group meetings, Ms. Jones invites students to use their dictionaries as a reference when they are stuck on a word. To support Martha's verb-tense understanding, Ms. Jones plans a mini-lesson focusing on the differences among past, present, and future tense, and preselects books that use one tense to build Martha's confidence in learning this aspect of grammar (*using the information*). She encourages Martha to add these words to her dictionary, too. As Ms. Jones continues her weekly running records, she has her book checklist and a verb-tense tally sheet to track Martha's progress (*how*). After a few days, Ms. Jones notes that Martha is able to read one verb tense correctly (*compiling, summarizing*, and *interpreting*), and she therefore adds reading material that includes another tense (*using the information*). Ms. Jones follows this process to assess and plan for all children with similar needs.

Interviewing Other Educational Professionals

Ms. Jones also enlisted the help of Martha's kindergarten teacher. Since Martha attended kindergarten in the same school, Ms. Jones has access to enrollment information provided by Martha's parents and her kindergarten report cards, Ms. Jones speaks with the kindergarten teacher to learn more about Martha's day-to-day progress (*what*). Through this conversation (*how*), she learns that the kindergarten teacher shared similar concerns but had seen Martha progress over the course of the school year, especially in her use of English and development of social skills. The teacher also mentions sharing her concerns with family members, who helped Martha by reading books in Spanish to her and reviewing her numbers (*compiling information*). The kindergarten teacher remains concerned, however, about Martha's limited gains in literacy and mathematics. Ms. Jones reviews Martha's portfolio for information about her mathematics learning and finds that Martha demonstrated grade-level proficiency at the end of kindergarten (*summarizing* and *interpreting*). Therefore, Ms. Jones decides to focus on improving Martha's literacy skills. She shares some of her observational notes with the other first-grade teachers in her building to brainstorm ideas of how to modify her language arts curriculum to support Martha's literacy learning better (*interpreting* and *using the information*). Ms. Jones decides that if her curriculum and instructional plans do not produce immediate gains, then she needs to seek assistance from the school psychologist.

Involving the Child

One frequently overlooked aspect of early childhood assessment is the role of children; the assessment cycle does not need to be the sole responsibility of the teacher. This goes beyond simply obtaining information from children and engages them in the assessment process (*how*). In doing so, it fosters children's metacognition (self-awareness of their own learning), and helps to ease the teacher's burden of ongoing assessment for an entire classroom of children. Keeping these ideas in mind, combined with her knowledge that Martha's learning struggles may impact her motivation (*what*), Ms. Jones asks Martha what activities she does well, what she enjoys most, and what is harder for her to do in mathematics (*how*). She creates activities in the math center that build on Martha's strengths and challenge her to learn (*using this information*). Since Ms. Jones only has a part-time assistant 2 days a week, she enlists the help of other students in the classroom who are strong in mathematics by pairing them with Martha to complete these activities (*compiling*). Both students fill out a card upon completion of the activity to indicate what they learned and what they still need some help with (*interpreting*). Other ways to involve young children in the assessment process include having children self-select work products for inclusion in their portfolio, using a checklist of criteria for making these choices (*compiling* and *summarizing*); having children show and explain their portfolios to their families during parent conferences (*interpreting*); having Martha and her reading buddy use a tally sheet to evaluate their paired read-aloud, which is recorded (*compiling* and *summarizing*) and listened to by Ms. Jones and other students (*compiling* and *summarizing*). Using these varied approaches to engage children actively in the assessment of their learning, Ms. Jones is surprised to see how delighted Martha is when recognizing her own achievements.

Communicating with the Family

Although young children spend the majority of their time in educational settings, prior to school entry they are most often surrounded by their families. Thus, relatives, typically parents, know their children well in the home and other out-of-school contexts. Given Ms. Jones's lack of experience with children growing up in culturally and linguistically diverse homes and communities, she decides to request some basic family background information by sending a survey home with children in the first month of the school year; she enlists the assistance of her Spanish-speaking colleague to translate it (*how*). As part of this survey, she also asks permission to contact families about scheduling a home visit. For a student like Martha, who is particularly puzzling, Ms. Jones believes that visiting Martha's home and talking with her parents will provide additional insight about Martha (*why*). She is also sensitive to the potential for home–school differences that may help to explain Martha's behavior in school. In addition, Ms. Jones brings a Spanish-speaking translator on the home visit to minimize any communication difficulties. When it is time for parent–teacher conferences, Ms. Jones finds that the relationship she established with Martha's parents during the home visit allowed them to have an honest conversation about Martha's struggles. Having Martha attend the conference also facilitated the communication and allowed everyone—Ms. Jones, Martha, and her parents—to plan what can be done at home and at school to assist Martha further.

Screening and Diagnosis

After reviewing Martha's portfolio, Ms. Jones notices improvement in Martha's fluency and vocabulary development. However, Martha is still performing below proficiency (*why*). Martha's parents verify that she communicates well at home but usually mixes Spanish and English when speaking. Ms. Jones decides to evaluate Martha's vocabulary development in English and in Spanish, using a language screening tool that can detect the possibility of a learning disability (*what*). Screening tools are most frequently used when teachers have concerns about a child's learning or development. Screening evaluations are conducted as needed, and as recommended by the teacher or parents. They can be comprehensive (covering multiple areas of learning) or focused in nature. Ms. Jones recognizes the importance of the screening and hopes this is the only time Martha will need to be screened (*when*). After receiving permission from Martha's parents, Ms. Jones enlists the assistance of the bilingual Latina school psychologist, who is trained in administering language assessment to young Spanish–English-speaking children. The school psychologist visits the classroom often in order to support another child with speech delays; thus, Martha has seen her many times and regularly greets the school psychologist in Spanish when she visits the classroom. Consequently, Martha feels at ease going with her to be screened. The school psychologist follows the screening instrument's manual for collecting and recording data (*how*), as well as *compiling, summarizing*, and *interpreting* the results. Ms. Jones depends on the bilingual trained professional to offer valuable insight into Martha's vocabulary development. The results of the screening indicate that Martha's Spanish and English are developing at typical rates for her age, and there are no signs of a learning disability. In Martha's case, the screening does not result in additional testing, and Ms. Jones returns to her ongoing assessments.

Monitoring Trends and Accountability

School districts and policymakers often have students take standardized tests to determine not only student performance but also the effectiveness of the school curriculum (*why*). Generally, these standardized tests evaluate young children's academic content skills (*what*) in third grade (*when*). Because Martha is in first grade, Ms. Jones must search for other standardized test results that might be available to her. Her district also administers a school readiness test 5 months prior to kindergarten entry (*when*) for evaluation and placement purposes (*why*). Ms. Jones has access to the results of the kindergarten readiness test, which measures letter-sound knowledge, counting to 20, and fine and gross motor development (*what*). After consulting with the kindergarten teacher (*how*), Ms. Jones learns that Martha showed general proficiency in all areas shortly after starting kindergarten. In addition, the kindergarten teacher states that Martha's prior preschool experience and parental support greatly influenced her learning (*compiling* and *summarizing*). Ms. Jones realizes this test yielded minimal information to assist Martha now (*interpreting*). Therefore, Ms. Jones must rely on her informal, ongoing assessment, especially observation, to learn more about Martha's abilities and to identify best practices to support her continued academic learning.

The assessment cycle provides Ms. Jones a framework to make decisions regarding the selection, implementation, and interpretation of assessments. Ms. Jones is surprised to learn that her ongoing assessments provide more valuable information regarding Martha's struggles than do formal measures. Ms. Jones's ongoing assessment practices offer immediate feedback that enables her to adjust her curriculum and instructional practice regularly. Yet she also understands the importance of screening and diagnosis for special needs, and the district required tests. Ms. Jones discovers that these assessments provide additional information about a child, but she relies on her ongoing assessments for curriculum and instructional planning. In adopting and following the assessment cycle, Ms. Jones appreciates how a continual system of tracking children's growth and learning is vital to successful classroom instruction. The information she has gained through this process helps her to know she is doing her best to support children's learning.

REFLECTIONS AND NEW DIRECTIONS

Early childhood assessments can have a significant positive impact on young children's development and educational learning opportunities. Assessments that benefit young children are age-appropriate and measure what they are intended to measure, they consider linguistic and cultural experiences, and they guide curriculum and instructional practices. Furthermore, these assessments are "well designed, implemented effectively, developed in the context of systematic planning, and are interpreted and used appropriately" (National Research Council, 2008, p. 12). The challenge encountered by researchers and educators stem from young children's episodic and rapid growth rates, and the diverse backgrounds and experiences they bring to educational settings. Therefore, teachers must have a strong foundation in child development, be familiar with good instructional practices, and know the standards or expected learning outcomes for development and academic content knowledge, as well as understand the key principles of assessments and the various methods and tools for creating and selecting measures. The strength of having numerous methods and tools for assessing young children also contribute to the challenge of identifying one measure to evaluate a particular skill.

Instead of having more time and support to learn about a child's family, personality, and cultural and linguistic experience, and to evaluate the child's abilities and performance fully, teachers frequently must administer high-stakes tests that measure a set of discrete skills that focuses on breadth rather than depth. Furthermore, these tests do not take into account family circumstances, limited school resources, or children's mood or health at the time of the test (Meisels, 2007; Pianta, 2007). To complicate the situation further, high-stakes tests do not inform instruction or consider how much children have learned since they took the test. Unfortunately, teachers feel pressured to "teach to the test," especially when decisions about their jobs, salary, and school funding, are based on children's test scores. High-stakes tests are not best practice for supporting and increasing the educational opportunities for young children, yet curriculum and instructional practices are heavily influenced by them.

With assessment purpose guiding the decision-making process (McAfee & Leong, 2011; NAEYC, 2003; National Research Council, 2008; Shepard et al., 1998), another challenge is the tension between how teachers and policymakers view assessment. Teachers need assessments that provide daily or weekly feedback regarding children's performance. Assessment is ongoing and continuously being revised and adjusted to children's learning and development. Policymakers are more interested in group trend performance, and they incorrectly assume that one test best represents what children know and predicts student performance. However, one test from one point in time cannot capture all that a child knows, determine whether a child needs intervention services, or predict how well a child will perform in the future. Even screening and diagnostic measures require multiple scores before a teacher refers a child for intervention services. What is needed is a comprehensive system of assessment for children and programs (Meisels, 2007) that includes a collection of child outcomes and an "examination of variations in children, families, teachers, and programs that may help explain differences in those outcomes" (p. 42). Predicting overall school success without keeping in mind the classroom context, along with other life factors (e.g., family, community, teacher education and preparation, school resources, and curriculum), leads to mislabeling, misplacements, and other adverse consequences for everyone involved.

Policymakers, researchers, and educators must keep the assessment principles in mind and have basic understanding of best practice when selecting, administering, scoring, and interpreting the results of any assessment. Teachers need to be involved in research examining their own assessment practices and to identify assessments that provide reliable and valid results for general education classrooms. Researchers can play a seminal role in helping classroom teachers to study and reflect on their assessment decision-making process through an action research approach. Teachers should participate in assessment development, including validity and reliability studies, and have input into the decision about which assessments are used. Teachers also require training and ongoing support in using assessments with young children (see the following section for specific suggestion). More research is needed for assessment development with typically developing children, particularly with culturally and linguistically diverse groups, and for examining the effectiveness of observations and their predictability (National Research Council, 2008), Early childhood assessment should guide teachers to provide the best educational opportunities for children and, ultimately, benefit the child.

PROFESSIONAL DEVELOPMENT ACTIVITIES

▪ Conducting and recording objective observations to document children's abilities.

▪ Converting information gathered about children into meaningful interpretations, and developing curriculum and instructional practices informed by state or national standards.

▪ Interpreting and sharing the results of standardized tests, including high-stakes tests, with colleagues and families.

▪ Using portfolios and technology to organize child assessment data and to involve children's families in the assessment process.

▪ Understanding the difference between children who require supplemental services and children who are developing a second language.

REFERENCES

Ackerman, D. J., & Coley, R. J. (2012). *State pre-K assessment policies: Issues and status*. Princeton, NJ: Educational Testing Service.

American Educational Research Association, American Psychological Association, & the National Council on Measurement in Education (AERA/APA/NCME). (1999). *The standards for educational and psychological testing*. Washington, DC: American Educational Research Association.

Bagnato, S. J., Smith-Jones, J., McComb, G., & Cook-Kilroy, J. (2002). *Quality early learning—key to school success: A first-phase 3-year program evaluation research report for Pittsburgh's Early Childhood Initiative (ECI)*. Pittsburgh, PA: SPECS Program Evaluation Research Team.

Bodrova, E. (2008). Make-believe play versus academic skills: A Vygotskian approach to today's dilemma of early childhood education. *European Early Childhood Education Research Journal, 16*(3), 357–369.

Bracken, B. A., & McCallum, R. S. (1998). *Universal Nonverbal Intelligence Test*. Chicago: Riverside.

Calfee, R. (1992). Authentic assessment of reading and writing in the elementary classroom. In M. J. Dreher & W. H. Slater (Eds.), *Elementary school literacy: Critical issues* (pp. 211–226). Norwood, MA: Christopher-Gordon.

California Department of Education. (2007). *Standardized testing and reporting*. Sacramento: Author.

California Department of Education. (2010). *Desired Results Developmental Profile Assessment Instruments*. Sacramento: Author.

Cronbach, L. J. (1990). *Essentials of psychological testing* (5th ed.). New York: Harper & Row.

CTB/McGraw-Hill. (1989). *Comprehensive Test of Basic Skills*. Monterey, CA: Author.

Daily, S., Burkhauser, M., & Halle, T. (2010). A review of school readiness practices in the states: Early learning guidelines and assessments. *Child Trends: Early Childhood Highlights, 1*(3), 1–12.

Dale, B. A., McIntosh, D., Rothlisberg, B. A., Ward, K. E., & Bradley, M. H. (2011). Profile analysis of the Kaufman Assessment Battery for Children, second edition, with African American and Caucasian preschool children. *Psychology in the Schools, 48*(5), 476–487.

Dichtelmiller, M. L., Jablon, J. R., Dorfman, A. B., Marsden, D. B., & Meisels, S. J. (2001). *The Work Sampling System*. New York: Pearson Early Learning.

Dodge, D. T., Colker, L. J., & Heroman, C. (2000). *The Creative Curriculum*. Washington, DC: Teaching Strategies.

Dunn, L. M., & Dunn, L. M. (1997). *Peabody Picture Vocabulary Test* (3rd ed.). Circle Pines, MN: American Guidance Service.

Fantuzzo, J., Hightower, D., Grim, S., & Montes, G. (2002). Generalization of the Child Observation Record: A validity study for diverse samples of urban, low-income preschool children. *Early Childhood Research Quarterly, 17,* 106–125.

Fuchs, L. S., & Fuchs, D. (2004). Determining adequate yearly progress from kindergarten through grade 6 with curriculum-based measurement. *Assessment for Effective Intervention, 29*(4), 25–37.

Gallant, D. J. (2009). Predictive validity evidence for an assessment program based on the Work Sampling System in mathematics and language and literacy. *Early Childhood Research Quarterly, 24,* 133–141.

Gaviria-Soto, J. L., & Castro-Morera, M. (2005). Beyond over-representation: The problem of bias in the inclusion of minority group students in special education programs. *Quality and Quantity, 39,* 537–558.

Gettinger, M. (2001). Development and implementation of a performance-monitoring system for early childhood education. *Early Childhood Education Journal, 29*(1), 9–15.

Gottlieb, M. (2006). *Assessing English language learners: Bridges from language proficiency to academic achievement.* Thousand Oaks, CA: Corwin Press.

Green, E. J. (1997). Guidelines for serving linguistically and culturally diverse young children. *Early Childhood Education Journal, 24*(3), 147–154.

Gullo, D. F. (2006). Alternative means of assessing children's learning in early childhood classrooms. In B. Spodek & O. N. Saracho (Eds.), *Handbook of research on the education of young children* (2nd ed., pp. 443–455). Mahwah, NJ: Erlbaum.

Hallam, R., Grisham-Brown, J., Gao, X., & Brookshire, R. (2007). The effects of outcomes-driven authentic assessment on classroom quality. *Early Childhood Research and Practice, 9*(2). Retrieved February 5, 2012, from *http://ecrp.uiuc.edu/v9n2/hallam.html.*

Hatch, J. A., & Grieshaber, S. (2002). Child observation and accountability in early childhood education: Perspectives from Australia and the United States. *Early Childhood Education Journal, 29*(4), 227–231.

Heath, S. B. (1983). *Ways with words: Language life, and work in communities and classrooms.* New York: Cambridge University Press.

High/Scope Educational Research Foundation. (1992). *Child Observation Record.* Ypsilanti, MI: Author.

High/Scope Educational Research Foundation. (1998). *High/Scope Program Quality Assessment.* Ypsilanti, MI: Author.

Hirsch-Pasek, K., Kochanoff, A., Newcombe, N. S., & De Villiers, J. (2005). Using scientific knowledge to inform preschool assessment: Making the case for "empirical validity." *Social Policy Report, 19*(1), 1–9.

Hoover, H. D., Dunbar, S. B., & Frisbie, D. A. (2001). *Iowa Tests of Basic Skills.* Rolling Meadows, IL: Riverside.

Invernizzi, M., Landrum, T. J., Teichman, A., & Townsend, M. (2010). Increased implementation of emergent literacy screening in pre-kindergarten. *Early Childhood Education Journal, 37,* 437–446.

Jablon, J. R., Dombro, A. L., & Dichtelmiller, M. L. (2007). *The power of observation for birth through eight* (2nd ed.). Washington, DC: Teaching Strategies, Inc.

Jones, J. (2004). Framing the assessment discussion. In D. Koralek (Ed.), *Spotlight on young children and assessment* (pp. 4–8). Washington, DC: National Association for the Education of Young Children.

Kaufman, A. S., & Kaufman, N. L. (2004). *Kaufman Assessment Battery for Children, Second Edition.* Circle Pines, MN: American Guidance Service.

Kettler, R. J., & Feeney-Kettler, K. A. (2011). Screening systems and decision making at the preschool level: Application of a comprehensive validity framework. *Psychology in the Schools, 48*(5), 430–441.

Kim, J., & Suen, H. K. (2003). Predicting children's academic achievement from early assessment scores: A validity generalization study. *Early Childhood Research Quarterly, 18*, 547–566.

LaParo, K. M., & Pianta, R. C. (2000). Predicting children's competence in the early school years: A meta-analytic review. *Review of Educational Research, 70*(4), 443–484.

Lightfoot, C., Cole, M., & Cole, S. R. (2012). *The development of children* (7th ed.). New York: Worth.

Macy, M. G., & Bricker, D. D. (2006). Practical applications for using curriculum-based assessment to create embedded learning opportunities for young children. *Young Exceptional Children, 9*(4), 12–21.

Mathematica Policy Research. (2006). *Implementation of the Head Start National Reporting System: Spring 2005 update.* Princeton, NJ: Author.

McAfee, O., & Leong, D. J. (2011). *Assessing and guiding young children's development and learning* (5th ed.). Upper Saddle River, NJ: Pearson Education, Inc.

McMillan, J. H. (2008). *Assessment essentials for standardized-based education* (2nd ed.). Thousand Oaks, CA: Corwin Press.

McNair, S., Bhargava, A., Adams, L., Edgerton, S., & Kypros, B. (2003). Teachers speak out on assessment practices. *Early Childhood Education Journal, 31*(1), 23–31.

Meisels, S. J. (2007). Accountability in early childhood: No easy answers. In R. C. Pianta, M. J. Cox, & K. L. Snow (Eds.), *School readiness and the transition to kindergarten in the era of accountability* (pp. 31 –47). Baltimore: Brookes.

Meisels, S. J., & Atkins-Burnett, S. (2005). *Developmental screening in early childhood: A guide.* Washington, DC: National Association for the Education of Young Children.

Meisels, S. J., & Atkins-Burnett, S. (2006). Evaluating early childhood assessments: A differential analysis. In K. McCartney & D. Phillips (Eds.), *Blackwell handbook of early childhood education* (pp. 533–549). Malden, MA: Blackwell.

Meisels, S. J., Atkins-Burnett, S., Xue, Y., Nicholson, J., Bickel, D. D., & Son, S.-H. (2003). Creating a system of accountability: The impact of instructional assessment on elementary children's achievement test scores. *Education Policy Analysis Archives, 11*(9). Retrieved February 5, 2012, from *http://epaa.asu.edu/epaa/v11n9.*

Meisels, S. J., Bickel, D. D., Nicholson, J., Xue, Y., & Atkins-Burnett, S. (2001). Trusting teachers' judgments: A validity study of a curriculum-embedded performance assessment in kindergarten to grade 3. *American Educational Research Journal, 38*(1), 73–95.

Meisels, S. J., Henderson, L. W., Liaw, F., Browning, K., & Have, T. T. (1993). New evidence for the effectiveness of the Early Screening Inventory. *Early Childhood Research Quarterly, 8*, 327–346.

Meisels, S. J., Liaw, F., Dorfman, A., & Nelson, R. F. (1995). The Work Sampling System: Reliability and validity of a performance assessment for young children. *Early Childhood Research Quarterly, 10*(3), 277–296.

Meisels, S. J., Marsden, D. B., Wiske, M. S., & Henderson, L. W. (1997). *The Early Screening Inventory Revised.* New York: Pearson.

Meisels, S. J., & Piker, R. (2001). *An analysis of early literacy assessments used for instruction* (Technical report). Ann Arbor, MI: Center for the Improvement of Early Reading Achievement (CIERA).

Meisels, S. J., Xue, Y., Bickel, D. D., Nicholson, J., & Atkins-Burnett, S. (2001). Parental reactions to authentic performance assessment. *Educational Assessment, 7*(1), 61–85.

Meisels, S. J., Xue, Y., & Shamblott, M. (2008). Assessing language, literacy, and mathematics skills with work sampling for Head Start. *Early Education and Development, 19*(6), 963–981.

Mindes, G. (2007). *Assessing young children* (3rd ed.). Upper Saddle River, NJ: Pearson Education, Inc.

National Association for the Education of Young Children (NAEYC). (2003). *Early childhood, curriculum, assessment, and program evaluation: Building an effective, accountable system in programs for children birth through age 8.* Washington, DC: Author.

National Association for the Education of Young Children (NAEYC). (2005). *Screening and assessment of young English-language learners*. Washington, DC: Author.

National Governors Association Center for Best Practices & Council of Chief State School Officers. (2010). *Common core state standards*. Washington, DC: Authors.

National Research Council. (2008). *Early childhood assessment: Why, what, and how* (C. E. Snow & S. B. Van Hemel, Eds.) (Committee on Developmental Outcomes and Assessments for Young Children, Board on Children, Youth, and Families, Board on Testing and Assessment, Division of Behavioral and Social Sciences and Education). Washington, DC: National Academies Press.

Newborg, J. (2004). *Battelle Developmental Inventory, Second Edition*. Rolling Meadows, IL: Riverside.

Payan, R. M., & Nettles, M. T. (2008). Current state of English-language learners in the U.S. K–12 student population. Retrieved from *www.ets.org/media/conferences_and_events/pdf/ellLsympsium/ell_factsheet.pdf*.

Pellegrini, A. D. (1992). Kindergarten children's social-cognitive status as a predictor of first grade success. *Early Childhood Research Quarterly, 7*, 564–577.

Pellegrini, A. D. (2001). Practitioner review: The role of direct observation in the assessment of young children. *Journal of Child Psychology and Psychiatry, 42*(7), 861–869.

Pianta, R. C. (2007). Early education in transition. In R. C. Pianta, M. J. Cox, & K. L. Snow (Eds.), *School readiness and the transition to kindergarten in the era of accountability* (pp. 3–10). Baltimore: Brookes.

Pianta, R. C., LaParo, K. M., & Hamre, B. (2007). *Classroom Assessment Scoring System*. Baltimore: Brookes.

Samson, J. F., & Lesaux, N. K. (2009). Language-minority learners in special education: Rates and predictors of identification for services. *Journal of Learning Disabilities, 42*(2), 148–162.

Schappe, J. F. (2005). Early childhood assessment: A correlational study of the relationships among student performance, student feelings, and teacher perceptions. *Early Childhood Education Journal, 33*(3), 187–193.

Shepard, L., Kagan, S. L., & Wurtz, E. (1998). *Principles and recommendations for early childhood assessments*. Washington, DC: National Education Goals Panel.

Stiggins, R. J. (2002). Assessment crisis: The absence of learning. *Phi Delta Kappan, 83*(10), 758–765.

Stipek, D. (2006). No Child Left Behind comes to preschool. *Elementary School Journal, 106*(5), 455–465.

Stullich, S., Eisner, E., & McCrary, J. (2007). *National Assessment of Title I, Final Report: Volume I. Implementation* (NCEE 2008-4012). Washington, DC: National Center for Education Evaluation and Regional Assistance, Institute of Education Sciences, U.S. Department of Education.

Teaford, P., Wheat, J., & Baker, T. (2010). *Hawaii Early Learning Profile* (2nd ed.). Palo Alto, CA: Vort Corporation.

U.S. Department of Education. (2001). *No Child Left Behind: Executive summary*. Washington, DC: Author.

U.S. Department of Health and Human Services, Administration for Children and Families (2010, January). *Head Start impact study: Final report*. Washington, DC: Authors.

VanDerHeyden, A. M., Witt, J. C., Naquin, G., & Noell, G. (2001). The reliability and validity of curriculum-based measurement readiness probes for kindergarten students. *School Psychology Review, 30*, 363–382.

Washington, J. A., & Craig, H. K. (1999). Performances of at-risk, African American preschoolers on the Peabody Picture Vocabulary Test–III. *Language, Speech, and Hearing Services in Schools, 30*, 75–82.

Wilson, M., & Adams, R. J. (1996). Evaluating progress with alternative assessments: A model for Chapter 1. In M. B. Kane (Ed.), *Implementing performance assessment: Promise, problems and challenges* (pp. 39–60). Hillsdale, NJ: Erlbaum.

Wilson, S. B., & Lonigan, C. J. (2009). An evaluation of two emergent literacy screening tools for preschool children. *Annals of Dyslexia, 59,* 115–131.

Woodcock, R. W., & Mather, N. (2000). *Woodcock–Johnson Psycho-Educational Battery—III.* Itasca, IL: Riverside.

Woodcock, R. W., & Muñoz-Sandoval, A. F. (1996). *Bateria Woodcock–Muñoz–R: Pruebas de aprovechamiento.* Itasca, IL: Riverside.

Wortham, S. C. (2008). *Assessment in early childhood education* (5th ed.). Upper Saddle River, NJ: Pearson Education, Inc.

Wright, R. J. (2010). *Multifaceted assessment for early childhood education.* Thousand Oaks, CA: Sage.

CHAPTER 17

ASSESSING THE EFFECTIVENESS
OF ENVIRONMENTS AND INSTRUCTION
IN EARLY CHILDHOOD SETTINGS

BRIDGET E. HATFIELD
ROBERT C. PIANTA

> One looks back with appreciation to the brilliant teachers, but with gratitude to those who touched our human feelings. The curriculum is so much necessary raw material, but warmth is the vital element for the growing plant and for the soul of the child.
> —CARL G. JUNG

> Our progress as a nation can be no swifter than our progress in education. The human mind is our fundamental resource.
> —JOHN F. KENNEDY

Francine nervously walks into her prekindergarten classroom before the children arrive for the day. Today is her annual principal's observation. Like many teachers, she has worked hard to prepare lessons and activities that build upon her students' current developmental levels, and she hopes they will be on their best behavior and show the principal what they have learned. From past experience, she knows that the principal's evaluation will be general and positive. But what she really hopes is that this observation experience provides her with specific strategies for improving her teaching practice, and not just general praise and observations. Simultaneously, her principal Janet sits down to review the observation protocol that her school has used for the past 10 years. Every year, she thinks to herself, "How do I know if this observation captures effective teaching strategies or is tied to student achievement? And, after receiving my feedback, do teachers make any needed improvements?"

The challenges and questions posed by Janet and Francine are similar to those currently facing school district personnel and teachers around the country. In this age of heightened accountability for teachers, it is imperative that educators use observational tools that (1) reliably measure effective teaching practices, (2) are linked to student achievement, and (3) provide teachers with targeted feedback that improves classroom instruction and practices. In this chapter, we review two standardized, valid, reliable observational measures—Early Childhood Environment Rating Scale (ECERS; Harms & Clifford, 1980; Harms, Clifford, & Cryer, 1998) and the Classroom Assessment Scoring System (CLASS; Pianta, LaParo, & Hamre, 2008)—that may be used to understand effective teaching in early childhood settings. Also, we describe for teachers and principals such as Francine and Janet the key characteristics of valid and reliable observational assessments and how both measures, ECERS and CLASS, discussed in this chapter are related to children's developmental and academic growth. Finally, we use the CLASS as an example of how one uses a tool to target professional development to individual teacher's needs.

This chapter draws from decades of experience using observation at scale in early childhood education to derive implications for administrative decisions, evaluation practices, and policymaking. The field has long embraced the value of observing classrooms and teacher–child interactions, and for early childhood education in particular, features of the settings in which children are served are the hallmarks of quality. *Standardized* observations of those features yield metrics used in state and federal policy, program improvement investments, and credentialing of professionals (Pianta, 2005).

This chapter also presents lessons we have learned from observation in early childhood education that may be helpful as states and districts begin implementing more rigorous observation protocols in the context of quality improvement efforts. These lessons focus on the importance of standardization, training of observers, methods for ensuring the validity and reliability of the instruments, and using observational measures as leverage to produce effective teaching. These lessons form the basis for a series of recommendations for policy, selection, and implementation related to observation of environments and instruction in early education settings.

What Research Says about the Large-Scale Use of Standardized Observation Protocols for Early Childhood Settings and Teachers

Children's development of knowledge and skills is fostered through everyday interactions and relationships with adults across the settings children experience in the years prior to school (Bronfenbrenner & Morris, 2006). Over time, children engage in elaborated and symbolically mediated interactions with caregivers (parents and teachers), in which emotion, cognition, behavior, and communication are intertwined and organized. This complex, dynamic process fosters the capacity, skills, and interest to read, understand, and produce written language; to self-regulate; to engage in academic activities; and to acquire knowledge of the world—the key components of readiness to learn and success in school (e.g., Dickinson, Anastasopolous, McCabe, Peisner-Feinberg, & Poe, 2003; Lonigan, Burgess, & Anthony, 2000; Morrison, Bachman, & Connor, 2003). In early care and education settings, adult–child relationships are a context for stimulating and organizing processes that are observed and assessed as school readiness skills.

Children's early experience within family and aspects of family structure is consistently a strong predictor of preacademic skills, as well as later academic achievement and cognitive functioning (McWayne, Hampton, Fantuzzo, Cohen, & Sekino, 2004; Morrison & Connor, 2002). Maternal education and family income are key elements of family structure associated with young children's academic outcomes, language development, and cognitive abilities (Burchinal, Peisner-Feinberg, Pianta, & Howes, 2002; Duncan

& Murnane, 2011; Vandell et al., 2010). In addition, aspects of the parent–child relationship, in particular, maternal sensitivity during parent–child play interactions, are especially robust predictors of children's academic competence in kindergarten and first grade, even after accounting for factors such as maternal education (National Institute of Child Health and Human Development [NICHD] Early Child Care Research Network [ECCRN], 2002a; Vandell et al., 2010). Relatedly, a stimulating home environment is another well-established element of the family associated with young children's academic and cognitive development (Bradley, Corwyn, Burchinal, McAdoo, & Coll, 2001). There is general consensus that early family context, in particular, parenting quality and the stimulation of language skills, tends to make a stronger contribution to children's development than other early childhood contexts (NICHD ECCRN & Duncan, 2003).

Early child care experiences, particularly high-quality care, also appear to enhance children's development of language and academic skills prior to school entry (Burchinal et al., 2002; Vandell et al., 2010), above and beyond the effects of the family environment as a "value-added" factor (NICHD ECCRN & Duncan, 2003). Across several naturalistic, longitudinal projects, including the Cost, Quality, and Outcomes Study, NICHD Study of Early Child Care, and the Multistate Study of Prekindergarten, findings consistently demonstrate that quality experiences in a child care context predict language, cognitive, and achievement outcomes, after researchers control for family selection factors such as socioeconomic status and parental sensitivity (Peisner-Feinberg et al., 2001; Vandell et al., 2010). Definitive evidence from quasi-experimental and experimental studies with samples of children who experience social and economic risks further indicates a positive effect of comprehensive, high-quality child care and children's cognitive ability and academic success from elementary school through adolescence (e.g., Pianta, Barnett, Burchinal, & Thornburg, 2009). Effects of the most thorough and concentrated of these early child care interventions are reported to be sustained into early adulthood, leading to positive academic achievement and increased rates of employment (Campbell, Ramey, Pungello, Sparling, & Miller-Johnson, 2002).

In summary, experiences with adults in the home, child care, preschool, and the early school grades are formative assets for the development of skills that translate into success in elementary school and beyond. Understanding, assessing, and ultimately strengthening the role and impact of young children's relationships and interactions with adults, at scale, become the critical tasks for professionals and policymakers hoping to foster the early school success of large numbers of children.

The following section describes large-scale work done in observation of teachers and classroom settings in early childhood education. First, we discuss two prominent observation systems, the ECERS (Harms & Clifford, 1980; Harms et al., 1998) and the CLASS (Pianta, LaParo, & Hamre, 2008). Then, we present explicit descriptions of how best to use an observational tool in early childhood settings, using the CLASS as an example of how to use this data in a professional development framework.

RESEARCH INTO PRACTICE: STANDARDIZED OBSERVATION OF EARLY EDUCATION AND CARE SETTINGS

Early Childhood Environment Rating Scale

The suite of environmental rating scales (ERS) developed by Richard Clifford, Thelma Harms, and colleagues, have been nothing short of foundational to the development of the early childhood education infrastructure in the United States and many countries around the world (Harms & Clifford, 1980). The ERS are observational tools that capture information on settings that serve young children, including physical safety, hygiene, nutrition, educational materials, program offerings (e.g., activity schedules), and general qualities of social and language interactions between adults and children. Observers are trained to a standard for agreement with master-coded examples and demonstrate specific levels of accuracy before using the system. The Early Childhood Environment Rating Scale—Revised (ECERS-R, Harms et al., 1998) is the most widely used metric for program quality in early childhood education settings such as Head Start, preschool, and subsidized child care. Nearly every single public investment in early childhood education—increasing access or slots in existing programs, opening new sectors of programming, or improving existing programming—has involved legislative or regulatory language related to ensuring quality, and ECERS has been the "gold standard."

The ECERS has been a ubiquitous presence in most major studies of early education quality as well as impacts on accreditation and licensing. The research studies, the majority of which were with large, diverse samples of children, teachers, and settings, provided not only data on the validity and use of these rating scales but also considerable experience in the development and deployment of regimens for training, quality control, and scoring. Nearly all of this research found a relation between higher scores on the ECERS and more positive child development outcomes in areas considered important for later school success, such as language development (Administration for Children and Families [ACF], 2006; Ludwig & Miller, 2007; Pianta et al., 2009). In more than 20 states, ECERS is one of the metrics (quality of the environment, teacher credentials, features of the curriculum, etc.) for Quality Rating and Improvement Systems (QRIS; Mitchell, 2009) that are combined to derive an overall rating of quality (e.g., three stars in a five-star system). States are investing in program improvements and professional development that purportedly are coupled with QRIS metrics. Thus, there are an abundance of examples of scaled-up use of the ECERS that aligns with policy initiatives and program development investments that touch many millions of children (Pianta et al., 2009). Features of early childhood programs specified by ECERS indicators are woven into professional licensure and credentialing systems, and license settings and the systems that credential professionals (American Public Health Association [APHA] & the American Academy of Pediatrics [AAP], 1992; Layzer & Price, 2008; National Association for Regulatory Administration [NARA], 2009).

Thus, in over two decades of investments in Head Start, ECERS scores gradually increased nationwide to the point that the mean score in nationally representative reports showed an overall quality level of 5 on the ECERS 7-point range (ACF, 2006). Features of quality measured by the ERS that include materials, the physical environment, hygiene, or program schedules primarily have accounted for the reported jumps in scores. These increases have undoubtedly improved the experiences of children, the safety of settings, and the overall quality of programs; in several cases these improvements appear also to have corresponded to improvements in some measured aspects of children's development (APHA & AAP, 1992; Layzer & Price, 2008; Pianta et al., 2009). In fact, one of the fundamental conclusions to be drawn from the widespread use of the ECERS is that observation can be embedded in accountability and improvement models, and actually drive change in observed indicators. Observations can be scaled; used in accountability, program development, and market-oriented policy tools; and generally over time produce change in features of programs assessed by these tools.

However, in recent studies, ERS-defined quality improvements have not directly led to improvements in children's school readiness skills. When programs lack educational materials or fail to operate with a daily schedule of learning activities (indicators on the ECERS), then a focus on these benchmarks translates into increments in children's outcomes. However, when nearly all programs advance these features of quality, and variation in these features declines (e.g., occurred in Head Start), links between programs' ECERS scores and child outcomes also appeared less strong. Further analysis suggests that other elements of observed program quality (e.g., teacher–child interactions) are potential candidates for more focused assessment.

Classroom Assessment Scoring System: Observing Interactions

The CLASS (Pianta, LaParo, & Hamre, 2008), a more recently developed observational instrument, is designed to measure features of teacher–child interaction in settings that serve children as young as infants and as old as high school age. The CLASS has been most widely used at scale in preschool classrooms (Mashburn et al., 2008; Pianta et al., 2009). The CLASS is based on developmental theory and research suggesting that interactions between children and adults are primary mechanisms of their development and learning.

The CLASS specially measures *interactions* between teachers and children and among children in classrooms; scoring is not determined by the presence of materials, the physical environment or safety, teacher education level, or the adoption of a specific curriculum. This distinction between *observed interactions* and physical materials or reported use of curriculum is important because materials and curriculum in most early elementary settings are usually prevalent and fairly well organized.

Domains of the CLASS

The CLASS complements the information gathered by the ECERS and assesses three broad domains of teachers' interactions with children—Classroom Organization, Emotional Support, and Instructional Support. Within each domain are several specific dimensions of teacher–child interaction (Figure 17.1).

CLASSROOM ORGANIZATION

Home and preschool settings in which *behavior, time,* and *attention* are well regulated through interactions with adults foster more positive gains on a range of school readiness outcomes (Cameron, Connor, & Morrison, 2005). These settings function best and children have the most opportunities to learn when expectations for children's behavior are embedded within developmentally appropriate expectations, when children consistently have things to do, and when children are interested and engaged in learning tasks (Pianta, Hamre, & Stuhlman, 2003). Consistent with constructivist theories that guide much of early childhood practice (Bruner, 1996; Rogoff, 1990; Vygotsky, 1979), when teachers provide activities in which there are multiple pathways for engagement, students are not just *passively* engaged in learning, they are *active* participants in it. Taken together, these types of behaviors that comprise the domain of Classroom Organization set the stage for learning.

EMOTIONAL SUPPORT

The ability to maintain caring and supportive relationships with students is crucial for all teachers of young students (Pianta, 1999). Sensitive teachers and teachers who create

CLASS Framework for Prekindergarten Classrooms

Domain	Dimension	Description
Emotional Support	Positive Climate	Reflects the overall emotional tone of the classroom and the connection between teachers and students. Considers the warmth and respect displayed in teachers' and students' interactions with one another as well as the degree to which they display enjoyment and enthusiasm during learning activities.
	Negative Climate	Reflects the level of expressed negativity, such as anger, hostility, or aggression, demonstrated by teachers and/or children. Low scores represent fewer instances of expressed negativity in the classroom.
	Teacher Sensitivity	Encompasses teachers' responsivity to students' needs and awareness of students' level of academic and emotional functioning. The highly sensitive teacher helps students see adults as a resource and creates an environment in which students feel safe and free to explore and learn.
	Regard for Student Perspective	The degree to which the teachers' interactions with students and classroom activities place an emphasis on students' interests, motivations, and points of view, rather than being very teacher driven. This may be demonstrated by teachers' flexibility within activities and respect for students' autonomy to participate in and initiate activities.
Classroom Organization	Behavior Management	Encompasses teachers' ability to use effective methods to prevent and redirect misbehavior, by presenting clear behavioral expectations and minimizing time spent on behavioral issues.
	Productivity	Considers how well teachers manage instructional time and routines so that students have the maximum number of opportunities to learn. Not related to the quality of instruction, but rather teachers' efficiency.
	Instructional Learning Formats	The degree to which teachers maximize students' engagement and ability to learn by providing interesting activities, instruction, centers, and materials. Considers the manner in which the teacher facilitates activities so that students have opportunities to experience, perceive, explore, and utilize materials.
Instructional Support	Concept Development	The degree to which instructional discussions and activities promote students' higher-order thinking skills versus focus on rote and fact-based learning.
	Quality of Feedback	Considers teachers' provision of feedback focused on expanding learning and understanding (formative evaluation), not correctness or the end product (summative evaluation)
	Language Modeling	The quality and amount of teachers' use of language-stimulation and language-facilitation techniques during individual, small-group, and large-group interactions with children. Components of high-quality language modeling include self and parallel talk, open-ended questions, repetition, expansion/extension, and use of advanced language.

FIGURE 17.1. CLASS framework for early childhood and elementary classroom quality.

a positive climate in their classrooms tend to be more familiar with the academic needs of individual students (Helmke & Schrader, 1988). These features of teacher–child interactions collectively and separately predict students' performance on standardized tests of literacy skills in PreK and first grade (NICHD ECCRN, 2003; Pianta, 2003); lower levels of mother-reported internalizing behaviors in kindergarten and first grade (NICHD ECCRN, 2003); and students' engagement in the classroom across all grade levels (NICHD ECCRN 2002b; 2003). Although these processes are important for all students, they may be particularly important for students at risk of school failure. For example, among a group of students that displayed significant behavioral and emotional problems in kindergarten, those placed in first-grade classrooms offering high levels of emotional support made academic progress at levels similar to those of their low-risk peers, while at-risk students placed in classrooms offering lower levels of emotional support fell further behind their low-risk peers (Hamre & Pianta, 2005).

INSTRUCTIONAL SUPPORT

Teachers of classrooms with high Instructional Support engage children in intentional activities designed to promote higher-order thinking skills, provide specific feedback geared to further a child's understanding, and afford opportunities to learn language and social skills. At core of Instructional Support is movement from rote memorization and simple recall to the creation of an environment where children learn to think, problem-solve, and create (Bransford, Brown, & Cocking, 1999; Mayer, 2002). Teacher-provided feedback is specific and directed at understanding why an answer is incorrect or correct, not whether it is "right" or "wrong." Finally, the teacher and children in the classroom engage in conversation, and the teacher may pose many open-ended questions designed to promote language use. These interactions within Instructional Support are intentionally crafted by the teacher and serve to promote understanding of facts within a real-world context; not memorization.

The CLASS in Early Childhood Settings

The CLASS, like the ECERS, is widely used in research and program development, as well as Head Start and QRIS systems. These uses require standardized training and reliability testing protocols, which we discuss in the next section. In the past 3 years, over 4,000 people across the country have been trained to use the CLASS reliably, thus documenting its scalability. It is evident from studies on training with CLASS and the ERS that large-scale (e.g., national) implementation and rollout of an observational assessment is possible, with combinations of live and Web-based training protocols to sustain training of thousands of observers to acceptable levels of agreement. A growing body of work now documents the ways in which CLASS observations of early education settings identify components of teacher–student interactions that contribute to students' social and academic development (Bill & Melinda Gates Foundation, 2010; Mashburn et al., 2008; Pianta et al., 2005). The pattern of results is quite consistent, with levels of teachers' Instructional Support (e.g., feedback, focus on conceptual understanding, rich conversational discourse) that not only are quite low but also forecast students' learning gains. Evidence links teachers' engagement with students and their instruction to student learning and development, and it has been demonstrated that these teacher behaviors can also be improved by professional development (Allen, Pianta, Gregory, Mikami, & Lun, 2011; Pianta, Mashburn, Downer, Hamre, & Justice, 2008).

CLASS is also used in a variety of high-stakes and program improvement applications. The recent federal legislation reauthorizing Head Start specifically mentioned that a standardized observation of teacher–child interaction was to be the metric for program monitoring and accountability. Every Head Start grantee is evaluated every 3 years, with CLASS observations conducted in a representative number of classrooms by a set of independent, trained evaluators. Cutoff scores have been established based on the accumulated empirical evidence on CLASS that designate levels of scores that are acceptable for continued operation, or that trigger the grantee having to recompete for Head Start funds. In parallel with this accountability-driven evaluation, the Office of Head Start has funded a network of training and technical assistance centers, early childhood specialists, and related personnel to focus on program improvements and human capital advancement, much of which focuses on CLASS and associated professional development demonstrated to improve CLASS scores. And like the ECERS, CLASS is also being used in QRIS models for preschool and child care programs in a variety of states.

Although it is too early to determine the extent to which high-stakes adoption of the CLASS in Head Start, or other large-scale uses of CLASS in early childhood accountability or program improvement systems, will result in an actual shift in program quality or in children's school readiness, it is quite evident that its use in this framework has driven requests for training and technical assistance. Thus, early childhood education is now very focused on teachers' instructional and socioemotional interactions. Clearly, between the ECERS and the CLASS, early childhood education has accumulated a wealth of experience in using standardized observations in policy and program improvement contexts, and in deploying observational protocols at scale.

Observation in Early Childhood Settings

Observations of teachers' interactions and classroom processes play a major role in helping to describe and identify effective practices and professional development to improve those practices. Thus observation can be an effective tool in building capacity for teaching and learning (Allen et al., 2011; Bill & Melinda Gates Foundation, 2010; Pianta, Mashburn, et al., 2008). Observing teachers' classroom interactions and practices is a potentially key lever for improvement. The use of standardized observations, if they reliably and validly measure classroom interactions that impact student learning, is a direct and effective mechanism for focusing on teachers' classroom interactions, with the potential to illuminate links between certain inputs (e.g., resources for teachers) and desired outcomes (e.g., optimized student learning). It also supports a common lens and shared language for technical assistance in QRIS stakeholders and Head Start staff who build the important lines of communication that are necessary to create improved teacher–child interactions.

The advantage of using measures that are standardized, reliable, and validated, such as the CLASS, to compare student outcomes is that with these kinds of observations, educators, mentors, and administrators know that their comparisons between and within programs use the same metric of comparison. Use of standardized, reliable, and valid tools in no way interferes with giving personalized feedback to teachers; rather, it allows for the provision of highly specific and personalized feedback with regard to clearly defined areas that are consistent across all teachers, and provides a strong background for interpretation and comparison of scores. Using standardized tools for which there is evidence of reliability and validity across various samples outweighs the disadvantages related to a highly customized approach in which every classroom, school, or district adapts an existing tool or develops a new one. These issues, examined in greater detail below, use the CLASS as an example for discussion.

Observation Procedure

It is important to select an observation system that provides clear instructions for use, in terms of how to set up and conduct observations, and how to assign scores. This is an essential component of a useful observation system: Without standardized directions to follow, different people are likely to use different methods, which severely limits the potential for agreement between observers when making ratings, thus hampering systemwide applicability (Bill & Melinda Gates Foundation, 2010; Pianta & Hamre, 2009). In this regard standardization is not the same as reliability or validity; it refers to the rules and procedures for observing and ensures consistency and quality control. These procedures include considerations of time of day; qualifications of observers; length of the observation; and other features, any of which could undermine the quality of data collected and, ultimately, the inferences drawn from these data.

There are three main components of standardization that users may consider evaluating in an observation instrument: (1) training protocol, (2) parameters around observation, and (3) scoring directions. The CLASS offers a 2-day training session with a CLASS-certified trainer, so that individuals can learn how to administer the CLASS. During the training, trainees watch and code five "gold standard" videos, with the prompting and assistance of the trainer. Finally, trainees take a reliability test; trainees who pass are certified for 1 year. Although not mandatory, it is also recommended that after certification, individuals complete calibration exercises (e.g., double-coding). These practices help to ensure that, throughout the year, an individual is not deviating from the CLASS standards for scoring.

Regarding observation parameters, an observation tool should offer standardization in terms of the length of observations, the start and stop times of observations, the time of day or specific activities to observe, whether observations are announced or unannounced, and related issues. The CLASS manual offers clear instructions for length of observation and under what circumstances one can end an observation early, as well as the suggestion that individuals observe for 2 hours in order to observe a range of activities and experiences in the classroom to obtain a score that is accurately representative.

With regard to scoring, users are advised to look for clear, consistent guidelines. The CLASS manual provides clear guidelines for observing and scoring. Observers watch and code in a cycle. One full cycle includes a 20-minute observation in the classroom, with the observer taking notes, and after the 20 minutes observation, scoring all 10 CLASS dimensions in less than 10 minutes. Then the observer starts another cycle. The observer assigns a score that is determined by the CLASS manual. The manual provides detailed descriptions for low-, middle-, and high-level teacher–child interactions for each dimensions.

Reliability and Validity of an Observational Tool

Reliability is a key consideration in selecting an observational assessment tool (Bill & Melinda Gates Foundation, 2010; Pianta & Hamre, 2009). *Reliability* is a property of any measurement tool that refers to the degree of error, or bias, in the scores obtained. It addresses the extent to which a tool measures those qualities consistently across a wide range of considerations that could affect a score (e.g., raters, length of the observation period, training). In observational assessments of classrooms, a reliable tool produces the same score for the same observed behaviors, regardless of features of the classroom outside of the scope of the tool, and regardless of who is making the ratings.

For example, three certified CLASS observers visit Classroom A on the same day and code four cycles together. Given that individuals have been deemed reliable based on CLASS standards, on average, they give the same score for each dimension; that is, if Observer A gives the classroom a 4 on Positive Climate, then Observers B and C are also likely to code that classroom a 4 on Positive Climate. Thus, the CLASS produces the same score for the same set of behaviors, regardless of who is observing the classroom. Further, the CLASS is also reliable between classrooms; that is, if Classroom B received a 4 on Positive Climate, the behaviors observed in Classroom B would be consistent with behaviors observed in Classroom A. This is an important consideration when a measure is used to compare results across classrooms; it emphasizes equity in expectations.

If there is very low agreement between two or more observers' ratings within a CLASS cycle, the degree to which the scores represent the teachers' behavior rather than the observers' subjective interpretations of that behavior or personal preferences is questionable. Conversely, if two independent observers can consistently assign the same ratings to the same patterns of observed behaviors, then this speaks to the fact that ratings truly represent objective attributes of the classroom as defined by the scoring system, as opposed to attributes of the observer.

Additionally, it is important to consider the stability of the measurement, or observations, over time. In classrooms, this usually translates to stability across a given school year. If ratings shift dramatically and/or randomly from one observation cycle or day or week to the next within a given classroom, these ratings are not likely to represent core aspects of the interactions or teaching practices in that classroom. Conversely, if scores are at least moderately consistent across time, they likely represent something stable about the set of skills that teachers bring into the classroom setting, and feedback and support around these behaviors are much more likely to resonate with teachers and to function as useful levers for helping them change their practice.

In studies that have used the CLASS and followed the standard protocols for training and observation described earlier, there is evidence that CLASS ratings capture features of teachers' behavior that are consistent from day to day, across times of year, and within the content area the teacher is teaching (e.g., Bill & Melinda Gates Foundation, 2010). For example, scores assigned in October and April to a classroom for Quality of Feedback, a dimension in the CLASS, will be similar.

Validity is the degree to which scores or metrics derived from the observation system are associated with student or teacher outcomes about which the observation is designed to provide information or to make predictions. Selecting instruments with demonstrated validity is critical to making good use of observational methodology because this information allows users to have confidence that the information they are gathering is relevant to the outcomes that interest them, and that the types of behaviors outlined in the system can be held up as goals for high-quality teacher practice. We must know that our assessment tools are directly and meaningfully related to our outcomes of interest before we begin using them in either professional development or accountability frameworks; without validity information, users have no such assurances.

If the user is interested in understanding how classroom teacher–student interactions and behaviors, which are organizational, emotional, and instructional in nature, relate to child academic and socioemotional outcomes, the CLASS serves as a reliable and valid tool to measure such observations. The CLASS domains (i.e., Classroom Organization,

Emotional Support, Instructional Support) are based on educational and developmental theory that serves to promote positive development in children and adolescents. Furthermore, the predictive ability of each domain aligns with theory and research on child development. In over 700 PreK classrooms in an 11-state study, higher levels of CLASS Instructional Support predicted children's language, literacy, and math gains, while Emotional Support predicted social skills, with effect sizes ranging from small or moderate, roughly accounting for changes of between 5 and 15 percentile points on standardized tests (Mashburn et al., 2008). Simply, instructional interactions predicted changes in literacy, language, and math, while increased Emotional Support (e.g., teacher is sensitive to children's needs, respects and promotes child's point of view) is related to social skills.

However, if a user has a particular observation tool that is well aligned with the questions he or she wants answered about classroom practice and meets the criteria summarized previously (e.g., standardized, reliable), there is always the possibility that no data will be available on validity for the particular outcomes the user is interested in evaluating. In these instances, it would certainly be possible to use the observation in a preliminary way and evaluate whether it is, in fact, associated with outcomes of interest. For example, a district or organization could conduct a pilot test with a subgroup of its teachers and students to determine whether scores assigned using the observation tool are associated with the outcomes of interest. This testing would provide some basis for using the instrument for accountability or evaluative purposes.

The importance of selecting an observation system that includes validity information cannot be overstated. If the teacher behaviors evaluated in an observation are known to be linked with desired student outcomes, teachers will be more willing to reflect on these behaviors and "buy in to" observationally based feedback; teacher educators and school personnel can feel confident establishing observationally based standards and mechanisms for meeting those standards; and educational systems, teachers, and students will all benefit (Allen et al., 2011; Bill & Melinda Gates Foundation, 2010; Pianta & Hamre, 2009). In the next section, we provide an overview of a professional development program based on the CLASS.

Improving Teacher–Student Interactions: MyTeachingPartner

The MyTeachingPartner (MTP) approach to professional development connects the features of emerging and promising professional development presented in the chapter's first section, and the focus on teacher–student interaction presented in the second, to provide teachers with professional development inputs that include the following:

1. Extensive opportunities to *observe* effective teacher–student interaction through analysis and viewing of multiple video examples.
2. *Skills training* in identifying effective and ineffective instructional, linguistic, and social responses to students' cues, and identifying the behavioral sequences connecting teacher responses to students' engagement and skills.
3. Repeated *opportunities for individualized feedback on* and *analysis of* one's own interactions with students.

The suite of MTP professional development supports contains three specific resources linked to the inputs: (1) a video library of annotated exemplars; (2) Web-mediated individualized coaching; and (3) a college course focused on the CLASS. All three rely on the

CLASS as the primary way to "see" or observe and define effective practice. This section of the chapter describes each of these approaches to professional development and the results related to improving teachers' effectiveness and children's learning.

MyTeachingPartner Video Library and Coaching

The MTP Web video library is an opportunity to observe others' effective interactions and provides over 400 video clips of teachers' effective interactions. Each clip is accompanied by a very detailed and specific description of the behaviors the teacher is engaging in that defines interaction as effective for fostering student learning and development. These 1- to 2-minute videos are organized (and searchable) by the CLASS dimensions and each includes an explicit, behavioral description of what is happening in the video footage that reflects a high-quality teacher–child interaction. Teachers are often isolated within their own classrooms and rarely have the opportunity to see authentic, real-time examples of effective interactions and teaching. The idea behind the MTP video library is to provide opportunities for these teachers to learn more about types of interactions that are important for student learning (knowing), and to understand exactly what these interactions look like when enacted by others (seeing).

MTP *coaching* involves observation-based analysis and feedback enacted through a regular cycle of Web-mediated interaction (both synchronous and asynchronous) between a teacher and coach (Figure 17.2). Every 2 weeks, teachers videotape their instruction in

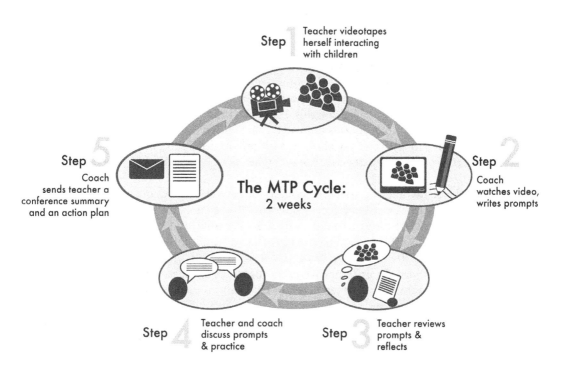

FIGURE 17.2. MyTeachingPartner cycle description.

literacy, language, and social skills, and send this footage to their coach. The coach edits the tape into three segments that focus on a specific CLASS dimension (e.g., concept development), that focus on (1) identification of instances of effective behavior, (2) analysis of alternatives, and (3) instruction. The segments and feedback (called "prompts") are posted to a secure website where teachers view the segments and comments and respond to prompts. The prompts focus attention on specific aspects of teacher–child interaction, such as "What did you do here to help Jaden pay attention, and what did he do in response?" and include links to clips of high-quality exemplars from the video library. Both the response to coach feedback online and the conversations during conferences are set up to encourage teachers' analysis and reflection of their own interactions. MTP coaching increases teachers' knowledge and skills to observe interactions with students, and awareness of their impact on student motivation, teacher–student relationships, and student learning.

EVIDENCE SUPPORTING MYTEACHINGPARTNER VIDEO LIBRARY AND COACHING

We tested these MTP professional development resources in a randomized controlled trial with over 240 state-funded PreK teachers to determine their impact on improved instruction and child outcomes (Pianta, Mashburn, et al., 2008). Two MTP resources were implemented and compared: (1) Teachers had access to the MTP video library, and (2) some received MTP coaching and access to the video library. Teachers assigned to coaching made significant gains compared teachers with access to the video library in reading and responding to students' cues, using a variety of formats to engage children actively in instruction, and intentionally stimulating language development (behaviors in the Instructional Support domain). These impacts were roughly on the order of one scale point on the CLASS rating system; for example, moving from a rating of 3 to 4 in one academic year. And in classrooms in which 100% of the children enrolled were from economically disadvantaged families, there were remarkable differences in teachers' rates of change in sensitivity and responsiveness, and in facilitation of engagement and enthusiasm in learning. When the teachers received coaching, the quality of these classrooms' interactions increased roughly 1.5 rating points on the CLASS scale. In addition, comparisons of child outcomes indicated that children in MTP coaching classrooms made greater gains in receptive vocabulary, task orientation, and prosocial assertiveness, scoring approximately 4–5 percentile points higher than children in the other conditions on standardized tests.

The evidence favored the coaching condition. However, hints in follow-up analyses suggested that teachers who had access only to video exemplars and made regular use of these exemplars were also observed to be more sensitive and responsive to children's needs, proactive and effective at managing behavior, and skilled at maximizing children's learning time. In short, for some teachers, just watching examples of effective teaching from the video library improved their practice. Children of those teachers who spent more time watching video exemplars online also experienced greater gains in social development during the PreK year. Interestingly, teachers who spent more time watching and analyzing their own classroom video footage online as part of coaching also had children who experienced greater gains in vocabulary development during the PreK year, with gains equal to approximately 5 percentile points.

Collectively, these findings suggest that the act of watching oneself and others interact with children in a classroom in and of itself may contribute to changes in instruction and children's learning. Additionally, focus groups with teachers at the end of the project indicated that many of the teachers, particularly those receiving coaching, felt that they could have taken better advantage of reflection work with their coach if they had had a greater understanding of what constituted effective teacher–child interactions at the beginning of the year. They needed more knowledge about these practices and more time to see what they looked like in classrooms.

We recently scaled up the MTP coaching model to 450 PreK teachers in 15 sites served by local consultants (Pianta, 2011), trained and supported by our team (all using standardized and manualized procedures). When evaluated in a randomized controlled trial the benefits of MTP coaching were confirmed. Teachers (in PreK programs) who received MTP coaching improved in nearly every feature of interaction assessed by the CLASS, particularly the dimensions of Instructional Support, with effects averaging approximately 1 point on the CLASS dimensions. This study not only replicated the value of MTP coaching for teachers but also demonstrated that the model of coaching can be replicated and extended through standardized training and support protocols. Importantly, although a 1-point magnitude difference on the CLASS 1- to 7-point rating scale may seem small, recall that prior research demonstrated that a 1-point difference in the quality of teachers' interactions, particularly in the instructional domain, was associated with increased achievement outcomes for children (Pianta, Mashburn, et al., 2008).

MTP College Course

The third professional development resource is the MTP course, a 3-credit college course that focuses on improving teachers' knowledge of effective interactions, their skills in identifying effective interactions, and applying those skills to their own classrooms (Hamre et al., 2012). This course, like the other MTP professional development resources initially developed for and evaluated in PreK classrooms, is entitled Support of Language and Literacy Development through Effective Teacher–Child Interactions and Relationships.

The course targeted two major clusters of belief, knowledge and skills—the first focused on effective teacher–student interactions, and the second specifically on teaching of literacy and language in early childhood classrooms. The course used the similar framework to that in the video library and MTP—professional development rooted in knowing, seeing, and doing—to make explicit links between classroom behaviors and intended benefits for children. For example, when learning about quality of feedback, teachers were encouraged to watch and analyze videos that highlighted the ways in which specific teacher behaviors led to children spending more or less time thinking about and analyzing a problem. The course also targeted teachers' skills in detecting effective teacher–child interactions though video analysis. We hypothesized that it was not sufficient for teachers to gain knowledge about effective interactions; they needed actual skills involving identification of effective interactions with a high degree of specificity to be most likely to transfer coursework into changes in their instructional practice (seeing). Therefore, a primary emphasis in the course was analysis of videotapes from real classrooms to develop the skill of identifying effective (and ineffective) interactions and articulating specific behavioral evidence to support these judgments.

In a large-scale randomized controlled trial, compared to teachers in the control condition, those in the course condition reported more intentional teaching beliefs, and demonstrated greater knowledge of and skills in detecting effective teacher–child interactions (Hamre et al., 2012). Teachers in the course condition also reported stronger beliefs about the importance of teaching children early literacy and language skills, and demonstrated greater knowledge about these skills. And those who took the course demonstrated more effective emotional and instructional practices in interactions with children. The magnitude of the impact of the course on teachers' observed classroom practices was between one-half and 1 scale point on the CLASS metric. Importantly, teachers' skills in detecting effective interactions partially accounted for the effects of the course on teachers' actual practices.

REFLECTIONS AND NEW DIRECTIONS

Effective teaching in early childhood education requires skillful combinations of explicit instruction, sensitive and warm interactions, responsive feedback, and verbal engagement or stimulation intentionally directed to ensure children's learning, while embedding these interactions in a classroom environment that is not overly structured or regimented. For children enrolled in preschool, effective teaching can boost development and school readiness skills, and can have longer term benefits to children and communities over time. However, effective teaching is not often discussed as a feature of program quality regulated by policy; instead, program features such as teacher qualifications or curriculum, which have much less influence on children, are considered. Teacher–child interaction and teachers' effective implementation of educational and developmental curricula, as features of program quality, are central ingredients responsible for program effects.

It is important to note that aspects such as effective teaching in early education settings can be improved with specific and focused training and support, and this will have expected effects on children's learning. As demonstrated with the MTP suite of professional development, the best, most successful approaches to professional development focus on providing teachers with (1) developmentally relevant information on skills, targets, and progressions, and (2) support for learning to skillfully use instructional interactions and effectively implement curricula. Effective professional development support allows direct tracing of the paths (and putative effects) of inputs to teachers and to children, and to children's skill gains. As reviewed in this chapter, there is very promising evidence that when such targeted, aligned supports are available to teachers, children's skill gains can be considerable. Unfortunately, preschool teachers are rarely exposed to these types of professional development programs, and at present, there is very little indication that the policy frameworks and resources are aligned with the most promising, evidence-based forms of effective professional development, such as MTP.

Current public policies for child care, Head Start, and state PreK fail to ensure that most American children attend highly effective preschool education programs. Some attend no program at all; others attend educationally weak programs. Children in families from the middle of the income distribution have the least access, but coverage is far from universal even for children in poverty. This state of affairs can have marked and deleterious effects on children, families, and communities. Increased provision of child care subsidies under current federal and state policies is particularly unlikely to produce any meaningful improvements in children's learning and development, and could have mild negative consequences. Increased public investment in effective preschool education programs for all children can produce substantial educational, social, and economic benefits, but only if the investments are in programs in which teaching is highly effective.

PROFESSIONAL DEVELOPMENT ACTIVITIES (AGES 3–5)

- Erika is the director of a small child care program. She has six classrooms (two infant, two toddler, two mixed age). Some teachers within her program complain that they are plagued with behavior problems, so they are especially concerned about better developing socioemotional competencies in their classrooms, while other teachers seem to have classroom behavior under control and express more interest in further developing their students' academic competencies. Erika has just received some funding to support the use of the MTP video library at her center, but she's not sure how to use these funds in ways that are most likely to help her individual teachers. How would you organize the teachers at the center, so that they get the most out of this professional development?

- You are planning to observe teachers in ECE settings to assess the quality of their interactions in the classroom and must choose an observational assessment. What three components of the assessment should you consider, so that you have data that are reliable and valid?

- Your assistant teacher asks the preschool children in the classroom many open-ended and cognitively stimulating questions. However, these questions are rarely posed in a warm, sensitive manner, nor do they consider the child's perspective. When you approach her about the delivery of her questions, the assistant teacher states, "I am asking the questions dictated in the curriculum. I don't see what I am doing wrong." Based on what you have read in this chapter, how would you help your assistant teacher understand that in order to be effective, her questions must occur in the context of a warm, sensitive relationship?

REFERENCES

Administration on Children and Families (ACF). (2006). *FACES findings: New research on Head Start outcomes and program quality.* Washington, DC: U.S. Department of Health and Human Services.

Allen, J. P., Pianta, R. C., Gregory, A., Mikami, A. Y., & Lun, J. (2011). An interaction-based approach to enhancing secondary school instruction and student achievement. *Science, 333,* 1034–1037.

American Public Health Association (APHA) & the American Academy of Pediatrics (AAP). (1992). *Caring for our children: National health and safety performance standards: Standards for out-of-home child care programs.* Washington, DC: Authors.

Bill & Melinda Gates Foundation. (2010). *Learning about teaching: Initial findings from the Measures of Effective Teaching Project.* Seattle, WA: Author.

Bradley, R. H., Corwyn, R. F., Burchinal, M., McAdoo, H. P., & Coll, C. G. (2001). The home environments of children in the United States, Part II: Relations with behavioral development through age thirteen. *Child Development, 72,* 1868–1886.

Bransford, J., Brown, A., & Cocking, R. (1999). *How people learn: Brain, mind, experience, and school.* Washington, DC: National Academy Press.

Bronfenbrenner, U., & Morris, P. A. (2006). The bioecological model of human development. In W. Damon & R. M. Lerner (Eds.), *Handbook of child psychology: Vol. 1. Theoretical models of human development* (6th ed., pp. 793–828). New York: Wiley.

Bruner, J. (1996). *The culture of education.* Cambridge, MA: Harvard University Press.

Burchinal, M., Peisner-Feinberg, E., Pianta, R., & Howes, C. (2002). Development of academic skills from preschool through second grade: Family and classroom predictors of developmental trajectories. *Journal of School Psychology, 40,* 415–436.

Cameron, C. E., Connor, C. M., & Morrison, F. J. (2005). Effects of variation in teacher organization on classroom functioning. *Journal of School Psychology, 43*, 61–85.

Campbell, F. A., Ramey, C. T., Pungello, E., Sparling, J., & Miller-Johnson, S. (2002). Early childhood education: Young adult outcomes from the Abecedarian project. *Applied Developmental Science, 6*, 42–57.

Dickinson, D. K., Anastasopolous, L., McCabe, A., Peisner-Feinberg, E. S., & Poe, M. D. (2003). The comprehensive language approach to early literacy: The interrelationships among vocabulary, phonological sensitivity, and print knowledge among preschool-aged children. *Journal of Educational Psychology, 93*, 465–481.

Duncan, G., & Murnane, R. (2011). *Whither opportunity: Rising inequality, schools, and children's life chances*. New York: Russell Sage Foundation.

Hamre, B. K., & Pianta, R. C. (2005). Can instructional and emotional support in the first grade classroom make a difference for children at risk of school failure? *Child Development, 76*, 949–967.

Hamre, B. K., Pianta, R. C., Burchinal, M., Field, S., LoCasale-Crouch, J. L., Downer, J. T., et al. (2012). Course on effective teacher–child interactions: Effects on teacher beliefs, knowledge, and observed practice. *American Educational Research Journal, 49*, 88–123.

Harms, T., & Clifford, R. M. (1980). *Early Childhood Environment Ratings Scale*. New York: Teachers College Press.

Harms, T., Clifford, R. M., & Cryer, D. (1998). *The Early Childhood Environment Ratings Scale: Revised Edition*. New York: Teaches College Press.

Helmke, A., & Schrader, F. W. (1988). Successful student practice during seatwork: Efficient management and active supervision not enough. *Journal of Educational Research, 82*, 70–75.

Layzer, J., & Price, C. (2008). *Closing the gap in the school readiness of low-income children*. Washington, DC: U.S. Department of Health and Human Services.

Lonigan, C. J., Burgess, S. R., & Anthony, J. L. (2000). Development of emergent literacy and early reading skills in preschool children: Evidence from a latent-variable longitudinal study. *Developmental Psychology, 36*, 596–613.

Ludwig, J., & Miller, D. L. (2007). Does Head Start improve children's life chances?: Evidence from a regression discontinuity design. *Quarterly Journal of Economics, 122*, 159–208.

Mashburn, A., Pianta, R., Hamre, B., Downer, J., Barbarin, O., Bryant, D., et al. (2008). Measures of classroom quality in pre-kindergarten and children's development of academic, language and social skills. *Child Development, 79*, 732–749.

Mayer, R. E. (2002). *The promise of educational psychology: Vol. 2. Teaching for meaningful learning*. Upper Saddle River, NJ: Prentice Hall.

McWayne, C., Hampton, V., Fantuzzo, J., Cohen, H., & Sekino, Y. (2004). A multivariate examination of parent involvement and the social and academic competencies of urban kindergarten children. *Psychology in the Schools, 41*, 1–15.

Mitchell, A. W. (2009). Models for financing state-supported prekindergarten programs. In R. Pianta & C. Howes (Eds.), *The promise of Pre-K* (pp. 51–64). Baltimore: Brookes.

Morrison, F. J., Bachman, H. J., & Connor, C. M. (2003). *Improving literacy in America: Lessons from research*. New Haven, CT: Yale University Press.

Morrison, F. J., & Connor, C. M. (2002). Understanding schooling effects on early literacy: A working research strategy. *Journal of School Psychology, 40*, 493–500.

National Association for Regulatory Administration (NARA). (2009). *The 2007 Child Care Licensing Study*. Lexington, KY: Author and National Child Care Information and Technical Assistance Center.

National Institute of Child Health and Human Development (NICHD) Early Child Care Research Network (ECCRN). (2002a). The interaction of child care and family risk in relation to child development at 24 and 36 months. *Applied Developmental Science, 6*, 144–156.

National Institute of Child Health and Human Development (NICHD) Early Child Care Research Network. (2002b). The relation of global first-grade classroom environment to structural classroom features and teacher and student behaviors. *Elementary School Journal, 102*, 367–387.

National Institute of Child Health and Human Development (NICHD) Early Child Care Research Network. (2003). Social functioning in first grade: Prediction from home, child care and concurrent school experience. *Child Development, 74*, 1639–1662.

National Institute of Child Health and Human Development (NICHD) Early Child Care Research Network, & Duncan, G. J. (2003). Modeling the impacts of child care quality on children's preschool cognitive development. *Child Development, 74*, 1454–1475.

Peisner-Feinberg, E. S., Burchinal, M. R., Clifford, R. M., Culkin, M. L., Howes, C., & Kagan, S. L., et al. (2001). The relation of preschool child-care quality to children's cognitive and social developmental trajectories through second grade. *Child Development, 72*, 1534–1553.

Pianta, R. C. (1999). *Enhancing relationships between children and teachers*. Washington, DC: American Psychological Association.

Pianta, R. C. (2003, February). *Teacher–child interactions: The implications of observational research for re-designing professional development*. Presentation to the Science and Ecology of Early Development (SEED), National Institute of Child Health and Human Development, Washington, DC.

Pianta, R. C. (2005). Standardized observation and professional development: A focus on individualized implementation and practices. In M. Zaslow & I. Martinez-Beck (Eds.), *Critical issues in early childhood professional development* (pp. 231–254). Baltimore: Brookes.

Pianta, R. C. (2011, April). *Coaching and coursework impacts on preschool teachers' interactions with children*. Presentation to the Society for Research in Child Development Annual Meeting, Montreal, Quebec, Canada.

Pianta, R. C., Barnett, W. S., Burchinal, M., & Thornburg, K. R. (2009). The effects of preschool education: What we know, how public policy is or is not aligned with the evidence base, and what we need to know. *Psychological Science in the Public Interest, 10*, 49–88.

Pianta, R. C., & Hamre, B. K. (2009). Conceptualization, measurement, and improvement of classroom processes: Standardized observation can leverage capacity. *Educational Researcher, 38*, 109–119.

Pianta, R. C., Hamre, B., & Stuhlman, M. (2003). Relationships between teachers and children. In W. Reynolds & G. Miller (Eds.), *Comprehensive handbook of psychology: Vol. 7. Educational psychology* (pp. 199–234). Hoboken, NJ: Wiley.

Pianta, R. C., LaParo, K., & Hamre, B. K. (2008). *Classroom Assessment Scoring System (CLASS)*. Baltimore: Brookes.

Pianta, R. C., Mashburn, A., Downer, J., Hamre, B., & Justice, L. (2008). Effects of web-mediated professional development resources on teacher–child interactions in pre-kindergarten classrooms. *Early Childhood Research Quarterly, 23*, 431–451.

Rogoff, B. (1990). *Apprenticeship in thinking: Cognitive development in social context*. New York: Oxford University Press.

Vandell, D., Belsky, J., Burchinal, M., Steinberg, L., Vandergrift, N., & the NICHD Early Child Care Research Network. (2010). Do effects of early child care extend to age 15 years?: Results from the NICHD Study of Early Child Care and Youth Development. *Child Development, 81*, 737–756.

Vygotsky, L. S. (1979). The genesis of higher mental function. In T. V. Wertsch (Ed.), *The concept of activity in Soviet psychology* (pp. 144–188). White Plains, NY: Sharpe.

PART IV

EFFECTIVE INSTRUCTION ACROSS THE CURRICULUM

CHAPTER 18

PROMOTING PHYSICAL LITERACY AND ACTIVITY IN YOUNG CHILDREN

JACQUELINE D. GOODWAY
JOHN C. OZMUN
SHANNON T. DIERINGER
JIHYUN LEE

Lack of activity destroys the good condition of every human being, while movement and methodical physical exercise save it and preserve it.

—PLATO

Jennifer has been in the "early childhood business" for over 20 years. She started working at a local day care as a senior in high school. She continued in that role while completing her degree in early childhood education. Upon graduation she opened her own day care center. During those two decades she also raised three children of her own, now all active adults. She and her husband, while not competitive athletes, certainly enjoyed watching their children grow up playing a variety of sports. By the time their children reached high school she was well aware that their physical fitness and successful sports participation did not just happen by chance. As their children grew up Jennifer and her husband provided them with multiple opportunities for active, unstructured play combined with structured skills instruction through a variety of youth sports programming. They also spent hours helping their children practice skills such as throwing, catching, and kicking. As Jennifer reflected on the many children for whom she cared, she recognized that other children were not as lucky as her own. They possessed few of the skills necessary for sports participation and had parents who were mostly inactive. As a result, Jennifer always made sure the children in her day care received daily structured and unstructured physical activity experiences that promoted motor skills development and an enjoyment of moving. She hoped these experiences would serve as the foundation for each of them to lead active lifestyles across their lifespans.

WHAT RESEARCH SAYS
ABOUT DEVELOPING THE PHYSICALLY LITERATE CHILD

A common focus of early childhood is the development of school readiness skills such as numeracy and literacy. However, as philosopher Jean-Jacques Rousseau said, one of the most important tasks of childhood is to skip, play, and run around all day long. It is a common misconception that children "just naturally" acquire fundamental motor skills (FMS) as a normal function of play and getting older. However, if we look at our preschool and elementary playgrounds and gymnasiums, it is clear that many young children are neither the physically active nor the competent and confident movers we would like them to be. Thus, the development of a child's movement skills must be taught and reinforced with as much care and attention as one would take in teaching the child to read, write, and do arithmetic. In recognition of the fundamental nature of nurturing a child's knowledge of and engagement in physical activity, the term *physical literacy* was coined recently to give appropriate attention to the need for children to be physically active.

The term *physical literacy* has been recently defined as the "motivation, confidence, physical competence, knowledge, and understanding to maintain physical activity throughout the lifecourse" (Whitehead, 2010, p. 5). Developing movement competence during the early years is paramount. Insufficient opportunities to develop their physical literacy can lead to devastating life consequences for children (Whitehead, 2010). As a result, all children should be provided with the necessary support and resources they need to develop physical literacy, FMS competence, and be physically active. Two important, but often discrete, bodies of research are pertinent to this chapter. The first deals with the development of FMS competence in young children and motor skills interventions to promote such FMS competence; the second focuses on what we currently know about the physical activity levels of preschoolers. It is impossible within this chapter to review all there is to know about these topics, but we identify key points, consider the practical implications of this research, and point the reader toward valuable resources for working with young children.

The Importance of FMS

One of the most critical skills sets children need to begin to acquire in early childhood is competence in FMS (Gallahue, Ozmun, & Goodway, 2012). FMS are the building blocks to future physical activities and sports. They are the movement equivalent of the ABCs in literacy. FMS comprise two groups of skills: (1) locomotor skills, such as running, jumping, and skipping; and (2) manipulation skills (also called object control skills), such as throwing, catching, and striking (Gallahue et al., 2012). Prominent models of motor development suggest that FMS are the foundation (Gallahue et al., 2012; Seefeldt, 1982) or basecamp (Clark & Metcalfe, 2002) of the mountain of motor development. Seefeldt (1982) hypothesized that a child who cannot run, throw, and catch with basic competence will be unlikely to break through the "FMS proficiency barrier" and engage successfully in sports and physical activities in which these skills are needed. A more recent model connects low motor competence in the early years to lower physical activity levels, and poor self-perceptions of motor competence (Stodden & Goodway, 2007; Stodden et al., 2008). The interaction of these factors strengthens over time and ultimately channels children into a "negative spiral of disengagement" from physical activity, placing them at higher risk of obesity. It is clear that developing basic FMS competence during early childhood is paramount. But how do these skills emerge? And what can we do as teachers to promote motor skills competence?

Sequential Development of FMS

As we look out at the playground and watch young children play it may seem that children run, throw, and jump in the same manner. But closer observation of their skills reveals that even children of the same age look very different in the way they perform motor skills (Gallahue et al., 2012). Whereas a younger child might show a stationary "chop throw," a girl might step and throw with the same hand and foot, and a boy might throw forcefully with wind-up of the arm and arm–leg opposition. We know from the motor development literature that children do not just naturally perform FMS with proficiency; they typically progress through a common sequence of movements that start with inefficient and unstable patterns of performance (Gallahue et al., 2012). With sufficient practice and feedback children develop more proficient patterns of performance and greater abilities to apply these skills to sports and games consistently (Gallahue et al., 2012; Stodden & Goodway, 2007). Research in motor development has identified developmental sequences for 10 FMS (Seefeldt, 1982) with anywhere between three and five stages of development per skill. Tables 18.1 and 18.2 describe these developmental sequences (for a more detailed description, see Gallahue et al., 2012). It is valuable for the early childhood educator to know that these developmental sequences as stages of development can inform teachers about developmentally appropriate physical activities for a given child. These stages can also serve as an assessment of a child's emerging FMS competence.

   Both girls and boys pass through the same sequence of motor skills development. However, gender differences can be found in FMS performance starting as young as the preschool years (Seefeldt & Haubenstricker, 1982; Thomas & French, 1985). Both boys and girls have similarities in locomotor skills such as running and jumping; however, boys typically outperform girls in manipulation skills (Goodway, Robinson, & Crowe, 2010; Seefeldt & Haubenstricker, 1982). It is not clear from the developmental literature why this might be, but some scholars have pointed to biological factors such as strength or sociocultural factors (e.g., unequal opportunities to be active, modeling, and feedback; Thomas & French, 1985).

Developmental Delays in FMS

Establishing habits that foster the development of proficient levels of FMS and healthy levels of physical fitness are critical events that take place during the early childhood years. However, there are disparities in the opportunity to do this. A growing body of research shows that young children who come from disadvantaged environments show significant developmental delays in their FMS, including locomotor (10th–17th percentile) and manipulation (16th percentile) skills (Goodway & Branta, 2003; Goodway, Crowe, & Ward, 2003; Goodway et al., 2010; Hamilton, Goodway, & Haubenstricker, 1999; Robinson & Goodway, 2009). This has been found to be true for African American and Hispanic children across geographic regions, and urban and rural environments (Goodway & Branta, 2003; Goodway et al., 2003, 2010; Hamilton et al., 1999; Robinson & Goodway, 2009). In a recent, large-scale study of the FMS of 275 children from Head Start, 85–92% of all children tested were developmentally delayed (Goodway et

TABLE 18.1. Summary of Locomotor Developmental Sequences

Fundamental motor skill	Stage 1	Stage 2	Stage 3	Stage 4
	Initial stage	Emerging stages		Proficient stage
Run	*Run—arms above head* Arms are high at head height. Flat-footed contact. Short, wide stride. Feet shoulder width apart.	*Run—arms midtrunk* Arms at midtrunk level. Vertical component of run still great. Legs near full extension.	*Heel–toe run—arms extended* Arms below waist. Arm–leg opposition with elbows nearly extended. Heel–toe contact.	*Run—pumping arms* Heel–toe contact (sometimes toe–heel when sprinting). Arm–leg opposition. Heel recovery close to buttocks. Elbow bent at 90 degrees.
Hop (1 foot to 1 foot)	*Hop—free foot in front* Non-support (free) foot in front of base leg with thigh parallel to floor. Body upright and hands at shoulder height.	*Hop—free foot by support leg* Non-support knee flexed with knee in front and foot beside support leg. Slight body lean forward. Both arms move together.	*Hop—free foot behind support leg* Nonsupport thigh alongside base support leg with free foot behind support leg, knee flexed. Body leans forward. Arms swing forward together.	*Hop—free leg pumps* Nonsupport leg is bent and knee pumps forward and back in a pendular action. Forward body lean. Arm opposition with swing leg.
Long jump (2 feet to 2 feet)	*Short jump—braking arms* Arms act as "brakes" moving forward then toward trunk on jump. Large vertical component. Legs not extended.	*Short jump—winging arms* Arms act as "wings" to side of body. Vertical component still great. Legs near full extension.	*Longer jump—arms swing to head* Arms move forward/elbows in front of trunk at take-off. Hands swing to head height. Take-off angle still above 45 degrees. Legs often fully extended.	*Long jump—full body extension* Complete arm and leg extension at take-off. Take-off near 45 degree angle. Thighs parallel to surface when feet contact for landing.
	Initial stage	Emerging stage	Proficient stage	
Gallop (step–together–step–together)	*Choppy run–gallop* Resembles rhythmically uneven run. Back leg crosses in front of lead leg during airborne phase and remains in front at touch down.	*Gallop—stiff back leg* Slow–moderate tempo, choppy rhythm. Black leg is stiff. Hips often turned sideways. Vertical component exaggerated.	*Gallop—smooth rhythmical* Smooth, rhythmical pattern with moderate tempo. Feet remain close to ground. Hips facing forward.	
Skip (step–hop–step–hop)	*Broken skip* Broken skip pattern or irregular rhythm. Slow, deliberate movement. Ineffective arm action.	*Skip—high arms and legs* Rhythmical skip pattern. Arms swing high and provide body lift. Excessive vertical component.	*Rhythmical skip* Arm action reduced/hands below shoulders. Easy, rhythmical movement. Support foot near surface on hop.	

Note. Based on Gallahue, Ozmun, and Goodway (2012).

TABLE 18.2. Summary of Manipulative Developmental Sequences

Fundamental motor skill	Stage 1	Stage 2	Stage 3	Stage 4	Stage 5
	Initial stage		Emerging stages		Proficient stage
Throw	*Front—chop throw* Feet stationary. Front facing. Arm "chop throws" from ear. No spinal rotation.	*Sideways—sling shot* Body turned sideways. Horizontal wind. "Sling shot throw" with block rotation of trunk. Arm swings across body.	*Step same arm–leg* High wind-up of arm. Ipsilateral (same arm–leg) step. Little spinal rotation. Follow-through across body.	*Step opposite arm–leg* High wind-up of arm. Contralateral (opposite arm–leg) step. Little spinal rotation. Follow-through across body.	*Arm wind-up* Arm swings downward and back. Contralateral step. Segmented body rotation. Arm–leg follow-through.
Two-handed catch	*Delayed reaction* Delayed arm action to ball. Arms straight in front until ball contact, then scooping action to chest. Feet stationary. Head often turns to side.	*Hugging* Arms encircle ball as it approaches. Ball is "hugged" to chest. Feet are stationary or may take one step.	*Scooping* Arms out and scoop ball to chest. Arms "scoop" under ball to trap it to chest. Single step may be used to step into the ball flight.	*Hand catch* Initial contact with ball is with hands only. Hand catch only if tossed to trunk. Feet stationary or limited to one step. Would not catch a ball tossed to side of body.	*Move to ball* Tracks flight of ball and moves body under ball flight. Catch with hands only. Fine adjustment of fingers to ball position as ball is caught.
	Initial stage		Emerging stages		Proficient stage
Kick	*Stationary—push* Stationary position. Little/no leg wind-up. Foot "pushes" ball. Often step backward after kick or poor balance.	*Stationary—leg swing* Stationary position. Free leg winds up behind base leg. Opposition of arms and legs.	*Moving approach* Moving approach to ball (1 step or several steps). Foot travels in a low arc. Arm/leg opposition. Steps past/beside ball on follow-through.	*Leap–kick–bop* Rapid approach to ball. Leaps before kick. Backward trunk lean during wind-up. Kicks hard. Hops after kick.	
Punt (drop ball and kick it)	*Stationary–yoke and push* Stationary position. No leg wind-up. Ball toss erratic "yoking." Push ball and often step back.	*Stationary leg swing* Stationary position. Free leg wind-up to rear. Yoking toss. Forceful kick attempt.	*Moving approach* Moving approach to ball. Some arm/leg yoking. Ball is tossed or dropped. Often steps beyond ball after kick.	*Leap–punt–bop* Rapid approach to the ball. Controlled drop of ball. Leap before ball contact. Kicks hard. Hop after ball contact.	
Strike (bat a ball)	*Chop strike* Feet stationary–front facing. Hand position on bat variable. "Chopping" downward strike pattern.	*Horizontal push* Sideways, feet stationary or small step. Horizontal push/ swing of bat. Trunk rotates as a block.	*Ipsilateral step and strike* Sideways orientation at start. Ipsilateral (same arm–foot) step. Diagonal downward swing of bat.	*Contralateral step and strike* Sideways orientation at start. Contralateral (opposite arm–leg) step. Segmented body rotation. Wrist rollover on follow-through.	

Note. Based on Gallahue, Ozmun, and Goodway (2012).

297

al., 2010). Like the findings cited earlier, locomotor skills of the girls and boys were the same (delayed), but the girls had significantly worse manipulation skills than boys. This is of particular concern considering that boys' skills were delayed, but girls' skills were even more delayed (Goodway et al., 2010). It is no wonder that, by adolescence, girls from these populations have some of the lowest physical activity rates of all children and youth (U.S. Department of Health and Human Services [USDHH], 1996, 2004). It is clear from the research evidence that a sizable number of disadvantaged preschool children are delayed in their FMS and require motor skills intervention to remediate the developmental delays reported.

Effects of Motor Skills Instruction

A growing number of scholars has begun to examine the influence of motor skill intervention on the FMS of disadvantaged preschool children. These studies showed that when motorically delayed preschool children received well-designed structured motor skills instruction, significant improvements in their FMS remediated developmental delays (Connor-Kuntz & Dummer, 1996; Goodway & Branta, 2003; Goodway et al., 2003; Hamilton et al., 1999; Martin, Rudisill, & Hastie, 2009; Robinson & Goodway, 2009). The time frame of these programs has typically been somewhere between 8 and 12 weeks (16–24 lessons), with 30–45 minutes per session. The majority of these programs has focused on manipulation skills, although some have also included locomotor skills. A variety of instructional approaches has been utilized to deliver the motor skills interventions, including (1) direct instruction (Connor-Kuntz & Dummer, 1996; Goodway & Branta, 2003; Goodway et al., 2003); (2) mastery motivational climate (Martin et al., 2009; Robinson & Goodway, 2009; Valentini & Rudisill, 2004; and (3) parents as teachers (Hamilton et al., 1999).

Direct instruction involves a teacher-led approach in which the teacher instructs each element of the lesson, clearly describes and demonstrates the task to be performed, and the children respond accordingly (Graham, Holt-Hale, & Parker, 2010). Mastery motivational climate (MMC) involves a more student-centered approach in which the teacher plans the lesson elements, but the children have high autonomy to complete tasks and activities based on their preferences (Robinson & Goodway, 2009; Valentini & Rudisill, 2004). MMC lessons are planned around manipulating within the lesson six "TARGET" structures; the acronym TARGET stands for Task, Authority, Reward, Grouping, Evaluation, Time (see Valentini, Rudisill & Goodway, 1999, for a detailed explanation). The rationale behind the MMC approach is that the instructional climate promotes students' motivation to engage in tasks and regulate their own pace of learning. The parents as teachers approach trains parents to instruct their children on FMS, while a lead teacher develops the lesson plans and acts as facilitator during lesson implementation (Hamilton et al., 1999).

All the motor skills intervention approaches previously identified have significantly impacted the FMS competence of disadvantaged preschoolers. In all of these interventions, high-quality instruction is provided, along with maximum opportunities to respond. Sufficient equipment is available and tasks are individualized to the child's own developmental needs. In many cases, the developmental changes were substantial, improving from the 10th–15th to the 60th–80th percentile (Goodway & Branta, 2003; Goodway et al., 2003, 2010; Hamilton et al., 1999; Robinson & Goodway, 2009).

Some general conclusions may be drawn from the studies identified earlier: (1) The children in the control groups who received typical preschool curricula in which physical activity opportunities were often nonfacilitated and play-based showed no improvements in FMS development; (2) disadvantaged preschool children were delayed in their motor skills and in need of intervention; and (3) children provided with structured, developmentally appropriate motor instruction made significant and often large gains in their FMS remediating their prior delays. In other words, current educational practices in relation to the development of FMS in schools and classroom are not meeting the needs of these children. This is a major long-term concern. If the status quo continues in schools and classrooms, children will not have the requisite skills to be physically active as adolescents and adults, and this is the very demographic (poor, African American, and Hispanic) that demonstrates the lowest levels of physical activity and the highest levels of obesity as adolescents and adults (USDHHS, 1996, 2004).

Physical Activity and Young Children

Growing scholarly attention has focused on the physical activity (PA) levels of young children. Much of this work has emanated from a worldwide epidemic of childhood obesity. Even among preschoolers, obesity rates have doubled over the past few decades, to the point that more than 10% of children ages 2–5 years are considered obese (Ogden & Carroll, 2010). Disparities exist, and obesity is disproportionately higher among our low-income preschool children. According to the Pediatric Nutrition Surveillance System (PedNSS; 2009), nearly one-third of 3.7 million low-income children (ages 2–4 years) surveyed were obese or overweight (Centers for Disease Control and Prevention [CDC], 2011). Childhood obesity increases the risk for additional health problems such as diabetes and hypertension, serving as a catalyst for social and behavioral issues that can be detrimental during the important early developmental years (Ward, 2010). As a result, many groups, including the American Academy of Pediatrics, CDC, and the National Association of Sport and Physical Education, highlight the importance of systematic strategies to increase PA during the early years as a means to reduce childhood obesity.

Most early childhood educators recognize the value of PA and attempt to promote PA and a healthy lifestyle in the children for whom they provide care. Despite these efforts, a growing body of research shows that young children spend much of their day (often as much as 80%) in sedentary behaviors and very little (as little as 3%) of the day in health-enhancing, moderate to vigorous physical activity (MVPA; Pate, McIver, Dowda, Brown, & Addy, 2008; Reilly, 2010). Overall, boys tend to have higher PA levels than girls (Finn, Johannsen, & Specker, 2002; Pate et al., 2008). As children get older, their MVPA declines (Jackson et al., 2003). It makes sense that children who have more media/screen time (e.g., TV, video games) also have less MVPA (Durant, Thompson, Johnson, & Baranowski, 1996; Pate et al., 2008). It also an established fact that PA levels of young children are influenced by the policies of the child care center where they spend most of their time (Dowda, Pate, Trost, Almeida, & Sirard, 2004; Kaphingst & Story, 2009). These sedentary patterns are compounded by the poor dietary habits found in low-income families and the lack of access to healthy foods in disadvantaged neighborhoods (Ogden & Carroll, 2010).

Child care centers and preschools are increasingly identified as "untapped resources" to promote PA (CDC, 2011; Kaphingst & Story, 2009). Many of these centers tend to have less structure and intentionality when planning PA. Active free play is generally planned for an outdoor playground or indoor gym/multipurpose space, but educational objectives such as the enhancement of FMS and physical fitness are rarely considered. Certainly early childhood educators face numerous obstacles when they consider promoting PA and motor competence in the development of their curricula. An analysis of multiple child care centers revealed that factors such as concerns about injury and safety, financial limitations, lack of staff training, and parental pressure to prioritize academic classroom learning over PA were pertinent issues when determining the amount and quality of physical literacy objectives (Copeland, Sherman, Kendeigh, Kalkwarf, & Saelens, 2012; Trost, Ward, & Senso, 2010). The American Academy of Pediatrics (2003) and the CDC (2011) have encouraged child care centers to promote, prioritize, and protect regular PA in young children. Ward, Vaughn, McWilliams, and Hales (2010) point out that consistent, structured PA programs can enhance the intensity and amount of PA that young children experience and result in children's improved motor skills. It has also been demonstrated that young children with more proficient in their locomotor skills tend to be involved in PA more frequently, adding further support for needed structured PA opportunities in early childhood settings (Robinson, Wadsworth, & Peoples, 2012). Overall, the PA levels of preschool children are low, and more evidence-based programs are needed to promote PA and motor competence within preschool settings.

RESEARCH INTO PRACTICE

Having summarized some of the major findings from the PA and FMS research on young children, we now turn our attention to the implications of this work for early childhood educators and those working with young children. The *Active Start* document developed by the National Association of Sport and Physical Education (NASPE; 2009), a highly valuable and practical resource for early childhood educators, provides national PA guidelines for children ages birth to 5 years.

National PA *Active Start* Guidelines and Promoting PA in Young Children

The national PA *Active Start* guidelines for children ages 0–5 years recommend that "All children birth to age 5 should engage in daily physical activity that promotes movement skillfulness and foundations of health-related fitness" (NASPE, 2009, p. iv). The guidelines are split into three age groups: infants (birth to onset of walking), toddlers (1–3 years), and preschoolers (3–5 years). For each age group there are five guidelines tied to promoting structured and unstructured PA, motor skills development, safe movement environments, and caregiver knowledge and engagement (see Figure 18.1). The *Active Start* PA guidelines and document are available from NASPE (2009).

Overall the *Active Start* document provides specific developmentally appropriate PA guidelines using the FITT approach:

- *Frequency*—how often the children should engage in PA
- *Intensity*—how hard or strenuous this activity should be for the child
- *Time*—the duration of the PA bout
- *Type*—the nature of the physical activities to be performed

For example under *frequency*, preschoolers should engage in one or more bouts of *structured* PA per day totaling at least 60 minutes. Examples of the types of structured PA include setting up a fundamental motor skills obstacle course; providing a range of developmentally challenging movement tasks in movement stations, where the child self-selects the difficulty of the task and the type of equipment, with caregivers acting as facilitators;

Guideline	Infant Guidelines
1	Infants should interact with caregivers in daily physical activities that are dedicated to exploring movement and the environment.
2	Caregivers should place infants in settings that encourage and stimulate movement experiences, and active play for short periods several times a day.
3	Infants' physical activity should promote skill development in movement.
4	Infants should be placed in an environment that meets or exceeds recommended safety standards for performing large-muscle activities.
5	Those in charge of infants' well-being are responsible for understanding the importance of physical activity and should promote movement skills by providing opportunities for structured and unstructured physical activity.
Guideline	**Toddler Guidelines**
1	Toddlers should engage in a total of at least 30 minutes of structured physical activity each day.
2	Toddlers should engage in at least 60 minutes—and up to several hours—per day of unstructured physical activity and should not be sedentary for more than 60 minutes at a time, except when sleeping.
3	Toddlers should be given ample opportunities to develop movement skills that will serve as the building blocks for future motor skillfulness and physical activity.
4	Toddlers should have access to indoor and outdoor areas that meet or exceed recommended safety standards for performing large-muscle activities.
5	Those in charge of toddlers' well-being are responsible for understanding the importance of physical activity, and promoting movement skills by providing opportunities for structured and unstructured physical activity, and movement experiences.
Guideline	**Preschooler Guidelines**
1	Preschoolers should accumulate at least 60 minutes of structured physical activity each day.
2	Preschoolers should engage in at least 60 minutes—and up to several hours—of unstructured physical activity each day, and should not be sedentary for more than 60 minutes at a time, except when sleeping.
3	Preschoolers should be encouraged to develop competence in fundamental motor skills that will serve as the building blocks for future motor skillfulness and physical activity.
4	Preschoolers should have access to indoor and outdoor areas that meet or exceed recommended safety standards for performing large-muscle activities.
5	Caregivers and parents in charge of preschoolers' health and well-being are responsible for understanding the importance of physical activity and for promoting movement skills by providing opportunities for structured and unstructured physical activity.

FIGURE 18.1. National *Active Start* PA guidelines for children from birth to 5 years. Reprinted from *Active Start: A Statement of Physical Activity Guidelines for Children from Birth to Age 5*, with permission from the National Association of Sport and Physical Education (NASPE), 1900 Association Drive, Reston, VA 20191, *www.NASPEinfo.org.*

or engaging in developmentally appropriate fitness activities, such as stretching and moving like different animals, to promote muscular strength and intermittent cardiovascular activities. Preschoolers should also have multiple opportunities each day to engage in *unstructured* PA. Examples of the types of unstructured PA include developing a motor skills center in the classroom and allowing children to move through this center when they choose; running to chase bubbles, rings, balls, hoops and other moving objects; playing on and around playground structures outside; or digging and building in a sandbox.

In terms of the *intensity* of movement sessions, caregivers should try to promote multiple bouts of MVPA, which is the type of activity most associated with positive health benefits. This intensity of activity causes children to breathe harder and increases their heart rate. Most young children can only maintain MVPA for 6–10 minutes each bout. At the end of bouts of MVPA caregivers can teach children typical bodily responses to exercise. For example, tell the children to put one hand on their heart and feel their heart beating, while holding the other hand up and opening and closing it to the beat of their heart. Teaching children that the heart is a muscle that needs to be exercised just like any other muscle in their body is an important concept. During unstructured PA, caregivers should encourage MVPA but ultimately allow children to be in charge of their own intensity of activity. We know from research that multiple shorter bouts of MVPA across the day in terms of *time* still promote positive health outcomes. Thus, caregivers can build bouts of structured PA into preschoolers' day, accumulating a total of at least 60 minutes daily. We have found that preschoolers are capable of engaging in 30–45 minutes of structured, developmentally appropriate motor activity at one time. Caregivers are also encouraged to provide multiple opportunities for inside and outside unstructured PA across the day, for a minimum of 60 minutes and up to several hours across the day.

Promoting FMS in Young Children

Like any academic skill, if motor skills are to be improved the following must occur: (1) thoughtful lesson planning of motor skills development and PA; (2) selection of a variety of high-quality tasks aligned with the developmental level of the children; (3) many individualized opportunities to practice a wide range of skills, with maximum opportunities to respond; (4) teacher instruction/facilitation and demonstration of skills; (5) individual feedback on performance; and (6) reward structures and/or other motivational techniques (NASPE, 2009). In terms of motivation, it is also helpful when children are allowed to make choices within the instructional environment, self-monitor, and engage in self-assessment.

Like all good teaching, the development of quality motor skills lessons starts with observation and evaluation of the current developmental level of the child. The FMS stages in Tables 18.1 and 18.2 are a valuable resource for lesson planning. High-quality lessons are developed as a result of collecting and analyzing student assessment data. Useful and psychometrically sound assessments to inform instructional planning include the Test of Gross Motor Development–2 (Ulrich, 2000) and the Peabody Developmental Scale (Folio & Fewell, 2000). From the results of assessment, teachers next identify the desired task or skill for the child to perform. For example, a child who is a Stage 2 catcher (hugger) would want to work toward hand catching (Stage 4), or a child who is hand catching would want to work toward moving his or her body to a ball tossed to the side (Stage 5). Next teachers should look closely at three areas (child, environment, task) that "constrain" or influence the child's emerging motor performance (Newell, 1986). In the

TABLE 18.3. Sample Child, Environmental, and Task Factors Influencing Catching

Child factors	Environmental factors	Task factors
• Poor ability to track ball in air • Poor fine motor control of hands • Cannot cross the midline with arms • Inability to control objects away from midline of the body	• Increase size of ball • Use large, soft (foam), brightly colored ball • Toss slowly from a close distance • Toss to child's midline (chest) • Cue the child "arms ready, reach, and pull" (ball to chest)	• Two-handed catching from a close distance—focus on hand contact. • As child improves, toss from further away; decrease the size of the ball; increase the speed of the ball; toss high, low or side to side.

example in Table 18.3 using catching, teachers should consider specific child factors such as tracking, environmental factors such as the size of the ball, and task factors such as the nature of the task. In this example the child lacks the ability to track the ball, manipulate objects finely, and catch outside the parameters of the body. In order to compensate for these factors, teachers can manipulate environmental and task factors to promote success by slowly tossing a soft, large ball from a close distance to the child, cueing the child to hand catch. As teachers observe the child's catching skills across time, they can continually manipulate both environmental and task factors to enhance the child's motor skills and provide developmentally appropriate, individualized, motor skills instruction.

Lessons Learned from SKIP

Over the past two decades, SKIP (Successful Kinesthetic Instruction for Preschoolers), a motor skills and PA program designed for disadvantaged African American and Hispanic preschoolers by Goodway and her colleagues (2006), has been implemented across the Midwest, the South, and southwestern regions of the United States in preschool and Head Start programs (see Figure 18.2).

For example, a SKIP lesson might be 30–45 minutes in length and look like this: (1) All children perform a 10-minute warm-up to music or a simple game to promote MVPA, instant activity, and increase heart rate; (2) children are divided into three groups and assigned to one of three skills stations (e.g., kick, catch, throw); (3) tasks at all stations are explained and demonstrated by the teacher; (4) after children go to the first station and

---

- Promote FMS competence.
- Improve children's perceptions of their motor competence.
- Engage in moderate to vigorous physical activity (MVPA).
- Teach the children the link between MVPA and a healthy lifestyle.
- Develop an understanding of bodily and movement principles.
- Learn to move in different environments, with different equipment and individuals.
- Develop an intrinsic desire to move, willingness to try and persist at new movement task, and an enjoyment of PA.

FIGURE 18.2. Goals of the SKIP program.

engage in 10 minutes of skills activity/development, the teacher provides feedback and refining tasks to meet children's needs; (5) children complete three 10-minute rotations, going to each station; and (6) at the end of the lesson, the teacher gathers the children for developmentally appropriate stretching, debriefing, and final feedback.

The initial development of this program utilized direct, teacher-centered instructional pedagogies. Core elements of the SKIP program include the following:

- Initial evaluation of the developmental motor status of children
- Developmental task analysis of each of the FMS (typically, catch, throw, kick, strike, bounce, roll, punt, run, gallop, skip, jump, hop, slide, leap) ranging from easy to more complex tasks in line with initial and ongoing motor assessments
- Inclusion of age-appropriate fitness elements, such as strength, flexibility and cardiovascular endurance, and movement elements, such as balance and weight transfer
- Innovative task design using manipulation of Newell's constraints perspective (child, environmental, task factors) to develop motivating tasks
- Individualized and inclusive instruction (tasks vary for each child)
- A focus on critical elements and cue words—children remember the words and coach themselves and each other
- Repetitive cycle of skills and tasks with opportunities to increase and decrease task complexity to meet learner needs
- Children as self- and peer coaches
- Child self-reflection and evaluation
- Use of "Motor Passports" by the children to track their own motor skills and physical literacy journey

As indicated earlier, use of the SKIP intervention has resulted in significant improvements in young children's FMS and perceived motor competence. More recently the SKIP program has embraced more student-centered pedagogies. The core elements of SKIP have been maintained, but the following more indirect child-centered instructional pedagogies have been utilized: Children participate in instructional decision making, choice of grouping, and an opportunity to self-govern, children have flexibility in the schedule or time at each task station—they can move where they want when they want; children have an option to establish or modify rules and choose from tasks with many difficulty levels built into them; children operate under their own direction, facilitated by the teacher and constrained by good instructional tasks; teachers place a greater emphasis on the process of learning; they teach children that their best effort and task persistence lead to a positive outcome and success; and children are the primary navigators of their own learning environment. Recent work comparing teacher-centered and child-centered versions of SKIP found that both versions brought about significant FMS motor outcomes (Robinson & Goodway, 2009). However, the child-centered version resulted in higher perceptions of motor competence than teacher-centered SKIP, suggesting that the child-centered SKIP program may in the long term be better for promoting a more intrinsic mastery orientation in young children (Robinson & Goodway, 2009).

SKIP continues to evolve specifically, in line with perspectives on physical literacy, and the role of parents and families in promoting motor competence. We have placed a greater emphasis on asking what children "feel in their inner selves" to get them to pay attention to kinesthetic and proprioceptive feedback from their bodies (we call these "muscle munchkins"). We ask children what happened after a movement, not to tell them what they did wrong but to examine the ways children relate to their bodies, and how motor intervention changes their perceptions of movement competence. We also see great potential in young children as agents of change or "boundary crossers" in their home and families. We are trying different approaches for promoting "movement homework" and parent–child activities within the home. Overall, we share the children's excitement and energy in the movement environment and hope to continue to support these young children in an active start to their lives.

REFLECTIONS AND NEW DIRECTIONS

There are many challenges ahead in promoting the physical literacy of young children and developing competent and confident movers across the lifespan. We still need to promote evidence-based motor skills development programs for young children. Child care centers (including in-home child care) and preschool programs seem to be the natural place for this to occur because so many of our nation's children spend their days in these programs. Significant policy issues need attention. The psychomotor domain is a significant part of children's development in the early years, yet many states do not require any coursework in motor development or physical education in order for early childhood teachers to become licensed. It is no wonder that early childhood educators identify knowledge and training as significant barriers to promoting PA (Kaphingst & Story, 2009). Clearly, few children across the country are meeting NASPE's *Active Start* guidelines, and attending to some of these policy issues may help in promoting more PA. From a research standpoint, there are still issues around accurately measuring a young child's PA because play includes activities, such as sliding and climbing, that cannot be accurately measured on accelerometers, one of the main ways we measure PA in young children (Jackson et al., 2003). We need to consider ways we can promote PA and motor competence outside of the child care facility and in children's homes—looking to ways we can educate and assist parents in promoting an active home environment. Ultimately we need to examine whether promoting motor competence and PA in the early years will help children to lead more active and healthy lifestyles over the long term. Although we believe this is the correct course, little research supports these claims.

We also need to develop and highlight model programs for PA and motor competence and share success stories within the early childhood community. SKIP is just one of many evidence-based movement programs, and various, useful resources to assist early childhood educators in providing developmentally appropriate PA instruction. For example, we recommend the following organizations:

- NASPE (*www.aahperd.org/naspe*)
- Physical education website—PE Central (*www.pecentral.org*)
- Head Start Body Start (*www.aahperd.org/headstartbodystart*)
- CDC (*www.cdc.gov*)

In conclusion, all children have the right to become physically literate, competent, confident, and motivated movers who engage in active lifestyles across the lifespan. We encourage all educators, child care providers, and parents to take on the many challenges that hinder physical activity and promote an active start for young children.

- Watch a child perform a FMS, such as catching, and identify the stage of the skill using the tables in this chapter.

- Observe all of the children in your class as they run across the playground, and identify the range of motor development using the developmental stages.

- Play an active game and ask the children to put their hand on their hearts and make a fist with the other hand every time their hearts beat. Talk about heart health and the importance of physical activity.

- Go to the Head Start Body Start website, download a lesson plan, and teach it to your class.

- Develop a physical activity homework assignment for the parents of children in your class, and ask them to do something active with their children.

REFERENCES

American Academy of Pediatrics. (2003). Prevention of pediatric overweight and obesity. *Pediatrics, 112*, 424–430.

Centers for Disease Control and Prevention (CDC). (2011). Obesity among low-income preschool children. Retrieved March 5, 2012, from *www.cdc.gov/obesity/downloads/pednssfactsheet.pdf*.

Clark, J. E., & Metcalfe, J. S. (2002). The mountain of motor development: A metaphor. In J. E. Clark & J. H. Humphrey (Eds.), *Motor development: Research and review* (Vol. 2, pp. 163–187). Reston, VA: NASPE Publications.

Conner-Kuntz, F., & Dummer, G. (1996). Teaching across the curriculum: Language-enriched physical education for preschool children. *Adapted Physical Activity Quarterly, 13*, 302–315.

Copeland, K. A., Sherman, S. N., Kendeigh, C. A., Kalkwarf, H. J., & Saelens, B. E. (2012). Societal values and policies may curtail preschool children's physical activity in child care centers. *Pediatrics, 129*, 265–274.

Dowda, M., Pate, R. R., Trost, S. G., Almeida, M. J., & Sirard, J. R. (2004). Influences of preschool policies and practices on children's physical activity. *Journal of Community Health, 29*(3), 183–196.

Durant, R. H., Thompson, W. O., Johnson, M., & Baranowski, T. (1996). The relationship among television watching, physical activity and body composition of 5 or 6 year old children. *Pediatric Exercise Science, 8*, 15–26.

Finn, K., Johannsen, N., & Specker, B. (2002). Factors associated with physical activity in preschool children. *Pediatrics, 140*, 81–85.

Folio, M. R., & Fewell, R. R. (2000). *Peabody Developmental Motor Scales: Examiners manual*, Austin, TX: Pro-Ed.

Gallahue, D. L., Ozmun, J. C., & Goodway, J. D. (2012). *Understanding motor development: Infants, children, adolescent and adults* (7th ed.). Boston: McGraw-Hill.

Goodway, J. D., & Branta, C. F. (2003). Influence of a motor skill intervention on fundamental motor skill development of disadvantaged preschool children. *Research Quarterly for Exercise and Sport, 74*, 36–47.

Goodway, J. D., Crowe, H., & Ward, P. (2003). Effects of motor skill instruction on fundamental motor skill development. *Adapted Physical Activity Quarterly, 20*, 298–314.

Goodway, J. D., & Robinson, L. E. (2006). *SKIP*ing toward an active start: Promoting physical activity in preschoolers. *Beyond the Journal: Young Children, 61*, 1–6.

Goodway, J. D., Robinson, L. E., & Crowe, H. (2010). Developmental delays in fundamental motor skill development of ethnically diverse and disadvantaged preschoolers. *Research Quarterly for Exercise and Sport, 81*, 17–25.

Graham, G., Holt-Hale, S. A., & Parker, M. (2010). *Children moving: A reflective approach to teaching physical education* (8th ed.). Mountain View, CA: Mayfield.

Hamilton, M., Goodway, J. D., & Haubenstricker, J. (1999). Parent-assisted instruction in a motor skill program for at-risk preschool children. *Adapted Physical Activity Quarterly, 16*, 415–426.

Jackson, D. M., Reilly, J. J., Kelly, L. A., Montgomery, C., Grant, S., & Paton, J. Y. (2003). Objectively measured physical activity in a representative sample of 3 to 4 year old children. *Obesity Research, 11*(3), 420–425.

Kaphingst, K. M., & Story, M. (2009). Child care as an untapped setting for obesity prevention: State child care licensing regulations related to nutrition, physical activity, and media use for preschool-aged children in the United States. *Preventing Chronic Disease: Public Health Research, Practice, and Policy, 6*(1), 1–13.

Martin, E. H., Rudisill, M. E., & Hastie, P. (2009). The effectiveness of a mastery motivational climate motor skill intervention in a naturalistic physical education setting. *Physical Education and Sport Pedagogy, 14*, 227–240.

National Association for Sport and Physical Education (NASPE). (2009). *Active Start: A statement of physical activity guidelines for children birth to five years* (2nd ed.). Oxon Hill, MD: American Alliance for Health, Physical Education, Recreation, and Dance Publications.

Newell, K. M. (1986). Constraints on the development of coordination. In M. G. Wade & H. T. Whiting (Eds.), *Motor development in children: Aspects of coordination and control* (pp. 341–360). Dordrecht, The Netherlands: Nijhoff.

Ogden, C., & Carroll, M. (2010). Prevalence of obesity among children and adolescents: United States, trends 1963–1965 through 2007–2008. *NCHS Health E-Stats.* Retrieved from *www.cdc.gov/nchs/data/hestat/obesity_child_07_08/obesity_child_07_08.htm.*

Pate, R. R., McIver, K., Dowda, M., Brown, W. H., & Addy, C. (2008). Directly observed physical activity levels in preschool children. *Journal of School Health, 78*(8), 434–444.

Reilly, J. J. (2010). Low levels of objectivity measured physical activity in preschoolers in child care. *Medicine and Science in Sports and Exercise, 42*, 502–507.

Robinson, L. E., & Goodway, J. D. (2009). Instructional climates in preschool children who are at risk: Part I. Object control skill development. *Research Quarterly for Exercise and Sport, 80*, 533–542.

Robinson, L. E., Wadsworth, D. D., & Peoples, C. M. (2012). Correlates of school-day physical activity in preschool students. *Research Quarterly for Exercise and Sport, 83*, 20–26.

Seefeldt, V., & Haubenstricker, J. (1982). Patterns, phases, or stages: An analytic model for the study of developmental movement. In J. A. S. Kelso & J. E. Clark (Eds.), *The development of movement control and co-ordination* (pp. 309–318). New York: Wiley.

Seefeldt, V. V. (1982). Concept of readiness applied to motor skill acquisition. In R. A. Magill, M. J. Ash, & F. L. Smoll (Eds.), *Children in sport* (2nd ed., pp. 31–37). Champaign, IL: Human Kinetics Publishers.

Stodden, D. F., & Goodway, J. D. (2007). The dynamic association between motor skill development and physical activity. *Journal of Physical Education, Recreation and Dance, 78*, 33–49.

Stodden, D. F., Goodway, J. D., Langendorfer, S. J., Roberton, M. A., Rudisill, M. E., Garcia, C., et al. (2008). A developmental perspective on the role of motor skill competence in physical activity: An emergent relationship. *Quest, 60*, 290–306.

Thomas, J. R., & French, K. E. (1985). Gender differences across age in motor performance: A meta-analysis. *Psychological Bulletin, 98*, 260–282.

Trost, S. G., Ward, D. S., & Senso, M. (2010). Effects of child care policy and environment on physical activity. *Medicine and Science in Sports and Exercise, 42*, 520–525.

Ulrich, D. (2000). *Test of Gross Motor Development–2.* Austin, TX: Pro-Ed.

U.S. Department of Health and Human Services (USDHHS). (1996). *Physical activity and health:*

A report of the surgeon general. Atlanta, GA: U.S. Department of Health and Human Services, Centers for Disease Control and Prevention, National Center for Chronic Disease Prevention and Health Promotion.

U.S. Department of Health and Human Services (USDHHS). (2004). Physical activity and fitness. Retrieved from *www.healthypeople.gov/data/2010prog/focus22/physicalfitnesspr.pdf.*

Valentini, N. C., & Rudisill, M. E. (2004). An inclusive mastery climate intervention and the motor skill development of children with and without disabilities. *Adapted Physical Activity Quarterly, 21*, 330–347.

Valentini, N. C., Rudisill, M., & Goodway, J. D. (1999). Incorporating a mastery climate into physical education: It's developmentally appropriate. *Journal of Physical Education Recreation and Dance, 7*, 28–32.

Ward, D. S. (2010). Physical activity in young children: The role of child care. *Medicine and Science in Sports and Exercise, 42*, 499–501.

Ward, D. S., Vaughn, A., McWilliams, C., & Hales, D. (2010). Interventions for increasing physical activity at child care. *Medicine and Science in Sports and Exercise, 42*, 526–534.

Whitehead, M. E. (2010). *Physical literacy: Throughout the lifecourse.* London: Routledge.

CHAPTER 19

NO FINE ART LEFT BEHIND
Creative and Expressive Education

SYLVIA MUNSEN

Imagination is more important than knowledge.
—ALBERT EINSTEIN

One can hear the voices of young children filling the air before entering the room and antici-pate the excitement. Boys and girls are seated on the floor singing a song and playing a vari-ety of African instruments. They are in the midst of a colorful and vibrant multicultural area in their classroom, filled with various artifacts from all around the world: instruments large and small, paintings, photographs, native costumes, scarves, and handcrafted toys. After the song is done, the teacher asks the children to describe the instruments they are play-ing. "What are the instruments made of? How is the sound created? What colors are used? Can you show me how you played the instrument?" Children excitedly take turns showing and describing their instruments—ranging from a gourd covered with a netting of seeds to a box with metal strips to pluck, to a "squeeze" or "talking" drum made with animal skin. The children view photographs of children from a choir in Uganda dressed in colorful native costumes of green and white, singing and playing instruments. They see drawings made by these Ugandan children as part of a tour to the United States. They view a video and see the members of the choir performing authentic dances and movement while singing. These dance movements help to portray everyday life experiences described in the song, from rowing a boat to picking fruit from a tree, to walking down a path.

What is everyday life like for these children? What can we learn about their lives through their music, art, dance, and drama? The children describe what they hear (the voices and the instruments), what they see (the moving and dancing; the construction of the instruments; the photos, paintings, and costumes), and what they feel (the expres-sions on their faces, the portrayal of everyday activities, their own responses to the artis-tic expression). The children in the class become immersed once again in a variety of

309

experiences in singing and playing, drawing and painting, moving and dancing, and portraying everyday life through drama. The arts represent a valuable way to understand themselves through experiencing the lives of other children halfway around the world.

As society faces the challenge of preparing its youth for life in the 21st century, one might ask, "What tools do we need to live a full, rich life? What kind of experiences should we provide to our children to grow and prosper as human beings? What is our responsibility as teachers, parents, and child care providers?" These and other questions are of significance as we consider the future of early childhood education in the 21st century.

Throughout the ages, educators and philosophers have advocated the development of the "whole child" in order to produce responsible and productive citizens with a rich quality of life. It is our collective social responsibility to provide the opportunities for all children to develop four domains of learning first identified by Piaget: cognitive, psychomotor, affective, and interpersonal. Historically, experience in the fine arts has been thought to provide the best avenue to develop students' affective domain. Gardner (2004) identifies musical intelligence as one of several discretely identifiable multiple intelligences. Indeed, in this age of increased mechanization, mass communication, and competition, we must ensure that our children are provided the opportunity to learn how to feel, as well as how to think and to do.

WHAT RESEARCH SAYS
ABOUT THE FINE ARTS AND EARLY CHILDHOOD EDUCATION

Moving into a new millennium provides an opportunity to reflect upon the artifacts of all cultures and history that remain as a record of human life. Throughout history, one of the many endeavors we share from one culture to another, from one generation to the next, is a record of humankind's artistic achievements: dance/movement, music, theater, and visual arts. These artistic achievements have been one of the primary methods of expressing or communicating our understanding of ourselves and the world around us. Therefore, it is the social obligation of parents and schools to share this cultural history with children. More important than the moral imperative of cultural transmission, however, is the opportunity for each child to participate directly in activities that can lead to aesthetic and artistic experience. If early childhood educators are truly committed to the growth and development of the "whole child," then the educational experiences of young children must include not only the cognitive and psychomotor but also the affective experiences in the fine arts. Regular engagement in the arts provides children necessary opportunities to learn how to express themselves and to share their feelings, expressions, and understandings with others. From experiences in the fine arts, children also learn to accept and value the contributions of all peoples and cultures throughout time.

Langer (1974) identified people's need to express their experiences through the use of symbols that distinguish them from other animals. Leonhard and House (1972, p. 114) stated that "man is unique among all creatures in the extent and quality of his potentials. He has physical, intellectual, ethical, and aesthetic potentials. If any aspect of his potential is neglected and undeveloped, he never attains his true stature as a human being." According to Broudy (1972, p. 58), "The quality of life is measured by the repertory of feelings which pervades it. Life is rich if the repertory of feelings is large and the discrimination among them is fine. Life is coarse, brutish and violent when the repertory is meager and undifferentiated." Reimer (1970, p. 38) asserted, "The arts are the most powerful tool available to man for refining and deepening his experience of feeling." Dewey (1916/1966, p. 238) stated that the arts "reveal a depth and range of meaning in experiences which otherwise might be mediocre and trivial. . . . They are not luxuries of education but emphatic expressions of that which makes any education worthwhile."

Arts education is grounded in the claim that the arts are unique for developing the human's aesthetic responsiveness. Leonhard and House (1972, p. 115) maintain that all humans are "responsive to music and can find satisfaction and meaning through experience with it." The goals and value of aesthetic education are to enrich the quality of people's lives by deepening their insights into the nature of human feeling. Since experience in the arts has been one of the most important avenues of expression of human feeling, it serves as a source of understanding humankind through the ages. Therefore, because the arts are of cultural and historical significance, and because they develop the unique human ability to feel a range of emotional responses, the arts should be an integral part of the educational process of young children.

Providing quality arts education for young children is always a challenge, largely due to a perpetual scarcity of funding and a near singular focus on the basics of reading, writing, and arithmetic in U.S. education. This is indeed unfortunate because a curriculum rich in the arts includes more concepts to be learned and skills to be developed than a narrowed basics curriculum mandates. And, as in all education, the quality of arts education is strongly related to the quality of arts teachers.

Creativity is identified as one central skill to preparing for life in the 21st century (Partnership for the 21st Century Project, 2009). Three such 21st-century "learning and innovation skills" apply directly to experiences in the arts: (1) creativity and innovation, (2) critical thinking and problem solving, and (3) communication and collaboration. Trilling and Fadel (2009, pp. 57–58) highlighted the importance of creativity as a skill for life in the 21st century when they wrote that "creativity and innovation can be nurtured by learning environments that foster questioning, patience, openness to fresh ideas, high levels of trust, and learning from mistakes and failures."

Maslow (1982) asserted that we need to develop "creative persons" equipped to deal with the challenges of a new century. He further challenged us to focus on developing the "creative person"—by focusing on the process, not just the product:

> Our era is more in flux more in process, more rapidly changing than any previous one in history. The rate of acceleration of accumulation of new scientific facts, of new inventions, of new technological developments, of new psychological happenings, of increased affluence, presents every human being today with a situation different from any than has ever happened before. Among other things, this new lack of continuity and stability from past to the present into the future makes all sorts of changes necessary which many people don't realize yet. . . . It is quite clear that we must teach them [people] to be creative persons, at least in the sense of being able to confront novelty, to improvise. They must not be afraid of change but rather must be able to be comfortable with change and novelty, and if possible (because best of all) even be able to enjoy novelty and change. . . . We must develop a race of improvisers, of "here–now" creators. . . . We must become more interested in the creative process, the creative attitude, the creative person, rather than in the creative product alone. . . . I consider nonverbal education so important, e.g., through art, through music, through dancing. I am not particularly interested in the training of arts because in any case this is done in a different way. Neither am I much interested in the children having a good time. . . . For that matter I

am not even interested in art education, per se. What I am really interested in is the new kind of education which we must develop which moves toward fostering the new kind of human being that we need, the process person, the creative person, the improvising person. . . . (pp. 93–96)

Harris (1998) identified creativity as an ability, an attitude, and a process. Dewey (1916/1966) emphasized the importance of process—of experiencing, undergoing, and doing. Maslow (1982) considered nonverbal education important for developing the creative attitude, the creative process. Gardner (2006) identified "the creating mind" as one of five minds. Bruner (1960/1978) advocated a new kind of "process of education"—one that emphasizes improvising, guessing, and creativeness. Leonhard and House (1972) highlighted the importance of providing opportunities for creativity and improvisation in (school) music programs. Creativity "is manifested both in the ability to create . . . and the ability to improvise and embellish" (p. 256).

As outlined in this section, it is important to include fine arts education in the lives of young children for a variety of reasons, as summarized in Table 19.1.

Experience in the fine arts is central to human experience, to quality of life. It is unique in its power to develop aesthetic responsiveness and to provide a record of human achievement from all cultures throughout the ages. A preponderance of evidence substantiates the value of an education rich with fine arts experience, which helps young children to develop fully, to reach their full potential as human beings. Embracing these tenets of the value of arts education can be challenging relative to time in the curriculum and funding. However, parents and schools must be committed to providing arts experience as part of each child's life to ensure full development, so that all children may lead richer lives.

RESEARCH INTO PRACTICE

How do teachers provide high-quality arts experiences for young children? Teachers can (1) choose the best works of art (movement/dance, music, theater, visual arts) for use in classroom activities, (2) focus on the artistic endeavor (i.e., have the children experience the arts directly by moving/dancing, speaking, singing, playing instruments, listening, exploring, creating, painting, acting), and (3) provide opportunities for children to

---

TABLE 19.1. Why Young Children Need Fine Arts Education

1. Each child has aesthetic potential, and it is the teacher's responsibility to develop that potential in each child to his or her highest level (Reimer, 1970).

2. Arts experience is central to our existence; it enhances the quality of life (Broudy, 1972; Dewey, 1916/1966; Reimer, 1970).

3. Education needs to include the development of the "whole child" (cognitive, psychomotor, affective, and interpersonal domains).

4. Creativity is critical to life in the 21st century—with a focus on problem solving, on process (not just product), and on learning to confront, accept, and learn about new and different things.

5. Works of art are the artifacts, the documentation of each culture and generation. Artifacts offer the opportunity to learn about and celebrate the unique aspects of each culture, and similarities and differences, which leads to understanding of self and others.

TABLE 19.2. Guidelines for Providing High-Quality Arts Experience in Early Childhood Classrooms

1. Choose the best works of art.
2. Focus on the artistic endeavor.
3. Provide opportunities to become more artistically sensitive and knowledgeable.

Note. Based on Reimer (1970).

become artistically sensitive and knowledgeable about the elements of each area of the fine arts (identifying, describing, labeling, sharing, comparing, feeling). As mentioned previously, feelings are central to human experience, to quality of life; they are unique in developing aesthetic responsiveness in humankind and provide a record of human endeavors throughout the ages.

The guidelines shown in Table 19.2 by Reimer (1970) may be used by teachers to answer the question "How do teachers provide high-quality arts experiences for young children?"

How does one select the best works of art for use with young children? By identifying and utilizing works that have survived the "test of time." Examples especially appropriate for young children include folk songs, folktales (which inspire acting, drawing, and moving activities), folk instruments from diverse cultures, and paintings from diverse traditions throughout time. Such sources invite immediate responses from children. They can sing, act, draw, and move in response to the works of art and create their own works of art. As guided by the teacher, the children are engaged as artists themselves.

"This Is the Way" (Figure 19.1), a Norwegian folk song, is an example of a good musical work that is appropriate for young children. This folk song has one of the standard forms, with repeated phrases and motives that children can experience and later identify as similar in quality and form to other composed songs and folk songs. In order to experience the artwork fully, children can be involved with the song by singing, playing instruments, creating new verses, and acting. The more engaged the child is with the work of art (in this case, a "classic" folk song), the more he or she will understand and know about that work.

Some of the engagement activities included with "This Is the Way" are (1) playing body percussion[1] and moving (walking, stomping, swaying) while singing the song; (2) creating new verses and acting them out ("This is the way that we pat our legs, brush our teeth, walk to school, jump up and down"); and (3) playing unpitched percussion[2] while singing the song. All of these activities provide children the opportunity to experience fully the work of art in relation to everyday experiences.

There are many illustrated books of familiar songs, primarily folk songs. These songs, which are appropriate for children, invite them to be involved with singing, playing instruments, moving, acting, and creating. In addition, the high-quality illustrations can serve to inspire visual art activities to represent their experience. Some examples include the following:

---

[1] Making sounds with clapping, snapping, patting legs, stamping feet, rubbing hands together, and so forth.

[2] Instruments that do not sound as a specific pitch, such as hand drums, wood blocks or wood sticks, tambourines, finger cymbals, maracas, guiros, and so forth; instruments that do sound as a specific pitch, such as xylophones, metallophones, glockenspiels, (resonator) bells, pianos, and so forth, are referred to as *pitched percussion*.

- *Cat Goes Fiddle-i-fee*, adapted and illustrated by Paul Galdone, ISBN 0-89919-705-1
- *Hush Little Baby*, illustrated by Aliki, ISBN 0-671-66742-4
- *Mary Wore Her Red Dress*, adapted and illustrated by Merle Peek, ISBN 0-89919-324-2
- *Roll Over!*, illustrated by Merle Peek, ISBN 0-395-58105-2
- *Old Macdonald had a Farm*, illustrated by Pam Adams, ISBN 0-85953-053-1

Participation: singing, playing, moving, creating, acting

Concepts: maintaining a steady beat; creating new verses; acting out actions

Materials: unpitched percussion

Sing the song and do appropriate body percussion (see footnote 1) and movement to a steady beat. The teacher and the children create new verses by playing body percussion, playing unpitched percussion (see footnote 2), identifying/acting out personal habits, moving in various ways, and so forth. Change words at end as desired (e.g., "here in Westside School" or "here in school each day").

Other verses to be created by the teacher and children who then sing and do can include:

"This is the way that we . . . "

- pat our legs, nod our head, touch our nose, pound a fist, etc. (body percussion)
- play the drums, play the woods, play the shakers, etc. (unpitched percussion)
- brush our teeth, comb our hair, wear a smile, etc. (personal habits)
- walk around, march along, slide around, jump up and down, etc. (movement)

FIGURE 19.1. "This Is the Way" (Norwegian folk song with English words by S. Munsen).

- *There Was an Old Lady Who Swallowed a Fly*, illustrated by Pam Adams, ISBN 0-85953-018-3
- *Five Little Ducks*, illustrated by Jose Aruego and Ariane Dewey, ISBN 0-517-58360-7
- *Shake My Sillies Out*, illustrated by David Allender, ISBN 0-517-56647-8
- *Twinkle Twinkle Little Star*, by Jannat Messenger, ISBN 0-689-71136-0
- *Today is Monday*, pictures by Eric Carle, ISBN 0-399-21966-8
- *This Land is Your Land*, paintings by Kathy Jakobsen, ISBN 0-316-39215-4
- *This Old Man*, illustrated by Carol Jones, ISBN 0-395-54699-0
- *The Wheels on the Bus*, adapted and illustrated by Paul Zelinsky, ISBN 0-525-44644-3

Children love to listen to and participate in storytelling. Folktales are examples of good works of art that inspire a variety of artistic responses from children. Another good example of a work of art is the African folktale *Why Mosquitos Buzz in People's Ears* (Aardema, 1978; see Figure 19.2). The children listen to the story as it is read aloud by the teacher and identify various characters (animals). They describe each character and are guided as to how each character might be represented with sounds, movement, colors, and expressions. The children select an instrument from a variety of unpitched percussion (drums, woods, bells, shakers, etc.) and create a pattern of sounds on that instrument to represent each character. They create masks or paint their faces and act expressively as one of the characters. The children may listen to the story repeatedly and be engaged by acting/moving as the various characters, making a sound representing each character, or playing the selected instrument that is appropriate each time a character is mentioned in the story. Finally, the children see examples of African jewelry and identify the colors and lines used to created these artworks. Then they can make their own African plate necklaces (Figure 19.3).

Many other high-quality books may be the basis for children portraying characters in artistic ways: identifying various characters; acting out the characters, including their movements, and painting faces; selecting an appropriate instrument representing each character to play whenever the character is mentioned in the story.

- *Hush!*, ISBN 0-531-09500-2
- *The Bremen-Town Musicians*, ISBN 0-06-443141-X
- *The Legend of the Bluebonnet*, ISBN 0-399-22411-4
- *The Legend of the Indian Paintbrush*, ISBN 0-399-21777-0
- *The Leopard's Drum*, ISBN 0-316-80466-5
- *Three Billy Goats Gruff*, ISBN 0-8234-1015-3
- *Aesop's Fables*

Other high-quality books have excellent illustrations with repeated words/phrases that invite a response with instruments. Children can suggest an appropriate instrument for these words/phrases to play when the word/phrase is read in the book.

- *Chicka Chicka Boom Boom*, ISBN 0-671-67949-X
- *In the Small, Small Pond*, ISBN 0-8050-2264-3
- *Old Black Fly*, ISBN 0-8050-3924-4
- *Thump, Thump, Rat-a-Tat-Tat*, ISBN 0-06443265-3

Participation: selecting/playing appropriate body and unpitched percussion, creating sounds, moving

Concepts: listening to a story and identifying characters; selecting/playing an appropriate unpitched instrument for each character and creating a rhythm pattern to represent each character

Materials: *Why Mosquitos Buzz in People's Ears* (Aardema, 1975), unpitched percussion

Characters: mosquito   iguana   python   rabbit   monkey

crow   Mother Owl   owlets   sun   King Lion   antelope

Ask the children to listen to the folktale and identify as many "characters" as possible and describe them with regards to their look, size, sound, and movement. The teacher reads the tale and makes a list of characters on the board/chart from the children's responses. What body percussion and what kind of movement would be appropriate? For example:

Mosquito: description: small, fast, soft but intense
        sounds/movement: soft (but intense) buzzing sounds in higher pitches
        instruments: finger cymbals, small maracas

Mother Owl and owlet(s): (compare mother–baby)
        description: larger vs. smaller, older vs. younger, louder vs. softer
        sounds/movement: vocal "whoo" louder/softer and lower/higher
        sounds instruments: "scraping" the head of a larger/smaller drum

King Lion: description: large, fast, loud
        sounds/movement: loud roar, fast movements
        instruments: conga drums or African "talking" drum

First, ask the children to create sounds (vocal and body percussion) and movements appropriate for each character as the teacher reads the story again. On another day, ask the children to recall and identify as many unpitched percussion as they know and place the instruments on the floor in addition to others that are available. Have children suggest a particular instrument that would be appropriate to represent each character. Depending on the size of the class, there might be one to three students playing the same kind of instrument (e.g., each playing a large drum for King Lion) as the story is read again. Encourage children to create sounds for the characters focusing on what would be appropriate: playing higher–lower, louder–softer, faster–slower instruments and instrument sounds.

   Older children can work in cooperative groups of two to three and create a pattern that would be representative of their character. For example, four loud beats could represent King Lion. Eight faster beats on the maracas could represent the mosquito. When reading the story, be sure to pause after each character is mentioned in the story so that the children have time to play their instrument, make the sounds, and/or do the movements. Read the story another day and have children play/move to represent a different character than before.

   Take the opportunity to discuss the "moral" of the tale. When there is a disagreement or misunderstanding between two people, how can the situation be resolved? Is it right to blame someone else for your actions? How does it feel to "blamed" for another person's inappropriate actions? What can you do?

FIGURE 19.2. *Why Mosquitoes Buzz in People's Ears.*

Participation: viewing photos and describing, painting, creating, gluing

Concepts: learn about the jewelry and life of other countries; making artwork from ordinary objects; work with liquid tempera paint

Materials: photos of women from various African countries with native dress and necklaces (*http://pinterest.com/p8ronella/africa-traditional-costumes*), paper plates, tempera paint, glue, scissors, beads/jewels/seeds/beads, and so forth.

Note: Necklaces made by children from *www.mrsbrownart.com/kindergarten.htm*.

Give one paper plate to each child. Children explore and share ways to use the paper plates and then identify things that could be made from the plates; share ideas. Show the children photos of women from various African countries wearing necklaces; children describe what they see and determine how necklaces can be made from the paper plate (children discover the need to cut the inside out and cut a small slice out to put around the neck). Identify various ways to decorate a necklace: various painting techniques with tempera paint, color schemes, adding "jewelry" such as shiny buttons, beads, seeds, and rhinestones. Provide the outside ring of a paper plate for each child with the small slice cut out. Move to tables with tempera paint. Children decide what colors to use. After it has dried, glue on decorations for the jewelry.

FIGURE 19.3. African plate necklaces. Adapted from *www.mrsbrownart.com/kindergarten.htm*.

A collection of animated, short classic works featuring art, dance, and music on DVDs, is appropriate, of high quality, and entertaining. It was produced by Amy Schatz for HBO.

- *Classical Baby: the Art show*, HBO
- *Classical Baby: the Dance show*, HBO
- *Classical Baby: the Music show*, HBO

Finally, many books based on classic music compositions include a high-quality CD of the music. These musical works of art lend themselves to creative movement and dramatic interpretation.

- *Peter and the Wolf*, retold and illustrated by Ian Bech, ISBN 0-689-80336-2
- *Peter and the Wolf*, retold and illustrated by Michele Lemieux, ISBN 0-688-09846-0
- *Pictures at an Exhibition*, by Anna Harwell Celenze and illustrated by JoAnn E. Kitchel, ISBN 1-57091-492-3
- *Carnival of the Animals* (by Saint-Saens), with commentary by Barrie Carson Turner, illustrations by Sue Williams, ISBN 0-8050-6180-0

In these previous examples, children have not only experienced good works of art but they also have been immersed in singing, playing, creating, moving, listening, acting, and painting along with, and in response to, those artworks. These modes of "doing" or "experiencing" support the second goal in providing high-quality works of art, which focuses on the art endeavor (Table 19.2). "The Wind and the Sun" (see Figure 19.4) invites children to focus on the "experiencing" inspired by another good work of art, a fable. Children are guided to listen to the tale, identify the "characters" in the tale (wind, sun, traveler), and to suggest ways to portray those characters with acting, body percussion (swishing hands, patting), and movement (walking, moving slowly). What kinds of actions, sounds, and movement would effectively portray each character? On another day, children are encouraged to explore sounds of various unpitched percussion instruments (hand drums, wood blocks, tambourines, etc.) in relation to the characters in the tale. Which instrument would effectively portray which character and why? Throughout the experience, children are engaged in focusing on the artistic endeavor. In addition, the moral of the story (essentially, "kindness is better than force") provides an opportunity to discuss appropriate behavior with one another.

Children love to wear costumes. The activity "Halloween" provides the opportunity to focus on the endeavor—this time with singing and creating, and wearing costumes as well (see Figure 19.5). Children enjoy creating their own solo about what they are wearing (costume and/or mask) and will be for Halloween.

Another example of an activity focused on the artistic endeavor is based on the traditional singing game, "Up on the Mountain" (see Figure 19.6). Children are engaged in singing, moving, and creating; they progress from making individual statues to making statues with a partner. Their "movement vocabulary" is expanded by viewing photos and paintings of famous statues, and by observing other children in the room making interesting shapes.

Children can engage in creating melodies to accompany the text of their favorite books; they can sing and dramatize the story. Books with texts that are conducive to

Participation: vocal sounds, playing, moving, creating, acting

Concepts: portraying a story through movement, acting, and playing unpitched percussion; exploring new ways to play unpitched percussion and then playing them when appropriate in the story

Materials: unpitched percussion (hand drums, finger cymbals, tambourines, wood blocks)

"The Wind and the Sun" (Aesop's fable)

The Wind and the Sun were disputing which was the stronger. Suddenly they saw a traveler coming down the road, and the Sun said: "I see a way to decide our dispute. Whichever of us can cause that traveler to take off his cloak shall be regarded as the stronger. You begin." So the Sun retired behind a cloud and the Wind began to blow as hard as he could upon the traveler. But the harder he blew the more closely did the traveler wrap his cloak around him, till at last the Wind had to give up in despair. Then the Sun came out and shone in all his glory upon the traveler, who soon found it too hot to walk with his cloak on.

"Kindness affects more than Severity."

Ask children to listen to the story and identify the main characters (wind, sun, traveler). What is the challenge? Who can get the traveler to take off his cloak? Read the story again and have children act out each character as the story progresses. Then divide children into three groups—one for each character—and act out again. Review story and create actions and vocal sounds for the three characters:

- wind (swishing hands, vocally making "blowing" sounds, etc.)
- sun (moving very slowly, making large circle with arms, etc.)
- traveler (patting legs or walking, clicking tongues, etc.)

Take turns being different characters.

Provide time to explore the sounds of various unpitched percussion (hand drums, wood blocks, triangles, tambourines, etc.). Encourage the children to consider which instruments could be played to reflect or portray each character. Play instruments and explore various beats and patterns to reflect or portray each character:

- wind (gently move fingers/hands over drum heads)
- sun (play triangles and tambourines as one chooses)
- traveler (play wood sticks or wood blocks)

Review the story with unpitched percussion taking turns to be different characters.

Lead a discussion regarding the moral of the story. ("Kindness works better than anger or force" might be more easily understood.) How does it apply to your life? What if you don't get the instrument you want to play today? (You will get to play it another time.) What if someone accidentally bumps into you? (It was an accident and that person should say "I'm sorry.") Ask the children to give other ideas of how it is better to be kind than angry to another person.

FIGURE 19.4. "The Wind and the Sun" (Arbuthnot, 1952, pp. 206–207).

Participation: chanting, singing, creating

Concepts: vocal exploration with singing; create melody for the answer

Materials: hand puppets, costumes

Hal-lo-ween, Hal-lo-ween, What will you be?   I'll be a pump- kin...

Chant the question phrase. Each child chants his or her own answer as a solo and the class echoes ("Joe will be a pumpkin"). On another day, sing the melody with questions (whole class) and answers (individual response and class echo). Children can be guided to create their own answer vocally singing on the two-three notes of the "question" but in a different order and creating a new melody. Wear costumes, use hand puppets, and/or create hand puppets painting on small paper sacks. Sing about the costumes or masks the children are wearing.

FIGURE 19.5. "Halloween" (chant).

singing a simple melody of two or three pitches, an improvised melody, or a known melody such as "Twinkle Twinkle Little Star" include the following:

- *Brown Bear Brown Bear What Do You See?*, ISBN 0-8050-1744-5
- *Baby Bear, Baby Bear, What Do You See?*, ISBN 0-8050-8336-7
- *Ten Little Rabbits*, ISBN 0-8118-2132-3
- *Ten Little Ladybugs*, ISBN 158117091-2
- *I Went Walking*, ISBN 0-15-238011-6

The last goal for providing a high-quality arts experience is for children to become more artistically sensitive and knowledgeable (Table 19.2). In the first example, "Create a Thunderstorm" (see Figure 19.7), children focus on listening to the sounds of a storm: rain, wind, cracks of lightning, and thunder. They are guided to create ways to replicate those sounds by playing body and unpitched percussion instruments and making vocal sounds. (Plan this activity in advance and use it on a stormy day, so that children have the direct experience of a real storm!) What sounds effectively portray the different parts of a storm? Which is softer–louder—raindrops or thunder? Which of these would involve higher or lower sounds? What about faster and slower? Creating a thunderstorm with vocal sounds and instruments provides the opportunity to discuss all of these artistic elements.

Through creating their own thunderstorm (with body and unpitched percussion instruments) and by experiencing the thunderstorm creations of others, children become more sensitive to the artistic aspects of each creation. They can articulate what they "liked" or thought was effective about each work (e.g., "I liked how this storm started and ended with the soft sounds of rain" or "I liked hearing the cracks of lightning all throughout the storm"). Listening, identifying, differentiating, and characterizing the qualities of the arts experience all lead to becoming more artistically sensitive and knowledgeable about sounds.

Participation: singing, moving, creating

Concepts: create various statues by self and cooperatively with a partner

Materials: photos and paintings of famous statues

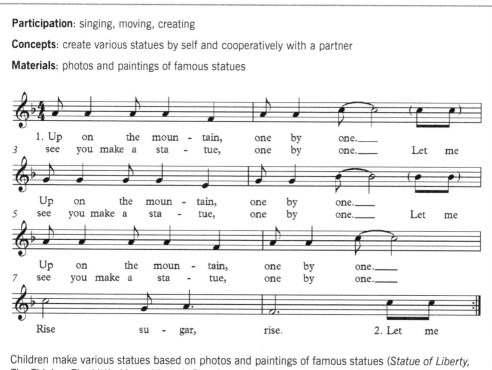

1. Up on the moun - tain, one by one.___

3. see you make a sta - tue, one by one.___ Let me

Up on the moun - tain, one by one.___

5. see you make a sta - tue, one by one.___ Let me

Up on the moun - tain, one by one.___

7. see you make a sta - tue, one by one.___

Rise su - gar, rise. 2. Let me

Children make various statues based on photos and paintings of famous statues (*Statue of Liberty, The Thinker, The Little Mermaid*, etc.). Practice making those statues and focus on standing still after the statue is created! Explore and create new statues. Half the group can make statues while the other half observes (to expand movement "vocabulary") and switch. Identify statues to have the whole class replicate. Sing Verse 1 while walking; make statues for Verse 2.

Explore and create making a statue with a partner. Identify several partner statues for replication by the whole class. Sing Verse 1 (now singing "two by two") walking around the room holding hands with partner. Sing Verse 2 and make a new statue with partner. When replicating an identified statue, sing "Oh, we can make that statue two by two."

FIGURE 19.6. "Up on the Mountain" (traditional singing game).

In addition children can experience the storm with painting activities. They can draw a picture of their own thunderstorm (dark clouds to represent thunder, a zigzag line for one crack of lightning, small raindrops progressing to large raindrops, more thunder and lightning, etc.). Each child can present his or her story with classmates and his or her family at home. Finally, children can take turns being the "conductor"—pointing to the various parts of the thunderstorm—and having their classmates make vocal sounds and/ or play instruments to represent the different parts of the storm as it progresses.

Going on a "Nature Field Trip" (see Figure 19.8) provides another opportunity for transforming what might be a fairly ordinary excursion into an artistic experience. Students are guided to see things they see everyday and create an artwork of that experience, one in which they can learn more about texture, line, shape, and the overall form of an artwork. In addition, they have created an artifact to share with their friends and family. It is interesting to note the differences and similarities between and among the "pathways" created by a group of children who all went on the same field trip. The artistic

Participation: playing body, unpitched and pitched percussion, vocal sounds, moving, creating a thunderstorm

Concepts: louder/softer, faster/slower, higher/lower (music and movement) choosing a color, thinner/thicker (visual art)

Materials: unpitched percussion, paper, crayons, paint

wind   rain   lightning   thunder

This is an appropriate activity to do on the day of a rainstorm or when teaching about rainstorms. Children identify what happens during a thunderstorm and do appropriate actions, sounds, and movement as a group:

- wind blows (vocal "blowing" sounds, swishing hands, etc., louder and softer)
- rain falls (snapping fingers, patting legs, tongue clicks, etc., louder and softer)
- lightning streaks across the sky with loud "crack" (move quickly and clap hands once very loudly)
- thunder rumbles (low vocal sounds and stamping feet on floor)

Divide children into four groups; assign each group a character: wind, rain, lightning, thunder. Teacher points to each character on a large chart to create a thunderstorm and the assigned group responds with appropriate actions, vocal sounds, and movement. Have a child be the leader and point to the various characters to create his or her thunderstorm. Point to characters individually and/or simultaneously.

Provide paper and crayons or paint for all children to create their own thunderstorm "map." Each map will be unique. One child might start his storm map with wind, another child with rain, and still another might hear the thunder first. The children suggest unpitched and pitched percussion to represent each character as a class. Perform several of the maps created by the children. Try these ideas and then have children create their own "sounds" to portray each character. Some suggestions might include:

- wind blows (rub hands on top of hand drums)
- rain falls (improvise with pitches C, D, E, G, and A on glockenspiels or bells)
- lightning streaks across the sky with loud "crack" (wood blocks)
- thunder rumbles (play large drums with mallets)

FIGURE 19.7. Create a thunderstorm.

Participation: moving, identifying, labeling, creating

Concepts: identify up to five different objects in nature on a field trip; portray trip's path in a visual art work; present story about the field trip

Materials: objects found on field trip (leaves, twigs, rocks, gravel, flowers, grass, seeds, trash, etc.), sack to collect the objects, glue, piece of construction paper (9" × 12", different colors), 18" pieces of yarn

Going on a field trip can be as simple as walking around the school or building where class is held. Determine a location where there are objects, which children can collect and bring back to the classroom. At tables, children lay all of their objects down. Each child chooses a piece of colored construction paper and a piece of yarn to use as the route or "map" of his or her field trip. The child glues the yarn in a meandering pattern, how he or she might have walked along discovering various objects in nature. Choose five objects and glue them down along the yarn "pathway" to create the "map" of one's experience. Present and describe one's trip to classmates and to families at home.

FIGURE 19.8. Nature field trip.

representations can be quite varied due to each child's unique experience, ability, and interests.

Embracing and enacting these guidelines to provide high-quality arts experiences in early childhood classrooms can be challenging, especially with diminishing funds for arts programs. Early childhood teachers need to ensure the continued inclusion of the arts in the curriculum. Also, experience suggests that the more training a teacher has received in fine arts education and in experiencing the fine arts directly, the higher the quality of the teaching. However, anyone with an interest in and commitment to quality education in the fine arts can successfully provide young children appropriate experiences in the fine arts. Despite the challenges of funding and training, early childhood educators must be committed to providing arts experiences as part of each child's daily classroom education.

Creativity is central to all fine arts education in early childhood. Leonhard and House (1972) highlight the importance of providing opportunities for creativity and improvisation in (school) music programs. Creativity "is manifested both in the ability to create . . . and the ability to improvise and embellish" (p. 255). The central premise of the Orff-Schulwerk approach to music and movement education is providing opportunities for children to explore and create. In this approach, children experience a variety of media in a creative setting: speech, singing, body percussion, movement, and instrumental play. Students are guided through a process that builds musical skills and concepts developmentally. The three developmental levels include imitation, exploration, and improvisation (Munsen, 1986). And, the goal is "to experience joy in music making" (*Guidelines for Orff-Schulwerk Training Courses Levels I, II, III*, 1980, p. 3). The consistent thread running through all these developmental levels or stages of improvisation (and creativity), moving from the known to the unknown, is applicable to all fines arts experience: dance/movement, music, theater, and visual arts.

Activities in all fine arts areas (dance/movement, music, theater, and visual arts) appropriate for early childhood classes have been presented as examples of how to provide high-quality arts experience. The activities are based on utilizing high-quality works of art that are appropriate for young children who are "immersed" in the art experience and given opportunities to become more artistically sensitive and knowledgeable. Young children can participate in a variety of ways in the fine arts: moving/dancing, singing, playing instruments, listening, exploring, creating, drawing, painting, and acting. Most activities include several experiential avenues simultaneously (moving, singing, and creating experience in one activity; singing, exploring, and acting in another; moving and painting in another; etc.).

The activities presented can serve as models for how to provide young children with high-quality arts experiences. Teachers using their imagination to create their own activities provides creative and expressive opportunities for all children. Children are motivated to participate in such activities as they enjoy playing, creating, exploring, and acting. It is exciting to learn along with children as they naturally suggest new and different ways to be involved in all areas of the fine arts. It is a privilege to share enriching experiences with them and to see everything through their eyes.

REFLECTIONS AND NEW DIRECTIONS

We are on a journey as human beings—teachers and children. Engaging in the arts helps us to enjoy the journey as teachers and children, to have special artistic experiences together. In conclusion, I offer a "top 10 list" that highlights how to work with children and to provide creative and expressive experiences in the early childhood classroom.

10. *Develop children's aesthetic potential* with experience in the arts, which is one of the best avenues for developing this potential.
9. *Provide artistic experiences for all children*, with the same opportunities in drama, dance/movement, music, and visual art on a daily basis as in all other curricular areas. These experiences can be integrated into the basic skills and content areas for early childhood.
8. *Choose art works of the highest quality* to share with children in the classroom.
7. *Guide children to be creative*; it is important for their full development; creativity is identified as one of the 21st Century Skills, and participation in the arts provides opportunities for children to be creative.
6. *Focus more on the process* than on the product.
5. *Motivate children to choose to participate* in creative activities.
4. *Learn* from one another—teachers and children are "colleagues."
3. *Plan* learning experiences carefully; however, be flexible and ready for change; be creative and ready to improvise.
2. *Serve as a role model* for children—as one who is excited about learning, passionate about life, and willing to try new things.
1. *Enjoy each and every day* with children; each child is special, has unique abilities, and is deserving of our time and best efforts.

PROFESSIONAL DEVELOPMENT ACTIVITIES

■ Work toward a degree (or an additional degree) in early childhood education, elementary education, and/or elementary education in one of the arts, or a collaborative arts program.

- Attend workshops and conferences offered through local universities and school districts and by organizations such as American Orff-Schulwerk Association, Early Childhood Music and Movement Association, KinderMusik, Organization of American Kodály Educators, Early Childhood Art Educators, National Art Education Association, National Dance Education Organization, International Drama/Theatre and Education Association, etc.

- Network via Facebook, Twitter, blogging, etc.

- Volunteer in a preschool, day care center, community center, or early elementary classroom, if you aren't working with children currently. (Volunteers may be subject to background checks.)

REFERENCES

Aardema, V. (1978). *Why mosquitos buzz in people's ears.* Hong Kong: South China Printing Company.

Arbuthnot, M. K. (Ed.). (1952). *Time for fairy tales: Old and new.* Chicago: Scott, Foresman.

Broudy, H. (1972). *Enlightened cherishing.* Urbana: University of Illinois Press.

Bruner, J. S. (1978). *The process of education.* Cambridge, MA: Harvard University Press. (Original work published 1960)

Dewey, J. (1966). *Democracy and education.* New York: Free Press. (Original work published 1916)

Einstein, A. Quotation. Retrieved June 20, 2012, from *www.einstein-quotes.com/creativity.html.*

Gardner, H. (2004). *Frames of mind: The theory of multiple intelligences.* New York: Basic Books.

Gardner, H. (2006). *Five minds for the future.* Boston: Harvard Business School.

Guidelines for Orff-Schulwerk Training Courses Levels I, II, III. (1980). Cleveland, OH: American Orff-Schulwerk Association.

Harris, R. (1998). Introduction to creative thinking. Retrieved December 30, 2011, from *www.virtualsalt.com.*

Langer, S. K. (1974). *Philosophy in a new key* (3rd ed.). Cambridge, MA: Harvard University Press.

Leonhard, C., & House, R. (1972). *Foundations and principles of music education* (2nd ed.). New York: McGraw-Hill.

Maslow, A. H. (1982). *The farther reaches of human nature.* New York: Penguin Books.

Munsen, S. C. (1986). *A description and analysis of an Orff-Schulwerk program of music education (improvisation).* University of Illinois at Urbana–Champaign. *ProQuest Dissertations and Theses* (303407977). Retrieved from *http://search.proquest.com/docview/303407977?accountid=14761.*

Partnership for 21st Century Skills. (2009). Framework for 21st century learning. Retrieved January 3, 2011, from *www.21stcenturysills.org/documents/framework_flyer_updated_april_2009.pdf.*

Reimer, B. (1970). *A philosophy of music education.* Upper Saddle River, NJ: Prentice Hall.

Trilling, B., & Fadel, C. (2009). *21st century skills.* San Francisco: Jossey-Bass.

CHAPTER 20

INSTRUCTIONAL DESIGN
THAT LEADS TO THE DEVELOPMENT
OF YOUNG SCIENTISTS

SUSAN A. KIRCH

> Children make the best theorists, since they have not yet been educated
> into accepting our routine social practices as "natural," and so insist on
> posing to those practices the most embarrassingly general and fundamental
> questions, regarding them with a wondering estrangement which we adults
> have long forgotten. Since they do not yet grasp our social practices as
> inevitable, they do not see why we might not do things differently.
> —TERRY EAGLETON, *The Significance of Theory* (1990, p. 34)

Although many early childhood and childhood educators and educational researchers claim to subscribe to Vygotsky's idea that learning is social, I find that the radical departure his theory took from behaviorist approaches is not fully appreciated. Here is an example of a recent exchange with a journal reviewer that captures a conversation I routinely have with preservice and inservice teachers and science education researchers:

AUTHORS: "Our knowing is deeply personal and constitutes part of whom we are. In school, learning is a process that can lead the development of a child and science learning can influence whether a child wants to be and become someone who engages in exploration, explanation and argumentation" (Kirch & Stetsenko, 2012, p. 45).

REVIEWER: Your statement, "Learning is a process that can lead the development of a child" is a huge claim! Perhaps you could revise it to read, "Learning is a process that contributes much to the development of a child."

AUTHORS: Our statement actually reflects a core idea in Vygotsky's theory of the relationship between learning and development, which he stated as: "The most essential feature of our hypothesis is the notion that developmental processes do not coincide with learning processes. Rather, the developmental process lags behind the learning process" (Vygotsky, 1978, p. 90). His point was that learning does lead development.

In this chapter, I demonstrate how an understanding of Vygotsky's point is essential for effective instruction in science and across the curriculum. Furthermore, understanding this point means acknowledging that "education is not about acquiring knowledge for the sake of knowing, but an *active project of becoming human*, a process that drives development and makes it possible" (Stetsenko, 2008, p. 487, original emphasis).

WHAT RESEARCH SAYS ABOUT EARLY CHILDHOOD SCIENCE TEACHING AND LEARNING

I have chosen two organizing principles for this chapter. First, I attempt to keep everything we know about early childhood science teaching and learning problematic, meaning that I am open to question and debate what we know because it is far from certain and settled. Second, I try to bring the perspectives of children to the fore. Using these two organizing principles, my goal is to encourage the reader to join the ongoing dialog, debate, and research in early childhood science education and learn about the work being conducted by early childhood educators worldwide. Early childhood science education in the United States currently operates on many untested assumptions. How does one write a chapter telling the reader what "researchers say" about science teaching and learning for young children and translating this "research into practice," when there is only a small body of reported knowledge to inform these discussions?

For this presentation about research and practice in early childhood science education, I employ a model articulated by the developmental psychologists Igor Arievitch and Anna Stetsenko (2000) over a decade ago. Figure 20.1 represents graphically their elegant model, which illustrates the interdependent relationships among teaching, learning, and development. The implications of this model are that if suitable theories of development guide practice, then the contingent educational practices should (and usually do) lead to desirable developmental outcomes (Figure 20.1a). However, if *inadequate* theories of development dominate decision making, then instructional educational practices that are contingent on those theories are likely to lead to poor student learning outcomes (Figure 20.1b). It is important to note that this model of development displays snapshots of learners in time—still images of specific developmental "outcomes" or "performances." Development, we know, is far from static; it is a "dynamical and fluid

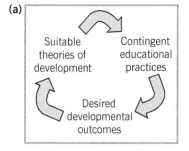 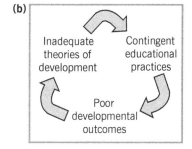

FIGURE 20.1. A graphic representation of Arievitch and Stetsenko's model illustrating the interdependent relationships between theories and practices of teaching, learning, and development. Figure 20.1a depicts a functional educational cycle and Figure 20.1b depicts a dysfunctional cycle. Based on Arievitch and Stetsenko (2000).

process . . . undergoing constant change and never following one preprogrammed path" (Stetsenko, 2008, p. 478). The tragic consequence of the inadequate theories of development we see playing out in our educational system is that poor instructional practices are developed, and the resulting poor developmental outcomes are interpreted to reinforce the inadequate theories of development. It is only when existing models are questioned, challenged, and tested that we have the opportunity to reset the cycle (a.k.a. reform, renewal, transformation). This questioning process sometimes reflects problem-posing actions that result from keeping knowledge and practices problematic, but they usually reflect the political tensions in education. To achieve my goal of keeping our knowledge and practices problematic, I question every part of this cycle for early childhood science education.

Two Worldviews on the Relationship between Teaching, Learning, and Development

One of the most influential theories on early childhood classroom practices in 20th century science education is an oversimplified version of Piaget's stage theory of cognitive development (Chapman, 1988), which implies that development (maturation) must precede learning. In other words, students can only learn when they are developmentally mature, and there is little to be gained from pushing them into tasks that require the assistance of an adult or more capable peer. The idea of a stage theory of cognitive development is that higher cognitive functions unfold concomitantly with development. In other words, as children grow and mature, so does their capacity to learn and attach adult meanings and concepts to natural phenomena. Older children, therefore, are more capable of higher mental functions than younger children, and specific types of instructional tasks or concepts should be reserved for children of an appropriate age. This view is gaining what looks like new evidentiary support: genetic and evolutionary explanations for identity and behavior. These views espouse that we are who we are and we do what we do because the genes we have inherited render us powerless in the face of relentless evolutionary mechanisms allowing only the fittest to survive. Although many scholars continue to object, "We are not our genes" (e.g., Lewontin, Rose, & Kamin, 1984; Noë, 2009; Stetsenko, 2008), the idea that a universal progression dictates human development is alive and well.

It has been well documented that simplified interpretations of Piaget's ideas have cemented into the decontextualized, topic-based, "hands-on" approach to learning that dominates the early childhood science landscape (and to a large extent the early adolescent landscape, too) (Metz, 1995). Activity-based, hands-on demonstration lessons allow students to recognize what they are already prepared to accept as true based on their personal, empirical (sensory) experiences of the world. When this recognition occurs, students are said to have learned the target concept. Thus, the problem with the idea that learning follows development (i.e., maturation must occur before a child can understand and construct a concept as an adult does) is that we cannot make definitive predictions about learning with this model. After exploratory, "hands-on" experiences without cultural mediation for internalization, students form either desired or undesired interpretations of phenomena. Students present either scientific or nonscientific conclusions about phenomena. The activity may serve as a limited exploration that is entertaining to the child but will result in either no cognitive growth or a cognitive growth spurt. Learners may demonstrate improved motor skills, but not necessarily. Learners will probably make little or no connection to scientific worldview and explanation. Learners may or may not recognize informative or relevant patterns needed for future learning or understanding consistent with scientific views. In fact, nothing is certain, and the student developmental outcomes are unpredictable if we support the theory that learning lags behind growth, as shown in Figure 20.2. Furthermore, according to this model, in which the ability to learn follows development, every failure is attributable to the absence of student development and not to the educational system or instructional practices. There is no incentive to question the theory because unpredictable (often poor) developmental outcomes are consistent with the theory. Commonly heard conclusions are: (1) students are not ready for the material; therefore, we should simplify the content further, and (2) students don't have the natural talent needed to understand, therefore we should not teach it.

What if we modify Figure 20.2 and assume that learning is the cause of development when cultural mediation in the form of intentional instruction is provided (Figure 20.3)? At this point, ignore the form that the mediation takes, that is, whether it is didactic vs. inquiry; systemic vs. decentralized; empirical vs. theoretical; or contextualized vs. decontextualized. Regardless of the form, the possible student learning gains are more hopeful. What student learning outcomes might we predict from this model? I propose that we can make some very specific predictions about learning using this model. First, the depth of student learning will be a measurable reflection of the quality of the mediation and, second, the content of student learning will be a measurable reflection of what the mediation orients the students to learn. Let's take the example of the popular lessons on classification. Depending on how the lessons are designed and mediated, a variety of predictable outcomes is possible. For instance, if students are oriented to learning how to classify plant seeds, we might predict they will know how to distinguish a particular group of seeds, but they will not necessarily know the principle or utility of classification or anything about seeds. Alternatively, if students study classification schemes in order to classify unknown objects (a practice of scientists), we might predict they have the potential to learn the language and rules of classification schemes, and the capacity to debate the uncertainties that arise in their process of identification with those schemes and how uncertainty is resolved in science (Kirch, 2010; Kirch & Siry, 2012). They may still not understand the point of identifying an unknown object or classifying objects as a way of exploring and expanding their knowledge of the world. However, if we can provide students with a theory of classification by revealing the origins and utility of the process, we might predict that students will see the power (and limits) of classification in general. In this case, they will gain a new tool for thinking about the world, which, in turn, will drive

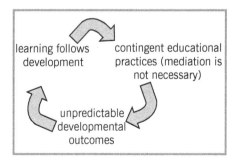

FIGURE 20.2. Consequences of the stage-theory of development and the notion that learning is development or learning lags behind development.

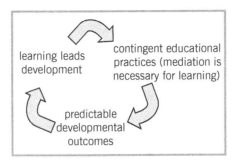

FIGURE 20.3. Consequences of Vygotsky's historical, sociocultural theory of development and the notion that learning can lead development.

their capacity to contribute to scientific practices as they become a scientist themselves. In this model (Figure 20.3), student developmental outcomes are more or less predictable, but the nature of those predictions depends heavily on understanding the instructional practices and theories of development used.

Most school efforts are increasingly dominated by ensuring that students are able to pass standardized tests of basic knowledge in mathematics, English language arts (ELA), and science. While science is tested far less frequently than ELA or math, the tests and the academic standards they claim to measure still exert a type of selective pressure on the curricula implemented in schools. As a researcher of instructional practices and curriculum developer I routinely ask what cognitive tools these standards and tests ask children to learn, and what tools are more or less likely to drive their development forward in a way that is beneficial to the child.

There are no national academic standards for PreK students, but there are plenty of national science content and performance standards in kindergarten and beyond. For the early childhood educator working with children ages 0–4 years, your state or local district may have documents that specify science knowledge and performance standards. These documents tend to vary quite dramatically from place to place, with some placing great emphases on tools for building scientific knowledge (a.k.a. "process skills" or "domain-general knowledge"), others emphasizing facts and ideas that children should know at the end of instruction (a.k.a., "science content knowledge" or "domain-specific knowledge"), and still others emphasizing both. For example, in my hometown (New York City) the Department of Education focuses on "scientific thinking" as a main goal within "Cognitive Development," which includes language and literacy development, mathematical thinking, and social studies. By the end of the PreK year it is expected that children will meet one performance standard; that is, they will "pose questions, seek answers, and develop solutions." In stark contrast to this broad goal, the Illinois State Board of Education detailed 10 knowledge and performance standards, with one to two "benchmarks" for each standard to be met at the end of preschool. All these standards and benchmarks are related to three overarching goals: (1) to understand the processes of scientific inquiry and technological design to investigate questions, conduct experiments, and solve problems; (2) to understand the fundamental concepts, principles, and interconnections of the life, physical, and earth/space sciences (e.g., know and apply concepts that explain how living things function, adapt, and change); and (3) to understand the relationships among science, technology, and society in historical and contemporary contexts.

These sound like laudable goals, but what are the implications for practice? What pedagogical practices has research identified that will make these goals attainable by teachers and learners? Furthermore, how can the required knowledge be learned in such a way that children can transform and use it to make new contributions now and in the future (Blackawton et al., 2011)? To answer these questions, I compare and evaluate two teaching vignettes designed to teach the standard "Know and apply concepts that explain how living things function, adapt and change," articulated in the Illinois preschool standards for science learning. Each vignette illustrates a specific type of instruction: activity-focused teaching and systemic–theoretical teaching (the latter is reviewed in Arievitch & Stetsenko, 2000). Vignette 2 illustrates what is necessary for instruction that is consistent with the model shown in Figure 20.3. Vignette 1, the most common but least effective form of instruction, is consistent with the model shown in Figure 20.2. Vignette 2 is designed to be a model for instruction that uses a theoretical view of teaching–learning that is quite different from all other forms of instruction presented in popular U.S. science curricular guides for early childhood educators. Vignette 2 presents a model consistent with Vygotksy's theory of learning, namely, that instruction should be organized so that learning leads (i.e., causes) the development of the child.

Vignette 1: Butterfly Lessons—An Example of Activity-Focused Teaching

For 2 weeks in the spring, preschool students are taught a series of lessons on butterflies. It is referred to among the teachers as the "Butterfly Unit." The students engage in a variety of activities related to the topic. In science, they observe caterpillars that are delivered to their classroom from a biological specimen clearinghouse. Students draw pictures of each stage and assemble them into a "life cycle" mural, poster, or mobile. Students are provided with diagrams of each stage in the life cycle and study the anatomy of the egg, caterpillar, pupa, and butterfly. They label each anatomical part (head, body, legs, antennae, wings, proboscis, etc.). In language arts, they read *Monarch Butterfly* by Gail Gibbons or *The Very Hungry Caterpillar* by Eric Carle (only two of about 100 books available for preschoolers on butterflies). Each writes a creative story of a butterfly, which he or she illustrates with drawings and paintings created in art. During math, they measure and record the length of the caterpillar over time and count the number of days it takes for the butterfly to complete each cycle stage. When the metamorphosis is complete, the students gather to release the butterflies during a Celebration of Spring party.

What can students learn by the end of such a teaching sequence? They may gain knowledge of the anatomical parts of the butterfly, and an ability to draw and illustrate butterflies. They may leave thinking the development of a butterfly is a mysterious process that moves in identifiable stages from something called an egg, to a larva, to a pupa, then to a butterfly. They may have knowledge of the time it takes the insect to traverse each developmental boundary, and of how large a caterpillar can grow before it reaches the pupal stage. Finally, they may learn that butterflies like release parties (i.e., Celebration of Spring party). These are very specific, highly probable predictions about what students will learn, and it is notable that they are not learning the content of the target learning standard, "Know and apply concepts that explain how living things function, adapt, and change." One might argue, "But the students studied the butterflies and observed the anatomical structures (legs, body, antennae, proboscis, winds, etc.) throughout the entire life cycle. They learned the functions of these parts by observing and recording." This may be true, but students did not engage in activities that were specifically about the function of these body parts or how these body parts evolved or may be evolving (that is what is meant by "change"). For example, what is it like to walk on six legs? How do the wings work? Why do the larva's legs look so different from the butterfly's legs? Why does the caterpillar go through metamorphosis at all? Why doesn't the caterpillar stay a caterpillar? Why doesn't a butterfly just hatch from the egg? How many animals metamorphose?

Another might argue, "The life cycle is a great example of how animals change. When the children compare the life cycle of the butterfly to how their own bodies are growing and changing, it is obvious that they are learning about change." This is true, but this conception of change is so superficial that it has no meaning or purpose. Who cares if animals and people both change over time?

This vignette illustrates a form of instruction that is very common in early childhood (and childhood) science education. It is purposeless, activity-focused teaching, which Wiggins and McTighe (1998) refer to as one of the "twin sins" of instructional design. This vignette also illustrates another common problem, a misalignment between the concept to be taught and the instructional design. The mismatch is so extreme in this case that the instruction does not actually address the intended learning goal. This common practice appears to have its roots in oversimplifications of Piaget's stage theory, and I highly recommend Kathleen Metz's (1995) analysis of this phenomenon in education, and her discussion with Deanna Kuhn (Kuhn, 1997; Metz, 1997).

How can we involve students as researchers and knowledge contributors in their classroom communities and beyond? How can we ensure that students understand the logic embedded in the concepts of change and adaptation? The next example, which illustrates a form of teaching that has yielded impressive gains in student learning, is called systemic–theoretical instruction.

Vignette 2: Change versus Adaptation—An Example of Systemic–Theoretical Teaching

No example I know of (in English) actually designs instruction for this standard using a systemic–theoretical approach to teaching, which is an alternative form of instruction I would like to introduce. The following fictional vignette, however, is an attempt at what might be necessary to fit this category of instruction and meet the goals for learning and development.

The first step in creating this vignette was to establish the origins and functions of the ideas in the target learning standard. To do this I asked and answered the following questions: Where did these ideas of function, adaptation, and change come from? and What intellectual work do these concepts help us do in science? These ideas probably have their modern scientific root in the observation, interpretation, modeling, and explanation of the geological record and biological diversity. Earth has clearly changed over time, and so have the living organisms on earth. Inanimate (nonliving) objects change but do not have the capacity to adapt to a changing environment. The types of changes that a rock undergoes over time are determined, fixed, and predictable by chemical and physical reactions. The types of changes that life can undergo are indeterminate, whether the organism is a microbe, bird, plant, insect, or mammal. Changes that are the product of a dynamic system of interactions between populations and environments are called *adaptations*, and there is no equivalent for nonliving objects. The core concepts underlying the learning goal we have been studying here are: How is change different for living versus nonliving things, and how can change be achieved when there are variations within populations and their interactions with the environment?

Given this understanding, we might begin by introducing students to these ideas and demonstrating how important they are in various familiar situations. Children will have to use variation and interaction as analytical tools to derive the fundamental concept of adaptation as one mechanism driving change of living organisms over time. This is a pretty tall order, but it is the literal interpretation of what is stated in the learning standard we are trying to reach. The reader should be thinking, as I am: Is this a learning goal we want to place in the early childhood standards? Nevertheless, the challenge is before us, so let's see how far we can get with the preschool or kindergarten child in mind before we object and call for a rewrite of the standard. Before beginning this unit, children need to have a firm grasp of the following tools for thinking: time, change, living and nonliving things, and reproduction (living things come from living things).

Proposed Week 1

Introduce children to the idea of change over time for nonliving and living objects and phenomena. The teacher starts by showing a few examples, then has children draw and show their own examples. Examples teachers and students might use include how the amount of light changes over the course of the day (night and day readings and discussions); how the temperature and weather change over the course of the year (regional seasons); how rocks change (erosion); how water changes (freezes, melts, evaporates); how we change over the course of a day (hungry, full, tired, sleepy, awake); how we change over the course of a year (grow taller, learn more); how our pets change; how trees change; how class caterpillars change into butterflies; how organisms in the fossil record changed; and so forth.

Proposed Week 2

Establish students as researchers of the processes of change and adaptation. Activities might include observing and describing what happens when rocks are frozen, rubbed, tumbled, blown on, soaked in water, and placed in running water; and when various combinations of these are applied. During these investigations the research question— Can a rock do anything to avoid these forces?—should be answered by the students. Students can perform more studies on other nonliving (including once-living) objects or move on to explore living objects. The research questions for living things can be much broader and include questions typically found in early childhood science handbooks (e.g., What kinds of adaptions would help an animal avoid being eaten? [camouflage studies]; What kinds of adaptations could help a plant control how much light it gets? [phototropism studies]; What kinds of adaptations would help a plant survive a drought? [seed studies, plant vascular system studies]; and What kinds of adaptations would help insects maximize their access to food sources? [life cycle and seasonal cycle synchrony studies]).

Proposed Week 3

By the end of research, many new questions should have been generated and recorded by the students and teachers, but the following patterns and ideas should be elicited from students in their research presentations: (1) The capacity for adaptation seems to be a property of living things but not nonliving things; (2) it appears that nonliving things cannot do anything to avoid interactions with the environment that cause them to change; and (3) it appears that living things can respond to their environment with behavioral adaptations to meet their required needs for food, water, shelter, and reproduction. For example, to avoid being eaten, animals can hide, flee, and fight predators. In order to eat, animals can chase, stalk, and catch prey. To find food, water, shelter, or a mate, animals can move from one environment to another (plants can also do this in the form of seeds). (4) It appears that some living things are already prepared to respond to their environment with physical or structural adaptations they already possess. For example, within a population of seeds some have a thicker coat than others, which allows these seeds to survive longer periods of drought compared to others in the population; and (5) it appears that living things have ways of repairing themselves if they are damaged, a property that is not shared by nonliving things.

At this point, it is very important to note that the target standard, "Know and apply concepts that explain how living things function, adapt, and change," is most likely referring to the modern evolutionary synthesis of the Darwinian model of evolution through variation and selection with the Mendelian model of inheritance of acquired traits. Our understanding of the mechanisms of function, adaptation, and change, however, are changing and have been for the last half-century as we find and need to explain many examples of non-Mendelian patterns of inheritance. In the past, I taught new teachers to be very careful with their explanations of adaptation and change, lest their students should develop a so-called "Lamarkian" view of evolution. To adequately prepare students for the dynamic work of developing evolutionary theory and for thinking about the complexity of adaptation and change, however, I now recommend handling the discussion in the form of further research projects. Specifically, students will need to follow up the four findings listed above. For example, if we believe the third finding and think that living things can respond to their environment with behavioral adaptations to meet their required needs for food, water, shelter, and reproduction, then we should ask: Where do these behaviors come from? Do living things learn these behaviors from siblings, peers, or parents? Do they reinvent them through their own independent trial-and-error work? Do they inherit these behaviors? In another research project related to the fourth finding, if we think that some living things are prepared to respond to their environment with physical or structural adaptations they already possess, then we must ask: Where did these physical traits come from? Could they disappear? If so, how? How come every organism is not born with these traits that put some in the population at an advantage? It is through these discussions that we cope with the reality that this standard oversimplifies a fundamental concept of biology. Interestingly, instructional approaches that incorporate and promote research like the one described here are one of the easier recourses in the face of the lack of curricular materials currently available.

Assessment

To assess students' understanding and progress, the teacher might show new pictures (or samples) of living and nonliving objects that the students have not studied. Students should be asked to explain their answers to the questions: Is the object in the picture able to adapt? Is the change in each example an adaptation or not? Pictures might include the following:

- Water on a sidewalk/ice on a sidewalk
- A pothole at time point X/a pothole at time point Y
- Building construction/building destruction
- Local animal inside a burrow or nest/local animal outside a burrow or nest

- Seagull catching and opening an oyster
- An octopus fleeing from a predator in front of an ink cloud

Students could work independently or in teams and present their results in various formats.

The instructional design in Vignette 2 fulfills the standard as written in the Illinois state standards for early childhood science used in this fictional example. All of the activities recommended in this systemic–theoretical teaching vignette have appeared in preschool classrooms (or are recommended for them). I have tried to design with the 4- or 5-year-old in mind, but meeting this standard will be a big challenge for teachers because of (1) the lack of instructional designs like the one illustrated in Vignette 2 and (2) the persistence of the widespread belief that activity-based instruction is effective.

I intended Vignette 2 to illustrate what I consider the most desirable form of instruction we currently have at our disposal, systemic–theoretical instruction (Arievitch & Stetsenko, 2000). In this approach learners are oriented toward a clear learning object (e.g., the problem illustrated by the learning standard); they are engaged in reflective performance and supported in the transition from material-dependent manipulation to mental manipulation. Learners are presented the learning object in a way that requires them to understand its origin or genesis (this means that passive demonstrations must be replaced by problem-posing and investigation). Students learn early to "distinguish essential characteristics of objects and phenomena, to form theoretical concepts . . . and use them as cognitive tools in further problem solving" (Arievitch & Stetsenko, 2000, p. 77). In Vignette 2 students learned why adaptation is a unique property of living organisms. Reflective practice in systemic–theoretical instruction requires that students (1) "discriminate among properties of the object or phenomenon" (p. 77; e.g., concept of change for living and nonliving objects), (2) "establish the basic unit of analysis of a particular property" (p. 77; e.g., the ability to adapt to environmental interactions), and (3) "reveal to the child the general rules . . . of how those units are combined into concrete phenomena" (p. 77; e.g., points elicited in the assessment and presentations). The transfer from material manipulation to mental manipulation in systemic–theoretical instruction must occur in the form of "students' active exploration of the studied subject under the guidance of a teacher. The method makes extensive use of symbolic and graphic models to represent basic relations between different properties of the object and the order of their systematic analysis" (p. 78). Symbol systems were not illustrated in this vignette but are discussed in Model 5 in the following section.

In this standards-based era of education, it is imperative to recognize that even though an instructional design claims to be oriented toward a big idea such as "living things function, adapt and change," it does not necessarily mean that a systemic approach has been developed or that the intended learning goal will be achieved. The systemic–theoretical form of instruction (and related versions called *developmental instruction*) was developed by Russian researchers, primarily Piotr Galperin and colleagues, working from the 1930s through the 1960s to test Vygotsky's ideas on the relationships among teaching, learning, and development. More than 800 teaching experiments conducted by these groups still have not been translated and reviewed by U.S. curriculum developers. The consequence is that this instructional model, with its impressive student learning gains, has not permeated our classroom practices, curricula, teacher preparation programs, or professional development efforts. Systemic–theoretical instruction requires that students be positioned as researchers, that they theorize what is happening around and within them (hooks, 1994), that they learn reflective performance and metacognitive activities, and that they discover the purpose of useful cultural tools and are provided opportunities to use these toward individual and collective goals. The opening quote from Terry Eagleton reminds us that the child's perspective is that of a theorist and researcher (which is a perspective aligned with the scientific disciplines).

RESEARCH INTO PRACTICE: DESIGNING EARLY CHILDHOOD SCIENCE INSTRUCTION

Developmental education or developmental instruction is a term currently used to describe the Galperin-inspired instructional approaches designed and tested by many researchers around the world, including Galperin (reviewed in the previous section), Davydov (1991), Aidarova (1982), Hedegaard (2005), Lompscher (1999), Zuckerman (Zuckerman, Chudinova, & Khavkin, 1998), Schmittau (2003), van Oers (2003), and Cobb (2001), among others. All assert that learning can lead development, and all have created and tested instructional approaches and learning pathways for students. These are the models I present to you now because I believe they best illustrate what we mean by systemic–theoretical instruction and how it differs from the "traditional instruction" or "activity-based instruction" commonly used throughout our educational system. Unfortunately, many of the models I am about to introduce address the upper ages of early childhood (grades K–2) and childhood (grades 1–6), and they do not all feature science, but that is why I call them "models." I believe they can serve as useful templates for developing and testing new curricula for use in early childhood science education and, at their core, these examples embody habits and practices relevant to science.

Model 1: Language Arts

What is a letter?: Galperin and Patina's lessons for 5- and 6-year-olds learning the Russian alphabet

How many ways can you teach a child to write the letters of an alphabet? In 1957, Patina published a quasi-experimental study comparing three teaching approaches, and demonstrated that the instructional decisions determined the speed and proficiency of learner work and accomplishment. Patina's systemic–theoretical instruction, based on the research of Vygotsky and designed in collaboration with Galperin, resulted in children who were able to reproduce not only any Russian letter faster than their peers in the other instructional environments but also any contour with high precision, whether it was letters of Latin, Arabic, or Armenian alphabets; blueprints; unfamiliar pictures; or stenographic symbols (reviewed in Arievitch & Stetsenko, 2000; Haenen, 2001). How was it possible?

In one of the comparison research groups, teachers used what Galperin and Patina called "traditional instruction." Patina asked the teachers to teach the alphabet by studying each letter, one at a time. They would show the students the letter and demonstrate how to write the letter while explaining what they were doing out loud. According to Arievitch and Stetsenko's (2000) translation, it sounded like this: "We begin at this point and draw the line downwards until here; then start to curve here to this point; and then turn upwards to approximately this point . . . " (p. 78). In this pedagogical approach, routinely used in the United States today (49 years after Patina's experiment), students were being asked to memorize each letter and how to draw it. Their attention was not

FIGURE 20.4. An example of the instructional tool developed and used by Patina to teach handwriting to elementary school children as well as how to reproduce symbols in general. Based on Haenen (2001).

directed toward the inherent logic of letters (or any written symbol, for that matter). This form of instruction does not acknowledge that there may exist any useful pattern to all written symbols students might encounter. A student's reasonable assumption might be, "This must be the easiest way to learn the alphabet because my teacher wouldn't make me learn how to write letters the most challenging way." Patina demonstrated that this is exactly what the teacher is doing when he or she teaches handwriting by this method.

Patina articulated a method that could make life for the young learner much easier and more interesting. Any letter or written symbol can be described as a pattern of critical points: the beginnings, the ends, the vertices, and the curves. This pattern could be taught to students through the use of one model letter (Figure 20.4). Once students could apply the method to the first letter, they could then generalize to any symbol. Teachers in this experimental working group were asked to teach students how to identify the pattern of critical points in any letter. They used one letter to model this initial lesson in pattern recognition, then, beginning with the second letter, students were asked to identify the critical points, construct the model of the letter, then copy the letter itself on another page. Patina and the teachers found that after the students mastered the set of critical points for any letter, they mastered letter writing quite quickly and were soon able to analyze and reproduce the letter visually, without putting the critical points on the paper first. In tests of transfer, Patina showed that students who had learned to study and analyze the Russian alphabet in this way were able not only to reproduce a variety of abstract symbols but also improved dramatically their solving of problems involving coordination in the plane and their counting ability (Patina, 1957, cited by Arievitch & Stetsenko, 2000).

Children are hungry for explanatory theories. In this case, Patina's teaching method helped them master a complex technical task (writing) quickly and nearly error free. If teachers and students can escape the tedium of learning by rote memorization, as in the traditional approach to writing described at the beginning, then they have more time for deep thinking about the meaning and use of the symbols themselves.

Model 2: Mathematics

Introducing multiplication as unit conversion rather than a special type of addition: Davydov's approach to teaching multiplication for 7-year-olds

Vasily Davydov (1991) noted that multiplication is typically taught immediately after addition and subtraction. Children learn that multiplication is just another way to express the sum of identical addends. He found that the topic was commonly introduced quickly as a particular arithmetical operation, then followed by learning multiplication tables.

In this approach, like the other traditional approaches discussed here, the learner's task is one of acceptance and memorization rather than of discovery and understanding. The learner is provided a very limited view of the purpose of multiplication.

When Davydov investigated the function and purpose of multiplication further, he found that mathematicians described multiplication very differently. According to Lebesgue, the most interesting (and maybe difficult) kind of question that results in multiplication is a "problem in changing the system of units" (Davydov, 1991, p. 30). Davydov realized that the "matter of the *change in units* is most often concealed" from the students, and he devised a new approach to teaching multiplication. As with all the examples in this chapter, I refer the reader to the original report, since I only provide a digest of the work next (Davydov, 1991).

Davydov (1991, p. 34) argued that the first instructional lessons should show the child the "necessity of changing the units of calculation (measurement)." First, the child was asked to perform the calculation (measurement) of an object with the aid of a deliberately small and inconvenient unit. A large jug of water was displayed, and students were asked to figure out how many rabbits could be given water to drink if each rabbit needs only a tiny glassful. The teacher insisted that the task be done even though it looked very difficult or even impossible to the children. Pouring the water from the large jug into the tiny glass was awkward because the jug was hard for the children to move, the water spilled, and the glass was so tiny that it took a very long time to find an answer. Soon the children saw that the task was difficult because it was very inconvenient to use the small glass (the unit with small dimensions). At that point, the teacher asked them to find another method to solve the problem. If the students did not think to use a larger measuring unit (e.g., a mug instead of a tiny glass), the teacher demonstrated the new method of counting that included multiplication. By pouring the water from the jug into the mug, students saw that the teacher could do this six times before the jug was emptied. Students explained that the jug held six "mugfuls" of water, and the teacher reminded them that their task was to find out how many "little glassfuls" of water were in the jar. How could they find out how many little glassfuls there were in the jug just by knowing how many mugfuls there were? If a student did not reveal the method, the teacher did. "We used the mug instead of a little glass—fine, this made our work easier, but we did not find how many glassfuls there are in one of those mugfuls. Can we find that out now? How?" (Davydov, 1991, p. 37). Usually students explained that they would have to pour water into the mug and measure it with the glass. The teacher did this, and the students counted how many glassfuls of water the mug held (e.g., five glassfuls). At this point the teacher was poised to walk the students through the solution.

Eight more lessons followed in which students (1) solved a problem similar to the rabbit water example—they calculated the number of oatmeal servings in the same jar filled with oatmeal; (2) were asked, "What will change in our notation if we have counted with other measures and found there are 20 little glassfuls in the mug and four mugfuls in the whole jar?"; (3) solved a new problem such as calculating the number of bricks in a picture of a brick wall without counting individual bricks; (4) used and learned to read multiplication formulas and symbols as they replaced the words "times" and "equals" with symbols; (5) used their discovered operations to solve a variety of problems with and without being provided with large units; (6) were taught how to compose formulas and graphic representations from text after learning to read multiplication formulas fluently (e.g., "Find how many links are in a paper chain made of eight large pieces, each of which consists of five links"); (7) constructed multiplication tables with the aid of the teacher; and (8) represented the basic laws of multiplication.

At the end of the instructional unit, Davydov gave the children five assignments to test their level of understanding of multiplication and the stability of their mastery after instruction. The results showed students could solve a series of two- and three-dimensional area problems that required them to display increasing amounts of reasoning.

This work done in the 1960s was translated into English in 1991. Recall the traditional method of instruction for multiplication outlined at the beginning of this description, which looks very similar to current U.S. curricula. When students are taught, through this method, that multiplication is just another way to express the sum of identical addends, they are denied a deeper level of understanding that allows them to soar in their problem-solving capacities and appreciation for the history, meaning, and purpose of mathematics.

Model 3: Language Arts

"We are going to study language": Aidarova's literacy lessons for 6- and 7-year-olds learning Russian language arts

In Lada Aidarova's experimental literacy curriculum for 6- to 7-year-olds, she emphasized not only individual operations of grammar, syntax, spelling, and so forth, but also how to learn in general (Aidarova, 1982). She designed her instruction so that her students could form a clear idea of not only what they were going to do, but also *how* and *why* they were going to do it. How was this possible? She asked, "How can children be given the general picture of the activities they are setting out to master [before they have mastered them]?" (p. 126). While this may sound like Aidarova is instructing teachers to introduce the main study topic, it is not the same as telling the students, "We are going to be studying something called grammar this year. Does anyone know what grammar is?" Her idea is much deeper. She presents the larger picture, as well as the how and the why in a brief introductory exchange with students that ends as follows: "You have been going to school for half a year now. You speak Russian and can read and write. Today we are going to take a look at the way our language is built and what laws govern our speech. Beginning today we will have special lessons to *investigate our native language*. Can we do that?" (p. 126, emphasis added).

In this brief introduction, Aidarova set the stage: The children would be investigators of their native language. In an introductory lesson, she worked with students to establish the concept of investigation. First, she began by asking the students to define *investigate* and the children explained that *to investigate* means "people study new things." Next, she asked them what or who is needed for an investigation. In the discussion they generated the following list of necessities: (1) an investigator or "an important person" "with spectacles" "thinking"; (2) a topic of investigation, such as space, plants, nature, ancient people, stones, sea, animals; (3) a means or method of research, including tools or instruments (e.g., telescope, stethoscope, spacesuits, rock hammers); and (4) an ability to distinguish between what is known and what is still unknown.

At the end of the discussion, Aidarova and her students generated a model for learning (investigation), and her students knew what they were going to do, as well as *how* and *why* they were going to do it. They were going to investigate the rules and conventions of their own language to find out what was known and still unknown. Aidarova's students (all in their first year of school and 6–7 years old) were already quite adept at using their language to communicate or to get information. They had not, however, compared different communication episodes and analyzed their characteristics, found criteria to distinguish between different communication episodes, or categorized various elements of communication (verbs, tenses, etc.). "When learning tasks are set for children as research problems, first-graders have to turn the material they know empirically, [from everyday sensory experiences], into a problem to be analyzed for the first time" (Aidarova, 1982, p. 139).

Once the students understood their learning goals and their role as investigators, they researched various questions over the remainder of the year. Through their research they learned the rules and conventions of their own language. Their study questions included the following: What is a word? What is the difference between a word and an object? Is a word the same thing as its model? What jobs does the word perform? What does the word communicate? How can we learn of what the word is built? What orthograms exist in words, and how can we check them? Why do we need synonyms? What is tense form in verbs? What forms of communication exist? Can the same meaning be expressed multiple ways? Can the same form express more than one distinct meaning? How is the same message received by different people? What was the nature of preverbal means of communication?

Based on my experience in elementary school classrooms and the fact that Aidarova's work is not widely referenced in the United States (or English-based research literature), I am confident that this is not how language and literacy instruction is typically approached anywhere in the country. Interestingly, Aidarova's first-grade students would probably have no trouble meeting all of the new Common Core State Standards for Language now required of our students (National Governors Association Center for Best Practices & Council of Chief State School Officers, 2010, pp. 25–27):

- Demonstrate command of the conventions of standard English grammar and usage when writing or speaking.
  - At the end of Aidarova's course, students could "single out all the morphemes in the given words; select and write out words that are similar to the original words in their semantic and formal features: (a) root meaning; (b) prefix form; (c) inflexion form and meaning" (Aidarova, 1982, p. 175) successfully at the beginning of second grade, and every year tested beyond.
- Determine or clarify the meaning of unknown and multiple-meaning words and phrases based on grade 1 reading and content, choosing flexibly from an array of strategies.
  - At the end of Aidarova's course, students could analyze foreign words and translate several Russian words into a corresponding foreign language when they were given the roots of each word in advance and used their method of analysis for unknown words.
- With guidance and support from adults, demonstrate understanding of word relationships and nuances in word meanings.
  - When asked to pick out homonyms and words with homonymous roots, suffixes, and inflections from a given text, or to determine whether there were any synonyms among a given list of words, students understood these tasks without trouble.

Aidarova positioned students as researchers and theorists at the beginning of their study of language. I periodically reread Aidarova's work for inspiration and to remind myself that with creative and bold instruction designed with her model in mind, children thrive when they are productively engaged in learning. While the outstanding performance of her students on myriad assessments over several years is notable, I am most impressed by the questions students posed during language learning: What language did primitive humans speak? How many languages are there in the world? What do various languages have in common, and how are they different? Can we use our scale to analyze all languages? Why are some languages written with pictures and others with letters? These questions indicate that Aidarova fostered student's curiosity and their willingness to conduct research for answers. These young people are consistently positioned to see themselves as capable explorers.

Model 4: Science

Growth versus development: Zuckerman, Chudinova, and Khavkin's science lessons for 7- and 8-year-olds

At the end of Zuckerman and colleagues' (1998) 4-week course designed for teaching and learning the theoretical notions of growth and development, students who participated in an experimental curriculum developed by the authors were able to explain how a given model was an example of growth, development, or a combination of the two. Students were given the following models to evaluate: (1) a picture showing an expanding family— first a married couple, then children arriving, one after another; (2) a graph representing the growth of an elementary school child's reading speed (an image already familiar to all the students); and (3) a picture showing changes in the number of teeth (three smiles were presented—the toothless smile of a baby, a complete set of teeth in a 3-year-old, and the loss of the front teeth in a 6-year-old). All 19 students in the experimental curriculum demonstrated understanding of qualitative and quantitative change (growth and development). How did they do it?

At the end of the monthlong unit on growth and development, which included growing plants, playing games, and solving puzzles, students were expected to reproduce the distinction between two fundamental ideas in science: growth and development. *Growth* was defined as an increase in size, whereas *development* was defined as "an irreversible temporal change of an observed object" that "is both the visible footprint of time and its measure" (Zuckerman et al., 1998, p. 213). The authors asserted that growth can be thought of as a quantitative change, and development can be thought of as a qualitative change. The reason these two concepts were taught together was to help students "construct the notions of life, evolution, turnover of matter and energy, and other fundamental concepts of life and its relation with the environment" (p. 213). Teachers wanted students to understand "the world as permanently changing and transforming" (p. 229). To this end, they developed the following sequence of activities, most of which the reader will probably recognize and has done with students in the past. Notice here, however, how the researchers in this study modified and organized these familiar activities into an instructional sequence that led students to construct very sophisticated understandings of growth and development.

Zuckerman and colleagues (1998) evoked children's curiosity with the game Ten Questions (also known as Twenty Questions and popularized in the United States in the late 1940s as a weekly radio quiz program of the same name). Children found winning strategies quickly (e.g., "Is it alive?" and if alive, "Is it an animal or a plant?"). Ten Questions was followed by a classification game (alive or not alive) to help students become aware of their own understanding of these ideas. Students were given easy objects to classify (earthworms, rocks), as well as provocative objects (wind, echoes, fire, seeds). Once debates arose in the classroom (the authors talked about how to manage debates and support student skepticism), teachers helped students to design and investigate questions that stimulated the most disagreement. For example, "How can we prove that the plant and its seeds are alive?" was reformulated to "Is the seed alive? How can we find the answer to this question?" In response to this question, a student stated a clear, testable hypothesis: "If a new plant can grow out of the bean, it is certainly alive. If not, it is dead." In the process of testing this hypothesis, new questions arose (e.g., "Where did the shoot and root appear from?," "Where does the seedling get the building material for growth?") and more student-designed investigations ensued.

After these practical–exploratory activities, the instructors had provided students a sufficient number of experiences to begin to develop, compare, and theorize concepts of growth and development. First, students were asked to draw the growth of the seed and the plant (as they observed it), then to translate this specific drawing into an abstract symbol that could represent the growth of the plant or any object. For example, the symbol in Figure 20.5a shows growth as a quantitative change. Students soon saw that their plants were not only increasing in size (growth) but also changing in appearance (leaf shape and number). Therefore, a new symbol for development was needed. Figure 20.5b depicts development as a qualitative change. In order to show growth and development linked together, students created a new symbol (Figure 20.5c). (All the symbol systems presented here were adapted from Figure 4 in Zuckerman et al., 1998, p. 219.)

After a series of intermediate games in which students created and evaluated word-to-pictogram relationships, they were placed on teams of two within groups of six players. Each team was given a position to defend: The first team was given the pictogram for growth (Figure 20.5a), the second was given development (Figure 20.5b), and the third was given growth and development linked together (Figure 20.5c). The three teams at the table then sorted a new pile of photo cards into categories "growth only," "development only," or "growth and development linked." The teacher did not overwhelm students with a larger number of photos, but instead supplied a small number of carefully selected, provocative photos that were bound to lead to debates over the possible categorizations. Ultimately, the students had to decide the criteria for categorization, and this led to questions that were used for further student inquiry.

Contrary to activity-based instruction common in early childhood science curriculum guides, students did not focus on learning plant anatomy or a series of facts about plants. Instead, the debates focused on theorizing about growth and development and what these concepts entail at the biological and/or anatomical level. The goal was not to arrive at "right answers"; in fact, there are no clearly right answers for each of these cases. Therefore, teachers and students have to be comfortable with some degree of indeterminacy and focus on being clear about their definitions, assumptions, caveats, evidence, and explanations. For example, members of the group representing the "growth" position claimed that the picture of the baby-to-toddler-to-schoolchild was an example of growth, and the evidence they cited in support of their position was that they knew they themselves were getting taller. They gave an example: When they were 3 years old they could not reach the elevator button, but when they were 7 years old, they could. Members of the group that took the "development" position, however, debated this; they agreed that growth was happening but argued that development was also happening. They also used their personal experience as evidence in support of their position: "My mind has also changed." In addition, those in the "development" position also argued that changes in

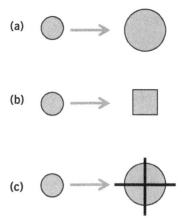

FIGURE 20.5. An example of an instructional tool developed and used by Zuckerman, Chudinova, and Khavkin (1998) to teach elementary school students about growth and development. Figure 20.5a depicts the type of symbol generated by students and teachers to represent growth as quantitative change; Figure 20.5b depicts development as qualitative change; and Figure 20.5c depicts concurrent growth and developmental change.

movement—such as crawling-to-walking-to-running—were also developmental changes because they were qualitative changes. Members of the "growth" position countered that the latter example represented only growth because the motions themselves did not change (babies make all the same motions), and there was only a change (an increase) in the amount of movement. This debate was worthy of a scientific conference presentation. After a whole-class discussion with student presentations, the teacher asked each group to develop a new picture, which they sent to other groups for classification and debate. Therefore, the student discourse in this peer cooperation format continued. In the weeks that followed the teacher introduced and taught a series of lessons related to the reversible and irreversible changes of inorganic and organic matter through the model of the growth and development of an island over a 200-year period, on which I do not elaborate here.

The common activities of growing seeds, having debates, playing games, and solving puzzles take on new meaning and purpose within this context in which students were responsible for learning a very different message (not the parts of a plant or seed, not how to graph and interpret growth under different conditions, and not to observe and describe the changes of specific organisms, but instead to get to the heart of the ways people contribute to the cultural–historical practices of science). One important tool to understand how the world works is to demonstrate how explanatory models provide predictive power. Understanding how one type of bean grows under certain conditions is interesting empirical knowledge that is fun to learn, but it is incomplete without a look at the larger processes and trends such as growth and development that have allowed scientists to generate powerful theories in fields such as evolutionary biology, genetics, astrophysics, and geology. Zuckerman and her colleagues (1998) presented a detailed curriculum plan, provided transcripts of 7- to 8-year-old students' questions, and presented the results of assessments from their quasi-experimental study, all of which serve as strong evidence that these students were thinking scientifically and engaged in learning.

Model 5: Philosophy of Science

What is scientific evidence?: The Scientific Thinker Project and Kirch, Stetsenko, and Milne's lessons on evidence for all ages

There have been repeated calls for learners to be critical thinkers, to participate in argumentation, and to understand the nature of scientific knowledge, but how can we achieve this in elementary school? In the Scientific Thinker Project we used the systemic–theoretical instruction framework to develop a new unit of instruction to teach third- and fourth-grade students concepts of evidence.

As in the other projects presented here, we began by searching for the basic unit of analysis on which we wanted students to focus in order to understand the relationship between scientific knowledge and evidence. This reflection led to the core question for the inquiry, which we believe is appropriate for learners of all ages: What do people mean when they say they *know* something in science? The answer(s) to this core question served as the basis for our curriculum unit design and exploration.

When people say they know something in science, it usually means they have done some type of investigation and have expended considerable intellectual effort to build a useful explanatory model. It means they are confident about an explanation, they believe others should trust what they say, and they believe their claim is testable. It means they can expect to be challenged and called to defend their position, and that their interpretation could eventually be proven "wrong" someday. It probably means they have standards that they meet in order to claim to know something. In addition to these practical implications, when an individual says *I know*, it reveals something about his or her worldview and experiences, maybe even individual motives and goals. In other words, knowledge is inherently personal. In school, learning is a process that can influence whether a child wants to be someone who engages in exploration, explanation, and argumentation (Kirch & Stetsenko, 2012).

The implications of this analysis of evidence and knowledge are that in order for students to rediscover the relationship between scientific inquiry and nature of scientific knowledge, it is essential that they understand the relationship between claims and evidence in the processes of knowledge production. Therefore, students need to become researchers of knowledge. They need to examine how we come to know what we know; when we trust what others say; how we test our knowledge; and when and how we challenge knowledge, defend or challenge a position, and make decisions. We organized the curriculum unit (3 weeks) around these questions, and preliminary analysis of pre- and postintervention tests shows that third- and fourth-grade participants developed sophisticated understandings of evidence and its use in knowledge production. Since we worked with elementary school-age students on this project, I do not elaborate on this unit further here, but instead direct interested readers to one presentation of the work published in *Science and Children* (Kirch & Stetsenko, 2012).

REFLECTIONS AND NEW DIRECTIONS

My organizing principles for this chapter were to keep what we know about early childhood science teaching and learning problematic and to bring to the fore the perspectives of children. The perspectives of children are best captured in systemic–theoretical instruction. Children ask big questions about history and origins. They want to know where things come from, how things work, why things are the way they are (Gallas,

1995; Lipman, Sharp, & Oscanyan, 1980). Research on curriculum development and testing reviewed here illustrates how these types of questions can engage students in deep learning (e.g., What is a mathematical unit? What is language? How do things grow and develop? What does it mean "to know"? How do I make the symbols of my language?).

In order to keep our knowledge about early childhood science pedagogy problematic, I have not reviewed many curricula and teaching methods that do not fall under the systemic–theoretical instruction model, which I currently find the most compelling form of instructional design for PreK–16 education. By providing the reader with tools to analyze science lessons and learning standards, I hope early childhood educators will keep everything problematic and begin (or continue) to revise their teaching to explore the systemic–theoretical model described here. Keeping our everyday practices as educators problematic is a game we can play (in all seriousness) for the sake of pushing our knowledge and understanding of early childhood and childhood science teaching and learning forward. The same can be done for our own personal funds of science-related knowledge— What do I think I know? How sure am I in what I know? What don't I typically ask about the world around me? What assumptions do I make about how things work? How can I learn children's perspectives and learn to look at the world as they might? The point here is that the transformation in early childhood science education I propose relies on educators who demand new curriculum designs and are willing to test them in their own classrooms with colleagues, parents, students, scientists, and educational research partners.

My aim in this chapter is to reach early childhood practitioners and researchers, but because of the lack of science resources for the early childhood educator, this chapter must also be a call for (1) translation of the 800 or so experiments conducted in Russia and reported in Russian during the last 50 years; (2) evaluation of existing early childhood curricula to identify existing examples of systemic–theoretical instruction designs; (3) a national, nonprofit organization dedicated to the production, testing, and dissemination of systemic–theoretical instructional practices through model programs; (4) preparation of future educators and teacher educators to use and test these models; and (5) reexamination of the standards for science learning in light of the types of instructional practices for internalization that we know are necessary for learning.

PROFESSIONAL DEVELOPMENT ACTIVITIES

Keeping knowledge about education problematic is a simple way we achieve many objectives:

- Revise instruction in order to position students as researchers (problem-posers and investigators).
- Ask students to debate and evaluate the evidence, positions, ideas, and theories that develop during their research.
- Conduct action research on teaching and learning with or without an educational researcher partner.
- Address weak or absent evidence for claims about early childhood teaching and learning that come from colleagues, supervisors, media, governments.
- Identify and revise specific personal beliefs, habits, and practices that can impede student learning.

REFERENCES

Aidarova, L. (1982). *Child development and education.* Moscow: Progress Publishers.

Arievitch, I. M., & Stetsenko, A. (2000). The quality of cultural tools and cognitive development: Gal'perin's perspective and its implications. *Human Development, 43*(2), 69–92.

Blackawton, P. S., Airzee, A., Allen, A., Baker, S., Berrow, A., Blair, C., et al. (2011). Blackawton bees. *Biology Letters, 7,* 168–172.

Chapman, M. (1988). *Constructive evolution: Origins and development of Piaget's thought.* New York: Cambridge University Press.

Cobb, P. (2001). Supporting the improvement of learning and teaching in social and institutional context. In S. M. Carver & C. Klahr (Eds.), *Cognition and instruction: Twenty-five years of progress* (pp. 455–478). Mahwah, NJ: Erlbaum.

Davydov, V. V. (1991). Psychological abilities of primary school children in learning mathematics. In L. P. Steffe (Ed.), *Soviet studies in mathematics education* (Vol. 6, pp. 9–85). Reston, VA: National Council of Teachers of Mathematics.

Eagleton, T. (1990). *The significance of theory.* New York: Blackwell.

Gallas, K. (1995). *Talking their way into science: Hearing children's questions and theories, responding with curricula.* New York: Teachers College Press.

Haenen, J. (2001). Outlining the teaching–learning process: Piotr Gal'perin's contribution. *Learning and Instruction, 11,* 157–170.

Hedegaard, M. (2005). *Radical–local teaching and learning: A cultural–historical approach.* Oakville, CT: Aarhus University Press.

hooks, b. (1994). *Teaching to transgress.* New York: Routledge.

Kirch, S. A. (2010). Identifying and resolving uncertainty as a mediated action in science: A comparative analysis of the cultural tools used by scientists and elementary science students at work. *Science Education, 94*(2), 308–335.

Kirch, S. A., & Siry, C. (2012). "Maybe the algae was from the filter": Maybe and similar modifiers as mediational tools and indicators of uncertainty and possibility in children's science talk. *Research in Science Education, 42*(2), 261–280.

Kirch, S. A., & Stetsenko, A. (2012). What does it mean to know?: Third-grade students research using claims and evidence in science. *Science and Children, 49*(9), 44–49.

Kuhn, D. (1997). Constraints or guideposts?: Developmental psychology and science education. *Review of Educational Research, 67*(1), 141–150.

Lewontin, R. C., Rose, S., & Kamin, L. J. (1984). *Not in our genes: Biology, ideology, and human nature.* New York: Pantheon Books.

Lipman, M., Sharp, A., & Oscanyan, F. (1980). *Philosophy in the classroom* (2nd ed.). Philadelphia: Temple University Press.

Lompscher, J. (1999). Activity formation as an alternative strategy of instruction. In J. Engeström, R. Miettinen, & R.-L. Punamäki (Eds.), *Perspectives on activity theory* (pp. 264–281). Cambridge, UK: Cambridge University Press.

Metz, K. (1995). Reassessment of developmental constraints on children's science instruction. *Review of Educational Research, 65*(2), 93–127.

Metz, K. (1997). On the complex relation between cognitive developmental research and children's science curricula. *Review of Educational Research, 67*(1), 151–163.

National Governors Association Center for Best Practices & Council of Chief State School Officers. (2010). Common Core State Standards for English language arts and literacy in history/social studies, science, and technical subjects. Retrieved September 2010 from *www.corestandards.org/assets/ccssi_ela standards.pdf.*

Noë, A. (2009). *Out of our heads: Why you are not your brain, and other lessons from the biology of consciousness.* New York: Hill & Wang.

Schmittau, J. (2003). Cultural–historical activity theory and mathematics education. In A. Kozulin, B. Gindis, V. Ageyev, & S. M. Miller (Eds.), *Vygotsky's educational theory in cultural context* (pp. 225–245). New York: Cambridge University Press.

Stetsenko, A. (2008). From relational ontology to transformative activist stance: Expanding Vygotsky's (CHAT) project. *Cultural Studies of Science Education, 3,* 465–485.

van Oers, B. (Ed.). (2003). *Narratives of childhood: Theoretical and practical explorations for the innovation of early childhood education.* Amsterdam: VU University Press.

Vygotsky, L. S. (1978). *Mind in society: The development of higher psychological processes.* Cambridge, MA: Harvard University Press.

Wiggins, G., & McTighe, J. (1998). *Understanding by design.* Upper Saddle River, NJ: Merrill/ Prentice Hall.

Zuckerman, G. A., Chudinova, E. V., & Khavkin, E. E. (1998). Inquiry as a pivotal element of knowledge acquisition within the Vygotskian paradigm: Building a science curriculum for the elementary. *Cognition and Instruction, 16*(2), 201–233.

CHAPTER 21

SOLVING PROBLEMS
Mathematics for Young Children

Douglas H. Clements
Julie Sarama

Two mothers happen to be visiting this classroom at the same time to determine whether they wish to send their 4-year-olds to the school. The following conversation with the teacher ensues.

MOTHER 1: I am so glad they are playing with blocks and not sitting down learning the three R's. Is that what your program is based on?

MOTHER 2: [before the teacher answers] Well, yes, I guess, but you *do* teach them reading and writing and math at some time, don't you?

TEACHER: I would answer "yes" to both of you, but I think I have to explain myself a bit more. We *do* teach literacy, science, and mathematics, and we do play. And we often do both at the same time.

MOTHER 1: I guess that's OK, if there's not organized group lessons.

TEACHER: Actually, organized lessons—short, fun whole- and small-group activities—are *also* a part of our day. That's why that girl was so articulate about needing a *rectangle block* and knowing that there is a block that is exactly the same length as two unit blocks. Short, focused, intentional activities enrich children's play.

MOTHER 2: But doesn't too much play mean they won't learn enough for school?

TEACHER: We have substantial free play because it really is a way for children to learn to apply and connect both school-type topics *and* develop social–emotional and other skills. But, you know, our focused activities are usually a type of play, too!

WHAT RESEARCH SAYS
ABOUT EARLY MATHEMATICS EDUCATION

Early Mathematics Education of Yesterday

A short historical review of early mathematics supports this teacher's approach. For example, Frederick Froebel invented kindergarten—originally a multiage early childhood education, so he invented present-day preschool into the primary grades. Froebel was a crystallographer. Almost every aspect of his kindergarten was crystallized into beautiful mathematical forms (Brosterman, 1997). Froebel used "gifts" to teach children the geometric language of the universe. Cylinders, spheres, cubes, and other materials were arranged and moved to show geometric relationships. His "occupations" with such materials included explorations (e.g., spinning the solids in different orientations; showing how, for example, the spun cube can appear as a cylinder), puzzles, paper folding, and construction. The triangles were used to teach concepts in geometry. Children covered the faces of cubes with square tiles and peeled them away to show parts, properties, and congruence. Many blocks and tiles were in carefully planned shapes that fit in the grid in different ways. Shapes, rings, and slats were used in plain view on the ever-present grid on the kindergarten table, arranged and rearranged into shifting symmetrical patterns or geometric borders.

Furthermore, structured activities that followed provided learning opportunities in basic arithmetic, geometry, and the beginning of reading. For example, the cubes children had made into the chairs and stoves would be made into a geometric design on the grid etched into every kindergarten table, and later laid into two rows of four each and expressed as "4 + 4." In this way, connections were key: The "chair" became a beautiful geometric design, which then became a number sentence.

Early Mathematics Education Today

Unfortunately, present-day early childhood settings often do not include this type of rich mathematics. Indeed, not much math learning at all happens in too many early childhood settings. As a result, math achievement of entering first graders is not substantially higher than that of entering kindergartners (Van den Heuvel-Panhuizen, 1996). Less than 3% of the preschoolers' day is spent on topics such as literacy and mathematics, and less than half of the children experienced these at all (Winton & Buysse, 2005). Kindergarten and first-grade teachers may spend too much time teaching children things they already know, and not enough time exploring more challenging mathematics, including problem solving (details on these and other findings can be found in Clements & Sarama, 2009a; Clements & Sarama, 2012a, 2012b).

Helping Students Learn Mathematics

What approaches show promise for teaching children challenging but achievable mathematics? One influential approach is to develop *learning trajectories* for specific domains in mathematics. As students learn about a mathematical topic, they progress through increasingly sophisticated *levels of thinking*. At each level, children can solve a new type of problem. These levels form a *developmental progression*. As an example of the significance of such research-based learning trajectories, authors of the *Common Core State Standards for Mathematics* (National Governors Association & Council of Chief State School Officers, 2010) started by writing brief learning trajectories for each major topic. These were used to determine what the sequence would be and were "cut" into grade-level specific standards.

A complete learning trajectory has three parts: a goal, a developmental progression of levels of thinking, and associated instructional activities. To attain a certain mathematical competence in a given topic or domain (the *goal*), students progress through several levels of thinking (the *developmental progression*), aided by tasks and experiences (the *instructional activities*) designed to help them attain the next level of thinking (Clements & Sarama, 2004). For example, one goal for young students is to learn to be competent counters. The developmental progression describes a typical trajectory that students follow in developing understanding and skill in counting. The first column in Figure 21.1 describes several levels of thinking in the counting learning trajectory. The second column provides an example of student behavior and thinking for each level.

The third, right-most, column in Figure 21.1 provides an example instructional task, matched to each of the levels of thinking in the developmental progression. These tasks are designed to help students move to a more advanced level of understanding by learning the ideas and skills needed to achieve that level of thinking; that is, as teachers, we can use these tasks to promote students' growth from one level to the next. More complete learning trajectories provide multiple illustrations of tasks for each level (e.g., see Clements & Sarama, 2009a), but the lists are by no means exhaustive because so many approaches are possible.

Teaching Use of Learning Trajectories

Learning trajectories' instructional tasks might offer a "sketch" of a curriculum—a sequence of activities. However, research suggests that they can and should offer more. They should support teachers' use of *formative assessment*—the ongoing monitoring of student learning to inform and guide instruction. Several reviews indicate that formative assessment is an effective teaching strategy (National Mathematics Advisory Panel, 2008; Shepard, 2005). However, the strategy is of no use unless teachers can accurately assess "where students are" in learning a mathematical topic and know how to guide them to the next level. Learning trajectories help to define the mathematical content that teachers have to know. The developmental progressions give teachers a tool to understand the levels of thinking at which their students are operating and provide direction concerning the *next* level of thinking that students should learn. Then the matched instructional tasks provide guidance as to what types of educational activities support that learning and help to explain why these activities would be particularly effective. Such knowledge helps teachers be more effective professionals. In the next section, we look at ways to put this all into practice.

RESEARCH INTO PRACTICE

Key to the use of formative assessment is knowing what standards or goals we are trying to reach, where the students are starting, and how to help them move from there to the goal. Notice that these three formative assessment questions align with the three components of learning trajectories, as follows:

Formative Assessment Questions	*Learning Trajectories' Components*
1. Where are you trying to go?	*The goal*—Describes the mathematical concepts, structures, and skills.
2. Where are you now?	*The developmental progression*—Helps to determine how the children are thinking now and on the "next step."
3. How can you get there?	*The instructional activities*—Provide tasks linked to each level of the developmental progression that are designed to engender the kind of thinking that forms the next level. Suggests feedback for specific errors.

Developmental Progression	Example Behavior	Instructional Tasks
Reciter *Verbal.* Verbally counts with separate words, not necessarily in the correct order.	Count for me. "One, two, three, four, six, seven."	Provide repeated, frequent experience with the counting sequence in varied contexts. *Count and Race.* Students verbally count along with the computer (up to 50) by adding cars to a racetrack one at a time.
Corresponder Keeps one-to-one correspondence between counting words and objects (one word for each object), at least for small groups of objects placed in a line.	Counts: ☐ ☐ ☐ ☐ "1, 2, 3, 4" But may answer the question "How many?" by recounting the objects or naming any number word.	*Kitchen Counter.* Students click on objects one at a time while the numbers from 1 to 10 are counted aloud. For example, they click on pieces of food and a bite is taken out of each as it is counted.
Counter (Small Numbers) Accurately counts up to five objects in a line and answers the **"How many?" question** with the last number counted. When objects are visible, and especially with small numbers, begins to understand cardinality.	Can you count these? ☐ ☐ ☐ ☐ "1, 2, 3, 4 . . . four!"	*How Many?* Tell students you have placed as many cubes (3, hidden) in your hand as you can hold. Ask them to count with you to see how many. Take out one at a time as you say the number word (so, when they say "two" they *see* two). Repeat the last counting number, "three," gesturing in a circular motion to all the cubes, and say, "That's how many there are in all." Challenge students to see how many they can hold during free time.
Counter and Producer (10+) Counts and counts out objects accurately to 10, then beyond (to about 30). Keeps track of objects that have been counted, even in different arrangements. Gives next number (usually to 20's or 30's). Separates the decade and the ones part of a number word, and begins to relate each part of a number word/numeral to the quantity to which it refers.	Counts a scattered group of 19 chips, keeping track by moving each one as it is counted.	*Road Race.* Students identify numbers of sides (three, four, or five) on polygons and move forward a corresponding number of spaces on a game board.

(continued)

FIGURE 21.1. Selected levels from the learning trajectory for counting. All figures adapted from Clements and Sarama (2009a). Copyright 2009 by Routledge. Adapted by permission.

Developmental Progression	Example Behavior	Instructional Tasks
Counter from N (N + 1, N − 1) *Verbal and Object.* Counts verbally and with objects from numbers other than 1 (but does not yet keep track of the *number* of counts).	Asked to "count from 5 to 8," counts: "5, 6, 7, 8!" Immediately determines numbers just after or just before. Asked, "What comes just before 7?" says, "Six!"	*One More!* Have the children count two objects. Add one and ask, "How many now?" Have children count on to answer. (Count from 1 to check the first time, or 2.) Add another, and so on, until they have counted to 10. Start again with a different starting amount. When children are able, warn them, "Watch out! I'm going to add more than one sometimes!" and sometimes add two, and eventually three, to the group. If children seem to need assistance, have a puppet model the strategy; for example, "Hmmm, there's fooour, one more makes it five, and one more makes it six. Six, that's it!"
Counter on Using Patterns *Strategy.* Keeps track of a few counting acts, but only by using numerical pattern (spatial, auditory, or rhythmic).	"How much is 3 more than 5?" Student feels 3 "beats" as counts, "5 . . . 6, 7, 8!"	*How Many in the Box Now?* Have the student count a small set of cubes. Put them in the box and close the lid. Ask the student how many cubes you are hiding. Then add one and ask again. When they answer, act incredulous, saying, "How do you *know* that? You can't even see them!" Have students explain their strategy, and count with them to emphasize the auditory rhythm. Repeat, adding 1, 2, and even 3 as they succeed.
Counter-on Keeping Track *Strategy.* Keeps track of counting acts numerically, first with objects, then by "counting counts." Counts up 1 to 4 *more* from a given number.	"How many is 3 more than 6?" "Six . . . 7 [puts up a finger], 8 [puts up another finger], 9 [puts up third finger]. 9." "What is 8 take away 2?" "Eight . . . 7 is one, and 6 is two. 6."	*Easy as Pie.* Students add two numerals to find a total number (sums of 1 through 10), and then move forward a corresponding number of spaces on a game board. The game encourages students to "count on" from the larger number (e.g., to add 3 + 4, they would count "4 . . . 5, 6, 7!").
Counter-Forward and Back *Strategy.* Counts "counting words" (single sequence or skip counts) in either direction. Recognizes that decades sequence mirrors single-digit sequence. Switches between sequence and composition views of multidigit numbers easily.	"What's 4 less than 63?" "62 is 1, 61 is 2, 60 is 3, 59 is 4, so 59." "What is 15 more than 28?" "2 tens and 1 ten is 3 tens. 38, 39, 40, and there's 3 more, 43."	*Math-O-Scope.* Students identify numbers (representing values that are 10 more, 10 less, 1 more, or 1 less than a target number) within the hundreds chart to reveal a partially hidden photograph.

FIGURE 21.1. *(continued)*

Using Learning Trajectories: An Example from Counting

Let's use an example from counting. We start by understanding the goal, the mathematics of counting. Initially, this may not seem necessary, but even "simple" mathematics is based on fundamental, deep ideas, and understanding these ideas explicitly helps us be effective teachers of mathematics.

The Goal

Here we take a brief look only at the mathematics of counting (for more, see National Research Council, 2009; Wu, 2011). Numbers help us solve problems by describing order or telling us specifically "how many" (e.g., 3 apples) or "how much" (1½ cups of applesauce) of something. The counting numbers can be thought about in two different ways. They form an ordered list, and they describe cardinality—"how many-ness." The idea of one-to-one correspondence connects these two concepts and helps to explain what cardinality is.

Numbers as a list can be used to describe order. Counting to anything but the smallest numbers requires a system to keep track. Our Hindu–Arabic numeral system is based on two ideas (Wu, 2011): (1) There are only 10 symbols called digits (0, 1, 2, 3, 4, 5, 6, 7, 8, 9); (2) all possible counting numbers are created by using these 10 digits in different places—the concept of place value. Any number, then, is the product of the "face" (digit) and the "place"; for example, 2,593 is 2 thousands, 5 hundreds, 9 tens, and 3 ones. When we count, we get up to 9, then signify the next number with the digit 1 in the tens place and the digit 0 as a "placeholder" in the ones place: 10. We have to work through 10 digits in the ones place, 10 to 19, when we run out again, so we put 2 in the tens place: 20. So 21 means we cycled through 0 to 9 twice, so we knew we counted 20 times plus one more time.

To use counting to tell how many or how much also requires the idea of one-to-one correspondence. Number is an abstraction—"two" describes how many eyes most people have, how many in a pair, how many wheels on bicycles, and so forth. This is so because every member in each of these collections can be matched in one-to-one correspondence with exactly one member of each of the other collections. For example, each shoe in a pair can be matched exactly with one of the wheels of a bicycle (so that no two shoes are matched with the same wheel, no two wheels are matched with the same shoe, and no shoes or wheels are left unmatched). Every set that can be similarly matched is a "set of two." This is the fundamental idea of cardinal number. (Note that one-to-one correspondence is an important concept in mathematics in its own right. It can be used to compare sets not only in the early years but also in the most advanced mathematics. For more details on concepts of math, see Clements and Sarama [2009a], the National Research Council [2009], and Wu [2011].)

Counting is a way to determine and label the number in any such collection. Counting makes a one-to-one correspondence between each member of any collection and the list of number words. See the example for the "Corresponder" level in Figure 21.1. Note also that the counting correspondence can be carried out in many different ways, starting at the left or the right, or in any other way, as long as an exact one-to-one correspondence is maintained.

And that is not the last of it, although the next idea is often underemphasized in classrooms. The last counting word used specifies the total number of items in a collection. Understanding and using this idea of numbers as an ordered list and a description of cardinality defines the next level of thinking in the learning trajectory; see the "Counter

(Small Numbers)" level in Figure 21.1. In this way, counting is a way to represent the abstract idea that all collections containing the same number of objects share a descriptive characteristic. When they are counted, the last counting word will be the same for all of them.

Another fundamental idea is that the next counting word tells how many units are in a collection that has *one more* unit. This links the higher levels of counting in Figure 21.1 to arithmetic, an idea to which we will return.

For now, that's our goal: Object counting with understanding.

The Developmental Progression

To understand the level(s) at which children are operating, we can use the developmental progression from the learning trajectory for counting presented in Figure 21.1. To assess where children are operating, teachers might use simple assessment tasks as described in the "Example Behavior" column in Figure 21.1. When asked to "count for me," does the child articulate each counting word, in order? The numbers "thirteen" and "fifteen," and the teens in general, are always challenging because of their atypical naming, so teachers can not only record any mistakes they hear but also see whether children see the *pattern* in the number system when they get to 20 and beyond. (A short note: This is why we call this competence "verbal counting" rather than "rote counting." The term *rote* may imply "mindless" learning, but knowing the numbers denote order and magnitude, even if only intuitively, and that there is a pattern or system involved, is decidedly not mindless.)

Let's say that a girl who just turned 4 years of age did well on this, counting past 10. We now have to check her use of one-to-one correspondence. First we use a simple situation of asking the child to count five objects laid out in a straight line. If the child can do this accurately, demonstrating one-to-one correspondence, we tentatively consider her to be at the Corresponder level or above. To check the next level, we ask, "How many are there?" Children at the Corresponder level often recount the objects rather than answering "five." A similar check for this level involves covering the objects and asking the question.

If the child quickly and confidently answers "five," we can lay out more objects, and eventually lay out objects not structured into a straight line (see the "Counter and Producer (10+)" level in Figure 21.1). Of course, with older students, one might use tasks further along the developmental progression as a starting point, working "up and down" the levels to ascertain where the student is.

Gathering information from structured interview assessments, such as those just described, near the beginning of the school year allows teachers to develop a clear picture of the skills and content knowledge of both the class and each individual, across multiple learning trajectories that are important for children in that age group. If teachers prefer, structured assessments are available that can aid that process. For example, the TEAM (Tools for Early Assessment in Math; Clements, Sarama, & Wolfe, 2011) is an interview tool that teachers administer using a flipbook, manipulatives, and a laptop or iPad. The teacher interacts with each child individually and records his or her responses and the strategies used to arrive at those responses. Thus, the teacher can see whether children understand and can explain their methods—critical goals for early mathematics learning (Fuson, 2004). At the conclusion of the assessment, the teacher automatically receives profiles of individual children, including summary scores and information (correctness and strategies) for each trajectory, as well as a report on the class as a whole. Finally, the TEAM report also prescribes instructional activities for each child, connected to a variety of curricula. Teachers are encouraged to readminister the TEAM midyear and at the end of the year.

The Instructional Tasks

The instructional tasks within the learning trajectories are, of course, not the only way to guide students through the levels of thinking and understanding. However, there is research evidence that in some cases certain tasks or sequences of activities are especially effective. For example, what if the child being assessed is at the "Corresponder" level only, unable to answer the "How many?" question. That child needs to develop the cardinality concept of the "Counter (Small Numbers)" level. Research suggests that one effective educational strategy is to help children connect their skills in counting with their skills in *subitizing*—their ability to recognize the number in a very small collection quickly, without counting. Many research-based approaches specifically guide and encourage students to develop the ability to see a small collection, such as three blocks, and tell almost instantly how many objects are in it (Clements & Sarama, 2009b). Because cardinality is built into subitizing, combining the two processes—subitizing and counting—is effective in encouraging the development of cardinality.

So, returning to our child who needs to develop cardinality in counting, we can see how the simple activity listed in Figure 21.1 (*How Many?*) builds, connects, and applies these competencies; that is, as children count with the teacher, who shows the blocks one at a time, saying the number word aloud, they *see*, and thus subitize, 1 when they say "one," and *see* 2 when they say "two," and so forth. This can imbue counting with quantitative (cardinal) meaning. At the end, repeating the last counting number "three," gesturing in a circular motion to all the cubes, and saying, "That's how many there are in all" emphasize that cardinal meaning. Again, many other activities may be used, but research suggests activities that similarly connect students' counting and subitizing will be particularly effective.

Similarly, in teaching students the "Counter on Using Patterns" level, the *How Many in the Box Now?* activity connects competencies from a previous level of the counting trajectory (e.g., count up starting at any number in the Counter from N (N + 1, N − 1) level) to other subitizing abilities (*rhythmic* subitizing—that is, feeling the "beat" of small numbers, e.g., "tah! tah! tah!" as 3) to the new activity of counting on to solve arithmetic problems. Research has shown that these competencies, when well developed, can be elicited by the teachers to support learning the strategy of counting on in a meaningful way.

In other cases, instructional tasks are simply illustrations of the broad type of activity that would be appropriate to encourage a student to reach that level of thinking. The highest level in Figure 21.1, for example, provides a worthwhile activity, but it is simply one of numerous problems that a teacher might present to encourage change in a student's level of thinking. Teachers need to use a variety of pedagogical strategies in teaching the content, such as presenting the tasks, guiding students in completing and practicing them, and orchestrating discussions and extensions. Teachers find it useful to observe students' answers and also their strategies, asking themselves the following specific questions (Shepard, 2005):

- What is the key error?
- What is the probable reason the student made this error?
- How can I guide the student to avoid this error in the future?

As an example of applying both the learning trajectory and these specific questions, a teacher working with a child at the "Reciter" level, working toward the "Corresponder" level, might note exactly if and how the child stumbles on maintaining one-to-one correspondence. If the key error is occasionally missing or double-counting an item, research indicates that the most probable reason is simple "rushing" and lack of appreciation of the importance of maintaining exact correspondence. To guide the child, emphasize the importance of accuracy and encourage the child to count slowly and carefully to "count each item exactly once" (Baroody, 1996). If that doesn't work, say, "Count with me," and gently guide the child's hand as you touch each item and say the correct counting word together, slowly walking the child through the counting. If, instead, the key error seems to be losing one-to-one correspondence only when objects are not arranged in a straight line, then the probable reason is the lack of a keeping-track strategy. To guide the child, suggest the strategy of physically moving items to a different pile or location. If they are not movable, make a verbal plan with the child, such as "Go from top to bottom. Start from the top and count every one"—then do so together (Baroody, 1996; Clements & Sarama, 2007). In difficult keeping-track situations, such as when objects are arranged in a circle, the specific guidance might be to stop children immediately when they try to recount previously counted objects and tell them that they counted that item already. Suggest that they start on an item they can remember (e.g., one at the "top" or "the corner" or "the blue one"—whatever makes sense in the activity; if there is no identifier, highlight an item in some way, for example, by placing a small object next to the starting item). These examples show how asking the three specific questions about errors helps teachers become considerably more effective (for more on these and other suggestions, see Clements & Sarama, 2007, 2009a).

Using Learning Trajectories in Teaching Arithmetic

Our second example is from the trajectories of addition and subtraction. A study of textbooks in California showed the importance of teaching root concepts and meaningful strategies for arithmetic, not simply "facts" (Henry & Brown, 2008). The learning trajectory should therefore include root knowledge, strategies, and skills.

The Goal

Mathematically, addition can be viewed as an extension of counting; that is, we can define addition in terms of counting (National Research Council, 2009; Wu, 2011). The *sum* 4 + 7 is the whole number that results from counting 7 numbers starting at 4, that is, 4, 5, 6, 7, 8, 9, 10, 11. As tedious as it would be to solve this way, the sum 56 + 895 is the number that results from counting 895 numbers starting at 56. In general, for any two whole numbers a and b, the sum $a + b$ is the number that results by counting b more numbers, starting at the number a (Wu, 2011). We can also skip count. If we skip count by 10's *ten times*, we have 100. Similarly, skip counting by 100's *ten times* results in 1000, and so forth. Thus, 47 + 30 can be solved by skip counting by 10s—47 . . . 57, 67, 77.

From the earliest levels, arithmetic depends on two properties: (1) the *associative law of addition* states that $(a + b) + c = a + (b + c)$, allowing mental addition strategies such as 5 + 3 + 7 = 5 + (3 + 7) = 5 + 10 = 15; (2) the *commutative law of addition* states that $a + b = b + a$; thus, an efficient mental strategy is 2 + 34 = 34 + 2, and so, 34, 35, 36. Young children use these properties, usually only intuitively, although many are explicitly aware of using commutativity in their counting-based strategies by starting to count at the larger number.

Subtraction does not follow these properties. Subtraction is defined mathematically as the inverse of addition; that is, subtraction is the *additive inverse* $-a$ for any a, such that $a + -a = 0$. Or, for $9 - 5$, the difference is the number that, when added to 5, results in 9. So, $c - a = b$ means that b is the number that satisfies $a + b = c$. In this example, $5 + 4 = 9$, so $9 - 5 = 4$. Another way of saying this is that because we know that subtraction and addition are inverses of each other, "$9 - 5 = \_\_$" means the same as $9 = 5 + \_\_$.

Subtraction can also be intuitively understood through counting: The *difference* $9 - 5$ is the whole number that results from counting *backwards* 5 numbers starting at 9—9 . . . 8, 7, 6, 5, 4. So, we have discussed two meanings. First, the difference $(9 - 5)$ is the whole number that results from counting backwards 5 numbers starting at 9—the "take away" notion of subtraction. Second, we saw that asking, "What is 9–5?" means the same as "What number added to 5 gives 9?" These notions are equivalent and may feel natural to us. To young children, seeing them all as the "same thing" takes time and repeated experience with many different examples.

This leads us to another important aspect of the goal of teaching early arithmetic. Children should learn to solve different kinds of problems. Of course, some problems are more difficult, simply because they involve larger numbers, and this is an important consideration. (Problems can be more difficult even with the larger *single-digit* numbers. This difficulty is, unfortunately, often much greater than it should be because too many curricula and teachers provide far more practice on problems with smaller digits and neglect the larger single-digit numbers. Teachers should ensure that students receive more balanced experiences.)

Beyond the size of the number, however, it is the *type*, or *structure* of the word problem that determines its difficulty. Type depends on the *situation* and the *unknown*. There are four different situations, shown in the four rows of Figure 21.2. For each of these categories, three quantities play different roles in the problem, any one of which can be the unknown. In some cases, such as the *Part unknown* of "Part–Part–Whole" problems, there is not a real difference between the roles, so this does not affect the difficulty of the problem. In others, such as the *Result unknown, Change unknown,* or *Start unknown* of "Join" problems, the differences in difficulty are large. *Result unknown* problems are easy, *Change unknown* problems are moderately difficult, and *Start unknown* problems are the most difficult. This is due in large part to the increasing difficulty children have in modeling, or "act outing," each type.

In summary, a main *goal* of the counting-based addition and subtraction learning trajectory is that children learn to solve arithmetic problems of the types in Figure 21.2. Addition and subtraction can be understood though counting, and that is one way children come to learn more about these arithmetic operations (for discussions of other ways, including place value, see Clements & Sarama, 2009a; Sarama & Clements, 2009).

The Developmental Progression

The second component of the learning trajectory is the developmental progression. The two major influences on these levels of thinking have already been discussed: the level of counting competence (along with other number knowledge, such as subitizing) and the type of problem (Figure 21.2). Selected levels for this learning trajectory are shown in the first column in Figure 21.3. Children develop increasingly sophisticated counting

Category	Start/Part Unknown	Change/Difference Unknown	Result/Whole Unknown
Join An action of joining increases the number in a set.	*Start unknown* □ + 6 = 11 Al had some balls. Then he got 6 more. Now he has 11 balls. How many did he start with?	*Change unknown* 5 + □ = 11 Al had 5 balls. He bought some more. Now he has 11. How many did he buy?	*Result unknown* 5 + 6 = □ Al had 5 balls and gets 6 more. How many does he have in all?
Separate An action of separating decreases the number in a set.	*Start unknown* □ − 5 = 4 Al had some balls. He gave 5 to Barb. Now he has 4. How many did he start with?	*Change unknown* 9 − □ = 4 Al had 9 balls. He gave some to Barb. Now he has 4. How many did he give to Barb?	*Result unknown* 9 − 5 = □ Al had 9 balls and gave 5 to Barb. How many does he have left?
Part–part–whole Two parts make a whole, but there is no action—the situation is static.	*Part unknown* [10 / ▢	6] 10 / (□ , 6) Al has 10 balls. Some are blue, 6 are red. How many are blue?	*Part unknown* [10 / 4	▢] 10 / (4 , □) Al has 10 balls; 4 are blue, the rest are red. How many are red?	*Whole unknown* [▢ / 4	6] □ / (4 , 6) Al has 4 red balls and 6 blue balls. How many balls does he have in all?
Compare The numbers of objects in two sets are compared.	*Smaller unknown* [7 / ▢	2] Al had 7 balls. Barb has 2 fewer balls than Al. How many balls does Barb have?	*Difference unknown* [7 / 5	▢] Al has 7 balls. Barb has 5. How many more does Al have than Barb?	*Larger unknown* [▢ / 5	2] Al has 5 balls. Barb has 2 more than Al. How many balls does Barb have?

FIGURE 21.2. Addition and subtraction problem types.

strategies to solve increasingly difficult problem types. For example, most children initially use a counting-all procedure. At the "Find Result +/−" level, given a situation of 6 + 2, such children count out objects to form as set of 6 items, then count out 2 more items, and finally count all those and say "8." Children use such counting methods to solve story situations as long as they understand the language in the story.

After children develop such methods, they eventually curtail them in favor of other methods. On their own, children as young as 4 or 5 years old may start "counting-on," solving the previous problem by counting, "Siiiiix . . . seven, eight. Seven!" The elongated pronunciation may be substituting for counting the initial set one-by-one. It is *as if* they counted a set of 6 items.

Children then move to the *counting-on-from-larger* strategy, which is preferred by most children once they invent it. Presenting problems such as 3 + 45, where the most "counting-on" work is saved by reversing the problem, often prompts children to start counting with the 45. See the "Counting Strategies +/−" level in Figure 21.3.

Developmental Progression	Example Behavior	Instructional Tasks
Small Number +/– Finds sums for joining problems up to 3 + 2 by counting-all with objects.	Asked, "You have 2 balls and get 1 more. How many in all?" Counts out 2, then counts out 1 more, then counts all 3: "1, 2, 3, 3!".	*Join Result unknown or Separate Result unknown* (take-away) problems, numbers < 5 (see Figure 21.1). "You have 2 balls and get 1 more. How many in all?" *Finger Word Problems.* Tell children to solve simple addition problems with their fingers. Use very small numbers. Children should place their hands in their laps between each problem. To solve the problems above, guide children in showing 3 fingers on one hand and 2 fingers on the other and reiterate: How many is that altogether? Ask children how they got their answer and repeat with other problems.
Find Result +/– Finds sums for joining (if you had 3 apples and get 3 more, how many do you have in all?) and part–part–whole (if there are 6 girls and 5 boys on the playground, how many children are there in all?) problems by direct modeling, counting-all, with objects. Solves take-away problems by separating with objects.	Asked, "You have 2 red balls and 3 blue balls. How many in all?" Counts out 2 red, then counts out 3 blue, then counts all 5. Asked, "You have 5 balls and give 2 to Tom. How many do you have left?" Counts out 5 balls, takes away 2, then counts remaining 3.	*Word Problems.* Children solving all the previous problem types using manipulatives or their fingers to represent objects. For *Separate, Result unknown (take-away),* "You have 5 balls and give 2 to Tom. How many do you have left?" Children might count out 5 balls, then take away 2, and then count remaining 3. For *Part–part–whole, Whole unknown* problems, they might solve, "You have 2 red balls and 3 blue balls. How many in all?" *Places Scenes (Addition)—Part–part–whole, Whole unknown problems.* Children play with toy on a background scene and combine groups. For example, they might place 4 tyrannosaurus rexes and 5 apatosauruses on the paper, then count all 9 to see how many dinosaurs they have in all.
Counting Strategies +/– Finds sums for joining (you had 8 apples and get 3 more . . .) and part–part–whole (6 girls and 5 boys . . .) problems with finger patterns and/or by counting-on.	Counting-on. "How much is 4 and 3 more?" "Fourrrrr . . . five, six, seven [uses rhythmic or finger pattern to keep track]. Seven!" Counting-up-to may solve missing addend (3 + __ = 7) or compare problems by counting-up (e.g., counts "4, 5, 6, 7" while putting up fingers), then counts or recognizes the 4 fingers raised.	*Teaching Counting-On Skills.* If children need assistance to use counting-on or do not spontaneously create it, explicitly teach the subskills. 1. Lay out the problem with numeral cards (e.g., 5 + 2). Count out objects into a line below each card. 2. Point to the last object of the first addend. When child counts that last object, point to numeral card and say, "See, this is 5 also. It tells how many dots there are here." 3. Solve another problem. If children counts the first set starting with one again, interrupt them sooner and ask what number they will say when they get to the last object in the first set. Emphasize that it will be the same as the numeral card.

(continued)

FIGURE 21.3. Selected levels from the learning trajectory for counting-based arithmetic.

Developmental Progression	Example Behavior	Instructional Tasks
Counting Strategies +/– *(continued)*	Asked, "You have 6 balls. How many more would you need to have 8?" Says, "Six, seven [puts up first finger], eight [puts up second finger]. Two!"	4. Point to first dot of set and say (e.g., for 5 + 2) "See, there are fiiiiive here, so this one (exaggerated jump from last object in the first set to first object in the second set) gets the number *six*. 5. Repeat with new problems. If children need more assistance, interrupt their counting of the first set with questions: "How many are here (first set)? So *this* (last of first) gets what number? And what number for *this* one (first of second set)"? *Double-Compare.* Students compare sums of cards to determine which sum is greater. Encourage children to use more sophisticated strategies, such as counting-on. *Join Result unknown* and *Part–part–whole, Whole unknown.* "How much is 4 and 3 more?" "See, there are 5 here, so this one (exaggerated jump from last object in the first set to first object in the second set) gets the number *six*. Repeat with new problems. If children need more assistance, interrupt their counting of the first set with questions: "How many are here (first set)? So *this* (last of first) gets what number? And what number for *this* one (first of second set)"?
Deriver +/–: Uses flexible strategies and derived combinations (e.g., "7 + 7 is 14, so 7 + 8 is 15") to solve all types of problems. Includes Break-Apart-to-Make-Ten (BAMT). Can simultaneously think of 3 numbers within a sum, and can move part of a number to another, aware of the increase in one and the decrease in another.	Asked, "What's 7 plus 8?" thinks: $7 + 8 \rightarrow 7 + [7 + 1] \rightarrow [7 + 7] + 1 = 14 + 1 = 15$. Or, using BAMT, thinks, $8 + 2 = 10$, so separate 7 into 2 and 5, add 2 and 8 to make 10, then add 5 more, 15.	*All types* of single-digit problems. *Tic-Tac-Total.* Draw a tic-tac-toe board and write the numbers 1 to 10. Players take turns crossing out one of the numbers and writing it on the board. Whoever makes 15 first wins (Kamii, 1985). 21. Play cards, where Ace is worth either 1 or 11 and 2 to 10 are worth their values. Dealer gives everyone 2 cards, including herself. On each round, each player, if sum is less than 21, can request another card, or "hold." If any new card makes the sum more than 21, the player is out. Continue until everyone "holds." The player whose sum is closest to 21 wins.

FIGURE 21.3. *(continued)*

Thus, counting skills—especially sophisticated counting skills—play an important role in developing competence with arithmetic. Counting easily and quickly predicts arithmetic competence in kindergarten and later. Knowing the next number (see the level "Counter from N (N + 1, N–1)" in Figure 21.1) predicts arithmetic achievement and addition speed in the primary grades.

Counting-on when increasing collections and the corresponding counting-back-from when decreasing collections are critical numerical strategies for children. However, they are only beginning strategies. In the case where the amount of increase is unknown, children use counting-up-to to find the unknown amount. If five items are increased, so that there are now nine items, children may find the amount of increase by counting and keeping track of the number of counts, as in "Fiiiive; 6, 7, 8, 9. 4!" And if nine items are decreased, so that five remain, children may count from 9 down to 5 to find the unknown decrease, as follows: "Nine; 8, 7, 6, 5. 4!" However, counting backwards, especially more than two or three counts, is difficult for most children unless they have consistent instruction. Instead, children might learn *counting-up-to* the total to solve a subtraction situation. For example, "I took away 5 from those 9, so 6, 7, 8, 9 (raising a finger with each count)—that's 4 more left in the 9."

The Instructional Tasks

As stated, instructional tasks in the learning trajectories are not the only way to guide children to achieve the levels of thinking embedded within the learning trajectories. However, in the last column of Figure 21.3 are specific examples of the type of instructional activity that helps to promote thinking at the subsequent level. Thus, teachers implement them, adapt them, or use them as a template to gauge the appropriateness and expected effectiveness of other lessons, including those in published curricula.

One of the main characteristics of the activities is the type of problem (Figure 21.2) that children can solve at each level. Furthermore, in many cases, there is evidence that certain aspects of the instructional tasks are especially effective. For example, although Figure 21.3 includes only samples of levels and activities, we included one elaborated example called *Teaching Counting-On Skills* in the "Counting Strategies" level. Based on theory and empirical work (El'konin & Davydov, 1975), these instructional procedures effectively teach counting on to children who have not yet developed this skill. After setting up the problem situation (Step 1), the teacher guides children to connect the numeral signifying the first addend (5 in the example—see Figure 21.3) to the five objects in the first set; students then learn to recognize that the fifth object is assigned the counting word "five" (Step 2 and, as necessary, Step 3). Afterward, the teacher helps the children understand that the first object in the second set will always be assigned the next counting number ("six"). These understandings and skills are reinforced with additional problems and a variety of specific, focused questions.

REFLECTIONS AND NEW DIRECTIONS

Learning trajectories, as well as assessment, curriculum development, and teaching, can support children's learning. Children whose teachers use research-based learning trajectories demonstrate higher levels of mathematical reasoning. Current research in learning trajectories points the way toward more effective and efficient, but still creative and enjoyable, mathematics.

However, many issues remain to be addressed. How can we scale up research-based professional development activities (see below)? There are different learning trajectories for each major mathematical topic. Is it more effective and efficient for math specialists to learn how to use learning trajectories? There is limited research on several mathematical topics upon which learning trajectories can be based. Are there valid developmental progressions for these topics? Finally, how can researchers and teachers work together to investigate these questions?

PROFESSIONAL DEVELOPMENT ACTIVITIES

- Develop knowledge of all three components of learning trajectories for each major topic of early mathematics: goals (the mathematics), developmental progressions, and instructional tasks. For example, read about these components for counting (Clements & Sarama, 2009a, Chapter 3); view videos of clinical interviews highlighting the type of thinking at each level; and, finally, discuss each level and how you might teach it using Figure 21.1 and videos of the instructional tasks listed, and discussing additional instructional tasks and teaching strategies.

- Provide professional development that is extensive, ongoing, reflective, grounded in particular curricular material, and situated partially in the classroom. For example, implement a particular curriculum, and after studying the learning trajectories in it, provide in-class coaching and sessions in which issues and problems emerging from the implementation are discussed.

- Give teachers continuous feedback from sources they trust about whether children are learning what they are taught and that this learning is valued. For example, have supervisors from the district observe teachers and children using fidelity instruments linked to the curriculum.

ACKNOWLEDGMENTS

This chapter was based on work supported in part by the Institute of Education Sciences (U.S. Department of Education) under Grant No. R305K05157. Work on the research was also supported in part by the National Science Foundation under Grant Nos. DRL-1019925 and DRL-1020118. Any opinions, findings, and conclusions or recommendations expressed in this material are those of the authors and do not necessarily reflect the views of the funding agencies.

REFERENCES

Baroody, A. J. (1996). An investigative approach to the mathematics instruction of children classified as learning disabled. In D. K. Reid, W. P. Hresko, & H. L. Swanson (Eds.), *Cognitive approaches to learning disabilities* (pp. 547–615). Austin, TX: Pro-Ed.

Brosterman, N. (1997). *Inventing kindergarten.* New York: Harry N. Abrams.

Clements, D. H., & Sarama, J. (2004). Learning trajectories in mathematics education. *Mathematical Thinking and Learning, 6,* 81–89.

Clements, D. H., & Sarama, J. (2007). *SRA real math building blocks PreK.* Columbus, OH: SRA/McGraw-Hill.

Clements, D. H., & Sarama, J. (2009a). *Learning and teaching early math: The learning trajectories approach.* New York: Routledge.

Clements, D. H., & Sarama, J. (2009b). Learning trajectories in early mathematics—sequences of acquisition and teaching. In R. S. New & M. Cochran (Eds.), *Encyclopedia of language and literacy development* (pp. 1–6). London, ON: Canadian Language and Literacy Research Network.

Clements, D. H., & Sarama, J. (2012a). Learning and teaching early and elementary mathematics. In J. Carlson & J. Levine (Eds.), *Instructional strategies for improving student learning: Focus on early mathematics and reading* (pp. 107–162). Charlotte, NC: Information Age.

Clements, D. H., & Sarama, J. (2012b). Mathematics learning, assessment, and curriculum. In R. C. Pianta, L. Justice, W. S. Barnett, & S. M. Sheridan (Eds.), *Handbook of early childhood education* (pp. 217–239). New York: Guilford Press.

Clements, D. H., Sarama, J., & Wolfe, C. B. (2011). *TEAM—Tools for Early Assessment in Mathematics*. Columbus, OH: McGraw-Hill Education.

El'konin, D. B., & Davydov, V. V. (1975). Children's capacity for learning mathematics. In L. P. Steffe (Ed.), *Soviet studies in the psychology of learning and teaching mathematics* (Vol. 7, pp. 1–11). Chicago: University of Chicago Press.

Fuson, K. C. (2004). Pre-K to grade 2 goals and standards: Achieving 21st century mastery for all. In D. H. Clements, J. Sarama, & A.-M. DiBiase (Eds.), *Engaging young children in mathematics: Standards for early childhood mathematics education* (pp. 105–148). Mahwah, NJ: Erlbaum.

Henry, V. J., & Brown, R. S. (2008). First-grade basic facts: An investigation into teaching and learning of an accelerated, high-demand memorization standard. *Journal for Research in Mathematics Education, 39*, 153–183.

Kamii, C. (1985). *Young children reinvent arithmetic: Implications of Piaget's theory*. New York: Teaching College Press.

National Governors Association & Council of Chief State School Officers. (2010). *Common core state standards for mathematics*. Washington, DC: Authors.

National Mathematics Advisory Panel. (2008). *Foundations for success: The final report of the National Mathematics Advisory Panel*. Washington, DC: U.S. Department of Education, Office of Planning, Evaluation and Policy Development.

National Research Council. (2009). *Mathematics in early childhood: Learning paths toward excellence and equity*. Washington, DC: National Academy Press.

Sarama, J., & Clements, D. H. (2009). *Early childhood mathematics education research: Learning trajectories for young children*. New York: Routledge.

Shepard, L. A. (2005). Assessment. In L. Darling-Hammond & J. Bransford (Eds.), *Preparing teachers for a changing world* (pp. 275–326). San Francisco: Jossey-Bass.

Van den Heuvel-Panhuizen, M. (1996). *Assessment and realistic mathematics education*. Utrecht, The Netherlands: Freudenthal Institute, Utrecht University.

Winton, P., & Buysse, V. (Eds.). (2005). NCEDL Pre-kindergarten study. *Early Developments, 9*.

Wu, H.-H. (2011). *Understanding numbers in elementary school mathematics*. Providence, RI: American Mathematical Society.

CHAPTER 22

READ ME A STORY

Reaping the Benefits of Reading for Young Children

LEA M. MCGEE

Christopher was sitting at his preschool writing center hard at work. A visitor to his classroom observed him for a few seconds then asked, "What are you writing?" Christopher replied, "I don't know yet. I'm not done." The visitor continued the conversation, "OK, be sure to put it in the writing rocking chair so you can share when you do finish. I can't wait to hear." A familiar routine in the classroom was for children to put any writing they accomplished during play in the teacher's rocking chair, so they could share it with the group at the end of center time. Christopher and eight other children placed their written messages in the chair, and the teacher asked each one to tell about their writing (Figure 22.1 shows Christopher's writing). Christopher announced, "I wrote a story but I didn't illustrate it yet. It says, 'The dog was bad.'" He read with emphasis, then glanced up from his paper at the other children, looking each one in the eye. Then he turned back to the paper and read at a rapid pace. "'It ate the mouse, it ate the cat, it ate the house, it ate the mommy.'" Then he slowed down and said very deliberately, "'It died, of course.'"

Christopher's story writing and pretend reading demonstrate many of the literate accomplishments expected of middle-class 4-year-olds, and expectations increasingly fostered in highly exemplary preschool programs for at-risk children. He was willing to pretend to write a story and did so using real and mock letters (mainly those found in his name). He wrote from left to right in lines of text. His story had six sentences, and his written text had six lines. In addition, he demonstrated his many experiences with having stories read aloud to him in engaging ways. He knew just when to look at his audience, how to use pacing to capture interest, and when to change his voice to indicate a critical part of the story. He also demonstrated knowledge of the plot line from the familiar traditional tale "I Know an Old Lady Who Swallowed a Fly." Indeed, reading stories and other genres of literature aloud was a critical component of his preschool program.

FIGURE 22.1. Christopher's writing.

WHAT RESEARCH SAYS
ABOUT READING ALOUD TO PRELITERATE CHILDREN

Many researchers for the last 30 or more years have investigated the benefits and nature of reading aloud to young children prior to the period when children can read for themselves. Because of space limitations, I focus specifically on research that has examined the benefits of reading aloud to children's language growth, comprehension development, and writing.

Reading Aloud and Its Benefits for Children's Language Development

Three meta-analyses of read-aloud research have confirmed that both parents' and teachers' read-aloud practices produce language gains for young children. Bus, van IJzendoorn, and Pellegrini (1995) found a moderate effect size for children's language growth, emergent literacy, and reading achievement based on the frequency of parent read-alouds. The National Early Literacy Panel (2008) found similar results in a review of preschool and kindergarten intervention programs that included a read-aloud component. Another meta-analysis using nearly twice as many studies as those included in the report of the National Early Literacy Panel found similar results: a moderate effect size for children's overall language growth (Mol, Bus, & de Jong, 2009). However, these researchers also documented two other critical findings. Interventions delivered by researchers produced greater effects than those presented by teachers. Interestingly, this result was confounded by group size because teachers were more likely to work with larger, whole groups, whereas researchers were more likely to work one-on-one or in small groups. Thus, the quality and likely the frequency of the interactive read-aloud is a critical variable (assuming that researchers are more skilled than teachers at interventions).

Examining individual studies within these meta-analyses that subsequently were published yields a gold mine of information about the nature of high-quality read-aloud sessions and their effects on specific language outcomes. In fact, in a critique of the findings of the National Early Literacy Panel report on the effects of read-aloud interventions, Schickedanz and McGee (2010) examined each study and found more nuanced outcomes. Thus, I review here a few individual studies of read-alouds, with an eye toward drawing practical implications.

Pappas and Brown (1987) examined how kindergartners' pretend readings changed after hearing a book read aloud three times. In a case study, researchers read a storybook aloud to a child and after each reading invited the child to read the book "her own way" or just to pretend to read. In pretend readings across the three read-alouds of the book, the child mentioned more of the actual story events in linguistic forms like those found in the book, and fewer ambiguous and misplaced ideas. The authors argued that the results demonstrate how children become familiar with the linguistic patterns authors use to convey their meanings in written stories (called the *written register*), which is critical for comprehension. While the pretend reading was used as a measurement in this study, a practical implication seems to be that if children engage in activities that extend their language experiences with the books after read-alouds, such as pretending to read the story, the benefits of using and understanding book language may increase.

Retelling a story (while looking at its illustrations) after hearing it read aloud was also examined in a study with older children. Penno, Wilkinson, and Moore (2002) were interested in vocabulary gains of first graders who listened to stories read aloud to them. Each book was read three times, and each time children retold the story. In one condition students heard word explanations for target words, whereas in the other condition no such explanations were provided. In the word explanation condition, the reader (1) slipped in a short verbal definition of the target word, (2) pointed to salient features in the illustrations related to a word's meaning, or (3) dramatized or role-played a word's meaning. Students in the word explanation condition made greater gains than those in the no-explanation condition as measured by a multiple-choice vocabulary test of the target words and the sophistication of students' use of the words in the retellings. Unfortunately the retellings were not analyzed for children's comprehension of the story events or use of the written register. Nonetheless, this study suggests that even as children approach the period in which they are learning to read, they still benefit from systematic read-alouds of stories, especially when readers provide information about vocabulary meanings without interrupting the reading. Again, retellings after the read-aloud probably boosted the benefits of learning vocabulary from the read-aloud.

A more recent study (Biemiller & Boote, 2006) used similar read-aloud procedures with and without word explanations with predominantly kindergarten, first-grade, and second-grade English learners (ELs). The findings showed that word meanings were learned to a greater degree in the word explanation condition. Furthermore, when the number of readings was increased from two to four readings, kindergarten children made greater gains. On the other hand, first and second graders made as many gains with two readings of a book as with four. These researchers conducted a second experiment in which books were read only two times, but twice the number of vocabulary words were taught (12–14 per book compared to six to eight). Teachers reviewed the meanings of target words after reading and on a subsequent day. The children learned twice as many words in this study, and these gains were sustained, as measured by a delayed posttest. Again, even older children in early elementary grades still benefit from multiple read-alouds of the same story with attention to teaching vocabulary words. It is important to note that review of the words after reading provided an additional boost in vocabulary learning. Older children need fewer book readings than kindergartners, but all children benefit from learning about a dozen targeted vocabulary words per book.

Two studies underscore how reading aloud provides benefits for two at-risk populations: children from underrepresented populations and ELs. Britto, Brooks-Gunn, and Griffin (2006) demonstrated that low-income African American mothers could produce higher language interactions during storybook reading when they engaged their preschool children in a conversation about a book before, during, and after reading than mothers who only read the book aloud. Roberts (2008) found that EL children who first heard storybooks read at home in their home language then heard their teacher read the book aloud in English learned as many English vocabulary words as children who heard the book in English both at home and at school. Family participation in the project nearly doubled when parents became aware that they could have access to school materials in their home language. These studies show that, with modification, parents of children in at-risk groups can be supportive and provide additional academic gains for their children through read-alouds.

Van Kleeck, Woude, and Hammett (2006) expanded research on reading aloud to consider the levels of children's language being targeted for instruction and measurement. Previous studies have primarily targeted receptive vocabulary (pointing to a picture when its name is spoken) or expressive vocabulary (saying the name of an object or action in a picture). This level of language is concerned with literal meaning, for example, when children are asked to identify an object or person in an illustration or to tell what is happening in an illustrated event. Higher level language focuses on inferential meaning rather than literal information. Children use inferential language as they infer character motivations and make connections among and between events in a story and their own life experiences. This language is elicited when children are asked questions such as "Why did the fox try to jump on Rosie?" or "What will happen if he catches Rosie?" The amount of this type of language use, which has also been called *analytic* talk, evoked in children during preschool read-alouds predicts their reading comprehension a year later (Dickinson & Smith, 1994).

In scripted read-alouds presented to language-impaired preschoolers, Van Kleeck and colleagues (2006) asked 25 questions, 70% at the literal level and 30% at the inferential level. Readers were provided scripted answers to the questions to give to children who failed to respond, in order to demonstrate both inferential and literal language and thinking. Children in the treatment group made greater gains on a standardized receptive language test and on assessments of both literal and inferential language use. The effects for inferential language gain were smaller than those for literal language gain but nonetheless positive. Thus, the types of questions teachers ask and their ability to model appropriate answers for children is a variable in high-quality read-alouds.

Finally, the genre of the book read aloud has been found to be influential in increasing children's language use. Price, Van Kleeck, and Huberty (2009) observed parent read-alouds of storybooks and expository (informational) books to preschoolers. Four levels of talk were coded. At Level 1 parents or children labeled objects or characters, or located them in illustrations. In Level 2, they described characteristics of objects or characters (noting size, color, shape, number) or described a scene in the illustrations. At Level 3 parents and children recalled information presented earlier in the book, made evaluations, or compared text events to the children's lives or to events in other books. At Level 4 children and parents engaged in reasoning as they made predictions, provided definitions, or made explanations. Expository text reading produced the greatest amount of Level 4 talk in both parents and children. Presumably these experiences provide to children demonstrations of and use of inferential language similar to what was scripted in the Van Kleeck and colleagues study (2006).

Two recent studies by Neuman and her colleagues (Neuman & Dwyer, 2011; Newman, Newman, & Dwyer, 2011) confirm that engaging children in activities that require sophisticated language use is an important component of a read-aloud program. These authors developed a curriculum around two units: living things and healthy habits (with a third unit on simple math in one study). During each topic teachers presented information in video clips, read informational books aloud, asked questions and presented challenges, reviewed information and vocabulary meanings, and engaged children in developmental writing (using whatever level of writing children were willing to use). The focus of the instruction went beyond merely learning new vocabulary such as *katydid*. Instead, children learned categorical information, such that a katydid is an insect because it has three body segments and six legs (targeting the vocabulary words *katydid, insect*, and *body segments*). The results demonstrated increases in children's vocabulary, as well as their ability to describe why words are placed in particular categories. Importantly, children displayed understanding of new words not taught in the curriculum when they were given information about the category of a new word. This study confirmed the need for information book read-alouds, and that reading books aloud on a single topic should be sustained across considerable time to allow for multiple and expanded understanding of concepts. Teachers should aim to develop vocabulary knowledge beyond mere definitions, but build understandings of categorical word knowledge.

In summary, a large body of research has suggested a wealth of effective read-aloud techniques. As summarized in Figure 22.2, teachers need to select books carefully and consider which vocabulary words to target for instruction. Teachers should read books more than once as they model how to comment about literal and inferential information. Books can be extended through retelling, pretend reading, writing, dramatic play, or hands-on science experiments.

Reading Aloud and Its Benefits for Children's Comprehension Development

Compared to the large body of research focusing on the relationship between reading aloud and young children's vocabulary growth, surprisingly few studies have attempted to improve children's listening comprehension of the stories being read or to transfer effects to general listening comprehension. Reese and Cox (1999) asserted that adults adopt different styles of reading aloud naturally (e.g., Britto et al., 2006; Dickinson & Smith, 1994), and argued that some of these styles may be more suited to developing comprehension than others. For example Dickinson and Smith (1994) found that one style of reading, which they called *performance-oriented* style, included more challenging comments and questions, and might therefore produce better comprehension gains. Reese and Cox (1999) also noted that another read-aloud style, which they called the *comprehender* style, includes comments and questions calling for reasoning and explanations that might also result in higher levels of listening comprehension for young children. Finally, they noted that a *describer* read-aloud style, which includes lower-level "what" questions, may not produce listening comprehension gains as effectively. Unfortunately, the results of their study examining the effects of three read-aloud styles did not bear out these assumptions. The describer style was the only reading style to influence outcomes, and these were linked to vocabulary and print outcomes. While the performance-oriented style produced the greatest mean gain in comprehension, the effect was not statistically significant. A closer look at the comments and questions used in the scripted read-alouds revealed no questions that required children to explain major events in relation to the story as a whole, which often is a critical component of higher level, inferential comprehension.

Stevens, Van Meter, and Warcholak (2010) found that reading aloud to kindergarten, first-grade, and primary-grade special education students, along with teaching them explicitly about story structure, improved their comprehension better than that of children who merely listened to the same stories. It is important to note that only free recall and answers to questions at the literal level, not answers to inferential questions, were scored.

- Select high-quality story and information books, and consider how best to introduce them. It is particularly important to introduce a story's problem because young children do not attend to this story element without being prompted.

- Prior to reading, select moderately challenging vocabulary to enhance children's understanding of the book (like the Tier 2 words recommended by Beck, McKeown, & Kucan, 2000). Target 10–12 words per book.

- Provide explanations of vocabulary while reading without interrupting the flow of the book. Engage children in conversation after reading in ways that foster inferential language and higher level thinking using target vocabulary.

- Read the book up to four times to preschool and kindergarten children, but fewer times to first and second graders.

- Teach children how to notice and to think about salient elements of stories. For example, as children learn to identify characters, they should also be taught to think about what motivates them and make inferences about what characters are thinking and feeling, and the effect this has on their actions.

- Provide follow-up activities that engage children in retelling or pretending to read the book. Engage children in writing or dramatic play activities.

- Plan for extended science or social studies units of study in which informational book read-alouds are embedded. Select multiple books about the topic; locate appropriate multimedia items and pictures to support conceptual learning.

- Select concepts to be developed using categories (e.g., insects) and their defining characteristics (all insects have three body segments and six legs), and teach these concepts with their vocabulary directly through explanation in read-alouds and in follow-up conversations and activities.

- Ask both higher-level inferential questions and lower-level literal questions, and model how to answer those questions. Model asking and answering the questions in a first read; ask questions and supporting multiple children as they attempt to answer the questions in the second and subsequent readings.

- Intersperse questions about nonfiction books during reading and conversation. Remember to use both literal and inferential questions.

FIGURE 22.2. Research-based implications for read-alouds.

Heisey and Kucan (2010) examined whether interspersing questions during a read-aloud or asking questions only after a read-aloud would improve first and second graders' understanding of nonfiction science books. Children recalled more information and were able to provide more justifications for their explanations when read-alouds were interspersed with questions than when questions were asked after read-alouds.

In summary, there is evidence that kindergartners and first graders improve comprehension of what is read to them and transfer this ability to other stories when the emphasis is primarily on literal recall. There is insufficient evidence at this time as to the best style of reading aloud to influence listening comprehension at higher levels of thinking; however, Figure 22.2 provides possible implications for teachers.

Effects of Read-Alouds on Children's Writing and Play

Research over two decades has shown that the literature children hear read aloud influences their writing content and style, but that highest quality literature has the most impact (e.g., Dressel, 1990). Fewer studies have examined how children's emergent and early writings are influenced by the literature they hear read aloud. Lancia (1997) described how his second graders used literature in their writing: borrowing an entire plot or a book's characters; plot devices, including settings or language patterns or titles; or genre devices, such as false leads in mysteries. Weisch (2008) found similar borrowings in children's pretend play in preschool. Rowe (1988) reported that young children often seek out toys to populate their play about books. She argued that selection of particular toys to use as characters in their play demonstrates that children as young as 2 years old comprehend character traits or characteristics that identify particular characters. Thus, while reading literature aloud has been shown to have a profound impact on older elementary children's writing, and much anecdotal evidence suggests it has this same effect on emergent and early writers, research evidence is lacking. However, children's play is clearly influenced by their experiences with literature that is read aloud.

In summary, reading aloud has an enormous influence on the development of a wide array of children's early literacy concepts, especially the development of oral language and listening comprehension. The remainder of this chapter focuses on two critical components that *require* reading literature aloud to children: higher level language use and comprehension. Because the effect of genre is influential, I first use the insights gained from research to put into practice reading aloud narratives or storybooks to preschoolers through second graders, and ways to extend these in follow-up activities such as writing, play, retelling, and pretend reading. Then I focus on describing high-quality reading of nonfiction, information books in rich and extended content units of study.

RESEARCH INTO PRACTICE:
QUALITY READ-ALOUDS THAT PROMOTE HIGH-LEVEL
ORAL LANGUAGE AND COMPREHENSION DEVELOPMENT

Reading Aloud Narratives or Storybooks

Narratives are stories that have, in the simplest sense, at least one well-developed character, an initiating event that reveals a problem, attempts to solve the problem (usually thwarted by obstacles), a resolution of the problem, and an ending that reveals the main character's reaction to the story resolution. The story takes place in a setting that provides either a backdrop for the story (e.g., the generic "once upon a time" settings for folktales) or an integral setting in which the specifics (time, location, conditions) are a critical element to the story plot. Furthermore, stories convey abstract themes that readers infer, based on their own understanding of the overall story in relation to their life's experiences.

Again, in the simplest sense, knowing about these elements (at least characters, setting, problem, attempts, and resolution) helps children better recall story information and enhances their overall listening comprehension for stories (Stevens et al., 2010). However, a story read aloud is enriched when teachers go beyond simple reading to examine a storybook in its richest form. Every element of a high-quality storybook contributes to its meaning: the title, the size and shape of the book, the endpapers, the color, perspective in the illustrations, and placement of text on a page, to name only a few design elements (Sipe, 2008). Cochran-Smith (1984) argued that teachers play the role of an ideal reader as they read aloud to children. Ideal readers notice design elements and consider a story in all its complexity. As ideal readers, teachers model for children what they are thinking and wondering as they read the book. They think aloud and make explicit what they are thinking, where they are looking, and what they are wondering about. This naturally includes literal information from the text and illustrations, as well as inferential thinking. The comments naturally include thinking at high levels of cognitive demand as teachers evaluate, make judgments, infer character traits, and connect ideas among story events. Thus, a high-quality read-aloud begins as teachers carefully look through books and say aloud to themselves what an ideal reader would likely be saying, perhaps mostly unconsciously.

Consider *Knuffle Bunny* by Mo Willems (2004). First, I look at the both the front and back covers and consider the title. The front cover shows a close-up of a little girl with a stuffed rabbit, walking with her father (who is seen only from the waist down). The back cover shows the little girl and rabbit in the daddy's arms as he walks with a mother holding a laundry basket filled with folded clothes. Everyone is smiling, and the perspective is much farther away, so that the setting of large brownstone buildings on a city street is very visible. The title, Knuffle Bunny, might refer to the girl or stuffed rabbit, either of which might be the main character around whom the problem is likely to be centered.

Next I look carefully at the end pages, frontispieces (illustrations before the title page), title page, and dedication, if there is one, in the opening pages. I check to see whether the front and back endpapers are the same (which they are in this book). The endpapers are a repetition of what looks like the door of a washing machine, with the stuffed rabbit inside with the bubbles, as if the rabbit is being washed. I am wondering if this might foreshadow the problem in some way. Three frontispieces show the daddy and mommy prior to the time of the story. The title page shows the girl hugging the bunny in front of washing machines at a laundromat. She looks blissful. I am wondering who Knuffle Bunny is and what the washing machine will have to do with the story.

Now I carefully read the story, looking at the illustrations before and after reading. After reading the first double-spread text, I know the little girl is Trixie, and I infer the errand they are going on is to wash clothes, presumably at the laundromat. The illustrations of the dad and Trixie break out slightly from the frame of illustration perhaps to signal that they are beginning a grand experience away from the safety of home. In the next two double spreads, I notice that as they walk down the block, through the park, past the school, and into the laundromat, Trixie and her dad are happy. Dad pays a great deal attention to Trixie (I infer that he is attentive to her), and she is being very good staying near her dad (I infer that she is a well-behaved child). Trixie seems very interested in all that is around her (I infer that she is curious).

There is a dramatic shift on the next page, where Trixie is dancing with pants on her head, swinging a bra, and illustrated with an exaggeratedly large, wide-open mouth (now I infer that she can be boisterous, loud, and silly). Dad seems tolerant and is looking at Trixie rather than what he is putting in the washing machine (I infer that Mom would never let Trixie get away with this behavior!). Dad lets Trixie put in the coin (he is letting Trixie have extra fun), and they walk away. I can see the bunny looking out from the washing machine. Seeing this triggers me to look back at the previous page and notice that the bunny is in the basket with the dirty clothes, and Dad isn't watching what he's putting in the washer. I infer this is the start of trouble (it will be important for children to notice what is going on in this and the following illustration). On the next page, Trixie is her curious self as she walks calmly home looking all around her, but then the text font enlarges on the words "realized something" and she is illustrated with great big eyes and a sad frown. The next two pages show Trixie trying to talk. She says nonsense words and I now realize the important fact I skipped over on the very first page of the story: "Not so long ago, *before she could even speak words*, Trixie went on an errand with her daddy. . . ." (I realize I will need to make sure children pay attention to this text early in the story). Her father replies to her as if he understands, but he does not. He thinks Trixie is talking about going home. On this page I infer that in Trixie's head she is saying, "No, no. Rabbit gone. RABBITT GONE." She must be very frustrated by her attempts to tell Daddy, but he cannot understand. It is so ironic that Trixie is "trying to use words" to solve the problem but cannot do so.

On the next two pages, Trixie continues to try and communicate without success, because Dad does not have a clue. She escalates into going boneless. I infer that, in Trixie's head, she is deciding not to go one step farther until she has her rabbit. Her daddy drags and carries her screaming the entire way home (she is very persistent). I infer how mad she is at her dad, and she keeps trying to say, "NO, rabbit gone." Daddy looks very angry (I can just hear him thinking, "What is the matter with Trixie? One minute happy, the next having a silly tantrum"). Just as he is unlocking the door, Mother asks, "Where is Knuffle Bunny?" Aha, I now know that the bunny is Knuffle Bunny and obviously it goes everywhere with Trixie. The expression on Trixie's face says, "I told you so." There are large zig zags in the illustrations coming from Dad's head emphasizing that he knows he is in trouble now. The family runs back to the laundromat. I can just hear the mom and dad thinking, "We better find Knuffle Bunny or there will be no living with Trixie."

When they get to the laundromat, there is a montage of four illustrations on one page showing the frenzy of their search inside, around, and behind all the washers, but they do not find Knuffle Bunny. Trixie is illustrated with quivering lips, so Daddy knows the search is not over. Now he looks determined (Trixie must get her persistence from him) and pulls all the clothes out of the machine. Trixie jumps for joy and says, "Knuffle Bunny." She talked! And the last page confirms that Trixie said her first words. So I know the end pages do foreshadow the loss of the bunny in the washing machine, and the back cover is the happy family returning home with the laundry clean and Knuffle Bunny safely found. I carefully look back at the pages where Dad is not looking as he puts in the laundry. It does not show him putting the bunny in the washing machine, but it is clear that he is not looking; I infer that this is how the bunny accidentally was put in the washer. I notice that the washer is labeled "M." On the next two pages, it is clear that the rabbit is in that washer, but neither Dad nor Trixie notices. On the search pages, they are looking inside the "M" washer but not deep enough.

After my first read, I consider the problem of the story, which is usually beyond the obvious, in this case that Knuffle Bunny is gone. The real problem is that Trixie cannot talk; she cannot communicate that the rabbit is gone. Dad does not understand what Trixie is trying to communicate. The solution occurs when Mom immediately recognizes the problem, and Dad gets serious about looking in the washer. One theme of this story is a caution for dads: "Always find a reason for a tantrum!" and Willems's subtitle confirms (*Knuffle Bunny: A Cautionary Tale*). This story might be about his own experiences with children (perhaps his own wife and child?).

Finally, I look back through the text to decide on important vocabulary words and phrases children might not know and that are important to understanding the story. I select the phrases *speak words* and *nowhere to be found*, and the words *errand, block, laundromat, machine, realized, bawled*, and *boneless*. I also decide to use and explain the words *persistent* and *communicate* because these were important to inferences about the story's meaning.

Only now am I ready to begin planning how to share this story with young children. I would want children of any age to notice by the second or third reading all the detail and inferences that I have revealed for myself. A portion of my plans for the first, second, and third reading of this story are shown in Figure 22.3. As shown, in the first read I make many comments. In the second read I ask questions related to comments I made on the first day. In the last read I usually ask children to reconstruct the story as I ask for clarifications and elaborations (McGee & Schickedanz, 2007). I show each illustration and ask, "What is happening here?"

Notice that my comments on the first read are based on the inferences I made as I read the book. After reading, I always ask one high-level question, which is intended to get children to reconsider an event within the context of the entire story. I use higher-level question stems that require children to reason with longer explanations that provide justifications. For example, questions I might ask about *Knuffle Bunny* are as follows:

- *Why* didn't Dad know where Knuffle Bunny was?
- *Why* didn't Trixie communicate to Dad?
- *How do we know* that Dad didn't realize Knuffle Bunny was missing?
- *How did we know* where Knuffle Bunny was?
- *What would happen if* Mom hadn't realized Knuffle Bunny was missing?
- *How* did Knuffle Bunny get lost?
- *How* is Knuffle Bunny like a best friend?

With children of all ages, I would follow up each reading with an activity that further extends children's understanding of the story, and their knowledge of the target vocabulary and story structure elements. I might place drama props (e.g., an item of clothing or an object associated with a character) in a dramatic play center. I might construct a chart of the major story parts and have children retell those parts of the story. Children could draw pictures of their favorite characters, then write about that character using emergent or invented spelling.

Older first and second graders could work in groups to prepare three other responses (Morrison & Wlodarczyk, 2009). Children could construct alpha-boxes by selecting a word or phrase from the book that begins with each letter of the alphabet. Or children could take a stand both for and against an issue related to the book and tell why they take this stand. For *Knuffle Bunny*, children could be asked: "Do you think the parents should have let Trixie take Knuffle Bunny to the laundromat?" Children answer "yes" or

	First read	Second read	Third read
Book introduction (front cover)	The title of this book is *Knuffle Bunny*. (Show front cover and point to title.) It is about Trixie (point to girl) and her dad (point to dad). Trixie gets lost. Something gets lost. Let's find out what gets lost and how they find it. Here are the end papers. I see washing machines. I predict a washing machine will be in this story. (Encourage comments about what children see and predict.)	Who can remember the title of this book? (Read title.) Trixie had a problem, didn't she? What was her problem? (Expand and clarify children's responses.) Look at the end papers. They help us know what the problem is going to be. How do they help?	Everyone, tell me the title of this story. What was the problem? (Have multiple children respond.) (Show end papers.) What is happening here on the end papers? Why did the illustrator make these end papers? (Expand and clarify children's responses.)
Title page	(Read title.) Here is Trixie in the laundromat, a store where you can wash your clothes. See all the washing machines. I am wondering who is Knuffle Bunny and why that is the title of this story.	Why is Trixie hugging that rabbit? Where are they? I think I know why the story's title is *Knuffle Bunny*. Who can tell me why this story is called *Knuffle Bunny*?	What is happening here? (Expand and clarify children's responses.) Why is *Knuffle Bunny* a good title for this story?
First double spread	(Read text.) Here are Trixie and her dad going on an errand, which means they have to do a job. I see a basket of clothes. I bet the errand is to wash clothes. Now remember Trixie is little, she can't even talk yet. Mom seems like she is going to enjoy reading a book and Trixie is excited, isn't she?	(Read text.) What was the errand Trixie and her dad had to go on? How do you know? What was the clue? What is important to remember about Trixie? Why is it important to know she can't talk?	What is happening here? (Expand and clarify children's responses then read text.)
Fourth double spread (inside the Laundromat)	(Read text.) It doesn't look like Trixie is helping at all. She is misbehaving, being bad. I don't think her mom would let her put clothes on her head. Look, I think she is yelling. Dad is watching Trixie. I think he is thinking, "That Trixie is so cute." Look, he isn't watching what he is doing. He is putting clothes in that machine, the one with M on it, but he isn't looking. (Demonstrate putting in clothes without looking.)	(Read text.) Is Trixie helping? Why do you think she is misbehaving? This is where the trouble begins. What is the trouble about to happen here?	What is happening here? (Expand and clarify children's responses then read text.) What will happen next?
Fifth double spread (when Trixie puts the money in the machine and they start to leave)	(Read text.) Oh no, look here. (Point to bunny ears and bunny face.) What got into the machine? I don't think Trixie knows. Do you think Dad knows? Trixie is just so happy she isn't noticing that her rabbit is gone. I think this might be trouble, don't you? Look at the bunny. I think he is shouting, "Don't leave me in here!!!"	(Read text. Oh no, I see trouble, what is it? Why is it a problem that the rabbit is in the washer? Do you think he is just dirty and needs a wash? Did Dad put him in the washer on purpose? Why didn't Trixie notice the rabbit is gone? What do you think the rabbit is feeling?	What is happening here? (Expand and clarify children's responses then read text.)

FIGURE 22.3. Plan for reading selected portions of *Knuffle Bunny* (Willems, 2004).

"no," then tell why or why not. In all extension activities, I would model use of the target vocabulary and provide supportive, positive feedback when children use these phrases and words independently.

Finally, I would plan ways to connect across stories. For example, *Knuffle Bunny* could be read before or after *Oonga Boonga* by Frieda Wishinsky (1998). In this story a baby cries and cries, and cannot communicate her problem—that she misses her brother. Thus, these books are linked by a similar problem. Children can compare and contrast how the children try to communicate and how the problems are solved in the two books.

Across a year's time I would be sure to cover each story's structure elements in depth. I would gradually reduce the number of explicit comments in the first read and ask more questions. I would select more challenging stories, with longer, more complex plots and texts. Similarly, I would select more challenging vocabulary.

Reading Aloud Nonfiction Informational Books

I would use a separate reading time to focus on nonfiction books. During the study of science or social studies topics, I would select book topics that follow content standards to read aloud. Once I selected a topic, keeping in mind the content standards to be covered, I would search for related nonfiction books to read aloud.

For example, on the topic of living things, I might focus on the nature of animal homes—specifically, the structure and building of bird nests. This is in line with content standards in life sciences (e.g., California Department of Education, 2000) in which kindergartners and first graders know and observe differences in behaviors and habitats of specific plants or animals. Furthermore, first graders are to know features of habitats and how animals use the habitats (e.g., for nesting) to thrive. There are several appropriate books for young children on nests and nest building, but I would begin with *Eyewitness BIRD* (Burnie, 2004) because it has the most information. It is too difficult to read aloud in its entirety to preschoolers or kindergartners, but I have found it to be an excellence resource for what I call "information book conversations," which occur when teachers tell children about a topic from an informational book using its illustrations as support. Occasionally parts of the text might be read aloud. I have found that information book conversations are much more powerful when conducted much like narrative read-alouds. I focus on the same content using the same book and other supporting activities or objects for 3 days. The first day I do much of the talking, with children doing activities and observing pictures, objects, and YouTube video clips. The second day I ask questions about material presented the first day and help children extend and expand their responses. On the third day I ask the same questions and make sure that most children have multiple chances to respond (by asking several children to answer the same question).

I have found that using five higher-level question stems helps me not only to pull the literal information from the information book but also to fill in inferential information not stated in the text or shown in the illustrations. I have found that posing the questions and searching for answers readily produces inferential-level thinking and identifies key vocabulary and concepts. These question stems are as follows:

- How—?
- Why—?
- How can we prove (or how do we know)?

- How is_____like (or different from)_____?
- What would happen if—?

For example, to plan a study of bird nests, I first pose the question (I underline vocabulary that will be highlighted), "How do birds build their nests?" I found that birds do two activities simultaneously: They gather *building materials* and *fashion the nests*. Most nests are *cup nests*, which are built from a variety of *natural materials* found in birds' *habitats*, including grass, *twigs*, leaves, animal hair and feathers, seeds, *moss*, and *lichen*. Birds also use *man-made materials* such as string, *tin foil*, paper, and tissues. Second, I pose the question, "Why do birds use each of these materials?" I found that grass, twigs, and leaves are used to *structure* the nest and that moss, feathers, animal hear and tissues are used for *insulation*. I naturally pose two more questions: "Why structure the nest with twigs, and so forth?" and "Why does the nest need insulation?" These questions are not answered directly in the text; however, they may be answered by looking at several illustrations that show drawings of birds standing on the edge of the nest feeding the baby birds. A series of photographs show the babies in the nest at 1, 3, 5, 9, and 13 days after *hatching*. These illustrations show that the babies are born without feathers and only gradually acquire them, and they showed how large the babies become (they *increase their weight 10 times* in 10 days!). I inferred that the nest must be built strong enough both to hold the parent and to *support the growing babies* as they increase their weight—thus, the need to use *sufficient* twigs and sticks. I also inferred the nest must be soft enough that the very *delicate newborns* will not be harmed, and provide enough insulation for the *featherless* babies to keep warm. Thus, nests need to be lined with very soft materials. I happened to think about a *baby crib* and how similar a nest is, with the need for soft *"bumper pads"* all around the *crib's rails*. This led to the question, "How can we prove that nests need soft materials?" I decided to plan an activity that compares rolling an egg around in a metal pan and in a pan full of cotton balls.

I found out that birds make the nest's round shape using a *circular movement*. First, birds bring the material and push it into the nest. Then they sit on the materials and turn around in a circular movement, pushing outward with their breasts. Thus, I inferred, this is why the nest is both circular and the shape of a cup (answering the question "How does a bird made the nest round?") Of course, I inferred the answer to "Why is the nest called a *cup nest*?" but needed to make it more explicit. Cup nests look like cups because they have an *indentation* in the center surrounded by *tall sides*. Again, I made the connection to a baby crib with those high railings × answering the question "How is a baby crib like a cup nest?"). This led to the next question: "Why are nests in the shape of a cup?" Neither the text nor the illustrations provided the answer, but the analogy to the baby crib suggests that the tall sides help keep the babies from falling out. A YouTube video I located showed for several minutes a single egg in a nest, in a tree that swayed back and forth in the wind. The egg rolls slightly but does not fall out from the nest, confirming that the indentation with its tall sides keeps the egg and babies from falling out. This made me pose the final question: "What would happen if the nest were not in the shape of a cup with its high sides? What would happen if the nest were flat like a plate?" The answer is simple, the egg or babies would roll out and not *survive*.

I am now ready to consider the order in which I present the information, the illustrations I show, which bits of text I might read, and what other materials and activities I should plan. I decided to get a picture of a baby crib (and my niece had a doll crib). I planned to take a trip around the edge of the schoolyard later to gather possible nest-making materials for a nest-making activity for preschoolers. I tore a trash bag full of newspaper strips for "building materials." Children gathered the material in their "beaks" placed it in the nest pile, and sat on it. Then they turned around in a circular motion. By the time each child worked on the nest, we would have a nest of newspaper. I also found plastic eggs that fit into a large teacup I brought along with a dinner plate (and each child experimented with swaying the cup or plate "nest" in the breeze). Finally, I gathered two real eggs, a metal baking pan, and lots of cotton balls.

On the first day I presented the informational content, focusing on the rich vocabulary and concepts, reading some text, and showing illustrations and the YouTube clip, as well as the baby crib. The children participated in the nest-making activity and experimented with the cup and plate nests. I conducted the experiment—"How can we prove that nests need soft materials?"—using the eggs and pan full of cotton. The second day I posed each of the questions I used in preparing for the first day and supported children's responses, especially helping them use the scientific vocabulary. I often expanded and clarified their responses. I interspersed asking the questions with doing the activities a second time. I sometimes used other information books to show illustrations or to read bits of text to support and extend our growing knowledge about bird nests. For preschoolers and kindergartners I asked questions on the third day but also helped children retell everything they knew about bird nests by asking, "Who can tell us something they know about bird nests?" I helped children use the scientific vocabulary in their informational retellings (Santoro, Chard, Howard, & Baker, 2008). For first and second graders, on the third day I shared additional books about bird nests and shared a writing chart of the important new vocabulary words. I invited children to retell all they knew about bird nests. Finally, children then drew cup nests and wrote about them in their science journals.

REFLECTIONS AND NEW DIRECTIONS

Reading aloud to young children benefits their vocabulary growth, understanding, acquisition, use of particular language structures found in written texts, and comprehension of both inferential and literal information. We have few studies showing that the style of reading aloud influences comprehension at different levels. Also, few studies have measured children's comprehension of individual stories or their listening comprehension in general as a result of reading aloud. This is a rich area for classroom implementation as research in action. I would have hoped for more teacher action research results published in professional journals such as *The Reading Teacher* or *Young Children*. For example, Gregory and Cahill (2010) describe a kindergarten program they developed to teach children how to use scheme and visualization, and to ask "I wonder" questions and make inferences. Unfortunately, they did not measure the results of their program or even providing anecdotal evidence.

Similarly, we have emerging evidence that reading aloud enriches children's pretend play, but we need more evidence of how reading aloud provides models for children's writing, especially in the emergent and early invented stages of writing. However, merely reading a book aloud will not produce these results. High-quality read-alouds are carefully planned and delivered to share with children the richness of a quality storybook and higher level knowledge related to content topics. This chapter has presented principles of reading aloud based on research and has provided richly descriptive illustrations of how teachers can plan engaging and effective read-alouds for all children, including those most at risk.

- Select a recently published storybook that is appropriate for a read-aloud to explore during a grade-level meeting. As you and your colleagues read the book, comment on what you are predicting and inferring. Focus on what the characters are thinking, what motivates them, and why they are acting as they do.

- Plan a read-aloud using many of the comments you and your colleagues discussed during the book-exploring session. If possible, have everyone conduct the read-aloud and tape-record the session. View the tapes together to look for evidence of your children's comprehension.

- Read the book aloud a second time, this time asking more high-level questions. Again video-tape and view the read-aloud for evidence of deeper understanding, especially in children you consider at risk.

- Find an appropriate book for an information book conversation. Plan with your colleagues what information you might share to answer the higher-order question stems provided in this chapter.

REFERENCES

Beck, I. L., McKeown, M. G., & Kucan, L. (2002). *Bringing words to life: Robust vocabulary instruction.* New York: Guilford Press.

Biemiller, A., & Boote, C. (2006). An effective method for building meaning vocabulary in primary grades. *Journal of Educational Psychology, 98,* 44–62.

Britto, P., Brooks-Gunn, J., & Griffin, T. (2006). Maternal reading and teaching patterns: Associations with school readiness in low-income African American families. *Reading Research Quarterly, 41,* 68–89.

Burnie, D. (2004). *Eyewitness BIRD.* New York: DK Publishing.

Bus, A., van IJzendoorn, M., & Pellegrini, A. (1995). Joint book reading makes for success in learning to read: A meta-analysis on intergenerational transmission of Literacy. *Review of Educational Research, 65,* 1–21.

California Department of Education. (2000). *Science Content Standards for California Schools K–12.* Sacramento, CA: Author.

Cochran-Smith, M. (1984). *The making of a reader.* Norwood, NJ: Ablex.

Dickinson, D., & Smith, M. (1994). Long-term effects of preschool teachers' book readings on low-income children's vocabulary and story comprehension. *Reading Research Quarterly, 29,* 104–122.

Dressel, J. (1990). The effects of listening to and discussing different qualities of children's literature on the narrative writing of fifth graders. *Research in the Teaching of English, 24,* 397–414.

Gregory, A., & Cahill, M. (2010). Kindergartners can do it, too!: Comprehension strategies for early readers. *The Reading Teacher, 63,* 515–520.

Heisey, N., & Kucan, L. (2010). Introducing science concepts to primary students through read-alouds: Interactions and multiple texts make the difference. *The Reading Teacher, 63,* 666–676.

Lancia, P. (1997). Literary borrowing: The effects of literature on children's writing. *The Reading Teacher, 50,* 470–475.

McGee, L., & Schickedanz, J. (2007). Repeated interactive read-alouds in preschool and kindergarten. *The Reading Teacher, 60,* 742–751.

Mol, S., Bus, A., & de Jong, M. (2009). Interactive book reading in early education: A tool to stimulate print knowledge as well as oral language. *Review of Educational Research, 79,* 979–1007.

Morrison, V., & Wlodarczyk, L. (2009). Revisiting read-aloud: Instructional strategies that encourage engagement with texts. *The Reading Teacher, 63,* 110–118.

National Early Literacy Panel. (2008). *Developing early literacy: Report of the National Early Literacy Panel.* Washington, DC: National Institute for Literacy. Available at *www.nifl.gov/ earlychilhood/nelp/nelpreport.html.*

Neuman, S., & Dwyer, J. (2011). Developing vocabulary and conceptual knowledge for low-income preschoolers: A design experiment. *Journal of Literacy Research, 43,* 103–129.

Neuman, S., Newman, E., & Dwyer, J. (2011). Educational effects of a vocabulary intervention preschoolers' word knowledge and conceptual development: A cluster-randomized trial. *Reading Research Quarterly, 46,* 249–272.

Pappas, C., & Brown, E. (1987). Learning to read by reading: Learning how to extend the functional potential of language. *Research in the Teaching of English, 21,* 160–184.

Penno, J., Wilkinson, I., & Moore, D. (2002). Vocabulary acquisition from teacher explanation and repeated listening to stories: Do they overcome the Matthew effect? *Journal of Educational Psychology, 94,* 23–33.

Price, L., Van Kleeck, A., & Huberty, C. (2009). Talk during book sharing between parents and preschool children: A comparison between storybook and expository book conditions. *Reading Research Quarterly, 44,* 171–194.

Reese, E., & Cox, A. (1999). Quality of adult book reading affects children's emergent literacy. *Developmental Psychology, 35,* 20–28.

Roberts, T. (2008). Home storybook reading in primary or second language with preschool children: Evidence of equal effectiveness for second-language vocabulary acquisition. *Reading Research Quarterly, 43,* 103–130.

Rowe, D. (1998). The literate potentials of book-related dramatic play. *Reading Research Quarterly, 33,* 10–35.

Santoro, L., Chard, D., Howard, L., & Baker, S. (2008). Making the *very* most of classroom read-alouds to promote comprehension and vocabulary. *The Reading Teacher, 61,* 396–408.

Schickedanz, J., & McGee, L. (2010). The NELP report on shared story reading interventions (Chapter 4): Extending the story. *Educational Research, 39,* 323–329.

Sipe, L. (2008). *Storytime: Young children's literary understanding in the classroom.* New York: Teachers College Press.

Stevens, R., Van Meter, P., & Warcholak, N. (2010). The effects of explicitly teaching story structure to primary grade children. *Journal of Literacy Research, 42,* 159–198.

Van Kleeck, A., Woude, J., & Hammett, I. (2006). Fostering literal and inferential language skills in Head Start children with language impairment using scripted book-sharing discussions. *American Journal of Speech–Language Pathology, 15,* 85–95.

Weisch, J. (2008). Playing with and beyond the story: Enhancing book-related pretend play. *The Reading Teacher, 62,* 138–148.

Willems, M. (2004). *Knuffle Bunny: A cautionary tale.* New York: Hyperion Books for Children.

Wishinsky, F. (1998). *Oonga Boonga* (C. Thompson, Illus.). New York: Dutton Children's Books.

CHAPTER 23

How Do You Write?
Writing for Young Children

STEVE GRAHAM
KAREN R. HARRIS

> If my doctor told me I only had six minutes to live,
> I wouldn't brood. I'd type a little faster.
> —ISAAC ASIMOV

Marco Alisdar is new to the teaching profession. In 2 months he will be teaching preschoolers. Like Isaac Assimov in the opening quote, he likes to write and plans to make writing an integral part of his class. Unfortunately, he is not sure how to make this happen. None of his college courses provided information on how to teach writing to very young children.

Celia Bowen teaches first grade. She is a 5-year classroom veteran and, by all accounts, a very good teacher. Just ask her principal; he claims that she is the best teacher in the school. Despite her success, Ms. Bowen is concerned about writing. Her students rarely write, and she devotes little to no time teaching this critical skill. Her state adopted the Common Core State Standards, and she realizes she will need to make writing an integral part of her class next year.

Ms. Bowen and Mr. Alisdar face two formidable challenges. How can they best teach writing to their young charges, so that they acquire the tools they need to write effectively now and in the future? How can they deliver such instruction so that their students come to value and enjoy writing? These are important goals because writing is a common tool for assessing what elementary and secondary youngsters know (e.g., essay tests, written reports). It provides a powerful mechanism for supporting students' learning because comprehension of material presented in class or text is enhanced when youngsters write about it (Bangert-Drowns, Hurley, & Wilkinson, 2004; Graham & Perin, 2007b). Teaching young children how to write also improves their ability to read and understand text (Graham & Hebert, 2011).

The importance of writing is further emphasized in the new Common Core State Standards (CCSS) adopted by 46 states (National Governors Association Center for Best Practices & Council of Chief State School Officers, 2010; *www.corestandards.org/the-standards/english-language-arts-standards*). The CCSS provide a road map for writing instruction in kindergarten through grades 12. While much of the guide concentrates on older students, the standards presented in kindergarten through grade 3 are relevant to early childhood writing instruction. These standards focus on the acquisition of foundational writing skills, such as handwriting and spelling, as well as the following four writing applications: (1) writing for multiple purposes (e.g., narrate, persuade, inform/explain); (2) producing and publishing well-organized text that is appropriate to task and purpose by increasingly applying processes that involve planning, revising, editing, and collaborating with others; (3) using writing to build knowledge about specific topics or materials read; and (4) applying writing to extend and facilitate learning in a range of discipline-specific subjects, as well as across purposes and audiences (beginning in grade 3). In addition, it is expected that, starting in kindergarten, students will apply digital writing tools to produce and publish their writing.

The implementation of CCSS writing standards requires that most K–3 teachers (including Mr. Alisdar) "up the ante," so to speak, if they are to meet these objectives. A recent national survey with grade 1 to grade 3 teachers (Cutler & Graham, 2010) found that children rarely write persuasive and informative text in the classrooms; they are not taught how to carry out essential writing processes, such as planning and revising; writing to extend and facilitate learning occurs infrequently; and the use of digital writing tools is almost nonexistent.

The purpose of this chapter is to provide road maps for evidence-based writing instruction with young children. Mr. Alisdar and Ms. Bowen will be our guides as we examine how they plan to teach writing next year. Their vision of preschool and first-grade writing instruction is based on the scientific study of writing development and effective writing instruction. Consequently, before examining Ms. Bowen and Mr. Alisdar's envisioned writing programs, we start our journey with a brief foray into writing research with young children.

WHAT RESEARCH SAYS ABOUT WRITING DEVELOPMENT AND INSTRUCTION

Writing Development

Writing is a complex and demanding task, even for those who are good writers. Skilled writing requires the skillful management of the writing environment; the constraints imposed by the writing topic; the intentions of the writer, and the processes, knowledge, and skills involved in composing (Zimmerman & Reisemberg, 1997). In essence, skilled writers are motivated, strategic, and knowledgeable about the craft of writing. Moreover, they have mastered a variety of skills for transforming ideas into acceptable sentences and for transcribing these sentences onto paper via handwriting, spelling, and typing (Graham, 2006).

These same four attributes (motivation, strategies, knowledge, and skills) play an important role in children's development in writing. In a review of the available scientific literature, Graham (2006) found that (1) better writers possess more of each attribute (e.g., knowledge about writing) than poorer writers, (2) children's mastery of each attribute increases with age and schooling, (3) individual differences in children's acquisition of each attribute predicts how well they write, and (4) instruction designed to increase a child's command of each attribute results in better writing.

Learning to write involves more than just acquiring the necessary motivation, skills, strategies, and writing knowledge. It is shaped by the social environment in which learning to write occurs. This includes routines that are established by teachers and children as they write and learn to write (Russell, 1997). To illustrate, writing development is more likely to flourish in an encouraging atmosphere, where children's writing efforts are supported in a positive manner.

Effective Writing Procedures

To develop their writing program for the upcoming year, effective teachers make it a priority to address how to enhance motivation (including creation of a positive writing environment), skills, strategies, and knowledge. They think that application of evidence-based writing practices provides the soundest way to accomplish this goal. Effective writing teachers rely on two types of evidence-based practices. This includes writing practices that were repeatedly effective in improving the writing of young children (4–10 years of age) in scientific studies (e.g., Graham, Kiuhara, McKeown, & Harris, 2012; Rogers & Graham, 2008), as well as writing practices identified through the scientific study of outstanding literacy teachers (Graham, 2010; Graham & Perin, 2007a). These evidence-based practices center around composing, teaching students to write, and supporting students' writing.

Composing

While it may seem obvious, children must write if they are to develop as writers. Surprisingly, young children today spend little time writing in school, about 20 minutes a day in the primary grades (Cutler & Graham, 2008), even though scientific studies show that increasing the amount of time students write enhances the overall quality of their writing (Graham et al., 2012).

For young beginning writers (especially in preschool through grade 1), writing is often interactive (Hall, 2012). Students may dictate compositions to their teacher or an aide (shared writing), or writing may be even more interactive, with teacher and children conjointly taking an active role in creating text. The text produced by young writers is also varied because it involves print (handwritten or digital), drawings, pictures, sounds, or some combination of these. There is also evidence that the writing of children in grades 1–3 improves over time when word processing is their primary mode for composing (Graham et al., 2012).

Teaching Students to Write

To develop as writers, children need to acquire special writing skills, strategies, and knowledge. Scientific studies demonstrate that young students' writing improves (Graham, Harris, & Hebert, 2011; Graham et al., 2012; Rogers & Graham, 2008) when they are taught the following:

1. Foundational writing skills such as handwriting, typing, spelling, usage, and sentence construction. The goal of such instruction is for students to be able to apply these skills correctly and in a facile manner.

2. Strategies for planning, revising, and editing their written products. Such instruction involves teaching general strategies, such as brainstorming, or more specific strategies, such as steps for writing a persuasive essay. In either case, the teacher models how to apply the strategy and provides assistance in using the strategy until children can apply it independently.

3. Structural characteristics of different types of text. This includes exploring the structure of both narrative and expository text. One way of teaching such knowledge is to provide students with model texts for a specific type of writing (e.g., narrative, explanations, descriptions, opinion), helping them to identify one or more basic structures in these models, then asking them to apply these elements in their own writing.

4. Attributes of good writing. One way of acquiring knowledge about these attributes is by teaching children to assess their own writing or the writing of their peers. For instance, they can be taught how to assess basic writing attributes such as organization, ideation, and word use.

Supporting Students' Writing

Because young students are still learning to write, they need support from their teachers and classmates. As noted earlier, teachers can support young students' writing efforts through shared and interactive writing activities. Six additional evidence-based practices for supporting young students' writing (Graham et al., 2011, 2012; Graham & Perin, 2007a; Rogers & Graham, 2008) follow:

1. Set specific goals for writing. Goals can be established by teachers or created by students. Examples of goals include adding three more ideas to a paper when revising or including specific elements in a piece of writing (e.g., at least three reasons to support one's belief in an opinion essay).

2. Establish a writing routine in which students are expected to plan, write, revise, and publish their compositions for authentic audiences and real purposes.

3. Encourage children to work together as they plan, write, edit, and revise their writing. Such collaborative efforts should be structured, with teachers providing explicit expectations for student behavior and actions within their cooperative groups or partnerships. For example, if the class is working on use of descriptive words in writing, one child might be assigned to give feedback to a peer, noting places in the text where such vocabulary enhances writing, as well as identifying places where more descriptive words are needed.

4. Engage students in prewriting activities that help them produce and organize their ideas. Examples of activities include tasks that encourage students to access what they already know, read about a topic to obtain more information, or arrange their ideas visually (e.g., graphic organizer) before writing.

5. Reinforce positive aspects of students' writing. This includes providing social praise, tangible reinforcers, or both, as a means of increasing specific writing behaviors.

6. Provide feedback on students' writing progress. This includes teachers providing feedback on students' progress in learning specific writing skills or strategies, as well as peers providing feedback to each other on their writing.

RESEARCH INTO PRACTICE

The Case of Mr. Alisdar

As Mr. Alisdar began to think about teaching writing to the children in his upcoming preschool class, a former Professor shared with him several chapters and articles about children's writing (Graham, 2006, 2010; Rowe, 2008; Rowe & Neitzel, 2010). Among other things, these sources provide information about how children's writing develops and a set of effective instructional tools for enhancing this development. The information in these texts is consistent with our earlier description of what research tells us about writing development and instruction.

Mr. Alisdar considers the instructional procedures contained in the borrowed text to be "potentially effective." One reason for this is that many of the practices identified in these sources were tested and validated with children in the primary grades. His preschool children are obviously younger. Another reason is that the rest of the identified practices in these texts were obtained by studying the instructional writing procedures applied by highly effective literacy teachers (both preschool and elementary-grade teachers). These practices were not scientifically tested through experimentation, so their impact on young children's writing development is uncertain.

In developing his preschool writing program, Mr. Alisdar decides his first step is to determine how to structure it. After some reflection, he decides to implement the following routines:

- Dedicate time for students to write each day.
- Involve students in various forms of writing over time.
- Teach writing each day, mixing whole-class instruction, teaching to small groups, and one-on-one interactions with individual students.
- Create multiple writing centers where students independently engage in writing.
- Create a writing storage shelf where children access a variety of writing materials and activities.
- Position writing within play activities.
- Use shared and interactive writing as vehicles for supporting students' writing skills, strategies, and knowledge.

Next, Mr. Alisdar considers how to support students' development of writing motivation, skills, strategies, and knowledge. He starts with motivation because previous experience has made it clear that young children like to write. For Mr. Alisdar, this is captured in a quote he recently read: "Children want to write. . . . This is no accident. Before they went to school they marked-up walls, pavements, newspapers with crayons, chalk, pen, or pencils (Graves, 1983, p. 3).

Motivation to Write

Mr. Alisdar decides that to make his class a motivating place for young writers, he needs to fill it with writing tools, materials, and activities. This includes stocking the writing centers and writing storage shelf with all kinds of writing tools, including pens, pencils, chalk, paint, crayons, dry-erase markers, and stamps. Writing materials includes lined and unlined paper, colored paper, notebooks, note pads, stationary, envelopes, colored paper, easels with large paper, magnetic slates, postcards, scissors, tape, and magazines with lots of pictures that students can remove and label. He does not need to worry about obtaining a chalkboard, a dry-erase board, or a computer—these are already in the classroom he will occupy. As he reconsiders what else he might need, Mr. Alisdar decides to obtain alphabet books, alphabet puzzles, toy mailboxes, letter templates, and magnetic letters. He makes a mental note to revisit this issue at the end of the first month of school because the need for additional tools, materials, and activities will be evident once instruction is under way.

He also decides that students are more likely to enjoy writing if choice is a part of the program. As a consequence, he plans to encourage students to write by themselves or with a peer on something of their own choosing several times a week. During this free writing time, he intends to direct students to work at a writing center or take writing materials from the writing shelf. He decides to design writing centers so that they involve play-based and social communication writing activities (Figure 23.1 provides examples of such writing centers).

To ensure further that the children in his class enjoyed writing, Mr. Alisdar decides to make the following procedures a regular part of his writing program:

- Praise children's varied writing efforts (e.g., pretend writing, scribbles, drawings, paintings, a string of letters, or conventional writing).
- Celebrate and post children's writing in the classroom.
- Provide children the opportunity to share their writing with others through reading, dramatization, role playing, and other forms of self-expression.
- Encourage children to share writing done at home at school, and vice versa.

Writing Skills

Mr. Alisdar next turns his attention to what writing skills to emphasize during the upcoming year and how to teach them. To help him think about this, he consults a report from the National Early Literacy Panel (Lonigan & Shanahan, 2009), locating information on early literacy skills typically acquired before age 5 that best predict later literacy success. For later writing success, the best early predictors are phonological awareness; recognizing, naming, and writing individual letters; and writing one's name. After reading a book by Marie Clay (1975), Mr. Alisdar realizes that preschool children need to learn about the basic conventions of print, too (e.g., writing moves from left to right and top to bottom; names start with a capital letter).

- **Story Writing Center**: stocked with story picture books; children are encouraged to draw one or more pictures for the story and act out the revised narrative.
- **Mail Center**: stocked with stationary, envelopes, postcards, and stamps; children are encouraged to write (or pretend to write) a letter to a classmate (deposited in the peer's cubby) or a family member (sent home in the child's backpack).
- **Gift Center**: stocked with a variety of writing utensils; children are encouraged to create a writing gift (e.g., a drawing, a cut-out picture that is labeled) for another classmate or a family member.

FIGURE 23.1. Examples of writing potential centers.

To teach basic phonological awareness skills, Mr. Alisdar decides to make activities such as the following a common feature of his class:

- Recite finger plays such as "Itsy-Bitsy Spider" and "I'm A Little Teapot," or sing songs such as "This Old Man" and "Teddy Bear, Teddy Bear" to promote sound awareness.
- Read simple, big books to the class, pointing to specific words as they are read.
- Read poems, nursery rhymes, and rhyming poems to the class.
- Play rhyming games in which the teacher says a word (i.e., *cat*) and children try to find a word that rhymes with it (e.g., *sat, rat, mat*).
- Clap out the syllable in words, then have the children clap out the syllables with you.
- Change the first and last sounds in words; for example, tell children that a rat went to sleep over night and woke up as a new animal who loves to purr. What is he now?

To teach children to recognize, name, and write individual letters (lowercase and capital), Mr. Alisdar plans to apply a variety of different activities. Examples of activities he means to use include reading alphabet books with the class; pointing out and naming individual letters as he reads big books to children; teaching his class the alphabet song; showing a letter card and asking students to name the letter; saying the name of a letter and asking students to identify a card containing the letter; modeling how to write the letter; asking students to trace the letter and copy it; and encouraging students to write the letter from memory. He further decides that he needs to remind himself to model and reinforce the use of correct pencil grip.

Another tool that Mr. Alisdar plans to use to teach letters is interactive writing. An example of how he intends to do this is presented in Figure 23.2.

To help his students learn to write their names, Mr. Alisdar plans to provide students with written models of their names, show them how to write each letter, and encourage them to trace the letters with their pencil (for some students he may focus only on one letter at a time). As the class participates in shared and interactive writing activities, he means to ask them to write their name or part of it on completed products. During such writing activities, Mr. Alisdar intends judiciously to decide which concepts of print

---

- The teacher asks students if they would like to taste an apple pie. This leads to a discussion about apples and where they come from. The teacher then reads out loud *The Apple Pie Tree* by Zoe Hall (1996), pointing out the letter *a* and other letters when appropriate. The reading of the book leads to further discussion about apple pies and how they are made.

- The next day, the class begins working on a written list of ingredients that are needed to make an apple pie. As the teacher and students brainstorm each ingredient, they orally stretch out the first sound of the word (AAAA-pples) and take turns writing the letter for the first sound, receiving help from the teacher as needed.

- As this process continues, some students contributed a picture, a letter, or a whole word to the class text. As this writing process is under way, the teacher highlights concepts of print such as spacing and directionality.

FIGURE 23.2. An example of interactive writing. Based on Hall (2012).

to highlight (e.g., capitalization, punctuation), and return to these concepts later when the class works on other shared and interactive writing assignments. As in any class of preschool children, some children acquire conventional writing skills more quickly than others. Mr. Alisdar plans to encourage and support such development because it provides good models of writing for the whole class.

Writing Strategies

A key to becoming a good writer is learning how to regulate the writing environment, one's writing behaviors, and the writing process (Zimmerman & Reisemberg, 1997). While Mr. Alisdar's students are taking their first steps on the road to becoming self-directed writers, he wants to be sure to help them get a good start down this path. An important part of learning to regulate the writing environment is getting, putting away, and taking care of the tools and materials used during writing. Mr. Alisdar plans not only to stress individual responsibility for each of these activities but also to assign helpers (on a rotating basis) who assist other class members as needed.

Mr. Alisdar further intends to stress two aspects of regulating writing behavior: (1) asking for help with writing when needed and (2) working productively. His approach to meet this first objective is to tell students that he wants them to ask for help when they need it, to model how to seek help appropriately, to provide students with practice in doing this correctly, and to praise and reinforce their help-seeking behavior. For his second objective, he plans to determine what students are thinking about doing during free writing time and to provide guidance as needed. He also means to conference with individual children who have trouble staying on task, to determine possible solutions.

In terms of regulating the writing process, Mr. Alisdar plans to emphasize strategies for planning and revising, which includes modeling how to plan and revise during interactive writing sessions. For example, during interactive writing session he intends to ask students to help him think about the purpose of the task and the audience. Over time, he means to model further how to set simple goals for such writing tasks, brainstorm ideas, and use drawing as a way to think, generate, or organize ideas. His ultimate goal is for students to share the responsibility for carrying out such planning activities during both shared and interactive writing.

Mr. Alisdar plans to use similar procedures to promote evaluation and revision. He intends to model making changes to what is planned or written during interactive writing, with students' increased sharing of this responsibility over the course of the year. He further intends to share his own writing with the class, asking students for suggestions to make what he writes better. Once students become comfortable sharing a written product with the class, he plans to ask class members to identify at least four things they liked about it and one thing they might change. The author would be encouraged to make the change if he or she agrees that it is a good idea.

Writing Knowledge

The primary mechanism that Mr. Alisdar means to use to increase students' knowledge about writing is reading. He intends to focus on three types of knowledge: concepts of print (this is also emphasized when the class engages in interactive writing), vocabulary (how word meanings are used in text), and the structural elements of specific types of text. As he reads books to students in his class, Mr. Alisdar plans to focus students' attention on specific aspects of the text. This includes, but is not limited to, how text moves from left to right and top to bottom, how spacing is used to separate letters and words, how the title of the book captures the reader's interest, how headings are used to provide structure to the composition, how highlighting brings special attention to words or a group of words, how pictures convey meaning and capture interest, how sentence patterns provide rhythm to the reading of the text, how words are put together to form vivid images, and how elements comprise a specific type of writing (e.g., stories tell what happen to one or more characters).

Not only will Mr. Alisdar stress reading with a "writer's eye" (Guth, 1987), but he means for his students to apply what they learn as they compose shared and interactive text. For example, after reading the "Little Red Hen," he intends for class members to compose their own version of the story, using the same word patterns but with characters who live at the zoo.

The Case of Ms. Bowen

To prepare for the upcoming school year, Ms. Bowen acquires the Common Core State Standards (CCSS) for writing in first grade (see Figure 23.3). These standards focus on three writing applications: (1) writing for multiple purposes (Text Types and Purposes); (2) supported production of text using traditional paper and pencil, as well as digital tools (Production and Distribution of Writing); and (3) supported use of writing as a tool for gathering and recalling information on specific topics (Research to Build and Present Knowledge). They also emphasize mastering a variety of handwriting, grammar, usage, and spelling foundational writing skills.

Motivation to Write

The first decision that Ms. Bowen makes for the upcoming year is to create a positive writing environment (applying the type of practices employed by highly effective literacy teachers [Graham, 2010] and supported by empirical research [Graham et al., 2012]). She reasons that her students are more likely to acquire the applications and skills emphasized in CCSS if they are learning to write in a pleasant, engaging, and supportive atmosphere. Figure 23.4 presents the eight procedures she intends to implement.

Writing Skills

Ms. Bowen finds the CCSS to be very helpful as she thinks about which writing skills to teach to her students next year. Similar to highly effective literacy teachers (Graham, 2010), she decides that the best skills instruction involves making it clear to students why they are learning a particular skill, modeling how to use it (multiple times if necessary), providing guided assistance as they practice applying the skill, and using the skill in context (when writing). For example, for handwriting she plans to teach lowercase letters first because students use these more often. She intends to teach two or three letters together that share similar formational characteristics, and to sequence these letter sets so that more common and easier letters are taught first (e.g., *l, i, t,* and *o, e, a*). For each set of letters, she plans for the class to review why it is important to learn these letters (i.e., so that others can read what students write, and so they can write down their ideas easily). Next, after Ms. Bowen models how to form each letter, students trace, copy, and write each letter from memory several times, then circle their very best letter. She further decides that this practice routine is to be repeated three or four times over the course of

Text Type and Purposes:

—Write opinion pieces in which they introduce the topic or name the book they are writing about, state an opinion, supply a reason for the opinion, and provide some sense of closure.

—Write informative/explanatory texts in which they name a topic, supply some facts about the topic, and provide some sense of closure.

—Write narratives in which they recount two or more appropriately sequenced events, include some details regarding what happened, use temporal words to signal event order, and provide some sense of closure.

Production and Distribution of Writing:

—With guidance and support from adults, focus on a topic, respond to questions and suggestions from peers, and add details to strengthen writing as needed.

—With guidance and support from adults, use a variety of digital tools to produce and publish writing, including in collaboration with peers.

Research to Build and Present Knowledge:

—Participate in shared research and writing projects (e.g., explore a number of "how-to" books on a given topic and use them to write a sequence of instructions).

—With guidance and support from adults, recall information from experiences or gather information from provided sources to answer a question.

Conventions of English:

—Demonstrate command of the conventions of standard English grammar and usage when writing: print all upper- and lowercase letters; use common, proper, and possessive nouns; use singular and plural nouns with matching verbs in basic sentences (e.g., He hops; We hop); use personal, possessive, and indefinite pronouns (e.g., *I, me, my*; *they, them, their, anyone, everything*); use verbs to convey a sense of past, present, and future (e.g., Yesterday I walked home; Today I walk home; Tomorrow I will walk home); use frequently occurring adjectives; use frequently occurring conjunctions (e.g., *and, but, or, so, because*); use determiners (e.g., articles, demonstratives); use frequently occurring prepositions (e.g., *during, beyond, toward*); produce and expand complete simple and compound declarative, interrogative, imperative, and exclamatory sentences in response to prompts.

—Demonstrate command of the conventions of standard English capitalization, punctuation, and spelling when writing: capitalize dates and names of people; use end punctuation for sentences; use commas in dates and to separate single words in a series; use conventional spelling for words with common spelling patterns and for frequently occurring irregular words; and spell untaught words phonetically, drawing on phonemic awareness and spelling conventions.

FIGURE 23.3. Common Core State Standards for writing in grade 1. From *www.corestandards. org/the-standards/english-language-arts-standards.*

a week, and that students will switch from tracing, copying, and writing individual letters (e.g., *o*) from memory to writing words (*loose*) and Hinky-Pinks (*Loosey-Goosey*) containing the letters. Once a week or more she intends for students to look at something written previously and correct malformed letters or create a sentence using the letters they are learning (e.g., for the letter *a*: "All ants are alike").

Her plan for spelling involves teaching students not only how to spell words they commonly use in their writing (taken from a list developed by Graham, Harris, & Loynachan, 1993) but also to increase their capacity to spell words in general. Every 2 weeks, she intends to contrast two spelling patterns (e.g., short vowels /a/ and /o/; short and long /a/; or long vowels /ay/ and /ai/). These patterns are to be introduced through a word-sorting activity, in which Ms. Bowen sorts words involving the two patterns into different piles and provides hints to students about why she places each card in one of the two piles (e.g., by emphasizing a specific sound in a word), leading students to discover and specifically state (with her help) the rule underlying the spelling patterns. During the next 2 weeks, she expects students to search for words in their reading and writing that fit the patterns; to learn to spell common words that fit the patterns by playing games (e.g., tic-tac-toe spelling); to build words with the patterns by adding consonants, blends, or diagraphs to rimes representing the patter (e.g., the rime "at" for short /a/); and to write something in less than 5 minutes that includes one or more of the pattern words.

Ms. Bowen decides to teach grammar and usage skills within the context of sentences. For example, to teach the use of commas to separate single words in a series (see Figure 23.3), she intends to write three sentence on the whiteboard (e.g., The dog is black. The dog is big. The dog is nice.), and model how to combine them into a single sentence (The dog is big, black, and nice). She expects to model the application of this skill several times with different sentences, then have students work together to combine several additional sets of sentences to practice this skill. Ms. Bowen plans for students to create several sentences of their own using commas to separate single words in a series, then share one of these with the class. Finally, she intends to ask students to look at something written previously and either make a revision involving this skill or add a sentence in which the skill is applied.

---

1. Reinforce students' writing accomplishments by having them share what they write with others, posting their work throughout the classroom and on a class Facebook page, and praising their writing attainments.

2. Structure the classroom so that students work together in positive and constructive ways while writing.

3. Create writing assignments that serve a real purpose, while providing students with a choice about writing topics and allowing them to modify assignments (to a reasonable degree), so that they are more interesting.

4. Give constructive feedback on students' writing but limit it to one to two items, while providing assistance (including teaching if needed) on how to address these concerns.

5. Create an enthusiastic and positive environment where children are encouraged to try hard, where they believe that the writing skills and strategies they are taught will help them be better writers, and where they attribute writing success to effort and the writing skills and strategies they are learning.

6. Provide students with just enough support that they can successfully carry out writing tasks and processes, but encourage them to act in a self-directed manner, doing as much as they can on their own.

7. Set clear goals for students' writing as well as high expectations, encouraging all students to surpass their previous writing efforts or accomplishments.

8. Adapt writing instruction and assignments to meet the needs of individual students.

FIGURE 23.4. Establishing a motivating writing classroom environment.

Writing Strategies and Knowledge

After carefully reviewing CCSS writing, Ms. Bowen decides to bundle writing strategies and knowledge together in planning next year's writing program. The CCSS for Text Types and Purposes (see Figure 23.3) emphasize three types of writing (persuasive, informative/explanatory, and narrative), with each primarily described in terms of basic structural elements for each type of text. For example, first-grade students are expected to write an opinion essay that introduces the topic, states an opinion supported by at least one reason, and provides some sense of closure. CCSS for Production and Distribution of Writing (see Figure 23.3), in contrast, emphasize writing processes needed to produce such papers. While the standards for writing process are pretty truncated at grade 1 (mostly involving topic focus and revision), Ms. Bowen decides that teaching her students' strategies to plan text that center around knowledge of structural elements makes good sense given that structural elements receive so much emphasis in CCSS and planning is critical to writing success (Graham, 2006).

In developing next year's writing program, Ms. Bowen decides to make two departures from CCSS in writing. First, the standards stress the use of a variety of digital tools to produce and publish writing, but there is only one computer in her classroom. She intends to encourage students to use this computer to publish their writing and to produce text with it whenever possible, but a single computer can only go so far (this is an issue for many teachers; Cutler & Graham, 2008). Second, CCSS emphasize that students' writing is to be produced with guidance and support from adults. While Ms. Bowen generally agrees with this idea, she does not want to do for children what they are capable for doing for themselves (see Figure 23.4). As a result, at the start of the year, she intends for students' planning, composing, and revising of text to be done with her through shared and interactive writing activities (see Figure 23.2). But by the second half of the school year, she expects to be teaching her students specific planning and revising strategies they can learn to apply independently. Figure 23.5 illustrates how she means to teach a writing strategy in one genre.

A major goal of CCSS is for students to use writing as a tool for both learning content material and comprehending the material read. In essence, students develop better understanding about a topic or specific text by writing about it (Graham & Perin, 2007b; Graham & Hebert, 2011). Ms. Bowen plans to make writing an integral tool to support learning and reading in her classroom. An example of an activity she intends to use is presented in Figure 23.6.

REFLECTIONS AND NEW DIRECTIONS

Mr. Alisdar and Ms. Bowen are to be commended for thinking about their writing programs so carefully and for deciding to implement evidence-based practices. Implementing such practices is not an easy task, though (Graham, 2013). Just because a writing practice is effective in a research study or used by highly effective literacy teachers does not guarantee that it will be effective in another teacher's classroom. There is rarely a perfect match between the conditions under which the writing practice is tested in research studies and the conditions in which it is subsequently put to use in classrooms. Even if the match were perfect, the safest course of action would be for teachers like Ms. Bowen and Mr. Alisdar to monitor the effects of the practice to be sure it works in their classrooms with their students.

Gaining knowledge about genre: A discussion with the class about the characteristics of good stories is initiated. As ideas are generated, they are listed on a whiteboard. The teacher provides a label for any common narrative elements identified, such as character and action. They teacher and the class read a story together and discuss what made the story enjoyable, listing and naming any new elements on the whiteboard. This is followed by a "story hunt" to find and discuss other story elements previously listed on the whiteboard. This process is repeated over several days until students are able to easily identify basic story elements in the material they are reading.

Teaching a genre specific strategy for planning/drafting text: Once students are familiar with all of the basic elements of a story, the teacher introduces a strategy in which students generate ideas before they start to write, using these elements as a prompt (Who are the characters in the story?). This includes generating prewriting ideas: who the story is about, when and where it takes place, what the main character wants to do, what happens, how the characters feel during the story, and how the story ends. The teacher models how to plan such a story (with help from the class), then they write the story together. The teacher continues modeling the strategy until the students are ready to apply it more independently with a peer (the teacher provides story writing partners, with assistance as needed). Finally, the teacher encourages students to write stories independently.

FIGURE 23.5. Teaching a story writing strategy for planning and drafting text. Strategies for planning, drafting, revising, and editing are available in *Writing Better* (Graham & Harris, 2005) and *Powerful Writing Strategies for All Students* (Harris, Graham, Mason, & Friedlander, 2008).

We currently do not know what combination or how much of evidence-based practice is needed to maximize writing development. There is evidence that using different evidence-based writing practices together can be beneficial (Sadoski, Wilson, & Norton, 1997), but teachers are mostly on their own to decide what dose and mixture is best. Once again, this makes it imperative that teachers monitor the effects of their writing program for each student in their class.

Before bringing this chapter to a close, it is important to recognize that we know very little about how to teach writing to preschool children. In fact, Mr. Alisdar had to rely heavily on research conducted with primary-grade children to plan his writing program. Finally, bringing children into the digital age of writing at school will remain a difficult task (as it was for Ms. Bowen), if we do not have enough 21st-century writing tools available in schools to make this a realistic possibility.

At the start of an earth science lesson about weather, the teacher asks students what the weather is like today. As students provide answers to questions, the teacher writes them on the blackboard. Next, she asks students to tell her what they think the weather will be like tomorrow (students draw and/or write their predictions in their science journals). They share their predictions with each other and discuss why they formed them. The next day, they again discuss the day's weather, revise their earlier prediction in their science journals, and make a new prediction for the next day. This is continued until the teacher judges that reasons the weather changes have been adequately explored.

FIGURE 23.6. Example of using writing to support content learning.

PROFESSIONAL DEVELOPMENT ACTIVITIES

- Pair with one or more teachers (or prospective teachers) in your school (or class). Select an age or grade level on which to focus. Determine how you will advance children's writing motivation, skills, strategies, and knowledge at the selected age or grade level.

- Form a study group with other teachers (or students in your class). Conjointly construct an interactive writing lesson, in which you and the children in your class first read something together, then write a response interactively that highlights an important writing skill.

- Develop an outline for how you will teach narrative, persuasive, or explanatory/informative text to students in your class (or practicum). Be as specific as possible. Then consider the students in your class and identify who is going to need extra assistance. Identify the supports and scaffolds you plan to put in place for these students and how you will modify what you are doing to ensure that they are successful.

REFERENCES

Bangert-Drowns, R. L., Hurley, M. M., & Wilkinson, B. (2004). The effects of school-based Writing-to-Learn interventions on academic achievement: A meta-analysis. *Review of Educational Research, 74,* 29–58.

Clay, M. (1975). *What did I write?: Beginning writing behavior.* Portsmouth, NH: Heinemann.

Cutler, L., & Graham, S. (2008). Primary grade writing instruction: A national survey. *Journal of Educational Psychology, 100,* 907–919.

Graham, S. (2006). Writing. In P. Alexander & P. Winne (Eds.), *Handbook of educational psychology* (pp. 457–478). Mahwah, NJ: Erlbaum.

Graham, S. (2010). Teaching writing. In P. Hogan (Ed.), *Cambridge encyclopedia of language sciences* (pp. 848–851). Cambridge, UK: Cambridge University Press.

Graham, S. (2013). Writing standards. In L. M. Morrow, K. K. Wixson, & T. Shanahan (Eds.), *Teaching with the Common Core Standards for English language arts, Grades 3–5* (pp. 88–106). New York: Guilford Press.

Graham, S., & Harris, K. R. (2005). *Writing better: Teaching writing processes and self-regulation to students with learning problems.* Baltimore: Brookes.

Graham, S., Harris, K. R., & Hebert, M. (2011). *Informing Writing: The benefits of formative assessment.* Washington, DC: Alliance for Excellence in Education.

Graham, S., Harris, K. R., & Loynachan, C. (1993). The basic spelling vocabulary. *Journal of Educational Research, 86,* 363–368.

Graham, S., & Hebert, M. (2011). Writing-to-read: A meta-analysis of the impact of writing and writing instruction on reading. *Harvard Educational Review, 81,* 710–744.

Graham, S., Kiuhara, S., McKeown, D., & Harris, K. R. (2012). A meta-analysis of writing instruction for students in the elementary grades. *Journal of Educational Psychology, 104,* 879–896.

Graham, S., & Perin, D. (2007a). What we know, what we still need to know: Teaching adolescents to write. *Scientific Studies in Reading, 11,* 313–336.

Graham, S., & Perin, D. (2007b). *Writing Next: Effective strategies to improve writing of adolescent middle and high school.* Washington, DC: Alliance for Excellence in Education.

Graves, D. (1983). *Writing: Teachers and children at work.* London: Heinemann.

Guth, H. P. (1987). *Essay 2: Reading with the writer's eye* (2nd ed.). Florence, KY: Wadsworth.

Hall, A. (2012). *Exploring the effectiveness of interactive writing in the Head Start preschool setting.* Unpublished doctoral dissertation, University of Kentucky, Lexington.

Hall, Z. (1996). *The apple pie tree*. New York: Blue Sky Press.

Harris, K. R., Graham, S., Mason, L., & Friedlander, B. (2008). *Powerful writing strategies for all students*. Baltimore: Brookes.

Lonigan, C., & Shanahan, T. (2009). Executive summary: Developing early literacy: Report of the National Early Literacy Panel. Retrieved from *http://lincs.ed.gov/publications/pdf/nelpsummary.pdf*.

National Governors Association Center for Best Practices & Council of Chief State School Officers. (2010). *Common Core State Standards*. Washington, DC: Author. Retrieved from *www.corestandards.org*.

Rogers, L., & Graham, S. (2008). A meta-analysis of single subject design writing intervention research. *Journal of Educational Psychology, 100*, 879–906.

Rowe, D. (2008). Social contracts for writing: Negotiating shared understandings about text in the preschool years. *Reading Research Quarterly, 43*, 66–95.

Rowe, D., & Neitzel, C. (2010). Interest and agency in 2- and 3-year olds' participation in emergent writing. *Reading Research Quarterly, 45*, 169–195.

Russell, D. (1997). Rethinking genre in school and society: An activity theory analysis. *Written Communication, 14*, 504–554.

Sadoski, M., Wilson, V., & Norton, D. (1997). The relative contribution of research-based composition activities to writing improvement in lower and middle grades. *Research in the Teaching of English, 31*, 120–150.

Zimmerman, B., & Reisemberg, R. (1997). Becoming a self-regulated writer: A social cognitive perspective. *Contemporary Educational Psychology, 22*, 73–101.

CHAPTER 24

LEARNING TO WORK IT OUT
Social Education for Young Students

LINDA S. LEVSTIK

Maybe our classrooms can be nicer than the outside world.
—VIVIAN PALEY (1993, p. 22)

A group of 4-year-olds gathers around Ms. Barrow as she places a colorful box on the world map rug on the floor. They have been locating continents, first on a color-coded puzzle map, then on inflatable globes and, finally, on the floor map. Ms. Barrow asks if anyone can tell her which continent lies under the box. The children chorus "Asia" and Ms. Barrow nods, lifting the box so all can see the continent label on the map. She explains that she is holding a continent box that contains cultural treasures from Asia. "The first Asian treasure, " she says, lifting a pair of chopsticks out of the box, "is . . . ?"

"Chopsticks!" several students call out.

Again, Ms. Barrow nods agreement. "Today I am going to read a story about chopsticks," she tells them, holding up *How My Parents Learned to Eat* (Friedman, 1987). She begins reading: "In my house, some days we eat with chopsticks and some days we eat with knives and forks. For me it's natural" (p. 1).

Mr. Kitts's first-grade class on the Santo Domingo Pueblo also uses children's literature to investigate how farming has changed over time. Because English is a second language for about 90% of his students, Mr. Kitts works with a translator in his classroom. As he introduces abstract concepts (chronology and technological change, for instance) he begins in English then asks the translator to explain in the students' home language. Careful attention to words and illustrations in the literature, followed by opportunities for students to illustrate important concepts through their own words and images, further reinforces new ideas. Rather than treat language differences in his classroom as a disadvantage, Mr. Kitts turns them into advantages. Sometimes, for instance, he asks students to back-translate—to tell him in English what the translator said in their home language. This comprehension check—students must understand the concept well enough to explain it in English—has the additional benefit of reinforcing students' bilingual expertise, while allowing the teacher and translator to make sure they are giving students the same information (Annenberg Foundation, 2001).

In a third classroom, two of Ms. Ruiz's kindergartners work in the peace center, using puppets to act out a dispute and negotiate a settlement based on the processes they learned and practiced during the very first week of school. Amelia uses a puppet to explain why Peter's "joke" made her feel hurt and angry, and Peter's puppet responds with an apology. Their negotiation goes smoothly—it is well into the year and they have had plenty of practice in reconciliation: sometimes apologizing, sometimes providing recompense ("I will replace the crayon I broke"), sometimes agreeing to a different work pattern ("We can take turns using the computer") (Angell, 2004; Berman, 1997; Bickmore, 2008).

In each of these classrooms, purposeful social education is a fundamental part of the curriculum. Indeed, social education has long been a significant feature of early childhood education. Ironically, however, the prevalence of social education in early childhood curricula has never elicited the kind of research attention given to other aspects of the curricular field with which it is most associated—social studies. Much can be gained, however, from a careful consideration of existing theory and research, beginning with a consideration of the purpose of social studies in early childhood settings.

WHAT RESEARCH SAYS ABOUT SOCIAL STUDIES

In considering the classrooms young children need, Patricia Cooper (2011) suggests that teachers consider "not only who young children are, but . . . who we can help them become" (p. 5). Although there are many things children *could* become, as members of a pluralist[1] democracy in an increasingly interconnected world we have a vested interest in helping all children become informed, participatory citizens, and social studies is one means to that end. From a social studies perspective, education supports students as they become increasingly "competent and confident learners and communicators . . . secure in their sense of belonging and in the knowledge that they make *a valued contribution to society*" (Hedges & Lee, 2008, p. 13, emphasis added). It is this latter emphasis on the individual *in community* that makes social studies such a crucial part of children's education because it focuses on developing respect for and willingness to work with diverse others, uniting that interest with democratic principles, and engaging students in dialogue about an increasingly humane and ever-evolving *common good* (Aitken & Sinnema, 2008; Barton & Levstik, 2004; Cooper, 2011; Iverson & James, 2011; Ladson-Billings, 2001; Paley, 1993). This is not a matter of indoctrinating young children in a single way of living in the world, but of inviting them to consider how to protect and celebrate diversity without losing the sense of connection and unity that makes sharing public spaces possible (Appiah, 2006; Barton & Levstik, 2004; Cooper, 2011; Selman, 2003).

---

[1]In this context, *pluralist* refers to the diversity of cultures in a single democracy and to that democracy's attempts to acknowledge, understand, and appreciate diversity.

Sharing Public Spaces

The deeply human tendency to create common ground for community interaction and community development can be traced from the earliest human communities to the present. Democracies rely on a variety of such public spaces, including schools, as laboratories for democracy (Dewey, 1916). Given that goal, social studies can best be seen as an *apprenticeship in democratic living* (Evans, 2010; Hahn, 2008; Levinson, 2012; Parker, 2008). It is worth remembering, however, that while every classroom embodies a system of values, goals, and purposes, some more closely resemble such an apprenticeship than others (Arthur, Davies, & Hahn, 2008; Hahn, 2008; National School Climate Center, 2012).

Early childhood educators are in the fortunate position of having long advocated practices associated with democratic classroom climates: emphases on connecting curricular content to children's lives outside of school, discussing individual and collective rights and responsibilities, and working together to achieve goals that contribute to the common good (Cooper, 2011; Hedges & Lee, 2008; Houser, 1996; James, 2012; Levstik & Barton, 2008). Social studies research also supports these practices in regard to three critical elements of a democratic apprenticeship: building equitable public spaces, engaging in social inquiry, and taking civic action (see Figure 24.1).

Building Equitable Public Spaces

Naming Difference

All the people like us are We, and everyone else is They.
—RUDYARD KIPLING (1926)

In his poem "We and They," Rudyard Kipling points out a common human tendency: noticing similarities and differences, and using these observations to distinguish between "we and they." At least initially, young children engage in this activity to figure out how members of the human community fit (or fail to fit) together: What differences make a difference? What are the rules of engagement across differences? How do people name difference, and what happens when they/we do? And, most crucially for a pluralist democracy, how do people negotiate differences that create discord? These are shark-infested waters for all of us, not least of all young children trying to live in community and struggling to name the differences they observe.

The power of naming has a long and troublesome history, especially in regard to race and ethnicity (Graham, 2009). Colonial powers not only renamed the places they colonized, they renamed the people, grouped them into races with specious "racial" traits, established hierarchies based on those traits, and used insulting names and images to maintain their hierarchies. Too often, insulting names follow children into classrooms with devastating consequences (Banks & Nguyen, 2008; Cooper, 2011; Ladson-Billings, 2001, 2009). Fortunately, educators can counter this legacy with one of the most powerful tools a democratic apprenticeship can offer, *respectful naming*. Respectful naming encourages children to see differences in healthy ways and to discuss them in an atmosphere of mutual respect and tolerance. This seems so self-evident that we sometimes forget how challenging it can be.

To begin with, young children may interpret words and phrases quite differently—and quite literally—relative to adult understandings. There's the 4-year-old who

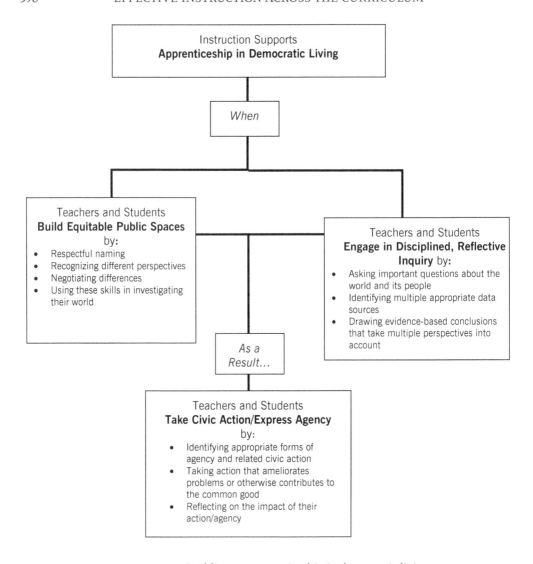

FIGURE 24.1. Building an apprenticeship in democratic living.

demonstrates "running for president" by running around the room or the 5-year-old who is amazed to learn that running for president involves a party. Another 5-year-old misunderstands the word *extinct* and refuses to enter a dinosaur exhibit because he fears it "stinked" (Levstik, 1994). As natural as these misconceptions are, they remind us how easily new vocabulary and especially metaphorical language can be misconstrued, and how much scaffolding is required to support any lasting conceptual change, even with relatively benign vocabulary.

Adults facing a more charged vocabulary may well be wary of naming or even seeing differences. You might recall the story of the emperor's new clothes. All the townspeople ignored what was obvious to a child—the emperor wore no clothes. A similar blindness occurs today when adults claim they "don't see race." In part they may hope that not noticing race suggests a lack of prejudice. Sometimes, too, they worry that they will misspeak if they name what they notice, but this kind of blindness and its accompanying silence have serious consequences for participatory democracy (Banks & Nguyen, 2008; Barton & Levstik, 2004; Ladson-Billings, 2009). It is extraordinarily difficult to discuss what we do not name. The concept of race is certainly problematic from a biological perspective, but it has deep historical roots and enormous social, cultural, political, and economic consequences (Mukhopadhyay, Moses, & Henze, 2007). Adults' silence about race warns children that some differences are so awful that even adults dare not name them, except in whispers, or even see them. Given race and ethnicity's intricate connection to children's identity development, such silences stymie a basic requirement of informed civic participation—a willingness to recognize perspectives other than one's own (Epstein, 2008; Swanson, Cunningham, Youngblood, & Spencer, 2009).

Perspective Recognition

Adults sometimes doubt children's ability to recognize others' perspectives, but over 20 years of research suggest otherwise (Davis, Yeager, & Foster, 2001; Knight, 1989; Levstik & Barton, 2008; Skolnick, Duhlberg, & Maestre, 2004).[2] From our earliest years we depend on our ability to read the people around us. Young children quickly learn that one parent may respond differently than the other, that siblings have interests that may or may not include them; that some people find a behavior amusing while others find it annoying; that facial expression and body language indicate people's feelings. In fact, a persistent *inability* to recognize others' perspectives is suggestive of neurological and psychological problems (Winner, 2002).

Just because children *can* recognize some perspectives, however, does not mean that they always care to do so or that their observations and interpretations are entirely accurate or consistent. In young children's "pretend" worlds we glimpse them imagining the thoughts and feelings of other people, sometimes as if others' thoughts and feelings match their own (a sympathetic response) and other times recognizing that others' perspectives might be quite different (an empathetic response). This is especially so when perspectives fall outside children's immediate experience or have negative associations of one kind or another (Cooper, 2011; Levstik & Groth, 2002). Fears, misinformation, and prejudices can confuse children's ability to recognize or take into account perspectives other than their own. Equitable, caring classroom communities provide a safe environment in which to counter misinformation and negotiate differences in pursuit of the community's common good (Angell, 2004; Claire, 2002; Furnam & Stacey, 2001; Houser, 1996; Levstik & Barton, 2010).

Fundamental to young children's ideas about the common good is the concept of *fairness* as equality (everyone gets the same thing). This concept has extraordinary influence in the classroom, but what happens when people need different things in order to produce reasonably equal opportunities? *Equity*—differential provisions to make equal opportunities possible—lies at the heart of some of the most difficult democratic decision making. Few begrudge a wheelchair ramp, a water fountain placed low enough for small children, handicapped seating on trains and busses, or safety seats for infants, but other accommodations involve considerably more negotiation, and this can be especially troublesome for young children so deeply attached to fairness as equality (Banks & Banks, 1995; Berman, 1997; MacNaughton, 2001). Although this is not an insurmountable

---

[2]Critical analysis of Piagetian approaches to perspective has a long history, including Donaldson (1978) and Gelman and Baillargeon (2006).

obstacle, as we see in the "Research into Practice" section, it does require explicit instructional attention.

Similarly, although children can usually identify both within-group and between-group differences in perspective in the context of stories, they may not draw on these literary insights in other contexts (Levstik & Groth, 2002). Researchers Janet Alleman and Jere Brophy (Alleman & Brophy, 2001, 2002, 2003; Brophy & Alleman, 2006, 2007, 2008) argue that one way to counter this tendency and to promote *conceptual transfer* (applying a concept learned in one context to another context) is to organize the primary social studies curriculum around cultural universals with which children already have some familiarity. *Cultural universals* refer to categories or patterns of learned behavior shared by people around the world (i.e., food, shelter, language, arts and recreation, familial, age, and gender relationships). Although behaviors vary considerably between places and across time, each variation makes sense in its cultural and historical context. As varied as Irish Gaelic, Incan Quechua, Khoisan, or American Sign Language might be, they have the same communicative functions. Similarly, an Amish horse and buggy is as much a form of transportation as a subway or jet plane—and just as much an expression of beliefs and values. As Alleman and Brophy's (2001) research makes clear, however, the fact that children participate in these cultural patterns does not mean that their ideas and understandings are necessarily well articulated. Alleman and Brophy argue that developing a broader, more connected, and better articulated understanding of pattern and variety in universal aspects of human experience can have a direct impact on children's success in making sense of their everyday lives. As a result, they suggest, cultural universals provide an important gateway for inquiry into the social phenomena that shape children's worlds and contribute toward their becoming more humane and informed citizens.[3]

Mediating Disciplined, Reflective Inquiry

In the context of social studies, *inquiry* refers to the process of investigating human experience using, primarily, concepts from history and the social sciences. At first blush this may sound rather grand in relation to young children. In fact, however, young children have considerable experience with informal social inquiry (Alleman & Brophy, 2001). As the "Research into Practice" section of this chapter points out, *disciplined, reflective inquiry* simply provides more refined tools for children's explorations, more practice in using these tools (the disciplined aspect of inquiry), more help in interpreting observations (the reflective aspect of inquiry), and more attention to taking action based on informed decision making (James, 2012; Levstik & Barton, 2010).

Inquiry in early childhood classrooms requires three levels of teacher mediation. The first focuses on the process of inquiry: helping children frame researchable questions, identify and use appropriate data sources, and build evidence-based interpretations (Cooper, 2002; Levstik & Barton, 2010; Levstik & Smith, 1997; MacDonell, 2006; Walker, Kragler, Martin, & Arnett, 2003). Question setting may take some time as children refine their ideas, and identifying and using data sources require direct instruction, but the biggest challenge is generally the final step—reporting evidence-based interpretations (Levstik & Smith, 1997; MacDonell, 2006; Swan, Hofer, & Levstik, 2007).

---

[3]In addition to Alleman and Brophy's (2001, 2002, 2003) work on cultural universals, Levstik and Barton's (2010) *Doing History* connects historical study to inquiries into cultural universals such as family and community.

Young children often invent highly imaginative explanations for social phenomena, especially for past events. Children tend, for instance, to assume that people in the past were ignorant—how else to explain old bathing costumes? Studies with older elementary students indicate that this perception moderates with explicit attention to how ideas and technologies develop over time. Alleman and Brophy (2001, 2002, 2003) note similar results in regard to cultural universals. Nonetheless, children may abandon their careful research when faced with crafting an interpretive narrative, opting for the familiar narrative arc of fiction rather than the less familiar evidence-based, nonfictional narrative (Barton & Levstik, 2004). With careful teacher mediation, however, children's explanations of social studies concepts, including cultural universals, become more explicit, more connected, and more accurate.

The second point of teacher mediation focuses on skills specific to the question under investigation and the disciplines informing inquiry: Do children need to locate places on a map or globe, identify pattern and variety in cultural universals, or sequence events in time order? Chronology, for instance, helps us make sense of the impact of past on present by clarifying some aspects of cause and effect. As children put events in chronological order, they begin to understand history as a way of describing change over time (Levstik & Barton, 2008). This need not involve serious attention to attaching numerical dates to past events, as this generally eludes children until about fourth grade. On the other hand, introducing chronology as sequence is well within the capabilities of most young children, especially if there are visual clues that include material culture and technology, or if events are structured in a strong narrative (Barton & Levstik, 2004; Levstik & Barton, 2008). Furthermore, with practice sequencing story elements (What came first? Next? Last?), as well as daily tasks (*before* and *after* categories help here), children become more and more adept at identifying time sequences. Although concepts of duration take longer to develop than sequence, young children's broad time categories (long, long ago; long ago; now) become more refined as they have more opportunities to connect visual time markers with time periods (Levstik & Barton, 2008).

The third point of mediation, *reflection*, is the "so what" of inquiry, an opportunity to consider how to apply students' investigations to the "outside world" in order to enhance the common good (MacDonell, 2006; Paley, 1993; Wade, 2007). Without reflection children may not recognize the significance of what they have learned, making it more likely that the cognitive gains they make will dissipate over time. As educators we are in a similar position. Without our reflection on social studies' humanitarian and democratic aims, research in the field is unlikely to result in an apprenticeship in more equitable democratic living for our students.

RESEARCH INTO PRACTICE: ENACTING AN APPRENTICESHIP IN DEMOCRATIC LIVING

Because early childhood classrooms remain one of the few places "small enough where you can pretend a good safe, fair world," early childhood educators are in the happy position of inviting young children to enter an *apprenticeship in democratic living* characterized by civic action in response to inquiry into human pattern and variety (Paley, 2000, p. 5). The remaining sections of this chapter suggest ways in which social studies research might help in that endeavor, beginning with classrooms as equitable public spaces.

Building Equitable Public Spaces

Naming Difference

Even though Max[4] is new to the United States and struggles with English names to describe his observations, he notices differences between himself and his new friend Kenneth. One day, when Kenneth's bus is late, Max asks his teacher when the "African bus" will arrive. His teacher tries to hush him, whispering to him that Kenneth's bus is just running late, but her worried response lets him know that something is wrong. Max may not catch on this time, but he soon will—and he may well internalize negative associations based on his teacher's fearful response. In contrast, a more ambitious, research-based approach to social studies might regard Max's observation as grounds for classroom inquiry, so that even the youngest children learn to name their observations more confidently and respectfully (Cooper, 2002; Grant, 2003; Grant & VanSledright, 2000).

Irene Cawley, a preschool teacher in a neighborhood with a recent influx of refugees from Africa and South America, notices how often her students comment on differences. Some describe new classmates as "talking funny" or "looking weird." Irene also overhears a heated debate about whether several of the refugee students are black or white. As an introduction to discussing such human variety, she decides to use Leo Lionni's (2006) *A Color of His Own*, about a chameleon who tires of blending into the background and wants a single color of his own. After reading the story, Irene wonders aloud whether she has a color of her own. Holding out her arm she says, "I think I see some brown and some black color in my skin. What do you think?" She picks up a brown crayon, asking if it is the same color of brown. As students agree that it is not quite right, Irene pulls out a variety of paints and puts a dab of one on her skin. "Not quite," she decides. "Try some of that one," a child says, pointing to a jar marked "chestnut." Soon the students want to find their own colors. "Some of you have more pink in your skin tone," Irene says and some children nod. "And others have different shades of brown and yellow," she says, prompting more nods. Irene blends spots of color on each child's arm until everyone agrees that the color is a good match ("Jaiden is mocha!"; "Eileen is a little peach and a little cinnamon"). During this conversation, children develop a rich and respectful vocabulary for describing physical differences. In fact, they delight in finding good descriptors not only in paint and crayon but also in the various books in their classroom. These words, Irene reminds them, should "make people feel good. Chestnut and black are both color names that make me feel good. Let's list the names that make you feel good." Irene writes these descriptive words on the class word wall for future reference, and the children create self-portraits to hang on the bulletin board in their classroom (Cooper, 2011; Ladson-Billings, 2009; Paley, 2000).

Ruby Yessin's first-grade class operates from a perspective of care that also supports respectful naming (Levstik, 1994; Levstik & Barton, 2008). Well aware of the hurtful power of words, she reminds students that "in this class we do not hurt living things" (Levstik & Barton, 2008, p. 59). This caring perspective includes rescuing a bee that is then released out a window, learning a "caring" greeting for guests when they enter the classroom, and using respectful names for each other. This approach permeates social studies content, where Ruby emphasizes historical and current examples of "care for

---

[4]All children's names in this chapter are pseudonyms. Where confidentiality agreements allow, I have used teachers' actual names. All other names are pseudonyms, and I have disguised or combined elements of classrooms in order to maintain anonymity. In all instances I am grateful for teachers' generosity in allowing me to observe in their classrooms and interview them about their practices.

others" and "making a difference" in the world. A biography of George Washington Carver, for instance, opens a conversation about "hope for the future," in which children investigate the ways Carver overcame hardships, used his curiosity, and became a scientist and inventor. As children name Carver's accomplishments, Ruby draws parallels to students. Carver "invented something used across the whole world," she notes, and "some people in this room remind me of George Washington Carver. They are inquisitive people who always ask lots of questions and are interested in all sorts of things" (Levstik & Barton, 2008, p. 36).

Similarly, Ruby discusses Dr. Martin Luther King in terms of a model of care for other people. "He thought of ways to make things better," she explains, reminding students that even though some people "still don't listen . . . one person can make a difference. . . . You as one person can make a difference in a lot of people's lives" (Levstik & Barton, 2008; pp. 37–38). Caring connections between past and present infuse almost every conversation in this classroom, whether describing how a "careful shipbuilder" might have worked on an explorer's ship in Columbus's time or on a spaceship today, or how "careful readers" in the past and in this class treat beautiful and fragile books. Over and over, Ruby and teachers like her strive for what Bardige (1988) identifies as "finely human" thinking:

> If we are to meet the challenge of educating in ways that help our children . . . become more human, then we must attend to and build on the "finely human" aspects of their thinking. As we help them to see and understand the realities, complexities and laws of the world, we must also help them to hang on to their moral sensitivities and impulses. (p. 104)

Such classrooms often begin with relatively simple "I Care" standards that include listening to each other, caring about other's feelings, and being responsible for one's own words and actions (*http://dbsschoolcounselor.blogspot.com/2011/10/i-care-language_07.html*). When enacted, these standards support the development of healthy patterns of friendship, sharing, and cooperation (Avery, 2002; Cooper, 2011; James, 2012). These patterns, in turn, establish the grounds for negotiating a classroom-based common good and for discussing how such standards might apply in the world outside the classroom. Care also makes possible a crucial feature of negotiating the common good: perspective recognition (Barton & Levstik, 2004).

Encouraging Perspective Recognition

Grace Wilkins works with 4- and 5-year-olds who are quite vocal about fairness. They count cookies at snack time and turns on the playground. Grace invites them into conversation about fairness by introducing the mathematical signs for equal (=) and unequal (< or >). Once children are comfortable using these signs, Grace introduces the concept of equity. First she explains that she has new socks, and it is only fair that everyone have two socks each. As she distributes the socks, however, students complain that this is not fair at all—the socks don't match and some are too big or too small. Grace responds with some puzzlement, "We all have the same number of socks! Isn't that fair?" After a chorus of disagreement, children explain that "matched pairs" rather than an equal number of socks would be most fair. As one child explains that he "needs a sock that fits," another comments that not everyone can wear the same socks because everyone has "different feet," and even if they were all the same size, they need "two of the same socks," and might prefer "different patterns on socks." "Ah," says the teacher, "some of you have different size feet and some of you have a different idea—a different perspective—about what kind of socks you like. Is that right?" When the students agree, the teacher leads a discussion about the source of such different ideas or perspectives. Grace suggests that "sometimes people don't always want or need the same thing. Some of you like socks with stripes, but some of you would rather have white socks and others might prefer longer socks, or socks with animal prints. And, if you lived on a beach, maybe you wouldn't want socks at all!" In the lively discussion that follows, the teacher suggests that they need a new rule—the Platinum Rule—to "remind us to think about others' ideas, about how they want or need to be treated" (Bennett, 1998, p. 209). "With this rule we will remember to pay attention to each others' different ideas . . . to our different perspectives." The children discuss differences in their own class, from people needing more or less quiet time, being more cautious about trying new things, or following different rules for what they can eat or wear. "When we pay attention to different perspectives," the teacher summarizes, "things may not be the same for everyone, but everyone may get what he or she really needs." With this foundation, when questions of fairness arise in Grace's class, discussion centers on whether a simple equal sign will do (we should all get the same thing) or the common good requires invoking the Platinum Rule (we may need different things) (Angell, 2004; Barton & Levstik, 2004; Bennett, 1998; Bickmore, 2008). As Grace's and Ruby's classes suggest, if it had no other merit, social studies would be crucial on these grounds alone: It remains the one part of the curriculum specifically designed to help diverse people build humane and democratic ways of sharing public spaces (Banks & Banks, 1995; Barton & Levstik, 2004; Cooper, 2011; Parker, 2002, 2008; Zong, Wilson, & Quashiga, 2008).

Sharing Safe and Equitable Public Spaces

As noted earlier, pretending that human differences aren't important leaves children unprepared for the demands of democratic citizenship. When children have too few opportunities to inquire into differences they often draw inaccurate and troubling conclusions. In these circumstances we hear an 8-year-old ask a classmate if her head will fall off if she removes her *hijab*, a 6-year-old wonder why the man she saw sleeping on a grate "forgot to go home," a 4-year-old Latina child crying because older children told her to "go back to your own country. We don't want you here." Such ill-informed responses to diversity strike at the very heart of "learning to work it out" in a pluralist democracy. When community tensions around immigration threatened to spill into Marisol Williams's school, she took action to create a safe public space in her preschool classroom.

From the very first day of school, Marisol greeted her students based on traditions in different parts of the world. At first there were not only some giggles but also curiosity about what was going on. Each day Marisol included discussions of culturally appropriate "good manners" and a picture, song, or artifact from the country of the week. One week, for instance, Marisol brought a *galimoto*—a homemade toy common to several African countries—and read a story about a boy who makes a truck from found objects (Williams, 1991). The children loved this new word *galimoto* and enjoyed making their own *galimotos* out of boxes, buttons, wheels, and straws. At other times guests from different parts of the world visited the class to share traditional clothing, foods, stories, and songs. Marisol encouraged children to draw on these experiences in their imaginative play, acting out interactions among people from different parts of the world. She also invited children to dictate stories based on their imaginative play, and used their stories as the basis for classroom discussion (Cooper, 2011). When she picked up on misconceptions,

Marisol might ask, "Do we know this is true?" or introduce other possibilities through literature, storytelling, and class investigations. She also helped her students develop a list of rights and responsibilities, "so we can live in an interesting and peaceful community." Over the course of the year Marisol's students learned a language of friendship and curiosity that inclined them to notice similarities, as well as differences, in perspective across cultures. They also had sufficient time to investigate both and to consider how to respond respectfully to differences (Field, 2003; Furnam & Stacey, 2001).

Marisol and the other teachers described in this chapter use a variety of children's literature to support students' investigations. Today, children's literature encompasses considerably more of the world than was the case even a few decades ago. As a result, it is easier to pair fiction with nonfiction to offer children important insight into how perspectives differ within as well as between groups.[5] *The Village of Round and Square Houses* (Grifalconi, 1986), set in Cameroon, and *Houses and Homes* (Morris, 1995), a world tour of family living, provide one example of such a pairing. In this case, kindergartners prepared for a visit from a Cameroonian guest by dictating observations and questions based on both books. Their questions helped their guest decide which pictures and artifacts could best help students understand different urban and rural communities in his country. This, in turn, led to a comparison of urban and rural communities in the United States, further expanding children's ideas about how customs and values vary within and between each country (Zong et al., 2008). The combination of paired literature (usually fiction and nonfiction) and firsthand experience is particularly powerful in regard to perspective recognition. In the case of cultural universals, for instance, well-chosen fiction and nonfiction introduce different perspectives, but at a slight remove. Firsthand experience—meeting someone from another culture—gives those differences an immediate, recognizable face. As they become more familiar, more often a topic of conversation, and more often associated with interesting people, ideas, and events, differences become less threatening and are more naturally the subject of the kind of disciplined, reflective inquiry that can inform democratic negotiation in the classroom and in the wider world. (See the list of Paired Literature/Literature Sets at the end of this chapter for additional suggestions.)

Mediating Inquiry

Disciplined Reflective Inquiry

Social studies inquiries need not be so complex or esoteric that young children cannot manage them. Rather, as a sizable body of research suggests, they can arise in response to children's questions about the form and function of cultural universals and draw on intellectually accessible resources, whether children's literature, studying material culture, or interviewing relevant community members (Alleman & Brophy, 2001; Cooper, 2002; Levstik & Barton, 2008). Sometimes associated with the "project method" (MacDonell, 2006), this kind of inquiry is *disciplined* in two senses. First, it is *systematic*, which refers to the processes children learn: articulating a researchable question, gathering and evaluating social data, organizing an appropriate response to their questions. Second, children's inquiry draws on *disciplined ways of knowing*—the kinds of questions and sources used in history and the social sciences.

---

[5]See the National Council for the Social Studies (NCSS) and the Children's Book Council bibliographies for social studies at *www.socialstudies.org/resources/notable*.

In the classroom, some questions arise naturally in the course of daily living; others develop in response to a teacher-initiated experience. The sources children use depend on their age and experience, as do the ways in which they share what they learn. A child's description of visiting a crowded, local farmers' market, for instance, led to a question about why the market was so popular. Children interviewed family, friends, and neighbors, invited an organic farmer to visit the class, discussed Paul Brett Johnson's (1997) *Farmer's Market*, and planned a trip to the market. Prior to the market visit, children investigated four products available at the market and appropriate for lunch: lettuce, tomatoes, cheese, and bread. They used a variety of children's fiction and nonfiction in their study and added their findings to a class mural showing the process of getting each product from farm to market. At the market they talked to farmers, purchased ingredients for sandwiches and salad, and came back to school to prepare their meal. For their "take action" project the class decorated heavy-duty paper market bags to encourage families and friends to "Buy Local," the market's slogan. Throughout their inquiry, children drew on the disciplines common to social studies, including geography, history, and economics. These disciplinary ways of knowing helped them think about important concepts, such as human–environmental interaction, change over time, and supply and demand.

Children also learn disciplined ways of thinking—distinguishing between fact and fiction, deciding on reliable sources, asking disciplinary questions. In a first-grade class, children distinguish among "for sure," "maybe," and "made up" facts as they examine historical myths about a range of people from Johnny Appleseed and Betsy Ross to Rosa Parks (Levstik, 1994; Levstik & Barton, 2008). In another class, children build a "history of our class" using weather observation, news from home, the day's activities, artifacts, and pictures. In both of these classes teachers introduce disciplinary ways of thinking, and suggest, for instance, that students "think like a geographer—ask questions about the environment," or "think like an archaeologist—ask questions about what different objects mean to people."

Some cautions apply here. Young children often invent highly imaginative explanations for social phenomena and are quick to assume that ignorance is an explanation for past people's ideas, choices, and cultures. Wise teachers use these explanations to motivate interest in finding out more about human experience. They draw on disciplinary thinking, not because children share all the practices of professional historians or geographers, but so that children can use disciplinary vocabulary and associated questions to help them better understand their world (Levstik, 1994). This requires explicit instructional attention. The rapid change in technologies and material culture even within children's own lifetimes provides one entry point for making sense of human ingenuity and intelligence (Ashby & Lee, 1987; Levstik & Henderson, 2011; MacDonell, 2006). Something as simple as a technological family tree helps to organize this instruction. Starting with a familiar tool or technology—bread making, for instance—children decide what resources and skills people had to possess to make this technology possible (types of grain, cooking systems, and accompanying rituals in different parts of the world). An array of excellent nonfiction, from Ann Morris's (1993) *Bread, Bread, Bread* (Foods of the World) and George Levenson's *Bread Comes to Life* (2008), to Gary Paulsen's *The Tortilla Factory* (1998), spur conversation about human ingenuity in this most basic of human endeavors, while suggesting civic action in response to hunger issues. Pot making is another technology that is accessible to young children. Not only can they experiment with making pots, they can use books such as Laban Hill's (2010) *Dave the Potter: Artist, Poet, Slave* and Byrd Baylor's (1987) *When Clay Sings*, and interview modern potters who may live and work in the community to investigate different techniques and social uses for this technology. A final project, "Soup for the World," might involve children inviting community members to fill children's hand-made bowls with donations to alleviate hunger locally, nationally, or internationally.

Reflection and Inquiry

If classroom investigations stopped with introducing children to the *disciplined* aspects of inquiry, children would still benefit. They acquire new and more accurate information, add to their understanding of different ways to describe their world, and refine disciplinary concepts that help them answer social questions. Without *reflection*, however, they may miss the significance of what they have learned, as well as the humanitarian and democratic potential in their social studies. And without *action* based on reflection, children may come to see citizenship as a spectator sport rather than a participatory endeavor. The class that visited the farmer's market, for instance, reflected on the relative advantages of local food from local markets and the wider selection available in grocery stores. They discussed the importance of farmers, the sources of their own food, and how people in a community rely on each other for so many things—and they decided on a democratic action in support of their community: making reusable market bags that reduce shoppers' environmental footprint, whether they shop at the local market or the grocery store. The decision to do so grew out of considerable debate about what was best for the community and what would best help their own families. It is this last step that addresses citizenship goals and makes social studies such an important part of all children's education.

REFLECTIONS AND NEW DIRECTIONS

This chapter began with Cooper's (2011) plea to consider who children are and who we can help them become (p. 5). Education in a pluralist democracy certainly benefits from children becoming "competent and confident learners and communicators . . . secure in their sense of belonging" but democracy also requires informed, active citizens committed not only to their own good but also a constantly negotiated, constantly evolving common good (Hedges & Lee, 2008, p. 13). The title of this chapter, "Learning to Work It Out," envisions social studies as a democratic apprenticeship in which teachers from different backgrounds help children from even more varied backgrounds work out democratic living in increasingly complex public spaces.

The teachers described in this chapter are committed to this work, oftentimes testing research findings by comparing the performance of older elementary students and much younger students. As their stories suggest, they are adept at "kid watching," adapting instruction on the basis of their observations as well as research findings, responding to community and school contexts, and constantly assessing the effectiveness of their adaptations. Their work takes place in an era marked by some troubling trends: a widening "civic empowerment gap" (Levinson, 2012) and reduced curricular attention to social studies (Alleman & Brophy, 2003). At a time when students' sense of civic empowerment divides sharply along racial, ethnic, and class lines, schools spend less and less time on social studies, the one curricular area most associated with citizenship education (Alleman & Brophy, 2003; Levinson, 2012). Students certainly deserve time to learn, but they also deserve learning based on a richer, deeper research base.

Existing research argues that young children possess the intellectual flexibility to recognize and respect other perspectives, to understand that perspectives change over time, to identify cultural pattern and variety, and to apply these understandings to real world issues. We need considerably more research on what conditions best support conceptual change in regard to these and other areas of the social studies. Unfortunately, persistent calls for attention to early childhood social studies have had little effect. We can continue on this well-trod path or exercise the civic powers that we mean to teach our students and advocate for social studies with school administrations, funding agencies, and organizations such as NCSS. Attending to the ways in which young children deepen their understanding of what it means to be human and humane, and using that understanding to "work out " a more equitable, informed, and participatory democracy must be fundamental not only to early childhood but also to all social studies education.

PROFESSIONAL DEVELOPMENT ACTIVITIES

- View one of the primary videos available at Annenberg's Social Studies in Action (*www. learner.org/resources/series166.html*). Use the questions that accompany the video to direct discussion about the social studies skills and concepts demonstrated in the classroom. Try a similar lesson in your own classroom and video-tape it, using the same questions to guide your self-evaluation.

- Read Rikki Levinson's *Watch the Stars Come Out* (1995). Identify a set of fiction and nonfiction books that would help children better understand human movement. Make sure the books represent different periods of time, and develop a set of questions that generates conversation about why people move and how movement might change over time.

- Work with colleagues to develop a peace center similar to the one described in the chapter. What would you include in the center? How would you have children learn to use the center? What kinds of rules might you post to help children remember how to use the center?

- Identify community members involved in working toward a common good. Work with your colleagues to develop a lesson to help students conduct oral interviews. Invite one community member to your class to be interviewed by your students. Video-tape this, so that you can identify problems students might have, additional supports you might need to develop, or types of preparation that might help the interviewee.

REFERENCES

Aitken, G., & Sinnema, C. (Eds.). (2008). *Effective pedagogy in social sciences/Tikanga a Iwi: Best evidence synthesis iteration.* Wellington: New Zealand Ministry of Education.

Alleman, J., & Brophy, J. (2001). *Social studies excursions, K–3. Book one: Powerful units on food, clothing, and shelter.* Portsmouth, NH: Heinemann.

Alleman J., & Brophy, J. (2002). *Social studies excursions, K–3. Book two: Powerful units on communication, transportation and family living.* Portsmouth, NH: Heinemann.

Alleman, J., & Brophy, J. (2003). *Social studies excursions, K–3. Book three: Powerful units on childhood, money, and government.* Portsmouth, NH: Heinemann.

Angell, A. (2004). Making peace in elementary classrooms: A case for class meetings. *Theory and Research in Social Education, 32*(1), 98–104.

Annenberg Foundation (Producer). (2001). Social studies in action: A teaching practices library, K–12. Retrieved from *www.learner.org/resources/series166.html#*.

Appiah, K. A. (2006). *Cosmopolitanism: Ethics in a world of strangers*. New York: Norton.

Arthur, J., Davies, I., & Hahn, C. (Eds.). (2008). *Sage handbook of education and democracy*. London: Sage.

Ashby, R., & Lee, P. (1987). Children's concepts of empathy and understanding in history. In C. Portal (Ed.), *The history curriculum for teachers* (pp. 62–88). London: Heinemann.

Avery, P. (2002). Teaching tolerance: What research tells us. *Social Education, 66*, 270–275.

Banks, C. M., & Banks, J. (1995). Equity pedagogy: An essential component of multicultural education. *Theory Into Practice, 34*(3), 152–158.

Banks, J., & Nguyen, D. (2008). Diversity and citizenship education: Historical, theoretical and philosophical issues. In L. S. Levstik & C. A. Tyson (Eds.), *Handbook of research in social studies education* (pp. 137–154). New York: Routledge.

Bardige, B. (1988). Things so finely human: Moral sensibilities at risk in adolescence. In C. Gilligan, J. V. Ward, & J. M. Taylor (Eds.), *Mapping the moral domain* (pp. 87–110). Cambridge, MA: Harvard University Press.

Barton, K. C., & Levstik, L. S. (2004). *Teaching history for the common good*. New York: Routledge.

Baylor, B. (1987). *When clay sings*. New York: Atheneum Press.

Bennett, M. (1998). *Basics concepts of intercultural communication*. London: Nicholas Brealey.

Berman, S. (1997). *Children's social consciousness and the development of social responsibility*. Albany: State University of New York Press.

Bickmore, K. (2008). Social studies and social justice. In L. Levstik & C. Tyson (Eds.), *Handbook of research in social studies education* (pp. 33–47). New York: Routledge.

Blyth, J. (1989). *History in primary schools*. London: Open University Press.

Brophy, J., & Alleman, J. (2006). *Children's thinking about cultural universals*. Mahwah, NJ: Routledge.

Brophy, J., & Alleman, J. (2007). *Powerful social studies for elementary students* (2nd ed.). Belmont, CA: Thomson/Wadsworth.

Brophy, J., & Alleman, J. (2008). Early elementary social studies. In L. Levstik & C. Tyson (Eds.), *Handbook of research in social studies education* (pp. 33–47). New York: Routledge.

Claire, H. (2002). Values in the primary history curriculum. In A. McCully & C. O'Neill (Eds.), *Values in history teacher education and research*. Lancaster, UK: History Teacher Education Network in collaboration with St. Martin's College.

Cooper, H. (2002). *History in the early years* (2nd ed.). London: Routledge/Falmer.

Cooper, P. (2011). *The classrooms all young children need: Lessons in teaching from Vivian Paley*. Chicago: University of Chicago Press.

Davis, O. L., Yeager, E., & Foster, S. (Eds.). (2001). *Historical empathy and perspective-taking in the social studies*. New York: Rowman & Littlefield.

Dewey, J. (1916). *Democracy and education*. New York: Macmillan.

Dickinson, A., & Lee, P. J. (1984). Making sense of history. In A. Dickinson, P. Lee, & P. Rogers (Eds.), *Learning history* (pp. 117–153). London: Heinemann.

Donaldson, M. (1978). *Children's minds*. New York: Norton.

Epstein, T. (2008). *Interpreting national history: Race, identity, and pedagogy in classrooms and communities*. New York: Routledge.

Evans, R. (2010). *Can getting young children civically engaged create actual civic change?* (National Children's Museum). Retrieved from *www.ncm.museum/learning-center/start/civic-engagement/can-getting-young-children-civically-engaged-create-actual-civic-change*.

Field, S. (2003). Using children's literature and the universals of culture to teach about Mexico. *The Social Studies, 96*, 123–127.

Friedman, R. (1987). *How my parents learned to eat*. Boston: Sandpiper/Houghton Mifflin.

Furnam, A., & Stacey, B. (2001). *Young people's understanding of society*. New York: Routledge.

Gelman, R., & Baillargeon, R. (2006). A review of some Piagetian concepts. In J. H. Flavell & E. M. Markman (Eds.), *Handbook of child psychology* (pp. 167–230). New York: Wiley.

Graham, L. (2009). *The power of names: Religion and mathematics.* Presented at the Philoctetes Center, New York. Retrieved from *http://philoctetes.org/news/the_power_of_names_religion_mathematics.*

Grant, S. G. (2003). *History lessons.* New York: Routledge.

Grant, S. G., & VanSledright, B. (2000). *Constructing a powerful approach to teaching and learning in elementary social studies.* Independence, KY: Wadsworth.

Grifalconi, A. (1986). *Village of round and square houses.* New York: Little, Brown.

Hahn, C. (2008). Education for citizenship and democracy in the United States. In J. Arthur, I. Davies, & C. Hahn (Eds.), *Sage handbook of education and democracy* (pp. 263–278). London: Sage.

Hedges, H., & Lee, D. (2008). Early childhood. In G. Aitken & C. Sinnema (Eds.), *Effective pedagogy in social sciences/Tikanga a Iwi: Best evidence synthesis iteration* (pp. 13–14). Wellington: New Zealand Ministry of Education.

Hill, L. C. (2010). *Dave the potter: Artist, poet, slave.* New York: Little, Brown.

Houser, N. (1996). Negotiating dissonance and safety for the common good: Social education in the elementary classroom. *Theory and Research in Social Education, 29,* 582–616.

Iverson, S., & James, J. H. (2011). Songs of citizenship: The use of music in the classroom. In J. K. Dowdy & S. Kaplan (Eds.), *Teaching drama in the classroom: A toolbox for teachers.* Rotterdam, The Netherlands: Sense Publishers.

James, J. H. (2012, May). *Critical service-learning and community building in the primary grades.* Paper presented at the annual meeting of CitizEd, York, UK.

Johnson, P. B. (1997). *Farmer's market.* London: Orchard Books.

Kipling, R. (1926). *Debits and credits.* Looe, UK: House of Stratus.

Knight, P. (1989). A Study of children's understanding of people in the past. *Educational Review, 41*(3), 207–208.

Ladson-Billings, G. (2001). *Crossing over to Canaan: The journey of new teachers in diverse classrooms.* Hoboken, NJ: Jossey-Bass.

Ladson-Billings, G. (2009). *The dreamkeepers: Successful teachers of African American children.* Hoboken, NJ: Jossey-Bass.

Levenson, G. (2008). *Bread comes to life: A garden of wheat and a loaf to eat.* Berkeley, CA: Tricycle Press.

Levinson, M. (2012). *No citizen left behind.* Cambridge, MA: Harvard University Press.

Levinson, R. (1995). *Watch the stars come out.* New York: Puffin Books.

Levstik, L. S. (1994). Building a sense of history in a first grade classroom. In J. Brophy (Ed.), *Research in elementary studies.* Greenwich, CT: JAI Press.

Levstik, L. S., & Barton, K. C. (2008). *Researching historical thinking.* New York: Routledge.

Levstik, L. S., & Barton, K. C. (2010). *Doing history: investigating with children in elementary and middle school* (4th ed.). New York: Routledge.

Levstik, L. S., & Groth, J. (2002). Scary thing, being an eighth grader: Exploring gender and sexuality in a middle school U.S. history unit. *Theory and Research in Social Education, 30*(2), 233–254.

Levstik, L. S., & Henderson, A. G. (2011, December). *Making sense of technological innovation.* Paper presented at the annual meeting of the College and University Faculty Assembly of the National Council for Social Studies, Washington, DC.

Levstik, L. S., & Smith, D. (1997). "I have learned a whole lot this year and it would take a lifetime to write it all": Beginning historical inquiry in a third grade classroom. *Social Science Record, 34,* 8–14.

Lionni, L. (2006). *A color of his own.* New York: Knopf.

MacDonell, C. (2006). *Project-based inquiry units for young children: First steps to research for grades pre-K–2.* Worthington, OH: Linworth.

MacNaughton, G. (2001). Equal opportunities: Unsettling myths. In T. David (Ed.), *Promoting evidence-based practice in early childhood education* (pp. 211–226). Oxford, UK: JAI Press.

Mukhopadhyay, C. C., Moses, Y., & Henze, R. (2007). *How real is race?: A sourcebook on race, culture, and biology.* Lanham, MD: Rowman & Littlefield.

Morris, A. (1993). *Bread, bread, bread.* New York: Mulberry Books.

Morris, A. (1995). *Houses and homes.* New York: HarperCollins.

National School Climate Center. (2012). *Guardian of democracy: The civic mission of schools.* Philadelphia: Leonore Annenberg Institute for Civics of the Annenberg Public Policy Center at the University of Pennsylvania and the Campaign for the Civic Mission of Schools. Retrieved from *www.schoolclimate.org/climate/documents/policy/guardian_of_democracy_web.pdf.*

Paley, V. (1993). *You can't say you can't play.* Cambridge, MA: Harvard University Press.

Paley, V. (2000). *White teacher.* Cambridge, MA: Harvard University Press.

Parker, W. (2002). *Teaching democracy: Unity and diversity in public life.* New York: Routledge.

Parker, W. (2008). *Knowing and doing in democratic education.* In L. Levstik & C. Tyson (Eds.), *Handbook of research in social studies education* (pp. 65–80). New York: Routledge.

Paulsen, G. (1998). *The tortilla factory.* London: Sandpiper Press.

Selman, R. (2003). *The promotion of social awareness: Powerful lessons from the partnership of developmental theory and classroom practice.* New York: Russell Sage Foundation.

Skolnick, J., Duhlberg, N., & Maestre, T. (2004). *Through other eyes: Developing empathy and multicultural perspectives in the social studies* (2nd ed.). Toronto: Pippin.

Swan, K. O., Hofer, M., & Levstik, L. S. (2007). And . . . action!: Students collaborating in the Digital Directors Guild. *Social Studies and the Young Learner, 19*(4), 17–20.

Swanson, D. E., Cunningham, M., Youngblood, J., & Spencer, M. B. (2009). Racial identity development during childhood. In H. Neville, B. M. Tynes, & S. O. Utsey (Eds.), *Handbook of African American psychology* (pp. 269–281). Thousand Oaks, CA: Sage.

Wade, R. (2007). *Community action rooted in history* (NCSS Bulletin 110). Silver Spring, MD: National Council for the Social Studies.

Walker, C., Kragler, S., Martin, L., & Arnett, A. (2003). Facilitating the use of informational texts in a 1st-grade classroom. *Childhood Education, 79,* 152–159.

Williams, K. L. (1991). *Galimoto.* New York: HarperCollins.

Winner, M. (2002). Assessment of social skills for students with Asperger syndrome and high-functioning autism. *Assessment for Effective Intervention, 27,* 73–80.

Zong, G., Wilson, A. H., & Quashiga, A. Y. (2008). Global education. In L. Levstik & C. Tyson (Eds.), *Handbook of research in social studies education* (pp. 197–218). New York: Routledge.

PAIRED LITERATURE/LITERATURE SETS

The books below can be paired or used in sets to support social studies teaching and learning.

Human Rights

Two United Nations Declarations represent international agreements regarding human rights in general and children's rights in particular. The first two books below offer versions of each Declaration to pair with any of the other three stories illustrating specific human/children's rights.

Castle, C. (2000). *For every child: The UN Convention on the Rights of the Child in word and picture.* New York: Fogelman Books (in association with UNICEF).—An array of artists illustrate 14 of the rights of the child. The text is child-friendly, and the varied illustrations offer opportunities to discuss the need for children's rights.

Hughes, L., & Collier, B. (Illus.). (2012). *I, too, am America.* New York: Simon & Schuster.—Beautiful collages representing African Americans' fight for a better future accompany Langston Hugh's poem, *I, Too, Sing America,* and suggest possibilities for children illustrating their own version of "I, too, am American." For older children, pair with Paula Shelton (2010). *Child of the Civil Rights Movement*. New York: Schwartz & Wade.

Robinson, M. (2008). *Every human has rights*. Washington, DC: National Geographic Children's Books.—Full-color photographs and children's poetry illustrate the UN Declaration on Human Rights. The beautiful photographic montages pair well with books illustrating human right issues.

Rumford, J. (2008). *Silent music: A story of Bagdad*. New York: Macmillan/Roaring Brook Press.—This gorgeously illustrated story encourages conversation about protecting children in a time of war. The artwork introduces important elements of Iraqi culture and history while emphasizing the right to literacy.

Williams, K. L., & Mohammed, K. (2007). *Four feet: Two sandals*. New York: Kendall Hunt.—A story of friendship and survival in a refugee camp in Pakistan addresses the importance of refugee status as a human right and emphasizes human resilience.

Cross-Cultural Differences

These books emphasize respectful naming in relation to various racial/ethnic and cultural differences, including skin color.

Deedy, C. A. (2010). *14 Cows for America*. Atlanta, GA: Peachtree Press.—Generosity and care cross cultural boundaries. In this lovely story, a group of Maasai in Kenya reach out to America in the aftermath of the 9/11 attacks. The illustrations capture the deep orange and ochre colors of the Kenyan landscape, as well as the globalization of Maasai culture. Paired with *A Life Like Mine, 14 Cows* moves children to think beyond cultural stereotypes.

Rayner, A. (Ed.). (2002). *A life like mine: How children live around the world*. New York: UNICEF.—Paired with *Shades of People, A Life Like Mine* puts skin color in rich cultural context. Each section provides a variety of respectful ways of naming cultural pattern and variety.

Rotner, S., & Kelly, S. M. (2009). *Shades of people*. New York: Holiday House.—Photographs from around the world illustrate variations in skin color and invite children respectfully to name their own skin color and celebrate the variety in their classroom, school, community, and world.

Building Community

Children benefit from different perspectives as they build their classroom community. These books can be paired to offer glimpses of shared spaces in neighborhood, school, and the wider world.

Miller, J. (2005). *Who's who in a neighborhood*. New York: Rosen.—Young children meet the diverse people who make up a neighborhood. The text highlights basic social studies concepts and related vocabulary, and could easily be used to initiate an inquiry into aspects of the neighborhood around the school.

Park, F., & Park, G. (2002). *Goodbye 382 Shin Dang Dong*. Washington, DC: National Geographic Children's Books.—Compelling enough to generate interest in, empathy for, and discussion about the immigrant experience—in this case, a young child prepares to leave her life in Korea for the United States. This story pairs well with *Who's Who in a Neighborhood*.

Polacco, P. (2012). *The art of Miss Chew*. New York: Putnam.—Miss Chew, an art teacher, recognized and celebrated Polacco's artistic talent while also helping her learn to read. This story's emotional depth is striking—typical of Polacco's work—and would pair nicely with *Goodbye 382 Shin Dan Dong* to illustrate how a variety of different children can share a classrooms "public space."

CHAPTER 25

TALK IT OUT
Building Oral Language

CHRISTINA YEAGER PELATTI
MARY BETH SCHMITT
LAURA M. JUSTICE

> Oral language development is a critical foundation for reading, writing,
> and spelling, and it is the "engine" of learning and thinking.
> —NATIONAL INSTITUTE FOR LITERACY (2009, p. 2)

Mrs. P. is in her second year of teaching preschool. Her school, funded by Head Start, private tuition fees, and endowments from the local university, serves young children from diverse cultural and socioeconomic backgrounds. Children from all funding sources are blended within each classroom in the center, making it one of the most diverse and inclusive preschools in the area. This diversity is reflected in Mrs. P.'s classroom: Some students are only now learning English, several students have significant disabilities, three students live in extreme poverty, and two students are from highly affluent backgrounds. She knows that each student enters her classroom with a range of previous exposure and experience with language, and she frequently thinks about how to ensure that all of her students benefit, if not thrive, from their experience in her classroom and graduate "ready" for kindergarten. Although Mrs. P. has attended workshops on how to provide high-quality instruction to all of her students, she is concerned that there is more that she can do in her classroom, particularly surrounding language development.

We start this chapter with an overview of recent research relevant to Mrs. P.'s desire to support her students' language development, with a particular emphasis on key constructs necessary to provide young children with high-quality language-learning environments. Next, we provide a description of best practices in early education classrooms, highlighting practical strategies and providing specific examples of ways that preschool teachers can actively and explicitly facilitate language development among young children in classroom settings. The chapter concludes with a discussion on future directions for both researchers and practitioners to consider as we learn more about appropriate practices in preschool classrooms. Our overall goal of this chapter is to highlight practical applications from the research literature that early educators, like Mrs. P., can immediately implement in their classrooms to ensure that they are providing the highest quality of support and instruction.

Language is a communicative system based on structured rules and abstract symbols. The five language domains—syntax, morphology, semantics, pragmatics, and phonology—are critical for effective communication, and encompass both spoken and written communication. Adequate knowledge across these five language domains is required for children to be competent users (Bryant, 2009). The five language domains are particularly important as young children learn how to communicate effectively. In addition, language provides young children the resources to learn across all academic content areas, and it plays a critical role as they become skilled readers and writers, applying knowledge of spoken language to written language.

WHAT RESEARCH SAYS
ABOUT ORAL LANGUAGE DEVELOPMENT

As the number of young children attending early education programs across the United States continues to rise each year, early educators are faced with the daunting task of ensuring that their students have access to high-quality preschool experiences (Barnett & Yarosz, 2004). The extant research literature indicates that children who have high-quality preschool experiences achieve greater academic outcomes than peers who do not have similar experiences (e.g., LoCasale-Crouch et al., 2007; Mashburn et al., 2008; Pianta et al., 2005). Despite the increased emphasis on promoting high-quality preschool education, there is no single universal definition of *high quality*. This lack of clarity inevitably leads to confusion about what it means to provide high-quality preschool instruction (i.e., Vandell & Wolfe, 2000). To some, quality is defined by meeting the minimum standards for the program infrastructure, including school financing, teacher training, years of experience, and/or child-to-teacher ratio (e.g., National Center for Education Statistics, 2003). To others, high-quality early childhood experiences may be based on the nature of child–teacher interactions, emphasizing both social and instructional aspects. In this chapter, our primary emphasis is largely on the latter premise that young children learn language, particularly complex vocabulary and sentence structure, through interactions with those who demonstrate use of these skills. Early childhood educators draw upon research findings to ensure that young children experience early environments characterized by a high quantity of complex language coupled with adult use of explicit language techniques (e.g., Justice, Mashburn, Hamre, & Pianta, 2008; Wasik, Bond, & Hindman, 2006).

This chapter is situated within various sociocultural theories of language development (e.g., Bruner, 1975; Chapman, 2000; Vygotsky, 1978). From this perspective, spoken language input from adults accelerates children's acquisition of language. In particular, adults provide input within each child's zone of proximal development (ZPD), or the difference between children's current level of language development and their language potential. As a result, language is developed through supported or scaffolded interactions with adults who engage in more advanced language usage (Vygotsky, 1978). Children have a better understanding of language once adults provide for them the techniques to support language acquisition. Through a social transmission process, young children begin to internalize the spoken language structures and incorporate them into their own higher mental functioning. According to sociocultural theoretical perspectives and recent research, three critical characteristics define high-quality language environments: (1) quantity of language, (2) complexity of language, and (3) techniques used to stimulate language acquisition. The overall premise is that children's exposure to language environments that provide high quantity and quality positively impacts their acquisition of increasingly complex language structures. Refer to Table 25.1 for key characteristics of high-quality language classrooms.

Quantity of Language

The amount of language input to which young children have access is related to their overall language growth. For example, Hoff-Ginsberg (1994) analyzed the utterances of 63 mothers with young children between the ages of 1 and 2½ years of age. Results revealed differences in both the mothers' use of language and their child's participation in conversation. Children who experienced more frequent language exposure produced more language, as well as more conversational turns per topic. Although this particular study was conducted in the home environment, the results highlight significant differences in the amount of young children's exposure to language. This finding has direct implications for preschool classrooms and highlights the need for early educators to provide their students with increased access to complex adult (teacher, aides, volunteer) talk.

Language Complexity

Language complexity is an important consideration when discussing early language development across the five language domains. Young children's language use may range from basic forms, such as simple sentences, and basic vocabulary words and communicative functions, to more sophisticated language, including complex sentences and abstract words, as well as the communicative functions of inferring and hypothesizing. At times, some adults may be tempted to use very simple language around young children; frequently they assume that simple language is easier for younger children to understand. However, the complexity of linguistic input or adult talk that children hear is associated with language growth across multiple linguistic dimensions, including grammar and

TABLE 25.1. Key Characteristics of High-Quality Language Classrooms

Characteristics of high-quality language classrooms	Strategy to facilitate language
Quantity	• Increase the amount of language input and use in classroom
Language complexity	• Cognitively challenging talk • Exposure to rare and varied vocabulary • Syntactically complex language
Language stimulation techniques	• Focused contrasts • Models • Event casts • Open questions • Expansions/recasts • Redirects/prompted initiations

vocabulary. For instance, children's rate of vocabulary development is associated with the average length of sentences used by their mothers (Hoff, 2003). Similarly, children's comprehension of complex sentences is associated with the extent to which preschool teachers use complex sentences in the classroom (Huttenlocher, Vasilyeva, Cymerman, & Levine, 2002). It is essential that adults stimulate young children's language development by exposing them to complex input and mature forms of language that expand their language development.

One aspect of linguistic complexity that has received more attention of late is the amount and nature of cognitively challenging talk. In other words, adult talk may refer to available perceptual aspects of the immediate environment (not considered to be very cognitively challenging because concrete referents are available in the environment) or to conceptual aspects outside the here and now (considered very cognitively challenging because no concrete referents are available). The evidence supports cognitively challenging talk as an essential feature of complex language environments (e.g., Smith & Dickinson, 1994; van Kleeck, Vander Woude, & Hammett, 2006). For example, van Kleeck and colleagues (2006) found that following an 8-week book-reading program in which teachers embedded cognitively challenging questions (e.g., "Why is the boy sad?"; "What do you think will happen next?"), children demonstrated increased abilities to use complex language. In summary, existing research highlights the need for early childhood educators to provide linguistically complex spoken language environments to facilitate language growth in their preschool students. See Table 25.2 for definitions and examples of complex language.

Language Stimulation Techniques

Language stimulation techniques include focused contrasts, models, event casts, open questions, expansions/recasts, and redirects/prompted initiations (Rice & Wilcox, 1995). Specific definitions and examples are provided in Table 25.3.

While some of these language stimulation techniques encourage children's active practice of complex language forms, others provide exposure to these advanced forms of language associated with adult language use (Bohannon & Bonvillian, 1997). Moreover, both are important to children's language development, and researchers describe strong relations between children's exposure to and interaction with adults who use complex language forms (i.e., Huttenlocher et al., 2002; McCartney, 1984). For example, children

TABLE 25.2. Language Complexity: Definition, Examples, and References

Domain	Definition	Example	References
Cognitively challenging talk	Talk that moves beyond the "here and now" to include past and future events	Tell me about a time when you went to a birthday party.	Massey (2004); Smith & Dickinson (1994)
Rare and varied vocabulary	Vocabulary that is not included in every day conversation	*Sloth, absorb*	Beals & Tabors (1995); Dickinson & Tabors (2002)
Syntactically complex language	Includes use of a variety of prepositional, noun, verb, and adjectival phrases and complex clauses	Before climbing into bed, the curly-headed boy finished reading his book about airplanes.	Huttenlocher et al. (2002)

TABLE 25.3. Language Stimulation Techniques: Definition and Examples

Technique	Definition	Example
Focused contrasts	Contrasts that provide input or feedback by giving two or more options for the appropriate response.	Child: "I falled off." Adult: "You *falled* off or you *fell* off?"
Models	Adults provide the child with a word or structure that the child may not be able to produce independently.	Adult: "Your *Tyrannosaurus rex* has big teeth." *Tyrannosaurus rex* is a type of dinosaur.
Event casts	Comments that provide ongoing commentary about a situation and may also be targeted to increase the quantity of input.	Adult: "You are pushing the car up the ramp. Uh oh! It flipped over."
Open questions	Questions or statements that do not require one specific answer; the child is able to provide a multitude of possible answers.	Adult: "What do you think is going to happen next?"
Expansions/recasts	Input that provides additional information by slightly altering yet preserving the overall meaning of the phrase or sentence.	Child: "Truck." Adult: "I want the big, red dump truck."
Redirects/prompted initiations	Prompts that encourage the child to initiate with a peer by directing their comment to them.	Adult: "Ask Johnny if you can play with the block. Try 'Johnny, can I play with the block?' "

Note. Based on Rice and Wilcox (1995).

who talk more have increased opportunities to practice sophisticated, complex forms of language use (Cabell et al., 2011). Because these children actively participate in conversation, they continue to develop advanced forms of language use, while their peers, who may not talk as much, do not have access to the same language development opportunities.

Despite the evidence highlighting the importance of providing high-quality language environments in preschool classrooms, including the aforementioned critical areas of quantity of complex language and language stimulation techniques, the research shows that there is considerable variability in the amount and complexity of adult talk and use of language stimulation strategies among early educators. For example, Justice and colleagues (2008) analyzed the language environments of 135 preschool classrooms using Classroom Assessment Scoring System (CLASS; Pianta, LaParo, & Hamre, 2004), an observational instrument used to rate the quality of early childhood classrooms. CLASS is organized into several broad domains and, of particular importance to this study, contains two scales: Language Modeling and Literacy Focus. The Language Modeling scale rates early educators' use of evidence-based strategies that accelerate language development (e.g., open-ended questions), while the Literacy Focus scale determines whether teachers incorporate literacy indicators. Results from Justice and colleagues (2008) revealed that over half (54%) of the teachers received the lowest rating of 1 or 2 on a 7-point scale, while only 4% were scored as providing the highest rating (6 or 7). Even more surprising is the finding that only a handful of the early childhood teachers in this study utilized the language stimulation techniques that have been shown to effectively accelerate the language development of preschoolers, including the use of open-ended questions, recasts, and extensions.

In summary, early childhood educators play a crucial role in the language development of young children. As we have discussed, three broad areas define high-quality language environments: (1) quantity of language, (2) complexity of language, and (3) techniques used to stimulate language acquisition. Despite the evidence, research indicates that some teachers have difficulty integrating techniques into practices to stimulate young children's language development. The rest of this chapter focuses on specific strategies that early educators can incorporate into their daily classroom routines to ensure that all preschool children have access to high-quality language environments.

RESEARCH INTO PRACTICE

As an early educator, you may ask yourself, "What does this research mean, and how can I ensure that my students receive high-quality instruction and are successful once they leave my preschool classroom?" Our goal in the next section is to translate the previously described research into practice; we provide practical strategies for early educators that can be immediately implemented in their classroom environment.

Quantity of Language

As previously described, research indicates that teachers' use of more language in early childhood classrooms results in better language outcomes for young students. Increasing the quantity of language in the classroom is a technique for the *teacher*; it is not contingent on the amount of child talk, although more child talk may be a by-product. Simply stated, teachers can increase the quantity of language by talking more about all classroom activities. In the following section, we discuss specific language stimulation techniques that help to expand both the amount and quality of language in the classroom. It is important for teachers to understand that increasing language quantity does not mean adding yet another lesson or content area to the daily instructional schedule. Teachers can use increased amounts of language during everyday routines, including snack and transition times.

Snack

Snack time tends to be highly motivating for children and absent of pressures to teach academic content. As such, this time can be an ideal opportunity to infuse more language into the daily schedule of activities. This can take many forms and may not occur the same way each time. For example, teachers may choose to talk about the snack itself and relate it to previous lessons (e.g., "Today we have crunchy foods for our snack. That's just like the bear in our story. He likes to eat crunchy foods, too"). Teachers can also model/encourage conversation (e.g., "Last night the thunder was so loud, it made my house shake. Who else heard the thunder?"). This might be a time to review the day and anticipate upcoming activities (e.g., "We have had a busy day so far. We played with our friends, we learned about forest animals, and we explored textures in science. Eat a good snack because we have more learning to do today"). As we have highlighted in each of these examples, teachers may embed increased language opportunities into conversation during snack time.

Transitions/Lining Up

Similarly, transitions offer another optimal opportunity to add adult language models into the school day. As with snack time, there are many possibilities for meaningful language input during transitions. For example, teachers can reinforce sequential concepts (e.g., "Julie is first in line; she is at the beginning, and Andrew is behind her. Molly is third, and Marian is fourth"). Also, teachers can highlight emergent literacy skills (e.g., "Molly and Marian are together in line. Both of their names start with the "M" sound"). Teachers might also increase the quantity of language by singing songs as the children line up and walk down the hall (with perhaps the added benefit of increasing focus and attention).

Although we have highlighted two specific examples of routine classroom activities in which the amount of language use may be increased, it is important to acknowledge that adult talk can and should occur throughout the daily routine, including circle time, center time, and free play. The critical component for teachers is to understand that they can single-handedly increase the amount of talk in the classroom; this, in turn, may have a positive impact on children's language acquisition. As previously described, although teachers may encourage their students to respond verbally to talk, this is not a necessity because young children also learn through exposure to adult language. It is important to caution teachers that the quantity of language in preschool classrooms is not the only consideration. At times, teachers may use an appropriate amount of language; however, it can become routine, repetitive, and not incorporate other key areas, such as rare words or linguistically interesting word forms, as we discuss in the following section.

Language Complexity

In addition to increasing the quantity of adult talk, research indicates that young children benefit from teacher input in areas related to language complexity, including cognitively challenging talk (e.g., Smith & Dickinson, 1994; van Kleeck et al., 2006), exposure to rare words (e.g., Beals & Tabors, 1995; Dickinson & Tabors, 2002), and syntactically complex speech (e.g., Huttenlocher et al., 2002). In this section, we discuss the three areas that encompass language complexity, then provide two specific contexts that exemplify how teachers can incorporate increased language complexity into the classroom.

The key component of cognitively challenging talk is shifting conversation from the "here and now" (i.e., discussion of people, objects, and events in the present context) to past and future events, ideas, or objects not currently visible. Activities that increase language complexity may be implemented in a variety of classroom contexts, including whole-class, small-group, and individual settings. Cognitively challenging talk may include explanations (e.g., "We need to practice our song, so we are ready for the school play next week"), descriptions (e.g., "I am thinking of an animal that has a long neck and many spots"), predictions (e.g., "I wonder if Curious George is going to get in trouble when the man comes back"), or personal narrative (e.g., "Last year for my birthday party . . .").

Teachers' use of rare vocabulary words, another key component associated with language complexity, includes using and defining a range of vocabulary words that are not typical of day-to-day teacher–student verbal interactions. Rare vocabulary words can be found across a range of contexts and word categories, including nouns (e.g., *constellation* instead of *stars*), verbs (e.g., *expand* instead of *grow*), and modifiers (e.g., *cautiously* instead of *carefully*). As suggested by Reutzel and Cooter (2008), language contexts, such as conversation and books, provide varying amounts of exposure to rare words. Last, language complexity involves the use of syntactically complex talk. Rather than using simple sentences (e.g., "It is story time"), teachers can increase their language complexity by using complex sentence structures (e.g., "Before we go to lunch, we are going to read a story"), prepositional phrases (e.g., "Make sure you sit *inside the circle*"), noun phrases (e.g., "Put your books on *the short, dark blue desk*"), and verb phrases (e.g., "Our classroom *has been getting* colder all day today").

Shared Book Reading

Shared book reading is one natural routine in which teachers can embed complex language. As an example, let us refer to the commonly read children's book *The Very Hungry Caterpillar* by Eric Carle (1969). Teachers can include cognitively challenging talk by encouraging young students to think about and discuss prior experiences with caterpillars (e.g., "I remember when Johnny found a caterpillar on the swing set yesterday") and make predictions (e.g., "Let's look at the pictures and predict what will happen next to our caterpillar"). Additionally, teachers can highlight rare vocabulary words in the book (e.g., *cocoon* and *salami*), concepts related to the book (e.g., *metamorphosis*), and comparisons between caterpillars and worms. As the teacher reads and makes predictions about the story, he or she may target syntactic complexity by intentionally including multiple-noun phrases and complex sentences (e.g., "First the caterpillar ate through *one red apple*, and then he ate through *two yellow pears*").

Dramatic Play

Dramatic play time is another routine during which teachers can increase use of complex language. While playing with peers, teachers can embed complex language in engaging contexts. For example, to a group of three students playing with airplanes and blocks, the teacher can introduce cognitively challenging talk by discussing past experiences (e.g., "That looks like the airplane I flew on to see my grandma") or predictions (e.g., "Oh no! What will happen if the blocks are in the way?"). This context of playing with airplanes and blocks may be a natural time to introduce rare vocabulary words (e.g., *hangar*, terms for more specific kinds of airplanes, *runway, air control tower*). It is important to understand that introducing such vocabulary words does not mean additional time or work for the teacher. Rather, new words can be used within the context of play (e.g., "You're building a place to keep the airplanes. That's called a hangar. It's kind of like a big garage for airplanes. Can I put my airplane into your hangar, too?"). Finally, syntactically complex language can be used throughout the interaction (e.g., "That is a big grey bomber" and "While my airplane is rolling down the runway, yours has already taken off").

Language Stimulation Techniques

Research supports the use of stimulation techniques to increase young children's acquisition of key language concepts (i.e., Rice & Wilcox, 1995). Specifically, language stimulation techniques are tools teachers can use to embed higher quantities of more complex language into early childhood classrooms. Whereas some techniques are designed solely to highlight new language opportunities for young children, others create more opportunities for children to talk. Regardless of the specific technique selected, a child's response is not the key area. Instead, teachers' use of these techniques (whether the child responds or not) is the critical component of creating high-quality language environments in the classroom. In the next section, we provide definitions and examples of each type of language stimulation technique, then highlight two situational examples that incorporate language stimulation techniques in early childhood classrooms.

Six language stimulation techniques include (1) focused contrasts, (2) models, (3) event casts, (4) open-ended questions, (5) expansions/recasts, and (6) redirects/prompted initiations (Rice & Wilcox, 1995).

1. *Focused contrasts* provide input or feedback when a child uses an incorrect word or grammatical form by giving two or more options for the appropriate response. For example, when a child says, "I falled off," the teacher can respond, "You *falled* down or you *fell* down?"

2. *Models* used by the teacher provide the child with a word or structure that may be new or unfamiliar. For example, "That dinosaur is called *Tyrannosaurus rex*. Your *Tyrannosaurus rex has* big teeth."

3. *Event casts* provide ongoing commentary about a situation and a natural way to add quantity, as well as complexity, to the language environment in the classroom. To use event casts, teachers talk about the surrounding environment. For example, while a child is playing with cars during free play, the teacher may comment, "You are pushing the car up the ramp. Uh oh! That yellow car flipped over. I hope that the driver isn't injured."

4. *Open-ended questions* do not have one specific—or correct—answer, and typically require an elaborated rather than just a one-word response, as with closed-ended or yes–no questions. Although typically in question form, open-ended questions may also be phrased as statements. For example, the teacher could ask, "What do you think is going to happen next?" or say, "Tell me what might happen."

5. *Expansions/recasts* provide additional input or information by slightly altering yet preserving the overall meaning in a phrase or sentence. For example, if a child says, "That's a truck." The teacher could respond, "Yes, that's a big, red dump truck."

6. *Redirects/prompted initiations* encourage a child to direct comments to a peer. For example, while playing with blocks, one child takes a block from another student. The teacher could say to the first child, "Ask Johnny if you can play with the block." If the child needs additional assistance, the teacher can prompt or provide the child with a response, such as "Try 'Johnny, can I play with the block?' "

To this point, we have provided a review of the existing research in regard to strategies and supports defined by Rice and Wilcox (1995) that facilitate language development in young children. Some of the strategies we recommended earlier may overlap. The point is not to isolate individual strategies but to make teachers become more conscious and intentional about their use of language stimulation techniques with young students. As previously described related to language quantity and complexity, language stimulation techniques can be easily incorporated into early childhood classroom routines throughout the day. In the next section, we provide two additional examples of ways to increase language input in early childhood classrooms.

Shared Book Reading

Shared book reading provides an ideal context for teachers to use sophisticated forms of language. In the following example, four students participate in a shared book reading of *The Gingerbread Man* by Eric Kimmel (1993). After reading the title and author of the book, the teacher may ask the students, "What do you think this book is about?" (open-ended question). The students say, "A cookie." The teacher explains, "Yes, this book is about a gingerbread man. Gingerbread is a type of cookie. It's my favorite flavor of cookie." (model and recast/expansion). The teacher continues, "I wonder what happens to the cookie in this book." One child says, "He eated by fox," to which the teacher responds, "Jack, was he *eated* by the fox or was he *eaten* by the fox?" (focused contrast). After reading the text on the first page, the teacher provides commentary reiterating the content (event casts). For example, the teacher says the following and points to the corresponding pictures,

> "First, the old man and the old woman made the gingerbread dough. Next they mixed all of the ingredients, rolled out the dough, cut the cookies, and set them on the baking pan. Then they put the pan in the oven. Once the cookies were finished baking, the old man and the old woman decorated them with two eyes, a mouth, and three buttons. Just then, the cookie jumped off the table and ran out the door. Uh oh! I wonder where the cookie is going."

Because this specific book utilizes a repetitive phrase, the teacher may encourage students to repeat it on each page. Additionally, the text of *The Gingerbread Man* incorporates several rare vocabulary words, including *pasture, grazing, sow*, and *sly*. While reading, the teacher can naturally highlight, ask questions, and encourage students to learn and use these words. The interactive nature of shared book reading continues until the book is finished. After the teacher and the children retell the story (the teacher may asks the open-ended question/comment, "Tell me about the story"), the teacher could say, "My favorite part is when the gingerbread man runs away from the old man and the old woman. Olivia, ask Peter about his favorite part of the story." (prompted initiation). As a general consideration while reading, teachers are encouraged to use at least one technique or strategy per page of text, as highlighted earlier. With this implementation, teachers are intentionally targeting the six language stimulation techniques while also providing complex language.

Free Play

As another example, two students are playing with Play-Doh. As the teacher approaches the pair, one student says, "Mrs. P., we play Play-Doh." The teacher responds, "Yes, Jacob you are play*ing* with three colors of Play-Doh" (recast/expansion). "Jane is rolling the Play-Doh into a pancake" (event cast). The teacher continues, "Jacob, tell me what are you making with your Play-Doh" (open-ended question). He says, "Snake," to which the teacher responds, "You are making a long, green snake. I hope that it doesn't bite us with its big teeth" (expansion, event cast). The teacher continues, "I wonder what Jane is making. Say, 'Jane, what are you making?'" (prompted initiation). As the children continue to play with the Play-Doh, the teacher may provide additional event casts, including "Jane is rolling the Play-Doh. Jacob is cutting the Play-Doh into a circle." Near the end of the interaction, the teacher says, "That Play-Doh is turquoise. Turquoise is a color that looks bright blue" (model). As with the previous book-reading example, we have provided specific suggestions to integrate language strategies into shared book reading and dramatic play. Through the integration of language stimulation techniques, teachers actively promote young children's language development.

Language Assessment

This chapter has highlighted research and practical strategies for early educators to implement into their daily classroom practices to facilitate language development for young students. Although not the primary focus of this chapter, an additional consideration is related to language assessments and how this information may inform teachers' use of stimulation techniques in the classroom. Historically, language sample analysis, the "gold standard," has been used to monitor students' language and capture growth over time (Heilmann et al., 2008). Recent literature suggests that because narrative analysis provides an authentic context, other language measures, such as the Narrative Assessment Protocol (NAP; Justice, Bowles, Pence, & Gosse, 2010) and Tracking Narrative Language Progress (TNL-Pr; Gillam & Gillam, 2009), may provide valuable information about students' language development and growth (Gillam & Justice, 2010). Importantly, speech–language pathologists demonstrate specific expertise in language development and serve as an invaluable resource for teachers, providing detailed information about language assessments and intervention. Early educators are strongly encouraged to consult with a speech–language pathologist, especially if they have questions about strategies to incorporate into classroom routines or concerns about the language development of individual students.

REFLECTIONS AND NEW DIRECTIONS

To this point in the chapter, we have provided both a summary of research and practical applications for teachers on how to implement language strategies in the classroom setting. One of our primary goals in this chapter is to highlight for teachers how the implementation of key strategies into the daily classroom routine is not overly time-consuming or difficult. However, it is important for teachers to be intentional about the input they provide, to ensure that their students are afforded high-quality language environments. As previously described, research shows significant variability in early educators' implementation of these language uses and strategies in their classrooms. For example, Turnbull, Anthony, Justice, and Bowles (2009) found that only 36% of the 5,017 teacher utterances included language stimulation techniques. In this study, modeling was the most common technique used (59.66%) while prompted initiation was the least (.99%).

Such research offers both implications for future research and professional development related to the language-learning environments in preschools. While research indicates that teachers infrequently use strategies related to language quantity, complexity, and language stimulation techniques in their classroom, the reason behind this finding remains unclear. Future research needs to identify gaps between research and practice related to high-quality environments, as well as mechanisms to support teachers' use of evidence-based techniques. While the strategies presented in this chapter are fairly straightforward, preschool teachers may benefit from additional professional development activities regarding practical ways to facilitate implementation to ensure high-quality language environments for young children.

PROFESSIONAL DEVELOPMENT ACTIVITIES

- As described in this chapter, research suggests that teachers need to be intentional about use of language in early childhood settings. Think about the language you use while interacting with your students. Do you incorporate language stimulation techniques into your classroom routine? Consider one context or activity in which you incorporate language stimulation techniques.

- Videotape a 5-minute interaction with your students. Watch the recording and use Table 25.3 as a checklist to determine the types and number of language stimulation techniques incorporated into this interaction.

- While reading a book with your students, use a minimum of one language stimulation technique per page.

- Prior to a book reading time with your students, predetermine at least three rare vocabulary words. While reading, how are you going to target these specific words with your students?

REFERENCES

Barnett, W. S., & Yarosz, D. J. (2004, August). Who goes to preschool and why does it matter? *Preschool Policy Matters, 8*, 2–16.

Beals, D. E., & Tabors, P. O. (1995). Arboretum, bureaucratic and carbohydrates: Preschoolers' exposure to rare vocabulary at home. *First Language, 15*, 57–76.

Bohannon, J., & Bonvillian, J. (1997). Theoretical approaches to language acquisition. In J. Berko Gleason (Ed.), *The development of language* (4th ed., pp. 259–316). Needham Heights, MA: Allyn & Bacon.

Bruner, J. S. (1975). The ontogenesis of speech acts. *Journal of Child Language, 2*, 1–19.

Bryant, J. B. (2009). Language in social contexts: Communicative competence in the preschool years. In J. B. Gleason & N. B. Ratner (Eds.), *The development of language* (7th ed., pp. 192–226). Boston: Pearson.

Cabell, S. Q., Justice, L. M., Piasta, S. B. Curenton, S. M., Wiggin, A., Turnbull, K. P., et al. (2011). The impact of teacher responsivity education on preschoolers' language and literacy skills. *American Journal of Speech–Language Pathology, 20*, 315–330.

Carle, E. (1969). *The very hungry caterpillar.* New York: Putman/Philomel.

Chapman, R. S. (2000). Children's language learning: An interactionist perspective. *Journal of Child Psychology and Psychiatry, 41*, 33–54.

Dickinson, D. K., & Tabors, P. O. (2002). Fostering language and literacy in classrooms and homes. *Young Children, 57*(2), 10–18.

Gillam, S., & Gillam, R. (2009). *Tracking Narrative Language Progress (TNL-Pr).* Seminar presented at the American Speech–Language–Hearing Association annual convention, New Orleans, LA.

Gillam, S. L., & Justice, L. M. (2010, September 21). RTI progress monitoring tools: Assessing Primary-grade students in response-to-intervention programs. *The ASHA Leader.* Retrieved from *www.asha.org/Publications/leader/2010/100921/RTI-Progress-Monitoring.htm.*

Heilmann, J., Miller, J., Iglesias, A., Fabiano-Smith, L., Nockerts, A., & Andriacchi, K. (2008). Narrative transcription accuracy and reliability in two languages. *Topics in Language Disorders, 28*, 178–188.

Hoff, E. (2003). The specificity of environmental influence: Socioeconomic status affects early vocabulary development via maternal speech. *Child Development, 74*, 1368–1378.

Hoff-Ginsberg, E. (1994). Influences of mother and child on maternal talkativeness. *Discourse Processes, 18*, 105–117.

Huttenlocher, J., Vasilyeva, M., Cymerman, E., & Levine, S. (2002). Language input and child syntax. *Cognitive Psychology, 45*, 337–374.

Justice, L. M., Bowles, R., Pence, K., & Gosse, C. (2010). A scalable tool for assessing children's language abilities within a narrative context: The NAP (Narrative Assessment Protocol). *Early Childhood Research Quarterly, 25*, 218–234.

Justice, L. M., Mashburn, A. J., Hamre, B. K., & Pianta, R. C. (2008). Quality of language and literacy instruction in preschool classrooms serving at-risk pupils. *Early Childhood Research Quarterly, 23*, 51–68.

Kimmel, E. (1993). *The gingerbread man.* New York: Holiday House.

LoCasale-Crouch, J., Konold, T., Pianta, R., Howes, C., Burchinal, M., Bryant, D., et al. (2007). Observed classroom quality profiles in state-funded pre-kindergarten programs and associations with teacher, program, and classroom characteristics. *Early Childhood Research Quarterly, 22*, 3–17.

Mashburn, A. J., Pianta, R. C., Hamre, B. K., Downer, J. T., Barbarin, O. A., Bryant, D., et al. (2008). Measures of classroom quality in prekindergarten and children's development of academic, language and social skills. *Child Development, 79*, 732–749.

Massey, S. L. (2004). Teacher–child conversation in the preschool classroom. *Early Childhood Education Journal, 31*, 227–231.

McCartney, K. (1984). The effect of quality of day care environment upon children's language development. *Developmental Psychology, 20*, 244–260.

National Center for Education Statistics. (2003). *Overview and inventory of state education reforms: 1900–2000.* Washington, DC: U.S. Department of Education, Institute of Education Sciences.

National Institute for Literacy. (2009). *Learning to talk and listen: An oral language resource for early childhood caregivers.* Washington, DC: RMC Research Corporation.

Pianta, R., Howes, C., Burchinal, M., Bryant, D., Clifford, R., Early, D., et al. (2005). Features of pre-kindergarten programs, classrooms, and teachers: Do they predict observed classroom quality and child–teacher interactions? *Applied Developmental Science, 9*(3), 144–159.

Pianta, R. C., LaParo, K., & Hamre, B. (2004). *The Classroom Assessment Scoring System Pre-K manual.* Unpublished manuscript, University of Virginia, Charlottesville.

Reutzel, D. R., & Cooter, R. B. (2008). Increasing reading vocabulary. In *Teaching children to read: The teacher makes the difference* (5th ed., pp. 190–231). Upper Saddle River, NJ: Pearson.

Rice, M., & Wilcox, K. (1995). *Language acquisition preschool: A classroom program for language facilitation.* Baltimore: Brookes.

Smith, M. W., & Dickinson, D. K. (1994). Describing oral language opportunities and environments in head start and other preschool classrooms. *Early Childhood Research Quarterly, 9*(3–4), 345–366.

Turnbull, K. P., Anthony, A. B., Justice, L. M., & Bowles, R. (2009). Preschoolers' exposure to language stimulation in classrooms serving at-risk children: Contribution of group size and activity context. *Early Education and Development, 20*, 53–79.

Vandell, D. L., & Wolfe, B. (2000). *Child care quality: Does it matter and does it need to be improved?* Madison: Institute for Research on Child Poverty, University of Wisconsin–Madison.

van Kleeck, A., Vander Woude, J., & Hammett, L. (2006). Fostering literal and inferential language skills in Head Start preschoolers with language impairment using scripted book-sharing discussions. *American Journal of Speech–Language Pathology, 15*(1), 85–95.

Vygotsky, L. S. (1978). *Mind in society: The development of higher psychological processes.* Cambridge, MA: Harvard University Press.

Wasik, B., Bond, M. A., & Hindman, A. (2006). The effects of a language and literacy intervention on Head Start children and teachers. *Journal of Educational Psychology, 98*, 63–74.

AUTHOR INDEX

SUBJECT INDEX

Page numbers followed by *f* indicate figure, *t* indicate table